World Economic Forum
Geneva, Switzerland 2001

Professor Klaus Schwab
President, World Economic Forum

Professor Michael E. Porter
Director, Institute for Strategy and Competitiveness
Harvard Business School &
Co-Director, Global Competitiveness Report

Professor Jeffrey D. Sachs
Director, Center for International Development
Harvard University &
Co-Director, Global Competitiveness Report

The Global Competitiveness Report 2001–2002

D0161409

Project Leaders:

Peter K. Cornelius
World Economic Forum

John W. McArthur
Center for International Development
Harvard University

New York • Oxford
Oxford University Press
2002

The *Global Competitiveness Report 2001–2002* is published by the World Economic Forum. The *Report* is the result of a collaboration between the World Economic Forum and the Center for International Development (CID) at Harvard University.

At the World Economic Forum:

Professor Klaus Schwab
President

Dr Peter Cornelius
Director

Yong Zhang
Economist

Fiona M Paua
Economist

At Harvard University:

Professor Michael Porter
Director, Institute for Strategy and Competitiveness
Harvard Business School

Professor Jeffrey Sachs
Director, Center for International Development
at Harvard University

John McArthur
Research Fellow, Center for International
Development at Harvard University

Dr Christian Ketels
Principal Associate,
Institute for Strategy and Competitiveness
Harvard Business School

Dr Weifeng Weng
Senior Research Associate,
Institute for Strategy and Competitiveness
Harvard Business School

Daniel Vasquez
Research Associate,
Institute for Strategy and Competitiveness
Harvard Business School

With thanks to Karine Burnet, Krzysztof Bulski, Alejandra Callejo, and Gilles Fumeaux for invaluable research assistance at the World Economic Forum and to Adrian Ma, Jorge-Edgar Marquez-Garcia, Dimitre Michev, Mannig Simidian, Padmesh Shukla, and especially Rebecca Thornton for invaluable research assistance at CID.

Oxford University Press

Oxford New York Athens Auckland
Bangkok Bogotá Buenos Aires Calcutta
Cape Town Chennai Dar es Salaam Delhi
Florence Hong Kong Istanbul Karachi
Kuala Lumpur Madrid Melbourne Mexico
City Mumbai Nairobi Paris São Paulo
Singapore Taipei Tokyo Toronto Warsaw

and associated companies in
Berlin Ibadan

Published by
Oxford University Press, Inc.
198 Madison Avenue,
New York, New York 10016
http://www.oup-usa.org

Oxford is a registered trademark of Oxford
University Press

ISBN 0-19-521837-X

Printing (last digit): 9 8 7 6 5 4 3 2 1

Printed in the United States of America on
acid-free paper

The term *country* as used in this report does not in all cases refer to a territorial entity that is a state as understood by international law and practice. The term covers well-defined, geographically self-contained economic areas that are not states but for which statistical data are maintained on a separate and independent basis.

Contents

Partner Institutes

Argentina
IAE, Management and Business School, Austral University
Professor Marcelo Paladino
Jose del Tronco, Research Assistant

Australia
Business Council of Australia, Melbourne
David Buckingham, Executive Director

Austria
University of Economics and Business Administration
Professor Dr. Christian Bellak

Bangladesh
Centre for Policy Dialogue
Professor Rehman Sobhan, Chairman
Dr. Debapriya Bhattacharya, Executive Director
Quazi Hasnat Shahriar, Research Associate
Ria Khan, Administrative Associate

Bolivia, Costa Rica, Ecuador, El Salvador, Guatemala, Honduras, Nicaragua, Panama
Latin American Center for Competitiveness and Sustainable
    Development (INCAE)
Roberto Artavia, Rector
Alberto Trejos, Dean

Bolivia
Universidad Católica Boliviana "San Pablo"
Dr. Carlos Alberto Gerke M., Rector – UCB
Lic. Marcela A. de Guzman, Directora Depto. Economía

Brazil
Fundacao Dom Cabral, Belo Horizonte
Professor Aldemir Drummond

Bulgaria
Center for Economic Development
Amelia Damianova, Senior Expert

Canada
Business Council of National Issues, Ottawa
Thomas P. d'Aquino, President and Chief Executive Officer

Chile
Universidad Adolfo Ibanez
Professor Gastón Galleguillos
Professor Dieter Wunder

China
Institute of Economic System and Management
State Council Office for Restructuring Economic Systems
Li Chen, Deputy Director
Dr. Yuanzheng Cao, Executive Vice President of
    BOC International Holdings
Dr. Shi-Ji Gao, Chief of International Comparative Systems

Colombia
National Planning Department, Bogota
Juan Carlos Echeverry, Vice-Director
Maria Isabel Agudelo, Project Manager

Czech Republic
CMC – Graduate School of Business, Celàkovice
Peter Loewenguth, President
Professor Dr. Jaroslav A. Jiràsek, Honorary Dean

Denmark
Copenhagen Business School
Professor Heather Hazard

Ecuador
Catholic University, and ESPOL
Juan Alvarado
Manuel del Valle

Egypt
Federation of Egyptian Industries
Dr. Abdel Moneim Seoudi, Chairman
Ahmed Ezz, Chairman
Loutfi Mazhar, Executive Director

Estonia
Estonian Chamber of Commerce, Tallinn
Mart Relve, Director General

France
Club de l'Expansion, Paris
Centre de Prévision de l'Expansion, Paris
Philippe Lefournier, Managing Director

Greece
Federation of Greek Industries, Athens
John Chryssanthacopoulos, Economist, Relations with the
    State and the Institutional Authorities
Antonis Tortopidis, Co-ordinator, Research and Analysis

Hong Kong
The Hong Kong General Chamber of Commerce
Ian Perkin, Chief Economist

Hungary
KOPINT-DATORG Economic Research, Budapest
András Köves, Deputy General Director
Gábor Oblath, Chairman
Agnes Nagy, Head of Section

Iceland
Samtok Atvinnulifsins
Confederation of Icelandic Employers, Reykjavik
Dr. Finnur Geirsson, President and CEO
Ari Edwald, Managing Director
David Stefansson, Project Manager

India
Confederation of Indian Industry
Tarun Das, Director General
TK Bhaumik, Senior Advisor – Policy

Indonesia
Boston Institute for Development Economies
Partnership for Economic Growth
Timothy S. Buehrer
Indonesian Chamber of Commerce and Industry, Jakarta
Dr. Tulus Tambunnan
Dr. Sjahrir

Ireland
Irish Management Institute
Barry Kenny, Chief Executive
Conor Hannaway, Director of Corporate Development
    Kevin Hannigan, Head of Economic Research
University College Cork, Department of Economics
Dr. Eleanor Doyle

Israel
Manufacturers Association of Israel, Tel Aviv
Moshe Nahum, Director, Foreign Trade and International
    Relations Division
Daniel Singerman, Economist

Italy
Ambrosetti Studi e Servizi Internazionali, Milan
Enrico Solimene, Managing Director

Japan
Keizai Doyukai (Japan Association of Corporate Executives)
International Affairs Department
Dr. Kiyohiko Ito, Deputy Managing Director

Jordan
Ministry of Planning, Competitiveness Unit
Nesreen Barakat, Director

Korea
Federation of Korean Industries
Seok-Joong Kim, Director
Chan-bok Lee, Economic Research Department

Latvia
Institute of Economics, Academy of Sciences, Riga
Raite Karnite
Stockholm School of Economics, Riga Campus
Dr. Karlis Kreslins

Lithuania
Statistikos Tyrimai – Statistical Surveys, Vilnius
Benonas Miksas, Director

Malaysia
Federation of Malaysian Manufacturers, Kuala Lumpur
Lee Cheng Suan, Chief Executive Officer
Lee Lee Ng, Assistant Manager International Division

Mauritius
Joint Economic Council of Mauritius, Port Luis
Raj Makoond, Director

Mexico
Ministry of the Economy, Office for the Coordination of Promotion
   of Trade and Investment
Eduardo J. Solis, Head

New Zealand
New Zealand Employers' Federation
   Anne Knowles, Chief Executive Officer

Nigeria
Nigerian Economic Summit Group
Professor Anya O. Anya, Director General & CEO
Dr. Mary Agboli, Associate Director & Head of Research
West African Institute for Financial and Economic Management, Lagos
Chris Itsede, Director

Norway
BI Norwegian School of Management
Department of Strategy
Professor Oivind Revang, Head of Department
Professor Torger Reve
Professor Erik W. Jakobsen

Peru
Centro de Desarrollo Industrial, Lima
Sociedad Nacional de Industrias
Dr. Luis Tenorio, Executive Director
Fany Sotelo, Project Manager
Liliana Arevalo, Project Assistant

Philippines
Makati Business Club, Makati City, Metro Manila
Guillermo M. Luz, Executive Director
Marc P. Opulencia, Deputy Director
Michael B. Mundo, Research Manager

Poland
Warsaw School of Economics
Professor Bogdan Radomski

Portugal
Instituto Superior de Estudos Empresariais da Universidade
   do Porto, Porto
Professor Rui Guimarães, Dean
AURN – Associaçao das Universidades da Regiao Norte, Porto
Professor Daniel Bessa

Romania
Romanian Center for Economic Policy, Bucharest
Professor Daniel Daianu, Co-founder
Alina Andrei, MBA, Economic Analyst

Russia
Institute for Private Sector Development and Socio-Economic
   Analysis, Moscow
Irina Evseyeva
Stockholm School of Economics, St. Petersburg Campus
Professor Carl F. Frey

Singapore
Economic Development Board, Singapore
Corporate Communications and Planning Division
Shirley Chen, Director, Corporate Services

Slovenia
Institute for Economic Research, Ljubljana
Dr. Peter Stanovnik, Director

South Africa
Business South Africa
Friede Dowie, Secretary General

Spain
High Council of Chambers of Commerce of Spain, Madrid
Fernando Gomez Avilés, President and Managing Director
José Manuel Fernández Norniella
Juan José de Lucio

Sri Lanka
Institute of Policy Studies of Sri Lanka
Ajith Colonne, Director of Administration & Corporate Affairs
Roshen Epaarachchi, Chief Research Officer for GCR Project

Sweden
Institute of International Business, Stockholm School of Economics
Professor Örjan Sölvell, Director
Vanja Ekberg, Administrative Director

Taiwan
Council of Economic Planning and Development, Taipei
Dr. P.K. Chiang, Chairman
Dr. Chi Schive, Vice Chairman
K.C. Lee, Vice Chairman
C.Y. Hu, Director, Economic Research Department
Chung-Chung Shieh, Economic Research Department

Thailand
National Economic and Social Development Board,
Economic Analysis and Projection Division
Arkhom Termpittayapaisith, Director

Ukraine
CASE - Ukraine, Kiev
Vladimir Dubrovskiy, Project Manager

Uruguay
ORT University, Montevideo
Professor Isidoro Hodora

Venezuela
CONAPRI, National Council for Investment Promotion, Caracas
Eugenia Labrador, Investment Manager
Gabriela Reveron, Business Analyst

Vietnam
Institute for Economic Research, Ho Chi Minh City
Nguyen Xuan Thanh, Research Fellow

Zimbabwe
Zimbabwe National Chamber of Commerce, Harare
Nhlanhla Masuku, President
Wonder Maisiri, Chief Executive
John Makamure, Chief Economist, Advocacy & Trade Manager

Preface

KLAUS SCHWAB

President, World Economic Forum

This year's *Global Competitiveness Report* appears at a time of exceptional uncertainty. Global economic activity has slowed substantially, stock markets have shown considerable volatility, and the world's major currencies have experienced significant fluctuations. In Europe, where the final steps toward monetary unification are about to be taken, output has declined considerably below the region's production potential. In Japan, there are serious concerns of a prolonged recession, and in several countries throughout the rest of Asia industrial production has shrunk markedly. Other emerging market economies have been subject to financial turmoil that reminds us of the severe crises in 1997 and 1998.

The greatest uncertainty, however, concerns the United States, whose economy has essentially come to a standstill in the second quarter of 2001. In the highly integrated world economy, the United States remains critical for global economic growth. Yet evidence will emerge only gradually regarding how the horrific tragedies of September 11 will affect this economy that was already experiencing a slowdown. In order to restore confidence, the US Federal Reserve, in concert with other central banks, has continued to lower interest rates while the federal government has developed a package for fiscal stimulus. It is extremely difficult to predict how fast a turnaround can be achieved, but the United States' underlying fundamentals will play the most important role in influencing its return to a sustained growth path. As this *Report* confirms, the United States' fundamentals remain highly competitive.

To be sure, as the global economy experiences this period of economic and political uncertainty, much is at stake. Calls for more protectionism have become louder. Commitments to international efforts urgently required to fight killer diseases as well as global climate change could be undermined. And, more generally, the recent backlash against globalization could gain increased momentum. There can be little doubt that these measures would hurt developing countries most.

Coping with the enormous challenges currently facing the global economy requires pursuing a prudent and proactive macroeconomic policy stance. More importantly, it requires strengthening the cross-border networks that promote private investment, entrepreneurship, and social progress around the world. In this endeavor, the *Global Competitiveness Report* remains an invaluable tool by identifying existing impediments to economic growth and thus helping in the design of policy measures to remove such obstacles as a precondition for advancing human well-being across the globe.

This year we have added not fewer than 17 countries to our analysis, reflecting the rising integration of developing countries into the global economy and ensuring that the *Global Competitiveness Report* remains the most comprehensive knowledge source for policymakers, the business community, and other key stakeholders. These new entrants are regionally diversified, with one economy from Africa (Nigeria), two from Asia (Bangladesh and Sri Lanka), five from central and eastern Europe (Estonia, Latvia, Lithuania, Romania, and Slovenia), and nine from the Western Hemisphere (Dominican Republic, Guatemala, Honduras, Jamaica, Nicaragua, Panama, Paraguay, Trinidad and Tobago, and Uruguay). As regards the latter, I would like to thank the Inter-American Development Bank for their excellent cooperation.

In the future, we will certainly continue to expand the list of countries covered by the *Global Competitiveness Report*. Although this *Report* remains our flagship publication, we plan to publish supplementary reports on specific regions, including one forthcoming study on Latin America and another on the transition economies in central and eastern Europe and the former Soviet Union.

We remain indebted to Professor Michael E Porter, director of the Institute for Strategy and Competitiveness at the Harvard Business School, and Professor Jeffrey D Sachs, Director of the Center for International Development at Harvard University, for their partnership and for acting as co-directors of the *Global Competitiveness Report*. We would also like to thank John W McArthur of the Center for International Development for managing this project on the Harvard side and for applying the rigorous standards to the data and analyses that ensure the ongoing excellence of the *Report*. Furthermore, heading the Global Competitiveness Program at the World Economic Forum, Dr Peter Cornelius has remained in charge of executing the Survey, coordinating the *Report*, and providing its intellectual driving force. Finally, we extend very special thanks to KPMG, our partner in this *Report*, for their support in this important venture.

Introduction

PETER K. CORNELIUS, World Economic Forum

JOHN W. MCARTHUR, Center for International Development at Harvard University

MICHAEL E. PORTER, Institute for Strategy and Competitiveness, Harvard Business School

JEFFREY D. SACHS, Center for International Development at Harvard University

KLAUS SCHWAB, World Economic Forum

Slowdown and Uncertainty: International Economic Networks in the Wake of September 11, 2001

October 5, 2001

The terrorist attacks of September 11, 2001, have led to numerous swift reactions in the political and security spheres. In the economic sphere, short-term reactions were severe: Through to September 25, an estimated US\$ 2 trillion were lost in world equity markets, 20 of the world's major stock market indexes dropped by more than 10 percent, and 32 national indexes dropped by at least 8 percent (see Table 1). Over the same period, at least 15 currencies saw their values drop by 4 percent or more relative to the US dollar, a tremendous amount over a short period (see Table 2). But many of these losses were later recouped: Between September 25 and October 3, more than $500 billion was regained of the $800 billion lost in US equity markets in the 14 days following September 11, and rebounds in other global markets were similar. Now, a few weeks after the attacks, attention is turning to the medium- and long-term impacts of September 11 on the global economy.

It is with these medium-term (roughly five years) economic trends that the *Global Competitiveness Report* is concerned. In September 2001, the world economy was already in the midst of a cyclical slowdown. In line with our stated objective of projecting countries' economic prospects independent of business cycles, this *Report* makes a key implicit assumption that global economic integration will continue in the years ahead, despite shocks such as the horrendous one of September 11. However, since the events of September 11 were of such potential significance to the world economy and because the *Report* had not yet gone to press at that date, we decided to add the following brief analysis of the post–September 11 world economy.

In the short term, the terrorist attacks have probably worked as a catalyst, pushing the world economy into a recession more quickly and more severely than would have been the case otherwise. Two factors are largely to blame. First, the terrorist attacks and the security precautions taken in their wake have made travel, trade, and communication more costly. Possible disruptions in transport networks threaten the functioning and efficiency of global production chains. Second, and more significant, business and consumer confidence took a significant blow. Before September 11, the resilience of US consumer spending was one of the few positive signs in an overall slowing world economy. Now there is more consumer uncertainty, leaving companies to wait and see what will happen next. Although it is highly probable that these two factors will dissipate over the next year, they could well place a drag on a global economic recovery.

In the longer term, the terrorist attacks will have a lasting negative impact if the policy responses trigger a reversal of the global economic integration that has characterized the past twenty years. The possibility of large-scale global conflict, terrorism, political backlash, and market uncertainty have the potential to raise the costs of cross-border business to levels not seen in decades, and thereby to limit the gains in economic well-being that global economic integration can yield. We therefore hope and believe that the responses to September 11 will be resolute and powerful, but that care will be taken to prevent them from derailing the benefits of global business.

Table 1: Fluctuations in equity markets across selected GCR economies

Country	Index	Change in value: Jan 1–Sep 10, 2001	Change in value: Sep 10–Sep 25, 2001
Argentina	Merval	−31.1%	−15.1%
Australia	All Ordinaries	0.9%	−8.8%
Austria	ATX	8.7%	−9.2%
Bangladesh	Bangladesh SE All Share Price Index	1.2%	−3.1%
Belgium	BEL–20	−9.7%	−9.6%
Brazil	Bovespa	−21.9%	−14.2%
Bulgaria	Bulgarian SE Sofia	−12.7%	−1.5%
Canada	TSE 300	−17.8%	−8.8%
Chile	IPSA	16.0%	−8.9%
China	Shanghai Composite	−10.5%	−3.4%
Colombia	Colombia SE Price Index	−0.3% *	−7.3%
Costa Rica	Costa Rica SE	11.4%	0.0%
Czech Rep	PX 50	−27.7%	−3.9%
Denmark	KFX	−13.0%	−12.7%
Ecuador	Quito–SE	6.1%	4.6%
Egypt	CMA	0.3%	−2.1%
Estonia	Talinn Stock Exchange	−16.7%	−3.5%
Finland	Helsinki General	−55.4%	5.4%
France	CAC 40	−26.0%	−11.0%
Germany	DAX	−27.4%	−14.2%
Greece	General Share	−25.1%	−14.7%
Hong Kong	Hang Seng	−31.3%	−11.2%
Hungary	Budapest (BUX)–Price Index	−20.6%	−0.2%
Iceland	Iceland SE ICEX All Share Price Index	−18.7%	−0.1%
India	BSE 30	−19.9%	−17.8%
Indonesia	Jakarta Composite	6.6%	−7.8%
Ireland	Ireland ISEQ	−2.5%	−13.2%
Israel	TA–100	−20.1%	−9.2%
Italy	MIBTEL	−24.7%	−15.0%
Jamaica	Jamaica SE	19.7%	−4.9%
Japan	Nikkei 225	−26.0%	−4.9%
Jordan	Amman SE Financial Market Price Index	20.5%	−8.3%
Korea	Seoul Composite	9.1%	−14.3%
Latvia	Latvia Dow Jones RICI (LVL) Price Index	9.0%	−4.3%
Lithuania	Lithuania Litin Price Index	−34.6%	−2.4%
Malaysia	KLSE Composite	2.3%	−12.8%
Mauritius	Mauritius SE SEMDEX Price Index	−6.5%	−2.8%
Mexico	IPC	3.6%	−9.4%
Netherlands	AEX General	−24.2%	−11.2%
New Zealand	NZSE 40	2.6%	−6.7%
Norway	Total Share	−14.9%	−15.8%
Panama	Panama SE General	−9.2%	−0.1%
Peru	Lima General	7.7%	−7.8%
Philippines	PSE Composite	−13.2%	−10.4%
Poland	Warsaw General Price Index	−27.9%	−7.5%
Portugal	BVL 30	−28.0%	−2.0%
Romania	BET 10	39.3%	−7.6%
Russia	Moscow Times	57.0%	−12.8%
Singapore	Straits Times	−19.1%	−17.8%
Slovak Republic	SAX	25.0%	2.4%
Slovenia	Slovenian Price Index (PIX)	−0.3%	−0.5%
South Africa	Johannesburg SE All Share 40 Price Index	2.6%	−8.6%
Spain	Madrid General	−14.9%	−7.4%
Sri Lanka	All Share	−8.9%	−1.7%
Sweden	Stockholmsborsen All Share Price Index	−27.8%	1.6%
Switzerland	Swiss Market	−24.7%	−8.3%
Taiwan	Taiwan Weighted	−9.6%	−18.5%
Thailand	SET	23.2%	−16.6%
Trinidad & Tobago	S&P/IFCF Trinidad & Tobago Price Index	2.5%	0.0%
Turkey	ISE National–100	0.9%	−20.2%
UK	FTSE 100	−19.1%	−7.4%
Ukraine	PFTS Index	−9.0%	−2.7%
United States	Dow Jones	−11.0%	−9.8%
Venezuela	IBC	9.6%	−5.1%
Zimbabwe	Zimbabwe Industrial	175.5%	−8.6%

*Since August 3, 2001

Sources: Yahoo Business News, Bloomberg, Datastream

Table 2: Exchange rate fluctuations across GCR economies

Country	Change in currency value relative to US Dollar: Jan 1–Sep 10, 2001	Change in currency value relative to US Dollar: Sep 10–Sep 25, 2001
Argentina	−0.1%	−0.1%
Australia	−7.7%	−5.8%
Austria	−3.9%	1.0%
Bangladesh	−5.2%	−3.7%
Belgium	−3.9%	1.0%
Bolivia	−5.1%	−4.2%
Brazil	−32.4%	−10.5%
Bulgaria	−4.2%	2.7%
Canada	−4.6%	−0.2%
Chile	−16.3%	−7.6%
China	0.0%	−0.1%
Colombia	−3.6%	−4.3%
Costa Rica	−4.5%	−4.0%
Czech Republic	−0.2%	0.0%
Denmark	−3.6%	1.1%
Dominican Republic	−1.7%	−4.2%
Ecuador	0.0%	0.8%
Egypt	−11.0%	0.1%
El Salvador	0.0%	0.1%
Estonia	−3.9%	1.7%
Finland	−3.9%	1.0%
France	−3.9%	1.0%
Germany	−3.9%	1.0%
Greece	−3.9%	1.0%
Guatemala	−3.4%	−2.9%
Honduras	−3.1%	−4.2%
Hong Kong SAR	0.0%	0.0%
Hungary	0.5%	−2.1%
Iceland	−17.2%	−2.6%
India	−1.2%	−1.5%
Indonesia	5.7%	−4.1%
Ireland	−3.9%	1.0%
Israel	−6.6%	−1.0%
Italy	−3.9%	1.0%
Jamaica	−1.0%	0.0%
Japan	−5.0%	2.1%
Jordan	−0.2%	−0.3%
Korea	−1.8%	−1.1%
Latvia	−0.8%	0.8%
Lithuania	0.0%	0.1%
Malaysia	0.0%	−0.1%
Mauritius	−6.4%	−0.5%
Mexico	3.0%	−0.3%
Netherlands	−5.5%	1.0%
New Zealand	−2.0%	−8.3%
Nicaragua	−5.6%	0.0%
Nigeria	−2.4%	−2.9%
Norway	−0.4%	0.8%
Panama	0.0%	0.0%
Paraguay	−23.5%	−4.0%
Peru	1.3%	−4.8%
Philippines	−2.8%	0.4%
Poland	−2.2%	−0.4%
Portugal	−3.9%	1.0%
Romania	−16.4%	−2.8%
Russia	−3.1%	0.0%
Singapore	−0.8%	−1.4%
Slovak Republic	−2.0%	−0.4%
Slovenia	−6.9%	−0.3%
South Africa	−11.6%	−3.3%
Spain	−3.9%	1.0%
Sri Lanka	−9.0%	0.0%
Sweden	−11.5%	−2.6%
Switzerland	−3.5%	4.1%
Taiwan	−5.0%	−4.4%
Thailand	−2.7%	0.4%
Trinidad and Tobago	2.9%	0.0%
Turkey	−110.9%	−11.4%
Ukraine	1.6%	0.1%
United Kingdom	−2.2%	0.1%
Uruguay	−17.9%	−1.2%
Venezuela	−6.8%	0.5%
Vietnam	−3.3%	−4.2%
Zimbabwe	−1.3%	−2.4%

Source: Oanda.com

Flash survey

To assess the magnitude of the effects of September 11 over the coming six months, between September 26 and October 1 we conducted a "flash survey" of 90 senior executives whose companies are members of the World Economic Forum. We asked them six questions about how their business operations had been affected by the terrorist attacks in the United States, soliciting their views on both their companies' operations and their general view of the world economy. Although the limited sample size prevents rigorous statistical analysis, the main results—and their consistency across regions and sectors—provide useful insights into the current thinking in global business.

Overall, the survey indicates that the terrorist attack has had a slightly but not overwhelmingly negative effect on business and consumer confidence. It suggests that the global economy is more resilient than many observers would suggest. Interestingly, the survey also revealed consistent business sentiments around the globe. The interconnectedness of the international economy appears to be yielding broadly similar responses to the current cyclical economic downturn and the events of September 11. In this sense, the terrorist attacks of September 11 hit not only the United States but also nations around the globe.

Changes to corporate investment

Of the executives surveyed, fully 64 percent foresaw no change in corporate investment plans due to the events of September 11. Meanwhile, 19 percent foresaw their company's investment decreasing by only 10 percent or less, and only 15 percent anticipated cutting back more than 10 percent on investment. Only 2 percent foresaw an actual increase in investment. Notably, there was no geographic trend among the companies anticipating large drops in investment. Indeed, those expecting the biggest decreases were companies with global operations spanning several continents. In sectoral terms, more than half of the manufacturing companies anticipated no change in their investment; nor did a full 75 percent of the financial firms. It is of note that these results were collected even before US interest rates dropped to their lowest point in four decades on October 2. Apparently, despite the headline-grabbing stories of massive cutbacks in a few industries, many if not most firms have stable investment plans, relatively robust to the aftereffects of September 11.

Anticipated changes in demand

On a 1-to-7 scale question where 1 = large increase in demand, 4 = no effect, and 7 = large decrease in demand, 20 percent of respondents anticipated no change in demand for their products, while 18 percent looked forward to an increase in demand. Meanwhile 62 percent anticipated a decrease, but more than two-thirds of them anticipated the drop in demand to be only minor (ie, a score of 5). The overall average response was 4.5, with little variation in mean scores across business sectors. Variation was also fairly limited geographically, with average scores ranging from 4.0 for companies operating in Latin America to 4.6 for companies operating in East Asia.

Effects of increased risk and costs of business

Perhaps the most obvious repercussion from the terrorist hijackings involves increased risks, and therefore costs, of doing business. These costs include, for example, increased insurance premia, increased shipping times and expenses, reduced business travel, and general trade disruptions. In a question that asked executives to rate on a 1-to-7 scale the effects and aftermath of terrorist attacks on business costs (1 = small effect, 7 = large effect), the mean response was 4.0. Companies operating in Asia, Sub-Saharan Africa, and the Middle East and North Africa were slightly more pessimistic than their counterparts operating in other regions, rating means responses of 4.3, 4.4, and 4.3, respectively. Interestingly, the average score for executives identifying their companies as being in the information technology (IT) sector was 4.7. In a sector already buffeted by declining demand, pessimism about the effect of the attacks was greater. Of course, the overall short-term impact of trends such as decreases in business travel might have some longer-term benefits. Becoming accustomed to the potential of videoconferencing and Internet-based communication technology could help many companies lower operating costs.

Effects of potential disruptions to supply chains

Anticipated disruptions to supply chains were significant but less severe than expected cost increases. On the same 1-to-7 scale (1 = small effect, 7 = large effect), the mean response across the sample was 3.0. Respondents from firms operating in Asia or the Middle East and North Africa were slightly more pessimistic than their peers, rating mean responses of 3.3 and 3.4 respectively, but there were no other discernible geography-based differences in responses. In sectoral terms, IT producers were again the most concerned about supply chain disruptions, with a mean score of 3.9 for that group.

Effects of potential disruptions in world oil markets

Of great interest to all markets is the possibility that world oil market disruptions will affect businesses' operating environments. The flash survey responses reflected this uncertainty, with the average score among respondents (with 1 = small effect and 7 = large effect) being 3.7. Economies operating in Sub-Saharan Africa had worse expectations, with an average score of 4.6, while companies operating in Latin America were slightly more optimistic, with an average response of 3.4. Across sectors, the average score to this question was quite constant, except for firms involved in IT, who were again slightly more pessimistic with an average score of 4.5.

Overall recession perceptions

Of the executives surveyed, none foresaw strong world-wide economic growth in 2002. Twenty-one percent predicted modest growth, but a full 79 percent predicted recession in the year ahead. Of significant interest, however, is that slightly more than half of those predicting a recession believed that such a downturn was likely even *before* September 11. In our sample, executives with operations in the Middle East and North Africa were slightly more likely to believe that the events of September 11 will cause a recession, while those operating in Latin America were somewhat more likely to believe a recession was already in the offing. Among executives with operations in Asia, Western Europe, and North America, roughly 45 percent believed a recession was already underway, approximately 35 percent perceived September 11 as a major cause of a coming recession, and the remaining 20 percent predicted modest global growth in the year ahead. The breakdown of responses was quite similar across sectors. In most areas of business, a large majority of respondents foresaw a recession in the year ahead and roughly half of those people thought a recession was already underway. The one exception was for firms in the financial industry, where slightly more executives (by a 3 to 2 margin) saw September 11 as a key element in causing a coming recession.

Together, these results paint an intriguing picture of the world economy. Both corporate investment and consumer demand will ebb at least slightly in the near future, but perhaps not by as much as predicted by early fears. The relative stability of planned investment and only minor anticipated drop in consumer and corporate demand suggest that executives do not see the events of September 11 as being cataclysmic for the world economy. The persistence of this sentiment will no doubt depend on future political and military developments.

Countries at greatest risk

The flash survey results provide interesting insights into global business perspectives, but they raise an equally important question. Which countries will be the most affected by the heightened uncertainty? We can identify four main, sometimes overlapping, groups of countries in terms of exposure.

First are those emerging market economies whose growth in output is most closely linked to the US business cycle. These economies were already suffering before September 11 and are likely to bear a heavy burden if the US economy requires an extended period to regain momentum. This is particularly relevant to the East Asian export-oriented economies. As indicated in Table 3, Singapore's exports to the United States in July 2001 were a full 30 percent less than for the same month in the previous year, while Taiwan's decreased by 24 percent. Since Singapore's exports to the United States accounted for 21 percent of its gross domestic product in 2000 and Taiwan's accounted for 13 percent, these drops represent major changes for those economies. Also affected are Korea, Malaysia, the Philippines, and Thailand, all of which saw roughly 20 percent drops in July-on-July exports to the United States. Many of these economies had already expe-

Table 3: July 2001 versus July 2000 exports to United States for selected GCR economies most dependent on US trade

Country	Exports to United States as % of GDP in 2000	Change in Exports to United States, July 2000 vs July 2001
Canada	33%	-5%
Trinidad & Tobago	30%	-8%
Malaysia	29%	-19%
Nigeria	26%	-16%
Nicaragua	24%	-8%
Mexico	24%	-6%
Dominican Republic	22%	-7%
Costa Rica	22%	-17%
Singapore	21%	-30%
Philippines	19%	-20%
Ecuador	17%	15%
Ireland	17%	37%
Venezuela	15%	-17%
El Salvador	15%	-4%
Guatemala	14%	-2%
Thailand	13%	-16%
Taiwan	13%	-24%
Sri Lanka	12%	4%
Israel	12%	-22%
Estonia	11%	-49%
China	9%	-6%
Korea	9%	-22%
Colombia	8%	-19%
Jamaica	8%	-27%
Hong Kong SAR	7%	-15%
Indonesia	7%	4%
Mauritius	7%	14%

Sources: US Census Bureau, IMF *World Economic Outlook May 2001*, and authors' calculations

rienced a major slump in demand for their information and communication technology-based exports as US firms continued to recover from the technology market bubble that burst in 2000.

Second are those economies with high levels of sovereign debt, particularly those with high debt-to-export ratios. Although interest rates have been lowered across the G-7 since September 11, 10-year US Treasuries have only decreased approximately 50 basis points, while the risk premia and long-term bond markets have expanded by nearly 100 basis points (and in some instances much more) in the weeks following the attacks. Economies such as Argentina, Bolivia, Brazil, Nicaragua, and Peru that have high debt-to-export ratios could be seriously strained in their ability to finance new debt or refinance old debt in the months ahead. Table 4 indicates some selected fluctuations in bond market risk spreads since September 11.

Third are the economies likely to be disrupted by interruptions to existing trade patterns, caused by increased insurance and freight costs, lengthened shipping times, and extended delays at customs. This will particularly affect economies reliant on ocean shipping and air cargo, again including the highly trade-dependent export-oriented economies of East Asia—notably Singapore, Taiwan, Korea, and Malaysia. But it is also likely to affect Canadian and Mexican firms facing longer delays at United States border crossings.

Fourth are those countries dependent on travel and tourism as significant sources of national income. The World Bank recently estimated that 65 percent of holidays to the Caribbean have been canceled for the short-term. It is difficult to predict how long this reluctance to travel will last and how long it will take for people to regain confidence in flying, but in the short term it will definitely

have an adverse impact for countries such as Jamaica, which had tourism receipts equivalent to nearly 18 percent of its gross domestic product in 1999, the most recent year for which World Bank data are available. Mauritius is similarly exposed to fluctuations in tourism, with tourist earnings equal to 13 percent of its GDP. The Dominican Republic and Costa Rica, two countries heavily dependent on US markets for their exports, are likewise dependent on tourism, with tourist receipts estimated at 9.6 and 6.6 percent of those economies, respectively. As noted in Table 5, tourism receipts account for more than 5 percent of GDP in several European countries as well, but visitors are less likely to stay away from those economies since air travel markets have been less disrupted in Europe than in North America and also because train service is an easier alternative means for travel in Europe.

What can be done?

With short-term real interest rates low, and corporate investment plans so far only mildly affected by September 11, the economic responses should include a set of confidence-building measures to stimulate consumer *and corporate* demand and help maintain the efficiency of international production networks. Amidst the formidable uncertainty, means are needed to ensure that the networks of the international economy continue to operate efficiently and with minimal disruption.

The main lesson of modern economic history is that we live in a globally networked economy, where major disruptions to global trade, finance, travel, and production have significant effects across the world economy. Even before September 11, this became evident once again. This year's global economic fallout from the bursting of the US financial bubble was already proving to be much sharper than originally predicted because the linkages across markets were stronger than had been commonly understood. Even economies such as Singapore and Taiwan, which rank very highly on our lead competitiveness Indexes, are being severely affected by this fallout. This does not imply that these economies are becoming less competitive, but rather that even the most competitive economies in the world are being affected by a cyclical downturn.

Policymakers must avoid confusing structural, cyclical, and short-term issues. When global demand picks up again, these competitive economies will be well positioned. The key is to ensure the stability of the networks and linkages that allow economies to interact with the greatest efficiency. Any central economic response to September 11, therefore, must involve bolstering the framework of globalization and recommitting governments around the world to making the world economy work for all nations, including the poorest. Without that, confidence in the international economic framework will remain dented.

Table 4: Selected sovereign bond risk spreads, September 10, 2001, versus October 2, 2001

	SEP 10, 2001	OCT 2, 2001
Sovereign Bond Risk Spreads		
Argentina	12.96	13.39
Brazil	10.14	11.85
Lebanon	5.31	6.72
Mexico	3.30	4.22
Philippines	6.82	8.10
South Africa	2.54	2.96
Brady Bond Risk Spreads		
Argentina	5.42	6.32
Brazil	7.52	9.13
Mexico	1.69	2.12
Venezuela	4.24	4.66
US Long-Term Interest Rates		
10-Year US Treasuries	4.84	4.51

Source: *Financial Times*

Table 5: Selected GCR economies for which tourism receipts represent a large share of national product

Country	Tourism Receipts as a % of GDP
Jamaica	17.9%
Mauritius	13.1%
Dominican Republic	9.6%
Bulgaria	7.1%
Costa Rica	6.6%
Hungary	6.5%
Greece	6.2%
Czech Republic	5.8%
Spain	5.5%
Thailand	5.4%
Austria	5.3%
Lithuania	5.2%
Slovenia	5.1%
Egypt	4.6%
Nicaragua	4.5%
Hong Kong SAR	4.5%

Source: World Bank, *World Development Indicators 2001*

Most importantly, policymakers need to continue pursuing the diplomacy needed to avoid large-scale global conflict. Military reprisals are a certainty, but for many reasons the biggest mistake would be to instigate the kind of response that sends the world into a wider military conflict. Although less important than the direct loss of lives, the economic costs would be horrendous.

Second, there needs to be confidence in the basic infrastructure of international trade and transport. Security at airports, seaports, and other nodes of commerce and travel should be enhanced.

Third, OPEC should continue making its supply decisions in a manner that avoids any disruptions in oil supplies or pricing. The OPEC member governments are among the most vulnerable to the current global crisis, and should readily commit to such an international pledge.

Fourth, the leading central banks must continue to ensure the ample supply of liquidity, as they have been doing since the attacks in the United States. With Japan already in recession, the Bank of Japan should take even more aggressive action to stabilize the economy by selling enough yen to prevent any further appreciation of the currency, and even some depreciation, as that is sorely needed for Japanese recovery.

Fifth, the world should launch a new trade round at the WTO Ministerial Meeting in November, to signal the intention of all member countries of the WTO to persevere in the path of free trade. It is time for the rich countries to respect the wishes of the poor in getting such a trade round off the ground. That would require proactive steps by the wealthy economies of the world to ensure that the developing country exporters have improved access to rich country markets (especially for apparel and agriculture exports) and to negotiate mutually acceptable solutions to poor countries' concerns about access to essential medicines.

Sixth, the United States should comprehensively revamp and expand its assistance efforts for the world's poorest nations. Lack of economic development is a root cause of social unrest and violence, so the United States and other rich countries need to recognize the overwhelming strategic benefits gleaned from supporting poor nations' economic development. Perhaps most crucially, the United States needs to provide more leadership and financing to provide debt relief and financial help for the world's poorest countries so that they can battle the disease epidemics of AIDS, malaria, and tuberculosis that are currently killing millions of poor people each year.

Concluding thoughts

The international economy has recently become characterized by unprecedented levels of interconnectedness in global production, communication, and transportation networks. Even prior to September 11, we were seeing how the linkages in those networks intertwine the fates of economies around the globe. In light of the unimaginable horror of the attacks of September 11, policymakers need to find ways to protect those networks amidst a climate of uncertainty and, in many instances, fear.

The consolidation and expansion of global networks requires ongoing policy attention both within and between borders. While policymakers will understandably focus on the international issues we have highlighted above, they must also continue to focus on the efforts to improve the underlying structures of their domestic economies. There can be little doubt that the continued development of economies around the world will play a pivotal role in reducing the anger and sense of fatalism that ferments terror and armed conflict. Moreover, even amidst the shock and horror we all feel in the aftermath of September 11, we must not forget or ignore the tremendous economic progress that has been made by dozens of countries in recent years, and that must be continued in order to reduce poverty and promote global living standards. To this end, we hope the information contained in this year's *Global Competitiveness Report* will prove useful for policymakers hoping to enhance continuously their economies' long-term capacity to support and promote the economic foundations of human well being. This is the only way to address security concerns successfully in the long run.

13

Table 1. Overall competitiveness rankings

GROWTH COMPETITIVENESS INDEX RANKING

Country	Growth Competitiveness Ranking 2001	Growth Competitiveness Ranking 2001 among GCR 2000 countries	Growth Competitiveness Ranking 2000
Finland	1	1	5
United States	2	2	1
Canada	3	3	6
Singapore	4	4	2
Australia	5	5	11
Norway	6	6	15
Taiwan	7	7	10
Netherlands	8	8	3
Sweden	9	9	12
New Zealand	10	10	19
Ireland	11	11	4
United Kingdom	12	12	8
Hong Kong SAR	13	13	7
Denmark	14	14	13
Switzerland	15	15	9
Iceland	16	16	23
Germany	17	17	14
Austria	18	18	17
Belgium	19	19	16
France	20	20	21
Japan	21	21	20
Spain	22	22	26
Korea	23	23	28
Israel	24	24	18
Portugal	25	25	22
Italy	26	26	29
Chile	27	27	27
Hungary	28	28	25
Estonia	29	—	—
Malaysia	30	29	24
Slovenia	31	—	—
Mauritius	32	30	35
Thailand	33	31	30
South Africa	34	32	32
Costa Rica	35	33	37
Greece	36	34	33
Czech Republic	37	35	31
Trinidad and Tobago	38	—	—
China	39	36	40
Slovak Republic	40	37	38
Poland	41	38	34
Mexico	42	39	42
Lithuania	43	—	—
Brazil	44	40	45
Jordan	45	41	46
Uruguay	46	—	—
Latvia	47	—	—
Philippines	48	42	36
Argentina	49	43	44
Dominican Republic	50	—	—
Egypt	51	44	41
Jamaica	52	—	—
Panama	53	—	—
Turkey	54	45	39
Peru	55	46	47
Romania	56	—	—
India	57	47	48
El Salvador	58	48	49
Bulgaria	59	49	57
Vietnam	60	50	52
Sri Lanka	61	—	—
Venezuela	62	51	53
Russia	63	52	54
Indonesia	64	53	43
Colombia	65	54	51
Guatemala	66	—	—
Bolivia	67	55	50
Ecuador	68	56	58
Ukraine	69	57	56
Honduras	70	—	—
Bangladesh	71	—	—
Paraguay	72	—	—
Nicaragua	73	—	—
Nigeria	74	—	—
Zimbabwe	75	58	55

CURRENT COMPETITIVENESS INDEX RANKING

Country	Current Competitiveness Ranking 2001	Current Competitiveness Ranking 2001 among GCR 2000 countries	Current Competitiveness Ranking 2000
Finland	1	1	1
United States	2	2	2
Netherlands	3	3	4
Germany	4	4	3
Switzerland	5	5	5
Sweden	6	6	7
United Kingdom	7	7	8
Denmark	8	8	6
Australia	9	9	10
Singapore	10	10	9
Canada	11	11	11
France	12	12	15
Austria	13	13	13
Belgium	14	14	12
Japan	15	15	14
Iceland	16	16	17
Israel	17	17	18
Hong Kong SAR	18	18	16
Norway	19	19	20
New Zealand	20	20	19
Taiwan	21	21	21
Ireland	22	22	22
Spain	23	23	23
Italy	24	24	24
South Africa	25	25	25
Hungary	26	26	32
Estonia	27	—	—
Korea	28	27	27
Chile	29	28	26
Brazil	30	29	31
Portugal	31	30	28
Slovenia	32	—	—
Turkey	33	31	29
Trinidad and Tobago	34	—	—
Czech Republic	35	32	34
India	36	33	37
Malaysia	37	34	30
Thailand	38	35	40
Slovak Republic	39	36	36
Jamaica	40	—	—
Poland	41	37	41
Latvia	42	—	—
Greece	43	38	33
Jordan	44	39	35
Egypt	45	40	39
Uruguay	46	—	—
China	47	41	44
Panama	48	—	—
Lithuania	49	—	—
Costa Rica	50	42	43
Mexico	51	43	42
Mauritius	52	44	38
Argentina	53	45	45
Philippines	54	46	46
Indonesia	55	47	47
Colombia	56	48	48
Sri Lanka	57	—	—
Russia	58	49	52
Dominican Republic	59	—	—
Ukraine	60	50	56
Romania	61	—	—
Vietnam	62	51	53
Peru	63	52	49
El Salvador	64	53	51
Zimbabwe	65	54	50
Venezuela	66	55	54
Nigeria	67	—	—
Bulgaria	68	56	55
Guatemala	69	—	—
Paraguay	70	—	—
Nicaragua	71	—	—
Ecuador	72	57	57
Bangladesh	73	—	—
Honduras	74	—	—
Bolivia	75	58	58

Executive Summary:
Competitiveness and Stages of Economic Development

MICHAEL E. PORTER, Institute for Strategy and Competitiveness, Harvard Business School

JEFFREY D. SACHS, Center for International Development at Harvard University

JOHN W. MCARTHUR, Center for International Development at Harvard University

This year's *Global Competitiveness Report* appears in the aftermath of the September 11 terrorist attacks in the United States. Although this *Report* was already at the editor on that watershed date, we felt it important to supplement the medium-term (five-year) analysis that is contained in the annual *Report* with a separate, shorter-term analysis of the world economy, which is included in the new Introduction. The *Report*'s underlying medium-term analysis is still relevant in the high likelihood that the world economy and the globalization process continue apace, despite the shock of this tragedy and the short-term uncertainties and dislocations created in its wake. Indeed, we regard the potential gains from globalization, if properly managed, as so vital to world welfare that we urge the international community to do all in its power to preserve the peaceful and deepening economic linkages around the world, and to best ensure that they serve to benefit all countries rich and poor.

The *Global Competitiveness Report* focuses on two distinct but complementary approaches to the analysis of economic competitiveness. The first, led by Professor Jeffrey D Sachs of the Center for International Development at Harvard University, focuses on global competitiveness as "the set of institutions and economic policies supportive of high rates of economic growth in the medium term." Prior to 2000, the *Report* presented an overall index based on this approach that was known simply as the Competitiveness Index. Starting with the 2000 *Report*, this measure was relabeled the Growth Competitiveness Index, or GCI. Building on the foundations of theoretical and empirical macroeconomics, the GCI represents a best estimate of 75 economies' underlying prospects for growth over the coming five years. This year's *Report* assesses the growth prospects in 17 countries not previously covered, including Bangladesh, Nigeria, Romania, Slovenia, Sri Lanka, and the three Baltic countries, as well as nine economies in Latin America and the Caribbean.

The *Report*'s second approach to competitiveness, led by Professor Michael E Porter of the Institute for Strategy and Competitiveness at the Harvard Business School, is embodied in the Current Competitiveness Index, or CCI, as first presented in last year's edition. The CCI uses microeconomic indicators to measure the "set of institutions, market structures, and economic policies supportive of high current levels of prosperity," referring mainly to an economy's effective utilization of its current stock of resources. This Index thus assesses the current productive potential of the same 75 economies. Together the GCI and CCI present distinct yet highly complementary insights into sources of national competitiveness.

Both the GCI and CCI combine hard data and unique survey data to assess competitiveness in a large sample of countries. Central to both Indexes is the Executive Opinion Survey, conducted annually by the World Economic Forum. The Survey is indispensable to the *Report*, since no reliable hard data sources exist for many of the most important aspects of an economy such as the efficiency of government institutions, the sophistication of local supplier networks, or the nature of competitive practices. Even where hard data are available, the data often do not cover all the countries in our sample. The Executive Opinion Survey records the perspectives of business leaders around the world by asking them to compare aspects of their local business environment with global standards, this year including more than 4,600 respondents. The business leaders surveyed actually make many of the investment and policy decisions that drive economic growth and development, so by recording their perspectives we obtain an incomparable, up-to-date knowledge base concerning the current state of economic affairs in each of the 75 countries assessed.

Transitions in economic development

This year's *Global Competitiveness Report* emphasizes an increasingly important theme confronting many nations: Countries face very different challenges and priorities as they move from resource-based to knowledge-based economies.[i] As an economy develops, so do its structural bases of global competitiveness. At low levels of development, economic growth is determined primarily by the mobilization of primary factors of production: land, primary commodities, and unskilled labor. As economies move from low- to middle-income status, global competitiveness becomes Investment-Driven, as economic growth is increasingly achieved by harnessing global technologies to local production. Foreign direct investment, joint ventures, and outsourcing arrangements help to integrate the national economy into international production systems, thereby facilitating the improvement of technologies and the inflows of foreign capital and technologies that support economic growth. In most economies, the evolution from middle-income to high-income status involves the transition from a technology-importing economy to a technology-generating economy, one that innovates in at least some sectors at the global technological frontier. For high-income economies at this Innovation-Driven stage of economic development, global competitiveness is critically linked to high rates of social learning (especially science-based learning) and the rapid ability to shift to new technologies.

The principal factors that contribute to global competitiveness, and thereby improve living standards, will therefore differ for economies at different levels of development. For some low-income economies, the main challenge is to get the basic factor markets—for land, labor, and capital—working properly. As countries advance, the basic challenge is to make connections with international production systems by attracting sufficient flows of FDI. Once reaching high-income status, the basic challenge facing countries is typically to generate high rates of innovation and commercialization of new technologies. The critical institutions in a country, and its barriers to continued growth, will therefore differ depending on that country's current position.

Successful economic development is thus a process of successive upgrading, in which businesses and their supporting environments co-evolve, to foster increasingly sophisticated ways of producing and competing. Seeing economic development as a sequential process of building not just macroeconomic stability but also interdependent factors such as quality of governance, societal capacity to advance its technological capability, more advanced modes of competition, and evolving forms of firm organizational structure, helps to expose important potential pitfalls in economic policy. To evolve successfully through different levels of development, key parts of the economic environment must change at appropriate times. Lack of improvement in any important area can lead to a plateau in productivity and stalled economic growth.

At low levels of development, government's main job is to provide overall political and macroeconomic stability and sufficiently free markets to permit the effective utilization of primary commodities and unskilled labor both by indigenous firms and through attracting foreign investment. Firms produce commodities or relatively simple products of long-standardized technology designed in other more advanced countries. Technology is assimilated through imports, foreign direct investment, and imitation. In this stage, companies compete on price and often lack direct access to consumers. They have limited roles in the value chain, focused on assembly, labor-intensive manufacturing, and resource extraction. A Factor-Driven economy is highly sensitive to world economic cycles, commodity price trends, and exchange rate fluctuations.

As development proceeds, government priorities need to focus increasingly on improvements in physical infrastructure (ports, telecommunications, roads) and regulatory arrangements (customs, taxation, company law) to allow the economy to integrate more fully with global markets. In this Investment-Driven phase, efficiency in producing standard products and services becomes a dominant source of global competitiveness. The products and services produced become more sophisticated, but technology and designs still largely come from abroad. Technology is accessed through licensing, joint ventures, foreign direct investment, and imitation. Nations in this stage not only assimilate foreign technology, however, but they also develop the capacity to improve on it. The national business environment supports investment in efficient infrastructure and modern production methods. Companies often produce under contract to foreign original equipment manufacturers (OEM), which control design and marketing. Gradually, companies extend capabilities more widely in the value chain. An Investment-Driven economy is concentrated on manufacturing and on outsourced service exports. It is susceptible to financial crises since it relies heavily on foreign capital flows, as well as external sector-specific demand shocks.

Perhaps the hardest transition is from technology-importing, efficiency-based development to innovation-based development. This requires a direct government role in fostering a high rate of innovation, through public as well as private investments in research and development, higher education, and improved capital markets and regulatory systems that support the start-up of high-technology enterprises. At this innovation stage, enterprises themselves become less hierarchical, with much more delegation of authority to sub-units within the enterprise. Buyers and suppliers and corporate sub-units are often linked together in flexible networking arrangements that facilitate innovations and rapid shifts in the division of labor within the organization. Firms invest heavily in the continual training and upgrading of their workforce. Compensation systems involve incentive payment schemes linked to the productivity of different parts of the enterprise. In the same way, the firms within an industry also become much more interactive, with deep industrial clusters characterized by a sophisticated division of labor, increasing flows of workers between enterprises, and a mix of fierce competition and cooperation among enterprises within an industry. Companies compete with unique strategies that are often global in scope. Such characteristics have been noted in American high-tech regions such as Silicon Valley, Route 128 in Boston, and the Research Triangle of North Carolina.

It is our hypothesis that many of the failures in economic development in recent years involve countries getting stuck at critical junctures of economic transition: Between Factor-Driven and Investment-Driven or between Investment-Driven and Innovation-Driven stages. For example, some countries successfully master the initial phase of Factor-Driven growth, but then fail to make the transition to technology imports and globalized production systems. Others effectively reach the investment phase of development, but then fail to progress to homegrown innovation. These transition points are indeed difficult to manage from both a macroeconomic and microeconomic perspective. The shift from one phase of development to the next often requires new ways of organizing governments, markets, and enterprises, so it is not altogether surprising therefore that many countries fail at making the appropriate transitions, or even fail to recognize that such a transition is needed. The transition from primary commodities to increased utilization of imported technologies to innovation requires changes in government priorities and spending patterns as well as in the internal structure and aims of business enterprises. Shifts in both macroeconomic policy and microeconomic business structure are necessary. Ironically, old strategies become the new weaknesses. A highly opportunistic corporate approach that worked well serving disparate OEM customers, for example, becomes a liability in making the long-term commitments required for advanced production processes and pursuing true innovations.

This framework helps to highlight why some countries enjoy significant economic progress for a period and then appear to stall in their development. When economies reach transition points, they require wholesale transformation of many interdependent dimensions. Successful Investment-Driven economies such as Taiwan and Singapore, for example, are finding that their reliance on sustained infrastructure investments, OEM manufacturing for multinationals, and government guidance of the economy to boost efficiency are insufficient to support very high levels of prosperity. Their current level of wages and domestic costs makes them vulnerable to competition from lower-wage countries such as China. Likewise Ireland, which has been tremendously successful in attracting foreign investment for manufacturing, now faces the need to justify higher wages and higher local costs without yet having developed a world-class innovative structure. In a more severe example, Argentina has become caught in the early Investment-Driven stage of development where it still has to compete on price, but its overvalued exchange rate and lack of technological sophistication and scientific innovative capacity are combining to keep the economy in crisis. The challenge for all these economies is to move to an Innovation-Driven economy with world-class technological capacities and the presence of deep clusters. To do so, companies need to move to new types of strategies, investment priorities must change, higher education must take on even greater importance, and government's role in the economy needs to shift.

One of the principal goals of the *Global Competitiveness Report* is to identify the policy challenges that face governments at various levels of development. As suggested earlier, some tasks are common to all governments: macroeconomic stability, provision of basic medical and health care, openness of the economy, and a competitive exchange rate that supports export growth. Some tasks are critical for countries attempting to move beyond a traditional primary commodity base: improvements of infrastructure, universal secondary education, improved technical education, and flexibility of labor markets. Finally, special tasks are required for countries attempting to move from technology-using to technology-innovating economies: for example, a venture capital sector as well as other improved financial and legal arrangements for new startups, increased government spending on R&D, and improved legal tools for intellectual property rights. Reflecting their complementary perspectives, the Growth Competitiveness Index and Current Competitiveness Index aim to shed light on the respective macro and micro priorities at various phases of economic development.

The Growth Competitiveness Index

Building on the latest developments in economic growth research, as well as the results from recent years' *Global Competitiveness Reports*, the Growth Competitiveness Index methodology has been updated since last year to provide a ranking of the underlying potential for medium-term (five years) growth that better accounts for the widely varying levels of development of the included countries. As outlined in detail in Chapter 1.1 by John W McArthur and Jeffrey D Sachs, the GCI divides the *Report*'s sample of 75 countries into two main groups based on their level of technological capacity. Using patenting as a measure of innovative capacity, the Growth Competitiveness chapter identifies the 21 Innovation-Driven economies in the world today, for which it uses the shorthand term *core* economies (a term with no moral judgments intended, simply a statement about innovation as the source of growth!). It then attempts to identify the specific factors in technological advancement among these core economies. At the same time, the GCI includes an entirely separate measure of technological advancement for the non-innovating (or *non-core*) economies, one that puts more weight on technological diffusion as these economies absorb and adapt production practices developed mainly by the innovating economies.

The GCI not only incorporates the differing forms of technological advancement that are linked to growth in the core and non-core economies, but also stresses the differing importance of technological advancement for these two groups of economies. The GCI is comprised of three subindexes: the level of technology in an economy, the quality of public institutions, and the macroeconomic conditions related to growth. Among the world's core economies, statistical evidence indicates that innovation plays a dominant role in medium-term economic growth. For these economies, the GCI thus places a weight of 1/2 on the technology index against weights of 1/4 each on public institutions and macroeconomic environment. Among the non-core economies, technological advancement, measured largely by the economies' performance in skill-based manufacturing exports, appears to play a more limited role relative to the other two factors. Thus, the GCI places a weight of 1/3 on each component index when calculating overall scores for the non-innovating economies. For the three economies that appear to be at the cusp of innovation-driven growth—Hong Kong SAR, Ireland, and Singapore—GCI values are calculated as an average of those economies' scores using the core and non-core formulas.

The new GCI results are listed in Table 1, which shows this year's overall rankings as well as the change in rankings among only those countries included in this and last year's *Reports*. Finland, for the first time, ranks first in the world, indicating that it now has the best prospects for growth over the next five years. This country's remarkable turnaround over the past decade serves as evidence of how quickly an economy's prospects can be transformed by strong political institutions, a focus on technology, and sound macroeconomic management. The United States ranks second. Although the United States is currently at risk of a recession, it is still far and away the world's technological leader and engine of economic growth in the medium term. Canada, the sixth-ranked economy in the 2000 GCI, rounds out the top three places, having moved up in the growth rankings mainly due to this year's weight accorded to tertiary education as a key factor in technological innovation. Australia and New Zealand, two other countries with strong measures of university-educated human capital, have jumped significantly in the growth rankings from 11th to 5th and 19th to 10th spots, respectively. Notably, and reflecting their looming challenges in making the transition from investment-based to innovation-based growth, Singapore has dropped from 2nd to 4th place, Ireland has dropped from 4th to 11th, and Hong Kong SAR has shifted from 7th to 13th. Meanwhile, Japan's ongoing economic stagnation is reflected in its continuing low position at 21st, down one slot from last year.

19

Other notable GCI results include the strong growth prospects of new entries Estonia, at 29th, and Slovenia, at 31st. Estonia's ranking is well ahead of the results for Baltic neighbors Lithuania (43) and Latvia (47). Results lower down the list are generally more stable, with the important exceptions of Turkey, which dropped six spots compared with last year, and Indonesia, which tumbled 10 places. Of additional importance are the newly included Latin American economies, most of which scored in the lower quintile of the growth rankings, frequently reflecting their difficulty in emerging from a Factor-Driven to an Investment-oriented stage of development. Brazil, nonetheless, has moved up five spots, ranking 44th in the expanded sample, while Chile holds steady in 27th. Other relatively bright spots in Latin America include new entrants Uruguay at 46th and the Dominican Republic at 50th.

Bangladesh and Nigeria, the two poorest economies in our sample, are included in this year's *Report* for the first time ever and, perhaps not surprisingly, rank near the very bottom of the GCI scale. This should not, however, be taken as a sign of pessimism about these economies. Indeed, the avid willingness of business people in those economies to participate in the Executive Survey reflected a remarkable interest in policy dialogue and subsequent economic transformation. As this *Report's* chapter on Growth Competitiveness also outlines, both Bangladesh and Nigeria have a tremendous opportunity for what economists call "catch-up" growth if those countries are able to continue to enhance their political and technological capacities under the auspices of stable macroeconomics.

The GCI's component indexes on technology, public institutions, and macroeconomic environment are reported within the same chapter and are presented here in Table 2. Careful assessment of these indexes and the variables they comprise reveals many of the relative strengths and weaknesses to growth within each economy. China and Korea provide two very brief examples. China ranks 6th on the macroeconomic environment index, but only 50th on the measure of public institutions and 53rd on the technology index, yielding an overall GCI ranking in 39th place. Korea, on the other hand, ranks 9th in technology and 8th for its macroeconomic environment, but 44th for its public institutions, producing a 23rd place score overall. Underlying these indexes are numerous subindexes that can be investigated in some detail, thereby providing policymakers and business leaders reading this *Report* with valuable information regarding how best to advance their economies' growth prospects.

Table 2. Rankings of growth competitiveness component indexes

Country	GCI Ranking	Technology Index Rank	Public Institutions Index Rank	Macroeconomic Environment Index Rank
Finland	1	3	1	10
United States	2	1	12	7
Canada	3	2	11	13
Singapore	4	18	6	1
Australia	5	5	8	17
Norway	6	7	16	5
Taiwan	7	4	24	15
Netherlands	8	14	5	9
Sweden	9	6	7	29
New Zealand	10	11	4	14
Ireland	11	28	18	2
United Kingdom	12	10	9	12
Hong Kong SAR	13	33	10	4
Denmark	14	12	3	31
Switzerland	15	24	13	3
Iceland	16	19	2	34
Germany	17	15	17	19
Austria	18	16	15	26
Belgium	19	13	22	24
France	20	17	20	22
Japan	21	23	19	18
Spain	22	27	23	11
Korea	23	9	44	8
Israel	24	26	14	61
Portugal	25	25	25	35
Italy	26	31	27	23
Chile	27	42	21	21
Hungary	28	21	26	38
Estonia	29	8	29	43
Malaysia	30	22	39	20
Slovenia	31	30	30	39
Mauritius	32	37	32	30
Thailand	33	39	42	16
South Africa	34	46	35	27
Costa Rica	35	32	37	42
Greece	36	38	40	32
Czech Republic	37	20	53	49
Trinidad and Tobago	38	52	36	25
China	39	53	50	6
Slovak Republic	40	29	38	64
Poland	41	35	41	50
Mexico	42	36	56	36
Lithuania	43	41	34	56
Brazil	44	49	47	33
Jordan	45	54	28	54
Uruguay	46	45	31	63
Latvia	47	34	48	59
Philippines	48	40	64	28
Argentina	49	48	55	40
Dominican Republic	50	44	54	46
Egypt	51	64	33	51
Jamaica	52	43	43	71
Panama	53	57	59	44
Turkey	54	51	46	68
Peru	55	62	45	58
Romania	56	47	52	67
India	57	66	49	45
El Salvador	58	58	60	47
Bulgaria	59	50	51	69
Vietnam	60	65	63	37
Sri Lanka	61	59	58	60
Venezuela	62	55	65	53
Russia	63	60	61	57
Indonesia	64	61	66	41
Colombia	65	56	57	66
Guatemala	66	68	70	52
Bolivia	67	67	62	70
Ecuador	68	69	68	62
Ukraine	69	63	71	73
Honduras	70	70	72	72
Bangladesh	71	74	75	48
Paraguay	72	73	74	65
Nicaragua	73	71	67	74
Nigeria	74	75	73	55
Zimbabwe	75	72	69	75

The Current Competitiveness Index

Whereas the Growth Competitiveness Index strives to estimate the underlying conditions for growth over the coming five years, the Current Competitiveness Index (CCI) evaluates the underlying conditions defining the *current* level of productivity in each of the 75 economies covered. Using a microeconomic approach focusing on the detailed conditions that support a high level of sustainable productivity, measured by GDP per capita, the CCI aims to move beyond the examination of broad, aggregate variables characteristic of most economic growth models. Using common factor analysis, the Current Competitiveness Index (CCI) is an aggregate measure of microeconomic competitiveness. This chapter also reports two subindexes, one focusing on company sophistication and the other on quality of the national business environment drawing on a complex array of variables with a demonstrated statistical relationship to GDP per capita.

This year's CCI rankings are shown in Table 1, while subrankings on the sophistication of company operating practices in each country and the quality of the business environment are presented in Table 3. For the second year, Finland edges out the United States to achieve the number one ranking. Advanced nations improving their current competitiveness ranking in 2001 include the Netherlands, Sweden, Australia, Austria, France, and Iceland. Advanced countries that experienced a decline in the rankings in 2001 include Germany, Denmark, and Belgium in Europe; and Singapore, Japan, and Hong Kong SAR in Asia. Developing nations that improved their current competitiveness rankings on a comparable sample basis include Hungary, India, Thailand, Poland, China, Russia, and Ukraine. Developing countries whose position has fallen include Chile, Malaysia, Turkey, the Czech Republic, Greece, Jordan, Mauritius, and Peru. As important as the overall ranking, however, is the subrankings and specific strengths and weaknesses presented in the *Report*. Taken together, they provide a concrete set of priorities for national action.

Table 3: Rankings on current competitiveness component indexes

Country	CCI Ranking	Company Operations and Strategy Ranking	Quality of the National Business Environment Ranking
Finland	1	2	1
United States	2	1	2
Netherlands	3	3	3
Germany	4	4	4
Switzerland	5	5	5
Sweden	6	6	6
United Kingdom	7	7	8
Denmark	8	9	10
Australia	9	24	7
Singapore	10	15	9
Canada	11	14	11
France	12	10	12
Austria	13	11	13
Belgium	14	12	14
Japan	15	8	18
Iceland	16	16	15
Israel	17	18	17
Hong Kong SAR	18	21	16
Norway	19	23	19
New Zealand	20	19	20
Taiwan	21	20	21
Ireland	22	17	22
Spain	23	22	23
Italy	24	13	24
South Africa	25	25	27
Hungary	26	33	25
Estonia	27	32	26
Korea	28	26	30
Chile	29	30	28
Brazil	30	29	32
Portugal	31	38	29
Slovenia	32	28	35
Turkey	33	44	31
Trinidad and Tobago	34	27	37
Czech Republic	35	41	33
India	36	43	34
Malaysia	37	37	38
Thailand	38	42	39
Slovak Republic	39	57	36
Jamaica	40	31	44
Poland	41	55	40
Latvia	42	35	43
Greece	43	51	42
Jordan	44	56	41
Egypt	45	36	46
Uruguay	46	48	45
China	47	39	47
Panama	48	40	49
Lithuania	49	47	48
Costa Rica	50	34	52
Mexico	51	46	53
Mauritius	52	49	50
Argentina	53	53	51
Philippines	54	45	54
Indonesia	55	50	57
Colombia	56	52	59
Sri Lanka	57	58	55
Russia	58	54	56
Dominican Republic	59	59	58
Ukraine	60	62	60
Romania	61	63	61
Vietnam	62	64	64
Peru	63	65	62
El Salvador	64	66	63
Zimbabwe	65	60	67
Venezuela	66	67	66
Nigeria	67	61	68
Bulgaria	68	70	65
Guatemala	69	69	69
Paraguay	70	68	71
Nicaragua	71	73	70
Ecuador	72	71	72
Bangladesh	73	72	73
Honduras	74	74	75
Bolivia	75	75	74

The CCI measures the level of GDP per capita that is sustainable in the long term. However, in the short and medium run, nations can over- or underperform their microeconomic fundamentals because of surges of inbound FDI, natural resource windfalls, and the like. The chapter compares a country's *expected* GDP per capita, given its current microeconomic competitiveness, with its actual GDP per capita. A positive gap signals upside potential, while a negative gap indicates vulnerability. Finland leads the advanced countries in upside potential, which is consistent with its high GCI ranking. Finland's stunning turnaround in microeconomic competitiveness is still far from being fully realized in terms of reported prosperity. Conversely, Norway, Iceland, and Ireland all continue to enjoy a level of prosperity that exceeds their microeconomic fundamentals. This suggests a challenge for these countries in maintaining their current success. To a lesser extent this is also true for the United States and Canada.

Turkey, Brazil, and South Africa are among the middle-income countries that should be able to support a higher GDP per but are currently underperforming for various reasons. The converse is true for Greece, Argentina, Russia, and Slovenia, which are among a group of countries whose levels of income will be unsustainable without substantial microeconomic reform. India heads the list of low-income countries with upside potential that could be unlocked by governmental and political reform.

Our findings make it clear that micro reforms must go beyond reducing the role of government and abolishing market distortions. Government also has a range of positive roles that are fundamental to prosperity—such as investing in specialized human resources, building innovative capacity, facilitating cluster development, and stimulating advanced demand via regulatory standards. Many nations need to move beyond first stage micro reforms and address these agendas.

In keeping with the overall theme of this year's *Report*, our results highlight the need to set a nation's economic priorities to be consistent with its level of development. Especially challenging are the difficult transitions between competitive stages. At the Factor-Driven stage, our findings suggest the core challenge for firms is to increase their efficiency, for example, by improving production process sophistication and beginning to delegate authority. Improving transportation and communications infrastructure, upgrading public education and the training of management, liberalizing trade, and reducing corruption are essential. These steps create a foundation of efficiency, transparency, and competitive pressure necessary to improve the productivity of Factor-Driven competition.

To move into middle income, the challenge is to make the transition to the Investment-Driven stage. The Investment-Driven stage depends on a high rate of investment in products, processes, and the acquisition of technology. Corporate priorities expand to include, for example, in-house product development, licensing the best foreign technology, connecting to foreign markets, and developing the capacity to improve technology. Among other things, reducing bureaucratic red tape and enhancing the legal system become important to enhance business efficiency, while local financial markets become much more necessary to mobilize debt and equity capital.

To reach high-income status, incremental improvements in quality and efficiency are no longer enough. To reach the Innovation-Driven stage, companies must innovate at the world technology frontier, develop unique product designs, sell globally, and create more decentralized and flexible organizational structures. Truly world-class research institutions must emerge, along with strong research collaboration with universities, venture capital availability, truly sophisticated demand conditions, and intense local competition.

The CCI and the GCI measure different but complementary dimensions of competitiveness. Figure 1 compares the two rankings for 2001 and reveals that they are highly correlated. Finland ranks first on both Indexes, while the United States ranks second. However, there are divergences in rankings that are potentially revealing about country economic prospects. Of the high-income countries, for instance, Norway and Ireland rank 10 or more positions higher on growth competitiveness than they do on current competitiveness. Significant micro reform will be a central challenge in these countries. Conversely, Germany and Switzerland rank 10 or more positions worse on growth competitiveness than they do on current competitiveness. Creating the vitality and assets required for growth looms as the fundamental challenge in already highly productive economies.

Of the medium-income countries, Mauritius, Costa Rica, Taiwan, and New Zealand rank significantly better on growth competitiveness than on current competitiveness. Turkey and Brazil, on the other hand, rank worse on growth competitiveness than on current competitiveness. Creating more dynamism and the capacity for change are the challenge for these countries. Of the low-income countries, Bulgaria, Bolivia, and the Dominican Republic are among the countries with higher ranks on growth competitiveness than on current competitiveness. India, Jamaica, Indonesia, Colombia, Ukraine, and Zimbabwe are facing lower growth prospects that lag their ranking on current competitiveness.

Figure 1: Growth and Current Competitiveness Index rankings

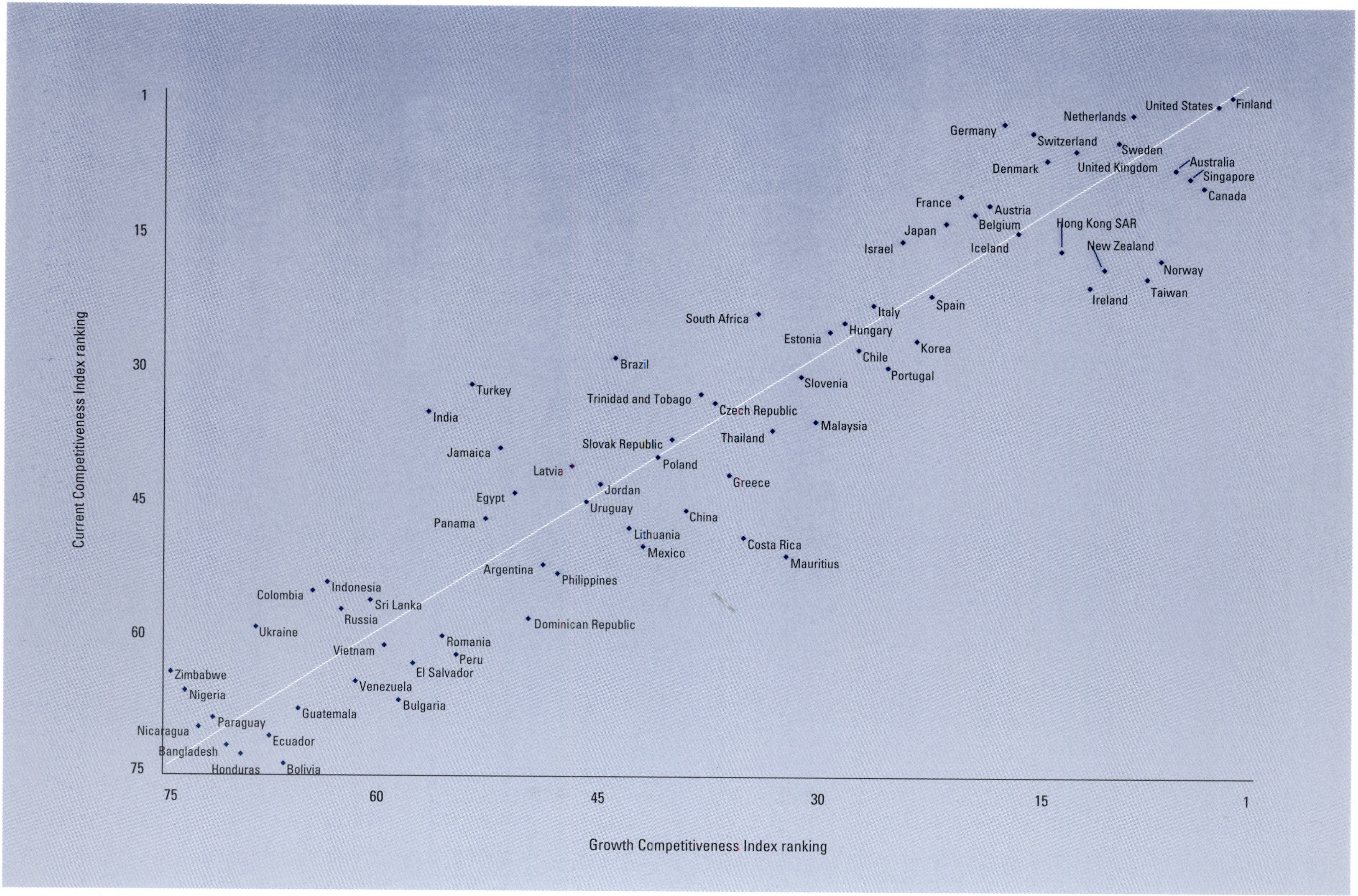

Structure of the Report

Just as the *Report* includes two distinct perspectives on competitiveness, it includes chapters on a range of other central issues relating to competitiveness and economic performance. In each case, authors have taken advantage of the Executive Opinion Survey's to inform their own research.

The chapter by Daniel Esty of Yale University and Michael E Porter on "Measuring National Environmental Regulation and Performance," explores the differences among countries in environmental performance and their link between environmental outcomes and national environmental policy choices. The chapter also explores the crucial question of whether environmental quality must come at the expense of competitiveness and economic development, as traditional economic theory has suggested. The findings are revealing: environmental performance varies systematically with the quality of a country's environmental regulatory regime. The statistical findings are then used to construct an index that ranks countries in terms of the quality of their environmental regulations. The research reveals that there is no evidence that higher environmental quality compromises economic progress. Environmental performance is positively and highly correlated to GDP per capita. The chapter presents preliminary evidence suggesting that countries with stricter environmental regulation than would be expected at their level of GDP per capita enjoy faster economic growth.

The chapter on "National Innovative Capacity" by Porter and Scott Stern of Northwestern University delves in detail into the conditions that allow a country to innovate at the global technology frontier. The findings reveal the striking degree to which the national circumstances actually explain differences across countries in innovative activity measured by US patenting. The statistical findings allow the construction of an overall innovative capacity ranking of the 75 countries, as well as comparisons across countries in important components of innovative capacity including availability of scientific and technical personnel, innovation-related policy choices, cluster vitality, and the quality of linkage mechanisms between basic research and the private sector.

The next chapter presents an update on "Economic Creativity" by Andrew M Warner of the Center for International Development at Harvard University. The concept of economic creativity was central to last year's overall Growth Competitiveness Index and moreover provided a methodological breakthrough that stimulated much of our research over the past year on how to quantify the distinct effects of innovation versus diffusion as contributors to economic growth.

The fourth chapter of Part 2 provides a new framework for assessing national trade performance at the sectoral level, as constructed by Cornelius along with International Trade Centre economists Friedrich von Kirchbach, Mondher Mimouni, Jean-Michel Pasteels, and Shilpa Phadke. Taking advantage of sophisticated United Nations data on the trade flows of all 75 GCR countries over the past five years, the authors are able to assess how countries' individual industries are performing compared with the same industries in other countries. They furthermore compare the future prospects for those industries, based on a range of factors that includes the current global demand trends for those industries.

In the next chapter of Part 2, Peter Cornelius and Yong Zhang of the World Economic Forum review recent developments in European labor markets and the context for ongoing structural reform in this area. Using questions from the Executive Opinion Survey, they then create a measure of labor market flexibility to compare countries across the European Union. The authors discuss how labor market restrictions have become an impediment to growth in the European Union, particularly since exchange rates have been removed as a macroeconomic adjustment mechanism.

The chapter on labor markets is followed by an update in which Warner joins Cornelius to assess the performance of the euro as of early 2001. Here the authors find some interesting shifts in European executives' assessment of the euro's prospects for stability.

Finally, Part 2 concludes with a review of the Executive Opinion Survey by Cornelius and McArthur, including a brief description of our surveying methodology, several descriptive statistics of our Survey sample, and a few key tests of the consistency and accuracy of the Survey results.

The third and final section of this *Report* is broken into two parts, country profiles and data tables. In the country profiles, we outline some key advantages and disadvantages drawn from the variables and methodologies used in constructing the Growth Competitiveness Index and the Current Competitiveness Index. We also include numerous strengths and weaknesses of each economy that are not directly included in the respective Indexes but might nonetheless be of interest to the reader. In the accompanying data tables, results are listed by country for most variables covered in the *Report*. These tables provide easy reference for the reader who wishes to look at each variable in detail. The data also provide a wealth of information for policymakers and business leaders who wish to compare their economies to others across a range of dimensions. For researchers and data enthusiasts hoping to gain a much deeper level of knowledge from the *Report*'s underlying data, a full electronic version of the Survey data is available as an accompaniment to this *Report*.

Notes

[i] We explored the stages of national competitive development in Michael E Porter, The Competitive Advantage of Nations. New York: The Free Press; London: Macmillan Press, 1990.

Part 1

The Competitiveness Indexes

The Growth Competitiveness Index: Measuring Technological Advancement and the Stages of Development

JOHN W. MCARTHUR and **JEFFREY D. SACHS,**
Center for International Development at Harvard University

A central objective of the *Global Competitiveness Report* is to assess the capacity of the world's economies to achieve sustained economic growth. We do this by analyzing the extent to which individual national economies have the structures, institutions, and policies in place for economic growth over the medium term, roughly a perspective of five years. These structural, institutional, and policy features of national economies are summarized in the Growth Competitiveness Index (GCI). We do not try to predict short-term business cycles, though we discuss short-term issues, especially as they affect the longer-term prospects for economic growth.

Economists' knowledge of the processes and policies that underpin economic growth has advanced tremendously over the past decade. With the increasing availability of cross-country macroeconomic data, the rapid evolution in theoretical and statistical methods, and the increasing sophistication of survey tools—including the Executive Opinion Survey that is conducted annually in preparation of this *Report*—economists have vastly increased their ability to test theories of economic growth. At least some of the ideological battles of the past are receding in the face of improved evidence.[i]

Of course, our knowledge remains imperfect. We do not know the exact mechanisms through which growth occurs, nor are we able to forecast future growth rates with absolute precision. Economic crises sometimes emerge somewhat out of the blue, as with Japan's decade long recession and the East Asian crisis in 1997. Research into the subject of economic growth is ongoing, and thus our understanding of the relevant technological, institutional, geographical, and societal factors improves with every year that passes. As a result, we are constantly updating the framework used in the Growth Competitiveness Index. This year's GCI is no exception.

This chapter on growth competitiveness contains two distinct sections. The first provides an outline of current knowledge concerning economic growth and the results for this year's GCI. The second proceeds in greater detail, describing the new GCI methodology and logic used in the construction of this year's Index.

ECONOMIC GROWTH AND GROWTH COMPETITIVENESS: THE FUNDAMENTALS

An overview of economic growth

Economists have identified three inter-related mechanisms involved in economic growth. The first is the efficient allocation of resources, based on market competition and a sophisticated division of labor. Adam Smith identified this factor already in 1776, and observed that international trade plays an enormously important role in achieving an efficient division of labor. The second mechanism is capital accumulation. When national saving is converted into increasing capital per worker, the output per worker also tends to rise. Economists have come to appreciate that productive capital includes not just the plant and equipment of business sector, but also the human capital that results from investments in education, health, and on-the-job training. The third mechanism in economic growth is technological advance. Improvements in technology (both new goods and better ways of producing goods) can be achieved by creating a truly new technology, or by adopting (and adapting) a technology that has been developed abroad. The first process is called *technological innovation*; the second, *technological diffusion.*

All three mechanisms—division of labor, capital accumulation, and technological advance—are important, but technological advance is probably the most fundamental of the three in modern history. Without technological advance, the benefits of an improved division of labor, or a higher rate of capital accumulation, push the economy to a higher standard of living but not to continuously high economic growth. For example, as capital is accumulated, the rate of return on new investment tends to fall over time unless the capital accumulation is accompanied by technological change, which creates new profitable investment opportunities. Thus, the Soviet Union accumulated capital at a high rate, but because civilian technology was nearly moribund, the rate of return to new investments fell to close to 0 by the 1980s, contributing to the collapse of the system.

Technological advance, on the other hand, has been self-perpetuating in the high-income countries. Each new technological innovation triggers yet further innovation, in a kind of chain reaction that fuels long-term economic growth. Thus, in the science-based, technologically advanced economies, economic growth has continued for nearly two centuries without running out of dynamism, or even slowing down.

There are, of course, volumes to be written about how the structural characteristics and economic policies of each economy affect economic growth. The division of labor is affected by trade policies, state versus private ownership, the legal system, and so forth. Capital accumulation is affected by the confidence in property rights, the rates of taxation, the faith in the judicial system, and the extent of macroeconomic stability or instability. Technological diffusion and innovation are affected by intellectual property rights, the size of the potential market for a new invention, government support for scientific research, the state of the higher education, and many other factors.

Economists have increasingly returned to another idea of Adam Smith's as well: that physical geography plays an important role in determining economic growth. When a poorer economy is close to a richer economy, the poorer neighbor can often benefit by absorbing technologies and capital from the richer neighbor. Economic growth then spreads "within the neighborhood" of the richer economy. A more distant economy, by contrast, may be less able to benefit from capital inflows and technological diffusion. Climatic factors can also affect long-term development, because of the effects of climate on disease, food productivity, and other sectors of the economy.

By virtue of their distinctive histories, geography, and social conditions, countries are at widely varying levels of income, technological sophistication, capacity to innovate, and overall capacity to achieve sustained economic growth. But perhaps the most significant global division today from the view of long-term economic growth is the one between countries that are able to achieve technological innovation at a high rate and those that are not. The main innovators in the world, as measured, for example, by the rate at which they patent new products and processes, are few in number. The United States and Canada, Western Europe, Japan, and a handful of other economies (Israel, Korea, Singapore, and Taiwan) account for the vast bulk of new patents each year. In 2000, these countries accounted for barely 15 percent of the world's population, but fully 99 percent of the patents issued for new inventions by the US Patent Office.

The world's technological divide was first incorporated into the growth competitiveness framework in last year's *Report* when our colleague Andrew Warner constructed the economic creativity index to distinguish empirically between growth stimulated by innovation and growth fueled by technology transfer. (An update on economic creativity by Dr Warner is included in Chapter 2.3 of this *Report*. Another chapter on innovation by Michael E Porter and Scott Stern appears as Chapter 2.2.) This year we build on the distinction between innovation and technology transfer by using the term *core economy* for a country that is a technological innovator; all the rest are said to be *non-core economies*. This classification system allows us to distinguish statistically how various factors affect growth at different stages of development. (The methodology section in the second half of this chapter describes exactly how this framework applies to our growth competitiveness calculations.) As an empirical matter, we define the core group as all economies that achieve

29

at least 15 patents per million population. The economies meeting this core criterion in 2000 are listed in Box 1. The core economies are, typically, the richest countries and typically have achieved sustained economic growth over the course of many years, indeed decades. Their economic growth is powered, fundamentally, by their capacity to innovate. The competition among the core economies is closely related to their relative capacities to innovate and to win new global markets for their technologically advanced products.

Box 1: Core innovators as of 2000

Countries with more than 15 US utility patents registered per million population in 2000.

Australia	Hong Kong SAR	New Zealand
Austria	Iceland	Norway
Belgium	Ireland	Singapore
Canada	Israel	Sweden
Denmark	Italy	Switzerland
Finland	Japan	Taiwan
France	Korea	United Kingdom
Germany	Netherlands	United States

We certainly don't want to be misunderstood by our use of terms. The use of *core* and *non-core* is not meant as a value judgment in any way, nor as a slight or insult to the non-innovating regions. It is meant only as a useful shorthand to describe the critical division in today's world economy between the innovating and non-innovating economies. The economic dynamics have been very different in these two groups of countries, and we highlight those differences in this *Report*. We also hope that the description will help more countries to develop the means for higher rates of technological innovation within their own economies.

The non-core economies often achieve very high rates of growth, indeed the world's very highest rates, by rapidly absorbing the advanced technologies and capital of the core economies. This process of "catch-up growth" has been extremely important for many developing countries. But we should highlight the fact that catch-up growth has its inherent limits. As a non-core economy narrows the income gap with the technological leaders, its ability to narrow the gap still further tends to diminish, or even disappear. In order to close the income gap fully, the non-core economy must become a technological innovator—in other words, it must become part of the core economy itself.

Globalization has generated new opportunities for countries, but also new challenges. By raising the mobility of financial capital, skilled workers, and new technologies, economies now have the capacity to grow at super-charged annual rates if they can become attractive magnets for investment and technological diffusion. But at the same time, globalization punishes the laggard economies far more harshly than in the past. When the business environment is poor, skilled workers and capital simply "pack up their bags" and leave for a more promising location. Thus, lawless governments impose a particularly high economic cost on their countries. Unfortunately, some of the losers today are suffering not for their sins, but for their poor geographical inheritance. Some distant locations (such as landlocked countries in Latin American, Africa, and Asia) are experiencing high rates of brain drain and capital outflow because their remoteness raises transport costs and diminishes the incentives for investment. Even here, however, investments in infrastructure (such as better roads and airports, and better Internet connectivity) can compensate for some of the inherent difficulties.

The most successful of the non-core economies in recent years have achieved fast growth by attracting high levels of foreign direct investment (FDI) from the high-tech multinational firms of the core economies. This FDI brings with it new technology, capital, export markets, and organizational know-how, all in one process. Thus, China, Singapore, Hong Kong, and more recently Ireland, Mexico, and Poland, have all achieved FDI-led growth at very rapid rates. Much of this FDI has been export oriented. The multinational firm has invested in these non-core economies not so much for the local market (though that can be important) but rather because it sees the economy as an export platform for the world market. Thus, the regions that have benefited most from this kind of FDI are those that have good access to global shipping lanes (eg, coastal regions) or land proximity to major markets (Mexico, Poland).

The boundaries between core and non-core economies are clearly not rigid. A technologically laggard country can become an innovator, but the breakthrough from non-core to core economy is not a simple one, and most places in the world have not accomplished the transition. That is, of course, why the group of core economies remains so small as a share of the world's population. Yet countries such as Iceland, Ireland, Hong Kong SAR, Korea, Singapore, and Taiwan have all achieved a breakthrough in innovative capacity, and have thereby become part of the "core" of the world economy (see Table 1). They are all growing rapidly based largely on their technological prowess. One of our goals in this *Report* is to identify some of the key factors that allow an economy to

Table 1: Core technology-innovating economies in the 1980s and in 2000

country	Average Annual US Utility Patents Granted per Million Population in 1980s*	1980s rank	US Utility Patents Granted per Million Population in 2000*	2000 rank
1980s Core technology innovators				
Switzerland	189.6	1	182.1	4
United States	165.8	2	308.7	1
Japan	101.2	3	246.6	2
Sweden	94.3	4	177.2	5
Germany	85.1	5	123.6	7
Netherlands	51.9	6	78.1	11
Canada	50.3	7	111.2	9
United Kingdom	43.2	8	60.6	16
France	43.0	9	64.4	14
Israel	42.1	10	135.0	6
Austria	40.3	11	62.1	15
Finland	37.0	12	119.4	8
Denmark	31.7	13	82.3	10
Belgium	26.4	14	67.8	13
Norway	22.6	15	55.1	18
Australia	21.4	16	36.7	20
Italy	16.4	17	29.7	22
New Zealand	15.2	18	28.0	23
1980s Non-core economies that became core innovators by 2000				
Taiwan	12.8	19	210.3	3
Iceland	9.0	21	61.6	17
Ireland	8.8	22	32.4	21
Hong Kong SAR	5.4	23	26.3	24
Singapore	2.4	26	54.3	19
Korea	1.3	28	70.1	12

*Note that Luxembourg averaged 71.7 US patents per million population in the 1980s and achieved 91.8 per million population in 2000 but is not included in our analysis.

become an innovator, in order to help more countries achieve the transition to innovation. These factors include: sizeable investments in higher education, a good information technology base, high levels of government spending on research and development, and effective intellectual property laws that promote research and development.

Another objective of this *Report* is to estimate as accurately as possible the different roles of technology at different stages of development. Each country's specific challenges posed by globalization depend importantly on its stage of economic and technological development. A very poor country with rudimentary levels of health and education will generally not be competing on the basis of technological innovation. Rather, the goal for that country will be to attract capital investment and discourage capital flight, and to use the proceeds of economic growth to invest in improved health, education, and infrastructure. For a country somewhat higher up the development ladder, the main goal is likely to be to speed up the process

of technological diffusion into the country, in part by attracting high-tech foreign direct investments. For the most advanced of the non-core economies, the goal is likely to be the transition from technological diffusion to technological innovation—in other words, the transition from being a non-core economy to being a core economy. Among the most advanced countries, the main competition is in high-tech markets. Success in high-tech innovation depends on scientific prowess, the translation of science into technology, and the commercialization of that technology, often through start-up businesses.

Just as the challenges of growth differ according to the stage of economic development, we have found that the explanatory power of our Growth Competitiveness Index is improved if we allow for different weightings of factors depending on the stage of development. For the core countries, for example, the weight accorded to technological indicators (relative to other factors) should be higher than for non-core economies. Similarly, the importance of innovation relative to diffusion is higher for the core economies than for the non-core economies. We verify through regression analysis that, as the stage of economic development changes, the relative importance of various sub-components of the GCI also changes.

Finally, it is important to say a bit about the macroeconomic environment. Government monetary and fiscal policies, and stability of financial institutions, have important effects on short-term economic dynamics as well as on the long-term capacity to grow. The key macroeconomic factors in long-term growth are budget balance, modest taxation, high rates of national saving, stability in the financial system, and a realistic level of the exchange rate that preserves the competitiveness of the export sector. When one or more of these macroeconomic factors is jeopardized (for example, by large budget deficits or a banking crisis), the short-term consequences can be stunning. Banking crises in Latin America and Asia during the 1990s resulted in a collapse of GNP of 5 percent or more in a single year in many countries. The medium-term growth prospects are also implicated, though less dramatically, since macroeconomic instability seriously damages capital accumulation and the efficient division of labor. Although the short-term macroeconomic convulsions are often highest in the minds of investors or businessmen planning this year's strategy, our concern remains focused on the medium-term implications of the macroeconomic environment.

The Growth Competitiveness Index 2001–2002

Results

The overall Growth Competitiveness Index (GCI) aims to measure the capacity of the national economy to achieve sustained economic growth over the medium term, controlling for the current level of economic development.

Using data from recent years' Executive Opinion Survey, and building on other economic research by ourselves and colleagues at the Center for International Development at Harvard University—especially Andrew Warner, who has played a leading role in this *Report*'s intellectual development—the GCI 2001 focuses on three pillars of growth: technology, public institutions, and the macroeconomic environment, each with its own index. This is slightly modified from last year's Growth Index, which focused on economic creativity (similar to this year's technology index), finance (closely linked to the new macroeconomic environment index); and internationalization (which is somewhat related to both the technology and macroeconomic indexes). We also, for the first time, present a unified Index that distinguishes between growth factors affecting the world's core innovator economies and those affecting the non-core technological adapters.

Despite the revisions in methodology and labeling, the reader should be aware that many of last year's underlying variables are still included in this year's overall Growth Index. Many have been re-categorized, however, and several have also been dropped in light of new evidence regarding the role of various factors at different stages of development. Broadly speaking, the technology index measures the capacity for innovation and diffusion of technology. The public institutions subindex mainly measures the role of politics and the bureaucracy in supporting market-based economic activity and the division of labor. The macroeconomic environment index measures variables related to capital accumulation and the efficiency of the division of labor.

This year's results are presented in Tables 2 and 3. Table 2 focuses on the overall rankings, comparing this year's placings to last year's for the 58 countries included in both GCIs. Table 3 presents the results for the technology, public institutions, and macroeconomic environment indexes that, together, form the overall GCI. As explained in more detail below, these component indexes are constructed and weighted somewhat differently for the core and non-core economies.

When looking at Table 2, the reader should note that, given the updates in this year's GCR methodology as well as the expanded coverage of 17 new countries, a precise comparison between this year's and last year's results is not recommended. The reader should also note that, due to its perennially small yield in our Executive Opinion Survey,

Table 2: Growth Competitiveness Index rankings and 2000 comparisons

country	GCI 2001 rank	GCI 2001 score	GCI 2001 rank among GCR 2000 countries	GCI 2000 rank
Finland	1	6.03	1	5
United States	2	5.95	2	1
Canada	3	5.87	3	6
Singapore	4	5.84	4	2
Australia	5	5.74	5	11
Norway	6	5.64	6	15
Taiwan	7	5.59	7	10
Netherlands	8	5.56	8	3
Sweden	9	5.55	9	12
New Zealand	10	5.53	10	19
Ireland	11	5.52	11	4
United Kingdom	12	5.51	12	8
Hong Kong SAR	13	5.47	13	7
Denmark	14	5.44	14	13
Switzerland	15	5.43	15	9
Iceland	16	5.40	16	23
Germany	17	5.39	17	14
Austria	18	5.33	18	17
Belgium	19	5.31	19	16
France	20	5.29	20	21
Japan	21	5.25	21	20
Spain	22	5.17	22	26
Korea	23	5.13	23	28
Israel	24	5.01	24	18
Portugal	25	4.92	25	22
Italy	26	4.90	26	29
Chile	27	4.90	27	27
Hungary	28	4.87	28	25
Estonia	29	4.87	—	—
Malaysia	30	4.83	29	24
Slovenia	31	4.70	—	—
Mauritius	32	4.60	30	35
Thailand	33	4.53	31	30
South Africa	34	4.50	32	32
Costa Rica	35	4.49	33	37
Greece	36	4.46	34	33
Czech Republic	37	4.41	35	31
Trinidad and Tobago	38	4.40	—	—
China	39	4.40	36	40
Slovak Republic	40	4.36	37	38
Poland	41	4.30	38	34
Mexico	42	4.29	39	42
Lithuania	43	4.27	—	—
Brazil	44	4.26	40	45
Jordan	45	4.24	41	46
Uruguay	46	4.22	—	—
Latvia	47	4.19	—	—
Philippines	48	4.16	42	36
Argentina	49	4.11	43	44
Dominican Republic	50	4.10	—	—
Egypt	51	4.03	44	41
Jamaica	52	3.92	—	—
Panama	53	3.88	—	—
Turkey	54	3.86	45	39
Peru	55	3.85	46	47
Romania	56	3.84	—	—
India	57	3.84	47	48
El Salvador	58	3.84	48	49
Bulgaria	59	3.82	49	57
Vietnam	60	3.77	50	52
Sri Lanka	61	3.74	—	—
Venezuela	62	3.70	51	53
Russia	63	3.70	52	54
Indonesia	64	3.69	53	43
Colombia	65	3.68	54	51
Guatemala	66	3.44	—	—
Bolivia	67	3.42	55	50
Ecuador	68	3.36	56	58
Ukraine	69	3.26	57	56
Honduras	70	3.11	—	—
Bangladesh	71	3.04	—	—
Paraguay	72	3.01	—	—
Nicaragua	73	3.01	—	—
Nigeria	74	2.99	—	—
Zimbabwe	75	2.81	58	55

Table 3: Growth Competitiveness Index component indexes

TECHNOLOGY			PUBLIC INSTITUTIONS			MACROECONOMIC ENVIRONMENT		
Country	Rank	Score	Country	Rank	Score	Country	Rank	Score
United States	1	6.42	Finland	1	6.59	Singapore	1	5.52
Canada	2	6.37	Iceland	2	6.56	Ireland	2	5.20
Finland	3	6.35	Denmark	3	6.42	Switzerland	3	5.18
Taiwan	4	6.19	New Zealand	4	6.33	Hong Kong SAR	4	5.12
Australia	5	6.05	Netherlands	5	6.29	Norway	5	5.08
Sweden	6	5.81	Singapore	6	6.27	China	6	5.04
Norway	7	5.77	Sweden	7	6.19	United States	7	4.97
Estonia	8	5.68	Australia	8	6.17	Korea	8	4.94
Korea	9	5.66	United Kingdom	9	6.14	Netherlands	9	4.88
United Kingdom	10	5.56	Hong Kong SAR	10	6.01	Finland	10	4.82
New Zealand	11	5.55	Canada	11	6.01	Spain	11	4.82
Denmark	12	5.54	United States	12	6.01	United Kingdom	12	4.81
Belgium	13	5.54	Switzerland	13	5.99	Canada	13	4.74
Netherlands	14	5.54	Israel	14	5.98	New Zealand	14	4.70
Germany	15	5.49	Austria	15	5.98	Taiwan	15	4.69
Austria	16	5.45	Norway	16	5.95	Thailand	16	4.68
France	17	5.44	Germany	17	5.93	Australia	17	4.68
Singapore *	18	5.44	Ireland	18	5.87	Japan	18	4.66
Iceland	19	5.41	Japan	19	5.76	Germany	19	4.65
Czech Republic	20	5.39	France	20	5.72	Malaysia	20	4.59
Hungary	21	5.39	Chile	21	5.69	Chile	21	4.56
Malaysia	22	5.36	Belgium	22	5.67	France	22	4.54
Japan	23	5.28	Spain	23	5.47	Italy	23	4.53
Switzerland	24	5.27	Taiwan	24	5.30	Belgium	24	4.48
Portugal	25	5.27	Portugal	25	5.25	Trinidad and Tobago	25	4.48
Israel	26	5.27	Hungary	26	5.20	Austria	26	4.46
Spain	27	5.23	Italy	27	5.05	South Africa	27	4.43
Ireland *	28	5.20	Jordan	28	5.04	Philippines	28	4.42
Slovak Republic	29	5.18	Estonia	29	4.99	Sweden	29	4.40
Slovenia	30	5.18	Slovenia	30	4.90	Mauritius	30	4.34
Italy	31	5.01	Uruguay	31	4.89	Denmark	31	4.28
Costa Rica	32	4.97	Mauritius	32	4.79	Greece	32	4.26
Hong Kong SAR *	33	4.93	Egypt	33	4.76	Brazil	33	4.24
Latvia	34	4.83	Lithuania	34	4.70	Iceland	34	4.24
Poland	35	4.75	South Africa	35	4.69	Portugal	35	4.24
Mexico	36	4.70	Trinidad and Tobago	36	4.63	Mexico	36	4.18
Mauritius	37	4.67	Costa Rica	37	4.56	Vietnam	37	4.15
Greece	38	4.62	Slovak Republic	38	4.54	Hungary	38	4.04
Thailand	39	4.54	Malaysia	39	4.53	Slovenia	39	4.02
Philippines	40	4.53	Greece	40	4.50	Argentina	40	3.99
Lithuania	41	4.46	Poland	41	4.40	Indonesia	41	3.96
Chile	42	4.45	Thailand	42	4.36	Costa Rica	42	3.94
Jamaica	43	4.43	Jamaica	43	4.30	Estonia	43	3.94
Dominican Republic	44	4.42	Korea	44	4.25	Panama	44	3.92
Uruguay	45	4.40	Peru	45	4.24	India	45	3.88
South Africa	46	4.39	Turkey	46	4.21	Dominican Republic	46	3.87
Romania	47	4.33	Brazil	47	4.21	El Salvador	47	3.87
Argentina	48	4.33	Latvia	48	4.18	Bangladesh	48	3.81
Brazil	49	4.33	India	49	4.11	Czech Republic	49	3.81
Bulgaria	50	4.32	China	50	4.10	Poland	50	3.75
Turkey	51	4.28	Bulgaria	51	4.07	Egypt	51	3.74
Trinidad and Tobago	52	4.10	Romania	52	4.06	Guatemala	52	3.73
China	53	4.05	Czech Republic	53	4.04	Venezuela	53	3.73
Jordan	54	3.99	Dominican Republic	54	4.02	Jordan	54	3.69
Venezuela	55	3.98	Argentina	55	4.01	Nigeria	55	3.68
Colombia	56	3.92	Mexico	56	3.99	Lithuania	56	3.66
Panama	57	3.89	Colombia	57	3.85	Russia	57	3.64
El Salvador	58	3.86	Sri Lanka	58	3.84	Peru	58	3.62
Sri Lanka	59	3.82	Panama	59	3.83	Latvia	59	3.58
Russia	60	3.78	El Salvador	60	3.79	Sri Lanka	60	3.56
Indonesia	61	3.76	Russia	61	3.68	Israel	61	3.55
Peru	62	3.71	Bolivia	62	3.67	Ecuador	62	3.45
Ukraine	63	3.68	Vietnam	63	3.58	Uruguay	63	3.38
Egypt	64	3.59	Philippines	64	3.53	Slovak Republic	64	3.35
Vietnam	65	3.56	Venezuela	65	3.40	Paraguay	65	3.31
India	66	3.54	Indonesia	66	3.35	Colombia	66	3.29
Bolivia	67	3.52	Nicaragua	67	3.33	Romania	67	3.14
Guatemala	68	3.38	Ecuador	68	3.30	Turkey	68	3.10
Ecuador	69	3.33	Zimbabwe	69	3.30	Bulgaria	69	3.09
Honduras	70	3.29	Guatemala	70	3.22	Bolivia	70	3.08
Nicaragua	71	3.21	Ukraine	71	3.15	Jamaica	71	3.05
Zimbabwe	72	3.20	Honduras	72	3.01	Honduras	72	3.02
Paraguay	73	2.98	Nigeria	73	2.84	Ukraine	73	2.95
Bangladesh	74	2.83	Paraguay	74	2.75	Nicaragua	74	2.48
Nigeria	75	2.44	Bangladesh	75	2.48	Zimbabwe	75	1.93

* = When calculated as core economy. See Table 6B for values when calculated as non-core.

33

Luxembourg is not included in this year's rankings, so all 2000 rankings below third place have been scaled up one spot relative to their published order in the *Global Competitiveness Report 2000*.

Although the GCI sample has been expanded and its methodology modified, there is a high correlation between the rankings for last year and this year.[ii] In our view, this has two main explanations. First, despite changes in our growth competitiveness methodology in recent years, our Index is robustly capturing the key underlying elements affecting medium-run economic growth. Second, the consistency in rankings suggests that the underlying processes affecting growth have themselves been changing only gradually over the past three to five years. *We urge appropriate caution in the interpretation of the rankings.* An index like this cannot finely distinguish between the growth prospects of countries that are very similarly ranked. The trends throughout Table 2 are informative, but one should not over-interpret a movement of a few slots in the ranking.

Nonetheless, reading through the GCI rankings, the most obvious changes have taken place in the top spots, where Finland, for the first time, ranks first in the world. This is a notable achievement for a small open economy that underwent a deep recession after the Soviet Union collapsed a decade ago. It also serves as evidence of how quickly an economy's prospects can be transformed by strong political institutions, a focus on technology (especially the prowess of Nokia and the rest of the ICT sector), and sound macroeconomic management. The United States, currently at risk of a recession but still the world's largest market, technological leader, and engine of economic growth, has slipped to second spot—an interesting yet marginal overall change. The United States is still, of course, the overwhelming powerhouse of the world economy in the high-tech industries. Canada, the sixth-ranked economy in the 2000 GCI, rounds out the top three places, having moved up mainly due to this year's weight accorded to tertiary education as a key factor in technological innovation.

Singapore, the second ranked economy in the 2000 GCI, has dropped two spots to fourth, due more to the increased weight on innovation in this year's Index than to shifts in the local economy. Similarly Ireland and Hong Kong SAR, still strong economies with impressive growth prospects, have dropped from 5th to 11th and 8th to 13th, respectively, because of evidence that they will need to become more innovative to maintain their current high growth rates into the future. These three fast-growing economies have each been highly successful in pursuing technology-diffusing, manufacturing-based export growth strategies. They have concurrently expanded their local scientific and innovation capacities so that each now easily surpasses our 15 patents per million population criterion

for the technological core. Yet despite their fast-pace growth and their development of local innovative capacities, they have not yet fully transformed their source of growth from diffusion to innovation. They appear to be, in a sense, between non-core and core economy status. In our final GCI rankings, we calculated their scores as both core and non-core economies, and then averaged the two. If we were to have calculated each solely as non-core economies, each would have had a higher overall ranking.[iii]

Norway marks another interesting shift in the rankings—this year up from 15th to 6th—having invested heavily in developing its information and communications technology (ICT) capacity, not unrelated to its Scandinavian neighbors' strength in this regard, while its government has concurrently enjoyed enviable macroeconomic conditions thanks to natural resource abundance and high oil prices. New Zealand has also scored a dramatic jump in the rankings, from 19th to 10th, reflecting its consistently stable macroeconomic and institutional environment and also its growing technological capacity that receives increased attention in this year's methodology. Iceland's move seven spots up, from 23rd to 16th, reflects the positive growth prospects for another country with one of the world's most advanced ICT infrastructures.

At the middle and lower ends of the rankings of countries covered in both this and last year's GCRs, results are more stable, with few countries experiencing dramatic shifts. For instance, Chile and South Africa are unchanged at 27th and 32nd spots respectively. Notable exceptions include Turkey, which was surveyed during the height of its economic crisis in the early months of 2001 and dropped six spots on the rankings. Even more dramatic was the drop for Indonesia, a country that has experienced ongoing political uncertainty while flirting with the prospect of major turmoil over the past year. It dropped 10 places, from 43rd to 53rd. Meanwhile, Mauritius climbed five spots from 35th to 30th, Jordan moved up from 46th to 41st, and Bulgaria jumped an impressive 8 places from 57th to 49th. Interestingly, Argentina has barely shifted since last year, improving one place from 44th to 43rd. Argentina is a bit of a paradox, of course. Many features of its economy are satisfactory, yet the economy remains trapped with an overvalued currency and unimpressive technological dynamics. Argentina may be a quintessential case of an economy that was fairly sophisticated 40 years ago but failed to develop its technological capacity.

On a less optimistic note, there is year-to-year consistency at the very bottom of the rankings, with three of the final four spots among the 58 countries covered in 2000 still occupied by Ecuador, Ukraine, and Zimbabwe, all countries facing ongoing macroeconomic disorder with

Figure 1: Partial regression results of GCI versus 1992–2000 GDP per capita growth, controlling for initial GDP level*

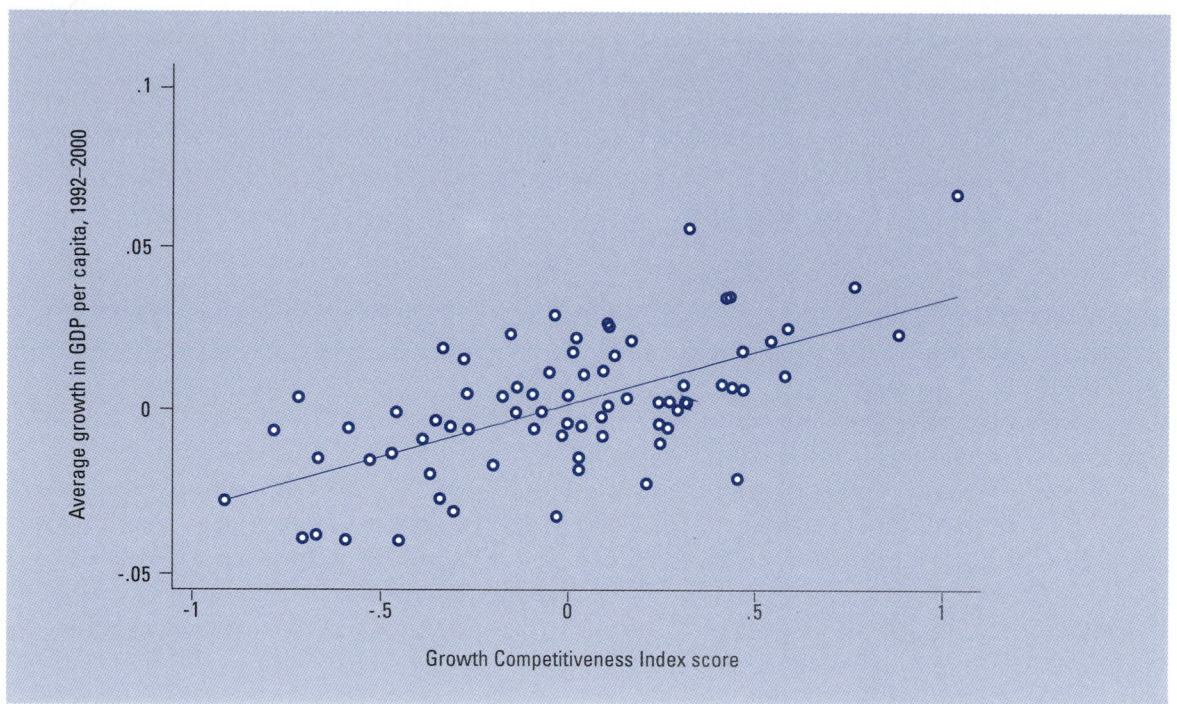

Growth Competitiveness Index score

*More precisely, growth here is measured as the average annual change in the GDP GAP with the United States from 1992 to 2000 (1995 to 2000 for transition economies), as explained in the methodology section of this chapter.

little positive growth prospect in sight. Joining Ukraine toward the bottom of list, Russia continues to suffer the consequences of decades of economic mismanagement under Soviet rule and the haphazard process of economic change since 1991. Although it has moved up two slots, it remains very low, and this year is in the 52nd position.

Looking at the 17 countries added to this year's expanded GCI sample, one finds some interesting results. The top-scoring new entrant is Estonia, ranking 29th overall and well ahead of its Baltic neighbors Lithuania at 43rd and Latvia at 47th. The Caribbean economies of Trinidad and Tobago and Jamaica also provide noteworthy results, ranking 38th and 52nd respectively. Romania, a new addition at 56th, comes slightly behind. The members of the largest geographic group of new additions to the GCR—Latin American economies—have their economic difficulties reflected in generally low rankings. Honduras at 70th, Paraguay at 72nd, and Nicaragua at 73rd occupy three of the bottom six rankings. Guatemala, at 66th, is not far ahead. The relative bright spots among the newly included Latin American countries are found in Uruguay (46th), the Dominican Republic (50th) and Panama (53rd). Interspersed among these rankings are Latin American economies included in previous years' *Reports*: El Salvador (58th), Venezuela (62nd), Colombia (65th), and Bolivia (67th).

The Growth Competitiveness Index and economic growth

The goal of the GCI is to capture important factors in economic growth over roughly a five-year perspective. Of course, we cannot test the GCI for 2001 based on future growth, so instead we examine whether the GCI helps to account for patterns of growth during the recent past and then extrapolate into the future. Specifically, we examine the relationship between the GCI and economic growth from 1992 to 2000. The basic test equation explains annual economic growth over this period as a function of the country's GCI score and its initial level of income in 1992 (on the grounds that poorer countries, all other things equal, will tend to grow faster). As shown in Figure 1, the GCI has a strong relationship with recent economic growth, controlling for initial income level. (The same test reveals, as expected, that countries that began the 1990s relatively poorer achieved faster average growth over the period than their wealthier counterparts.) Of course, the real proof of the pudding for the GCI will be whether the Index helps account for future rather than past growth!

35

Interpreting the Growth Competitiveness Index

Although changes in the GCI rankings are informative, several points need to be established in order to ensure proper interpretation of the Index. First, as mentioned, the underlying methodology of the Index has been updated since last year, so year-to-year comparisons are not exact. Second, as also outlined above, the growth prospects of an economy depend not only on the GCI score but also on the level of per capita income. The catch-up effect is not included within the GCI itself, so a poor country with a low GCI might still have good growth prospects because it has room to "catch up" relative to a richer country with a somewhat higher GCI score.

Third, GCI rankings should not be confused with GCI scores. The difference in growth prospects for economies, say, five spots apart from one another on the rankings are not the same at all points on the GCI distribution. For instance, Finland's top GCI score of 6.03 is roughly 0.3 greater than Australia's 5th place score, whereas New Zealand's 10th place score of 5.53 is only 0.1 greater than Switzerland's 15th ranked value of 5.43. In an even tighter bunching, Panama's 53rd place score of 3.88 is barely different from El Salvador's value five slots lower at 3.84.

Fourth, the maximum possible score on the GCI is 7; the lowest is 1. All component variables, whether taken from the GCR Executive Opinion Survey or from hard data sources, have been re-based so that the "top" score is always equal to 7 and the "lowest" score is always to 1. Based on our statistical analysis, for two economies at the same level of per capita income, an increase of one point in GCI score (on the 1-to-7 scale) is linked, on average, to a rise of the growth rate of slightly more than 3 percentage points per annum. Conversely, the GCI implies that two economies with similar scores but different starting income levels will have different growth rates. For example, an economy with GDP per capita of $10,000 and a GCI score of 5 is predicted to grow, on average, nearly 2 percentage points faster per year than an economy with GDP per capita of $20,000 and the same GCI score of 5.

Fifth, although we and our colleagues at the Center for International Development at Harvard have spent a great amount of time studying such important growth factors as climate and proximity to markets, these geographical factors are not directly included in the GCI. Geographical factors do appear indirectly, because they affect industrial structure and other economic variables that are included in the Index. We want to stress, however, the importance and relative neglect of these geographical factors. The Baltic countries, for instance, with their seaport access and proximity to Western European markets, have an intrinsic advantage—independent of their policies—over land-locked economies in South America or economies such as Nigeria that have ample ocean access

but no major export markets nearby. Similarly, Mexico has an intrinsic growth advantage over Argentina, and Poland over Romania. At the same time, New Zealand has very strong institutional, macroeconomic, and technological prospects for growth, as evidenced by its top-10 ranking on this year's Index, but it is located thousands of miles from most major markets, with the minor exception of Australia. We hope in future studies to incorporate these factors more directly in the GCI.

Sixth, there are fundamental limitations to the statistical analysis of medium-term growth. Regression tools allow us to capture and estimate the effects of numerous factors across a wide range of economies, but the range of countries with available data is inherently small and the period available for analysis is unfortunately short. Individual countries have specific characteristics that will inevitably be missed in our cross-sectional research, which relies on averages and trends. Also, our unit of analysis—the national economy—is blunt. The economies in our sample range from small and homogeneous societies such as Iceland, with a population of fewer than 300,000, to the massive and diverse countries of India and China, each with more than one billion people and an incredible internal diversity. The GCI does not account for these internal variations in growth prospects.

Finally, one must be sure not to confuse the last places on the GCI ranking with the worst growth prospects in the world. There are more than 150 countries around the world with populations of greater than one million. In this study we cover only 74 of those plus Iceland. We do not yet include the other 75 economies due to problems in collecting data, problems that are often highly related to the lack of economic development and growth competitiveness. The countries that occupy the last few spots of the GCI are far from lost causes—they merely represent the economies with the most policy work to do among our sample of countries. They also represent the countries with the greatest opportunity for "catch-up" growth as described above. Nigeria, for example, as the most populous country in Africa, stands truly at the dawn of a new economic and political era and, despite its fragile policy environment, could make great strides in economic development with good domestic policies and international help. Rather than seeing a low score on the ranking as cause for despair, we would instead hope that policymakers and business leaders will view the information contained in this report as a useful means to identify policy priorities and, in the future, to benchmark the success of new initiatives. Indeed, regardless of national income level, we aim for the information contained in the GCI to help policymakers and private-sector representatives in every country identify their national priorities as they seek to enhance their citizens' levels of economic welfare.

A brief comment on the United States

With the United States in slowdown, all eyes are on the country for clues about economic prospects in the coming few years. Will the United States go into a deep and prolonged slump, as Japan did after the bursting of its financial bubble in the early 1990s? Will it recover fairly quickly and resume its dynamic growth of the second half of the 1990s? Although we are reluctant to make short-term forecasts, especially given the purposes of the GCI, we stress that the underlying competitiveness of the United States economy remains very strong, auguring well over a five-year perspective. Of course, there are some notable blemishes that merit our attention.

The United States is in a slowdown now related to the end of a huge wave of investment in ICT capital stock. There are three reasons for the slowdown. First, after an enormous building period in information technology, companies are taking a breather in their ICT investments. They have no need to keep accumulating IT equipment as rapidly as they did in the second half of the 1990s. Second, the roll out of high bandwidth applications is certainly proceeding more slowly than expected just a few years ago. Third, the United States experienced a financial bubble when optimism about the IT revolution led to a euphoric overpricing of the technology sector. The risks of the US bubble have been evident for years, even before the stock market crash of 2000–2001. In mid-1998, the *Global Competitiveness Report* warned about the apparent overvaluation of the stock market.[iv] The worry was repeated in the 1999 GCR, when we wrote, "Everybody with sufficient stock market holdings feels rich and very clever. . . . Our best guess is that they will feel a little less clever in a year's time,"[v] a view that was vindicated by the subsequent end of the bubble beginning in the spring of 2000.

Does the bursting of the bubble undermine the case for the competitiveness of the United States? Not really, if we take a view over five or more years. The dynamism of the US economy remains tremendous. The flexibility of labor markets, ease of startups, technological prowess, and fiscal balance are all very strong. The financial sector appears to be sound, even after the collapse of the bubble, though undoubtedly there will be a stream of bad news as some heavily indebted enterprises go under. It seems unlikely to us that the United States will therefore enter into a prolonged slump of the sort that afflicted Japan in the 1990s. It is notable that Japan's competitiveness ranking has always been much lower than that of the United States in the past five years, and continues to be much lower in this year's *Report*.

The United States does have its relative weaknesses, however. Although the United States ranks second overall, this is a reflection of extraordinary strength in technology, combined with notably lower scores on the other two GCI component indexes. On the macroeconomic environment index, it rates seventh, somewhat behind the top countries of Singapore and Ireland. On the public institutions index, it ranks even lower, placing 12th, with a score roughly comparable with those of Hong Kong SAR and Israel. On more specific points, the dollar is surely overvalued relative to the euro. The rule of law is not as strong as Americans sometimes assume, as evidenced by 11th place ranking on the US corruption subindex and 17th place ranking on its measure of contracts and law. The low placing on the latter measure is due to poor scores on Executive Opinion Survey questions relating to government neutrality in public contracts and policy (18th overall) and a 22nd place ranking on the business costs imposed by organized crime. Note that this latter ranking is roughly the same as last year's, when the United States scored 25th on the same question.

Perhaps most notably, and somewhat notoriously, the United States is an unequal society, with huge perceived (and likely quite real) discrepancies between services enjoyed by the rich and the poor. In our Executive Opinion Survey question that asks about the difference in health care availability for the rich and poor, the United States scores 27th, behind Estonia and just ahead of Malaysia. In a parallel question that asks about discrepancies in schools available for rich versus poor children, the United States ranks even worse at 43rd, after Russia and barely above Uruguay. These Survey results highlight the inequalities in the United States when compared with inequalities in other countries, especially those in Western Europe, where the social welfare state is far more inclusive and therefore the quality of public services compared with private services also considered to be quite high. It is notable that Finland, the top country in this year's GCI, ranks best in the world on the measure of perceived educational equality and third on the measure of health care equality. Thus, Finland has achieved a technologically sophisticated economy with a high degree of social equality as well.

37

METHODOLOGY BEHIND THE GROWTH COMPETITIVENESS INDEX

As outlined in the previous section, because of the different growth trajectories that economies typically face at different levels of development, a fundamental issue must be considered when assessing growth competitiveness around the world: Different growth factors play different roles at different stages of development.[vi] Our research has suggested that public institutions, for instance, play a more crucial role at low and middle levels of development than they do at high levels, where economies tend to have less variation in institutional quality and a satisfactory threshold of organizational efficiency has already been met. Likewise, once overall macroeconomic stability is achieved, including sustainable fiscal balances and a healthy banking system with broad access to credit, "increased" stability becomes difficult to measure and its benefits become less pronounced.

Technology plays a key role in all stages of development. But again, the means through which technological progress occurs, and the conditions conducive to its advance, will vary at different levels of development. At low levels of development, growth competitiveness is achieved mainly through the effective exploitation of land, primary commodities, and unskilled labor. As economies move from low- to middle-income status, competitiveness is increasingly achieved by harnessing global technologies to local production. Foreign direct investment, joint ventures, and outsourcing arrangements help to integrate the national economy into international production systems, thereby facilitating the improvement of technologies and the inflows of foreign capital that support economic growth. The transition from middle-income to high-income status involves a transition from a technology-importing economy to a technology-generating economy, from technological adoption to innovation. At high levels of income, global competitiveness depends on innovation, high rates of social learning, and rapid adaptability to new technologies.

By adding 17 countries to our analysis since last year's GCR, we have significantly expanded our competitiveness research capacity. Most of the economies added to the GCR are middle-income developing countries, so including them provides more information about economic growth in the non-core economies. We should reiterate that the inherently backward-looking nature of empirical economic research poses a fundamental limitation in projecting future growth rates. The patterns that typified growth in the 1990s are not exactly the same as those that characterized growth in the 1960s or even the 1970s, and one can never fully predict what future technological innovations or revolutions will transform economic dynamics around the world. Despite these limitations, we

have found growth trends from the past decade that are strikingly clear and thus not likely to change dramatically over the coming five years. These are the trends that inform our analysis and give rise to the growth forecast represented by the GCI.

The steps of our methodology in uncovering and determining relative weights for these trends are as follows:

1. First, for our 1990s economic analysis, we divided our sample of 75 economies into core and non-core groups based on an objective measure of their level of technological sophistication: the 1980s average annual number of utility patents registered in the United States per million population. This variable has strengths and weaknesses as a general indicator of technology, but it does help to provide a clear grouping of the economies that were registering technological advances—at an international standard—at the beginning of the 1990s. By this criterion, we identified 18 core economies with more than 15 US utility patents granted per million population in the 1980s. These were Switzerland, the United States, Japan, Sweden, Germany, the Netherlands, Canada, the United Kingdom, France, Israel, Austria, Finland, Denmark, Belgium, Norway, Australia, Italy, and New Zealand. Table 1 lists the economies included in the 1980s core and also those that achieved the core criterion by 2000 and were hence counted as core economies in calculations for this year's GCI.

2. As a second step, we calculated the 1992 and 2000 levels of Gross Domestic Product (GDP) per capita, measured at purchasing power parity (PPP), for all 75 countries in our sample, with the exception of the former Eastern Bloc transition economies, for which we calculated 1995 levels. We then calculated the ratio of each country's GDP per capita PPP to US GDP per capita PPP in both 1992 (1995 for the transition economies) and 2000, and calculated the average annual change in the ratio over that period as our measure of economic growth. As a shorthand, we call this ratio to US GDP the *GDP GAP*. We chose 1992 as a starting point, since it marks the end of the last major industrialized world recession and removes business cycle fluctuations that might otherwise distort the analysis of growth rates. For the transition economies, we selected 1995 in order to avoid incorporating the general negative growth that occurred during the first years of those economies' post-communism adjustment period.

3. Third, drawing on the economic growth literature and our own research at CID, we constructed more than a dozen subindexes to test their links with economic growth (as defined above). The indexes were typically comprised of both "hard" and "soft" data, the latter coming from the results of the Executive Opinion Survey. Using these subindexes, and testing them in a variety of specifications, we created indexes for three broad factors that were linked to economic growth in the 1990s: the quality of public institutions, the macroeconomic environment, and technology. As we have already stressed, these three factors are interwoven—strong institutions, for example, are needed for technological development to occur; a sophisticated technology base will contribute greatly to macroeconomic stability—but they do each have close and statistically distinct relationships with recent trends in economic growth. Measurements for each of these three pillars of growth, as well as their weightings in the GCI, are given below.

4. We then combined the component indexes into the overall GCI. For the core economies, our statistical analysis suggested we should place extra emphasis on the role of innovation and technology. Accordingly, the weightings for the core economies were as follows:

> Core GCI = 1/2 technology index
> + 1/4 public institutions index
> + 1/4 macroeconomic environment index.

Meanwhile, for the non-core economies, our statistical analysis suggested a more balanced weighting between technology, institutions, and macroeconomic conditions. We therefore calculated GCI values for these countries as a simple average of the three component indexes:

> Non-core GCI = 1/3 technology index
> + 1/3 public institutions index
> + 1/3 macroeconomic environment index.

As noted above, for Ireland, Singapore, and Hong Kong SAR—economies in transition from non-core to core status—we averaged their core GCI and non-core GCI scores to calculate an overall score.

Fourth, we examined the relationship between the GCI and growth during 1992 to 2000 using the following growth equation:

$$\text{Average Annual Change in GAP} = ß_0 + ß_1 \times GCI + ß_2 \times \text{natural log (percentage GDP GAP in 1992)}^{\text{vii}}$$

The results of this regression equation were displayed in Figure 1.[viii] We now turn to a more detailed discussion of the subcomponents of the overall Index.

Technology

Capturing the various processes of technological development forms a central challenge of our competitiveness research. Constructing measures that are precise enough to represent trends in specific countries yet broad enough to allow global comparability is a long-term research endeavor in which we are still in the early stages. Nonetheless, in the preparation of this year's *Report* we have investigated and developed technology indicators that provide a crucial advance in the evolution of global competitiveness comparisons. Since the core and non-core technology economies follow distinctly different processes of technological development, we have developed respective measures of technology that are used in competitiveness calculations for each group.

Technology in the core economies

For the core economies, the technology index is a simple average of an innovation subindex and an information and communication technology (ICT) subindex, both of which are comprised of hard and soft data. (The reader should note that the innovation subindex presented here is different from the "innovative capacity index" constructed by Michael E Porter and Scott Stern in Chapter 2.2 of this *Report*. That measure seeks to explain the underlying factors that contribute to innovation as measured by patents. The innovation subindex here seeks to explain the elements of innovation, such as patents, that are linked measurably to growth.) Using a simple linear transformation, the hard data were converted to a 1-to-7 scale so that they could be easily merged with the Executive Opinion Survey questions, most of which have possible responses on a range of 1 to 7, with 1 being the low score and 7 the high score.[ix] The precise composition of the technology index is outlined in Box 2.

Box 2: Technology index components

Technological core economies

core technology index = 1/2 innovation subindex
+ 1/2 ICT subindex.

Technological non-core economies

non-core technology index = 1/8 innovation subindex
+ 3/8 technology transfer subindex
+ 1/2 ICT subindex.

1. Innovation subindex

innovation subindex = 1/4 Survey data + 3/4 hard data.

innovation Survey questions

3.01 What is your country's position in technology relative to world leaders?

3.02 Does continuous innovation play a major role in generating revenue for your business?

3.06 How much do companies in your country spend on R&D relative to other countries?

3.09 What is the extent of business collaboration in R&D with local universities?

innovation hard data

3.16 US Utility Patents Granted per million population in 2000

3.19 Gross Tertiary Enrollment Rate in 1997*

2. Technology transfer subindex

technology transfer subindex = 1/2 technology transfer
Survey question
+ 1/2 technology-in-trade residual.

3.04 Is foreign direct investment in your country an important source of new technology?

3.23 Technology-in-trade residual in 1999*

* Or latest available year.

3. Information and communication technology subindex

ICT subindex = 1/3 ICT Survey data + 2/3 ICT hard data

ICT Survey questions

4.03 How extensive is Internet access in schools?

4.07 Is competition among ISPs sufficient to ensure high quality, infrequent interruptions and low prices?

4.08 Is ICT an overall priority for the government?

4.09 Are government programs successful in promoting the use of ICT?

4.11 Are laws relating to ICT (electronic commerce, digital signatures, consumer protection) well developed and enforced?

ICT hard data

4.13 Number of mobile telephone users per capita

4.14 Number of Internet users per capita

4.15 Number of Internet hosts per capita

4.16 Number of telephone mainlines per capita

4.17 Number of personal computers per capita

Innovation subindex

When considering economic growth, a measure of innovation is central to measuring levels of technological sophistication in the core economies. Innovation is a product of many factors, but foremost among these are skilled human resources, well-developed market incentive structures for science, and intensive interaction between scientific and business sectors. The innovation measure aims to capture many of these processes through the use of hard and Survey data. On the hard side, we include two variables: US utility patents granted per million population and gross tertiary enrollment rates.

Patents are not a perfect measure of innovation, since they do not distinguish between very minor innovations that are simply technological refinements and major innovations that revolutionize a field. However, on average they present a very useful measure of innovation intensity in an economy and, to some extent, of the frequency with which innovations are taken to market rather than simply left in a laboratory. Tertiary education enrollment rates form a similarly broad but useful measure. They do not tell us the specific skill composition of a workforce, nor the precise number of product and process innovators in an economy, but they do provide a sound indication of a country's capacity to develop new technology and products at all levels of its economy. In fact, when performing statistical tests in which different variables were assessed in terms of their relationship with 1990s growth in the core economies, tertiary enrollment rates were found to be the variable most closely linked to high growth in the 1990s. We hence placed a greater weighting on it (3/4) than on patents (1/4) in the construction of the hard data portion of the innovation subindex.

The Survey questions incorporated in the innovation subindex form broad indicators of technological sophistication and product development. As shown in Box 2, the innovation subindex blends the hard data score with average country Survey scores from questions on the overall level of technology in the economy, the role of continuous innovation in generating revenue, company R&D spending relative to international peers, and private sector R&D collaboration with local universities. The overall innovation subindex places a 3/4 weight on the hard data and 1/4 weight on the soft data.

Innovation subindex scores and rankings are listed for the full sample in Table 4 and for only the core in Table 6A. In both tables, one sees that Canada is ranked first among the core economies, just slightly ahead of the United States, while Hong Kong, Iceland, and Ireland occupy the bottom positions. The greatest driving factor on these rankings is gross tertiary enrollment, a measure on which Canada's 88 percent ratio is the highest in the world by a significant margin.[x] The United States has the second-highest ratio at 81 percent and Australia the

Table 4: Innovation subindex

innovation subindex = 3/4 hard data score + 1/4 Survey data score

Country	Innovation Subindex	Rank	Country	Innovation Hard Data Score	Rank	Country	Innovation Survey Data Score	Rank
Canada	6.51	1	Canada	6.84	1	Finland	6.14	1
United States	6.50	2	Taiwan*	6.76	2	United States	6.11	2
Taiwan	6.37	3	United States	6.63	3	Sweden	5.99	3
Finland	6.12	4	Australia	6.24	4	Switzerland	5.93	4
Australia	5.96	5	Finland	6.12	5	Germany	5.89	5
Korea	5.46	6	Korea	5.69	6	Israel	5.79	6
Norway	5.27	7	Norway	5.34	7	France	5.73	7
Belgium	5.19	8	New Zealand	5.27	8	Japan	5.72	8
Sweden	5.17	9	Belgium	5.07	9	Netherlands	5.70	9
New Zealand	5.11	10	Sweden	4.89	10	Singapore	5.70	10
United Kingdom	5.02	11	United Kingdom	4.84	11	United Kingdom	5.55	11
France	5.01	12	France	4.78	12	Belgium	5.54	12
Germany	4.98	13	Germany	4.67	13	Canada	5.51	13
Netherlands	4.88	14	Denmark	4.66	14	Austria	5.38	14
Denmark	4.83	15	Austria	4.62	15	Denmark	5.35	15
Austria	4.81	16	Netherlands	4.61	16	Ireland	5.32	16
Japan	4.74	17	Spain	4.45	17	Iceland	5.27	17
Israel	4.71	18	Italy	4.44	18	Taiwan	5.19	18
Singapore	4.48	19	Japan	4.42	19	Australia	5.10	19
Spain	4.48	20	Israel	4.35	20	Norway	5.06	20
Italy	4.47	21	Ireland	4.13	21	Hong Kong SAR	4.79	21
Switzerland	4.44	22	Singapore	4.08	22	Korea	4.77	22
Ireland	4.43	23	Iceland	4.04	23	South Africa	4.76	23
Iceland	4.35	24	Greece	3.99	24	New Zealand	4.63	24
Greece	3.95	25	Switzerland	3.94	25	Hungary	4.63	25
Estonia	3.94	26	Estonia	3.80	26	Czech Republic	4.61	26
Slovenia	3.80	27	Russia	3.73	27	Italy	4.58	27
Russia	3.72	28	Slovenia	3.65	28	Spain	4.56	28
Hong Kong SAR	3.67	29	Argentina	3.55	29	Chile	4.40	29
Argentina	3.61	30	Portugal	3.49	30	Brazil	4.38	30
Portugal	3.58	31	Ukraine	3.47	31	Estonia	4.34	31
Costa Rica	3.51	32	Hong Kong SAR	3.29	32	Slovak Republic	4.30	32
Ukraine	3.48	33	Bulgaria	3.29	33	India	4.29	33
Chile	3.41	34	Costa Rica	3.25	34	Poland	4.29	34
Hungary	3.30	35	Chile	3.08	35	Costa Rica	4.28	35
Latvia	3.29	36	Latvia	3.05	36	Slovenia	4.24	36
Panama	3.24	37	Panama	3.03	37	China	4.23	37
Czech Republic	3.24	38	Hungary	2.85	38	Malaysia	4.23	38
Bulgaria	3.19	39	Venezuela	2.80	39	Trinidad and Tobago	4.14	39
South Africa	3.10	40	Uruguay	2.79	40	Philippines	4.02	40
Uruguay	3.03	41	Czech Republic	2.78	41	Latvia	4.02	41
Venezuela	3.01	42	Poland	2.55	42	Thailand	3.98	42
Poland	2.98	43	South Africa	2.55	43	Indonesia	3.91	43
Slovak Republic	2.97	44	Slovak Republic	2.53	44	Jamaica	3.87	44
Philippines	2.80	45	Bolivia	2.46	45	Portugal	3.86	45
Dominican Republic	2.78	46	Dominican Republic	2.46	46	Panama	3.85	46
Thailand	2.77	47	Lithuania	2.46	47	Greece	3.82	47
Lithuania	2.76	48	Philippines	2.39	48	Mexico	3.80	48
Brazil	2.66	49	Peru	2.38	49	Jordan	3.79	49
Malaysia	2.64	50	Thailand	2.36	50	Argentina	3.79	50
Peru	2.62	51	Romania	2.33	51	Dominican Republic	3.75	51
Mexico	2.61	52	Mexico	2.21	52	Uruguay	3.74	52
Romania	2.51	53	Egypt	2.15	53	Russia	3.68	53
Bolivia	2.50	54	Malaysia	2.11	54	Vietnam	3.68	54
Egypt	2.47	55	Turkey	2.09	55	Lithuania	3.64	55
Turkey	2.45	56	Brazil	2.08	56	Nigeria	3.64	56
Colombia	2.39	57	Colombia	2.03	57	Zimbabwe	3.63	57
Jamaica	2.29	58	Ecuador	2.01	58	Sri Lanka	3.63	58
Ecuador	2.25	59	Jamaica	1.76	59	Venezuela	3.62	59
Jordan	2.25	60	Jordan	1.73	60	Mauritius	3.56	60
India	2.16	61	El Salvador	1.73	61	Turkey	3.53	61
El Salvador	2.08	62	Honduras	1.64	62	Ukraine	3.50	62
China	2.07	63	Guatemala	1.58	63	Colombia	3.47	63
Indonesia	2.06	64	India	1.44	64	Egypt	3.44	64
Guatemala	2.00	65	Indonesia	1.44	65	Peru	3.34	65
Honduras	1.96	66	Nicaragua	1.40	66	Guatemala	3.26	66
Trinidad and Tobago	1.94	67	China	1.35	67	El Salvador	3.14	67
Nicaragua	1.83	68	Paraguay	1.32	68	Nicaragua	3.11	68
Sri Lanka	1.81	69	Trinidad and Tobago	1.21	69	Romania	3.05	69
Vietnam	1.77	70	Sri Lanka	1.21	70	Bangladesh	3.01	70
Zimbabwe	1.75	71	Vietnam	1.14	71	Paraguay	3.00	71
Paraguay	1.74	72	Zimbabwe	1.12	72	Ecuador	3.00	72
Mauritius	1.71	73	Mauritius	1.10	73	Honduras	2.92	73
Nigeria	1.66	74	Bangladesh	1.09	74	Bulgaria	2.89	74
Bangladesh	1.57	75	Nigeria	1.00	75	Bolivia	2.61	75

*Note that Taiwan's hard data innovation score is based solely on patent levels, since gross tertiary enrollment data comparable with the other countries is not available.

Table 5: Information and communications technology subindex

ICT subindex = 2/3 hard data score + 1/3 Survey data score

Country	ICT Subindex	Rank	Country	ICT Hard Data Score	Rank	Country	ICT Survey Data Score	Rank
Finland	6.58	1	Norway	6.83	1	Finland	6.37	1
Iceland	6.47	2	Iceland	6.83	2	Singapore	6.06	2
Sweden	6.45	3	Sweden	6.77	3	Sweden	5.82	3
Singapore	6.40	4	United States	6.70	4	Iceland	5.75	4
United States	6.34	5	Denmark	6.69	5	United States	5.63	5
Norway	6.28	6	Finland	6.68	6	Canada	5.55	6
Denmark	6.25	7	Switzerland	6.63	7	Hong Kong SAR	5.47	7
Canada	6.23	8	Netherlands	6.62	8	Estonia	5.45	8
Netherlands	6.20	9	Australia	6.60	9	Denmark	5.37	9
Hong Kong SAR	6.19	10	Canada	6.57	10	United Kingdom	5.37	10
Australia	6.15	11	Singapore	6.56	11	Netherlands	5.36	11
Switzerland	6.10	12	Hong Kong SAR	6.56	12	Austria	5.33	12
Austria	6.09	13	Japan	6.52	13	Australia	5.26	13
United Kingdom	6.09	14	Taiwan	6.48	14	Norway	5.18	14
Germany	6.01	15	Austria	6.48	15	Ireland	5.16	15
Taiwan	6.01	16	Germany	6.46	16	Korea	5.15	16
New Zealand	5.99	17	United Kingdom	6.46	17	Germany	5.11	17
Ireland	5.97	18	New Zealand	6.45	18	France	5.09	18
Belgium	5.90	19	Ireland	6.38	19	Taiwan	5.07	19
Estonia	5.88	20	Belgium	6.36	20	New Zealand	5.06	20
France	5.87	21	Israel	6.30	21	Switzerland	5.05	21
Korea	5.87	22	France	6.26	22	Belgium	4.97	22
Israel	5.83	23	Korea	6.23	23	Israel	4.88	23
Japan	5.82	24	Portugal	6.15	24	Spain	4.86	24
Portugal	5.68	25	Italy	6.15	25	Portugal	4.73	25
Spain	5.63	26	Estonia	6.10	26	Hungary	4.60	26
Italy	5.55	27	Slovenia	6.07	27	Czech Republic	4.59	27
Slovenia	5.47	28	Spain	6.01	28	India	4.57	28
Czech Republic	5.45	29	Czech Republic	5.88	29	Chile	4.57	29
Hungary	5.30	30	Greece	5.85	30	Jordan	4.56	30
Slovak Republic	5.26	31	Slovak Republic	5.69	31	Malaysia	4.49	31
Chile	5.20	32	Hungary	5.66	32	Brazil	4.49	32
Malaysia	5.16	33	Uruguay	5.62	33	Japan	4.42	33
Uruguay	5.15	34	Chile	5.51	34	Slovak Republic	4.40	34
Greece	5.14	35	Malaysia	5.50	35	Italy	4.37	35
Latvia	5.02	36	Latvia	5.48	36	Slovenia	4.27	36
Poland	4.90	37	Poland	5.46	37	South Africa	4.27	37
Brazil	4.86	38	Argentina	5.31	38	Egypt	4.24	38
Argentina	4.84	39	Mauritius	5.29	39	Uruguay	4.21	39
South Africa	4.80	40	Lithuania	5.22	40	Jamaica	4.11	40
Mauritius	4.77	41	Costa Rica	5.15	41	Latvia	4.09	41
Costa Rica	4.69	42	Trinidad and Tobago	5.11	42	Philippines	4.07	42
Lithuania	4.67	43	South Africa	5.07	43	China	3.96	43
Trinidad and Tobago	4.64	44	Turkey	5.05	44	Colombia	3.95	44
Turkey	4.61	45	Brazil	5.04	45	Thailand	3.94	45
Mexico	4.60	46	Mexico	4.99	46	El Salvador	3.93	46
Jamaica	4.57	47	Bulgaria	4.94	47	Argentina	3.92	47
Venezuela	4.51	48	Venezuela	4.85	48	Panama	3.86	48
Panama	4.48	49	Romania	4.84	49	Dominican Republic	3.86	49
Bulgaria	4.45	50	Jamaica	4.81	50	Venezuela	3.84	50
Colombia	4.40	51	Panama	4.79	51	Mexico	3.82	51
Jordan	4.26	52	Russia	4.66	52	Costa Rica	3.78	52
Thailand	4.23	53	Colombia	4.62	53	Poland	3.77	53
Russia	4.16	54	Thailand	4.37	54	Turkey	3.75	54
Philippines	4.12	55	Peru	4.23	55	Mauritius	3.73	55
China	4.04	56	Philippines	4.14	56	Greece	3.71	56
Dominican Republic	4.02	57	Jordan	4.10	57	Trinidad and Tobago	3.71	57
Peru	4.01	58	Dominican Republic	4.10	58	Lithuania	3.58	58
Romania	4.00	59	China	4.08	59	Peru	3.57	59
El Salvador	3.93	60	Ukraine	4.01	60	Bulgaria	3.48	60
Egypt	3.82	61	El Salvador	3.92	61	Indonesia	3.44	61
Ukraine	3.77	62	Paraguay	3.90	62	Sri Lanka	3.43	62
Ecuador	3.62	63	Ecuador	3.88	63	Ukraine	3.29	63
Paraguay	3.56	64	Bolivia	3.87	64	Vietnam	3.24	64
Bolivia	3.52	65	Guatemala	3.77	65	Nigeria	3.17	65
Guatemala	3.50	66	Egypt	3.61	66	Russia	3.15	66
Indonesia	3.44	67	Indonesia	3.44	67	Ecuador	3.11	67
India	3.43	68	Sri Lanka	3.41	68	Nicaragua	3.05	68
Sri Lanka	3.42	69	Honduras	3.36	69	Guatemala	2.97	69
Honduras	3.22	70	Nicaragua	3.29	70	Bangladesh	2.94	70
Nicaragua	3.21	71	Zimbabwe	3.21	71	Zimbabwe	2.94	71
Zimbabwe	3.12	72	India	2.86	72	Honduras	2.92	72
Vietnam	2.84	73	Vietnam	2.64	73	Paraguay	2.89	73
Nigeria	2.16	74	Nigeria	1.66	74	Bolivia	2.80	74
Bangladesh	1.96	75	Bangladesh	1.47	75	Romania	2.34	75

42

third-highest at 80 percent. Finland, the top European country in this regard, is next at 74 percent. Hong Kong has the lowest ratio among core economies at 22 percent, anchoring it in a low innovation ranking. On the patent measures, the United States and Japan are clearly the world leaders, with 309 and 246 respective US patents granted per million people in 2000. Canada ranks 9th among patent recipients, with 111 per million population in the same year. On the Survey measures of innovation, Finland comes out on top, followed closely by the United States and Sweden. Italy, New Zealand, and Korea meanwhile fill out the bottom side of the same scale, indicating low levels of firm-based innovation and university-business research collaboration in those countries.

Information and communications technology subindex
The ICT subindex is comprised of 2/3 hard data and 1/3 Survey data. The hard data include simple per capita measures of telephone lines, personal computers, Internet usage, Internet hosts, and mobile phone users, as published by the International Telecommunications Union. These data were again combined into an overall 1-to-7 scale that was in turn merged with Survey questions regarding ICT usage and government policies, as outlined in Box 2.

Table 5 shows the ICT subindex scores, with the Scandinavian countries occupying three of the top six positions. Finland takes the top spot by virtue of its highest average score on the Survey questions along with a high ranking on the hard measures of ICT, reflecting the overall prioritization of communications technology in that economy. Notably, Norway has the highest combined score on the hard ICT variables, followed closely by Iceland and Sweden. Last among the core economies on the overall ICT scores are Israel, Japan, and Italy, each of which have a low ranking among the core on hard measures of connectivity. These three countries score particularly poorly, however, on the survey measures of ICT, suggesting less of an emphasis on ICT in the public policies of these economies.

To form the overall core-economy technology index, the ICT subindex is averaged with the innovation subindex. The results are presented in Table 6A, which lists technology rankings for the core separately from the non-core. The United States ranks as the global technological leader, followed by Canada, Finland, and Taiwan. Note that this ranking represents a broad measure of technology, reflecting current ICT infrastructure, recent history of scientific innovation and product innovation, human resource potential for future innovation, and the policy environment for future scientific and product discovery. Several western European economies, including Germany, France, Austria, and Belgium, are tightly clustered in the middle of the group, all lagging behind their Scandinavian neighbors. Impressively, Korea and Taiwan, two countries

that were not among the core in the 1980s, both rank among the top 8 economies on this measure in 2001. Singapore, with its large push to develop local technological capacity, ranks just behind France. Further behind are Hong Kong and Ireland, two economies that, despite their fast growth, have not yet reached the top global tier of technological innovation processes.

Technology in the non-core economies

For countries that have not yet reached the stage of global technological competitiveness, one needs a measure of how quickly they are absorbing and implementing internationally competitive production technologies from the most sophisticated economies. To do this, we used the United Nations' COMTRADE database and also Statistics Canada's *World Trade Analyzer* to create a variable that measures the extent of manufacturing technology in the export structure of non-core economies. Countries with a technology-based export sector are judged to be more adept, in general, at absorbing technologies from abroad than economies with a primary commodity–based export structure. Regression analysis confirms strongly that, all other things equal, primary commodity–based economies indeed grew less rapidly in the past decade (and since 1970) than did more technology-based export economies.

To construct the technology-in-trade variable, we first calculated the average value of non-primary product exports as a proportion of GDP throughout the 1990s. To ensure the broadest possible reference base, we calculated this not just for the GCR sample, but also for the more than 100 countries for which detailed international trade data are available. Non-primary exports were defined to include most processed textiles and manufactured goods, but not mining products or processed raw materials.[xi] We then regressed the natural logarithm of the average 1990s value of non-primary exports as a percent of GDP on the natural logarithm of national population in the same period, and then converted the residual to a 1-to-7 scale, as with our other hard data.[xii] This *trade residual* term is important because small economies are inherently more open to trade, so when measuring extent of trade one needs to control for the size of an economy to understand the underlying variation in its trade performance.

The technology transfer subindex was created by averaging the technology-in-trade variable with a Survey question on the extent to which foreign direct investment "is an important source of new technology." This technology transfer subindex was then given a 3/8 weight against a 1/8 weight for the innovation subindex and a 4/8 weight for the ICT subindex to create non-core values on the overall technology index. The rationale for the various technology weightings merits a brief explanation. In our simple least squares regression analysis, we found that,

Table 6A: Technological core economies

Country	Technology Index	Core Rank	Country	Innovation Subindex	Core Rank	Country	ICT Subindex	Core Rank
United States	6.42	1	Canada	6.51	1	Finland	6.58	1
Canada	6.37	2	United States	6.50	2	Iceland	6.47	2
Finland	6.35	3	Taiwan	6.37	3	Sweden	6.45	3
Taiwan	6.19	4	Finland	6.12	4	Singapore	6.40	4
Australia	6.05	5	Australia	5.96	5	United States	6.34	5
Sweden	5.81	6	Korea	5.46	6	Norway	6.28	6
Norway	5.77	7	Norway	5.27	7	Denmark	6.25	7
Korea	5.66	8	Belgium	5.19	8	Canada	6.23	8
United Kingdom	5.56	9	Sweden	5.17	9	Netherlands	6.20	9
New Zealand	5.55	10	New Zealand	5.11	10	Hong Kong SAR	6.19	10
Denmark	5.54	11	United Kingdom	5.02	11	Australia	6.15	11
Belgium	5.54	12	France	5.01	12	Switzerland	6.10	12
Netherlands	5.54	13	Germany	4.98	13	Austria	6.09	13
Germany	5.49	14	Netherlands	4.88	14	United Kingdom	6.09	14
Austria	5.45	15	Denmark	4.83	15	Germany	6.01	15
France	5.44	16	Austria	4.81	16	Taiwan	6.01	16
Singapore	5.44	17	Japan	4.74	17	New Zealand	5.99	17
Iceland	5.41	18	Israel	4.71	18	Ireland	5.97	18
Japan	5.28	19	Singapore	4.48	19	Belgium	5.90	19
Switzerland	5.27	20	Italy	4.47	20	France	5.87	20
Israel	5.27	21	Switzerland	4.44	21	Korea	5.87	21
Ireland	5.20	22	Ireland	4.43	22	Israel	5.83	22
Italy	5.01	23	Iceland	4.35	23	Japan	5.82	23
Hong Kong SAR	4.93	24	Hong Kong SAR	3.67	24	Italy	5.55	24

Table 6B: Technological transition economies

Country	Technology Index	Rank Among Non-core Economies	Country	Innovation Subindex	Rank Among Non-core Economies	Country	ICT Subindex	Rank Among Non-core Economies	Country	Technology Transfer Subindex	Rank Among Non-core Economies
Singapore	6.26	1	Singapore	4.48	1	Singapore	6.40	1	Singapore	6.67	1
Ireland	5.96	2	Ireland	4.43	3	Hong Kong SAR	6.19	2	Ireland	6.46	3
Hong Kong SAR	5.93	3	Hong Kong SAR	3.67	8	Ireland	5.97	3	Hong Kong SAR	6.32	4

among the technology variables, ICT was linked to approximately half of the variation in average annual growth, so we gave it a corresponding weight in the technology index. Calculating the remainder of technology transfer and innovation subindexes was slightly more complicated. Using a statistical tool known as nonlinear least squares, we estimated the relative weights on innovation relative to technology transfer, and found an almost perfectly symmetrical result for the core and non-core. With the average annual 1992 to 2000 change in the per capita GDP GAP still as the dependent variable, for the core economies we found our measure of innovation to merit a weighting of 0.85 relative to technology transfer. This result and other statistical tests not reported here supported our emphasis on innovation in the core technology index.[xiii] For the non-core economies, we found that technology transfer merited a weighting of 0.81 relative to innovation. Given the small sample, the relatively short time period covered in this assessment, the other variables affecting growth that are not included in our model, and our general hesitation to place too much emphasis on any single factor in the development process, we scale back the coefficient on technology transfer to 0.75 in our GCR calculations.

In Table 6B, we present the technology index results obtained for the technological transition economies—Hong Kong SAR, Ireland, and Singapore—when they are considered non-core economies. In clear contrast to their rankings on the innovation-based core technology index, these economies score significantly ahead of the rest of the non-core economies when a technology transfer approach is used to assess their technological competitiveness. In Table 6C, we rank only the non-core economies as defined by 2000 patent levels. Notable on this list are the countries ranked 1st through 3rd: Estonia, the Czech Republic, and Hungary. Each of these economies has adopted manufacturing-based export-led growth strategies, and the success of those policies is clearly reflected in their index scores.

Portugal and Spain are also of significant interest. Both of these economies have enjoyed average real per capita growth rates of more than 3 percent over the past five years, but neither has been a tremendously successful innovator. Neither has a sufficient patenting rate to be included among the European core economies, and neither ranks among the top 15 non-core skilled manufacturing exporters. Through their close links with the rest of Western Europe, these economies do have high ICT scores, results that bolster their overall technology scores.

Table 6C: Technological non-core economies

Country	Technology Index	Non-core Rank	Country	Innovation Subindex	Non-core Rank	Country	ICT Subindex	Non-core Rank	Country	Technology Transfer Subindex	Non-core Rank
Estonia	5.68	1	Spain	4.48	1	Estonia	5.88	1	Malaysia	6.54	1
Czech Republic	5.39	2	Greece	3.95	2	Portugal	5.68	2	Hungary	6.19	2
Hungary	5.39	3	Estonia	3.94	3	Spain	5.63	3	Czech Republic	6.03	3
Malaysia	5.36	4	Slovenia	3.80	4	Slovenia	5.47	4	Estonia	5.98	4
Portugal	5.27	5	Russia	3.72	5	Czech Republic	5.45	5	Costa Rica	5.84	5
Spain	5.23	6	Argentina	3.61	6	Hungary	5.30	6	Slovak Republic	5.81	6
Slovak Republic	5.18	7	Portugal	3.58	7	Slovak Republic	5.26	7	Philippines	5.65	7
Slovenia	5.18	8	Costa Rica	3.51	8	Chile	5.20	8	Thailand	5.56	8
Costa Rica	4.97	9	Ukraine	3.48	9	Malaysia	5.16	9	Mexico	5.53	9
Latvia	4.83	10	Chile	3.41	10	Uruguay	5.15	10	Mauritius	5.52	10
Poland	4.75	11	Hungary	3.30	11	Greece	5.14	11	Dominican Republic	5.50	11
Mexico	4.70	12	Latvia	3.29	12	Latvia	5.02	12	Romania	5.37	12
Mauritius	4.67	13	Panama	3.24	13	Poland	4.90	13	Portugal	5.28	13
Greece	4.62	14	Czech Republic	3.24	14	Brazil	4.86	14	Slovenia	5.24	14
Thailand	4.54	15	Bulgaria	3.19	15	Argentina	4.84	15	Poland	5.15	15
Philippines	4.53	16	South Africa	3.10	16	South Africa	4.80	16	Vietnam	5.12	16
Lithuania	4.46	17	Uruguay	3.03	17	Mauritius	4.77	17	Latvia	5.08	17
Chile	4.45	18	Venezuela	3.01	18	Costa Rica	4.69	18	Sri Lanka	5.01	18
Jamaica	4.43	19	Poland	2.98	19	Lithuania	4.67	19	Jamaica	4.96	19
Dominican Republic	4.42	20	Slovak Republic	2.97	20	Trinidad and Tobago	4.64	20	Spain	4.96	20
Uruguay	4.40	21	Philippines	2.80	21	Turkey	4.61	21	Indonesia	4.76	21
South Africa	4.39	22	Dominican Republic	2.78	22	Mexico	4.60	22	Lithuania	4.74	22
Romania	4.33	23	Thailand	2.77	23	Jamaica	4.57	23	China	4.73	23
Argentina	4.33	24	Lithuania	2.76	24	Venezuela	4.51	24	Bulgaria	4.51	24
Brazil	4.33	25	Brazil	2.66	25	Panama	4.48	25	Turkey	4.45	25
Bulgaria	4.32	26	Malaysia	2.64	26	Bulgaria	4.45	26	Bangladesh	4.41	26
Turkey	4.28	27	Peru	2.62	27	Colombia	4.40	27	El Salvador	4.37	27
Trinidad and Tobago	4.10	28	Mexico	2.61	28	Jordan	4.26	28	South Africa	4.27	28
China	4.05	29	Romania	2.51	29	Thailand	4.23	29	Jordan	4.21	29
Jordan	3.99	30	Bolivia	2.50	30	Russia	4.16	30	Brazil	4.17	30
Venezuela	3.98	31	Egypt	2.47	31	Philippines	4.12	31	Greece	4.15	31
Colombia	3.92	32	Turkey	2.45	32	China	4.04	32	India	4.14	32
Panama	3.89	33	Colombia	2.39	33	Dominican Republic	4.02	33	Trinidad and Tobago	4.09	33
El Salvador	3.86	34	Jamaica	2.29	34	Peru	4.01	34	Argentina	3.88	34
Sri Lanka	3.82	35	Ecuador	2.25	35	Romania	4.00	35	Bolivia	3.86	35
Russia	3.78	36	Jordan	2.25	36	El Salvador	3.93	36	Uruguay	3.85	36
Indonesia	3.76	37	India	2.16	37	Egypt	3.82	37	Honduras	3.84	37
Peru	3.71	38	El Salvador	2.08	38	Ukraine	3.77	38	Chile	3.80	38
Ukraine	3.68	39	China	2.07	39	Ecuador	3.62	39	Colombia	3.78	39
Egypt	3.59	40	Indonesia	2.06	40	Paraguay	3.56	40	Zimbabwe	3.78	40
Vietnam	3.56	41	Guatemala	2.00	41	Bolivia	3.52	41	Nicaragua	3.69	41
India	3.54	42	Honduras	1.96	42	Guatemala	3.50	42	Peru	3.67	42
Bolivia	3.52	43	Trinidad and Tobago	1.94	43	Indonesia	3.44	43	Guatemala	3.66	43
Guatemala	3.38	44	Nicaragua	1.83	44	India	3.43	44	Egypt	3.66	44
Ecuador	3.33	45	Sri Lanka	1.81	45	Sri Lanka	3.42	45	Ukraine	3.63	45
Honduras	3.29	46	Vietnam	1.77	46	Honduras	3.22	46	Venezuela	3.60	46
Nicaragua	3.21	47	Zimbabwe	1.75	47	Nicaragua	3.21	47	Panama	3.32	47
Zimbabwe	3.20	48	Paraguay	1.74	48	Zimbabwe	3.12	48	Ecuador	3.31	48
Paraguay	2.98	49	Mauritius	1.71	49	Vietnam	2.84	49	Russia	3.30	49
Bangladesh	2.83	50	Nigeria	1.66	50	Nigeria	2.16	50	Nigeria	3.06	50
Nigeria	2.44	51	Bangladesh	1.57	51	Bangladesh	1.96	51	Paraguay	2.62	51

Other interesting stories are found further down the non-core technology rankings. With the exception of Mexico, Uruguay, and the Dominican Republic, most Latin American economies rank among the bottom half of the list. Argentina, one of the wealthiest countries in the non-core group, ranks 24th, just ahead of Brazil, which has a per capita GDP (PPP) nearly 50 percent smaller. Like much of Latin America, Argentina is an economy that needs to develop its technological base in order to grow.

Public institutions

Although technology provides a key pillar of economic growth, so too does the quality of the public institutions. Institutions are crucial for their role in ensuring the protection of property rights, the objective resolution of contract and other legal disputes, efficiency of government spending in public services, and transparency in all levels of government.[xiv] All of these factors underpin the division of labor, and therefore the efficiency of resource allocation. They are also fundamental in establishing the societal stability required for growth. Although the quality of institutions has been difficult to measure historically, in recent years the *Global Competitiveness Report*'s Executive Opinion Survey has played an important role in developing new techniques to quantify institutional quality across countries.[xv]

As with technology, institutions play different roles at different stages of economic development. Our regressions have shown evidence that once a threshold of institutional development has been met, it is very difficult to detect the growth effects of further modest improvements in institutional quality. (This is of course a working hypothesis that could be disproved with the development of more sophisticated measures of institutional quality.) Our regressions also show that institutional quality is closely linked to economic growth in the non-core countries. This is why we place a weight of 1/3 on the public institutions index in the non-core GCI calculations and a weight of only 1/4 in the core GCI calculations.

Box 3: Public institutions index

public institutions index = 1/2 contracts and law subindex
+ 1/2 corruption subindex.

contracts and law subindex Survey questions

6.01 Is the judiciary independent from the government and/or parties to dispute?

6.02 Are financial assets and wealth clearly delineated and well protected by law?

6.04 Is your government neutral among bidders when deciding upon public contracts?

6.12 Does organized crime impose significant costs on business?

corruption subindex Survey questions

7.01 How common are bribes paid in connection to import and export permits?

7.02 How common are bribes paid when getting connected to public utilities?

7.03 How common are bribes paid in connection with with annual tax payments?

The public institutions index (PII) is based entirely on Survey data and has two main components, as outlined in Box 3. The first is a measure of contract and law enforcement. It consists of economies' average score on questions concerning neutrality in government procurement, judicial independence, clear delineation and respect for property rights, and costs related to organized crime. The second element of the public institutions index is a subindex of corruption, or the abuse of public service positions for personal financial gain. This subindex measures the pervasiveness of bribery in three key public service areas: imports and exports, connection to public utilities, and tax collection.

Results for the PII and its main components are listed in Table 7. Finland, Iceland, Denmark, and New Zealand rank as the countries with the four top scores for overall institutional quality. Bangladesh, Paraguay, Nigeria, and

Honduras have the lowest scores. It is further interesting to note the countries that score significantly better or worse than one might expect based on their GDP per capita. The Czech Republic and Argentina, for instance, score 53rd and 55th, despite the fact that they have the 29th and 31st highest respective incomes per capita in the world. And even though it has grown to be the 24th richest economy today, Korea still rates almost as poorly at 44th. On the positive side, Egypt rates 33rd on the PII, contrasting with its 64th place ranking in per capita wealth. Jordan also ranks at 28th and Uruguay 31st on the PII, compared to 58th and 41st, respectively, on income per person.

Looking at the subindexes of the PII, Finland, Iceland, and Denmark cover the top three places on *both* the contracts and law measure and the corruption subindexes. These closely linked rankings suggest that the three countries have strong overall public and legal institutions relative to the rest of the world. Indeed, looking through the rest of the sample in Table 7, one finds that for the most part there is a strong similarity between countries' rankings on the two subindexes. This suggests that the subcomponents are capturing similar information about the rule of law in society.

Some important information may also be found when countries have significantly different rankings on the two subindexes. Among the high-income countries, for instance, Canada ranks 6th on corruption but 19th on contracts and law. Switzerland's case is nearly the exact opposite, rating 6th on contracts and law but 20th on corruption.

Lower down the list, at income levels where our research shows that differences in institutional quality play a much larger role in economic development, is where the most important information seems to be found. Consider Egypt. Its legal system of contracts and government neutrality scores in 24th place, which is high relative to its income level. Unfortunately, corruption seems to be weakening its institutions tremendously, according to the views of the business community, as indicated by its 54th place ranking on that subindex. India shares a similar problem, ranking 33rd on contracts and law but right near the bottom, at 66th, on corruption. Likewise, Thailand ranks 34th and 59th, Romania 39th and 64th, and Vietnam 49th and 71st on the respective subindexes. These are countries where effective anti-corruption measures could dramatically improve the prospects for growth.

Conversely, in many instances corruption is much less of a problem than weaknesses in contracts and law. Lithuania achieves a high score at 17th on frequency of bribery, but it ranks near the bottom at 59th on the measure of law and property rights. The pattern is similar in Peru (30th and 60th), Bulgaria (34th and 64th), and Colombia (40th and 67th). Dramatic institutional reforms

Table 7: Public institutions index

public institutions index = 1/2 contracts and law subindex + 1/2 corruption subindex

Country	Public Institutions Index	Rank	Country	Contracts and Law Subindex	Rank	Country	Corruption Subindex	Rank
Finland	6.59	1	Finland	6.35	1	Iceland	6.98	1
Iceland	6.56	2	Denmark	6.21	2	Finland	6.83	2
Denmark	6.42	3	Iceland	6.14	3	Denmark	6.62	3
New Zealand	6.33	4	Netherlands	6.09	4	New Zealand	6.61	4
Netherlands	6.29	5	New Zealand	6.05	5	Singapore	6.56	5
Singapore	6.27	6	Switzerland	5.97	6	Canada	6.52	6
Sweden	6.19	7	Singapore	5.97	7	Sweden	6.51	7
Australia	6.17	8	Germany	5.89	8	Australia	6.49	8
United Kingdom	6.14	9	Austria	5.89	9	Netherlands	6.48	9
Hong Kong SAR	6.01	10	Sweden	5.87	10	United Kingdom	6.42	10
Canada	6.01	11	Australia	5.86	11	United States	6.38	11
United States	6.01	12	United Kingdom	5.86	12	Hong Kong SAR	6.38	12
Switzerland	5.99	13	Israel	5.78	13	Chile	6.35	13
Israel	5.98	14	Ireland	5.71	14	Japan	6.29	14
Austria	5.98	15	France	5.69	15	Norway	6.28	15
Norway	5.95	16	Hong Kong SAR	5.64	16	Israel	6.18	16
Germany	5.93	17	United States	5.64	17	Lithuania	6.07	17
Ireland	5.87	18	Norway	5.62	18	Austria	6.07	18
Japan	5.76	19	Canada	5.50	19	Ireland	6.02	19
France	5.72	20	Belgium	5.41	20	Switzerland	6.01	20
Chile	5.69	21	Jordan	5.27	21	Germany	5.98	21
Belgium	5.67	22	Spain	5.23	22	Taiwan	5.98	22
Spain	5.47	23	Japan	5.23	23	Belgium	5.92	23
Taiwan	5.30	24	Egypt	5.15	24	France	5.75	24
Portugal	5.25	25	Portugal	5.06	25	Spain	5.71	25
Hungary	5.20	26	Chile	5.03	26	Hungary	5.69	26
Italy	5.05	27	Uruguay	5.01	27	Italy	5.56	27
Jordan	5.04	28	Mauritius	4.91	28	Portugal	5.44	28
Estonia	4.99	29	Hungary	4.70	29	Estonia	5.42	29
Slovenia	4.90	30	Taiwan	4.62	30	Peru	5.31	30
Uruguay	4.89	31	Estonia	4.55	31	Slovenia	5.29	31
Mauritius	4.79	32	Italy	4.55	32	South Africa	5.21	32
Egypt	4.76	33	India	4.54	33	Slovak Republic	5.13	33
Lithuania	4.70	34	Thailand	4.53	34	Bulgaria	5.12	34
South Africa	4.69	35	Costa Rica	4.52	35	Trinidad and Tobago	5.10	35
Trinidad and Tobago	4.63	36	Slovenia	4.50	36	Malaysia	4.97	36
Costa Rica	4.56	37	Greece	4.44	37	Jordan	4.81	37
Slovak Republic	4.54	38	Poland	4.32	38	Uruguay	4.78	38
Malaysia	4.53	39	Romania	4.30	39	Latvia	4.73	39
Greece	4.50	40	South Africa	4.17	40	Colombia	4.73	40
Poland	4.40	41	Trinidad and Tobago	4.15	41	Jamaica	4.70	41
Thailand	4.36	42	Malaysia	4.10	42	Mauritius	4.67	42
Jamaica	4.30	43	Korea	4.09	43	Costa Rica	4.60	43
Korea	4.25	44	Turkey	3.98	44	Greece	4.57	44
Peru	4.24	45	Brazil	3.97	45	Poland	4.48	45
Turkey	4.21	46	Slovak Republic	3.95	46	El Salvador	4.47	46
Brazil	4.21	47	Jamaica	3.89	47	Dominican Republic	4.46	47
Latvia	4.18	48	Czech Republic	3.85	48	China	4.46	48
India	4.11	49	Vietnam	3.77	49	Brazil	4.45	49
China	4.10	50	Argentina	3.75	50	Turkey	4.44	50
Bulgaria	4.07	51	China	3.74	51	Korea	4.41	51
Romania	4.06	52	Sri Lanka	3.66	52	Mexico	4.40	52
Czech Republic	4.04	53	Latvia	3.62	53	Russia	4.38	53
Dominican Republic	4.02	54	Dominican Republic	3.59	54	Egypt	4.37	54
Argentina	4.01	55	Mexico	3.58	55	Argentina	4.28	55
Mexico	3.99	56	Philippines	3.54	56	Bolivia	4.26	56
Colombia	3.85	57	Panama	3.41	57	Panama	4.26	57
Sri Lanka	3.84	58	Indonesia	3.35	58	Czech Republic	4.23	58
Panama	3.83	59	Lithuania	3.34	59	Thailand	4.19	59
El Salvador	3.79	60	Peru	3.16	60	Guatemala	4.12	60
Russia	3.68	61	El Salvador	3.11	61	Venezuela	4.05	61
Bolivia	3.67	62	Bolivia	3.08	62	Sri Lanka	4.03	62
Vietnam	3.58	63	Zimbabwe	3.01	63	Ecuador	3.91	63
Philippines	3.53	64	Bulgaria	3.01	64	Romania	3.82	64
Venezuela	3.40	65	Nigeria	2.98	65	Nicaragua	3.76	65
Indonesia	3.35	66	Russia	2.97	66	India	3.67	66
Nicaragua	3.33	67	Colombia	2.96	67	Honduras	3.64	67
Ecuador	3.30	68	Nicaragua	2.91	68	Zimbabwe	3.58	68
Zimbabwe	3.30	69	Bangladesh	2.84	69	Philippines	3.51	69
Guatemala	3.22	70	Ukraine	2.84	70	Ukraine	3.47	70
Ukraine	3.15	71	Venezuela	2.76	71	Vietnam	3.39	71
Honduras	3.01	72	Paraguay	2.72	72	Indonesia	3.35	72
Nigeria	2.84	73	Ecuador	2.70	73	Paraguay	2.77	73
Paraguay	2.75	74	Honduras	2.37	74	Nigeria	2.70	74
Bangladesh	2.48	75	Guatemala	2.31	75	Bangladesh	2.13	75

are still needed in these countries in order to advance economic development, but on the more optimistic side, the somewhat lower perceived extent of corruption may indicate an opening for increasing transparency and objectivity in key areas of governance and law.

Let us reiterate that these measures are not objective standards, but rather perceptions among business executives. We believe that governments should take these perceptions seriously, not just dispute their exactitude.[xvi] These kinds of perception indexes, in our studies and in many other studies, have helped account for differences in economic growth, with countries with high perceived corruption suffering lower growth.

Macroeconomic environment

The third and final pillar of the GCI is formed by an index of the macroeconomic environment. This index has three main elements: hard data to measure the overall stability of a country's macro economy, Survey data to assess the short-term outlook of private agents in the economy, and a measure of the share of government expenditures as a percentage of GDP.

The hard data components of the macroeconomic stability subindex, as outlined in Box 4, include the real exchange rate relative to the United States,[xvii] the interest rate spread between deposits and loans, the general government budget balance as a percent of GNP, consumer

price inflation in 2000, and the national savings rate. These variables, which as always are rescaled to 1-to-7 scores for index calculations, are each evenly weighted with two Survey questions, one asking about prospects for recession in the coming year and another asking about the tightening of credit over the past year.

Table 8 reviews the results of the macroeconomic stability subindex. Singapore, with its high savings rates, sound financial system, and strong history of fiscal responsibility, rates first again on this measure. Norway, which last year enjoyed a general government surplus of nearly 15 percent, ranks 2nd. Next are Finland, the Netherlands, Sweden, and Switzerland, each of which has healthy macroeconomic environments at the moment. The United States, largely due to its low savings rate and expectations of recession, has the lowest of all its subindex rankings here, placing 42nd in the sample. Most unstable are the economies with headline-grabbing fiscal histories in recent years, including Bolivia, Nicaragua, and Zimbabwe.

To calculate the overall macroeconomic environment index, the stability subindex is given a 1/2 weighting against the broad measure of a country's current macroeconomic situation provided by the *Institutional Investor's* country credit rating, which receives a 1/4 weight, and government expenditure as a percent of GNP, which also receives a 1/4 weight.[xviii] Many studies have shown that high levels of government expenditure relative to GNP are associated with low economic growth.[xix] This is probably because high rates of taxation are then required to pay for the government expenditures, and the high rates of taxation have a depressing effect on economic growth. The most heavily taxed region in the world, Western Europe, probably suffers a reduced rate of economic growth as a consequence.

We recognize that the optimal level of government expenditures is a much more complex issue than suggested by our approach. It certainly would not be correct to infer that economic growth would be maximized at zero government expenditures (though our equation has that perverse property). When government spending is too low, then governments do not meet even the core needs for education, health, and public services needed to underpin economic growth. This is the case, for example, in Guatemala, which has extremely low government spending—too low to meet even the basic health and education needs of the population. Higher levels of government spending, as in Western Europe, may be justified by the services provided or by the benefits for social equality even if they come at some price in terms of economic growth. These are difficult political, economic, philosophical tradeoffs. We hope in future studies to develop a more sophisticated evaluation of different types of government spending and their effects on competitiveness, stability, and other dimensions of economic performance.

Box 4: Macroeconomic environment index

macroeconomic
environment index = 1/2 macroeconomic stability subindex
+ 1/4 country credit rating in March 2001
+ 1/4 general government expenditure in 2000

Macroeconomic stability subindex

macroeconomic
stability subindex = 5/7 macroeconomic hard data
+ 2/7 macroeconomic survey data

Macroeconomic environment hard data

2.28 Inflation in 2000
2.30 Lending – borrowing interest rate spread in 2000
2.29 Real exchange rate relative to the United States in 2000 (1990–95 = 100)
2.24 General government surplus in 2000
2.26 National savings rate in 2000

Macroeconomic environment Survey questions

2.01 Is your country's economy likely to be in a recession next year?
2.03 Has obtaining credit for your company become easier or more difficult in the past year?

Table 8: Macroeconomic environment index

macroeconomic environment index = 1/2 stability subindex score + 1/4 country credit rating score + 1/4 government expenditure score

Country	Macroeconomic Environment Index Score	Rank	Country	Macroeconomic Stability Subindex	Rank	Country	Country Credit Rating Score	Rank	Country	Government Expenditure Score	Rank
Singapore	5.52	1	Singapore	5.37	1	Switzerland	7.00	1	Guatemala	7.00	1
Ireland	5.20	2	Norway	5.35	2	Germany	6.92	2	Dominican Republic	6.70	2
Switzerland	5.18	3	Finland	5.25	3	Netherlands	6.87	3	Thailand	6.34	3
Hong Kong SAR	5.12	4	Netherlands	5.13	4	France	6.83	4	China	6.29	4
Norway	5.08	5	Sweden	5.13	5	United States	6.82	5	El Salvador	6.17	5
China	5.04	6	Switzerland	5.13	6	United Kingdom	6.79	6	Bangladesh	6.13	6
United States	4.97	7	Korea	5.03	7	Norway	6.67	7	Hong Kong SAR	6.10	7
Korea	4.94	8	Spain	5.03	8	Austria	6.57	8	Philippines	6.07	8
Netherlands	4.88	9	France	5.01	9	Canada	6.48	9	Venezuela	5.77	9
Finland	4.82	10	Italy	4.98	10	Denmark	6.47	10	Indonesia	5.66	10
Spain	4.82	11	Austria	4.91	11	Finland	6.42	11	Costa Rica	5.65	11
United Kingdom	4.81	12	Ireland	4.91	12	Japan	6.40	12	Mexico	5.49	12
Canada	4.74	13	Belgium	4.90	13	Belgium	6.38	13	Argentina	5.39	13
New Zealand	4.70	14	Canada	4.89	14	Sweden	6.35	14	Vietnam	5.28	14
Taiwan	4.69	15	China	4.83	15	Singapore	6.29	15	Mauritius	5.22	15
Thailand	4.68	16	Germany	4.83	16	Ireland	6.29	16	Korea	5.20	16
Australia	4.68	17	Hong Kong SAR	4.77	17	Spain	6.19	17	Chile	5.06	17
Japan	4.66	18	Denmark	4.74	18	Italy	6.17	18	Ecuador	5.05	18
Germany	4.65	19	Vietnam	4.70	19	Portugal	5.97	19	Peru	5.05	18
Malaysia	4.59	20	Trinidad and Tobago	4.66	20	Australia	5.78	20	Singapore	5.03	20
Chile	4.56	21	Nigeria	4.65	21	New Zealand	5.62	21	South Africa	5.03	20
France	4.54	22	Hungary	4.64	22	Taiwan	5.56	22	Sri Lanka	5.03	20
Italy	4.53	23	New Zealand	4.61	23	Iceland	5.34	23	Trinidad and Tobago	4.92	23
Belgium	4.48	24	Malaysia	4.60	24	Greece	5.18	24	Malaysia	4.89	24
Trinidad and Tobago	4.48	25	Greece	4.60	25	Hong Kong SAR	4.86	25	Brazil	4.88	25
Austria	4.46	26	United Kingdom	4.60	26	Chile	4.76	26	Paraguay	4.82	26
South Africa	4.43	27	Taiwan	4.53	27	Slovenia	4.63	27	Ireland	4.71	27
Philippines	4.42	28	South Africa	4.53	28	Korea	4.51	28	United States	4.71	27
Sweden	4.40	29	Japan	4.52	29	Israel	4.49	29	Bolivia	4.66	29
Mauritius	4.34	30	Russia	4.52	30	Czech Republic	4.38	30	Panama	4.58	30
Denmark	4.28	31	Brazil	4.50	31	Hungary	4.35	31	Colombia	4.42	31
Greece	4.26	32	Slovenia	4.41	32	Poland	4.28	32	Egypt	4.33	32
Brazil	4.24	33	Portugal	4.41	33	Malaysia	4.25	33	India	4.29	33
Iceland	4.24	34	Thailand	4.39	34	China	4.22	34	Nigeria	4.29	33
Portugal	4.24	35	Australia	4.39	35	Mexico	4.13	35	Lithuania	4.22	35
Mexico	4.18	36	Estonia	4.39	36	Estonia	3.81	36	Australia	4.15	36
Vietnam	4.15	37	Iceland	4.33	37	Mauritius	3.74	37	Taiwan	4.12	37
Hungary	4.04	38	Philippines	4.28	38	Trinidad and Tobago	3.66	38	Honduras	4.08	38
Slovenia	4.02	39	Indonesia	4.26	39	Uruguay	3.65	39	Jordan	3.99	39
Argentina	3.99	40	Chile	4.20	40	South Africa	3.62	40	New Zealand	3.95	40
Indonesia	3.96	41	Mauritius	4.20	41	Thailand	3.59	41	Jamaica	3.86	41
Costa Rica	3.94	42	United States	4.17	42	India	3.40	42	Uruguay	3.84	42
Estonia	3.94	43	Czech Republic	4.12	43	Egypt	3.38	43	Ukraine	3.84	42
Panama	3.92	44	Israel	4.04	44	Latvia	3.25	44	Russia	3.69	44
India	3.88	45	Latvia	4.03	45	Slovak Republic	3.23	45	Turkey	3.61	45
Dominican Republic	3.87	46	Jordan	4.03	46	Panama	3.22	46	Romania	3.54	46
El Salvador	3.87	47	Slovak Republic	4.00	47	Costa Rica	3.14	47	Nicaragua	3.47	47
Bangladesh	3.81	48	Poland	3.98	48	Lithuania	3.11	48	Switzerland	3.45	48
Czech Republic	3.81	49	Panama	3.95	49	Brazil	3.09	49	United Kingdom	3.25	49
Poland	3.75	50	India	3.91	50	Turkey	3.09	49	Japan	3.22	50
Egypt	3.74	51	Argentina	3.88	51	Philippines	3.05	51	Estonia	3.18	51
Guatemala	3.73	52	Ecuador	3.75	52	Colombia	2.85	52	Spain	3.04	52
Venezuela	3.73	53	Lithuania	3.66	53	Argentina	2.79	53	Latvia	3.00	53
Jordan	3.69	54	Egypt	3.63	54	El Salvador	2.71	54	Iceland	2.98	54
Nigeria	3.68	55	Bangladesh	3.62	55	Jordan	2.70	55	Bulgaria	2.97	55
Lithuania	3.66	56	Romania	3.56	56	Peru	2.70	55	Norway	2.92	56
Russia	3.64	57	Mexico	3.55	57	Venezuela	2.49	57	Poland	2.74	57
Peru	3.62	58	Costa Rica	3.49	58	Bulgaria	2.43	58	Canada	2.71	58
Latvia	3.58	59	Bulgaria	3.48	59	Sri Lanka	2.40	59	Greece	2.65	59
Sri Lanka	3.56	60	Ukraine	3.45	60	Dominican Republic	2.38	60	Czech Republic	2.61	60
Israel	3.55	61	Sri Lanka	3.40	61	Guatemala	2.25	61	Slovenia	2.61	60
Ecuador	3.45	62	Peru	3.37	62	Paraguay	2.05	62	Hungary	2.53	62
Uruguay	3.38	63	Venezuela	3.32	63	Bolivia	1.97	63	Netherlands	2.38	63
Slovak Republic	3.35	64	El Salvador	3.30	64	Jamaica	1.94	64	Finland	2.37	64
Paraguay	3.31	65	Honduras	3.22	65	Vietnam	1.94	64	Portugal	2.18	65
Colombia	3.29	66	Dominican Republic	3.21	66	Romania	1.92	66	Slovak Republic	2.17	66
Romania	3.14	67	Jamaica	3.20	67	Bangladesh	1.85	67	Germany	2.04	67
Turkey	3.10	68	Paraguay	3.18	68	Russia	1.82	68	Italy	1.97	68
Bulgaria	3.09	69	Uruguay	3.02	69	Indonesia	1.68	69	Belgium	1.76	69
Bolivia	3.08	70	Colombia	2.94	70	Honduras	1.59	70	Zimbabwe	1.71	70
Jamaica	3.05	71	Turkey	2.85	71	Ecuador	1.26	71	Israel	1.62	71
Honduras	3.02	72	Guatemala	2.84	72	Nigeria	1.14	72	Austria	1.44	72
Ukraine	2.95	73	Bolivia	2.84	73	Ukraine	1.08	73	France	1.33	73
Nicaragua	2.48	74	Nicaragua	2.72	74	Nicaragua	1.01	74	Denmark	1.17	74
Zimbabwe	1.93	75	Zimbabwe	2.50	75	Zimbabwe	1.00	75	Sweden	1.00	75

49

CONCLUSION

As the world becomes increasingly interconnected but the disparities between wealthy and poor countries become ever starker, policymakers, business leaders, academics, and other globally minded citizens all require a much keener understanding of the forces contributing to economic growth in both the medium and long term, and how the importance of those forces changes at different stages of economic development. This chapter has focused on the central processes underpinning medium-term economic growth, with particular emphasis on technological advancement.

Marking a new direction in competitiveness research, we outlined key empirical distinctions between technological diffusion and innovation as pertains to economic growth. In so doing, we estimated not just the changing nature of technological advancement that typically accompanies economic development, but also the increasing importance of technology as economies create a sustainable capacity for innovation.

By dividing our sample of GCR countries into two groups, core and non-core technological innovators, we were able to estimate the respective growth-related effects of innovation and diffusion in the 1990s. Our evidence indicates that innovation matters substantially more than diffusion in the core economies, and that diffusion matters proportionately more in the non-core ones. Our evidence furthermore suggests that public institutions and the macroeconomic environment remain more important for economic growth within the non-core economies than within the core economies. This is partly due to the limited variation in institutional quality and macroeconomic factors among core economies. It is also likely due to a threshold effect, whereby economies that have attained a certain level of quality in institutions and macroeconomic policymaking yield increasingly small benefits from marginal improvements in those areas.

All of these findings are incorporated in the new Growth Competitiveness Index, which blends core and non-core measures of technological advancement with measures of institutional quality and the macroeconomic environment to create a unified competitiveness ranking across 75 countries. GCI scores represent our best estimate at the underlying growth prospects for each country, once their current level of GDP is taken into account. Of equal importance, rankings in the GCI's three component indexes of technology, public institutions, and macroeconomic environment provide important insight into each economy's specific sources of growth competitiveness.

References

Barro, Robert J. "Economic Growth in a Cross-Section of Countries." *Quarterly Journal of Economics*, CVI: 407–443 (1991).

———. *Determinants of Economic Growth: A Cross-Country Empirical Study*. Cambridge, MA: MIT Press, 1997.

The Institutional Investor Online. "Country Credit Ratings," accessed at http://www.iimagazine.com/premium/rr/ countrycredit/ccr/2001.htm on August 12, 2001.

The International Monetary Fund. *World Economic Outlook: May 2001*. Washington, DC: The International Monetary Fund, 2001.

International Trade Centre and United Nations Statistics Division. *PC-TAS Trade Analysis System, 1995–1999* (CD-ROM). December 2000.

Kaufman, Daniel and Shang-jin Wei. "Does 'Grease Money' Speed Up the Wheels of Commerce?" NBER Working Paper No. 7093, 1999.

Knack, Stephen and Philip Keefer. "Institutions and Economic Performance: Cross-Country Tests Using Alternative Institutional Measures," *Economics and Politics*, VII (1995), 207–220.

Mauro, Paolo. "Corruption and Growth," *Quarterly Journal of Economics*, CX: 681–713 (1995)

Sachs, Jeffrey D. "Ten Trends in Global Competitiveness in 1998," *Global Competitiveness Report 1998*. Geneva: World Economic Forum, 1998.

Sachs, Jeffrey D and Andrew M Warner. "Year in Review," *Global Competitiveness Report 1999*. Geneva: World Economic Forum, 1999.

Statistics Canada. *World Trade Analyzer: 1980–1996* (CD-ROM), Ottawa: Statistics Canada, 1998.

United Nations. *Human Development Report 1990*. New York: Oxford University Press, 1990.

Warner, Andrew M. "Economic Creativity," *Global Competitiveness Report 2000*. New York: Oxford University Press, 2000.

Wei, Shang-jin. "Why is Corruption So Much More Taxing Than Tax? Arbitrariness Kills," NBER Working Paper No. 6255, 1997.

World Bank Task Force on Education. *Higher Education in Developing Countries: Peril and Promise*. Washington, DC: The World Bank, 2000.

The World Bank. *World Development Indicators 2001* (CD-ROM). Washington DC: The World Bank, 2001.

Notes

[i] Much of the empirical knowledge today was stimulated by Robert J Barro's seminal work, "Economic Growth in a Cross-Section of Countries," *Quarterly Journal of Economics* CVI (1991): 407–443.

[ii] The simple correlation coefficient between the rankings for the two years is 0.97.

[iii] Specifically, Singapore would jump from 4th to 2nd overall on the GCI, Ireland would shift from 11th to 8th, and Hong Kong SAR would leap from 13th to 6th—compared with their 2000 overall rankings of 2nd, 4th, and 7th, respectively.

[iv] See Jeffrey D Sachs, "Ten Trends in Global Competitiveness in 1998," *Global Competitiveness Report 1998*, (Geneva: World Economic Forum, 1998) p.18.

[v] Jeffrey D Sachs and Andrew M Warner "Year in Review," in *Global Competitiveness Report 1999*, (Geneva: World Economic Forum, 1999) p.21.

[vi] Indeed, there is strong evidence that even the catch-up effect occurs only once a minimum threshold of economic development has been met. For instance, of the 36 countries ranked as having "high" human development in the United Nations' 1990 *Human Development Report*, 35 achieved rising living standards from 1990 to 1998 and the entire group averaged 2.3 percent average annual economic growth over the same period. At the same time, the 34 middle-development countries achieved a slightly lower average growth rate of 1.9 percent per year, with 7 experiencing declines in GDP per capita. Meanwhile, low-development countries averaged 0 percent economic growth, with 15 of 34 experiencing an outright decline in living standards.

[vii] Again, the GDP GAP term is measured as a country's GDP per capita (PPP) as a percentage of the United States GDP per capita (PPP) in 1992, *ie*, all values in 1992 were between 0 and 1. We then calculated the natural logarithm of those values for the regression estimates. In parallel fashion, the dependent variable in this equation was calculated as the average annual change in the GDP GAP with the United States from 1992 to 2000. As mentioned in the text, for transition economies 1995 was used as the base year rather than 1992.

[viii] The regression results for the overall GCI, with the average annual change in GDP GAP relative to the United States as the dependent variable, are as follows:

Variable	Coefficient	Standard Error
ln (Initial GDP GAP)	−.028	.005
GCI	.033	.005
Constant term	−.187	.026

Number of observations = 75; Adjusted R^2 = 0.41

[ix] The standard formula for converting each hard variable to the 1-to-7 scale was:

$$6 \times \frac{(\text{Country Value} - \text{Sample Minimum})}{(\text{Sample Maximum} - \text{Sample Minimum})} + 1$$

In some instances, minor adjustments were made to account for extreme outliers in the hard data.

[x] Gross tertiary enrollment data were taken from the World Bank's *World Development Indicators 2001* and the World Bank Task Force on Education's *Higher Education in Developing Countries: Peril and Promise* (Washington, DC: World Bank, 2000). Most of these figures are for 1995 and 1996. The most recent are for 1997. Many national enrollment rates have undoubtedly changed substantially since then, but data for more recent cross-country analysis are simply not available.

[xi] Specifically, we included all exports falling under the United Nations' Standard Industrial Trade Classification codes 54, 57, 58, 65, 7, 81, 82, 83, 84, 85, 87, 88, 893, 894, 898, 8996, and 95.

[xii] Note that we again used the 1995–99 values for the transition economies to match our analysis of the average growth rate over the same period.

[xiii] The specific results of the nonlinear least squares regression were as follows, with the average annual percentage change in GDP GAP relative to the United States still as the dependent variable in the following equation:

Growth =   Constant + B_1 x 1980s non-core x {N_1 {0.5
             x ICT subindex + 0.5 [(1 − N_2) innovation subindex
             + N_2 x technology transfer subindex]}
             + (1 − N_1) (macroeconomic index + institutional index)}
             + B_2 x 1980s core x {C_1 {0.5 x ICT subindex
             + 0.5 [C_2 x innovation subindex
             + (1 − C_2) technology transfer index]}
             + (1 − C_1) (macroeconomic index + institutional index)}
             + G x (GDP GAP in 1992),

where B_1, C_1, C_2, G, N_1, and N_2 are the coefficients to be estimated.

The variables "1980s non-core" and "1980s core" take a 0 or 1 value depending on an economy's status in that period. The regression results are as follows:

Variable	Coefficient symbol	Coefficient value	Standard error
Initial GDP GAP in 1992	G	−.027	.007
Non-core Index weight	B_1	.029	.005
Core Index weight	B_2	.032	.007
Non-core technology weight	N_1	.642	.116
Non-core diffusion weight over innovation	N_2	.808	.257
Core technology weight	C_1	.896	.268
Core innovation weight over diffusion	C_2	.849	.397
Constant term	—	−.213	.033

Number of observations = 75

Adjusted R^2 = 0.50

[xiv] Stephen Knack and Philip Keefer, "Institutions and Economic Performance: Cross-Country Tests Using Alternative Institutional Measures," *Economics and Politics*, VII (1995): 207–220; Paolo Mauro, "Corruption and Growth," *Quarterly Journal of Economics*, CX: 681–713 (1995); Robert J Barro, *Determinants of Economic Growth: A Cross-Country Empirical Study* (Cambridge, MA: MIT Press, 1997.

[xv] See, for example, Shang-jin Wei, "Why Is Corruption So Much More Taxing Than Tax? Arbitrariness Kills," NBER Working Paper No. 6255, 1997; Daniel Kaufman and Shang-jin Wei, "Does 'Grease Money' Speed Up the Wheels of Commerce?" NBER Working Paper No. 7093, 1999.

[xvi] Nonetheless, in one noteworthy example of the robustness of the Survey results, we find that national scores on the public institutions index remain almost exactly the same when half the Survey responses from the sample are randomly excluded. For more details on the consistency of Executive Opinion Survey results and the possibility of national-level perception bias, consult the final chapter of this *Report*.

[xvii] For the real exchange rate measure, the average value from 1990 to 1995 is set to 100, except for the transition economies where we set 1995 values to 100. To avoid excessive complication, real exchange rates were converted to simple scores on the standard 1-to-7 scale. Values of less than 80, ie, those that are strongly overvalued, were given a score of 1. Those with values of less than 100 and greater than 80 were given a score of 2.5. Values of 100–120, 120–140, and 140 and above were given scores of 4, 5.5, and 7 respectively.

[xviii] The *Institutional Investor*'s country credit ratings are taken from http://www.iimagazine.com/premium/rr/countrycredit/ccr/2001.htm.

[xix] Most prominent among these studies is Barro 1997, *op cit*.

Enhancing the Microeconomic Foundations of Prosperity: The Current Competitiveness Index[i]

MICHAEL E. PORTER, Institute for Strategy and Competitiveness, Harvard Business School

Competitiveness has become a central preoccupation of both advanced and developing countries in an increasingly open and integrated world economy. Despite its acknowledged importance, the concept of competitiveness is often misunderstood. Here, we define competitiveness concretely and show its direct relationship to a nation's standard of living. The Current Competitiveness Index provides a conceptual framework and a data-rich basis to analyze the fundamental competitiveness of countries in a comparative context.

Much discussion of competitiveness has focused on the macroeconomic, political, and legal circumstances that underpin a successful economy. These circumstances are becoming increasingly well understood. A stable set of political institutions, a trusted legal context, and sound fiscal and monetary policies contribute greatly to a healthy economy. However, these macroeconomic conditions are necessary but not sufficient. They provide the opportunity to create wealth, but do not by themselves create wealth. Wealth is actually created in the microeconomic foundations of the economy, rooted in company operating practices and strategies as well as in the quality of the inputs, infrastructure, institutions, and array of regulatory and other policies that constitute the business environment in which a nation's firms compete. Unless there is appropriate improvement at the microeconomic level, political, legal, and monetary and fiscal reforms will not bear full fruit.

Beginning in 1998, we began an effort to examine statistically the microeconomic foundations of competitiveness and prosperity across a wide array of countries. The microeconomic approach focuses on the detailed conditions that support a high level of sustainable productivity and prosperity, measured by GDP per capita. The approach aims to move beyond the examination of broad, aggregate variables characteristic of most economic growth models, such as marginal savings and investments rates, and examines the complex array of national circumstances that support productivity. These microeconomic differences between nations prove to account for a very high proportion of the variation across countries in the level GDP per capita.[ii] The approach also recognizes that improvement in competitive potential and prosperity is not a simple linear process in which nation's progress on a constant set of dimensions. Instead, successful economic development involves the successive focus on competing on increasingly sophisticated dimensions. This year's *Report* highlights especially the shifting priorities that arise at different stages of economic development.

In the *Global Competitiveness Report 2001–2002*, we again present separate indexes for current (sustainable) competitiveness and growth competitiveness. These indexes focus on different dimensions of the challenge of improving prosperity, and provide greater insight into the strengths and challenges of nations than is possible in a single index.

The Current Competitiveness Index examines the microeconomic bases of a nation's GDP per capita. While nations can over- or underperform their fundamentals in the short and medium run, the index provides insights into the level of GDP per capita that is sustainable in the long term. The Growth Competitiveness Index looks at the more macroeconomic sources of GDP per capita growth, and generates predictions about the ability of a country to improve its per capita income over time at more/less than the convergence growth rate. Although the sustainable level of current GDP per capita and the rate of growth are correlated in the long term, each requires its own distinctive agenda.

This year's Current Competitiveness Index includes further enhancements in country coverage, variables measured, and methods compared with previous years. We are particularly pleased to have added more countries, bringing the total to 75, up from 58 last year. The countries added are all developing countries, providing a much richer platform for exploring the earlier stages of development.

Despite the significant expansion of the sample, the statistical findings are remarkably stable compared with the 2000 *Report*. The results again provide strong support for the importance of microeconomic competitiveness for prosperity and economic development. Our findings also verify the striking and regular pattern of microeconomic changes that accompany economic development.

This chapter presents six sets of results: First, we analyze the impact of individual microeconomic indicators on the level of GDP per capita to verify statistical validity, and test for the functional form of the relationship.

Second, we create an aggregate measure of microeconomic competitiveness, the Current Competitiveness Index (CCI), together with two subindexes focusing on company sophistication and the quality of the national business environment. We analyze the impact of these overall indexes on GDP per capita.

Third, we use the statistical models to generate strengths and weaknesses for each country as well as insights into the overall patterns of competitive development in the world economy.

Fourth, we investigate the variations in the causes of prosperity at different stages of economic development. This allows us to highlight the most salient challenges for low-income, middle-income, and high-income nations and the major challenges those nations face in making the transition from one stage to another.

Fifth, we briefly analyze the impact of microeconomic indicators on economic growth and the relationship of imbalances between actual and predicted income levels with growth of GDP per capita.

Finally, we utilize the Index to generate the country current competitiveness rankings (see Table 1) and identify those countries whose current competitiveness will support higher incomes and who may be poised for improvement, as well as those countries whose current performance is ahead of their measured competitiveness and may face challenges in sustaining it.

As in any such investigation of a complex topic in a large number of countries, the data and the methods that are available are far from perfect. There are simply no available "hard" data on most of the salient dimensions of competitiveness, especially for a broad array of countries. Another challenge is establishing causality, because a strong statistical association does not prove the direction in which causality proceeds. We proceed pragmatically, while aiming to improve the effort each year. What is heartening is the consistency of the findings over time, and the remarkable robustness of the results to sensitivity analysis.

We believe strongly that insights into the microeconomic correlates of rising prosperity are important even if causality remains unproven. Although there may be a natural tendency for some microeconomic conditions to improve as GDP per capita grows, such improvement is clearly far from automatic. Along virtually all dimensions, microeconomic circumstances *can be influenced markedly* by purposeful action in both government and the private sector. It will be many years before definitive tests of causality will be possible, but this does not diminish the importance of understanding the microeconomic changes that accompany successful development and the patterns by which nations improve them.

Our results again highlight the pressing need to incorporate microeconomic and competitive thinking better into efforts to stimulate economic growth. In advanced countries, which have largely gotten their macro policies right, it is micro reform that holds the key to reversing unemployment problems and translating economic growth into a rising standard of living. The process of microeconomic reform also needs to move to a new stage: In countries such as New Zealand and the United Kingdom, microeconomic reforms so far have been focused on the

Table 1: The Current Competitiveness Index

Country	CCI Ranking				Company Operations and Strategy Ranking				Quality of the National Business Environment Ranking				2000 GDP per Capita (ppp adjusted)
	2001	2000	1999	1998	2001	2000	1999	1998	2001	2000	1999	1998	
Finland	1	1	2	2	2	3	7	8	1	1	2	2	24,864
United States	2	2	1	1	1	2	1	2	2	2	1	1	33,886
Netherlands	3	4	3	3	3	7	8	5	3	3	3	4	25,598
Germany	4	3	6	4	4	1	5	1	4	6	5	8	24,931
Switzerland	5	5	5	9	5	5	2	3	5	10	9	10	28,518
Sweden	6	7	4	7	6	6	3	4	6	11	7	9	23,884
United Kingdom	7	8	10	5	7	11	13	9	8	9	8	5	23,197
Denmark	8	6	7	8	9	8	9	10	10	4	6	7	27,120
Australia	9	10	13	15	24	20	19	22	7	7	10	12	25,758
Singapore	10	9	12	10	15	15	14	12	9	5	12	6	23,000
Canada	11	11	8	6	14	16	12	15	11	8	4	3	27,783
France	12	15	9	11	10	9	6	6	12	15	11	13	24,032
Austria	13	13	11	16	11	12	10	11	13	12	13	17	26,314
Belgium	14	12	15	19	12	10	11	13	14	13	15	18	26,958
Japan	15	14	14	18	8	4	4	7	18	19	19	19	25,796
Iceland	16	17	22	24	16	14	21	28	15	16	21	23	29,167
Israel	17	18	20	21	18	13	18	21	17	20	20	20	19,577
Hong Kong SAR	18	16	21	12	21	23	24	17	16	14	18	11	24,448
Norway	19	20	18	14	23	21	23	14	19	18	16	15	29,500
New Zealand	20	19	16	17	19	22	16	19	20	17	14	16	20,010
Taiwan	21	21	19	20	20	18	17	16	21	21	22	21	17,223
Ireland v	22	22	17	13	17	19	20	18	22	22	17	14	25,200
Spain	23	23	23	22	22	24	22	23	23	23	23	22	19,202
Italy	24	24	25	26	13	17	15	20	24	26	27	27	23,304
South Africa	25	25	26	25	25	26	28	33	27	25	25	25	9,189
Hungary	26	32	33	31	33	34	36	39	25	31	33	31	12,335
Estonia	27	—	—	—	32	—	—	—	26	—	—	—	9,178
Korea	28	27	28	28	26	25	27	24	30	28	30	28	17,311
Chile	29	26	24	23	30	27	26	25	28	24	24	24	9,187
Brazil	30	31	35	35	29	29	32	27	32	32	37	39	7,389
Portugal	31	28	29	33	38	35	37	48	29	27	26	30	16,882
Slovenia	32	—	—	—	28	—	—	—	35	—	—	—	17,127
Turkey	33	29	31	29	44	28	33	26	31	29	32	29	6,870
Trinidad and Tobago	34	—	—	—	27	—	—	—	37	—	—	—	8,771
Czech Republic	35	34	41	30	41	41	55	31	33	34	36	33	13,721
India	36	37	42	44	43	40	48	50	34	37	43	42	2,403
Malaysia	37	30	27	27	37	30	25	34	38	30	31	26	8,924
Thailand	38	40	39	37	42	47	43	37	39	40	39	36	6,469
Slovakia	39	36	48	36	57	31	51	40	36	36	47	37	11,035
Jamaica	40	—	—	—	31	—	—	—	44	—	—	—	3,657
Poland	41	41	37	41	55	36	38	38	40	41	38	40	8,971
Latvia	42	—	—	—	35	—	—	—	43	—	—	—	6,838
Greece	43	33	36	38	51	32	45	32	42	33	34	38	16,326
Jordan	44	35	32	32	56	46	44	42	41	35	28	32	4,079
Egypt	45	39	43	40	36	44	49	47	46	39	42	35	3,602
Uruguay	46	—	—	—	48	—	—	—	45	—	—	—	8,904
China	47	44	49	42	39	38	31	35	47	45	50	44	3,953
Panama	48	—	—	—	40	—	—	—	49	—	—	—	6,169
Lithuania	49	—	—	—	47	—	—	—	48	—	—	—	6,999
Costa Rica	50	43	38	—	34	39	35	—	52	42	41	—	9,236
Mexico	51	42	34	39	46	42	30	29	53	43	35	41	8,914
Mauritius	52	38	30	—	49	37	29	—	50	38	29	—	9,512
Argentina	53	45	40	34	53	45	39	30	51	44	40	34	12,314
Philippines	54	46	44	45	45	43	34	41	54	46	46	45	3,956
Indonesia	55	47	53	51	50	51	47	52	57	47	52	51	3,014
Colombia	56	48	52	49	52	48	40	43	59	48	53	49	5,923
Sri Lanka	57	—	—	—	58	—	—	—	55	—	—	—	3,512
Russia	58	52	55	46	54	33	42	45	56	53	55	47	8,213
Dominican Republic	59	—	—	—	59	—	—	—	58	—	—	—	5,962
Ukraine	60	56	56	52	62	52	50	51	60	56	56	52	3,693
Romania	61	—	—	—	63	—	—	—	61	—	—	—	6,309
Vietnam	62	53	50	43	64	50	41	36	64	52	49	43	1,974
Peru	63	49	46	47	65	53	56	49	62	51	44	46	4,797
El Salvador	64	51	47	—	66	57	46	—	63	50	48	—	4,477
Zimbabwe	65	50	45	48	60	56	54	46	67	49	45	48	2,697
Venezuela	66	54	51	50	67	49	53	44	66	55	51	50	5,677
Nigeria	67	—	—	—	61	—	—	—	68	—	—	—	871
Bulgaria	68	55	54	—	70	54	52	—	65	54	54	—	5,469
Guatemala	69	—	—	—	69	—	—	—	69	—	—	—	3,784
Paraguay	70	—	—	—	68	—	—	—	71	—	—	—	4,396
Nicaragua	71	—	—	—	73	—	—	—	70	—	—	—	2,396
Ecuador	72	57	57	—	71	55	57	—	72	58	57	—	3,068
Bangladesh	73	—	—	—	72	—	—	—	73	—	—	—	1,561
Honduras	74	—	—	—	74	—	—	—	75	—	—	—	2,469
Bolivia	75	58	58		75	58	58		74	57	58		2,408

opening of markets and reducing the role of the government. Microeconomic reforms need to move to a second stage in which investments are made to upgrade the business environment and enhance the productivity of clusters.

Developing countries, again and again, are tripped up by microeconomic failures. With global capital markets, countries can engineer spurts of growth through macroeconomic and financial reforms that bring floods of capital and cause the illusion of progress as construction cranes dot the skyline. Such reforms allow countries to exploit current comparative advantages. Unless firms are fundamentally improving their operations and strategies and competition is moving to a higher level, however, growth will be snuffed out as jobs fail to materialize, wages stagnate, and returns to investment prove disappointing. Capital flows and attention then shifts elsewhere. The austerity that results from such cycles is at the core of the backlash against globalization that is becoming perhaps the most important global economic problem.

Successful economic development requires progress on multiple fronts simultaneously. Reform efforts also need to be tightly connected to the current stage of each country's development. As an economy progresses, the constraints to continued advancement shift. Also, at strategic points in the development process, the whole basis of national competitiveness must be transformed. This requires a change in many aspects of company strategy as well as new requirements for the national business environment. We investigate these inflection points in this chapter.

What is competitiveness?

Despite widespread acceptance of its importance, competitiveness remains a concept that is not well understood. The most intuitive definition of *competitiveness* is a country's share of world markets for its products. This makes competitiveness a zero-sum game, because each country's gains come at the expense of others. This view of competitiveness is used to justify intervention to skew market outcomes in a nation's favor, as well as policies to hold down local wages and devalue the nation's currency to expand exports. In fact, it is still often said that devaluation "makes a nation more competitive." Business leaders are prone to the market share view, because the policies seem to help solve their short-term problems in coping with international rivals.

The market share view of competitiveness, however, is deeply flawed. Where this thinking is entrenched, it becomes a principal reason why nations fail to progress economically. The goal of economic development is a rising standard of living. The need for low wages reveals a lack of competitiveness rather than competitive strength. Devaluation means that a nation takes a collective pay cut by discounting its products and services in world markets and paying more for the goods it purchases abroad. Nations with substantial export shares are often poor, while those with focused positions are often prosperous.

To understand competitiveness, it is necessary to move beyond the misleading metaphor of direct market competition and relate competitiveness to the sources of a nation's prosperity. A nation's standard of living is determined by the productivity of its economy, which is measured by the value of goods and services produced per unit of the nation's human, capital, and natural resources. Productivity depends both on the *value* of a nation's products and services, measured by the prices they can command in open markets, and the efficiency with which they can be produced.

True competitiveness, then, rests on productivity. This reveals the fundamental flaw in market share–based thinking. Productivity allows a nation to support a strong currency, and with it a high standard of living. Productivity is the goal, not exports per se. Exports of low-priced products, which support only subsidence wages, are not sufficient to make a nation prosperous. It is the productivity to manufacture high-quality products that support rising wages that really matters. The productivity underpinnings of competitiveness also make it clear that the entire economy matters for standard of living, not just the traded sector. The productivity of domestic industries has a major influence on the cost of living and the cost of doing business, not to mention the level of wages in the domestic economy.

The world economy is not a zero-sum game. Many nations can improve their prosperity if they can improve productivity and specialize in the products and services where they are most productive.

The central challenge in economic development, then, is how to create the conditions for rapid and sustained productivity growth. Stable political/legal institutions and sound macroeconomic policies create the potential for improving national prosperity. But wealth is actually created at the microeconomic level—in the ability of firms to create valuable goods and services using productive methods. Only in this way can a nation support high wages and attractive returns to capital. Political and legal institutions coupled with macroeconomic policies set the overall context, yet prosperity depends on improving a nation's capabilities at the microeconomic level (see Figure 1).

Figure 1: Determinants of productivity and productivity growth

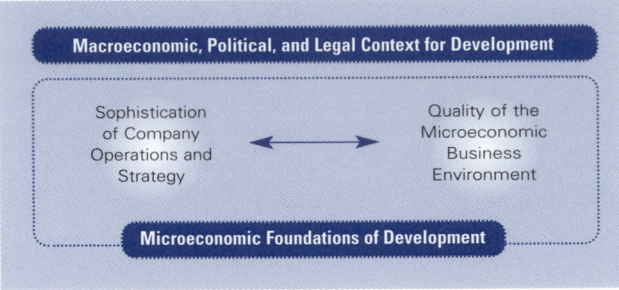

The microeconomic foundations of productivity rest on two interrelated areas: (1) the sophistication with which companies or subsidiaries based in the country compete, and (2) the quality of the microeconomic business environment. National productivity is ultimately set by the productivity of a nation's companies. An economy cannot be competitive unless companies operating there are competitive, whether they are domestic or subsidiaries of foreign companies. However, the sophistication of companies is inextricably intertwined with the quality of the national business environment. More sophisticated strategies by companies require more highly skilled people, better information, improving infrastructure, more advanced institutions, and stronger competitive pressure.

To support rising prosperity, companies must transform their ways of competing. The types of competitive advantages a nation's companies enjoy must shift from comparative advantages (low-cost labor or natural resources) to competitive advantages due to more distinctive products made with more productive methods. The transitions in goals, operating practices, and strategies required for successful development are described in detail in previous years' *Reports*. What were strengths in competing at earlier stages become weaknesses at more advanced levels of development. Rapid copying of foreign technology, for example, must give way to internal development of indigenous technology. Changes are often resisted by the corporate sector, because past approaches were profitable and because old habits are deeply ingrained in companies.

Moving to more sophisticated ways of competing depends on parallel changes in the microeconomic business environment. The business environment can be understood in terms of four interrelated influences: the quality of factor (input) conditions, the context for firm strategy and rivalry, the quality of demand conditions, and the presence of locally related and supporting industries (see Figure 2).

Government plays an inevitable role in economic development because it affects many aspects of the business environment. Government shapes the quality of factor conditions, for example, through its training and infrastructure policies. The sophistication of home demand derives in part from regulatory standards and processes, consumer protection laws, government purchasing, and openness to imports. Similar policy influences are present in all four parts of the business environment (sometimes referred to as the diamond). There are distinct roles for government in improving the business environment at the national, state, and local levels as well as in coordinating policies with neighboring countries. A concerted effort to improve the business environment is needed at all these governmental levels.

In addition to government, however, many other institutions in an economy have a role in economic development. Universities, schools, infrastructure providers, standard-setting agencies, and a myriad of other organizations contribute in some way to the microeconomic business environment. Such institutions must not just develop and improve themselves, but must also become more connected to the economy and better linked with the private sector.

The private sector itself is not only a consumer of the business environment but can and must play a role in shaping it. Individual firms can take steps such as establishing schools, attracting suppliers, or defining standards that not only benefit themselves but also improve the overall environment for competing. Collective industry bodies, such as trade associations and chambers of commerce, also have important roles to play in improving infrastructure, upgrading training institutions, and the like, that are often not recognized. The private sector can also take collective steps to enhance the ability of individual companies to improve operating practices and strategies.

Figure 2: The microeconomic business environment

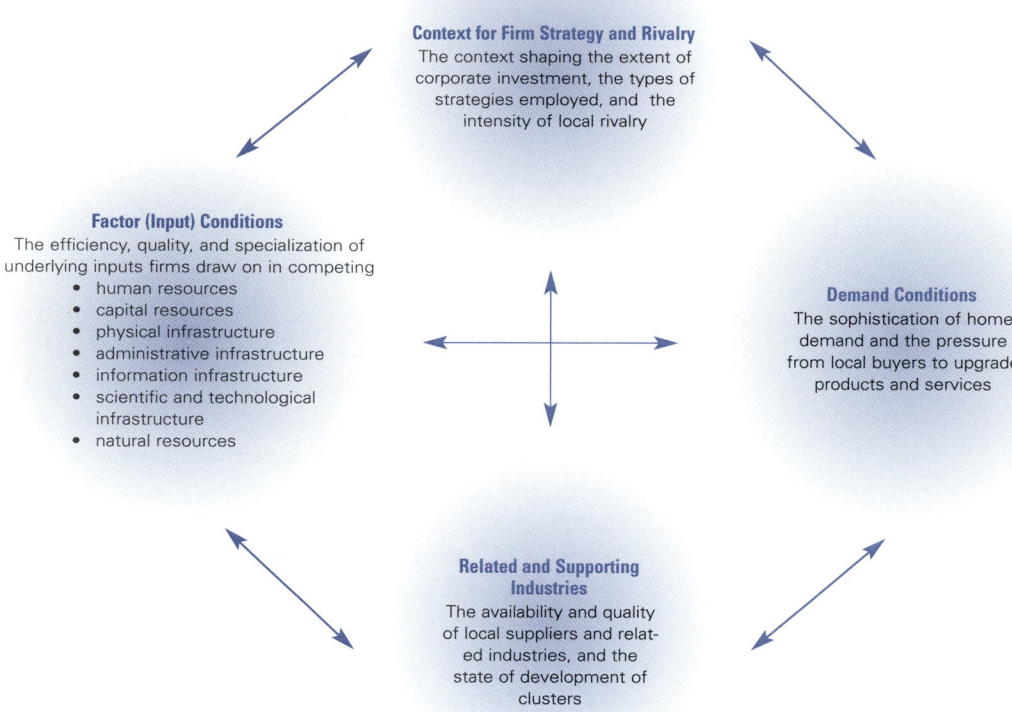

Economic development

Successful economic development is a process of successive upgrading, in which the *business environment in a nation evolves to support and encourage increasingly sophisticated and productive ways of competing*. Nations at different levels of development face distinctly different challenges. The succession of improvements in the microeconomic environment that accompany successful development were explored in detail in previous years' *Reports*.

Seeing economic development as a sequential process of building interdependent microeconomic capabilities, evolving the modes of competing, improving incentives, and increasing rivalry also exposes important pitfalls in economic policy. The influence of one part of the microeconomic business environment depends on others. Lack of improvement in any important area can lead to a plateau in productivity growth and stalled development. Worse yet, it can undermine the whole reform process. When well-trained college graduates cannot find appropriate jobs because companies are still competing based on cheap labor, a backlash against business is created.

This analysis makes it clear why macroeconomic policy alone is insufficient. Macroeconomic policies fostering high rates of capital investment will not translate into rising productivity, for example, unless the forms of investment are appropriate, the company skills and supporting industries are present to make the investments efficient, and strong competitive pressures and adequate corporate governance provide the needed market discipline. In Asia, for example, it was weaknesses in these areas that brought down economies that looked solid in terms of macroeconomic indicators. Moreover, high rates of public investment in human capital will not pay off unless a nation's microeconomic circumstances create the demand for skills in companies. Removing distortions in exchange rates and other prices will eliminate impediments to productivity, but microeconomic foundations must be in place if productivity is actually to increase. The prudence of foreign debt levels depends on exactly what the capital is invested in, together with the microeconomic fundamentals surrounding its deployment and governance. Regulating overall debt levels is less important, in many ways, than improving the microeconomic foundations. For sound policies at the macroeconomic level to translate into an increasingly productive economy, then, parallel microeconomic improvements must take place.

Figure 3: Stages of economic development

As nations develop, they progress through a number of stages in terms of their characteristic competitive advantages and modes of competing (see Figure 3).[iii] In the Factor-Driven stage, basic factor conditions such as low-cost labor and access to natural resources are the dominant sources of competitive advantage and international products. Firms produce commodities or relatively simple products designed in other, more advanced countries. Technology is assimilated through imports, foreign direct investment, and imitation. In this stage, companies compete on price and lack direct access to consumers. They have limited roles in the value chain, are focused on assembly, labor-intensive manufacturing, and resource extraction. A Factor-Driven economy is highly sensitive to world economic cycles, commodity price trends, and exchange rate fluctuations.

In the Investment-Driven stage, efficiency in producing standard products and services becomes the dominant source of competitive advantage. The products and services produced become more sophisticated, but technology and designs still largely come from abroad. Technology is accessed through licensing, joint ventures, foreign direct investment, and imitation. However, nations in this stage not only assimilate foreign technology, but also develop the capacity to improve on it. The national business environment supports heavy investment in efficient infrastructure and modern production methods. Companies largely serve OEM customers and extend capabilities more widely in the value chain. An Investment-Driven economy is concentrated on manufacturing and on outsourced service exports. It is susceptible to financial crisis and external, sector-specific demand shocks.

In the Innovation-Driven stage, the ability to produce innovative products and services at the global technology frontier using the most advanced methods becomes the dominant source of competitive advantage. The national business environment is characterized by strengths in all areas together with the presence of deep clusters. Institutions and incentives supporting innovation are well developed. Companies compete with unique strategies that are often global in scope. An Innovation-Driven economy has a high service share, and is resilient to external shocks.

This analysis also begins to make it clear why countries find the transition to a new stage of development so difficult. Such inflection points require wholesale transformation of many interdependent dimensions of competition. In Asia, for example, successful Investment-Driven economies such as Taiwan and Singapore are finding that their reliance on sustained infrastructure investments, OEM manufacturing for multinationals, and government guidance of the economy to boost efficiency are insufficient to support higher levels of prosperity. Yet their current level of wages and domestic costs makes them vulnerable to competition from lower-wage countries such as China. The challenge for both Taiwan and Singapore is to move to an Innovation-Driven economy with a presence of deep clusters. To do so, however, companies need to move to new types of strategies, investment priorities must change, and government's role in the economy needs to shift.

Measuring microeconomic competitiveness

The Current Competitiveness Index (CCI) is constructed from measures of microeconomic competitiveness based primarily on Survey data drawn primarily from senior business leaders and, to a much lesser extent, from government officials. Only through a detailed survey can textured measures of the competitive environment and company practices be assembled across many countries. Although quantitative measures are available for some variables for some countries, a consistent ranking of a large number of countries is simply impossible at this time without the Survey. Moreover, the informed judgments of thousands of actual participants in the economies or companies are important in their own right.

This year's Survey involves more than 4,600 respondents from 75 countries. Approximately 37 percent of the respondents were from largely domestic companies, 34 percent were from significant exporters, 15 percent were from multinationals operating in the country, and 4 percent were from government. Survey data from the various categories of respondents in a country were quite similar, and the Survey findings have been quite consistent from year to year.

Appendix A lists the questions included in this year's Survey about the sophistication of company operations and strategy and the quality of the microeconomic business environment, grouped by part of the diamond. Questions on company operations and strategy were similar to 2000. New questions were added on the willingness to delegate authority and the extent of incentive compensation.

To assess the microeconomic business environment better, new questions were added in all four parts of the business environment: In the area of factor conditions, we added questions on the quality of math and science education and the availability of scientists and engineers. To measure demand conditions, we added questions on the extent of government procurement of advanced technology products and the laws relating to information technology. A series of new questions measured cluster depth and vitality. We added questions on the extent of product and process collaboration, the local availability of components and parts, the local availability process machinery, local access to specialized research and training services, and local information technology services. In the area of the context for firm strategy and rivalry, we added a question on the extent of cooperation in labor-employee relations.

The questions aim to capture the state of practice or the quality of capabilities in a nation, but do so in way that is meaningful for Survey respondents. For example, we get at the stock of basic human capital with a question on the quality in public schools because this is something that respondents can compare more readily across countries. The quality of schools, a flow measure, will be highly correlated with the stock of basic skills.

The sample of 75 countries extends our previous sample by adding almost 20 countries. The countries included in this year's Index are shown in Table 1. In Appendix B, we report the results for the same set of countries as last year's Index to facilitate comparisons.

To estimate the CCI, the principal dependent variable used is the level of GDP per capita in 2000, adjusted for purchasing power parity (PPP). GDP per capita is the broadest measure of national productivity and is tightly connected over time to a nation's standard of living.[iv] It is the best single, summary measure of current competitiveness available across all countries.[v] Purchasing power parity adjustments for 2000 are not yet available. To derive the 2000 GDP per capita figures used in our models, we started with the 1999 GDP per capita adjusted for purchasing power parity, grew it at the growth rate of real GDP per capita in each country, and adjusted for inflation using the US GDP deflator.

In our analysis, we sometimes explored differences across countries at different income levels. Three groups of countries were defined based on their purchasing power–adjusted US-dollar GDP per capita in 2000: 28 low-income countries with a GDP below $6,500; 28 middle-income countries with a GDP per capita between $6,500 and $23,000; and 19 high-income countries with a GDP per capita above $23,000. The cut-off points were selected based on an analysis of Survey reply patterns.

Elements of microeconomic competitiveness

To construct an overall index of competitiveness, we must identify the most important individual dimensions of microeconomic capability and validate their statistical relationship to GDP per capita. In this section, we identify the most important explanatory variables.

Table 2 shows the bivariate relationships between the available set of microeconomic variables in this year's Survey and GDP per capita. We also include US patents per capita for each country, a measure of scientific and technological prowess that is available for all countries. The variables are grouped into those measuring the sophistication of company operations and strategy and variables measuring the quality of the national business environment. Included in the table is the slope of the regression relationship, an indication of statistical significance, and the adjusted R^2 (or proportion of variation in GDP per capita explained adjusted for statistical degrees of freedom).[vi]

All the reported variables are highly statistically significant in the full set of countries. A wide range of company practices and multiple dimensions of the business environment prove strongly related to competitiveness. Of the new indicators available from this year's Survey, all are statistically significant. These findings are highly consistent with results from the earlier *Global Competitiveness Reports*. The stability of the results provides an important indication that the relationship between microeconomic circumstances and GDP per capita is robust and not an artifact of a single year or set of respondents.

Among the company variables, production process sophistication, the nature of the competitive advantage of a nation's companies and subsidiaries, the extent of training, and the extent of marketing have the strongest bilateral association with per capita GDP. By itself, the measure of whether competitive advantage rests on cheap labor/natural resources versus innovative products and processes explains a remarkable 75 percent of the variance in GDP per capita. The overall competitive approach of local companies thus represents a powerful indicator of the state of economic development. Of the new company variables, the measure of willingness to delegate authority has a very strong association (R^2 of 70 percent) with GDP per capita.

Table 2: Bivariate regression results, dependent variable: 2000 GDP per capita (PPP-adjusted)

	All Countries (N = 75)		Low GDP Countries GDP per capita < $6,500 (N = 28)		Moderate GDP Countries GDP per capita > $6,500 and < $23,000 (N = 28)		High GDP Countries GDP per capita > $23,000 (N = 19)	
	Slope	Adj. R^2	Slope	Adj. R^2	Slope	Adj. R^2	Slope	Adj. R^2
I. COMPANY OPERATIONS & STRATEGY								
Production Process Sophistication	8184.71**	0.806	964.66	0.087	4621.84**	0.323	1027.15	0.017
Nature of Competitive Advantage	6111.00**	0.754	997.38*	0.117	3496.76**	0.484	-136.85	0.002
Extent of Staff Training	8263.19**	0.751	797.71	0.065	3922.71**	0.243	2088.32*	0.157
Extent of Marketing	8091.45**	0.716	1003.97**	0.176	4158.14**	0.271	727.71	0.011
n Willingness to Delegate Authority	8141.51**	0.700	953.76	0.081	4017.67**	0.236	1206.29	0.098
Capacity for Innovation	7396.04**	0.687	782.33	0.066	3910.86**	0.343	248.71	0.004
Company Spending on R&D	7606.92**	0.677	-187.31	0.003	4158.02**	0.374	598.79	0.031
Value Chain Presence	6746.92**	0.673	590.42	0.034	3264.57**	0.281	-316.66	0.009
Breadth of International Markets	6329.62**	0.665	416.97	0.030	3249.32**	0.348	-940.91	0.065
Uniqueness of Product Designs	8023.89**	0.658	365.66	0.011	2903.52*	0.121	-131.17	0.001
Degree of Customer Orientation	9746.03**	0.653	637.65	0.061	4767.19**	0.230	3734.92*	0.170
Control of International Distribution	10553.50**	0.647	646.69	0.032	5578.89**	0.288	646.10	0.013
Extent of Branding	7194.89**	0.638	921.85*	0.101	4262.93**	0.336	-273.10	0.006
Reliance on Professional Management	7456.50**	0.543	102.92	0.002	2822.89**	0.145	1141.45	0.060
n Extent of Incentive Compensation	8365.11**	0.528	56.64	0.000	4652.96**	0.339	322.74	0.006
Extent of Regional Sales	6866.33**	0.516	190.83	0.007	575.87	0.009	-2283.83	0.067
Prevalence of Foreign Technology Licensing	6337.95**	0.251	351.02	0.037	3878.54**	0.199	-1400.29	0.044
II. NATIONAL BUSINESS ENVIRONMENT								
A. FACTOR (INPUT) CONDITIONS								
1. Physical Infrastructure								
Overall, Infrastructure Quality	5380.61**	0.740	1149.16**	0.367	3017.68**	0.333	744.41	0.066
a. Basic								
n Road Infrastructure Quality	7314.57**	0.308	468.29	0.027	1734.43	0.043	41.37	0.000
Railroad Infrastructure Development	3548.73**	0.413	42.73	0.001	1739.60**	0.224	-519.64	0.085
Port Infrastructure Quality	5657.46**	0.621	694.93**	0.156	2345.19**	0.211	375.47	0.011
Air Transport Infrastructure Quality	5751.99**	0.519	1015.18**	0.353	1514.00*	0.109	1150.81	0.043
b. Advanced								
Telephone/Fax Infrastructure Quality	4960.14**	0.494	652.94**	0.337	2708.61**	0.250	769.29	0.007
Availability and Cost of Cellular Phones	7021.03**	0.361	863.67**	0.206	2437.21**	0.144	-450.81	0.001
Speed and Cost of Internet Access	6259.46**	0.647	1938.23**	0.571	2223.78**	0.182	597.99	0.037
2. Administrative Infrastructure								
Police Protection of Businesses	5419.61**	0.680	439.55	0.085	3123.24**	0.496	1434.99	0.084
Judicial Independence	5046.87**	0.631	93.67	0.004	2485.05**	0.273	1014.93	0.053
Administrative Burden for Start-Ups	5731.16**	0.331	-77.02	0.001	1786.74*	0.105	878.64	0.065
Adequacy of Public Sector Legal Recourse	5787.16**	0.680	91.44	0.003	2696.93**	0.239	1137.59	0.041
Extent of Bureaucratic Red Tape	13206.03**	0.476	-115.34	0.001	4547.71**	0.168	1873.19	0.045
3. Capital Availability								
Ease of Access to Loans	7688.69**	0.692	355.72	0.019	3610.15**	0.253	1473.22	0.094
Financial Market Sophistication	5885.85**	0.657	653.75	0.086	2022.18**	0.155	403.85	0.012
Local Equity Market Access	4769.81**	0.407	-383.55	0.086	1973.30**	0.199	891.39	0.022
Venture Capital Availability	7005.05**	0.718	-186.27	0.004	3815.33**	0.403	865.22	0.052
4. Human Resources								
Quality of Public Schools	5006.30**	0.673	714.45**	0.184	2276.11**	0.277	528.01	0.012
n Quality of Math and Science Education	5148.26**	0.413	421.90	0.085	2027.69**	0.164	-1532.57	0.098
n Availability of Scientists and Engineers	6548.85**	0.355	371.78	0.050	3055.10**	0.166	2217.21	0.101
Quality of Management Schools	6351.34**	0.485	442.69	0.047	1469.08	0.057	1004.14	0.070
5. Science & Technology								
Patents per capita (2000)	107.32**	0.520	2544.00**	0.198	54.12**	0.277	16.50**	0.228
Quality of Scientific Research Institutions	7726.51**	0.660	34.59	0.000	4367.60**	0.357	1531.69	0.090
University/Industry Research Collaboration	7849.99**	0.685	61.71	0.001	4257.33**	0.364	809.44	0.020
B. DEMAND CONDITIONS								
Buyer Sophistication	7864.18**	0.735	39.98	0.000	5400.97**	0.529	1768.98	0.074
Consumer Adoption of Latest Products	8553.92**	0.693	498.01	0.036	4813.38**	0.413	1687.84	0.069
Presence of Demanding Regulatory Standards	7132.39**	0.805	860.26*	0.123	4886.87**	0.422	1410.50	0.036
Stringency of Environmental Regulations	6170.81**	0.809	991.30**	0.165	4005.35**	0.425	998.22	0.058
n Government Procurement of Advanced Technology Products	9967.47**	0.528	167.40	0.004	5362.12**	0.384	561.55	0.004
n Laws Relating to Information Technology	7368.22**	0.742	880.41*	0.121	3800.17**	0.393	993.97	0.027

(cont'd.)

Table 2: Bivariate regression results, dependent variable: 2000 GDP per capita

	All Countries (N = 75)		Low GDP Countries GDP per capita < $6,500 (N = 28)		Moderate GDP Countries GDP per capita > $6,500 and < $23,000 (N = 28)		High GDP Countries GDP per capita > $23,000 (N = 19)	
	Slope	Adj. R^2	Slope	Adj. R^2	Slope	Adj. R^2	Slope	Adj. R^2
II. QUALITY OF THE BUSINESS ENVIRONMENT (cont'd.)								
C. RELATED AND SUPPORTING INDUSTRIES								
Local Supplier Quantity	11287.11**	0.580	582.40	0.030	4903.60*	0.129	-26.16	0.000
Local Supplier Quality	9400.61**	0.767	1785.27**	0.257	4253.02**	0.178	992.45	0.019
State of Cluster Development	7797.84**	0.490	604.81	0.046	1909.25	0.078	-539.17	0.012
n Extent of Product and Process Collaboration	10177.43**	0.583	882.13	0.053	3405.46**	0.156	546.58	0.009
n Local Availability of Components and Parts	5144.44**	0.226	674.23**	0.143	1215.54	0.029	-613.71	0.033
n Local Availability of Process Machinery	4904.12**	0.262	441.17	0.065	1104.88	0.027	3.39	0.000
n Local Availability of Specialized Research and Traning Services	8286.02**	0.603	714.08	0.059	2201.04	0.085	839.70	0.026
n Local Availability of Information Technology Services	8666.74**	0.585	386.07	0.022	2824.35*	0.114	1380.16	0.046
D. CONTEXT FOR FIRM STRATEGY AND RIVALRY								
Favoritism in Decisions of Government Officials	7621.17**	0.642	755.78*	0.102	4344.58**	0.403	-217.08	0.002
Extent of Irregular Payments	7275.30**	0.719	1337.44**	0.350	3229.07**	0.255	1888.55	0.077
Extent of Distortive Government Subsidies	6557.01**	0.275	317.55	0.013	3278.33**	0.215	-1048.91	0.082
Decentralization of Corporate Activity	6597.65**	0.545	234.49	0.016	2509.01*	0.140	1158.65	0.085
n Cooperation in Labor-Employer Relations	6150.76**	0.247	540.74	0.033	2098.02	0.092	410.53	0.018
Tariff Liberalization	9260.09**	0.590	585.41	0.045	4475.84**	0.276	-2517.04	0.079
Hidden Trade Barrier Liberalization	6695.28**	0.664	898.09*	0.124	3318.45**	0.321	-927.23	0.038
Intellectual Property Protection	6446.12**	0.834	1185.60**	0.248	4550.83**	0.505	1018.75	0.035
Intensity of Local Competition	8366.32**	0.374	-188.15	0.006	2295.62	0.045	667.94	0.012
Extent of Locally Based Competitors	7539.95**	0.334	-58.87	0.001	1787.01	0.038	825.18	0.019
Effectiveness of Anti-Trust Policy	7473.45**	0.726	1432.50**	0.230	3603.66**	0.355	358.22	0.006
Efficacy of Corporate Boards	7344.27**	0.430	946.92*	0.125	2256.99*	0.111	996.55	0.081

NOTE: * denotes $p < 0.10$, ** denotes $p < 0.05$, n denotes new question infroduced into model in 2001.

61

Moving to the measures of the quality of the business environment, the findings again provide strong support for the relationship between all four dimensions of the competitive context and economic performance. Among factor conditions, overall infrastructure quality, venture capital availability, quality of public schools, adequacy of legal recourse, police protection of business, and university-business research collaboration have the strongest bilateral association with GDP per capita. Many of the most important influences are in institutions and rules, not in sheer accumulation of assets.

Measures of local demand conditions (IIB) perform particularly strongly in explaining the variation in GDP per capita. They range from buyer sophistication to consumer adoption of the latest products to the presence of stringent regulatory standards. These results run counter to the perceived wisdom that local demand and local markets are irrelevant in a global economy. Linkages among related industries and cluster development (IIC) are also important. These results suggest a powerful role of cluster linkages in competitiveness. Connections *across* entities and industries prove important to competitiveness, as do conditions within firms themselves. Finally, the rules and context governing competition itself are strongly related to measured productivity. The strongest are intellectual property protection and the application of antitrust that are particularly potent.

Of the new business environment variables, the quality of laws relating to IT has particularly great explanatory power. The local availability of components and parts proves to be an especially powerful predictor of GDP per capita in the low-income country group.

As in previous years, many of the individual variables are quite highly correlated with each other. This suggests that economic progress involves multiple dimensions of competitiveness moving together. Also evident is that individual elements have different influences at different levels of development, a subject we will turn to later in this chapter.

As with previous years' results, it is important to acknowledge that causality can be argued in both directions for some of the variables, though the Survey questions were worded to avoid spurious reverse causality. Note that the same causality issue applies in macroeconomic and economic growth analyses. The quality of scientists and engineers or the sophistication of buyers, for example, could be partly the result of high per capita GDP and not the cause. We provide provocative evidence of causality from microeconomic conditions to GDP per capita later in this chapter, but more years of surveying will be required to establish definitive cause and effect relationships.

Table 3: Significant changes in microeconomic conditions, 1998–2001

	Improving International Microeconomic Conditions No. of countries	Worsening International Microeconomic Conditions No. of countries
Sophistication of Company Operations and Strategy	Reliance on Profess. Management .... 34 .... l,m,h Extent of Regional Sales .... 28 .... l,m,h Extent of Marketing .... 23 .... h Degree of Customer Orientation .... 21 .... h Uniqueness of Product Designs .... 11 .... m Breadth of International Markets .... 8 .... l,m,h	Value Chain Presence .... 27 .... l,m Breadth of International Markets .... 21 .... l,m,h Extent of Branding .... 20 .... l,m Control of International Distribution .... 15 .... h Uniqueness of Product Designs .... 10 .... m
Quality of the Business Environment	Quality of Scientific Research Institutions ...... 37 .... l,m,h Overall, Infrastructure Quality .... 33 .... m,h Availability and Cost of Cellular Phones .... 31 .... l,m,h Road Infrastructure Quality .... 30 .... l,m,h Railroad Infrastructure Development .... 30 .... l,m,h Financial Market Sophistication .... 26 .... m,h Extent of Locally Based Competitors .... 22 .... h Port Infrastructure Quality .... 21 .... m,h Air Transport Infrastructure Quality .... 19 .... l,m University/Industry Research Collaboration ..... 18 .... m Effectiveness of Anti-Trust Policy .... 17 .... m Quality of Management Schools .... 17 .... m Administrative Burden for Start-Ups .... 17 .... m,h Quality of Public Schools .... 17 .... l,m,h Local Equity Market Access .... 15 .... m Efficacy of Corporate Boards .... 13 .... h Intensity of Local Competition .... 13 .... h Venture Capital Availability .... 12 .... l,m,h Favoritism in Decisions of Gov. Officials .... 12 .... h	Venture Capital Availability .... 17 .... l,m,h Extent of Distortive Government Subsidies ...... 15 .... h Intellectual Property Protection .... 15 .... l,m Quality of Public Schools .... 12 .... l,m,h

NOTE: l (low), m (medium), and h (high) indicates 8 or more countries from this income group included in the total number

Patterns of competitive development in the global economy

Now that there are several years of consistent Survey data, analysis of the overall patterns of change in the individual dimensions of competitiveness between the 1998 Survey and the 2001 Survey are possible.[vii] Table 3 identifies those areas where substantial changes in company practice and the quality of the business environment (either positive or negative) were reported in eight or more countries (about 10 percent). These data provide a picture of the evolution of microeconomic capability in the world economy. Overall, there is clear upgrading in national business environments, which means that the bar is rising. Among company operations and strategy, there are clear areas of broad progress, but signs of the growing intensity of competition.

The standard that must be met in terms of national business environments is clearly rising. The quality of physical infrastructure, especially, is improving in countries at all development stages. Nations at all income levels are working to improve research institutions. In middle-income countries, there are widespread improvements in antitrust policy, the sophistication of financial markets, the quality of management education, and the extent of

research collaboration between industry and universities. In high-income countries, there is widespread improvement in the vigor of local competition, upgrading of corporate boards, and improvements in the fairness and transparency of government.

Two areas of the business environment represent fault lines where some countries are progressing while others fall behind. The quality of public schools and the availability of venture capital are increasingly dividing countries. Broader challenges include the following: In low- and medium-income countries, protection of intellectual property rights is perceived as worsening in relative terms as competition moves to more knowledge-based activities. In high-income countries, the extent of distortive government subsidies is on the rise as governments are struggling to cope with international competition.

Companies are working to professionalize management in increasingly competitive markets, the single most widespread global development. Companies in nations at all levels of development are expanding sales within neighboring countries. In high-income countries, stepped-up marketing and a greater customer orientation are the rule.

While companies are improving in some respects, they are struggling to cope with tough international competition. Companies in many countries report a decreasing breadth of international markets. In low- and medium-income countries, companies are reporting narrower presence in the value chain and have difficulty building brands. Uniqueness of product designs is a strong differentiating factor in medium-income countries, with about an equal number of countries gaining versus falling back. In high-income countries, control of international distribution is weakening.

Measuring overall microeconomic competitiveness

To compute an overall measure of current competitiveness, we combine all the individual dimensions using common factor analysis to provide a single composite picture of the relative microeconomic competitiveness of each country.[viii] Because many of the dimensions of company sophistication and the quality of the business environment tend to move together, the relatively small sample size means that the impact of individual variables cannot be statistically distinguished. Hence we use common factor analysis instead of multiple regressions.

One dominant factor was present that captured 69 percent of the covariance among the variables, representing a robust composite picture of the overall microeconomic environment. The first factor score is defined as the Current Competitiveness Index (CCI). Regressing the CCI against GDP per capita explains a very high 84.2 percent of the variance across countries. The explained variance is up slightly from the 83.8 percent from previous years' *Reports*, in spite of the addition of 17 developing countries to the sample. We again find a strong relationship between microeconomic circumstances and current national prosperity.

Figure 4 plots the CCI against 2000 GDP per capita for each country in the sample. The line through the center of the country data points is the regression line, while the bands above and below the regression line delineate the 95 percent confidence forecast region.[x] The fit is tight, with only two countries (Norway and India) falling just outside the forecast region.

Countries lying above the regression line (overperformers) are those whose current GDP per capita *exceeds* that predicted by their microeconomic competitiveness, as measured by the CCI factor. This is a danger sign, because it means that a country's per capita income may be unsustainable.

Reasons for country overperformance seem to vary. For example, Norway, Iceland, Bolivia, and Canada have natural resource endowments that may be supporting unsustainable income levels. Ireland has had extraordinary recent income growth due to investments by multinationals, while the United States has extraordinary size, resources, and world influence. Greece and Argentina are experiencing deteriorating microeconomic conditions that will likely be reflected in future GDP per capita.

Countries lying below the regression line are those whose microeconomic competitiveness is *stronger* than current GDP per capita (underperformers). Underperformance bodes well for the future, because the platform is in place to support higher GDP per capita if macroeconomic, political, or other constraints can be eased.

The reasons for underperformance also seem to vary. Macroeconomic or political challenges such as in Turkey, Thailand, or Brazil are one reason. Egypt and Jordan face challenges due to regional turmoil in the Middle East. More encouragingly, rapidly improving nations such as Estonia or Finland experience lags in GDP per capita improvement that should correct themselves.

To analyze each country's competitive circumstances further, we computed separate common factors for those variables related to company operations and strategy and those variables related to the microeconomic business environment.[xi] One of the central tenets of our theoretical framework is that the sophistication of company operations and strategies depend on the quality of the microeconomic business environment and vice versa. Statistical analysis supports this relationship—the correlation between the two subfactors is 0.929.

To explore the relative state of company sophistication versus the quality of the microeconomic business environments in countries, the normalized factors are plotted against each other in Figure 5. Company sophistication is plotted on the vertical axis and the quality of the business environment on the horizontal axis. Countries lying above the 45-degree line are those whose companies are more advanced than the state of their business environment, while those below the line are countries whose business environment is more advanced than the average sophistication of local companies and subsidiaries.

Figure 4: The relationship between current competitiveness and GDP per capita

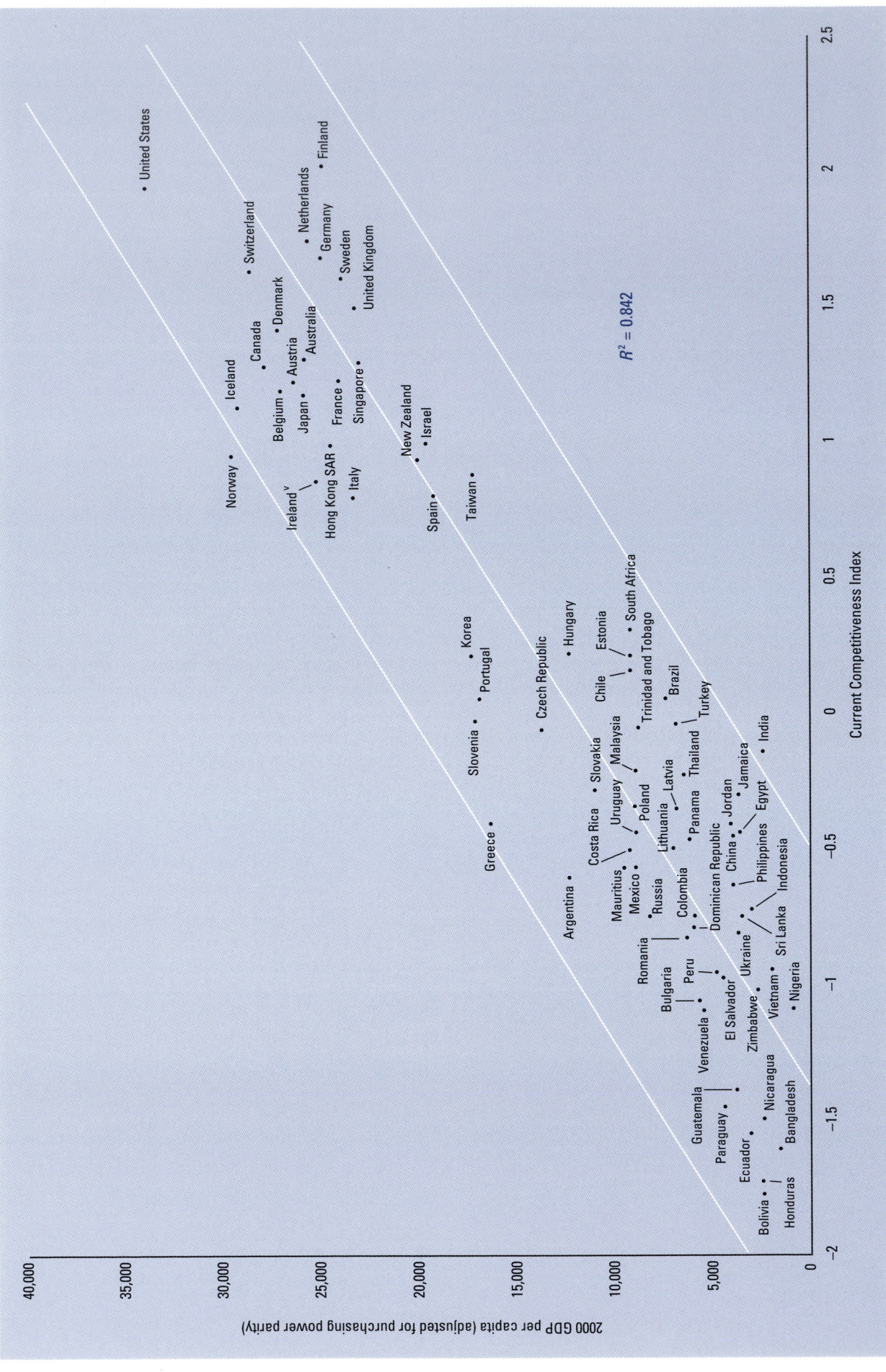

Figure 5: The relative development of companies and the microeconomic business environment

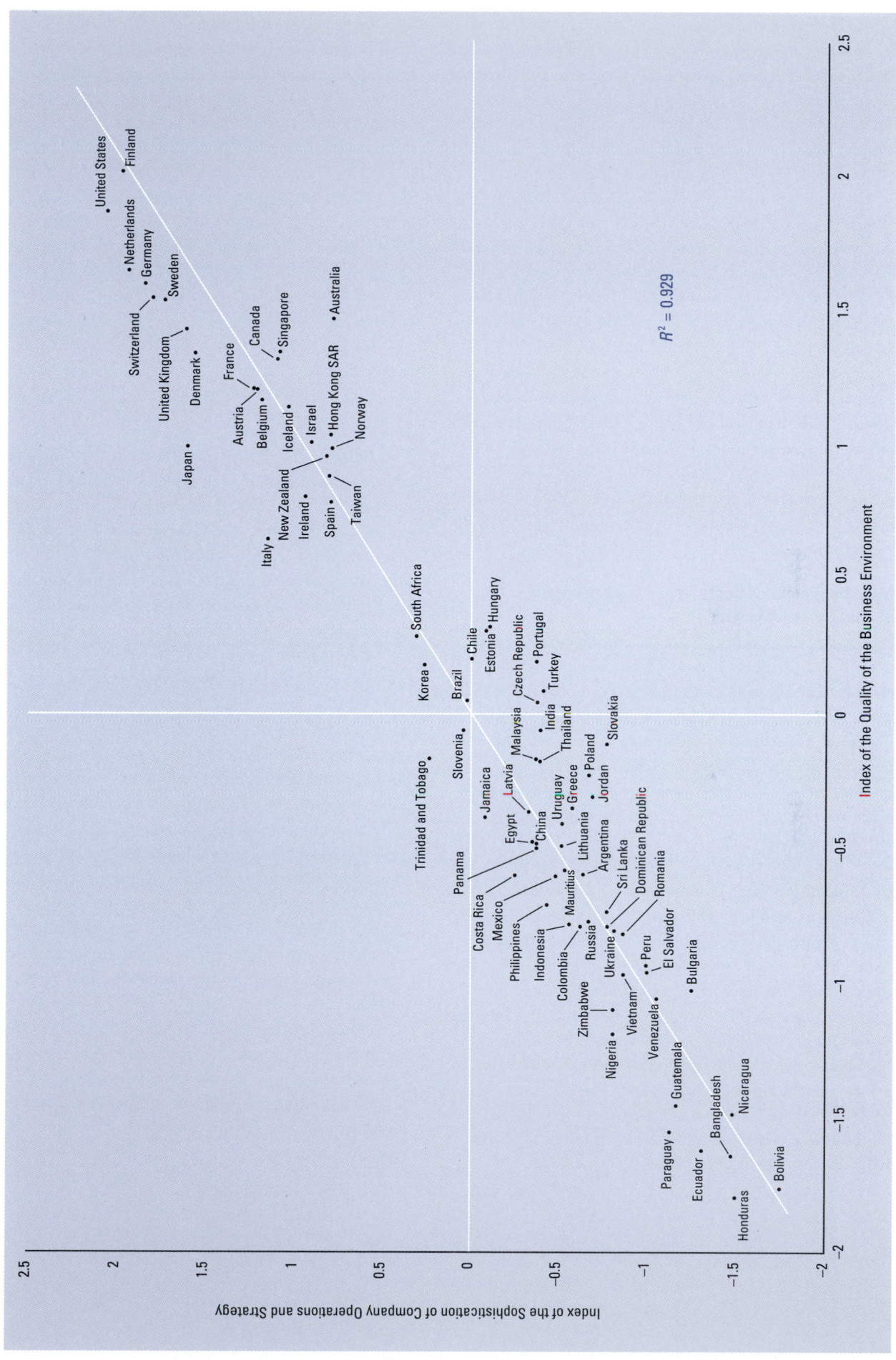

$R^2 = 0.929$

Index of the Sophistication of Company Operations and Strategy

Index of the Quality of the Business Environment

Countries whose company development is ahead of the business environment include Japan, Italy, Paraguay, and, to a lesser extent, Switzerland, Germany, and Sweden. Significant changes in public policy are necessary in these countries to underpin future prosperity. Japan remains the country with the most glaring weaknesses in the business environment. The consequences for Japan's economic growth have been severe.[xii] The business environments of Thailand, Sweden, and Hungary have improved most in relative terms compared to the 2000 *Report*, while those of Greece, Singapore, and Denmark have worsened.

Countries whose business environment is ahead of company practice include Australia, Slovakia, Portugal, Singapore, Hong Kong, Canada, and New Zealand. Many of the leading companies in these countries are still heavily involved in natural resource extraction (eg, Australia, Canada, and New Zealand), while others (Singapore and Hong Kong) depend heavily on OEM production and the subsidiaries of foreign multinationals. Efforts to improve entrepreneurial and managerial practice as well as business education are high priorities in these countries.

Microeconomic competitiveness and the state of country development

The appropriate company strategy and operations practices, as well as the influence of particular elements of the business environment, will differ for countries at different levels of income (and productivity). We expect the transition to be particularly challenging as economies shift from Factor-Driven to Investment-Driven to Innovation-Driven, because the stages involve different bases of competitive advantage and modes of integration with the global economy.

To examine these issues, we divide the countries in the sample into three groups based on per capita GDP: low income, medium income, and high income. While the reported variables are statistically significant across the entire sample and strongly distinguish countries *across* the three groups, the question is which variables have the strongest influence *within* groups. Unfortunately, however, our ability to distinguish these differences faces statistical hurdles. Limitations on sample size and in the variation in the dependent variable within groups reduce statistical power in the low-income and high-income subgroups. Within these subgroups, only the most robust variables will rise to the level of statistical significance.

We proceed with a number of approaches. The right hand side of Table 2 presents regressions within the subgroups. We explore both the statistical significance of each variable as well as the differences in slope even where variables do not achieve statistical significance. We also examine alternative functional forms of the relationships in the entire sample to see which has the best fit. An exponential relationship implies a greater effect at higher levels of a variable, while a semi-log relationship implies a greater effect at lower levels. This provides some indication of which variables are particularly important earlier in development and which ones take greater prominence at later stages.

What follows is our composite interpretation of all this evidence.

Low-income countries

The ability to move beyond competing solely on cheap labor/natural resources is the essential company challenge in the low-income countries, as revealed in the regressions. In other words, the challenge is to become increasingly efficient as a Factor-Driven economy. To do so, improving production process sophistication, introducing marketing and brand development, and beginning to delegate authority are important steps in enhancing company sophistication. Advancing other dimensions of corporate strategy and operations is premature at this stage.

Supporting priorities in terms of improving the business environment at the low-income stage with a positive relationship with GDP per capita are improving transportation and communications infrastructure, improving public education and training of management, liberalizing trade, reducing corruption, protecting intellectual property, and introducing a meaningful antitrust policy. Improving the quality of suppliers and introducing tighter regulatory standards are also important, as is beginning to improve corporate governance via effective corporate boards. All these steps create a foundation of efficiency, transparency, and competitive pressure to improve Factor-Driven competition.

Plotting the regressions of Survey respondents by subgroup for each variable helps reveal these patterns, and Figures 6 through 9 provide some representative examples. Improving buyer sophistication and scientific research institutions are not yet important in low-income countries, for example.

Figure 6: Prevalence of foreign technology licensing

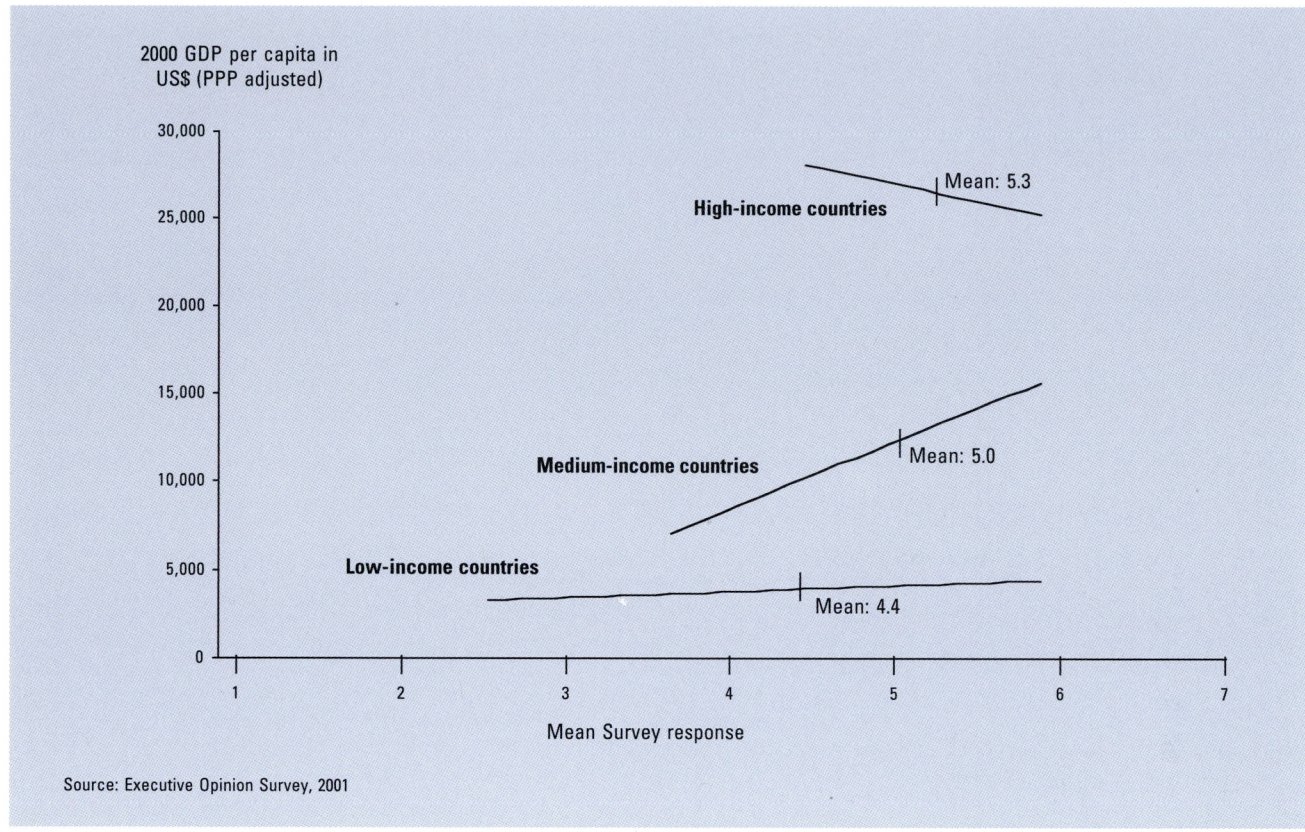

2000 GDP per capita in
US$ (PPP adjusted)

High-income countries — Mean: 5.3

Medium-income countries — Mean: 5.0

Low-income countries — Mean: 4.4

Mean Survey response

Source: Executive Opinion Survey, 2001

Figure 7: Buyer sophistication

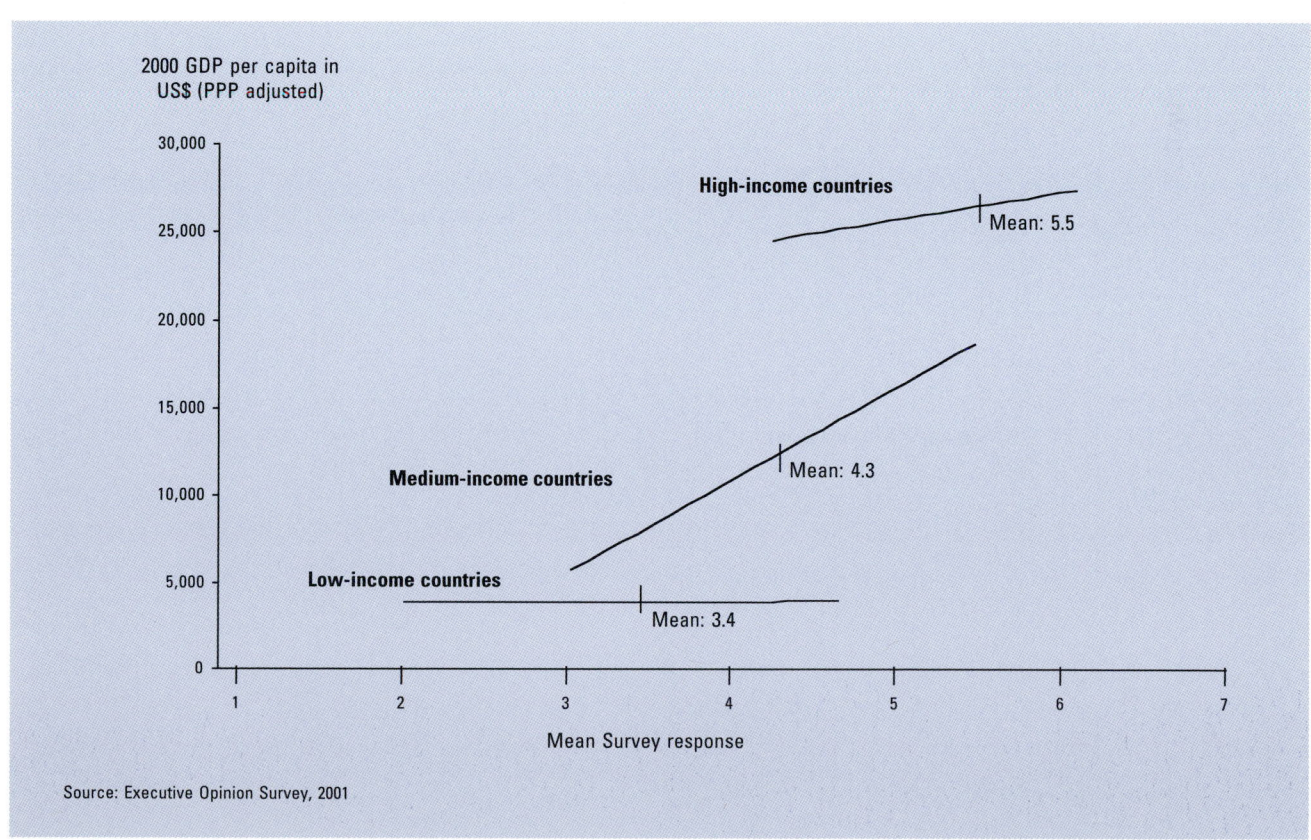

2000 GDP per capita in
US$ (PPP adjusted)

High-income countries — Mean: 5.5

Medium-income countries — Mean: 4.3

Low-income countries — Mean: 3.4

Mean Survey response

Source: Executive Opinion Survey, 2001

Figure 8: Quality of scientific research institutions

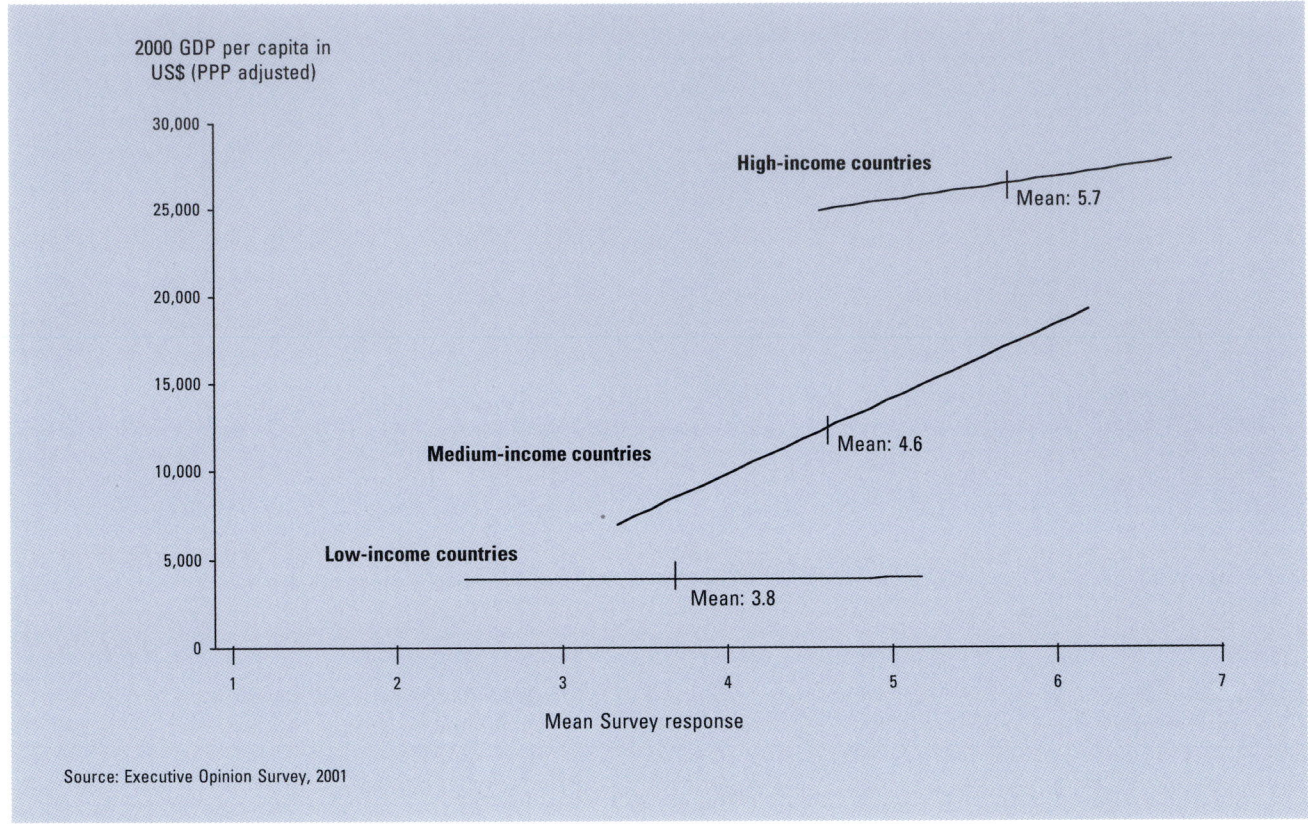

Figure 9: Venture capital availability

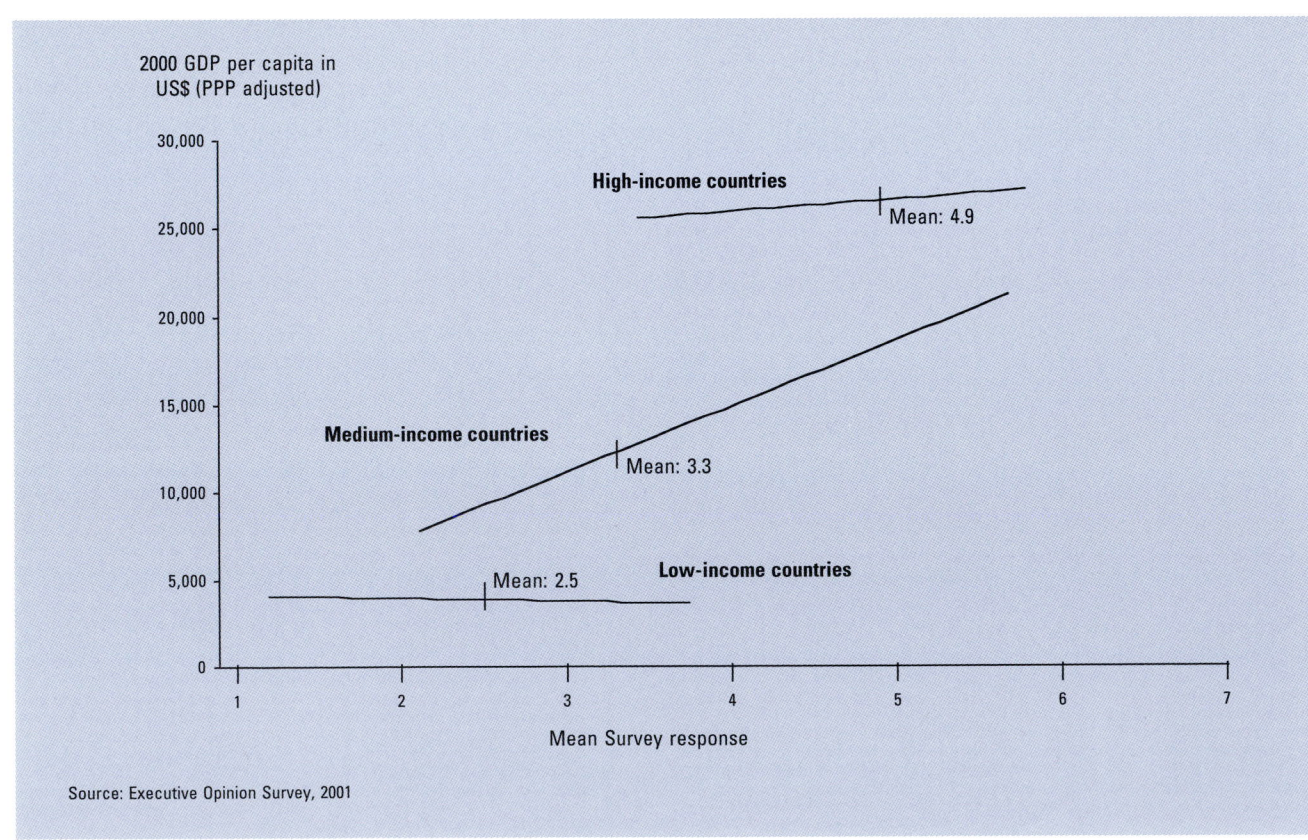

Medium-income countries

Moving into middle income, a series of new dimensions becomes essential. The challenge is to move beyond the Factor-Driven stage to the Investment-Driven stage. The regressions suggest the following patterns: Corporate priorities expand to include the greater orientation to customers versus the previous stage where products were either commodities or designed by foreign OEMs. Licensing foreign technology (Figure 6), developing the capacity to improve technology, and company spending on R&D become important. Gaining control of international distribution is essential to moving beyond the role of passive commodity or labor exporter. Introducing employee training is also important to enhance efficiency.

The Investment-Driven stage also creates new demands on the business environment. Reducing bureaucratic red tape and enhancing the legal system become important to enhance business efficiency. The financial markets become much more important to mobilize debt and equity capital. The Investment-Driven stage depends on a high rate of investment in products, processes, and acquisition of technology. Improving demand conditions are important to pressure improvements in producer quality (Figure 7). Full cluster development is needed to support higher levels of efficiency. As nations reach upper middle income, companies must utilize the best available foreign technology, produce products with quality levels at world standards, and organize at very high levels of efficiency.

High-income countries

To reach high-income status, further improvements in quality and efficiency are no longer enough. The hurdle is to move to the Innovation-Driven stage. The patterns of regressions suggest the following priorities: Companies must innovate at the world technology frontier, develop unique product designs, and sell globally. Reliance on foreign technology must fall in importance (Figure 6). In order to implement this transformation, a series of organizational changes becomes necessary. One is the complete professionalization of management, with a break from the family orientation common in the previous stage. Another organizational priority is the widespread adoption of incentive compensation to encourage risk taking. The ability to delegate authority remains important to whether a nation's firms achieve full Innovation-Driven capability.

Supporting enhancements in the business environment are also needed to achieve the Innovation-Driven stage. Some of the most important priorities are the emergence of truly world-class research institutions (Figure 8), strong research collaboration with universities, an improving supply of scientists and engineers, venture capital availability (Figure 9), truly sophisticated demand conditions, and intense local competition.

Microeconomic competitiveness and improvement in GDP per capita

The focus of the CCI is on measuring sustainable current competitiveness. However, many of the same microeconomic fundamentals also bear on the rate of productivity growth. Measures of the vitality of local competition, the environment for innovation, and demand side pressure, for example, boost current competitiveness as well as productivity growth. For example, the most influential single variable, not surprisingly, is the intensity of local competition, which was strongly associated with differences in GDP per capita growth across countries, especially in low- and high-income countries (not reported).

We briefly examined how *changes* in microeconomic conditions relate to changes in national income. We regressed the absolute change in GDP per capita 1997 to 2000 on *absolute changes* in microeconomic conditions between 1997 and 2000. A rising intensity of local competition has the strongest associations with increases in GDP per capita.

Finally, we explore the extent to which overperformance and underperformance versus microeconomic competitiveness relate to subsequent GDP per capita growth. A test of the causal influence of microeconomic conditions on GDP per capita is shown in Table 4. We calculated a measure (GAP), which is the difference between a country's *predicted* level and its *actual* level of 1997 GDP per capita based on its current competitiveness index for that year. In other words, GAP measures the degree to which a country was "overperforming" or "underperforming" its microeconomic fundamentals in 1997.

If microeconomic fundamentals cause GDP per capita, GAP should be related to GDP per capita growth in subsequent years. Countries with negative GAP, which were overperforming their fundamentals in 1997, would be expected to experience slower growth between 1997 and 2000, controlling for 1997 GDP per capita. The reverse should be true for countries underperforming their fundamentals in 1997. Hence we expect a positive sign. The strength of the effect may be modest, however, because of the relatively short time period and the susceptibility of GDP per capita growth to a myriad of transient and other disturbances.

Table 4: The relationship between predicted and actual income and change in subsequent GDP per capita

Source	SS	df	MS
Model	0.037313189	2	0.018656595
Residual	0.236362426	44	0.005371873
Total	0.273675615	46	0.024028468

Number of obs	=	47
$F(2, 44)$	=	3.47
Prob > F	=	0.0398
R^2	=	0.1363
Adj R^2	=	0.0971
Root MSE	=	0.07329

GDP pc growth, 1997–2000	Coefficient	Std. Error	t	P > |t|	[95% Conf. Interval]	
GAP, 1997	0.00000499	0.00000303	1.65	0.107	−0.0000081	0.0000348
GDP pc level, 1997	0.00000386	0.00000147	2.61	0.012	−0.0000725	0.0000304
Constant	0.0067456	0.0244175	0.28	0.784	−0.1603345	0.2846049

The results are consistent with the notion that micro-economic conditions *determine* the level of GDP per capita. Regressing 1997 to 2000 GDP per capita growth on GAP for the countries that have been included for all four years yielded positive coefficients overall and for all income categories. The coefficient was statistically significant at virtually the 90 percent level for the overall sample and is close to significant for low-income countries (not reported). Among low-income countries, GAP accounts for 21 percent of the variation in the subsequent change in GDP per capita, controlling for initial level. These results provide a tentative indication of causality from microeconomic conditions to changes in income.

Ranking microeconomic foundations

As noted earlier, competitiveness is not a zero-sum game. Many countries can improve productivity and prosperity. The Current Competitiveness Index tracks the performance of countries on this absolute level. However, the Index also supports comparisons among countries in their progress in building a productive economy, and hence has a relative component as well.

This year's overall CCI rankings are shown in Table 1, along with the last three years' rankings. Also included are the rankings across countries in company sophistication and the quality of the business environment. The inclusion of 17 new countries makes year-to-year comparisons difficult, especially for developing countries. Appendix B gives comparative rankings for the countries common to this and last year.

Finland again tops the United States as the leader in the CCI ranking, though the United States regained the number one company ranking. Advanced nations improving their current competitiveness rankings include the Netherlands, Sweden, Australia, Austria, France, and Iceland. Advanced countries slipping in the rankings include Germany, Denmark, Singapore, Belgium, Japan, and Hong Kong.

Developing nations improving their current competitiveness rankings on a comparable sample basis include Hungary, India, Thailand, Poland, China, Russia, and the Ukraine. Those falling in current competitiveness include Chile, Malaysia, Turkey, the Czech Republic, Greece, Jordan, Mauritius, and Peru.

Of the newly added countries, Estonia and Slovenia are the top-ranked performers. Estonia shows particular promise for future improvements in GDP per capita because it is underperforming its microeconomic potential. Bangladesh and several newly added Latin American countries register the greatest competitiveness challenges among our population of countries.

While each of the improving countries is different, there are some striking commonalities if one examines individual country patterns. Improving countries are ones where the effectiveness of antitrust policy is increasing, distortive government subsidies are declining, and weaknesses in physical infrastructure are being addressed. In the gaining countries, companies are becoming more customer oriented and more marketing savvy, improving the uniqueness of product designs, and upgrading production processes.

The countries that lost position exhibit a number of common characteristics: They are countries in which distortive government subsidies are becoming more prevalent, the quality of overall infrastructure is losing ground, the local supplier base is shrinking, and the extent of competition is falling. Companies in countries losing ground exhibit weakening regional sales, eroding control of their international distribution channels, and less distinctiveness in brands and product designs.

Please refer to the Country Profiles section of this *Report* for detailed descriptions of the competitive advantages and disadvantages of each country.

Further insight into the potential of each country can be gained from the analysis of overperformance and underperformance discussed previously. Table 5 lists countries in order of the divergence between actual GDP per capita and the expected GDP, given their microeconomic competitiveness. Underperforming countries are those with potential to improve GDP per capita over time—we term this *upside potential*. Countries whose actual and predicted GDP per capita are similar are termed *neutral*. Countries where predicted GDP per capita is lower than current GDP per capita are termed *overachievers*. Note that countries whose current competitiveness ranking has slipped modestly could still have upside potential, and vice versa.

Finland leads the advanced countries with upside potential. Its stunning turnaround in microeconomic competitiveness is still far from realized in terms of reported prosperity. Conversely, Norway, Iceland, and Ireland all continue to enjoy a level of prosperity that exceeds their microeconomic fundamentals. To a lesser extent this is also true for the United States and Canada.

Turkey, Brazil, and South Africa are among the middle-income countries that should be able to support a higher GDP per capita given their microeconomic fundamentals. The converse is true for Greece, Argentina, and Russia, which are among a group of countries whose levels of income will be unsustainable without substantial microeconomic reform. India heads the list of low-income countries with microeconomic capability that could be unlocked by microeconomic and political reform.

Table 5: GDP per capita relative to current competitiveness

	Advanced Countries	Middle Countries	Developing Countries
UPSIDE POTENTIAL			
Current competitiveness would support a higher per capita income	Finland Sweden United Kingdom	South Africa Brazil Turkey Chile Taiwan Hungary Israel Malaysia	India Egypt Jordan China Thailand Indonesia Philippines Vietnam Ukraine Zimbabwe
NEUTRAL			
Income and competitiveness are balanced	Germany Netherlands France Switzerland Australia Denmark	Singapore New Zealand Poland Spain Slovakia	Colombia
CURRENT OVERACHIEVERS			
Per capita income is high relative to current competitiveness	Norway Iceland Ireland United States Canada Belgium Italy Hong Kong SAR Austria Japan	Greece Argentina Portugal Korea Russia Mauritius Czech Republic Mexico Costa Rica	Bolivia Ecuador Bulgaria Venezuela Peru El Salvador

Conclusions

National prosperity depends on *competitiveness*, which reflects the productivity with which a nation uses resources. Competitiveness is rooted in a nation's microeconomic fundamentals and manifested in the nature of company operations and strategy and in the quality of the microeconomic business environment. Political stability and sound macroeconomic policies, accompanied by market opening and privatization, have long been considered the cornerstone for economic development. The results here suggest that they are necessary but not sufficient. We find strong evidence that microeconomic upgrading is a sequential process in which countries at different levels of development face distinctly different challenges.

While institutions such as the IMF have strongly encouraged macro reforms, our findings suggest that micro reforms are equally if not more important. Without micro reforms, growth in GDP induced by sound macro policies will be unsustainable and will not translate into improvements in GDP per capita. Appropriate micro reforms, which boost productivity and productivity growth, can also greatly ease the challenge of meeting government's fiscal obligations and reducing macroeconomic distortions.

A greater focus on microeconomic reforms will pay another essential dividend. While macro reforms almost inevitability inflict hardship in the short and medium run through raising interest rates and prices while cutting public expenditures, micro reforms can produce tangible and visible benefits for citizens. Breaking up local cartels and monopolies, for example, can lower the cost of food, housing, electricity, telephone service, and other costs of living. Regulatory reform can rapidly begin to ease inefficiencies, reduce pollution, raise product and service quality, and improve unsafe practices. Bold steps to improve education and training are particularly important, because they offer the hope of a better life for children. If citizens see businesses reforming themselves and having to confront tough competitive challenges, they themselves will be more willing to live with personal sacrifices and less likely to side with anti-reform interest groups. The political will and public support to make real economic change is elevated.

Our results again challenge the notion that microeconomic improvement is automatic if proper macroeconomic policies are instituted. While there may be a tendency for microeconomic conditions to improve because GDP per capita rises, *such improvement appears to be far from automatic*. Moreover, the rate of improvement in current competitiveness *can be affected* markedly by purposeful action in both government and the private sector. Microeconomic conditions can move ahead of or fall behind current GDP per capita, and we find evidence that this has an influence on subsequent economic growth.

Our findings indicate that it is unwise to view micro reforms only in terms of reducing the role of government and abolishing market distortions. Such steps remain a critical challenge for many countries to master. Yet government has a range of positive roles that are fundamental to prosperity, such as investments in human resources, building innovative capacity, and stimulating advanced demand via regulatory standards. Many nations need to move beyond first stage reforms and address these agendas. Also, the private sector has an important role in improving a nation's competitive platform through collective activities and cluster development initiatives. Second-stage micro reforms require a new perspective on the role of the private sector.

Our results also highlight the need to set a nation's economic priorities to be consistent with its level of development. We describe how the challenges are different for low-, medium-, and high-income countries. Especially challenging are the difficult transitions between development stages. Countries that have been very successful in one stage of development, such as Taiwan and Singapore in the Investment-Driven stage, need to recognize the multifaceted adjustments needed to manage the transition to the Innovation-Driven stage.

If there is to be continued momentum for economic reform in nations around the world, there is a pressing need to move to the next level of thinking and practice. Approaches centered largely on responding to international financial markets and ceding choices to impersonal global forces are producing a backlash that erodes the consensus for global economic progress and encourages populist national policies that are fundamentally self-defeating. Protests at international meetings should be a wake-up call that economic reform must move beyond now standard approaches and embrace domestic competition, stringent environmental standards, and policies that meaningfully boost the skills and opportunities of citizens.

Countries are converging on macroeconomic policies, and strong market forces penalize any nation that fails to reform in this arena. The central challenge to the world economy is now microeconomic reform, but reform that moves beyond past approaches. Progress in improving the sophistication of companies and the quality of the business environment is the only way to produce real improvements in efficiency, product quality, new business opportunities, and a rising standard of living for citizens.

References

Barro, Robert J. "Economic Growth in a Cross Section of Countries," *Quarterly Journal of Economics* 106, no. 2 (May 1991): 407–443.

Competitiveness Policy Council. "Lifting All Boats: Increasing the Payoff from Private Investment in the US Economy," Report of the Capital Allocation Subcouncil, Washington, DC: Competitiveness Policy Council, 1995.

Enright, Michael J, Antonio Francés, and Edith Scott Saavadra. *Venezuela: El Reto de la Competitividad*. Caracas, Venezuela: Ediciones IESA, 1994.

Fairbanks, Michael and Stace Lindsay. *Plowing the Sea: The Challenge of Competitiveness in the Developing World* Boston: Harvard Business School Press, 1997.

Ghemawat, Pankaj, Michael E Porter, and U Srinivasa Rangan. "A New Vision for Indian Economic Development: The Corporate Agenda," working paper, October 17, 1995.

Hall, Robert E and Charles I Jones. "Why Do Some Countries Produce So Much More Output per Worker than Others?" March 1998 draft, forthcoming in *Quarterly Journal of Economics*.

Hirschman, Albert O. *The Strategy of Economic Development*. New Haven: Yale University Press, 1958.

Ingham, Veronica H. "The Competitiveness of Argentina: From Sheltered Markets to Global Rivalry." Ph.D. diss., Fletcher School of Law and Diplomacy, Tufts University, May 1995.

Lucas, Robert E, Jr. "On the Mechanics of Economic Development," *Journal of Monetary Economics* 22 (July 1988): 3–42.

Mankiw, N Gregory, David Romer, and David N Weil. "A Contribution to the Empirics of Economic Growth," *Quarterly Journal of Economics* 107, no. 2 (May 1992): 407–437.

Mankiw, N Gregory. "The Growth of Nations," *Brookings Papers on Economic Activity* 1, no. 1 (August 1995): 275–310.

Nordhaus, William D. "Climate and Economic Development," in *Proceedings of the World Bank Annual Conference on Development Economics 1993*. Washington, DC: The International Bank for Reconstruction and Development/The World Bank, 1994: 355–376.

North, Douglass C. *Institutions, Institutional Change and Economic Performance: Political Economy of Institutions and Decisions*. Cambridge: Cambridge University Press, 1990.

Panayotou, Theodore and Jeffrey R Vincent. "Environmental Regulation and Competitiveness," in *The Global Competitiveness Report 1997*. Geneva, Switzerland: World Economic Forum, 1997.

Porter, Michael E. "Attitudes, Values, Beliefs, and the Microeconomic of Prosperity," in Lawrence E Harrison, Samuel P Huntington (eds.), *Culture Matters*, New York: Basic Books, 2000: 14–28.

———. "Introduction," *The Competitive Advantage of Nations: With a New Introduction*. New York: The Free Press, 1998a.

———. "Clusters and Competition: New Agendas for Companies, Governments, and Institutions," in *On Competition*. Boston: Harvard Business School Press, 1998b.

———. "What is Strategy?" *Harvard Business Review* 74, no. 6 (November–December 1996): 61–78.

———. "Comment on 'Interaction Between Regional and Industrial Policies: Evidence From Four Countries,' " by J Markusen, in *Proceedings of The World Bank Annual Conference on Development Economics 1994*. Washington, DC: The International Bank for Reconstruction and Development/The World Bank, 1995: 303–307.

———. *The Competitive Advantage of Nations*. New York: The Free Press; London: Macmillan Press, 1990.

Porter, Michael E, with Graham T Crocombe, and Michael J Enright. *Upgrading New Zealand's Competitive Advantage*. Auckland, New Zealand: Oxford University Press, 1991.

Porter, Michael E, Pankaj Ghemawat, and U Srinivasa Rangan. "A New Vision for Indian Economic Development," working paper, March 17, 1995.

Porter, Michael E, Scott Stern, and Council on Competitiveness. *The New Challenge to America's Prosperity: Findings from the Innovation Index*, Washington, DC, March 1999.

Porter, Michael E., Council on Competitiveness, and Monitor Group, *Clusters of Innovation Initiative: San Diego Report*, Washington, DC, May 2001.

Porter, Michael E and Hirotaka Takeuchi with Mariko Sakakibara. *Can Japan Compete?* Basingstoke, England: Macmillan, 2000; and New York: Basic Books, 2000.

Porter, Michael E and Claas van der Linde. "Toward a New Conception of the Environment-Competitiveness Relationship," *Journal of Economic Perspectives* 9, no. 4 (1995): 97–118.

Romer, Paul M. "Endogenous Technological Change," *Journal of Political Economy* 98, no. 5 (October 1990): S71–S102.

Sachs, Jeffrey and Andrew Warner. "Economic Reform and the Process of Global Integration," *Brookings Papers on Economic Activity* 1, no. 1 (August 1995): 1–118.

Sakakibara, Mariko and Michael E Porter. "Competing at Home to Win Abroad: Evidence from Japanese Industry," *Harvard Business School Working Paper 99-036*, September 4, 1998.

Solow, Robert M. "A Contribution to the Theory of Economic Growth," *Quarterly Journal of Economics* 70, no. 1 (February 1956): 65–94.

Notes

i Elisabeth de Fontenay, Christian Ketels, Daniel Vasquez, and Weifeng Weng I would like to thank for their major role in the analyses reported here. Lyn Pohl provided able supervision of the final production of the paper.

ii The proportion has grown modestly over the last several years as the model has been improved.

iii Stages were first introduced in Michael E Porter, *The Competitive Advantage of Nations*, Macmillan Press, 1990.

iv GDP per worker is employed as a productivity measure in some studies. We used the broader measure here because GDP per worker can be increased by high unemployment or low workforce participation, which do not increase wealth. Also, holders of capital, not only workers, contribute to national productivity. In comparing the United States and France, for example, the United States has absorbed a huge influx of new workers (higher workforce participation) over the last decade, while France has maintained high GDP per worker but with high unemployment and a large student population not counted as part of the potential workforce.

v In the case of Ireland, we used GNP instead of GDP because of the size of dividend outflows to foreign investors. Ireland's GDP is about 20 percent higher than its GNP.

vi Statistical significance at ** = 5 percent and * = 10 percent (all two-tailed tests) is noted in the table.

vii This analysis covers the questions that have been common over the three years, which comprise the great majority of questions.

viii Common factor analysis is a statistical technique for summarizing data by accounting for the common variance among all included variables. An alternative approach using a principal components analysis yielded similar qualitative results.

ix No other factor accounted for more than 4.6 percent of the covariance.

x The forecast region has wider bands than a 95 percent mean confidence region. The latter provides a confidence interval for a given level of competitiveness over repeated observations. The forecast region method, in contrast, reflects a higher degree of inherent uncertainty in predicting a single observation. As a result, interpretation of the proximity of data points to the regression line should be undertaken with appropriate caveats. Note that the forecast region widens slightly as it moves away from the "center" of the graph. The center is the point located at the intersection of the mean GDP per capita level and mean factor score.

xi In each case, a statistically significant, dominant factor again explains the great majority of the variance (77.4 percent for company operations and strategy and 67.6 percent for the business environment).

xii For a more detailed examination of Japan's competitive situation, see Porter et al (2000).

Appendix A: Survey Questions

I. COMPANY OPERATIONS & STRATEGY

Production Process Sophistication
Nature of Competitive Advantage
Extent of Staff Training
Extent of Marketing
Willingness to Delegate Authority . . . . New question
Capacity for Innovation
Company Spending on R&D
Value Chain Presence
Breadth of International Markets
Uniqueness of Product Designs
Degree of Customer Orientation
Control of International Distribution
Extent of Branding
Reliance on Professional Management
Extent of Incentive Compensation . . . . New question
Extent of Regional Sales
Prevalence of Foreign Technology Licensing

II. NATIONAL BUSINESS ENVIRONMENT

A. FACTOR (INPUT) CONDITIONS

1. Physical Infrastructure

Overall, Infrastructure Quality

a. Basic

Road Infrastructure Quality
Railroad Infrastructure Development
Port Infrastructure Quality
Air Transport Infrastructure Quality

b. Advanced

Telephone/Fax Infrastructure Quality
Availability and Cost of Cellular Phones
Speed and Cost of Internet Access

2. Administrative Infrastructure

Police Protection of Businesses
Judicial Independence
Administrative Burden for Start-Ups
Adequacy of Public Sector Legal Recourse
Extent of Bureaucratic Red Tape

3. Capital Availability

Ease of Access to Loans
Financial Market Sophistication
Local Equity Market Access
Venture Capital Availability

4. Human Resources

Quality of Public Schools
Quality of Math and Science Education . . . . New question
Availability of Scientists and Engineers. . . . . New question
Quality of Management Schools

5. Science & Technology

Patents per capita (2000)
Quality of Scientific Research Institutions
University/Industry Research Collaboration

II. NATIONAL BUSINESS ENVIRONMENT *(Cont'd.)*

B. DEMAND CONDITIONS

Buyer Sophistication
Consumer Adoption of Latest Products
Presence of Demanding Regulatory Standards
Stringency of Environmental Regulations
Government Procurement of Advanced
    Technology Products . . . . New question
Laws Relating to Information Technology . . . . New question

C. RELATED AND SUPPORTING INDUSTRIES

Local Supplier Quantity
Local Supplier Quality
State of Cluster Development
Extent of Product and Process Collaboration . . . . New question
Local Availability of Components and Parts . . . . New question
Local Availability of Process Machinery . . . . New question
Local Availability of Specialized Research
    and Traning Services . . . . New question
Local Availability of Information Technology Services. . . . New question

D. CONTEXT FOR FIRM STRATEGY AND RIVALRY

Favoritism in Decisions of Government Officials
Extent of Irregular Payments
Extent of Distortive Government Subsidies
Decentralization of Corporate Activity
Cooperation in Labor-Employer Relations . . . . New question
Tariff Liberalization
Hidden Trade Barrier Liberalization
Intellectual Property Protection
Intensity of Local Competition
Extent of Locally Based Competitors
Effectiveness of Anti-Trust Policy
Efficacy of Corporate Boards

Appendix B: The Current Competitiveness Index (Constant Country Sample)

Country	CCI Ranking				Company Operations and Strategy Ranking				Quality of the National Business Environment Ranking				2000 GDP per Capita (ppp adjusted)
	2001	2000	1999	1998	2001	2000	1999	1998	2001	2000	1999	1998	
Finland	1	1	2	2	2	3	7	8	1	1	2	2	24,864
United States	2	2	1	1	1	2	1	2	2	2	1	1	33,886
Netherlands	3	4	3	3	3	7	8	5	3	3	3	4	25,598
Germany	4	3	6	4	4	1	5	1	4	6	5	8	24,931
Switzerland	5	5	5	9	5	5	2	3	5	10	9	10	28,518
Sweden	6	7	4	7	6	6	3	4	6	11	7	9	23,884
United Kingdom	7	8	10	5	7	11	13	9	8	9	8	5	23,197
Denmark	8	6	7	8	9	8	9	10	9	4	6	7	27,120
Australia	9	10	13	15	22	20	19	22	7	7	10	12	25,758
Singapore	10	9	12	10	15	15	14	12	10	5	12	6	23,000
Canada	11	11	8	6	14	16	12	15	11	8	4	3	27,783
Austria	12	13	11	16	11	12	10	11	13	12	13	17	26,314
France	13	15	9	11	10	9	6	6	12	15	11	13	24,032
Belgium	14	12	15	19	12	10	11	13	14	13	15	18	26,958
Japan	15	14	14	18	8	4	4	7	18	19	19	19	25,796
Iceland	16	17	22	24	16	14	21	28	15	16	21	23	29,167
Israel	17	18	20	21	18	13	18	21	17	20	20	20	19,577
Hong Kong SAR	18	16	21	12	21	23	24	17	16	14	18	11	24,448
Norway	19	20	18	14	24	21	23	14	19	18	16	15	29,500
New Zealand	20	19	16	17	19	22	16	19	20	17	14	16	20,010
Taiwan	21	21	19	20	20	18	17	16	21	21	22	21	17,223
Ireland[v]	22	22	17	13	17	19	20	18	22	22	17	14	25,200
Spain	23	23	23	22	23	24	22	23	23	23	23	22	19,202
Italy	24	24	25	26	13	17	15	20	24	26	27	27	23,304
South Africa	25	25	26	25	25	26	28	33	26	25	25	25	9,189
Hungary	26	32	33	31	29	34	36	39	25	31	33	31	12,335
Korea	27	27	28	28	26	25	27	24	29	28	30	28	17,311
Chile	28	26	24	23	28	27	26	25	27	24	24	24	9,187
Portugal	29	28	29	33	33	35	37	48	28	27	26	30	16,882
Brazil	30	31	35	35	27	29	32	27	32	32	37	39	7,389
Turkey	31	29	31	29	38	28	33	26	30	29	32	29	6,870
Czech Republic	32	34	41	30	35	41	55	31	31	34	36	33	13,721
India	33	37	42	44	37	40	48	50	33	37	43	42	2,403
Malaysia	34	30	27	27	32	30	25	34	35	30	31	26	8,924
Thailand	35	40	39	37	36	47	43	37	36	40	39	36	6,469
Slovakia	36	36	48	36	49	31	51	40	34	36	47	37	11,035
Poland	37	41	37	41	46	36	38	38	37	41	38	40	8,971
Greece	38	33	36	38	43	32	45	32	39	33	34	38	16,326
Jordan	39	35	32	32	48	46	44	42	38	35	28	32	4,079
Egypt	40	39	43	40	31	44	49	47	40	39	42	35	3,602
China	41	44	49	42	34	38	31	35	41	45	50	44	3,953
Costa Rica	42	43	38	—	30	39	35	—	45	42	41	—	9,236
Mauritius	43	38	30	—	41	37	29	—	42	38	29	—	9,512
Mexico	44	42	34	39	40	42	30	29	44	43	35	41	8,914
Argentina	45	45	40	34	45	45	39	30	43	44	40	34	12,314
Philippines	46	46	44	45	39	43	34	41	46	46	46	45	3,956
Indonesia	47	47	53	51	42	51	47	52	47	47	52	51	3,014
Colombia	48	48	52	49	44	48	40	43	49	48	53	49	5,923
Russia	49	52	55	46	47	33	42	45	48	53	55	47	8,213
Ukraine	50	56	56	52	51	52	50	51	50	56	56	52	3,693
Vietnam	51	53	50	43	52	50	41	36	53	52	49	43	1,974
Peru	52	49	46	47	53	53	56	49	51	51	44	46	4,797
El Salvador	53	51	47	—	54	57	46	—	52	50	48	—	4,477
Zimbabwe	54	50	45	48	50	56	54	46	56	49	45	48	2,697
Venezuela	55	54	51	50	55	49	53	44	55	55	51	50	5,677
Bulgaria	56	55	54	—	56	54	52	—	54	54	54	—	5,469
Ecuador	57	57	57	—	57	55	57	—	57	58	57	—	3,068
Bolivia	58	58	58	—	58	58	58	—	58	57	58	—	2,408

Part 2

Selected Issues of Competitiveness

Ranking National Environmental Regulation and Performance: A Leading Indicator of Future Competitiveness?

DANIEL C. ESTY, Yale University

MICHAEL E. PORTER, Harvard Business School and Director, Institute for Strategy and Competitiveness

Environmental performance, encompassing the control of pollution and stewardship of natural resources, is of growing concern in both advanced and developing economies. Environmental quality plays a major role in quality of life, with a direct impact on the health and safety of a nation's citizens as well as its attractiveness as a place to live. It is becoming increasingly clear, however, that environmental performance has a further, more indirect, effect on living standards through its impact on a nation's capacity to sustain economic growth. The ability to grow requires resources and places strains on the environment that can drive up costs, especially in the longer run. But a growing body of research suggests that economic competitiveness and environmental performance are compatible, if not mutually reinforcing. Low pollution and efficient energy use are a sign of the highly productive use of resources. Policies that stimulate improvements in environmental quality, then, may actually foster improvements in competitiveness that underpin a rising standard of living in the long run.

Despite growing concern for the environment across almost all countries, and protestors from Seattle to Genoa demanding more emphasis on pollution control and natural resource management, environmental policymaking remains more an art than a science. Statistical analyses of the determinants of environmental performance across nations have been rare—indeed, almost nonexistent. Research in the environmental realm has traditionally relied heavily on anecdotal evidence and case studies. There are precious little systematic data on which to base environmental judgments at both the public policy and corporate levels. This may explain why the environmental field remains mired in deep controversies over the best path forward, with debate often dominated by emotional claims and heated rhetoric. We believe that more sophisticated use of environmental indicators and statistical tools to develop objective ways to gauge progress offer a constructive way out of the current stasis.

This chapter builds on our previous effort to investigate statistically the causes of environmental performance and to use the findings to rank countries in terms of environmental outcomes and environmental policies.[i] In particular, we seek to explain differences in national environmental outcomes—as measured by levels of air pollution (particulates and SO_2) and energy use—based on national policy choices in environmental regulation as well as in broader economic, political, and legal structures. We also explore empirically the question of whether strong environmental performance must come at the expense of competitiveness and economic development, as traditional

Figure 1: Determinants of environmental performance

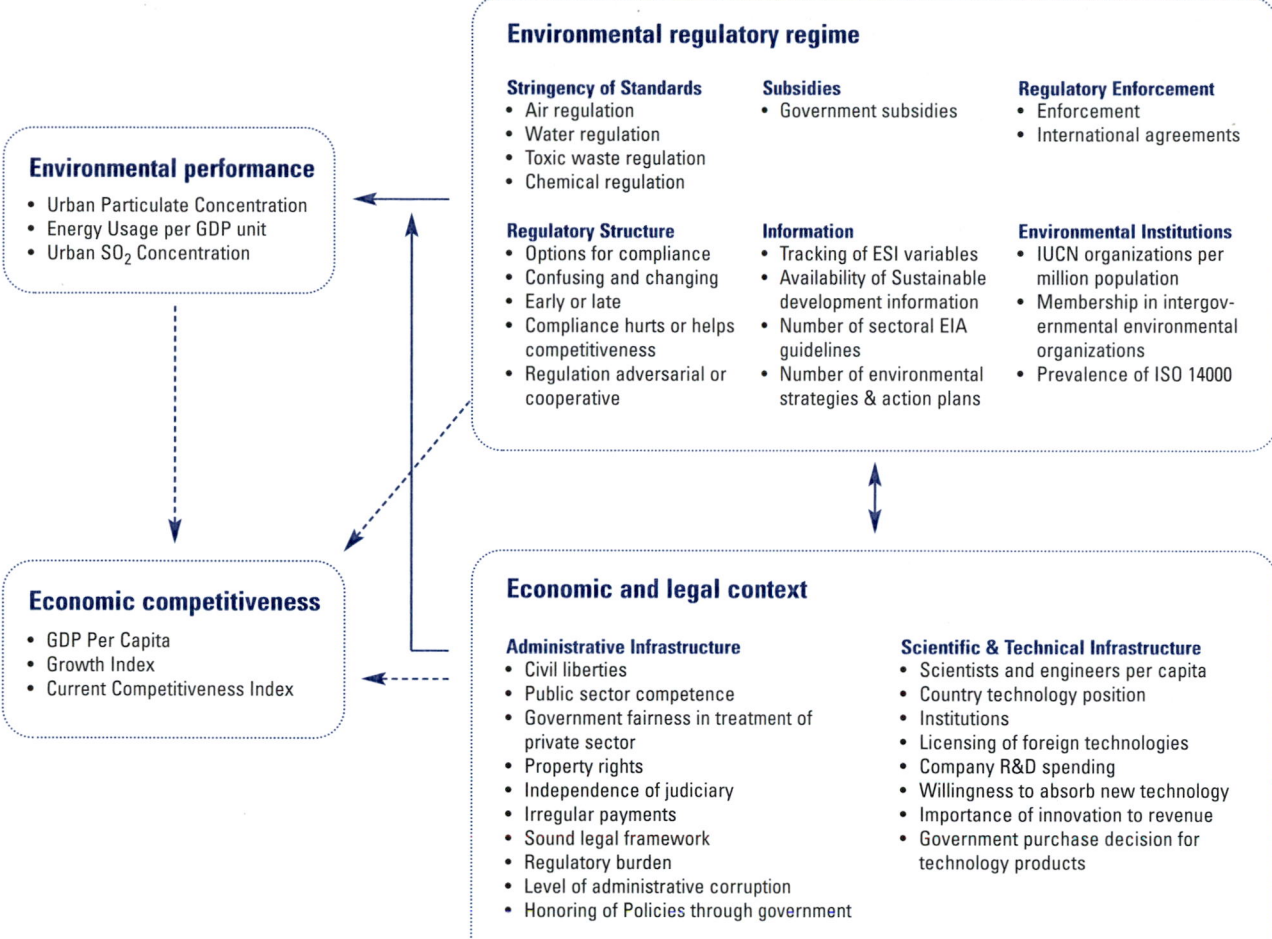

Environmental regulatory regime

Stringency of Standards
- Air regulation
- Water regulation
- Toxic waste regulation
- Chemical regulation

Subsidies
- Government subsidies

Regulatory Enforcement
- Enforcement
- International agreements

Regulatory Structure
- Options for compliance
- Confusing and changing
- Early or late
- Compliance hurts or helps competitiveness
- Regulation adversarial or cooperative

Information
- Tracking of ESI variables
- Availability of Sustainable development information
- Number of sectoral EIA guidelines
- Number of environmental strategies & action plans

Environmental Institutions
- IUCN organizations per million population
- Membership in intergovernmental environmental organizations
- Prevalence of ISO 14000

Environmental performance
- Urban Particulate Concentration
- Energy Usage per GDP unit
- Urban SO_2 Concentration

Economic competitiveness
- GDP Per Capita
- Growth Index
- Current Competitiveness Index

Economic and legal context

Administrative Infrastructure
- Civil liberties
- Public sector competence
- Government fairness in treatment of private sector
- Property rights
- Independence of judiciary
- Irregular payments
- Sound legal framework
- Regulatory burden
- Level of administrative corruption
- Honoring of Policies through government

Scientific & Technical Infrastructure
- Scientists and engineers per capita
- Country technology position
- Institutions
- Licensing of foreign technologies
- Company R&D spending
- Willingness to absorb new technology
- Importance of innovation to revenue
- Government purchase decision for technology products

79

economic theory has suggested (Jaffee et al 1995). More broadly, we also aim to put environmental decision-making on a firmer analytic footing and to encourage further efforts to generate better data and improve statistical methods.

Although hampered by imperfect data, a lack of time-series data that would permit more definitive tests of causality, and the need to utilize relatively crude methods, we find substantial evidence that environmental performance varies systematically with both the quality of a country's environmental regulatory regime and its broader economic and legal context. We utilize our model to create a framework for measuring the quality of national environmental regulation and to rank countries on both the quality of regulation and on environmental performance (see Table 8). We find a significant correlation between income and environmental performance, suggesting that alleviating

poverty should be seen as a priority for environmental policymakers. However, dramatic differences in environmental performance occur among countries at similar economic levels. This finding implies that environmental improvement is not merely a function of economic development but benefits from conscious policy choices. Our analysis suggests that a country's broader economic, legal, and other institutional underpinnings are also important in determining environmental performance. On the tradeoff between green and competitive, we find no evidence that improving environmental quality compromises economic progress. In fact, strong environmental performance appears to be positively correlated with competitiveness.

Modeling environmental performance and its causes

We employ three measures of environmental performance (environmental "output") that are available with broad country coverage: the level of urban particulates, urban SO_2 concentrations, and energy usage per unit of GDP.[ii] These measures constitute the dependent variables for the analysis.

Building on theoretical work in the economic, legal, regulatory, and environmental domains, we then assemble data on policy variables that potentially determine environmental outcomes.[iii] The framework for the analysis is shown in Figure 1. Environmental performance is hypothesized to result from two broad sets of independent variables. One set, which we term the *environmental regulatory regime*, is comprised of measures of various aspects of a country's environmental regulatory system including standards, implementation and enforcement mechanisms, and associated institutions. These variables capture regulatory elements that directly affect pollution control and natural resource management.

The second set of independent variables, which we term *economic and legal context*, are indicators of a country's more general administrative, scientific, and technical institutions and capabilities. These include measures of the extent of the rule of law, protection of property rights, and technological strength. The hypothesis is that a nation's environmental regulatory regime will be more effective in producing the desired outcomes if the economic and legal context is sound. Hence context indirectly (but perhaps importantly) determines environmental performance.

The dotted arrows in Figure 1 represent the final stage of the analysis, in which we examine the connection between environmental performance and economic success. We explore, in particular, the relationship between our environmental quality measures and GDP per capita, as well as the relationship between an index measuring the overall environmental regulatory regime (the environmental regulatory regime index (ERRI)) and GDP per capita. We also examine the relationship between the ERRI and the Current Competitiveness Index reported in Chapter 1.2. These relationships shed light on the longstanding debate over the extent of the tradeoff between environmental progress and economic success—a question of particular interest in the developing world.

Environmental Outcomes

Environmental output data are notoriously spotty, unreliable, and uneven, as are data on the characteristics of national regulatory regimes. Hence, establishing a sufficient database for a broad empirical analysis is no small undertaking. The performance measures used in this study are drawn from data assembled for the World Economic Forum's Environmental Sustainability Index (ESI) Project.[iv]

Three measures of environmental performance emerge as reliable enough and available in a large enough number of countries to utilize in our analysis. The first is urban particulate concentration, derived from World Bank and World Health Organization (WHO) data sources. This measure provides the mean total suspended particulate concentrations in the air (airborne dust) normalized by a country's urban population. A higher concentration indicates more pollution and thus worse air quality.

The second performance measure is mean SO_2 concentration normalized by urban population. This measure is also drawn from World Bank and WHO data. Again, higher figures represent worse air pollution.

The third environmental performance measure gauges energy efficiency. Using US Department of Energy data, we measure total energy consumption per unit of a country's GDP. Higher figures represent more energy consumed per unit of economic output and thus greater energy inefficiency. In comparing this measure across countries, we need to account for the fact that Russia and the countries of the former Soviet bloc operated for decades under an energy regime with prices set well below market prices. This history has left a legacy of energy inefficiency in these countries that is only slowly being corrected. We therefore include a dummy variable in our model to control for this history, which proves to be highly significant statistically.

Table 1 provides absolute rankings by country for each of the three environmental performance measures. Urban particulate data are available for just 42 of the 75 countries covered by the *Global Competitiveness Report 2001–2002* (GCR). The United States and the United Kingdom track particulates, but on a more refined basis than the rest of the world; thus their particulate rankings are not comparable, so they are therefore excluded from the urban particulate analysis.[v] Sweden and Norway are at the top of the particulate ranking, with China and Honduras at the bottom.

Table 1: Absolute environmental performance by country

Urban Particulate Concentration*
(Per City Population)

Rank	Country	Annual Mean
1	Sweden	9.0
2	Norway	10.3
3	France	14.2
4	Iceland	24.0
5	New Zealand	27.3
6	Switzerland	30.7
7	Canada	31.3
8	Netherlands	40.0
9	Australia	43.2
10	Germany	43.3
11	Japan	43.6
12	Austria	45.7
13	Finland	49.9
14	Argentina	50.0
15	Portugal	50.4
16	Venezuela	53.0
17	Czech Republic	58.4
18	Denmark	61.0
19	Hungary	63.7
20	Slovak Republic	64.5
21	Spain	72.7
22	Romania	82.0
23	Korea	83.8
24	Italy	86.9
25	Malaysia	91.6
26	Latvia	100.0
27	Russia	100.0
28	Brazil	106.2
29	Lithuania	114.3
30	Colombia	120.0
31	Ecuador	125.7
32	Greece	178.0
33	Bulgaria	199.2
34	Philippines	200.0
35	Thailand	223.0
36	Costa Rica	244.5
37	Indonesia	271.0
38	Guatemala	272.3
39	India	277.5
40	Mexico	279.0
41	China	310.8
42	Honduras	320.0

* Not all data were available for all countries.

Urban SO$_2$ Concentration*
(Per City Population)

Rank	Country	Annual Mean
1	Argentina	1.02
2	Lithuania	2.10
3	New Zealand	3.49
4	Finland	4.38
5	Iceland	5.00
6	Sweden	5.23
7	Latvia	5.36
8	Norway	5.47
9	Denmark	7.00
10	Portugal	9.22
11	Netherlands	10.00
12	Romania	10.00
13	Spain	11.00
14	Thailand	11.00
15	Switzerland	11.34
16	Germany	12.80
17	Canada	12.87
18	Australia	13.17
19	Austria	13.21
20	France	13.89
21	United States	15.43
22	Italy	15.55
23	Ireland	18.89
24	Singapore	20.00
25	Malaysia	20.49
26	Belgium	21.02
27	Ecuador	21.52
28	United Kingdom	21.96
29	South Africa	22.37
30	Slovak Republic	22.66
31	Japan	24.33
32	Czech Republic	27.34
33	India	27.55
34	Chile	29.00
35	Philippines	33.00
36	Venezuela	33.00
37	Greece	34.00
38	Hungary	37.33
39	Costa Rica	38.84
40	Korea	52.41
41	Bulgaria	52.45
42	Poland	54.72
43	Egypt	69.00
44	Mexico	74.00
45	Brazil	75.78
46	China	97.07
47	Russia	97.55

* Not all data were available for all countries.

Energy Usage
(Per Mil. $ GDP)

Rank	Country	Bil. BTU
1	Denmark	4.84
2	Switzerland	5.19
3	Japan	6.55
4	Italy	6.66
5	Ireland	6.85
6	Austria	7.09
7	Germany	7.28
8	France	7.39
9	Finland	8.37
10	United Kingdom	8.59
11	Spain	8.73
12	Honduras	8.97
13	Mauritius	9.11
14	Sweden	9.14
15	Israel	9.96
16	Peru	10.81
17	Netherlands	11.01
18	Slovenia	11.26
19	Australia	11.46
20	Guatemala	11.52
21	Portugal	11.77
22	Belgium	11.83
23	Norway	12.17
24	Argentina	12.22
25	Uruguay	12.86
26	Greece	12.95
27	Bangladesh	13.15
28	United States	13.41
29	Sri Lanka	13.70
30	El Salvador	13.75
31	Brazil	14.01
32	Iceland	14.49
33	New Zealand	15.09
34	Paraguay	15.32
35	Estonia	16.09
36	Costa Rica	16.13
37	Chile	16.63
38	Canada	17.54
39	Mexico	17.72
40	Korea	17.91
41	Bolivia	18.41
42	Dominican Republic	18.68
43	Panama	18.70
44	Thailand	19.29
45	Philippines	19.74
46	Singapore	20.41
47	Zimbabwe	22.34
48	Malaysia	22.88
49	Indonesia	22.96
50	Nigeria	23.66
51	Colombia	23.98
52	Latvia	25.01
53	Ecuador	27.57
54	India	28.13
55	Egypt	31.03
56	Hungary	32.29
57	Jordan	34.52
58	Jamaica	35.58
59	Nicaragua	36.46
60	South Africa	37.92
61	China	39.10
62	Venezuela	44.11
63	Poland	45.05
64	Lithuania	54.92
65	Czech Republic	56.22
66	Romania	58.39
67	Bulgaria	60.71
68	Slovak Republic	63.95
69	Vietnam	64.57
70	Russia	74.19
71	Ukraine	96.53

Figure 2: Relationship between urban particulate concentration and GDP per capita

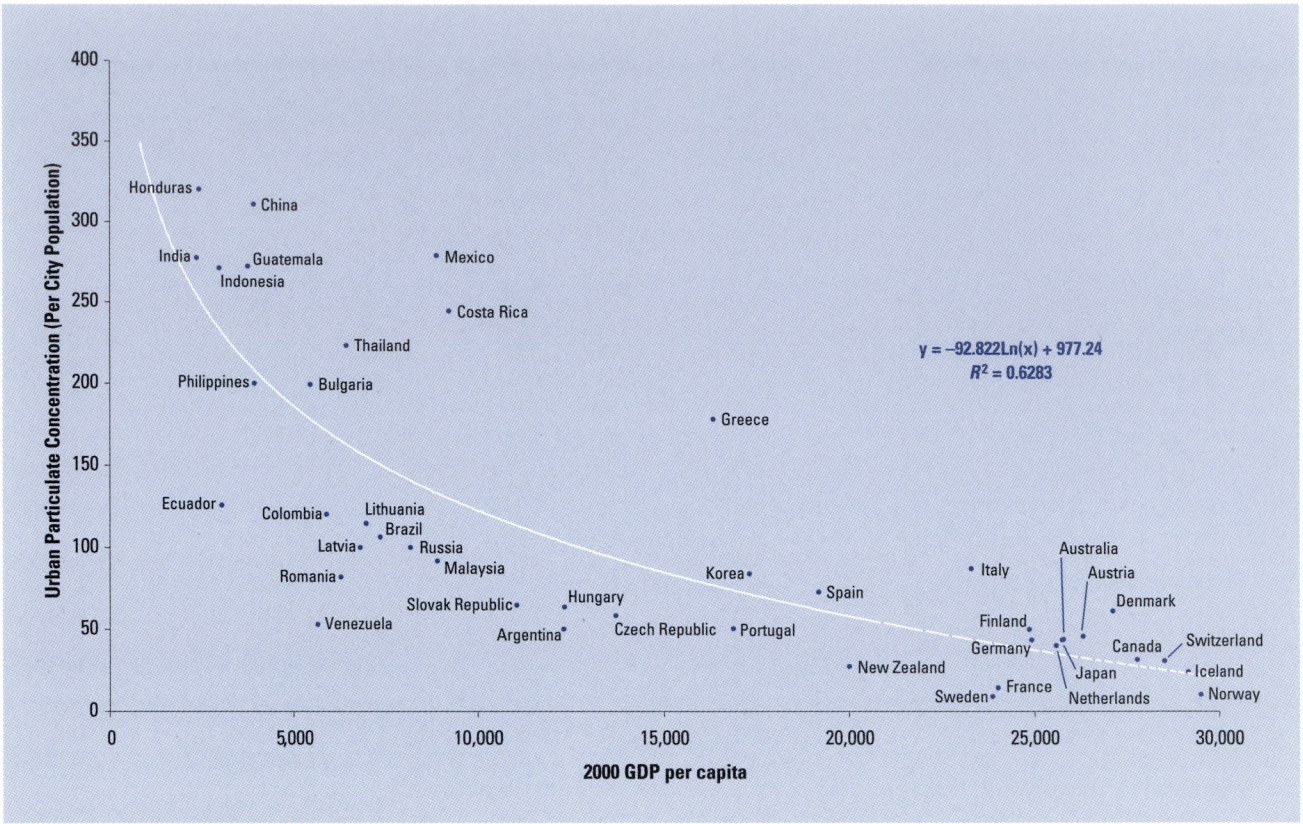

Figure 3: Relationship between urban SO₂ concentration and GDP per capita

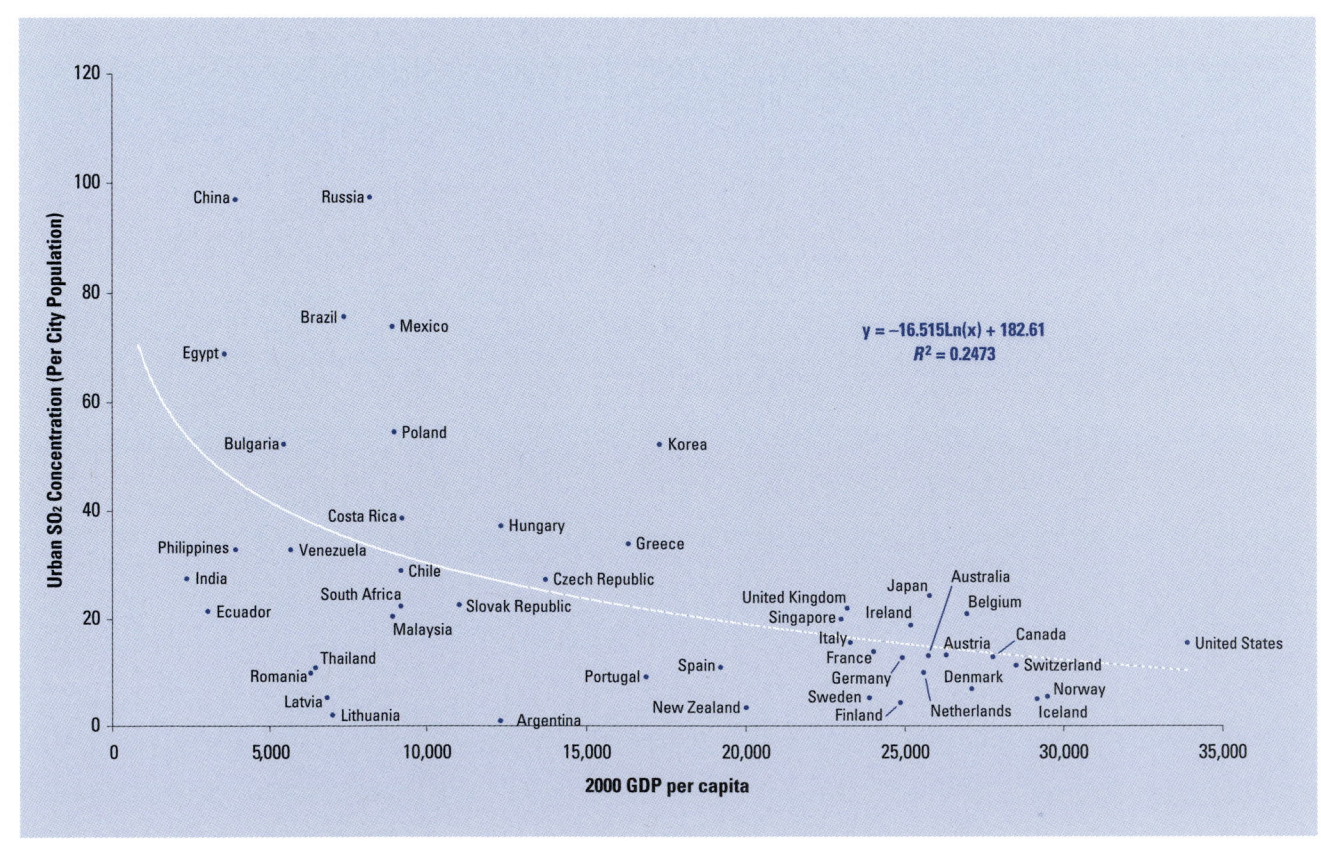

Figure 4: Relationship between energy usage and GDP per capita (log model)

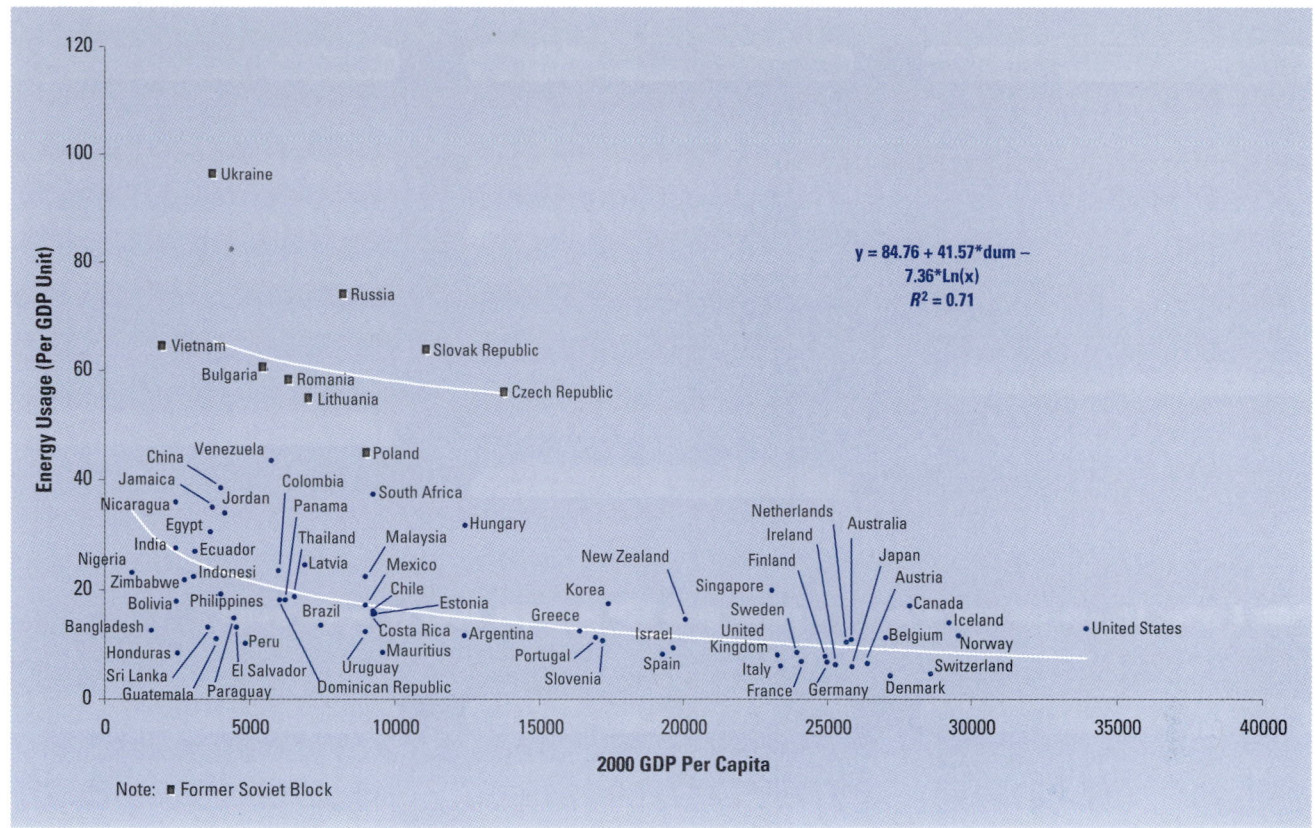

$$y = 84.76 + 41.57 \cdot dum - 7.36 \cdot Ln(x)$$
$$R^2 = 0.71$$

Note: ■ Former Soviet Block

Table 2: Energy usage relative to expected given GDP per capita, listed by income groups

Low-Income Countries (≤ $6,500)			Middle-Income Countries ($6,500–$23,000)			High-Income Countries (≥ $23,000)		
Rank	**Country**	**Residual**	**Rank**	**Country**	**Residual**	**Rank**	**Country**	**Residual**
1	Honduras	−18.29	1	Hungary	−24.70	1	Denmark	−4.78
2	Bangladesh	−17.48	2	Poland	−14.29	2	Italy	−4.08
3	Guatemala	−12.60	3	Mauritius	−8.22	3	Switzerland	−4.06
4	Peru	−11.57	4	Lithuania	−6.24	4	Japan	−3.44
5	Nigeria	−11.28	5	Brazil	−5.19	5	Ireland	−3.31
6	Sri Lanka	−10.96	6	Uruguay	−4.96	6	France	−3.12
7	El Salvador	−9.13	7	Spain	−3.44	7	Germany	−2.96
8	Bolivia	−9.04	8	Argentina	−3.21	8	Austria	−2.75
9	Paraguay	−7.69	9	Israel	−2.06	9	United Kingdom	−2.18
10	Zimbabwe	−4.27	10	Slovenia	−1.74	10	Finland	−1.89
11	Philippines	−4.05	11	Estonia	−1.51	11	Sweden	−1.42
12	Romania	−3.53	12	Costa Rica	−1.42	12	Netherlands	0.96
13	Indonesia	−2.84	13	Portugal	−1.34	13	Australia	1.46
14	Bulgaria	−2.26	14	Chile	−0.96	14	Belgium	2.16
15	Dominican Republic	−2.09	15	Greece	−0.41	15	Norway	3.17
16	Panama	−1.82	16	Mexico	−0.09	16	Iceland	5.41
17	Thailand	−0.88	17	Czech Republic	0.02	17	United States	5.43
18	India	0.67	18	New Zealand	3.24	18	Canada	8.10
19	Ecuador	1.90	19	Korea	4.98			
20	Colombia	3.17	20	Malaysia	5.08			
21	Egypt	6.55	21	Latvia	5.25			
22	Nicaragua	8.98	22	Slovak Republic	6.14			
23	Jordan	10.96	23	Singapore	9.58			
24	Jamaica	11.21	24	Russia	14.20			
25	China	15.30	25	South Africa	20.33			
26	Venezuela	22.98						
27	Ukraine	30.66						
28	Vietnam	35.66						

Table 3: Urban particulate concentration relative to expected given GDP per capita, listed by income groups

Low-Income Countries (≤ $6,500)

Rank	Country	Residual
1	Venezuela	−121.87
2	Ecuador	−106.27
3	Romania	−83.06
4	Colombia	−50.93
5	Philippines	−8.40
6	Bulgaria	20.92
7	India	22.78
8	Indonesia	37.35
9	Guatemala	59.80
10	Thailand	60.26
11	Honduras	67.85
12	China	102.36

Middle-Income Countries ($6,500–$23,000)

Rank	Country	Residual
1	Latvia	−57.59
2	Argentina	−52.99
3	Slovak Republic	−48.69
4	Brazil	−44.20
5	Malaysia	−41.31
6	Lithuania	−41.17
7	Russia	−40.59
8	Hungary	−39.10
9	Czech Republic	−34.57
10	New Zealand	−30.61
11	Portugal	−23.31
12	Spain	10.93
13	Korea	12.41
14	Greece	101.19
15	Costa Rica	114.79
16	Mexico	146.02

High-Income Countries (≥ $23,000)

Rank	Country	Residual
1	Sweden	−32.50
2	France	−26.77
3	Norway	−11.65
4	Iceland	1.05
5	Canada	3.80
6	Netherlands	4.93
7	Switzerland	5.62
8	Germany	5.75
9	Australia	8.73
10	Japan	9.28
11	Finland	12.13
12	Austria	13.20
13	Denmark	31.29
14	Italy	43.13

Table 4: Urban SO_2 concentration relative to expected given GDP per capita, listed by income groups

Low-Income Countries (≤ $6,500)

Rank	Country	Residual
1	Ecuador	−28.49
2	Romania	−28.10
3	Thailand	−26.69
4	India	−26.49
5	Philippines	−12.81
6	Venezuela	−6.84
7	Bulgaria	11.99
8	Egypt	21.64
9	China	51.25

* Not all data were available for all countries.

Middle-Income Countries ($6,500–$23,000)

Rank	Country	Residual
1	Lithuania	−34.29
2	Latvia	−31.41
3	Argentina	−26.04
4	New Zealand	−15.54
5	Portugal	−12.63
6	Malaysia	−11.88
7	South Africa	−9.52
8	Spain	−8.72
9	Slovak Republic	−6.21
10	Chile	−2.89
11	Czech Republic	2.07
12	Singapore	3.26
13	Costa Rica	7.03
14	Hungary	10.30
15	Greece	11.60
16	Poland	22.43
17	Korea	30.98
18	Brazil	40.29
19	Mexico	41.61
20	Russia	63.80

High-Income Countries (≥ $23,000)

Rank	Country	Residual
1	Finland	−11.07
2	Sweden	−10.89
3	Iceland	−7.81
4	Norway	−7.16
5	Denmark	−7.02
6	Netherlands	−4.97
7	Germany	−2.60
8	France	−2.12
9	Switzerland	−1.85
10	Australia	−1.70
11	Austria	−1.31
12	Italy	−0.97
13	Canada	−0.75
14	Ireland	3.67
15	United States	5.09
16	United Kingdom	5.37
17	Belgium	6.91
18	Japan	9.49

The SO₂ rankings cover 47 countries. Argentina and Lithuania rank at the top on this measure. China and Russia face the most severe SO₂ problems.

Energy usage data are available for 72 countries. Denmark and Switzerland rank highest in energy efficiency. Russia and the Ukraine emerge as the most energy inefficient countries.

Figures 2, 3, and 4 plot the relationship between each measure of environmental performance and GDP per capita. One pattern that is immediately discernable across all three measures is that richer countries achieve better results than poorer ones. The improvement of environmental performance as income rises is most pronounced with regard to urban particulates and energy efficiency, and least strong for SO₂ emissions. Among lower-income countries, the variance on all three measures is particularly high relative to more prosperous countries. This suggests that environmental performance can be *substantially improved* in many low-income countries independent of the gains that come with economic development.

The regression relationship between environmental performance and GDP per capita provides an interesting perspective on how each country performs *relative* to its wealth. Countries above the regression line in Figures 2, 3, and 4 exhibit weaker environmental results on the particular performance measure than would be expected given their level of GDP; those countries below the regression line demonstrate better performance. These results are shown in Tables 2, 3, and 4.

With regard to particulate levels, Italy, Greece, Mexico, Costa Rica, China, and Denmark are notable laggards relative to income. Sweden, Norway, Argentina, Latvia, Ecuador, and Venezuela show relatively strong performance. In terms of SO₂ performance, Russia, Brazil, Mexico, Korea, China, Egypt, Japan, and Belgium lag relative to income. The United States is also a weak performer. Iceland, Finland, Sweden, Argentina, Latvia, Lithuania, Thailand, Romania, and Ecuador show relatively strong results.

In energy efficiency, Denmark, Switzerland, Japan, Italy, Hungary, Poland, Honduras, and Bangladesh, among others, appear to be more energy efficient than would be expected given their level of income. The United States, Canada, Singapore, Russia, South Africa, Venezuela, the Ukraine, and Vietnam emerge as relatively poor performers relative to income. As can be seen in Figure 4, the dummy variable for former Soviet bloc countries is highly significant, suggesting that the countries that faced artificially low energy prices suffered a common fate of huge inefficiency.

Taken together, these findings are consistent with established theory that suggests that pollution control improves with economic development (World Commission on Environment and Development 1987). Our data do not, however, reveal an inverted U-shaped environmental "Kuznets curve." A number of other studies have found such a pattern, characterized by rising emissions in the early stages of development and improving environmental performance after middle-income levels have been reached (Grossman and Krueger 1995; Harbaugh et al. 2000). Our results may be explained by the fact that our sample of countries contains relatively few countries in the "early industrialization" stage of development in which emissions and energy usage would be low and rising, especially for the air pollution measures.

The relationship between environmental performance and level of development supports several preliminary but important policy conclusions. First, the evidence that poorer countries uniformly perform less well on all three environmental quality measures supports an emphasis on alleviating poverty as a core policy goal from the perspective of environmental progress.

Second, the wide variations in environmental performance among countries at a similar level of economic development suggest that income or development stage affects, but does not alone determine, environmental outcomes. Some rich countries seem to have learned how to advance environmental quality ahead of their economic progress; others have not. Similarly, some developing countries appear to have achieved far better environmental quality relative to their level of development, while other countries seem to be sacrificing environmental goals in the pursuit of economic growth. We explore whether this approach is effective later in this chapter.

Third, it is notable that environmental performance gains with income emerge most quickly for the most localized problem (particulates), least rapidly with regard to environmental impact (energy usage) that generates the harms (CO₂ emissions from fossil fuel burning) most widely spread over space and time.[vi] Intermediate results occur for the variable (SO₂) that arises on an intermediate spatial and temporal scale. This pattern comports with the theoretical prediction that the geographic and temporal spread of an environmental issue represents critical policy variables. Where harms have a trans-boundary or inter-temporal dimension, they constitute "super externalities," which raise special collective action problems and often prove especially difficult to address (Dua and Esty 1997).

Determinants of environmental performance

Data on the environmental regulatory regime and the broader economic and legal context are drawn from both the ESI project and the *Global Competitiveness Report 2001–2002* annual Survey of business and government leaders.[vii] We categorize the determinants of environmental performance in two broad groups: measures related to a country's environmental regulatory regime, and measures of its economic and legal context. The full list of variables along with their definitions and sources can be found in Appendix A.

For the purposes of analysis, we divide the environmental regulatory regime variables into a number of categories representing different aspects of a country's regulatory approach:

- stringency of environmental pollution standards
- sophistication of regulatory structure
- quality of the environmental information available
- extent of subsidization of natural resources
- strictness of enforcement
- quality of environmental institutions

The stringency of standards category includes measures of the perceived rigor of a nation's air pollution, water pollution, toxic waste, and chemical regulations. This information is drawn from the GCR Survey. We expect a negative relationship between each of the measures of regulatory stringency and our dependent variables, since more rigorous standards should lead to lower levels of urban particulates, lower SO_2 concentrations, and lower energy usage per unit of GDP.

The regulatory structure category measures the degree to which a nation's environmental regulations are flexible, clear, consistent, progressive, structured to help competitiveness, and designed to promote cooperative versus adversarial business-government relations. In each case, we anticipate a negative relationship between variables and our measures of environmental performance because a more refined and sophisticated regulatory structure is expected to produce less pollution and energy usage. In this category, we have introduced two new variables this year drawn from the GCR Survey: (1) a measure of whether regulatory structure helps or hurts competitiveness; and (2) a variable capturing the degree of cooperation versus adversarial behavior characteristic of the regulatory approach.

The information category attempts to measure the degree to which a nation has a sufficient data foundation for policymaking and to support enforcement of environmental regulations. There are no direct measures of the quality of the information underlying each country's environmental regime, and we rely on four proxy variables drawn from the ESI data set: (1) the degree to which a country collects data in the 65 categories tracked by the ESI analysis; (2) the extent of sustainable development information and the existence of plans to support national environmental decision-making (as called for in the Rio Earth Summit's Agenda 21 process); (3) the prevalence of guidelines for sectoral environmental impact assessments; and (4) the breadth of environmental action plans. The last two of these measures are new and reflect the ESI project's ongoing effort to get a better grasp of the quality of environmental information across countries. All of these information indicators are relatively crude, but should provide some basis for gauging whether a nation seeks to make environmental judgments on an analytically rigorous basis. We expect a negative relationship between these information variables and our environmental performance measures.

The subsidies measure is derived from the GCR Survey data on the extent of a country's subsidization of energy and other materials. Where price signals are distorted, we expect to see greater inefficiency and higher levels of pollution. Thus we anticipate a positive relationship between the level of subsidies and particulate levels, SO_2 concentrations, and energy usage.

The strictness of enforcement measures are drawn from the GCR Survey. The first measure gauges how aggressively a nation's environmental regulations are enforced, and the second provides a gauge of the depth of a country's commitment to treaty requirements and other international environmental obligations. We expect a negative relationship between these measures of enforcement rigor and our dependent variables, as those countries that take environmental regulations (whether domestic or international) seriously should experience better pollution control and energy usage.

The final regulatory regime category, institutional quality, seeks to measure the degree to which intergovernmental (international) organizations and nongovernmental entities (environmental groups, community organizations, business associations, and other elements of civil society) reinforce governmental environmental efforts. The mechanisms for such reinforcement are diverse (Esty 1998). In some cases, these entities directly undertake environmental activities and thus substitute for government action. Environmental groups, for instance, may identify harms, highlight issues that demand attention, undertake data gathering and analyses, or throw a spotlight on poor environmental performers who should be pursued. NGOs may also strengthen a society's capacity for pollution control by providing environmental education to the public or technical assistance to polluters. Of course, such entities may also play counterproductive roles as well, especially if they pursue extreme positions and utilize solely adversarial approaches, unnecessarily increasing cost.

Our capacity to measure the degree of institutional quality is limited, and the variables in this category are, of necessity, somewhat crude proxies. We use data from the ESI database (a new variable) on the number of entities (scaled by population) that participate in the World Conservation Union (IUCN), an umbrella organization of environmental NGOs and research centers. We also draw on ESI data that provide a measure of the breadth of a country's engagement with intergovernmental environmental bodies. A third institutional quality variable comes from the GCR Survey and gauges the extent to which a nation's companies utilize the ISO 14000 certification process for environmental management. We expect a negative relationship between these measures and our dependent variables gauging environmental outcomes.

The second broad group of independent variables tracks potentially significant dimensions of a country's economic and legal context. We analyze this broader set of societal variables based on a growing theoretical literature, which suggests that a country's underlying political, legal, and economic structures may contribute as much to environmental protection as the details of its regulatory regime (Esty 1997; Sachs 1998; Esty and Porter 2000).

Under the economic and legal context, there are two categories of variables. First, we analyze what we call *administrative infrastructure*. In this category, we assemble data on civil and political liberties drawn from the ESI and measures (from the GCR Survey) of public sector competence, degree of governmental favoritism, how vigorously private property is protected, the independence of the judiciary, demands for irregular payments as a price for doing business, the extent of the rule of law, burdensome regulations, corruption, and the degree to which new governments honor the obligations of prior administrations. For each of these variables, we would anticipate a negative relationship vis-à-vis our particulates, SO_2, and energy usage measures. The last three datasets represent new information developed in the 2001 GCR Survey.

The second group of variables under legal and economic context addresses various aspects of a country's technical capacity. It is again hard to measure scientific and technological sophistication directly, so we rely upon a series of proxies. These include ESI data on the number of scientists and engineers (scaled by population) in each country and GCR Survey data that provide a gauge of a country's technology position, the strength of its scientific community, the degree to which foreign technology is commonly licensed, intellectual property protection, research and development spending, willingness to absorb new technologies, business commitment to innovation,

and governmental commitment to technology development and innovation. We expect each of these measures of technical capacity to be negatively correlated with environmental impacts, as greater technical strength should lead to better environmental performance. The last three variables in this category are new datasets drawn from the 2001 GCR Survey.

As noted above, the independent variables are far from perfect measures of the potential determinants of national environmental outcomes. These variables are, however, the best ones currently available, and represent, in some cases, a significant improvement over prior efforts to model the policy levers and other drivers of environmental performance. Despite their limitations, the data allow us to begin to identify empirically the variables that determine a nation's success in controlling pollution and improving energy efficiency.

Statistical methodology

Our analytic approach unfolds in several stages. First, we use bilateral regressions (Tables 5, 6, and 7) to explore whether there is a statistically significant relationship between each independent variable and energy usage, urban particulate levels, and SO_2 concentrations. Because many of the independent variables are collinear and the degrees of freedom are limited, multiple regression techniques cannot be used to examine the joint influence of all the variables. Instead, as a second stage of analysis, we "roll up" the significant independent variable in each category into a subindex using common factor analysis. Then, we regress these subindexes against the dependent variables.[viii] Appendix B reports the percentage of covariance explained by the first factor and the first factor coefficient for each index variable. Finally, the statistically significant category subindexes are rolled up into an overall environmental regulatory regime index (ERRI) and an overall economic and legal context index (ELCI).

In light of the significant association between per capita GDP and environmental performance, we also analyze performance relative to a peer group of countries defined by income level. We regress ERRI against GDP per capita (graphed in Figure 5) and calculate the residuals (distance above or below the regression line) for each country (Table 9). This provides a way of analyzing how each country performs against expectations established by its income level. We also examine the relationship between the ELCI and ERRI, and the relationship between ELCI and GDP per capita.

Table 5: Bilateral regressions: energy usage

	(ß)	R^2	Sig.	df
2001 Dependent Variable: Energy Usage (Per Unit GDP)				
ENVIRONMENTAL REGULATORY REGIME INDEX	−5.281	0.67	0.000	68
Stringency Subindex	−5.632	0.68	0.000	68
Air Regulation	−4.044	0.69	0.000	68
Water Regulation	−3.859	0.68	0.000	68
Toxic Waste Regulation	−3.576	0.67	0.000	68
Chemical Regulation	−3.902	0.68	0.000	68
Overall Regulation	−3.917	0.67	0.000	68
Regulatory Structure Subindex	−4.480	0.64	0.002	68
Options for Compliance	−4.005	0.60	0.102	68
Confusing and Changing	−4.982	0.65	0.001	68
Early or Late	−4.058	0.67	0.000	68
Compliance Hurts or Helps Competitiveness	−6.094	0.62	0.016	68
Regulation Adversarial or Cooperative	−6.355	0.63	0.007	68
Information Subindex	−2.507	0.61	0.081	68
ESI–Variables %–available	−0.271	0.62	0.020	68
Sustainable Development Info	−1.009	0.58	0.764	41
Number of Sectoral EIA Guidelines	0.041	0.59	0.923	68
Number of Environmental Strategies & Action Plans	−0.197	0.59	0.815	68
Subsidies Subindex	0.43	0.33	0.00	39
Government Subsidies	7.065	0.66	0.000	68
Regulatory Enforcement Subindex	−4.466	0.65	0.001	68
Enforcement	−3.890	0.65	0.001	68
International Agreements	−3.976	0.64	0.002	68
Environmental Institutions Subindex	−4.740	0.65	0.001	68
IUCN	−1.392	0.60	0.300	68
Memberships	−0.699	0.65	0.001	67
Prevalence of ISO 14000	−3.994	0.63	0.011	68
ECONOMIC AND LEGAL CONTEXT INDEX	−4.836	0.65	0.001	68
Administrative Infrastructure Quality Index	−5.647	0.68	0.000	68
Civil Liberties	−5.190	0.75	0.000	68
Public Sector Competence	−2.383	0.59	0.333	68
Gov't Favor Private Sector Firms	−4.200	0.64	0.003	68
Property Rights	−4.756	0.71	0.000	68
Independent Judiciary	−3.426	0.66	0.000	68
Irregular Payments	−4.973	0.68	0.000	68
Legal Framework	−3.880	0.66	0.000	68
Regulatory Burden	−5.144	0.63	0.006	68
Level of Administrative Corruption	−5.695	0.69	0.000	68
Honoring of Policies through Gov. Transition	−4.558	0.65	0.001	68
Scientific and Research Infrastructure Index	−3.788	0.63	0.008	68
Scientists and Engineers	−0.003	0.64	0.004	64
Technology Position	−3.636	0.66	0.000	68
Institutions	−3.341	0.62	0.018	68
Licensing of Foreign Technology	−3.692	0.61	0.055	68
Company R & D Spending	−4.207	0.64	0.002	68
Willingness to Absorb New Technology	−3.803	0.62	0.033	68
Importance of Innovation to Revenue	−6.158	0.62	0.020	68
Gov't Purchase Decisions for Tech. Products	−2.962	0.60	0.160	68

*Refer to Appendix A for definitions of variables.

Table 6: Bilateral regressions: urban particulates

	(ß)	R^2	Sig.	df
2001 Dependent Variable: Urban Particulates (Per City Pop)				
ENVIRONMENTAL REGULATORY REGIME INDEX	−58.19	0.44	0.000	40
Stringency Subindex	−67.58	0.52	0.000	40
Air Regulation	−46.86	0.52	0.000	40
Water Regulation	−46.44	0.53	0.000	40
Toxic Waste Regulation	−45.10	0.52	0.000	40
Chemical Regulation	−46.24	0.51	0.000	40
Overall Regulation	−47.54	0.51	0.000	40
Regulatory Structure Subindex	−52.54	0.35	0.000	40
Options for Compliance	−89.06	0.33	0.000	40
Confusing and Changing	−60.31	0.42	0.000	40
Early or Late	−45.23	0.47	0.000	40
Compliance Hurts or Helps Competitiveness	−61.14	0.17	0.007	40
Regulation Adversarial or Cooperative	−46.15	0.12	0.028	40
Information Subindex	−56.07	0.22	0.002	40
ESI–Variables %–available	−3.86	0.15	0.011	40
Sustainable Development Info	−58.76	0.18	0.028	25
Number of Sectoral EIA Guidelines	−0.99	0.00	0.825	40
Number of Environmental Strategies & Action Plans	4.94	0.01	0.525	40
Subsidies Subindex				
Government Subsidies	65.95	0.31	0.000	40
Regulatory Enforcement Subindex	−58.31	0.43	0.000	40
Enforcement	−52.79	0.45	0.000	40
International Agreements	−49.93	0.38	0.000	40
Environmental Institutions Subindex	−47.86	0.29	0.000	40
IUCN	−16.40	0.05	0.150	40
Memberships	−6.40	0.22	0.002	39
Prevalence of ISO 14000	−47.01	0.25	0.001	40
ECONOMIC AND LEGAL CONTEXT INDEX	−58.94	0.40	0.000	40
Administrative Infrastructure Quality Index	−57.48	0.39	0.000	40
Civil Liberties	−42.67	0.37	0.000	40
Public Sector Competence	−42.49	0.07	0.095	40
Gov't Favor Private Sector Firms	−53.99	0.36	0.000	40
Property Rights	−45.62	0.48	0.000	40
Independent Judiciary	−32.47	0.30	0.000	40
Irregular Payments	−59.91	0.46	0.000	40
Legal Framework	−40.45	0.35	0.000	40
Regulatory Burden	−47.93	0.15	0.013	40
Level of Administrative Corruption	−54.64	0.38	0.000	40
Honoring of Policies through Gov. Transition	−43.16	0.24	0.001	40
Scientific and Research Infrastructure Index	−58.15	0.38	0.000	40
Scientists and Engineers	−0.04	0.42	0.000	39
Technology Position	−42.94	0.40	0.000	40
Institutions	−57.57	0.36	0.000	40
Licensing of Foreign Technology	−56.20	0.15	0.010	40
Company R & D Spending	−49.65	0.32	0.000	40
Willingness to Absorb New Technology	−75.25	0.41	0.000	40
Importance of Innovation to Revenue	−63.51	0.15	0.012	40
Gov't Purchase Decisions for Tech. Products	−68.82	0.26	0.001	40

*Refer to Appendix A for definitions of variables.

Table 7: Bilateral regressions: urban SO₂ concentration

	(ß)	R^2	Sig.	df
			2001 Dependent Variable: Urban SO_2 (Per City Pop)	
ENVIRONMENTAL REGULATORY REGIME INDEX	**−11.351**	**0.21**	**0.001**	**45**
Stringency Subindex	**−13.857**	**0.28**	**0.000**	**45**
Air Regulation	−9.407	0.27	0.000	45
Water Regulation	−9.592	0.28	0.000	45
Toxic Waste Regulation	−9.283	0.27	0.000	45
Chemical Regulation	−9.538	0.27	0.000	45
Overall Regulation	−9.839	0.27	0.000	45
Regulatory Structure Subindex	**−9.686**	**0.16**	**0.005**	**45**
Options for Compliance	−9.312	0.05	0.130	45
Confusing and Changing	−11.905	0.20	0.002	45
Early or Late	−10.105	0.28	0.000	45
Compliance Hurts or Helps Competitiveness	−11.584	0.09	0.038	45
Regulation Adversarial or Cooperative	−11.128	0.11	0.022	45
Information Subindex	**−10.206**	**0.10**	**0.029**	**45**
ESI–Variables %–available	0.207	0.00	0.662	45
Sustainable Development Info	−21.624	0.25	0.004	29
Number of Sectoral EIA Guidelines	−0.708	0.01	0.464	45
Number of Environmental Strategies & Action Plans	0.722	0.00	0.732	45
Subsidies Subindex				
Government Subsidies	12.301	0.15	0.008	45
Regulatory Enforcement Subindex	**−10.989**	**0.18**	**0.003**	**45**
Enforcement	−8.960	0.17	0.004	45
International Agreements	−10.221	0.19	0.003	45
Environmental Institutions Subindex	**−6.921**	**0.08**	**0.053**	**45**
IUCN	−6.270	0.10	0.030	45
Memberships	−0.684	0.04	0.194	44
Prevalence of ISO 14000	−8.027	0.10	0.034	45
ECONOMIC AND LEGAL CONTEXT INDEX	**−11.738**	**0.19**	**0.002**	**45**
Administrative Infrastructure Quality Index	**−12.815**	**0.23**	**0.001**	**45**
Civil Liberties	−12.206	0.47	0.000	45
Public Sector Competence	−3.364	0.01	0.553	45
Gov't Favor Private Sector Firms	−10.056	0.15	0.008	45
Property Rights	−9.644	0.27	0.000	45
Independent Judiciary	−7.166	0.18	0.003	45
Irregular Payments	−12.413	0.26	0.000	45
Legal Framework	−9.343	0.23	0.001	45
Regulatory Burden	−9.259	0.10	0.032	45
Level of Administrative Corruption	−12.877	0.27	0.000	45
Honoring of Policies through Gov. Transition	−8.685	0.11	0.021	45
Scientific and Research Infrastructure Index	**−10.010**	**0.14**	**0.009**	**45**
Scientists and Engineers	−0.006	0.09	0.038	45
Technology Position	−7.931	0.18	0.003	45
Institutions	−8.883	0.11	0.025	45
Licensing of Foreign Technology	−11.980	0.08	0.049	45
Company R & D Spending	−7.802	0.12	0.020	45
Willingness to Absorb New Technology	−15.067	0.20	0.002	45
Importance of Innovation to Revenue	−15.770	0.13	0.011	45
Gov't Purchase Decisions for Tech. Products	−9.316	0.06	0.109	45

*Refer to Appendix A for definitions of variables.

Figure 5: Relationship between the environmental regulatory regime index and GDP per capita

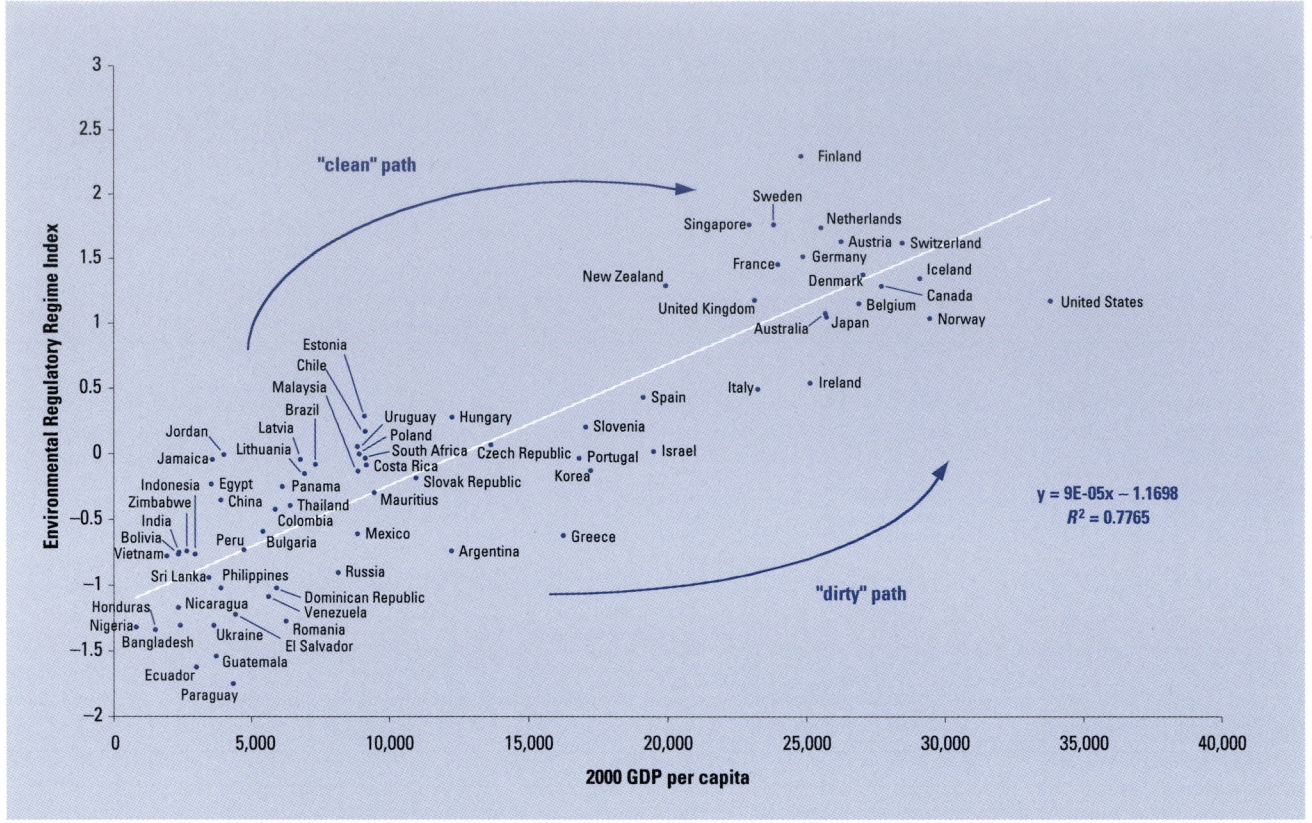

Figure 6: Relationship between the environmental regulatory regime index and economic and legal context index

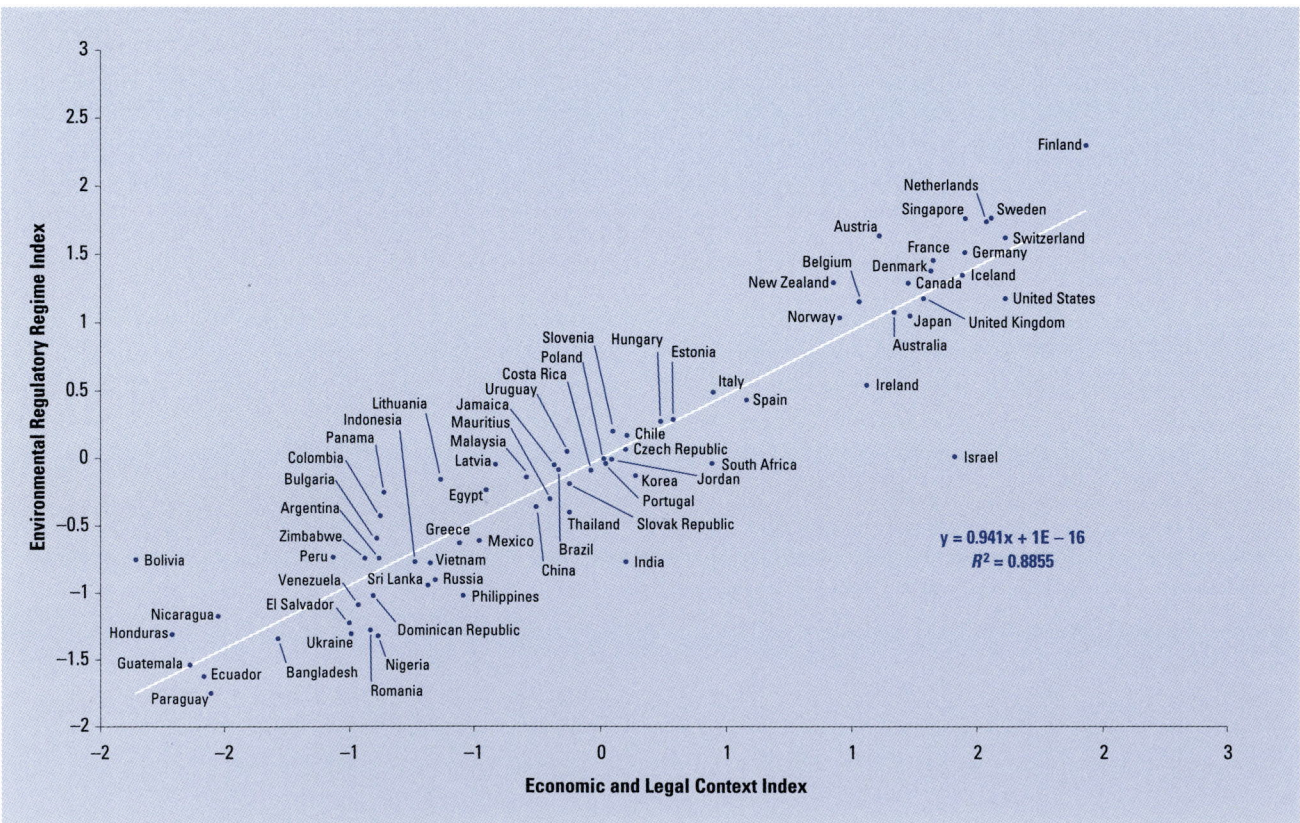

Results for individual measures and indexes

The bilateral regression results are shown in Tables 5, 6, and 7. The energy efficiency regressions are shown in Table 5. A large number of the independent variables show a statistically significant relationship with energy usage, with the expected negative sign and a reasonable degree of explained variance. All of the elements of the regulatory stringency category show particular significance, as do the enforcement variables. Most of the regulatory structure measures also prove to be highly significant. These categories of variables account for the highest amount of explained variance. The subsidies variable is highly significant and has the expected positive sign. This result suggests, consistent with economic theory, that mispriced resources will be inefficiently used, and that subsidies represent a major policy error.

The information and institutions measures perform less strongly. In the information category, one variable (percentage of ESI variables available) emerges as significant while the other three measures do not. In the institutional category, IUCN membership fails to show significance while the other two measures of institutional capacity are significant.

Among the economic and legal context variables, all but one (public sector competence) emerge as highly significant with the expected negative sign. The new variables measuring corruption and whether new governments honor the commitments of prior administrations prove to be statistically significant. In the scientific and technical capacity category, all of the variables except one (government commitment to technology development and innovation) show a reasonable degree of significance and the expected negative sign.

To build the subindexes and indexes, we employ only the statistically significant variables. All of the subindexes are highly significant in explaining energy usage, have the expected negative sign, and account for substantial explained variance. The ERRI and ELCI register similarly high levels of significance with the expected negative signs and a substantial degree of explained variance.

Although preliminary, the latter results provide some empirical support for the hypothesis that a nation's underlying economic and legal structure may be as important to environmental success as the specific details of its environmental regulatory regime. This conclusion argues for more attention to "fundamentals"—such as eliminating corruption and building functioning market economies—and to "governance"—such as strengthening the rule of law and developing mechanisms to protect property rights—in setting development priorities and in targeting development assistance. Interestingly, this is the direction that the recent policies of the United Nations Development Programme are taking.

The ERRI and the ELCI prove to be highly correlated and show similar levels of significance and explained variance. Hence it appears that environmental regulation and overall economic and legal context generally improve in parallel. We explored the joint influence of ERRI and ELCI on environmental performance. In practice, the high correlation between the two indexes (as shown in Figure 7) means that their effects on energy usage could not be distinguished statistically.

Table 6 presents the second set of bilateral regressions for urban (air) particulate concentrations. Again, the vast majority of variables are significant with the expected sign and account for a reasonable degree of explained variance. All of the measures of regulatory stringency and structure are highly significant, with the stringency variables accounting for the greatest level of explained variance. The subsidies measure is highly significant, has the anticipated positive sign, and accounts for a reasonable degree of explained variance.

In the information category, two variables emerge as significant with the expected negative sign, but do not account for as high a degree of explained variance. In the institutional reinforcement category, the number of IUCN memberships is again not significant, while the other two variables (participation in intergovernmental environmental bodies and corporate participation in environmental management systems) emerge as highly significant.

The regulatory stringency, regulatory structure, information enforcement, and institutional subindexes all emerge as highly significant with the expected negative sign, as does the cumulative ERRI. Across all of these subindexes, however, the degree of explained variance is somewhat lower in the urban particulate regressions than in the energy usage ones. Two of the subindexes—information foundations and institutional reinforcement—perform notably less well than the others. This may reflect the fact that these variables are imperfect proxies or that information and institutions play more mixed roles.

All of the variables in the economic and social context regression emerge as significant in the urban particulates regulations. All have the expected negative sign, with many accounting for a substantial degree of explained variance. The administrative infrastructure and technical capacity subindexes both show very high levels of significance, the expected negative sign, and a high degree of explained variance. The ELCI similarly emerges as highly significant. It accounts for almost as much explained variance as the ERRI. However, both the ERRI and the ELCI explain a somewhat smaller proportion of variations in urban particulate concentrations than energy usage. Again, the independent effects of ERRI and ELCI could not be distinguished statistically.

Figure 7: Relationship between the environmental regulatory regime index and current competitiveness

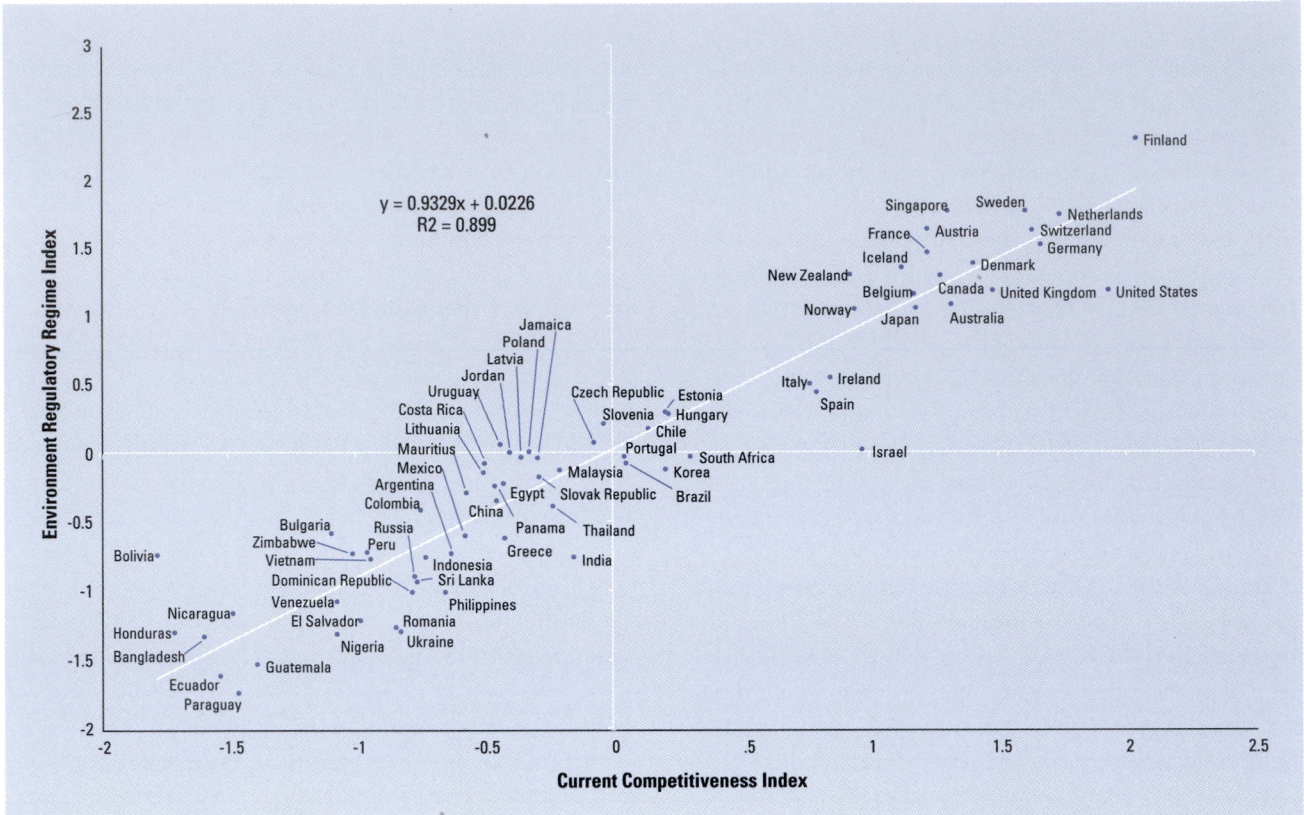

The SO_2 regression results are presented in Table 7. Most of the independent variables are once again significant with the expected negative sign. The degree of explained variance is, however, generally much lower for SO_2 than for either energy usage or particulate concentrations. This finding may reflect the fact that the benefits of SO_2 control (reduced acid rain) accrue downwind—frequently beyond the territorial boundaries of the jurisdiction undertaking regulatory action. Thus, from a cost-benefit perspective, the regulating entity has less to gain than it has in the control of particulates or with investments in energy efficiency, both of which provide more localized benefits.

The subsidies measure again shows a high level of significance and the expected positive sign, but accounts for a lower amount of variance than with the other measures of pollution. In the information category, three of the four measures are not statistically significant. Again, the looser fit may suggest that even a well-informed government that is serious about environmental protection has less of an incentive to address SO_2, given its geographic dispersion, than other more localized issues.

All of the environmental regulatory regime subindexes are significant and have the expected negative sign in the SO_2 regressions. Only the regulatory stringency subindex accounts, however, for a reasonable degree of explained variance. ERRI once again proves to be highly significant, although the degree of explained variance is not high. As a general matter, the regression fit for SO_2 appears weaker than for particulates or energy usage, perhaps reflecting the more limited regulatory payoffs noted above.

Among the variables in the economic and legal context grouping, all but one (public sector competence) emerge with high statistical significance and the expected negative sign in the SO_2 regressions. Some of the measures account for a reasonable degree of explained variance (eg, civil liberties, property rights, and irregular payments). In general, the administrative infrastructure variables show greater significance and higher degrees of explained variance than the technical capacity measures. The administrative infrastructure subindex is highly significant with a reasonable degree of explained variance. The technical capacity subindex shows a high degree of significance but does not account for an especially large amount of explained variance. The overall ELCI is significant and explains a reasonable amount of the variance in SO_2 concentrations.

Ranking environmental regulatory quality

The bilateral, subindex, and index regressions establish a statistically significant relationship between the various policy measures and environmental performance. The next stage in the analysis is to use ERRI to explore the differences across countries in environmental regulatory quality.

Table 8 presents a ranking of countries ranked by absolute ERRI scores. This index (combining the always significant regulatory stringency, structure, subsidies, and enforcement subindexes) represents a summary performance measure of the quality of the environmental regulatory system in a country. Among the top-ranked countries are Finland, Sweden, and Singapore. Countries at the bottom include Guatemala, Ecuador, and Paraguay.

Given the significant relationship between level of development and environmental performance, we would expect a similar relationship with environmental regulatory quality. What is most interesting in Table 8, then, is not so much the fact that Finland outranks Paraguay on the stringency of environmental regulation, but the reasons why countries with similar incomes perform so differently. For instance, why does Costa Rica (36th place) do better than Panama (42nd place) and Peru (50th place)? Similarly, why do Spain (21st) and Portugal (31st) so dramatically outperform Greece (49th)? Likewise, Chile (25th) distinctly outperforms Argentina (51st), and Poland (29th) comes in way ahead of Russia (57th). The last two pairings reveal a general pattern suggesting that more aggressively market-oriented economies (Chile and Poland) may outperform those (Argentina and Russia) where a more interventionist economic tradition persists.

To control for income differences and hence the level of economic development, Table 9 ranks countries by their residuals from the regression of ERRI and GDP per capita (plotted in Figure 5). This relative ranking represents a measure of environmental regulatory quality relative to expectations established by income level. Among the low-income countries, Jordan and Jamaica come out on top, while Ecuador and Paraguay trail. Among middle-income countries, Singapore, Estonia, and New Zealand rank high. Israel, Argentina, and Greece lag. Among the wealthiest nations, Finland, Sweden, and the Netherlands lead, while Italy, Norway, and Ireland rank low. The United States occupies the bottom rung of the high-income group ladder.

Table 8: Environmental regulatory regime index by country, absolute ranking

Environmental Regulatory Regime Index

Rank	Country	Score	Rank	Country	Score
1	Finland	2.303	37	Korea	−0.121
2	Sweden	1.772	38	Malaysia	−0.127
3	Singapore	1.771	39	Lithuania	−0.146
4	Netherlands	1.747	40	Slovak Republic	−0.177
5	Austria	1.641	41	Egypt	−0.224
6	Switzerland	1.631	42	Panama	−0.242
7	Germany	1.522	43	Mauritius	−0.290
8	France	1.464	44	China	−0.348
9	Denmark	1.384	45	Thailand	−0.389
10	Iceland	1.354	46	Colombia	−0.416
11	New Zealand	1.299	47	Bulgaria	−0.584
12	Canada	1.297	48	Mexico	−0.602
13	United Kingdom	1.185	49	Greece	−0.619
14	United States	1.184	50	Peru	−0.722
15	Belgium	1.159	51	Argentina	−0.732
16	Australia	1.083	52	Zimbabwe	−0.732
17	Japan	1.057	53	Bolivia	−0.743
18	Norway	1.045	54	Indonesia	−0.758
19	Ireland	0.546	55	India	−0.759
20	Italy	0.498	56	Vietnam	−0.770
21	Spain	0.437	57	Russia	−0.895
22	Estonia	0.296	58	Sri Lanka	−0.936
23	Hungary	0.283	59	Philippines	−1.014
24	Slovenia	0.209	60	Dominican Republic	−1.014
25	Chile	0.177	61	Venezuela	−1.079
26	Czech Republic	0.073	62	Nicaragua	−1.164
27	Uruguay	0.059	63	El Salvador	−1.215
28	Israel	0.021	64	Romania	−1.268
29	Poland	0.005	65	Ukraine	−1.297
30	Jordan	0.002	66	Honduras	−1.300
31	Portugal	−0.028	67	Nigeria	−1.314
32	South Africa	−0.029	68	Bangladesh	−1.331
33	Latvia	−0.036	69	Guatemala	−1.532
34	Jamaica	−0.037	70	Ecuador	−1.616
35	Brazil	−0.077	71	Paraguay	−1.743
36	Costa Rica	−0.078			

As noted earlier, ERRI and ELCI are highly correlated, as shown in Figure 6. Nevertheless, it is evident that some countries have an economic and legal context that outpaces their environmental regulatory quality, while others have advanced environmental regulation faster than context. In Israel, India, Ireland, the United States, South Africa, the Philippines, and Nigeria, environmental regulation lags overall context, while in Finland, Austria, New Zealand, Panama, and Bolivia, environmental regulatory quality is ahead of improvements in the broader economic and legal context. The divergence between ERRI and ELCI, however, was not statistically associated with differences in environmental outcomes. This may be due to the high correlation of ERRI and ELCI in the sample.

Table 9: Environmental regulatory regime index relative to expected results given GDP per capital, listed by income groups

Low-Income Countries (≤ $6,500)

Rank	Country	Residual
1	Jordan	0.794
2	Jamaica	0.793
3	Egypt	0.612
4	China	0.455
5	Panama	0.355
6	Vietnam	0.216
7	Colombia	0.204
8	Bolivia	0.204
9	India	0.188
10	Zimbabwe	0.187
11	Thailand	0.180
12	Indonesia	0.132
13	Bulgaria	0.078
14	Peru	0.002
15	Sri Lanka	−0.092
16	Philippines	−0.211
17	Nicaragua	−0.217
18	Nigeria	−0.225
19	Bangladesh	−0.307
20	Honduras	−0.359
21	Dominican Republic	−0.397
22	Venezuela	−0.436
23	El Salvador	−0.461
24	Ukraine	−0.470
25	Romania	−0.684
26	Guatemala	−0.714
27	Ecuador	−0.730
28	Paraguay	−0.981

Middle-Income Countries ($6,500–$23,000)

Rank	Country	Residual
1	Singapore	0.806
2	Estonia	0.614
3	New Zealand	0.612
4	Latvia	0.499
5	Chile	0.494
6	Brazil	0.407
7	Uruguay	0.402
8	Lithuania	0.374
9	Poland	0.343
10	Hungary	0.308
11	South Africa	0.288
12	Costa Rica	0.235
13	Malaysia	0.214
14	Mauritius	−0.003
15	Czech Republic	−0.031
16	Slovak Republic	−0.032
17	Spain	−0.175
18	Slovenia	−0.211
19	Mexico	−0.259
20	Portugal	−0.426
21	Russia	−0.487
22	Korea	−0.558
23	Israel	−0.626
24	Argentina	−0.705
25	Greece	−0.964

High-Income Countries (≥ $23,000)

Rank	Country	Residual
1	Finland	1.165
2	Sweden	0.725
3	Netherlands	0.541
4	France	0.404
5	Germany	0.377
6	Austria	0.368
7	United Kingdom	0.202
8	Switzerland	0.154
9	Denmark	0.037
10	Canada	−0.112
11	Australia	−0.138
12	Japan	−0.168
13	Belgium	−0.173
14	Iceland	−0.184
15	Italy	−0.495
16	Norway	−0.523
17	Ireland	−0.623
18	United States	−0.792

Table 10: Environmental regulatory stringency and economic growth

Variable	Model 1 Dependent Variable: Annual Percentage Growth Rate of GDP per Capita, 1995–2000			Model 2 Dependent Variable: Annual Percentage Growth Rate of GDP per Capita, 1995–2000		
	Parameter Estimate	t Value	Prob > |t|	Parameter Estimate	t Value	Prob > |t|
Intercept	1.577	3.62	0.001	−2.352	−1.91	0.060
GDP per Capita, 1995 (thousand, ppp)	0.056	1.77	0.082	0.092	2.78	0.007
General Government Spending, 2000				−0.043	1.62	0.111
Gross Fixed Investment (as % of GDP)				0.226	5.17	<0.0001
Environment Regulatory Regime Index Relative to Expected Given GDP per Capita	0.830	1.51	0.135	0.795	1.66	0.102

The relationship between environmental performance and competitiveness

Finally, we turn to the question of whether environmental regulatory stringency detracts from or contributes to economic progress. Figure 7 shows that the quality of a nation's environmental regulatory regime is strongly and positively correlated with its competitiveness as measured by the Current Competitiveness Index, or CCI (see Chapter 1.2). Many of the nations with top-tier competitiveness rankings also have strong environmental performance scores. Finland, for example, ranks at the top of the ERRI and at the top of the CCI. The United States stands out as an exception, with a high competitiveness rank and a relatively low environmental regulation score. Figure 5 tells a similar story about how high levels of per capita income and economic development correlate with high environmental regulatory quality.

The correlations revealed in Figures 5 and 7 do not, of course, prove causation. But the finding that a strong environmental regulatory regime is not inconsistent with top-tier economic performance is itself interesting. Indeed, the fact that the top environmental performers do not appear to have suffered economically strongly supports the "soft" version of the "Porter hypothesis," which argues that environmental progress can be achieved without sacrificing competitiveness (Porter 1990 and Porter and van der Linde 1995). Testing the "hard" version of this hypothesis—that countries with forward-leaning environmental policies and programs will actually enhance their competitiveness—requires time-series data that are not yet available.

Figure 5 highlights the development policy choice that every nation faces. Countries would like to move from the lower left corner of the chart (which represents low levels of environmental performance and low national income) to the upper right quadrant (which represents high levels of environmental performance and high income). The question is what path to take. Or, to put it differently, must the environment be sacrificed to achieve economic progress? Those countries above the regression line can be seen as having chosen a "clean" development trajectory in which environmental regulatory quality advances ahead of economic advancement. Those below the line have chosen a relatively "dirty" path to growth, with relatively lax environmental regulation in the hope of growing faster.

In addressing this choice, we are able to provide a crude test using the available data. We regress a number of control variables on GDP per capita growth between 1995 and 2000, including the initial level of GDP per capita, gross fixed capita formation as a percent of GDP, and government spending as a percent of GDP. We then introduce a variable, which measures the residual from the regression of ERRI on GDP per capita (Table 10). Countries with positive residuals have ERRI scores that are higher than would be expected given their income, and vice versa. The residual has a positive sign with significance at virtually the 90 percent level. Countries that pursue a stringent regulatory regime appear to achieve more rapid growth. Although tentative, this result suggests the possible superiority of the "clean" model. However, more years of data and better controls will be necessary to validate this finding.

Conclusion

The results presented here must be seen as preliminary. The data available suffer from many limitations, narrowing the feasible statistical approaches. Precise causal linkages remain unproven. Indeed, a central conclusion of our research is that better environmental data are required at the global, national, local, and corporate levels if a more systematic approach to environmental improvement is to be implemented. As the world community looks toward the Sustainable Development Summit in Johannesburg in 2002, a worldwide commitment to improved environmental data should be adopted as a priority initiative.

With these caveats, however, the relationships that do emerge as statistically significant are striking. The analysis provides considerable empirical evidence that cross-country differences in environmental performance are associated with the quality of the environmental regulatory regime in place. We find that the rigor and structure of environmental regulations have particular impact, as does emphasis on enforcement. The damaging effect of subsidies is also clear. Although developing a strong and sophisticated regulatory regime that fully internalizes externalities presents real challenges, ending price-distorting, inefficiency-creating, and pollution-inducing subsidies is within the policy grasp of every nation. Environmental performance appears to improve with certain kinds of information and also to improve to the extent that a nation's environmental regime is reinforced by an environmentally oriented private sector and broad-based relationships with international environmental bodies. Information and institutions have some but less impact on environmental performance, based on our analysis. This finding may, in part, be due to weaknesses in the available data.

Our results also suggest that environmental performance requires improvements in a country's institutional foundations. In practice, a nation's economic and legal context and its environmental regulatory regime go hand in hand. This association demands further exploration. But the preliminary evidence developed here suggests that countries would benefit *environmentally* from an emphasis on developing the rule of law, eliminating corruption, and strengthening their governance structures.

The strong association between income and environmental performance also carries important implications. Among other things, it provides powerful corroboration for a policy emphasis on poverty alleviation and the promotion of economic growth as a key mechanism for improving environmental results.

The empirical evidence developed here suggests that the anti-globalization arguments of the environmental protestors in the streets at every recent major international gathering are off the mark. Limiting trade and the engagement of developing countries with the rest of the world is a recipe for environmental failure, not environmental success. Rather, the more fully a country moves to modernize its economy, institutional structures, and regulatory system, the more quickly its environment performance appears to improve—along with improvements in per capita income.

The country rankings that emerge from our analysis seem largely to square with observed reality. The variations in performance highlight the fact that countries vary widely in their environmental outcomes and policy choices, even after controlling for level of income. There are clearly better and worse ways to approach pollution control and natural resource management. The data provided here offer some important clues as to where the search for "best practices" should begin. Moreover, our findings suggest that the environment need not be sacrificed on the road to economic progress. Quite to the contrary, the countries that have the most aggressive environmental policy regimes also seem to be the most competitive and economically successful. We also find preliminary evidence that a stringent environmental regime relative to income may speed up economic growth rather than detract from it.

This study highlights the fact that the environmental domain need not rely on guesswork. The results here show that a more analytically rigorous approach to policy-making could pay real dividends. More fundamentally, our analysis strongly supports the notion that the uncertainties that plague environmental decision-making can be reduced, and that current levels of policy contention could be reduced as well.

Our preliminary efforts to use statistical methods to explain environmental successes and failures seem to confirm some aspects of the prevailing wisdom. For example, poverty emerges as a source of serious environmental degradation and thus deserves ongoing policy attention. Subsidies appear not only to skew prices and distort trade; they also lead to inefficient production and unnecessary pollution. But some new priorities also emerge from this research. Notably, there appear to be significant gains to be had by moving environmental laggards toward the best practices of those jurisdictions whose performance is top tier. This argues for much greater strategic emphasis on information development and dissemination. Likewise, the significance of economic and legal context to environmental results argues for a new focus on governance as the foundation for both environmental and economic progress. The results here suggest that there are ways to move beyond the ideological and emotional obstacles that stand in the way of faster environmental progress.

References

Dua, André and Daniel C Esty. 1997. *Sustaining the Asia-Pacific Miracle: Environmental Protection and Economic Integration*. Washington DC: Institute for International Economics.

Esty, Daniel C and Michael E Porter. 2000. "Measuring National Environmental Performance and Its Determinants." In *The Global Competitiveness Report 2000* (Michael E Porter and Jeffrey D Sachs et al, eds), New York: Oxford University Press.

Esty, Daniel C 1998. "NGOs at the World Trade Organization: Cooperation, Competition, or Exclusion." *Journal of International Economic Law* Vol. 1, No. 1 (March).

———— 1997. "Environmental Protection During the Transition to a Market Economy." In *Economies in Transition: Asia and Europe* (Wing Woo, Stephen Parker, Jeffrey Sachs, eds.), Cambridge: MIT Press.

Grossman, Gene M and Alan B Krueger. 1995. "Economic Growth and the Environment." *Quarterly Journal of Economics* 110, No. 2 (May): 353–375.

Harbaugh, William, Arik Levinson, and David Wilson. 2000. "Re-examining the Empirical Evidence for an Environmental Kuznets Curve." NBER Working Paper No. 7711 (May).

Jaffee, Adam B, Steven R Peterson, Paul R Portney, and Robert N Stavins. 1995. "Environmental Regulation and the Competitiveness of U.S. Manufacturing: What Does the Evidence Tell Us?" *Journal of Economic Literature* 33, No. 1 (March): 132–161.

Porter, Michael E. 1990. *The Competitive Advantage of Nations*. New York: Free Press.

Porter, Michael E and C van der Linde. 1995. "Green and Competitive: Ending the Stalemate," *Harvard Business Review* 73, No. 5 (September/October): 120–155.

Sachs, Jeffrey. 1998. "Globalization and the Rule of Law," *Yale Law School Occasional Papers* 2d series, No. 4.

World Commission on Environment and Development. 1987. *Our Common Future*. Oxford: Oxford University Press.

World Economic Forum. 2001. Global Leaders for Tomorrow Environmental Task Force, 2001, *Environmental Sustainability Index 2001* (Geneva: World Economic Forum) (available at www.yale.edu/envirocenter/esi).

Notes

[i] This study builds on Daniel C Esty and Michael E Porter, "Measuring National Environmental Performance and Its Determinants," in Michael E Porter, Jeffrey Sachs, et al., *Global Competitiveness Report 2000* (New York: Oxford University Press). As is explained in the pages that follow, the present analysis incorporates new data and a variety of new variables, but utilizes statistical model similar to that of the GCR 2000 study.

[ii] For a further discussion of the data gaps that plague the environmental domain, see World Economic Forum Global Leaders for Tomorrow Environmental Task Force, 2001, *Environmental Sustainability Index 2001* (Geneva: World Economic Forum) (available at www.yale.edu/envirocenter/esi).

[iii] Again, the lack of systematic environmental data gathering in many countries and the limited information available with regard to a number of key issues constrains our model. Filling these data gaps— both in terms of depth and breadth—should be a policy priority. Better data remains a prerequisite for a more analytically rigorous approach to environmental decision making.

[iv] This project, undertaken by the World Economic Forum's Global Leaders for Tomorrow Environmental Task Force, with the support of the Yale University Center for Environmental Law and Policy and the Center for International Earth Science Information Network (CIESIN) at Columbia University, ranks 122 countries on their "environmental sustainability" based on performance in 22 categories building on a dataset of 65 underlying variables. The Environmental Sustainability Index (ESI) report and details on the ESI dataset can be found at www.yale.edu/envirocenter/esi.

[v] Both the United States and the United Kingdom track smaller particulates than the rest of the world. The United States and the United Kingdom emphasis follows the most recent medical evidence, which suggests that it is the smaller particles that penetrate deep into the lungs and present a real health threat.

[vi] Energy usage also has highly localized effects insofar as efficiency directly affects competitiveness and some of the harms (particulates and other local air pollutants) do not spread geographically.

[vii] The 2001 Survey, undertaken jointly by the World Economic Forum and Harvard University's Center for International Development and Institute for Strategy and Competitiveness, builds on questionnaire responses from more than 4,000 business, government, and non-governmental organization (NGO) leaders in 75 countries.

[viii] In developing the category subindexes, we use only those variables that appear appropriately grouped based on Eigen Value analysis, as shown in the factor analysis results given in Appendix B. Thus, in developing the regulatory stringency subindex, we drop the overall regulation measure. The sectoral EIA guidelines measure and the environmental strategies and action plans measure drop out of the information subindex. The measures of civil liberties, public sector competence, irregular payments, and regulatory burden are all dropped from the administrative infrastructure subindex. The scientists/engineers, licensing of foreign technology, and business innovation measures fall out of the technical capacity subindex.

Appendix A: Description of variables

Variable	Definition	Measurement	Source (WEF/ESI)
ENVIRONMENTAL PERFORMANCE			
Energy use	Energy Usage, 1997 (High = More inefficient)	Total energy consumption per unit of country GDP	ESI
Urban SO₂	Urban SO₂ concentration, 1990–96 (High = More particulates)	Average normalized mean of total SO2 per unit of city population	ESI
Urban particulates	Urban particulates concentration, 1990–96 (High = More particulates)	Average normalized mean of total suspended particulates per unit of city population	ESI
ENVIRONMENTAL REGULATORY REGIME			
Stringency of Standards			
Air regulation	Stringency of air regulations (High = More stringent)	Survey data (scale1–7)	WEF
Water regulation	Stringency of water regulations (High = More stringent)	Survey data (scale1–7)	WEF
Toxic waste regulation	Stringency of toxic waste regulations (High = More stringent)	Survey data (scale1–7)	WEF
Chemical regulation	Stringency of manufacturing chemical use regulations (High = More stringent)	Survey data (scale1–7)	WEF
Overall regulation	Stringency of overall environmental regulation (High = More stringent)	Survey data (scale1–7)	WEF
Regulatory Structure			
Flexibility	Options for achieving compliance in environmental regulations (High = Many options)	Survey data (scale1–7)	WEF
Stability	Environmental regulations in your country are confusing and frequently changing (High = Stable)	Survey data (scale1–7)	WEF
Early or late	Environmental regulations are enacted ahead or much later than other countries (High = Ahead)	Survey data (scale1–7)	WEF
Compliance hurts or helps competitiveness	Complying with environmental standards hurts/helps competitiveness (High = Helps)	Survey data (scale1–7)	WEF
Regulation adversarial or cooperative	Environmental gains are achieved through adversarial means or government-business cooperation (High = Cooperative)	Survey data (scale1–7)	WEF
Information			
ESI Variables–%	Percentage of ESI variables in publicly available data sets	% of total ESI variables (n=64)	ESI
Sustainable development info	Availability of sustainable development information at the national level		ESI
Number of sectoral EIA guidelines	Numer of sectoral EIA guidelines		ESI
Number of environmental strategies & action plans	Number of environmental strategies & action plans		ESI
Subsidies			
Government subsidies	Government subsidies in your country encourage inefficient use of energy or materials or there are no subsidies (High = High subsidies)	Survey data (scale1–7)	WEF
Regulatory Enforcement			
Enforcement	Environmental regulations are not enforced or enforced erratically or are enforced consistently and fairly (High = Consistently and fairly)	Survey data (scale1–7)	WEF
International agreements	Compliance with international agreements is a high priority in your country's government (High = Agree)	Survey data (scale1–7)	WEF
Environmental Institutions			
IUCN	Number of IUCN membership organizations, 1998	(per million population)	ESI
Memberships	Number of memberships in environmental intergovernmental organizations, 1998	frequency count	ESI
Prevalence of ISO 14000	How many Companies utilize environmental management system such as ISO 14000 (High = Most)	Survey data (scale1–7)	WEF

(cont'd.)

Appendix A: Description of variables *(cont'd.)*

Variable	Definition	Measurement	Source (WEF/ESI)
ECONOMIC AND LEGAL CONTEXT			

Administrative Infrastructure Quality

Variable	Definition	Measurement	Source (WEF/ESI)
Civil and political liberties	Index ranging from 1 (Low levels of liberties) to 7 (High levels)		ESI
Public sector competence	The competence of personnel in the public sector is higher or lower than in the private sector (High = Higher than private sector)	Survey data (scale1–7)	WEF
Favoritism	Public sector officials tend to favor well-connected private firms and individuals (High = Disagree)	Survey data (scale1–7)	WEF
Property rights	Property rights are unclear and unprotected by law or are clearly delineated and protected by law (High = Clearly delineated and protected)	Survey data (scale1–7)	WEF
Independent judiciary	The judiciary in your country is independent and not subject to interference by the government and/or parties to the dispute (High = True)	Survey data (scale1–7)	WEF
Irregular payments	Irregular payments connected with import-export permits, business licenses, exchange controls, tax assessments, etc. (High = Never occur)	Survey data (scale1–7)	WEF
Trusted legal framework	A trusted legal framework exists in your country for private business to challenge the legality of government actions and/or regulations (High = True)	Survey data (scale1–7)	WEF
Regulatory burden	Administrative regulations in your country are burdensome//not burdensome (High = not)	Survey data (scale1–7)	WEF
Level of administrative corruption	Do other firm' unfair or corrupt activities impose costs on your firm (High = No costs)	Survey data (scale1–7)	WEF
Honoring of policies through Gov't transition	Do new governments honor the contractual commitments and obligations of previous regimes (High = honor)	Survey data (scale1–7)	WEF

Administrative Infrastructure Quality

Variable	Definition	Measurement	Source (WEF/ESI)
Scientists and engineers	Research and development scientists and engineers	(per million population)	ESI
Technology position	Country's position in technology generally lags behind most countries or is a leader (High = Leader)	Survey data (scale1–7)	WEF
Institutions	Scientific research institutions in your country are not internationally reputable (High = World class)	Survey data (scale1–7)	WEF
Licensing foreign technology	Licensing of foreign technology is uncommon or is a common means to acquire new technology (High = Common)	Survey data (scale1–7)	WEF
Intellectual property protection	Intellectual property in your country is or is not adequately protected (High = Well protected)	Survey data (scale1–7)	WEF
Company R & D spending	Companies in your country do or do not spend much on R & D relative to international peers (High = Spend heavily on R & D)	Survey data (scale1–7)	WEF
Willingness to absorb new technology	Companies in your country are not interested//aggressive in absorbing new technology (High = Aggressive)	Survey data (scale1–7)	WEF
Importance of innovation to revenue	In your business, continuous innovation plays a major role in generating revenue not true/true (High = True)	Survey data (scale1–7)	WEF
Gov't purchase decisions for tech. products	Government purchase decisions for technology products are based solely on price / on technology and encourage innovation (High = On technology)	Survey data (scale1–7)	WEF

Appendix B: Factor Analysis Results

	FIRST FACTOR			
	First Eigen Value	Difference from Second EV	Percent of Variance Explained	Score Coefficient
Stringency Subindex	3.97	3.95	99.16	
Air Regulation				0.251
Water Regulation				0.251
Toxic Waste Regulation				0.251
Chemical Regulation				0.251
Overall Regulation				*
Regulatory Structure Subindex	4.05	3.60	81.08	
Options for Compliance				0.216
Confusing and Changing				0.239
Early or Late				0.221
Compliance Hurts or Helps Competitiveness				0.224
Regulation Adversarial or Cooperative				0.210
Information Subindex	1.15	0.29	57.31	
ESI-Variables %-available				0.660
Sustainable Development Info				0.660
Number of Sectoral EIA Guidelines				*
Number of Environmental Strategies & Action Plans			*	
Regulatory Enforcement Subindex	1.93	1.86	96.38	
Enforcement				0.509
International Agreements				0.509
Environmental Institutions Subindex	1.59	1.19	79.72	
IUCN				*
Memberships				0.560
Prevalence of ISO 14000				0.560
Administrative Infrastructure Quality Index	5.35	5.14	89.09	
Civil Liberties				*
Public Sector Competence				*
Gov't Favor Private Sector Firms				0.172
Property Rights				0.178
Independent Judiciary				0.179
Irregular Payments				*
Legal Framework				0.180
Regulatory Burden				*
Level of Administrative Corruption				0.176
Honoring of Policies through Gov. Transition				0.175
Scientific and Research Infrastructure Index	4.52	4.32	90.38	
Scientists and Engineers				*
Technology Position				0.214
Institutions				0.212
Licensing of Foreign Technology				*
Company R & D Spending				0.212
Willingness to Absorb New Technology				0.210
Importance of Innovation to Revenue				*
Gov't Purchase Decisions for Tech. Products				0.203

ROLLUP OF SUBINDICES

	First Eigen Value	Difference from Second EV	Percent of Variance Explained	Score Coefficient
Environmental Regulatory Regime Index	3.46	3.06	86.56	
Stringency Subindex				0.279
Regulatory Structure Subindex				0.274
Government Subsidies				−0.238
Regulatory Enforcement Subindex				0.281
Economic and Legal Context Index	1.90	1.79	94.81	
Administrative Infrastructure Quality Index				0.513
Scientific and Research Infrastructure Index				0.513

Note: * means that variable is not included in the corresponding index

National Innovative Capacity

MICHAEL E. PORTER, Institute for Strategy and Competitiveness, Harvard Business School

SCOTT STERN, Northwestern University and the Brookings Institution

Introduction

The defining challenge for competitiveness has shifted, especially in advanced countries. The challenges of a decade ago were to restructure, lower cost, and raise quality. Today, continued operational improvement is a given, and companies in many countries are able to acquire and deploy the best current technology. In advanced nations with relatively high labor costs and equal access to global markets, producing standard products using standard methods will not sustain competitive advantage. Instead, advantage must come from the ability to create and then commercialize new products and processes, shifting the technology frontier as fast as their rivals can catch up.

Although R&D investments are undertaken in all countries, a small number of geographic locations tend to dominate the process of global innovation in specific sectors and technological areas. For example, though biomedical research takes place throughout the world, more than three-fourths of all biotechnology pharmaceutical patents have their origin in a handful of regional clusters in the United States.

Overall innovative activity also concentrates in a relatively small, though growing, number of countries. From the early 1970s through the late 1980s, the United States and Switzerland maintained a per capita "international" patenting rate well in excess of all other economies (Figure 1). The rate of growth of international patenting has varied dramatically among OECD countries. The Scandinavian nations, Japan, and emerging East Asian economies have registered sharp increases, while Western European nations such as France and the United Kingdom have realized a relatively constant rate of innovation.

Why does the intensity of innovation vary across countries? How does innovation depend on location? On the one hand, firms and the private sector are the ultimate engines of innovation. On the other hand, the innovative activities of firms within a country are strongly influenced by national policy and the presence and vitality of public institutions. In other words, innovation intensity depends on an interaction between private sector strategies and public sector policies and institutions. Competitiveness advances when the public and private sectors together promote a favorable environment for innovation.

Figure 1: International patents per capita, leading countries, 1975–2000

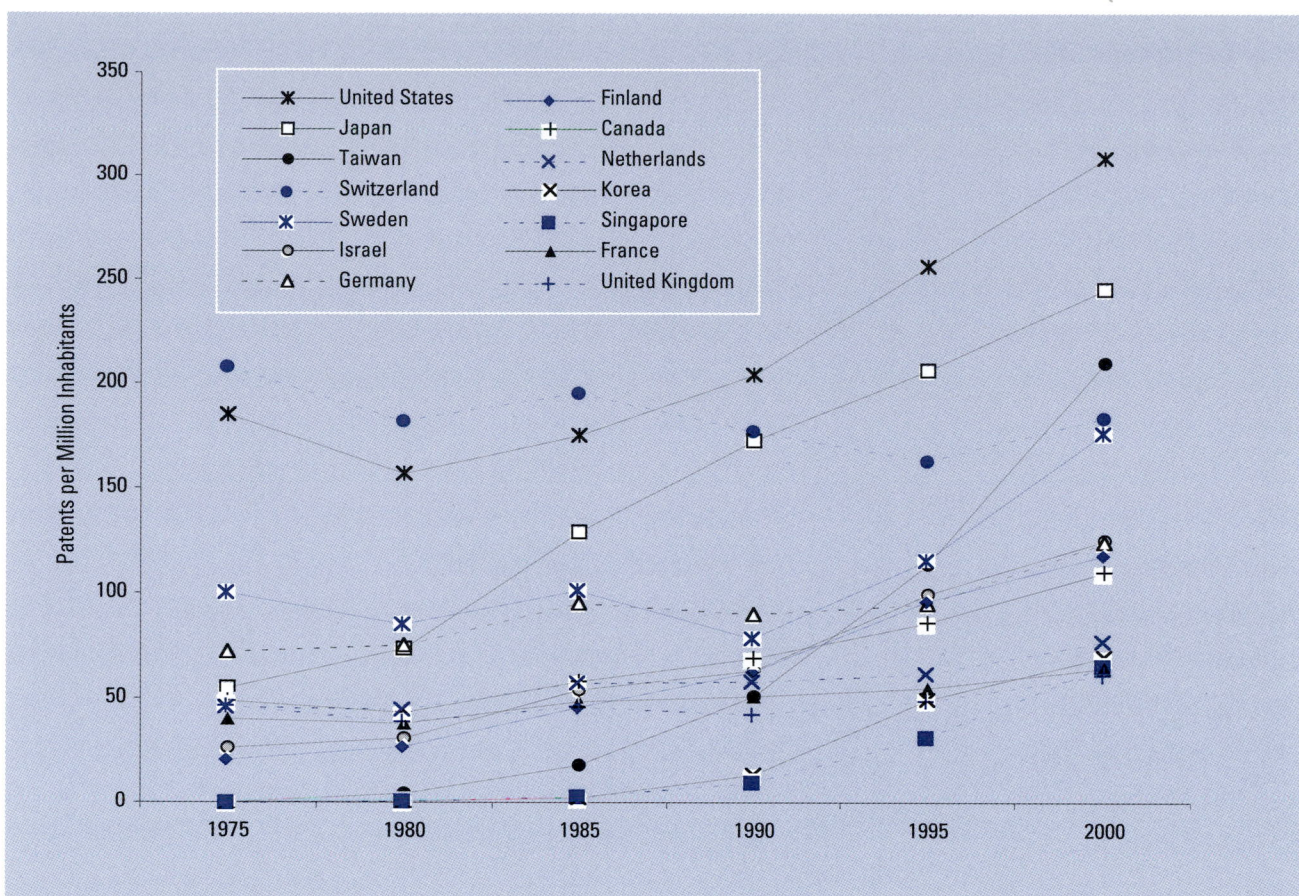

Understanding the role of innovation in competitiveness and economic development has become increasingly important. As advanced nations face the prospect of declining population growth and the completion of the structural reforms that have propelled OECD economies over the past two decades, a stepped-up rate of innovation is needed to drive the faster productivity growth that will be required to sustain healthy economic growth rates. A higher rate of innovation in one nation need not come at the expense of others. Increasing the rate of innovation in many nations can improve their productivity and prosperity and collectively speed the rate of world economic growth.

Ultimately, innovation also holds the potential to address our most pressing social and human challenges. Many policy discussions assume the existence of a sharp tradeoff between goals such as health, environment, safety, and short-term economic growth. However, a healthy rate of innovation increases the likelihood that new technologies will emerge that substantially temper or even eliminate such tradeoffs.

Over the last several years, we have undertaken a series of research projects aimed at evaluating the role of location in innovation and the ways in which the geographic distribution of innovation has shifted over time.[i] In this paper, we first review our framework for understanding national differences in the intensity of innovation. Then we extend our prior studies by drawing on new data and more nuanced measures available from the 2001 *Global Competitiveness Report* (GCR). We use these data to rank countries in terms of national innovative capacity along a series of dimensions (see Table 1).

Table 1: Innovation capacity index and subindexes

COUNTRY	Innovative Capacity Index		Proportion of Scientists and Engineers Subindex		Innovation Policy Subindex		Cluster Innovation Environment Subindex		Linkages Subindex	
	RANK	INDEX	RANK	INDEX	RANK	INDEX	RANK	INDEX	RANK	INDEX
United States	1	30.3	6	4.3	1	8.1	1	10.9	1	7.1
Finland	2	29.1	7	4.2	4	7.3	2	10.9	3	6.7
Germany	3	27.2	11	4.1	7	7.0	4	9.9	10	6.1
United Kingdom	4	27.0	18	3.9	13	6.8	3	10.0	9	6.3
Switzerland	5	26.9	13	4.0	15	6.7	5	9.9	7	6.3
Netherlands	6	26.9	23	3.8	3	7.4	14	9.2	4	6.6
Australia	7	26.9	8	4.2	10	6.8	9	9.4	5	6.5
Sweden	8	26.9	2	4.5	21	6.1	6	9.8	6	6.5
France	9	26.8	9	4.1	6	7.1	10	9.3	8	6.3
Canada	10	26.5	14	4.0	5	7.3	12	9.2	11	6.1
Israel	11	26.5	19	3.9	14	6.8	15	9.1	2	6.7
Japan	12	26.4	1	4.5	12	6.8	7	9.7	21	5.4
Singapore	13	26.0	17	3.9	2	7.4	17	8.9	15	5.8
Taiwan	14	26.0	16	4.0	9	6.9	8	9.6	17	5.6
Belgium	15	25.4	15	4.0	11	6.8	19	8.8	14	5.8
Ireland	16	25.4	12	4.0	16	6.6	16	9.1	16	5.7
Austria	17	25.3	29	3.5	8	6.9	11	9.3	18	5.5
Norway	18	25.3	5	4.3	18	6.4	21	8.6	12	5.9
Denmark	19	25.2	10	4.1	19	6.4	20	8.8	13	5.9
Iceland	20	24.8	4	4.3	20	6.2	18	8.8	20	5.5
Spain	21	23.4	30	3.5	17	6.5	23	8.4	28	5.0
Italy	22	23.3	31	3.5	23	6.0	13	9.2	30	4.7
Korea	23	22.9	22	3.9	24	5.6	24	8.3	24	5.1
New Zealand	24	22.1	28	3.6	35	5.0	27	8.0	19	5.5
Portugal	25	21.6	35	3.3	22	6.0	33	7.7	31	4.7
Czech Republic	26	21.3	36	3.2	26	5.5	29	7.9	29	4.7
Estonia	27	21.2	25	3.8	36	5.0	36	7.4	27	5.0
Hungary	28	21.1	34	3.3	25	5.6	38	7.2	25	5.0
South Africa	29	21.0	38	3.1	40	4.7	26	8.1	26	5.0
Russia	30	20.6	3	4.4	52	4.1	30	7.8	42	4.3
Slovenia	31	20.4	20	3.9	32	5.2	50	6.8	33	4.5
Ukraine	32	20.3	21	3.9	56	4.1	28	7.9	35	4.4
Brazil	33	20.1	48	1.9	27	5.4	25	8.2	32	4.6
Slovakia	34	20.0	26	3.7	49	4.5	35	7.6	44	4.2
Chile	35	19.7	42	2.6	31	5.4	34	7.6	45	4.2
Poland	36	19.6	32	3.5	50	4.5	37	7.2	36	4.4
Lithuania	37	19.2	24	3.8	55	4.1	45	6.9	34	4.4
India	38	18.9	59	1.2	39	4.8	31	7.8	23	5.2
Costa Rica	39	18.8	41	2.7	38	4.8	42	7.0	38	4.3
Trinidad and Tobago	40	18.6	49	1.9	41	4.7	32	7.7	39	4.3
Latvia	41	18.5	37	3.1	51	4.2	43	7.0	47	4.1
Greece	42	18.4	39	3.0	33	5.1	60	6.3	50	4.0
China	43	18.1	44	2.3	46	4.6	44	6.9	41	4.3
Turkey	44	17.8	46	2.1	34	5.0	49	6.8	55	3.9
Panama	45	17.4	55	1.5	42	4.7	39	7.2	51	4.0
Thailand	46	17.4	60	0.8	30	5.4	40	7.1	49	4.1
Mauritius	47	17.2	45	2.1	43	4.7	59	6.4	52	4.0
Egypt	48	17.2	43	2.3	44	4.7	66	5.9	43	4.3
Argentina	49	17.0	40	2.9	54	4.1	48	6.8	68	3.3
Bulgaria	50	16.9	27	3.7	64	3.6	67	5.8	56	3.8
Uruguay	51	16.8	51	1.8	47	4.6	52	6.7	58	3.8
Malaysia	52	16.8	63	0.7	28	5.4	54	6.5	46	4.2
Mexico	53	16.8	50	1.8	45	4.6	46	6.9	63	3.5
Indonesia	54	16.4	47	1.9	48	4.6	58	6.4	62	3.5
Romania	55	16.3	33	3.4	65	3.6	53	6.6	73	2.7
Philippines	56	15.8	58	1.2	62	3.8	47	6.8	53	3.9
Sri Lanka	57	15.5	56	1.4	60	3.9	62	6.1	48	4.1
Venezuela	58	15.2	54	1.5	57	4.0	61	6.1	60	3.6
Colombia	59	15.1	53	1.5	58	3.9	63	6.1	61	3.5
Peru	60	14.3	52	1.6	71	3.4	65	6.0	64	3.3
Vietnam	61	13.8	70	0.0	69	3.5	55	6.5	57	3.8
Dominican Republic	62	13.6	68	0.0	61	3.9	57	6.4	65	3.3
Guatemala	63	13.2	66	0.4	70	3.5	64	6.0	66	3.3
Paraguay	64	13.1	64	0.7	66	3.6	68	5.8	72	2.9
Zimbabwe	65	13.0	69	0.0	63	3.6	71	5.5	54	3.9
Nicaragua	66	12.7	62	0.8	72	3.2	70	5.5	69	3.1
El Salvador	67	12.5	71	-0.2	59	3.9	69	5.8	71	3.0
Honduras	68	11.9	65	0.4	67	3.6	72	5.4	75	2.6
Ecuador	69	11.9	61	0.8	73	3.2	74	4.9	70	3.0
Bangladesh	70	11.6	67	0.1	74	3.0	73	5.2	67	3.3
Bolivia	71	11.6	57	1.4	75	2.8	75	4.8	74	2.6
Hong Kong SAR	NA	NA	NA	NA	29	5.4	22	8.6	22	5.2
Jamaica	NA	NA	NA	NA	53	4.1	51	6.7	37	4.3
Jordan	NA	NA	NA	NA	37	4.8	56	6.4	40	4.3
Nigeria	NA	NA	NA	NA	68	3.6	41	7.0	59	3.7

Our findings reveal the striking degree to which the national environment matters for success in innovative activity, and they highlight sharp differences in the environment for innovation across both OECD and emerging economies. The analysis suggests that subtle aspects of a country's institutional and microeconomic environment play an important role in determining the productivity of investments in innovation. Though our results are subject to caveats common to any quantitative study focusing on the causes and consequences of innovation, the findings provide a consistent set of implications for policymakers attempting to enhance the locational foundations of innovation, and, with it, international competitiveness.

The determinants of national innovative capacity

The vitality of innovation in a location is shaped by *national innovative capacity*. National innovative capacity is a country's potential—as both a political and economic entity—to produce a stream of commercially relevant innovations. This capacity is not simply the realized level of innovation but also reflects the fundamental conditions, investments, and policy choices that create the environment for innovation in a particular location or nation. National innovative capacity depends in part on the technological sophistication and the size of the scientific and technical labor force in a given economy, and it also reflects the array of investments and policy choices of the government and private sector that affect the incentives for and the productivity of a country's research and development activities. National innovative capacity is also distinct from both the purely scientific or technical achievements of an economy, which do not *necessarily* involve the economic application of new technology.

The national innovative capacity framework aims to identify the factors enabling a region to innovate at the global frontier. Although the framework was created for application at the national level, it can also be employed to evaluate innovative capacity at the regional or local level.

National innovative capacity depends on three broad elements that capture how location shapes the ability of companies in a particular location to innovate at the global frontier (see Figure 2). Of course, taking advantage of the national environment for innovation is far from automatic, and companies based in the same location will differ markedly in their success at innovation. Nevertheless, sharp differences in innovative output in different locations suggest that location exerts a strong influence.

Figure 2: Elements of national innovative capacity

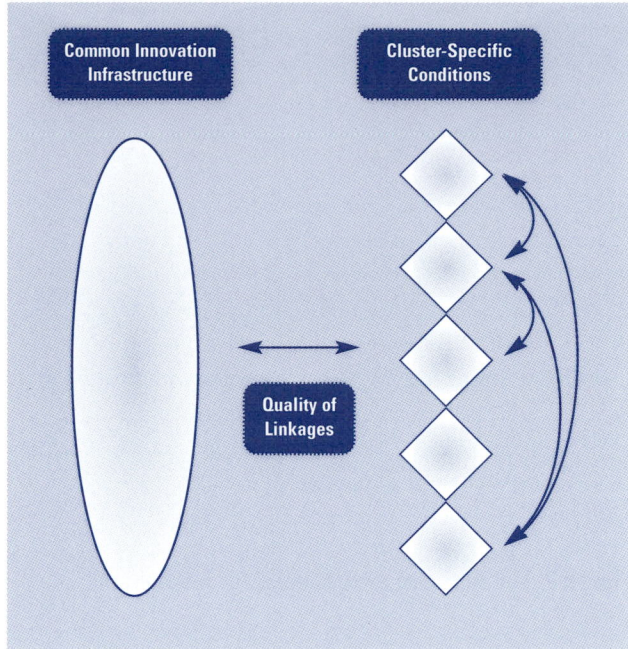

The common innovation infrastructure

A nation's *common innovation infrastructure* is the set of crosscutting investments and policies supporting innovation throughout an entire economy. This set includes the overall human and financial resources a country devotes to scientific and technological advances, the public policies bearing on innovative activity, and the economy's level of technological sophistication. The foundation of a nation's common innovation infrastructure is its pool of scientists and engineers available to contribute to innovation throughout the economy. A strong common innovation infrastructure is also built on excellence in basic research, which advances fundamental understanding and is at the root of much new commercial technology, where government funding remains essential in virtually every country. Crosscutting innovation policy areas include the protection of intellectual property, the extent of tax-based incentives for innovation, the degree to which antitrust enforcement encourages innovation-based competition, and the openness of the economy to trade and investment. Overall, a strong common innovation infrastructure requires a set of national investments and policy choices stretching over decades.

105

The cluster-specific environment for innovation

Although the common innovation infrastructure sets the basic conditions for innovation, it is ultimately companies that introduce and commercialize innovations. Innovation and the commercialization of new technologies take place disproportionately in clusters—geographic concentrations of interconnected companies and institutions in a particular field. The cluster-specific innovation environment is captured in the "diamond" framework (see Figure 3).[ii] Four attributes of a location's microeconomic environment affect the rate of innovation in a cluster as well as its overall competitiveness—the presence of high-quality and specialized inputs, a context that encourages investment coupled with intense local rivalry, pressure and insight gleaned from sophisticated local demand, and the local presence of related and supporting industries.

Figure 3: The national environment for innovation

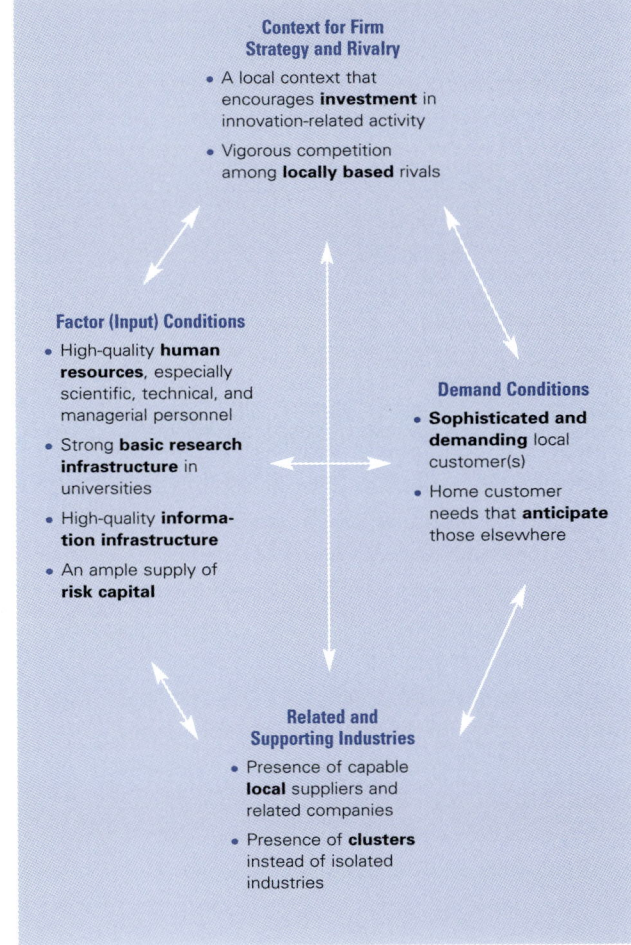

Clusters reflect important externalities in innovation that are contained in particular geographic areas. Presence within a cluster offers potential advantages to firms in perceiving both the need and the opportunity for innovation. Equally important, however, are the flexibility and capacity in clusters to act rapidly to turn new ideas into reality. A company within a cluster can often more rapidly source the new machinery, services, components, and other elements to implement innovations. Local suppliers and partners can and do get involved in the innovation process; the complementary relationships involved in innovating are more easily achieved among participants that are nearby. Reinforcing these advantages of clusters for innovation is the sheer pressure—competitive pressure, peer pressure, customer pressure, and constant comparison—that is inherent within a concentrated group of firms in the same field. We focus on clusters (eg, information technology) rather than individual industries (eg, printers), then, because of powerful spillovers and externalities across discrete industries that are vital to the rate of innovation.

The global competitiveness of a cluster depends importantly on its innovation orientation. For example, the Finnish pulp-and-paper cluster benefits from the multiple advantages of pressures from demanding domestic consumers and paper companies, intense local rivalry, and Finnish process-equipment manufacturers that are top of the line, with companies such as Kamyr and Sunds leading the world in the commercialization of innovative bleaching equipment. This is only one example out of many. A strong innovation environment within national clusters is the foundation for innovation-based competitive advantage in many fields, from pharmaceuticals in the United States to semiconductor fabrication in Taiwan.

The quality of linkages

The relationship between the common innovation infrastructure and a nation's industrial clusters is reciprocal: Strong clusters feed the common infrastructure and also benefit from it. A variety of formal and informal organizations and networks—which we call "institutions for collaboration"—can link the two areas. An especially important example is a nation's university system, which provides a particularly strong and open bridge between technology and companies. Without strong linkages, a nation's upstream scientific and technical advances can diffuse to other countries more quickly than they can be exploited at home. For example, although early elements of VCR technology were developed in the United States, it was three companies in the Japanese consumer electronics cluster that successfully commercialized this innovation on a global scale in the late 1970s.

Measuring national innovative capacity

To assess the sources of differences in innovative capacity across countries, we extend our prior research using new data and measures drawn from the GCR Survey. Using country-level data on innovative output, we identify elements of the national innovation environment with a statistically significant relationship to innovation. These elements are then used to calculate rankings reflecting how countries fare along each of the major dimensions of innovative capacity, as well as to construct an overall national innovative capacity ranking.

National innovative capacity is inherently difficult to measure for several reasons. First, measures of innovative output are imperfect (only certain types of innovation can be measured) and subject to some random fluctuations. Second, traditional data sources make it difficult to develop measures associated with the more nuanced drivers of innovative capacity, such as innovation policy and the cluster-specific innovation environment.

Because our focus here is on innovation at the technology frontier and on comparing innovation across nations, the single most useful measure of innovation is "international" patenting, measured by the number of patents the US Patent and Trademark Office (USPTO) granted to foreign and US inventors in 1999 and 2000. Over the past quarter century, there has been a dramatic increase in the rate of international patenting—from fewer than 25,000 per year in the late 1970s to more than 100,000 by the late 1990s.

We used USPTO patents as a measure of realized national innovative performance for several reasons. When a foreign inventor files a US patent, it is a sign of the innovation's potential economic value because of the costs involved. Also, the use of US patents helps ensure a standard of technological excellence that is at or near the global technology frontier. Of course, no single measure of innovation is ideal. In our related research, we have explored several alternative measures of innovation success, such as the pattern of exports in international high-technology markets. Overall, however, international patents constitute the best available measure of innovation that is consistent across time and location.[iii]

We employ regression analysis to evaluate the relationship of international patenting to nuanced measures of the innovation environment. The regression analysis allows us to assign the *relative* weights to individual elements in our innovative capacity rankings. This procedure provides a level of confidence that our country-level assessments of innovative capacity are clearly tied to long-term measures of international innovative performance.

Assessing innovative capacity across countries

To examine the linkage between realized innovation and measures associated with national innovative capacity, the analysis proceeds in three steps. First, we control for population and historical technological sophistication, and include a measure of the commitment of human resources to innovative activity.[iv] To do so, we regress the national level of international patenting in a sample of 75 countries in 1999 to 2000 on total population, the proportion of scientists and engineers employed within the nation, and a metric of the "stock" of international patents generated by a country between 1985 and 1994.[v] This baseline analysis includes each country's historical patenting in order to account for past differences in the ability of countries to innovate at the international frontier, as well as differences in their propensity to patent their inventions in the United States. The control for population allows us to focus on per capita rates of international patenting, which should relate most closely to a nation's standard of living.[vi] The patent stock number varies substantially across countries and time, as does the number of technological personnel, which is affected by a set of national human resource policies. For example, though their living standards are similar, the percentage of the workforce who are scientists and engineers is three times higher in Japan than in Italy or Spain.

Strikingly, over 80 percent of the total variance in international patenting across the world, controlling for population, can be explained by these two determinants of national innovative intensity. In other words, countries vary significantly in their historical ability to produce global innovation. They also vary significantly in their current resource commitment to innovative activity.

Creating subindexes

This regression becomes the baseline for further analysis. Of the baseline variables, the one that is most affected by current policy is the number of scientists and engineers. To assess national innovative capacity, then, we include the proportion of scientists and engineers in the workforce as the first measure. We use this measure to construct a scientific and technical personnel subindex.

The ranking of countries using this subindex is shown in the second column of Table 1. Japan ranks number 1, followed by Sweden. A number of smaller countries, such as Norway and Finland, rank highly. The United States is number 6, well below its overall innovative capacity ranking. This reveals a shortage of scientific and technical graduates that represents a real issue for the United States. Russia ranks higher on this subindex despite a relatively low overall ranking, as do a number of other former Soviet bloc countries. This reflects a legacy of technical training that could emerge as an important strength if other dimensions of competitiveness and innovative capacity can be improved.

Using the baseline regression as a foundation, we then systematically explore the role of innovation-related public policy, the cluster innovation environment, and the strength of linkages on innovation performance. Consider Table 2. For each country, we calculate the difference between the actual and predicted level of international patenting based on the baseline factors, and calculated the percentage gap relative to actual patenting. Some countries—such as the United States, Japan, and Korea—have a patenting level well above that predicted by the baseline model. Others, such as Spain and Russia, are substantially below the benchmark. In the remainder of this paper, we focus on whether measures drawn from the Survey can help explain this gap between predicted and realized international innovation performance.

Table 2: Residuals of the baseline regression model

Country	Standardized Residuals (%)*
United States	94
Paraguay	93
Japan	87
Taiwan	82
Honduras	82
Korea	81
Germany	77
Dominican Republic	72
Canada	66
Malaysia	66
United Kingdom	61
Slovenia	59
France	58
Thailand	52
Bolivia	49
Israel	49
Singapore	48
Sweden	46
Italy	45
Switzerland	44
Netherlands	44
Ukraine	41
Finland	33
Belgium	31
India	28
Costa Rica	28
Austria	25
Denmark	25
Mauritius	13
Guatemala	11
Australia	5
El Salvador	0
New Zealand	−19
Panama	−28
Norway	−28
Uruguay	−34
Brazil	−34
Mexico	−34
Ecuador	−35
Iceland	−37
Spain	−40
Venezuela	−42
Ireland	−53
Argentina	−94
Chile	−96
China	−123
Greece	−131
South Africa	−142
Egypt	−152
Colombia	−158
Philippines	−165
Peru	−236
Sri Lanka	−248
Czech Republic	−259
Romania	−274
Russia	−290
Turkey	−331
Portugal	−335
Indonesia	−381
Hungary	−445
Poland	−454
Trinidad and Tobago	−457
Bulgaria	−5925

*Note: After removing logs and obtaining the residuals, we standardize them by dividing by the actual values.

There are 24 Survey measures that are closely related to innovative capacity and that can be classified into three distinct groupings: innovation-related public policy, the cluster innovation environment, and the strength of innovation linkages. The variables in each of these groupings and the bilateral regressions are listed in the first column of Appendix A. Elements of the innovation policy environment, for example, include such measures as the "effectiveness of intellectual property," "the level of research in public research institutions," and the "effectiveness of competition policy in promoting efficiency." Similarly, measures of the cluster innovation environment include the "presence and depth of clusters," "the sophistication and pressure of local buyers," "the quality of suppliers," and the "availability of specialized research and training services."

We introduced each of these variables, one at a time, into the baseline specification. The results are striking. Out of the 24 measures, 23 proved to be positive as expected and statistically significant.[vii] In other words, even after controlling for the size of a country, the aggregate level of human resources devoted to innovation, and the stock of past ideas to build on, nuanced measures of the national environment are closely associated with the level of innovation realized by a country. This strongly supports the need to go beyond the more aggregate measures available in most of the previous economic literature, and reveals the importance of utilizing surveys and other means to assemble data on hard-to-measure dimensions of national economies.

To build an innovative capacity index, it was not feasible to include all 24 variables in a multivariate regression analysis. The reason is straightforward: Nearly all of the measures are themselves highly correlated with each other. In nearly all cases, the correlation is extremely high (particularly given that our analysis relies on a single cross-section of 75 countries). For measures drawn from similar portions of the GCR Survey (eg, the domestic competition component), the correlation sometimes reaches over .9. Therefore, rather than attempt to disentangle the distinct effects associated with each measure, we created a parsimonious specification using a few variables from each subgroup.

The innovation policy subindex

To assess a nation's innovation public policy environment, three measures were selected, each with a strong and robust relationship to international patenting controlling for population, the patent stock, and the number of scientists and engineers in the workforce:

- The effectiveness of intellectual property protection
- The ability of a country to retain its scientists and engineers
- The size and availability of R&D tax credits for the private sector

To calculate the subindex, we added these three variables to the baseline regression. All the subindex results are reported in Appendix B. Each measure is statistically significant, and each is predicted to have a substantial impact on the level of international patenting. For example, increasing the Survey response on intellectual property protection from 4 to 5 on a scale of 7 (less than one standard deviation) is associated with a 50 percent increase in a country's level of international patenting. The innovation policy subindex for each country is calculated as the weighted sum of the three measures, with the weights determined by the regression coefficients of each measure in the specification presented in Appendix B.

The third column of Table 1 presents the innovation policy subindex ranking. The United States registers the highest ranking, followed by Singapore, the Netherlands, Finland, Canada, and France. Surprisingly, a number of non-OECD economies, including Singapore as well as Taiwan and Israel, register rankings in the top 20, while large OECD economies, including Italy and Korea, lag behind. Sweden is notably weak on this subindex, which pulls down its overall ranking.

Latin American economies register surprisingly weak rankings; Brazil, Chile, and Costa Rica record the best showings, though all are outside the top 25. Though economies such as Mexico and Brazil have shown promising improvements in international competitiveness over the past decade, they have not developed the type of innovation policy environment that supports innovation at the world technology frontier.

Perhaps even more interesting are the results for India and China. Though often cited as emerging innovator countries, both register innovation policy rankings far below that of the main OECD economies. These countries have also not achieved the quality of innovation policy environment found in other emerging economies such as Singapore and Israel. Nevertheless, as will be evident in later analysis, their innovative capacity is more advanced than would be predicted by their current level of income.

The cluster innovation environment subindex

A similar calculation underlies the cluster innovation environment subindex. After exploring a number of the measures, we selected three measures of the cluster innovation environment to use to rank countries:

- The sophistication and pressure to innovate from domestic buyers
- The presence of suppliers of specialized research and training
- The prevalence and depth of clusters

As before, each of these measures is statistically significant and has a quantitatively significant impact on the rate of international patenting, even after controlling for population, the historical propensity to innovate, and the size of the R&D workforce. The cluster innovation environment subindex is calculated by adding together these three factors, using the weights calculated in the regression.

The fourth column of Table 1 reports the results. Finland is virtually tied with the United States as offering the best cluster environment for innovation. Relative to their policy rankings, the United Kingdom, Germany, Switzerland, Sweden, and Japan register relatively high rankings on the cluster innovation environment, while Singapore, the Netherlands, Canada, and France lag on this dimension. These patterns reflect important differences in innovative potential across countries, which are often misunderstood by analyses that focus only on policy indicators. Such weaknesses are also obscured by looking only at short-term innovative performance. Innovative performance is not simply a result of aggregate policy but also of the development and growth of clusters in the private sector. Finland and Germany, for example, have made long-term commitments to nurturing clusters; this commitment is an important source of the continuing competitive advantage held by companies in these countries in technology-intensive sectors.

Among the emerging economies, Israel, Taiwan, Singapore, and Ireland each possess a cluster innovation environment comparable with that of mainstream OECD economies, and outdistance countries such as Spain and Korea along this dimension. Once again, China and India are associated with only a modest cluster innovation environment relative to the most innovative countries. However, China and India are well positioned when compared with most Eastern European and Latin American economies, which have cluster innovation environments that are not yet developed. Brazil and Costa Rica are countries in Latin America that have a higher ranking along this dimension compared with that of their peers.

The linkages subindex

The fourth and final subindex measures the strength of linkages between the common innovation infrastructure and a country's clusters. As discussed earlier, this is perhaps the most difficult area in which to find measures, since it depends on relatively subtle forms of interaction between public sector institutions and private sector initiatives. The subindex is based on two Survey measures that capture important dimensions of the process by which a country's innovation resources are directed toward the needs of individual clusters:

- The overall quality of scientific research institutions
- The availability of venture capital for innovative but risky projects

The overall quality of scientific research institutions (as perceived by managers within a country) highlights the importance of universities and other institutions for collaboration in fostering linkages.[viii] The availability of venture capital reflects the importance of risk capital in translating basic research into commercializable innovation. Each measure is statistically and quantitatively significant in its predicted impact on the rate of international patenting, even after controlling for the baseline variables. The linkages subindex is the weighted sum of the two measures, with the weights determined by the regression coefficients as in the prior subindexes.

The fifth column of Table 1 reports the results. The United States is comfortably at the top of the ranking in this area, followed by Israel and Finland. Relative to the other subindexes, Japan registers a dramatically lower ranking, falling out of the top 20. Australia and Sweden improve their relative positions.

These results suggest that countries vary widely in their ability to build universities and other open research institutions, and in their ability to foster collaboration between them and the private sector. This area is particularly slow and challenging, and requires attitudinal shifts and a sustained policy commitment. Whereas Israel's innovation policy has largely succeeded because of initiatives aimed at fostering linkages (Trajtenberg forthcoming), Japan continues to suffer from a relative lack of world-class research institutions and collaboration between such institutions and the private sector. This will limit Japan's ability to become a stronger innovator across a wide variety of industrial areas.

No emerging economy except Israel registers in the top ten on the linkages subindex. Singapore, Taiwan, and Ireland all show relative weakness in this difficult and slow-to-build area. As before, the OECD economies of Italy and Spain have significant disadvantages in this area, as do the Latin American and Eastern European economies.

The national innovative capacity index

All four subindexes are combined into an overall innovative capacity index. The overall index is calculated as the unweighted sum of the subindexes.

The first column of Table 1 reports the results. The United States is ranked first, followed by Finland. Germany, the United Kingdom, Switzerland, the Netherlands, Australia, Sweden, and France round out the first tier. The overall ranking accords well with our earlier research and that of others on the patterns of international innovation. Over the past quarter century, the set of top-tier innovator economies has expanded to include many of the Northern European countries. More recently, Australia, Japan, Israel, and Taiwan have moved to high levels. Singapore has also moved to a high level, though its performance is partly the result of an abundance of US multinationals who have located there. This convergence in innovation achievement among a set of OECD economies is strongly tied to a substantial upgrading in the environment for innovation.

One interesting difference from previous work that emerges in this study is the ranking of Japan. Our earlier research revealed that Japan was developing the elements associated with first-tier level of innovative capacity. We see that here in Japan's strength in scientific and technical personnel. However, this study reveals Japan's weaknesses in innovation policy and in establishing strong linkages, resulting in a lower ranking in the overall innovative capacity index. Japan will need to progress in these areas if it is to become a more broadly based Innovation-Driven economy.[ix]

Overall, the OECD is responsible for the great majority of global innovation, reflecting a more favorable environment for innovation in these advanced economies. However, some of the Asian economies—most notably Taiwan and Singapore, as well as Israel outside Asia—have achieved the conditions to support innovation at a rate consistent with many Western European economies.

Many other areas of the world lag badly behind in innovative capacity. China and India are still at a quite early stage of development in terms of global innovation, though they are progressing well relative to their current level of per capital income. Some Asian economies, such as Indonesia, Malaysia, and Thailand, are far behind their Asian peers in innovative capacity, a major challenge.

Despite impressive improvements in macroeconomic stability over the past two decades in Latin America and positive political change in Eastern Europe, these areas of the world still do not offer environments that support innovation at the global frontier. Similarly, African nations are lagging: none is ranked above 29. South Africa, however, has an innovative capacity index that is higher than expected, given its overall level of economic development.

Corporate practices and innovation

Successful innovation depends not just on a favorable business environment but also on supportive company operating practices and strategies. National innovative capacity in the business environment and corporate behavior tend to move together. Companies must adjust their competitive approaches to attain higher levels of innovative output. Our Survey data allow us to characterize some of the shifts in corporate practices that are associated with countries that produce the highest output of international patents.

The GCR Survey includes 19 measures of the types of corporate strategies and operating practices that are characteristic of each country. We include each of these variables individually in the baseline model, and test for the size and significance of the influence. Again, the relatively high correlation among most of the variables precludes a meaningful multivariate analysis.

Abbreviated results of this analysis are shown in Table 3. First and foremost, the results reveal that firms in innovator countries have strategies that aim for unique products and processes rather than relying on low cost labor or natural resources. Firms in these countries are willing to invest heavily in R&D, and have moved beyond extensive use of technology licensing. Companies focus on building their own brands, controlling international distribution, and selling globally, all of which are complementary to innovation-based strategies. Organizationally, firms from innovator countries engage in extensive training of employees, delegate authority down the organization, and make greater use of incentive compensation than firms in countries with lower innovation output. We will explore the corporate correlates of innovative capacity more fully in subsequent reports.

Table 3: Operations and strategy variables—regressions

Dependent Variable	Coef.	t	Adj. R^2
Nature of Competitive Advantage	0.955	6.50	0.8959
Value Chain Presence	0.984	5.89	0.8874
Extent of Branding	0.928	4.50	0.8669
Uniqueness of Product Designs	1.063	4.24	0.8629
Production Process Sophistication	1.229	6.02	0.8892
Extent of Marketing	1.068	4.53	0.8673
Degree of Customer Orientation	0.927	3.26	0.8484
Control of International Distribution	1.218	3.98	0.8590
Prevalence of Foreign Technology Licensing	0.018	0.07	0.8212
Company Spending on R&D	1.263	6.86	0.9005
Extent of Regional Sales	0.443	2.21	0.8348
Breadth of International Markets	0.875	5.02	0.8747
Extent of Staff Training	0.987	4.59	0.8683
Willingness to Delegate Authority	0.939	4.40	0.8654
Extent of Incentive Compensation	0.923	3.97	0.8589
Reliance on Professional Management	0.399	1.53	0.8280
Quality of Management Schools	0.225	1.04	0.8244
Efficacy of Corporate Boards	0.401	1.63	0.8289
Internet Use leading to Inventory Cost Reduction	0.820	3.30	0.8491

*Note: Patents regressed on baseline and individual company operations and strategy variables.

Innovative capacity, competitiveness, and prosperity

Having developed the innovative capacity index, we examine the relationships between the index and our overall assessment of overall competitiveness (the Current Competitiveness Index) with the economy-wide prosperity (GDP per capita) in Figures 4 and 5.

The innovative capacity index and the Current Competitiveness Index are highly correlated (see Figure 4). Improving innovative capacity is integral to achieving the high levels of productivity necessary to achieve and sustain overall competitiveness. Most countries track the regression line from the overall sample. Those countries that diverge from the regression line tend to fall into a number of categories. One category is the countries of the former Soviet bloc (eg, Russia, the Ukraine, and Bulgaria), whose high proportion of scientists, engineers, and research institutions makes their innovative assets more advanced than their overall business environments. A second category of countries that diverge from the overall relationship are those that have access to particularly favorable natural resources or low labor costs relative to their level of economic sophistication (eg, Chile, New Zealand, South Africa, Turkey, and Malaysia). These other sources of competitiveness give these countries Current Competitiveness Index rankings that are significantly higher than their innovative capacity. A final category of countries departing from the typical relationship between innovative capacity and competitiveness are those with an unusual focus on innovation (eg, the United States, Israel, Taiwan, and Costa Rica).

Figure 4: The relationship between innovative capacity and the Current Competitiveness Index

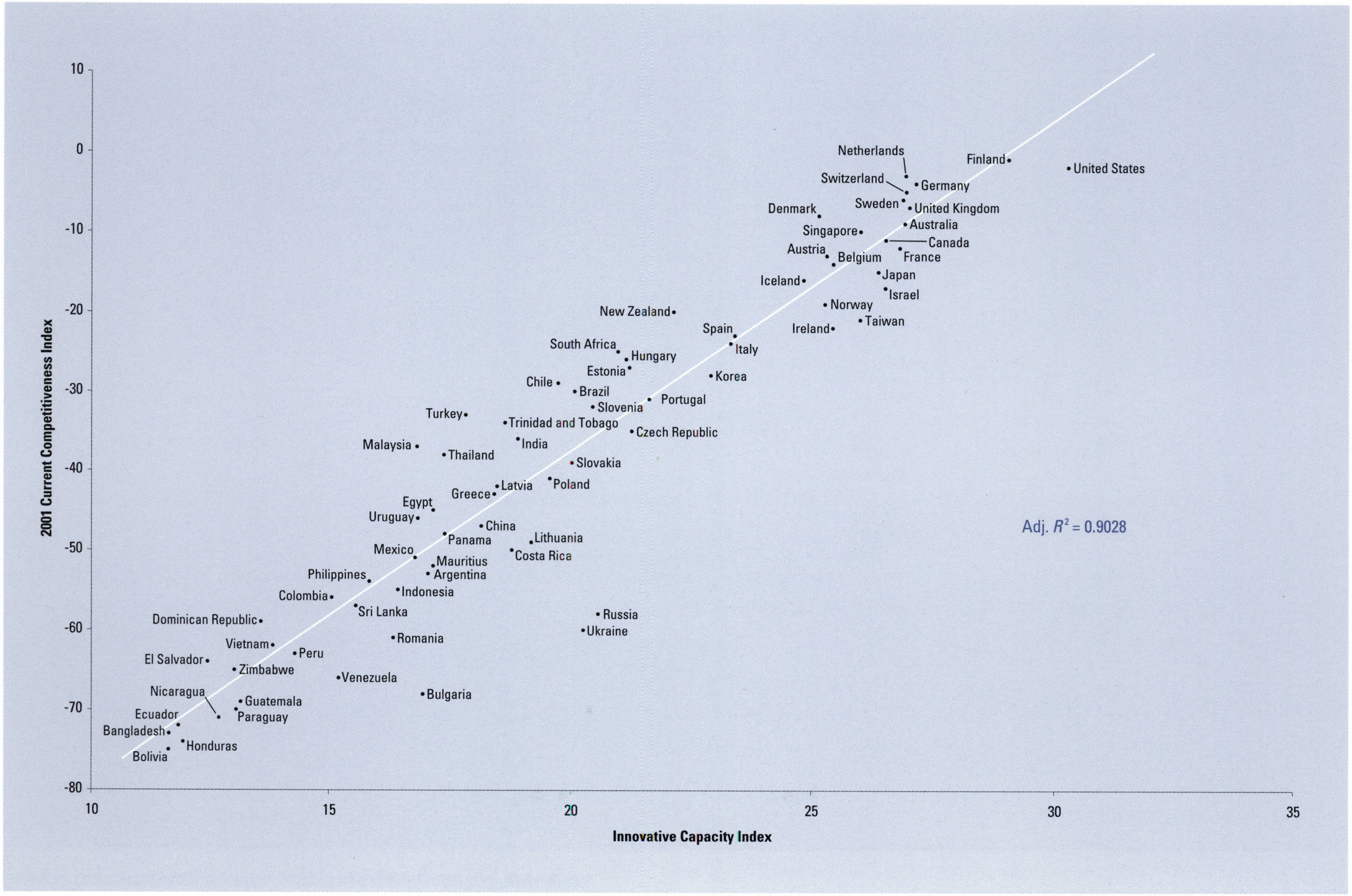

Adj. $R^2 = 0.9028$

113

Figure 5: The relationship between innovative capacity and GDP per capita

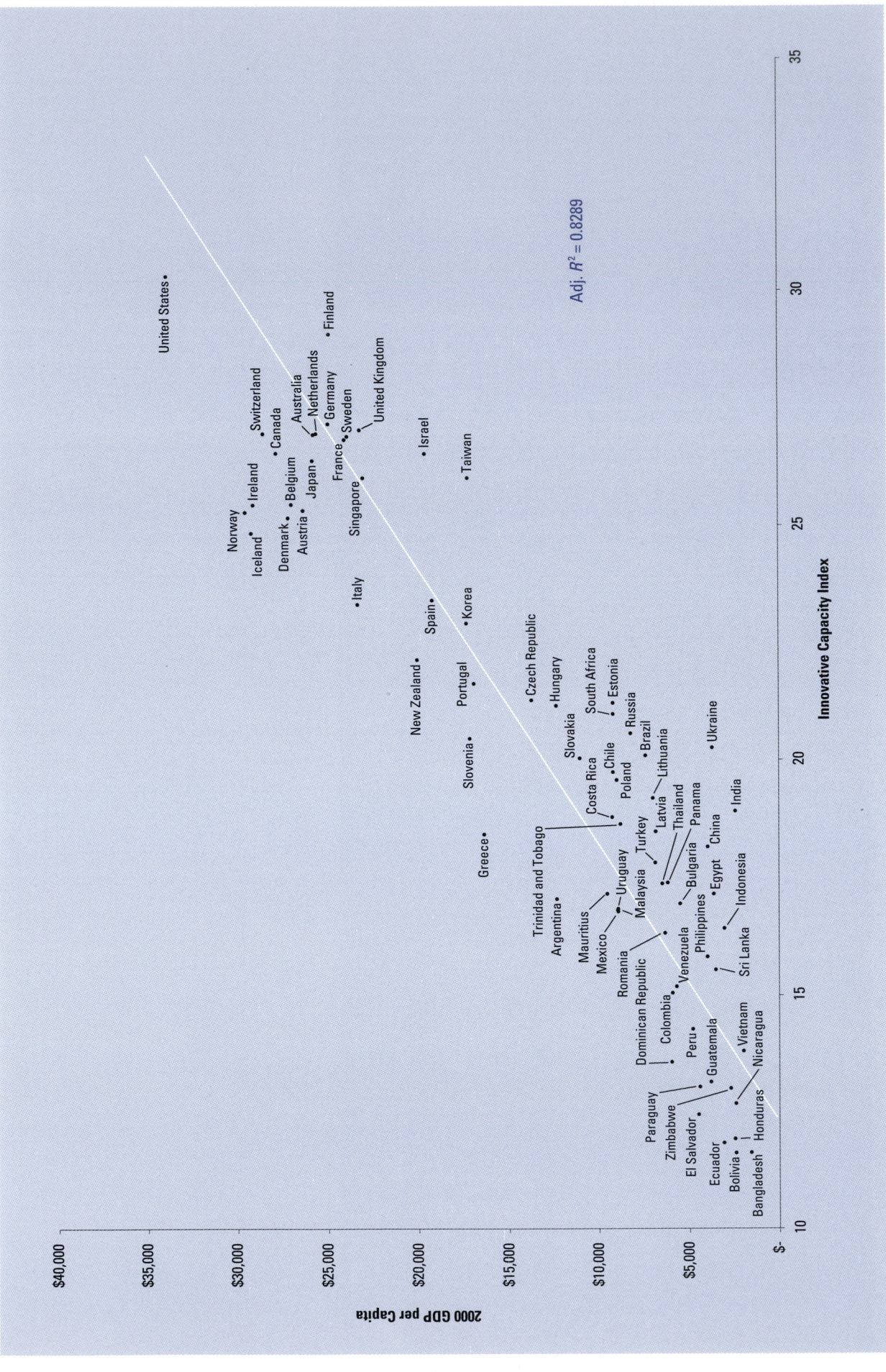

The relationship between innovative capacity and GDP per capita (Figure 5) is also revealing. The correlation is again high, but noticeably lower than the correlation with overall competitiveness. Analysis of the particular countries that are near, above, or below the regression line is suggestive of a number of economic development models. The first model, represented by countries falling on or near the regression line, is what might be termed "balanced development." Innovative capacity grows in parallel with overall competitiveness to produce a rising standard of living. Over time, successful countries move along the regression line to higher levels of income. A second model, represented by the countries above the regression line, involves reliance on natural resources or a favorable geographic location vis-à-vis other nations to produce a higher standard of living than would be justified by innovative capacity. Countries such as Norway, Iceland, Denmark, Greece, and Argentina fall into this group. Italy's position on the figure may be distorted by the sharp differences between the north and the south.

The United States, interestingly, falls above the regression line even though it is the leader in innovative capacity. This means that the United States' lead in innovative capacity is not great enough to explain its high income. This could reflect a disequilibrium in which US per capita income comes under pressure. More likely, however, is that high US income reflects the fact that the United States also enjoys abundant natural resources, a huge economy, and extraordinary political power in the world.

A third development model, represented by countries falling well below the regression line, is to grow innovative capacity *ahead* of the sophistication of the overall economy to pull the economy forward. China, India, Taiwan, Israel, and Finland are examples of this group of countries. Countries of the former Soviet bloc may be outliers not because of an innovation led national strategy, but because of a legacy of training scientists and engineers and building research institutions.

The consequences of each of model for the rate of economic growth are intriguing. Countries following the innovation-led model tend to be faster growing than those relying on natural endowments. Countries differ in their initial assets, however, which also affects their success. We will explore these issues in subsequent *Reports*.

Conclusions

Innovation has become perhaps the most important source of competitive advantage in advanced economies, and building innovative capacity has a strong relationship to a country's overall competitiveness and level of prosperity. We have offered a framework for analyzing national innovative capacity, drawing on our previous research, and used it to construct an innovative capacity index that allows us to rank countries on overall innovative capacity as well as its important components. Although the data available and statistical procedures face real limitations, the rankings both square with knowledge about individual countries and are revealing of strengths and challenges facing each country surveyed.

Those economies, such as Finland and Taiwan, that have proactively built innovative capacity, have prospered. In contrast, limited focus on innovative capacity will constrain the progress of countries such as Greece and Norway as well as many countries in Latin America and Eastern Europe. Building national innovative capacity will represent the fundamental development challenge facing many countries for years to come.

References

Dosi, G, K. Pavitt, and L. Soete (1990). *The Economics of Technical Change and International Trade*. New York: New York University Press; distributed by Columbia University Press.

Eaton, J. and S. Kortum (1996). "Trade in Ideas: Patenting & Productivity in the OECD," *Journal of International Economics*, 40(3–4), 251–278.

Eaton, J. and S. Kortum (1999). "International Technology Diffusion: Theory and Measurement," *International Economic Review*. 40(3), 537–570.

Evenson, R. (1984). "International Invention: Implications for Technology Market Analysis," in Zvi Griliches, ed., *R&D, Patents, and Productivity*. Chicago (IL): University of Chicago Press: 89–126.

Furman, J. L. M. E. Porter, and S. Stern (2001). "The Determinants of National Innovative Capacity," *Research Policy*, forthcoming.

Griliches, Z. (1984). *R&D, Patents, and Productivity*. Chicago (IL): University of Chicago Press.

Griliches, Z. (1994). "Productivity, R&D, and the Data Constraint," *American Economic Review*, 84(1), 1–23.

Griliches, Z. (1990). "Patent Statistics as Economic Indicators: A Survey," *Journal of Economic Literature*, 92, 630–653.

Jones, C. (1995). "R&D Based Models of Economic Growth," *Journal of Political Economy*, 103, 739–784.

Jones, C. (1998). *Introduction to Economic Growth*. New York (NY): W.W. Norton & Co.

Nelson, R., ed. (1993). *National Innovation Systems: A Comparative Analysis* New York (NY): Oxford University Press.

Porter, M. E. (1990). *The Competitive Advantage of Nations*. New York (NY): Free Press.

Porter, M. E.. (1998). "Clusters and Competition: New Agendas for Companies, Governments, and Institutions," *On Competition*. Boston (MA): Harvard Business School Press.

Porter, M. E., S. Stern, and Council on Competitiveness (1999b). *The New Challenge to America's Prosperity: Findings from the Innovation Index*. Washington (DC): Council on Competitiveness.

Porter, M. E. and S. Stern (2000). "Measuring the 'Ideas' Production Function," NBER Working Paper 7891.

Porter, M E, H Takeuchi, and M Sakakibara (2000). *Can Japan Compete?* London: MacMillan Press.

Romer, P. (1990). "Endogenous Technological Change," *Journal of Political Economy*, 98, S71–S102.

Schmookler, J. (1966). *Innovation and Economic Growth*. Cambridge (MA): Harvard University Press.

Solow, R.M. (1956). "A Contribution to the Theory of Economic Growth," *Quarterly Journal of Economics*, 70, 65–94.

Trajtenberg, M. (1990). "Patents as Indicators of Innovation," *Economic Analysis of Product Innovation*. Cambridge (MA): Harvard University Press.

Trajtenberg, M. (2002). "R&D Policy in Israel: A Review and Reassessment," *Innovation Policy and the Economy*, eds. A. Jaffe, J. Lerner, and S. Stern, MIT Press, forthcoming.

Notes

i For a complete exposition of the framework, see J Furman et al, "The Determinants of National Innovative Capacity," *Research Policy*, forthcoming, as well as M E Porter et al (1999), *The New Challenge to America's Prosperity: Findings from the Innovation Index*. Briefly, this framework synthesizes and extends three areas of prior theory: ideas-driven endogenous growth (Romer 1990), cluster-based national industrial competitive advantage (Porter 1990), and national innovation systems (Nelson 1993).

ii For a more complete exposition of the diamond framework and its role in understanding the origins of national competitive advantage, see Porter (1990; 1998).

iii For a more thorough discussion of the use of patenting and international patenting data (and alternatives) in studies of the causes and consequences of innovation, see J Furman et al, "The Determinants of National Innovative Capacity," *Research Policy*, forthcoming. Trajtenberg (1990) provides a thorough discussion of the role of patents in understanding innovative activity, stretching back to their use by Schmookler (1966) and noting their ever-increasing use by scholars in recent years (eg, Griliches 1984; 1990; 1994). The use of international patents also has precedent in prior work comparing international inventive activity (see Dosi et al 1990; Eaton and Kortum 1996).

iv This specification is simply the "ideas" production function, as developed in endogenous growth theory (Romer 1990). See Porter and Stern (2000) for a full derivation of our empirical formulation.

v We employ the natural logarithm (or a function of the logarithm) of all of these variables, to smooth out the variation in country size and also to provide for easily interpretable coefficient estimates. Science and engineering resources are drawn from several data sources, as summarized in *World Development Indicators*. Specifically, data for OECD countries are drawn from the OECD Main Science and Technology Indicators, Latin American data are drawn from the RICYT, and the Asian data are drawn primarily from the science and technology statistics from individual countries. We were unable to establish a reasonable baseline measure of resources devoted to innovation for four countries, and so we exclude these countries from the regression analysis (though we do include them as available in the rankings).

vi It would also have been possible to control for differences across countries in their overall level of prosperity by including GDP per capita as a variable in this baseline specification. Though we have used this formulation in our related work (see Furman et al 2001 for more details), our focus here is on *explaining* the drivers of prosperity, and so we focus our analysis on measures more closely related to the microeconomic foundations of competitiveness in our analysis.

vii It is important to note that the close relationship between each of the 24 measures and international patenting is not a statistical artifact. We explored a wider set of Survey measures (40 in all) with some conceivable relationship with innovation. Those variables most distant from the national innovative capacity framework (such as the overall quality of government) were not significantly related to the level of international patenting.

viii We also experimented with a measure of extent of collaboration between the private sector and leading research institutions. The quality of scientific research institutions measure was marginally more significant and highly correlated with the collaboration measure, so we included it in the subindex.

ix These findings are consistent with our in-depth study of Japan reported in Porter et al, *Can Japan Compete?*, MacMillan Press, 2000.

Appendix A: Subindex regressions

Dependent Variable = Log of US Patents, 1999–2000	Baseline			Innovation Policy Variables			Cluster Variables			Linkages Variables		
Independent Variables	Coef.	t-stat	Adj. R^2	Coef.	t-stat	Adj. R^2	Coef.	t-stat	Adj. R^2	Coef.	t-stat	Adj. R^2
Baseline Model												
			0.824									
Log of Patent Stock Metric (patents issued between 1985 and 1994)	3.141	7.070										
Log of Population in 2000	0.231	1.810										
Log of Proportion of Full-time Employed Scientists and Engineers	0.507	2.490										
Controlling for the Baseline Model												
Intellectual Property Protection				0.816	4.220	0.863						
Quality of Math and Science Education				0.114	0.550	0.822						
Attractiveness of National Environment for Retaining Scientists and Engineers				0.776	4.000	0.859						
Company Spending on R&D				1.263	6.860	0.901						
Government Subsidies for R&D				0.669	3.000	0.845						
Government R&D Tax Credits				0.660	3.590	0.853						
Government Procurement of Advanced Technology Products				0.916	2.730	0.841						
Presence of Demanding Regulatory Standards				1.065	4.210	0.863						
Effectiveness of Anti-Trust Policy				0.746	3.150	0.847						
Stringency of Environmental Regulations				0.882	4.220	0.863						
Buyer Sophistication							0.959	3.950	0.859			
Local Supplier Quality							1.144	4.530	0.867			
Consumer Adoption of Latest Products							0.897	3.370	0.850			
State of Cluster Development							0.978	4.390	0.865			
Local Availability of Specialized Research and Traning Services							1.205	4.350	0.865			
Extent of Product and Process Collaboration							1.514	4.960	0.874			
Manufacturing of Information Technology Hardware							0.751	4.950	0.874			
Uniqueness of Product Designs							1.063	4.240	0.863			
Production Process Sophistication							1.229	6.020	0.889			
Inventory Cost Reductions Due to Internet							0.820	3.300	0.849			
Absorption of New Technology										1.246	4.270	0.863
Quality of Scientific Research Institutions										1.107	3.860	0.857
University/Industry Research Collaboration										0.894	3.520	0.852
Venture Capital Availability										0.746	3.830	0.857

Appendix B: Subindex regression models

INNOVATION POLICY SUBINDEX

Regression Statistics

Adj. R^2	0.8841
Standard Error	1.0396
Observations	64

	Coef.	Std. Error	t-stat	P-value
Intercept	−11.6892	2.1325	−5.4815	0.0000
Log (Patent Stock Metric)	1.7808	0.4512	3.9465	0.0002
Log (S&E Proportion)	0.3085	0.1705	1.8099	0.0756
Log (Population)	0.4434	0.1219	3.6388	0.0006
Intellectual Property Protection	0.4707	0.2101	2.2402	0.0290
Attractiveness of Natl. Env. for Retaining S&E	0.4204	0.2070	2.0309	0.0469
Government R&D Tax Credits	0.4600	0.1703	2.7003	0.0091

CLUSTER INNOVATION ENVIRONMENT SUBINDEX

Regression Statistics

Adj. R^2	0.8891
Standard Error	1.0169
Observations	64

	Coef.	Std. Error	t-stat	P-value
Intercept	−12.1029	2.2140	−5.4665	0.0000
Log (Patent Stock Metric)	1.8455	0.4408	4.1866	0.0001
Log (S&E Proportion)	0.3517	0.1190	2.9547	0.0045
Log (Population)	0.1162	0.1786	0.6503	0.5181
Buyer Sophistication	0.4582	0.2495	1.8364	0.0715
State of Cluster Development	0.5519	0.2361	2.3373	0.0230
Local Avail. of Spec. Research and Training Services	0.8034	0.2713	2.9616	0.0045

LINKAGES SUBINDEX

Regression Statistics

Adj. R^2	0.8618
Standard Error	1.1351
Observations	64

	Coef.	Std. Error	t-stat	P-value
Intercept	−10.6576	2.2179	−4.8054	0.0000
Log (Patent Stock Metric)	1.9583	0.4862	4.0276	0.0002
Log (S&E Proportion)	0.4063	0.1213	3.3500	0.0014
Log (Population)	0.2854	0.1922	1.4850	0.1430
Quality of Scientific Research Institutions	0.6728	0.3790	1.7753	0.0811
Venture Capital Availability	0.4407	0.2572	1.7135	0.0920

Economic Creativity: An Update

ANDREW M. WARNER, Center for International Development at Harvard University

This chapter provides an update to the economic creativity index, which attempts to gauge economies' involvement in new technologies, combining pure innovation with transfers of technology and startups. This index was first introduced in last year's *Report*. It formed part of last year's growth competitiveness rankings (see *The Global Competitiveness Report 2000*, p 28) and obtained some additional publicity through the international media (see, for example, *The Economist*, September 23rd, 2000). This year, many of the ideas in the economic creativity index are included in what is now called the *technology index*. However, whenever there are slight changes in methodology, there is always an interest is seeing how the rankings would compare had there been no such change. Therefore this chapter provides the reader with a comparison of this year's and last year's economic creativity index, using the exact same methodology. The index is reported in Table 1. What follows is a brief review of the ideas behind the index.

The index gives credit to economies for being technologically sophisticated and innovative, but recognizes that innovation alone is not always sufficient for rapid growth. The experience of Japan and Germany during the past decade, during which both experienced relatively poor growth despite being international technological leaders in several fields, makes it difficult to argue that revving the innovation engine is enough. It is also true that even for larger samples of countries, innovation indicators sometimes do not correlate strongly with rates of economic growth, even after a number of controls are introduced for the level of development and macroeconomic conditions.

These facts may seem at odds with long-standing beliefs that technology is fundamental to economic success and competitiveness. But recent experience and statistical evidence indicate instead that a focus on primary innovation is too narrow. There are generally two additional considerations that need to be brought together to get a complete picture of what it takes to mold technological prowess into economic success.

The first consideration is to recognize that there are a number of ways in which countries benefit economically from new technologies apart from inventing them. There is considerable scope for importing new technologies through imitation, direct foreign investment, or licensing arrangements. Furthermore, the economic benefit of new technologies can be enhanced by adapting and improving the new technologies for local conditions. Therefore we need to measure not only primary innovation but also this process of technology transfer. Countries such as Singapore, Korea, and Ireland have been more successful than others at such transfers and it shows in their growth rates.

To take this into account, the second part of the economic creativity index is a technology transfer index. But the technology transfer index is incorporated into the economic creativity index in a somewhat unusual manner. Countries are given credit either for being highly innovative or for being good at transfers, not both. The idea here is to recognize that, for practical purposes, innovation and transfer can substitute for each other since they are both alternative means of acquiring new technologies. If a country excels at one, it is not so crucial to do the other well. In practical terms, what the EC index does is first to standardize both innovation and technology transfer indexes on a comparable scale, and then to give countries credit for the score of whichever index is higher. A country that ranks higher on innovation than technology transfer will be credited with the score of the innovation index, not the technology transfer index.

What this procedure excludes is the possibility—and it is a debatable point—that innovation and transfer complement each other. Wouldn't Korea's excellence at inward transfers of technology be enhanced if it developed its own homegrown innovative capacity too? Wouldn't the new industries in an innovative country benefit from actively importing related technologies? The answer to both questions is yes, in theory. But the problem is that the data do not offer any proof. We have not found any positive evidence that we can account for recent international growth patterns any better by adopting this complements approach rather than the either/or approach mentioned above.

In this year's *Report*, the technology index does something similar to this aspect of the economic creativity index by dividing the world into core and non-core countries, based on patent data. The underlying idea continues to be to separate innovators from transfer countries, to allow for the fact that countries tend to specialize in one of these two aspects of incorporating technology.

The second consideration that is important in translating new technologies into economic success is to recognize what is needed to complement technological prowess. The process of enhancing and adapting the new technologies for local conditions may itself be enhanced by economic policies. There are a number of possibilities. A sophisticated educational base is needed to absorb and upgrade primary innovations and foreign technologies effectively. Flexible labor markets and management practices may be needed to alter work norms to adapt to new technologies and to mobilize labor to new industries and sectors. Low barriers to entrepreneurship and startup ventures, as well as liberal bankruptcy rules, may be needed to facilitate experimentation with new techniques in commercial settings away from the rules and regulations of large established firms.

Table 1: Economic Creativity Index

Current Ranking	Country	This Year	Last Year	Change
1	Finland	1	2	1
2	United States	2	1	-1
3	Singapore	3	3	0
4	Taiwan	4	16	12
5	Sweden	5	4	-1
6	Netherlands	6	7	1
7	Israel	7	5	-2
8	Switzerland	8	11	3
9	Hong Kong SAR	9	10	1
10	United Kingdom	10	8	-2
11	Germany	11	13	2
12	Canada	12	14	2
13	Iceland	13	9	-4
14	Belgium	14	17	3
15	Denmark	15	12	-3
16	Norway	16	22	6
17	France	17	18	1
18	Malaysia	18	23	5
19	Australia	19	15	-4
20	Ireland	20	6	-14
21	Hungary	21	20	-1
22	Japan	22	19	-3
23	Austria	23	27	4
24	Poland	24	24	0
25	New Zealand	25	21	-4
26	Chile	26	32	6
27	Egypt	27	33	6
28	Brazil	28	30	2
29	Estonia	—	—	—
30	India	29	37	8
31	Portugal	30	31	1
32	Thailand	31	39	8
33	Italy	32	38	6
34	Spain	33	29	-4
35	South Africa	34	25	-9
36	Korea	35	26	-9
37	Trinidad and Tobago	—	—	—
38	Philippines	36	35	-1
39	Sri Lanka	—	—	—
40	Czech Republic	37	40	3
41	Slovenia	—	—	—
42	Argentina	38	44	6
43	Jordan	39	46	7
44	Venezuela	40	53	13
45	China	41	47	6
46	Turkey	42	28	-14
47	Romania	—	—	—
48	Vietnam	43	49	6
49	Slovak Republic	44	41	-3
50	Mexico	45	34	-11
51	Panama	46	48	2
52	Mauritius	47	43	-4
53	Costa Rica	—	—	—
54	Jamaica	—	—	—
55	Indonesia	48	42	-6
56	Nigeria	—	—	—
57	Latvia	—	—	—
58	Greece	49	36	-13
59	Uruguay	—	—	—
60	El Salvador	50	52	2
61	Lithuania	—	—	—
62	Zimbabwe	51	45	-6
63	Russia	52	51	-1
64	Colombia	53	55	2
65	Peru	54	50	-4
66	Ukraine	55	54	-1
67	Paraguay	—	—	—
68	Guatemala	—	—	—
69	Honduras	—	—	—
70	Nicaragua	—	—	—
71	Kazakhstan	—	—	—
72	Bulgaria	56	56	0
73	Bangladesh	—	—	—
74	Ecuador	57	57	0
75	Bolivia	58	58	0

121

The testing we have done in the background for this *Report* suggests that startups do a better job at distinguishing economies that are successful at benefiting from technologies than other kinds of businesses. Hence for the economic creativity index we calculate a startup index and introduce it into the index in such a way that it gives credit to economies that, in addition to being either highly innovative or technology importers, also have good conditions for startups.

In the EC ranking reported in Table 1, Finland has taken the lead over the United States, switching places from number 2 to number 1. Finland ranks first in startups and second in innovation. Singapore is third, as it was last year. Singapore tops the technology transfer rankings and combines this with a relatively high ranking on startups (number 11). Other countries that are ranked as world leaders in technology transfer are Malaysia, Hungary, and the special administrative republic of Hong Kong.

The big mover since last year is Taiwan, which increased by 12 positions in the rankings. Taiwan owes its position to high rating on startups, at number 3, along with relatively high ratings on innovation, at number 8, and technology transfer, at number 15. The reason for the large change in Taiwan's rank is a big improvement in the startup index, of 9 places. Looking back over past *Global Competitiveness Reports*, Taiwan's ranking last year at number 12 in startups was unusually low for that country, suggesting that last year's ranking, not this year's, was unusual for Taiwan. Therefore this change appears to be a return to a more representative ranking on this score for Taiwan.

Reading further down the list of countries, it is clear that most of the rankings are similar to those of last year. However, Ireland dropped by 14 places. This reflects an interesting shift, where Ireland's rating on technology transfer declined while its rating on innovation increased slightly. Since Ireland was so highly rated on technology transfer last year, this decline on technology transfer hurt its ranking. This may, however, represent a beneficial switch for the future of the Irish economy if its recent growth and the accompanying high wages are making Ireland uncompetitive as a technology transfer country.

The highest newcomer into the rankings is Estonia at number 29. Estonia combines a moderate ranking on innovation and technology transfer, 31 and 32 respectively, with a somewhat higher ranking on startups at number 21. Other newcomers are Trinidad and Tobago at number 37 and Sri Lanka at number 39. Several Central American, Latin American, and Eastern European countries remain at the bottom of the rankings. These low rankings are generally driven by low scores on the technology indicators along with data that indicate that the startup environment continues to be very difficult.

CHAPTER 2.4

Sectoral Trade Performance

PETER K. CORNELIUS, World Economic Forum

FRIEDRICH VON KIRCHBACH, International Trade Centre

MONDHER MIMOUNI, International Trade Centre

JEAN-MICHEL PASTEELS, International Trade Centre

SHILPA PHADKE, International Trade Centre

Foreign trade serves as an important growth engine. Open economies are generally found to outperform less open ones (see, eg, Sachs and Warner 1995). Gains from trade can be substantial (Frankel and Romer 1999), presumably a key reason why an increasing number of countries have liberalized their trade policies. According to the IMF's May 2001 *World Economic Outlook* (2001, p 77), almost 100 countries are classified as open economies today, compared with only around 40 in the 1980s. Virtually all of these newly open economies are emerging market countries. This opening has been accompanied by a rapid increase in world exports, which have grown significantly faster than world income.

International trade—as well as foreign investment—can help improve a country's productivity by allowing it to specialize in those industries and segments of industries where its companies are more productive and to import where its companies are less productive. No nation can be competitive in everything, of course, and international advantage is often concentrated in particular segments. Although classical theory explains the success of nations in particular industries based on factor endowments, this theory has been overshadowed by the globalization of competition and the power of technology (Porter 1998, p 162). Competing successfully abroad requires competitive pressure at home, however, a process in which rivalry among locally based producers drives firms to improve constantly. High R&D intensity reveals greater opportunities for innovation (Sakakibara and Porter 2001). This applies especially to industrialized countries, whereas less developed countries may find it more appropriate to adopt new technology from abroad.

In this paper, we take a closer look at the trade performance of individual countries in specific sectors. In so doing, we use United Nations COMTRADE data in highly disaggregate format and employ a novel approach recently developed by the International Trade Centre (a joint subsidiary organ of the United Nations Conference on Trade and Development [UNCTAD] and the World Trade Organization [WTO]). This approach, referred to as the *trade performance index* (TPI), allows us to examine a country's trade performance both as a snapshot in a particular year and in terms of its evolution over a five-year period. In both cases, the approach is based on a number of different dimensions, taking into account not just export growth or net exports, but also the extent to which trade is diversified in terms of the geographical distribution and across individual products.

We make no attempt, however, to "explain" the sectoral trade performance by analyzing the relative importance of potential right-hand side variables, such as trade restrictions, exchange rates, degree of rivalry, and so on. Nor do we intend to suggest that the different trade performance rankings represent an alternative measure of competitiveness. Rather, our analysis aims to provide new insights into the competitive advantages of countries in specific sectors, complementing the *Report*'s main objective—namely, to assess the ability of individual countries to achieve sustained economic growth over the medium term.

Export sectors in which countries have competitive advantages

Although it has become popular to judge a country's competitiveness in terms of its ability to produce goods and services that meet the test of international competition (Tyson 1991), trade-related measures, such as a country's export growth or trade balance, may be highly misleading as an overall indicator of competitiveness (Krugman 1994). Indeed, few would describe the United States as uncompetitive just because its trade deficit has widened substantially in the second half of the 1990s. As a matter of fact, the US economy has outperformed the economies of virtually all other industrialized countries, having enjoyed its longest upswing since official statistics have been available.

Moreover, for the United States, as well as for other major economies, foreign trade has only a relatively small impact on real GDP growth. Rather, increases in living standards are almost entirely driven by domestic productivity growth. As a result, they are not to any significant degree in economic competition with each other. In fact, if the United States is doing well, this helps the rest of the world by providing it with larger markets and selling its goods of superior quality at lower prices. International trade is not a zero-sum game—as we have seen in the late 1990s when the world economy was flying on one engine. When productivity rises in the United States, the main result is a rise in US real wages; there is nor reason to assume that European or Japanese wages should be affected.

Although trade-based variables may thus be misleading to examine a country's overall competitiveness, foreign trade does provide useful information about the sector-specific competitive advantages. These can be captured by a series of complementary indicators. With respect to the *current* trade performance, major criteria are (1) the share of the country's export sector in world trade, (2) the sectoral trade balance (net exports) and, in order to control for the size of the economy, (3) per-capita exports. In addition, export competitiveness is related to the ability to (4) differentiate export products within a given sector and (5) diversify export markets. These five indicators are summarized in the *trade performance current index*.

From a dynamic perspective, the change in the country's sector-specific share in world exports is obviously significant. Similarly, the ability of exporters to increase their sectoral trade surplus or reduce their deficit sheds light on the evolution of competitive advantages. In addition, the degree of specialization in particularly dynamic products within a given sector is closely related to trade competitiveness. Moreover, changes in product differentiation and market diversification capture the dynamics of trade competitiveness. The *trade performance change index* synthesizes these five criteria (for details, see Box 1).

Based on these criteria, the trade performance index positions 14 broad export sectors in 184 countries on a global ladder of sector-specific trade competitiveness. The overall findings are shown in Table 1, which presents the rankings of both the current and the change index for 14 sectors of each of the 75 countries covered in the GCR. The following sections provide an overview of the current situation and discuss the evolution of the competitive advantage in a number of key trade sectors and subsectors.

Box 1. Measuring Trade Performance

General concept

The trade performance index (TPI) is based on the following general concepts:

- **Global coverage**: The TPI assesses trade performance in the global market place. Export and import performance is benchmarked against structure and trends in world trade.

- **Sectoral focus**: By definition, a country's comparative advantage differs across product sectors. Similarly, competitive advantages—even when independent of comparative advantage in the classical sense—are not evenly spread across sectors. For this reason, the TPI takes a sectoral approach. For this *Report*, merchandise trade has been classified into 14 major product sectors.[i] The trade performance of all 184 countries is calculated separately for each of these sectors, although in Table 1 we show the results only for the 75 GCR countries.

- **Distinction between the current position and changes**: The TPI distinguishes between the current trade performance and changes in performance over the most recent five-year period. This distinction is particularly important for capturing the life cycle of sector-specific trade performance of countries.

- **Values and rankings**: Rankings faciliate comparative assessment. Performance indicators are therefore presented as a ranking compared to all other countries, with 1 being the most desirable position.

Performance indicators

For the assessment of the *current position* of the country and sector under review, five criteria are taken into account:

1. **Value of net exports**
   Net exports are defined as exports less imports. A country's net exports are an interesting indicator of its position in the world market for three reasons: First, they show whether local production can meet local demand and generate, in addition, an exportable surplus or not. Second, the indicator takes into account the fact that a growing share of inputs for exports is imported and often belongs to the same product category (eg, chemicals, electronics). Third, the concept of net exports helps to eliminate re-exports.

2. **Per capita exports**
   Per capita exports is one of the most significant indicators of the degree of outward orientation of an economy and the per capita income derived from international trade. It is independent of the size of the economy.

3. **Share in world exports**
   The share in world exports is probably the single most important indicator for the overall competitive position of the export sector in the country under review. By taking an aggregated national approach, it complements per capita exports.

4. **Product diversification**
   Export product diversification within a given sector provides a measure of the complexity of the sector under review. It sheds light on the sector's capacity for product differentiation. Diversification also reduces the vulnerability to product-specific shocks in external markets. Product diversification is measured in terms of the equivalent number of products of equal value and by the spread of export markets (see also Appendix 1).

5. **Market diversification**
   Similarly, export market diversification measures the success in pursuing a truly global marketing approach. Export market diversification also diminishes the dependence on shocks in any given target market. Similar to product diversification, market diversification is measured in terms of the equivalent number of target markets and the spread of export markets.

Five additional indicators are taken into account for the assessment of *change* in trade performance:

6. Change in world market share

The change in world market share is the most obvious indicator for assessing the dynamics of sectoral export performance. It brings out to what extent countries are gaining or losing out in global markets. It is expressed as the percentage change in market share (not percentage points). In view of the importance of this indicator, it is further decomposed into four elements, which add up to the total change in world market share (see Appendix 1 on methods of calculation):

- First, the *competitiveness effect* reflects the change in world market share due to changes in competitiveness.

- Second, the *initial geographical specialization* captures the positive or negative effect of the differences in import growth of the exporting country's initial partner countries. Exporting to a large but stagnating neighboring country, for instance, tends to pull down overall export growth, even if the market share in this target market remains stable.

- Third, the *initial product specialization* may have similar positive or negative effects on the change in market share. An initial specialization in a product that turns out to be in high demand over the five-year period under consideration will increase the world market share for the exporting country's sector under review.

- Fourth, the *adaptation effect* sheds light on the ability of export (marketing) managers in the country and sector under review to anticipate and prepare for changes in international demand, whether they are emerging target markets or products. This component captures the success or failure in increasing market share in growing markets and reducing the market share in declining markets.

7. Trend in the coverage of imports by exports

This indicator assesses the ability of exporters in the sector under review to increase the sectoral trade surplus, or reduce the deficit, of exports over imports. It is calculated as the least square trend of the sector-specific export coverage of imports over the five years under review.

8. Specialization in the most dynamic products within a sector

This indicator measures the specialization on products for which world demand is rapidly growing. It helps to see whether countries focus on sunrise or sunset sectors. The indicator is calculated as the rank correlation between the share of specific products within the exporting country's sector under review, on the one hand, and the global growth trend of world imports in the sector, on the other.

9. Change in product diversification

Changes in product diversification provide a view of the evolution of the breadth of integration into the international division of labor. They are measured as average annual variations in the number of equivalent export products and the spread of export products.

10. Change in market diversification

Changes in market diversification are measured as average annual variations in the number of equivalent export markets and the spread of target markets.

Current index and change index

Based on the above indicators, the TPI provides two composite indexes: the current index and the change index.

The current index is essentially a snapshot of country- and sector-specific trade performance at a given point in time. It is calculated on the basis of the average ranking of the first five performance indicators mentioned above.

The change index examines the trade performance from a dynamic perspective. It is based on the subsequent five dynamic indicators. Each of the five factors has been given the same weight (see Appendix 1).

Data sources

The TPI is based on the world's largest database of trade statistics—COMTRADE of the United Nations Statistics Division. The data are derived from some 100 reporting countries and cover over 90 percent of world trade. Calculations are made at the 5-digit level of the SITC—ie, for about 3,500 products—and aggregated to the 14 sectors distinguished in this chapter.

Thanks to the good coverage of COMTRADE, exports and imports of nonreporting countries are estimated on the basis of partner country data (mirror approach). This allows an extension of the coverage to 184 countries.

The data for the current index refer to 1999; the data for the change index cover the years 1995 to 1999.

Limitations of the trade performance index

The TPI's strength and limitation is that it is based entirely on quantitative data and does not capture any qualitative aspects of trade competitiveness. It also excludes services simply because comparable data on trade in services are not available. Moreover, the quality of the TPI hinges on the quality of the trade data for the country concerned. For instance, the mirror statistics for nonreporting countries do not capture trade with other nonreporting countries.

Table 1: Trade performance index

Current Index (Cu.I.) and Change Index (Ch.I.) on export competitiveness of 75 countries in 14 sectors (position 1 being the most competitive)

Sector	Transport equipment		Chemicals		Non-electronic machinery		IT & consumer electronics		Electronic components		Minerals		Basic manufactures		Miscellaneous manufactures		Fresh food		Processed food		Wood products		Clothing		Textiles		Leather products	
No. of exp countries	87		123		93		68		87		144		124		122		168		141		115		118		112		82	
World exp 1999 US$ bn	679		553		544		528		482		482		394		374		233		232		195		175		142		60	
Index	Cu.I.	Ch.I.	Cu.I.	Ch.I.	Cu.I.	Ch.I.	Cu.I.	Ch.I.	Cu.I.	Ch.I.	Cu.I.	Ch.I.	Cu.I.	Ch.I.	Cu.I.	Ch.I.	Cu.I.	Ch.I.	Cu.I.	Ch.I.	Cu.I.	Ch.I.	Cu.I.	Ch.I.	Cu.I.	Ch.I.	Cu.I.	Ch.I.
ARGENTINA	51	65	44	48	46	11	—	—	58	56	17	7	42	74	53	49	7	144	6	83	55	78	—	—	74	78	27	79
AUSTRALIA	33	52	34	63	21	75	30	59	29	77	1	54	14	92	26	25	3	121	5	18	47	25	29	66	32	36	39	27
AUSTRIA	20	28	24	33	11	53	20	22	14	28	54	91	8	68	23	77	46	49	29	74	3	39	25	20	16	91	29	34
BANGLADESH	—	—	123	123	—	—	9	50	10	51	—	—	118	104	94	22	118	129	—	—	—	—	27	19	58	88	45	42
BELGIUM-LUXEMBOURG	7	68	3	49	12	43	45	2	39	86	13	103	5	82	9	94	25	26	4	63	26	33	93	41	4	84	4	8
BOLIVIA	66	10	112	74	65	15	—	—	—	—	69	133	103	109	92	10	77	37	76	72	80	35	—	—	95	26	67	46
BRAZIL	18	37	40	92	41	82	55	51	43	86	57	52	23	108	48	45	14	43	13	48	17	52	15	27	35	81	19	23
BULGARIA	56	27	37	109	36	85	51	2	48	48	78	30	31	110	43	16	42	96	41	104	38	19	57	35	54	108	36	24
CANADA	11	25	33	58	31	47	29	26	47	13	8	90	22	41	36	41	9	99	30	45	10	87	57	35	40	17	—	—
CHILE	58	51	56	54	72	67	8	58	—	—	41	135	25	94	64	102	17	52	16	125	15	95	2	59	65	62	7	18
CHINA	9	4	29	50	39	45	58	—	23	33	52	32	17	43	15	88	20	48	27	24	46	74	59	102	12	51	22	60
COLOMBIA	60	20	62	60	55	58	32	23	63	41	42	94	55	2	54	55	34	112	57	14	59	11	61	61	48	79	43	29
COSTA RICA	—	—	55	43	64	30	31	30	52	25	118	70	62	19	55	11	30	72	23	75	53	59	26	97	70	8	21	58
CZECH REPUBLIC	10	32	27	82	15	48	23	40	25	31	49	117	15	60	28	73	57	69	39	79	29	50	19	22	18	59	30	12
DENMARK	8	34	10	20	6	73	17	—	15	40	20	85	28	7	5	63	4	94	3	102	29	40	44	23	21	13	35	3
DOMINICAN REPUBLIC	80	64	99	45	—	—	—	—	51	23	—	—	95	117	56	97	97	44	95	107	—	—	90	18	102	19	—	—
ECUADOR	80	64	87	21	58	—	37	12	—	—	68	95	84	24	84	15	28	73	33	12	58	42	73	85	81	50	60	71
EGYPT	—	—	71	59	—	—	—	—	72	8	66	113	68	95	73	58	96	139	87	68	—	—	79	30	38	53	66	40
EL SALVADOR	—	—	73	6	72	—	11	5	53	37	119	8	76	3	68	2	90	161	77	16	72	21	36	26	57	60	26	6
ESTONIA	44	44	39	24	29	32	37	—	18	16	44	84	40	23	39	40	71	123	44	40	16	6	48	111	29	2	—	—
FINLAND	26	83	19	23	8	60	7	31	2	66	47	78	6	79	8	101	58	67	35	92	2	101	11	86	34	66	—	—
FRANCE	1	77	6	64	5	65	11	43	1	73	24	51	16	54	14	89	2	103	2	98	13	65	16	101	5	98	9	36
GERMANY	2	75	1	73	1	86	13	—	31	43	16	119	1	58	1	23	21	111	17	88	8	67	28	77	21	21	12	63
GREECE	38	55	28	16	30	24	38	8	80	19	26	79	34	91	32	86	31	89	36	122	41	68	78	74	39	33	31	43
GUATEMALA	—	—	64	11	—	—	42	66	—	—	132	65	73	17	79	78	39	7	47	55	75	38	98	58	64	80	61	17
HONDURAS	—	—	100	52	59	83	18	3	38	79	124	4	112	77	99	118	72	141	90	3	76	47	32	57	103	92	33	—
HONG KONG SAR	36	73	82	108	44	35	48	4	24	44	87	61	64	86	30	118	—	—	60	82	70	115	—	38	41	101	—	10
HUNGARY	52	82	25	34	51	72	26	60	27	15	80	86	41	33	31	98	12	87	11	86	32	—	17	82	33	40	62	—
ICELAND	23	79	92	39	42	80	3	4	46	83	15	33	59	80	46	109	37	133	25	96	6	13	7	91	69	85	—	—
INDIA	35	5	41	71	61	6	21	9	40	12	35	83	56	116	25	75	24	56	40	139	44	46	55	44	20	102	13	38
INDONESIA	43	38	31	27	20	23	27	17	—	15	31	115	45	1	12	27	22	29	26	58	21	30	18	53	11	42	—	—
IRELAND	63	50	13	22	24	28	22	4	15	17	29	118	48	28	24	4	10	105	9	47	35	90	1	96	31	72	—	—
ISRAEL	12	67	12	41	2	84	4	9	3	65	55	82	49	36	6	117	36	81	45	111	—	46	55	44	37	46	—	—
ITALY	—	—	17	76	7	93	1	68	4	76	51	14	3	64	4	105	33	41	7	78	21	30	60	53	1	93	1	65
JAMAICA	96	47	96	47	—	—	—	—	3	14	76	104	101	113	72	1	85	57	66	31	35	90	60	46	13	95	—	—
JAPAN	7	84	7	88	3	7	1	—	—	—	—	—	4	90	—	—	—	—	50	51	106	55	87	48	92	48	—	—
JORDAN	5	—	52	9	66	7	54	20	—	—	—	—	97	84	72	—	135	23	—	—	—	—	—	—	—	—	—	—

Sector	Transport equipment		Chemicals		Non-electronic machinery		IT & consumer electronics		Electronic components		Minerals		Basic manufactures		Miscellaneous manufactures		Fresh food		Processed food		Wood products		Clothing		Textiles		Leather products	
KOREA	4	19	11	62	16	69	2	41	8	63	56	33	7	8	16	61	68	92	55	41	40	14	4	67	3	20	3	73
LATVIA	46	39	79	85	47	20	43	42	54	27	93	35	67	34	51	48	106	119	63	50	34	34	47	15	28	27	49	69
LITHUANIA	32	3	50	97	32	40	46	56	48	64	59	17	53	10	44	69	53	62	42	62	33	48	23	51	27	35	23	22
MALAYSIA	27	11	23	37	25	27	6	44	21	7	9	25	32	4	11	44	41	136	12	90	4	41	31	65	14	6	—	—
MAURITIUS	—	—	85	38	63	70	—	—	—	—	112	72	114	25	52	72	139	137	62	129	—	—	24	50	72	28	37	25
MEXICO	25	24	45	67	48	8	16	11	34	10	38	97	51	46	42	21	62	63	61	56	50	17	33	13	47	58	14	21
NETHERLANDS	16	57	2	99	10	31	14	53	11	72	18	112	26	47	2	31	1	68	1	110	24	92	22	55	6	41	16	49
NEW ZEALAND	49	13	51	42	26	14	39	24	35	30	84	66	46	39	41	18	5	154	8	49	19	85	71	73	66	44	75	67
NICARAGUA	—	—	—	—	—	—	—	—	—	—	122	46	—	—	107	87	47	61	93	36	92	60	—	—	106	106	75	67
NIGERIA	—	—	—	—	—	—	—	—	—	—	28	73	—	—	—	—	—	—	—	—	—	—	—	—	—	—	76	70
NORWAY	19	70	32	30	14	38	19	38	20	29	5	50	12	61	27	57	11	50	19	105	31	93	88	81	30	31	46	16
PANAMA	—	—	89	10	—	—	—	—	—	—	115	37	110	9	120	110	54	54	88	38	81	8	103	9	—	—	—	—
PARAGUAY	—	—	107	115	—	—	—	—	—	—	—	—	—	—	—	—	61	145	85	17	68	75	72	24	93	65	46	16
PERU	—	—	63	15	60	19	27	18	45	5	30	136	47	71	86	14	48	53	34	112	91	31	41	88	50	89	38	51
PHILIPPINES	50	17	65	8	27	64	47	7	36	21	82	41	70	38	59	96	82	71	78	99	69	76	21	98	63	38	34	33
POLAND	29	29	30	75	33	25	40	46	28	57	53	125	36	49	38	91	44	9	24	33	20	20	3	80	42	10	11	52
PORTUGAL	37	61	42	55	35	44	60	14	59	47	70	129	39	50	33	68	65	91	43	120	7	69	12	56	23	47	18	20
ROMANIA	31	46	48	104	34	46	35	17	30	58	77	92	24	51	57	92	59	126	82	64	28	9	53	21	46	90	47	32
RUSSIAN FEDERATION	15	36	15	53	37	57	34	54	33	20	4	116	11	29	22	32	75	95	75	95	18	86	66	84	45	49	15	39
SOUTH AFRICA*	22	69	21	36	18	74	4	67	13	52	3	47	13	105	13	42	13	34	18	60	12	28	39	71	43	14	28	72
SINGAPORE	13	72	4	2	23	54	36	1	41	26	10	34	30	59	19	100	19	84	28	115	22	63	30	61	25	57	5	56
SLOVAK REPUBLIC	28	31	36	91	22	39	33	16	12	46	81	24	19	62	35	82	78	39	52	84	11	29	38	105	36	70	41	7
SLOVENIA	39	60	20	35	19	79	24	33	17	49	98	29	30	65	18	54	89	101	38	27	5	51	37	63	24	74	28	72
SPAIN	6	26	18	44	77	22	63	63	60	49	25	38	10	89	21	56	8	25	15	61	27	22	9	33	17	56	5	56
SRI LANKA	—	—	77	32	3	61	5	27	7	45	95	98	92	83	45	60	29	18	97	114	86	105	46	39	62	29	41	7
SWEDEN	3	74	14	14	4	87	25	55	5	71	23	44	2	70	10	76	38	30	31	65	1	99	43	93	22	22	53	44
SWITZERLAND	24	71	9	65	17	90	12	47	6	32	32	69	27	20	3	112	67	114	21	87	30	57	14	78	9	96	17	64
TAIWAN	17	62	22	101	28	36	23	39	22	4	63	26	9	42	7	107	18	85	53	59	36	98	6	114	7	39	2	35
THAILAND	34	14	26	4	62	33	51	13	37	42	39	12	38	15	20	120	122	36	10	54	14	5	82	104	10	76	8	53
TRINIDAD AND TOBAGO	65	12	53	87	40	18	52	29	61	78	19	59	57	81	50	38	16	8	37	23	51	72	8	92	—	—	24	11
TURKEY	30	33	35	72	49	77	10	48	43	53	61	13	20	32	49	65	51	83	14	53	39	12	56	17	8	37	53	44
UKRAINE	45	30	38	111	9	71	—	—	61	68	43	31	21	100	74	59	51	83	54	103	56	23	20	110	78	63	17	64
UNITED KINGDOM	21	66	8	77	83	51	15	52	16	81	2	71	18	69	13	95	15	46	20	73	23	89	68	107	19	83	25	74
URUGUAY	57	23	74	26	13	59	—	—	—	18	125	89	85	75	85	81	6	138	32	37	74	49	45	79	59	105	59	74
USA	14	22	5	78	—	—	50	6	19	68	22	87	35	76	17	70	109	28	22	81	25	107	91	116	26	64	—	—
VENEZUELA	69	85	54	46	69	2	—	—	64	36	21	53	37	73	—	—	35	28	86	89	71	56	35	54	—	—	6	4
VIETNAM	73	35	91	29	89	49	50	6	64	36	74	58	71	5	40	9	35	38	58	4	67	24	35	54	60	1	6	4
ZIMBABWE	—	—	90	31	—	—	—	—	—	—	64	19	61	93	95	116	26	65	84	109	82	53	91	116	84	104	51	26

Notes: Colour codes indicate 5 quintiles in rankings: most competitive > > > > least competitive

*South African Customs Union

For full explanatory notes see: http://www.intracen.org/mas

Source: International Trade Centre UNCTAD/WTO

Transport and equipment

International trade in the transport and equipment sector is estimated at around US$ 850 billion in 1999 or about 15 percent of world trade. The bulk of foreign trade in this sector concerns passenger cars and automotive components and accessories, accounting for about 75 percent of total trade in this sector. Other broad categories include trucks, motorcycles, railway vehicles, ships, and aircraft and parts.

As can be seen from Table 2, foreign trade in automotive components and accessories is dominated by the industrialized countries, with the G-7 countries alone holding a combined world market share of around two-thirds. However, there exist a number of emerging market economies that have enjoyed rapid export growth, particularly Mexico, China, and the Czech Republic. Korea, Taiwan, and Brazil are also important exporters of automobiles and components thereof, although their market share has stagnated or even shrunk in recent years.

Possessing a world market share of more than 5 percent, Mexico represents the seventh largest car exporter in value terms, reflecting its strategic role in the NAFTA area. The country has become home to direct investment not only from all the major companies in the United States, but also from Japan, Korea, and the EU. As a result, Mexico's car production rose from 250,000 units in 1990 (of which 42 percent were exported) to 675,000 units in 1999 (of which 68 percent were exported). This trend appears as if it will continue, with expected investments in Mexican operations on the rise.

Rising shares in world trade in the automotive industry are also recorded for China and the Czech Republic, with the former becoming increasingly competitive in exporting automotive components such as wheels and brake systems. However, China is a minor exporter of cars (exports were worth US$ 14 million in 1999) and the Chinese automotive industry remains largely oriented toward producing cars for the domestic market. In 2000, 1.8 million vehicles were produced in China (largely by state-owned companies), of which only one third were passenger cars.

The rapid export growth in the Czech Republic reflects, to a large extent, huge FDI inflows, primarily from Germany, which have brought about rapid expansion, product innovation, modernization, and improvements in business strategies, distribution network access, and employment. After Volkswagen purchased the Czech car manufacturer Skoda, the share of exports in Skoda's sales went up from 34 percent in 1990 to 80 percent in 1999. In 1998, Skoda's contribution to Czech total exports was 10 percent accounting for 76 percent of the country's total auto exports. However, FDI flows to eastern Europe has not been confined to the Czech Republic. Poland, for example, has enjoyed considerable investment from Fiat, GM, and Daewoo, and is itself quickly becoming a major car and component production center. Hungary's export success stems directly from auto manufacturing, which has benefited greatly from FDI flows from a number of foreign investors, including Suzuki, Opel-General Motors, Ford, and Audi-Volkswagen. Before independence, Hungary's domestic car industry was limited to the production of buses (Ikarus) and trucks (Raba).

The increased integration of emerging-market producers into the global production process of cars and car components is reflected in the TPI change index, which, as explained above, is a comprehensive index of measuring improvements or deteriorations in a country's overall trade performance in a particular country. Whereas traditional producers, such as Germany, France, and Japan, retain the top three ranks in terms of their *current* performance, they are clearly outdone by the Czech Republic and China in terms of performance *change*. To a somewhat lesser extent, this also applies to Mexico, whose market share, however, is already more than twice the combined share of the Czech Republic and China.

Table 2: Automotive components and accessories

Country	Share in world exports 1999	TPI Current Index	Change in world export share	TPI Change Index
USA	18.70%	26	0%	12
Germany	13.60%	1	3%	24
Japan	10.70%	3	−8%	40
France	8.40%	2	−1%	36
Canada	5.60%	25	−1%	14
United Kingdom	5.20%	14	3%	5
Mexico	5.20%	30	11%	6
Italy	4.70%	6	2%	35
Spain	4.10%	16	5%	17
Belgium–Luxembourg	2.90%	5	−3%	30
Sweden	2.20%	4	3%	9
Korea	1.70%	11	1%	18
Austria	1.70%	13	3%	15
Netherlands	1.50%	8	−4%	39
Taiwan	1.40%	10	−2%	29
Brazil	1.30%	20	−2%	38
China	1.20%	15	14%	3
Czech Republic	1.20%	9	55%	2
Portugal	1.01%	22	3%	8
Hungary	0.79%	19	29%	25

Notes: World trade in the sector is estimated at US$ 235 billion in 1999, with 40 exporting countries. Rankings range from 1 (strong performance) to 40 (poor performance).

Source: ITC

Table 3: Industrial machinery and equipment

Country	Share in world exports 1999	TPI Current Index	Change in world export share	TPI Change Index
Germany	19.50%	1	0%	36
USA	15.60%	12	2%	22
Japan	11.90%	13	−5%	39
Italy	8.90%	4	2%	35
France	6.60%	2	3%	20
United Kingdom	5.80%	3	2%	29
Switzerland	3.20%	5	−2%	34
Belgium–Luxembourg	2.70%	9	−2%	32
Canada	2.60%	19	2%	9
Netherlands	2.20%	7	0%	6
Sweden	2.10%	6	−4%	18
Austria	1.95%	10	0%	13
Taiwan	1.68%	20	−6%	38
Korea	1.57%	17	2%	27
Spain	1.55%	14	4%	31
Singapore	1.45%	15	−3%	21
Denmark	1.43%	11	−1%	26
Finland	1.20%	8	3%	14
Mexico	1.11%	35	11%	2
China	1.11%	22	11%	8

Notes: World trade in the sector is estimated at US$ 310 billion in 1999, with 39 exporting countries. Rankings range from 1 (strong performance) to 39 (poor performance).

Source: ITC

Industrial machinery

The non-electrical machinery and machine tool sector is comprised of a wide range of products including engines and turbines, agricultural machinery, machinery for the manufacturing industry (textiles, processed food, steel, wood, etc), and construction and civil engineering equipment. Together, international trade in these goods represents around 12 percent of total world trade in manufactures. Industrialized countries account for more than 85 percent of world trade in industrial machinery, which is to a considerable degree explained by the sector's high technological intensity and well-developed clusters comprising engineering industries as providers of direct inputs for machine-tool manufacture. A number of European countries hold particularly strong positions in the TPI current index, especially Germany, France, and the United Kingdom (Table 3). The combined share of these three countries in these product categories amounted to almost one-third of world exports.

Nevertheless, some newly industrialized countries—in particular Korea, Singapore, and Taiwan—are among the top 20 exporters in this area, thanks to their success especially in the fields of agricultural, textile, food processing, and metalworking machinery. Although Mexico's and China's shares in global trade in industrial machinery still remains in the 1-percent range, both countries have been able to penetrate new markets and enjoy rapid increases in their shares. At the same time, they have become more diversified, both in terms of markets and products, which is reflected in their high rankings in the TPI change index. As far as Mexico is concerned, NAFTA has no doubt played an important role: A substantial percentage of exports are in fact re-exports of products assembled in the *maquiladora* sector (assembly plants for re-exports), located on the Mexican-US border.

Computers, consumer electronics, and telecommunication equipment

Encompassing computers (including large components such as storage and input-output devices), typewriters, calculators, photocopiers, radio, television receiver sets, cameras, video recorders, and telecommunication equipment (including cellular phones, switching and transmission equipment), this sector represented more than 10 percent of total world trade in 2000.[ii] With the exception of a few branches of this sector (such as television and radios), where world trade has been fairly stable in value terms, most product categories have enjoyed spectacular growth. The expansion of world trade in telecommunication equipment has been particularly fast, with the total export value having ballooned by around 50 percent between 1995 and 1999—this is compared with only a 12-percent increase for total merchandise world trade during that period. There exist a number of factors that have contributed to this increase. Among these factors is the boom in cellular phones and the development of Internet connections and wireless technology for mobile communications—facilitated by the privatization and liberalization of the telephony sector—and the reduction of trade barriers and related issues, such as mutual acceptance of technological standards.

Table 4: Telecommunication equipment

Country	Share in world exports 1999	TPI Current Index	Change in world export share	TPI Change Index
USA	14.90%	7	−2%	15
United Kingdom	11.40%	1	22%	4
Germany	8.90%	5	−2%	27
Japan	8.80%	4	−12%	32
Sweden	8.40%	2	11%	12
France	6.60%	6	13%	24
Finland	6.00%	3	33%	1
Canada	4.30%	11	1%	26
China	2.70%	26	6%	3
Taiwan	2.60%	9	0%	31
Mexico	2.59%	21	18%	7
Korea.	2.50%	19	0%	29
Israel	2.46%	12	−3%	25
Netherlands	1.90%	16	4%	19
Italy	1.85%	20	11%	13
Ireland	1.81%	10	23%	10
Belgium–Luxembourg	1.67%	8	−7%	20
Singapore	1.64%	14	−5%	30
Malaysia	1.56%	15	−4%	6
Denmark	1.18%	18	17%	11

Notes: World trade in the sector is estimated at US$ 95 billion in 1999, with 33 exporting countries. Rankings range from 1 (strong performance) to 33 (poor performance).

Source: ITC

Table 5: Image, sound equipment, and accessories

Country	Share in world exports 1999	TPI Current Index	Change in world export share	TPI Change Index
Japan	20.32%	2	−0.03%	35
USA	9.62%	12	0.01%	31
China	7.90%	9	0.10%	9
Mexico	6.66%	18	0.12%	15
Malaysia	5.56%	3	−0.04%	19
Germany	5.18%	7	−0.01%	10
United Kingdom	5.01%	10	0.02%	34
Singapore	4.98%	1	−0.08%	26
Netherlands	4.61%	4	0.01%	27
Korea	3.69%	6	−0.07%	29
Ireland	3.15%	11	7.71%	17
France	2.98%	16	3.98%	22
Belgium-Luxembourg	2.76%	5	1.26%	28
Taiwan	2.53%	8	−2.12%	24
Thailand	2.37%	15	2.77%	18
Austria	1.46%	14	1.79%	11
Spain	1.29%	23	17.13%	2
Hungary	1.27%	20	83.17%	1
Italy	1.00%	17	−1.74%	14
Indonesia	0.89%	22	−5.15%	16

Notes: World trade in the sector is estimated at US$ 130 billion in 1999, with 35 exporting countries. Rankings range from 1 (strong performance) to 35 (poor performance).

Source: ITC

132

The United States continues to maintain the largest share in world trade in telecommunication equipment, followed by the United Kingdom, Germany, and Japan (see Table 4). Their combined share amounted to almost 45 percent in 1999. With the exception of the United Kingdom, however, the top performers have been losing ground in recent years, with their TPI change indexes ranging only from 15 to 32. Finland, in the form of the company Nokia, held a share of 6 percent in terms of world exports in 1999, but was by far the best performer in terms of gaining market shares abroad. In fact, it outperformed Sweden, through Eriksson, by a wide margin— as reflected in the TPI change index—although the latter still enjoyed a considerably larger share in world exports in telecom equipment in 1999. Another overachiever is Ireland, whose share in world exports rose by almost one-quarter in the second part of the 1990s.

The rankings confirm that international companies continue to produce telecom equipment, which is extremely research-intensive, to a large extent in industrialized countries. However, there exist a number of emerging market economies where exports of these products have risen considerably as of late. This group again includes Mexico and China, which have a combined share in world exports that has remained fairly small, but which also have enjoyed rapid export growth—a growth mirrored by their TPI change rankings.

China and Mexico have already established a substantial export base in the image, sound equipment, and accessories sector, with a total export value of around 130 billion US dollars in 1999 (Table 5). Their world export shares amounted to around 8 and 6.5 percent, respectively. Mexico, benefiting from NAFTA, has become the leading exporter of TV receiver sets. However, with the geographical distribution of Mexico's exports largely concentrated on the United States, the country's ranking in the TPI change index has remained in the double digits. This double-digit ranking also applies to a number of Asian countries, namely Malaysia, Singapore and Korea, which have been very successful in exporting image and sound equipment, outperforming most industrialized countries in this area.

Apart from particular trade arrangements, such as NAFTA, an important reason for the relatively stronger performance of emerging market economies in this area— as opposed to the telephony sector—may be sought in the fact that the market is more mature and companies have been relocating their manufacturing base in the low-end products to developing countries. Japan is a case in point. It is still the leading exporter (with 20 percent of market share), but it is ranked at the bottom (among the leading trading nations) in terms of change, reflecting intense production relocations in Southeast Asia.

Chemicals, plastics, synthetic fibers, and rubber products

The chemical sector includes plastics, organics, fertilizers, coloring substances, synthetic fibers and rubber, pharmaceuticals, and cosmetics; it represented more than 10 percent of world trade in 2000. The turnover of the chemical industry worldwide was estimated at some US$ 1.5 trillion in 2000, with world trade in this sector amounting to an estimated one-third of total output. The triad (the US, the EU, and Japan) accounts for around 80 percent of global production and 70 percent of world trade (see Table 6). Other major players are the Asia-Pacific region and Switzerland (especially in pharmaceuticals).

Economies of scale are important in this sector, given the high degree of competition through product innovation requiring sophisticated research. This is particularly true in the pharmaceuticals industry, which represents around 20 percent of world trade in chemicals, and where only 30 firms account for nearly half of world sales. Research and development costs in the pharmaceuticals industry are estimated at around 10 percent of total costs.

Globalization has had a significant impact on the chemical sector in the last decade, as indicated by a considerable number of cross-border mergers and acquisitions and joint venture developments. Globalization has been particularly intense in the polymer industry, where standardized materials are increasingly required by major customers, such as manufacturers in the electronics and automotive industries, in need of identical materials in all of their remote operations.

Although industrialized countries continue to represent the major players, some Southeast Asian countries have assumed an increasingly important role in world trade in chemicals. Singapore is a case in point. The chemical industry in Singapore has grown rapidly in the last 10 years, both in terms of size and in range of products, and it now ranks 12th in export values in the chemical sector. The pharmaceuticals industry has expanded substantially in recent years due to massive inward foreign investment. Indeed, chemicals are Singapore's second biggest investment sector, surpassed only by electronics, with a 30 percent share of total investment in 2000.

One of the most dramatic developments in the chemicals sector in the 1990s concerns the collapse of market shares of the transition economies in central and eastern Europe. Russia remains the only country among the top 20 of world exporters of organic and inorganic chemicals (see Table 6). However, with its share having already declined to only 1.2 percent in 1999, Russia is ranked only 47 in the TPI change index. This reflects Russia's poor performance in many areas, such as chemical fibers, plastics articles, household chemicals, film and photo material, although there are noteworthy exceptions largely limited to tires, polyethylene, and sodium hydroxide.

Table 6: Organic and Inorganic Chemicals (*)

Country	Share in world exports 1999	TPI Current Index	Change in world export share	TPI Change Index
USA	15.10%	5	−1%	37
Germany	12.50%	1	−3%	48
Japan	7.70%	6	−1%	34
Ireland	6.80%	8	28%	6
United Kingdom	6.50%	2	−1%	45
France	6.00%	10	−1%	21
Netherlands	5.80%	3	−2%	12
Belgium–Luxembourg	5.50%	9	−2%	40
Switzerland	3.50%	4	−2%	31
Italy	3.20%	13	0%	24
China	3.20%	11	7%	9
Canada	2.20%	22	−2%	17
Korea	2.10%	19	6%	25
Singapore	1.80%	7	1%	5
Spain	1.30%	15	0%	18
Russian Federation	1.20%	24	−3%	47
Australia	1.18%	33	−2%	36
Taiwan	1.10%	26	−1%	38
India	0.98%	36	17%	22
Brazil	0.94%	29	1%	32

Notes: (*) Chemical sector in the strict sense, excluding pharmaceuticals, fertilizers, coloring substances, synthetic fibers and rubber.

World trade in the sector is estimated at US$ 215 billion in 1999, with 48 exporting countries. Rankings range from 1 (strong performance) to 48 (poor performance).

Source: ITC

Metals and other basic manufacturing

Including iron and steel products (such as flat-rolled products), base metals (aluminum, copper, zinc, etc), tools and cutlery, cement, clay and construction materials, glassware and pottery, this sector represents more than 8 percent of global trade. Within this sector, the most important goods in value terms are flat-rolled products (25 percent of world trade value of the sector), tubes, pipes, bars and other steel shapes (12 percent), aluminum (10 percent), copper (7 percent), glass and glassware (7 percent) and tools and cutlery (7 percent).

Industrialized countries still account for around 60 percent of world trade in the whole sector (see Table 7 for metal and metal products). In the steel industry, their share in world production decreased only slightly, from 50 percent to 48 percent, between 1992 and 1999. A considerably sharper fall in steel exports was recorded for the transition economies in central and eastern Europe, with their combined share having shrunk to 16 percent from 22 percent during this period. Russian exporters account for around one-third of this share, thanks not least to the country's abundant supply of energy, a key factor in the production process. By contrast, the emerging market economies outside that region enjoyed a significant increase in their share, growing to 36 percent from 28 percent. China and Korea, in particular, have become substantially more integrated in this area, a change that is mirrored in their TPI change index rankings. More recently, the steel industry has seen increased cross-border M&A

Table 7: Metal and metal products

Country	Share in world exports 1999	TPI Current Index	Change in world export share	TPI Change Index
Germany	11.00%	1	0%	38
Japan	7.80%	3	−1%	40
USA	6.40%	23	2%	14
France	6.40%	5	−1%	21
Belgium–Luxembourg	5.50%	2	−4%	52
Russian Federation	5.30%	15	0%	27
Canada	4.80%	12	0%	37
United Kingdom	4.30%	6	−2%	39
Italy	4.20%	17	0%	43
Korea	3.90%	7	6%	3
China	3.00%	24	12%	1
Netherlands	2.90%	11	−4%	44
Spain	2.20%	13	0%	42
Taiwan	2.18%	21	6%	28
Austria	2.15%	10	3%	18
Sweden	2.02%	4	−2%	36
Brazil	1.96%	26	−5%	55
Australia	1.86%	14	−2%	26
Norway	1.64%	16	1%	23
Chile	1.64%	18	2%	47

Notes: World trade in the sector is estimated at US$ 265 billion in 1999, with 56 exporting countries. Rankings range from 1 (strong performance) to 56 (poor performance).

Source: ITC

Table 8: Electronic components and equipment

Country	Share in world exports 1999	TPI Current Index	Change in world export share	TPI Change Index
USA	17.30%	8	1%	4
Japan	14.40%	2	−7%	17
Singapore	10.90%	1	2%	15
Korea	10.00%	6	1%	21
Malaysia	7.60%	5	−1%	16
Taiwan	7.10%	3	5%	6
Philippines	5.40%	9	22%	5
Germany	4.50%	10	−1%	18
France	4.20%	4	9%	11
United Kingdom	3.30%	14	−8%	24
Netherlands	3.19%	13	6%	12
Thailand	1.87%	15	0%	3
Canada	1.75%	24	1%	8
Hong Kong	1.37%	16	0%	9
Ireland	1.34%	7	20%	1
China	1.14%	19	36%	7
Mexico	1.04%	23	9%	23
Italy	0.70%	21	−5%	25
Belgium–Luxembourg	0.59%	11	−6%	27
Malta	0.56%	20	−4%	2

Notes: World trade in the sector is estimated at US$ 200 billion in 1999, with 27 exporting countries. Rankings range from 1 (strong performance) to 27 (poor performance).

Source: ITC

activity, resulting in a major re-organization of the production process. For example, the Usinor group has made important acquisitions not only in Europe (with the acquisitions of Fafer, Magona & Arvedi, Cockerill, and sales of Valdunes, RTM, Unimetal, Ascometal, Sogérail) but also worldwide, notably in Brazil and Poland.

China has also been gaining market shares in the area of basic manufacturing, notably in glassware, metallic tubes and pipes, cutlery, nails and screws, household equipment, and other manufactured base metals. Mexico has performed well, especially in areas such as ceramics (tiles, cubes, and articles for sanitary purposes), where Italy has traditionally been a world leader. Mexican firms have also performed well in the glass, cutlery, nails and screws, and metallic structures industries.

Electronic components and equipment

Electronic components and equipment have a wide range of applications, from consumer goods such as computers, mobile phones, and transport vehicles to communication equipment such as satellites. Semiconductor components include microprocessors; logic, memory, bipolar digital, analog, and discrete devices; and also include some electrical devices based on the SITC 3 system of classification. Thus defined, the export value of the electronics and electrical industry in 1999 was approximately US$ 450 billion, representing a share of around 8 percent in total world trade. Trade in electronic components and equipments totaled about US$ 200 billion in 1999 (see Table 8), of which transistors and valves constitute a substantial 43 percent.

Accounting for an export share of 17.3 percent, the United States remains the leading exporter of electronic components and equipment, followed by a number of Asian suppliers whose combined share accounts for more than half of global exports in this category. By comparison, Thailand, Hong Kong, and China are still lagging behind this group. However, Thailand has been quite successful in diversifying its exports, both geographically and in terms of products, a success that is mirrored in the country's high TPI change ranking. China has enjoyed particularly strong growth of its exports of electronic components and equipment, albeit from a still relatively low base.

A considerable part of Asia's outstanding export performance in this area reflects not only intra-industry, but also intra-firm trade. As a result, Asia has been hit particularly hard by the more recent downturn in the United States, as evidenced most dramatically in the sharp correction of "new-economy" stock prices. Notwithstanding these adverse developments, however, Asia appears set to continue to increase its export share, and according to some estimates, more than 40 percent of trade in semiconductors, excluding parts, could come from that region by the end of this decade.

Although Asia's integration has been outstanding, one of the fastest increases in world export shares is accounted for by Ireland. Indeed, although the country's absolute share in world exports of electronic components and equipment is still fairly small, it is top-ranked in terms of the TPI change index.

Textiles and clothing

Trade in textiles and clothing amounted to US$ 340 billion in 1999, or about 8 percent of global trade. Clothing makes up the bulk of this sector, that is, around 55 percent. Textile apparels make up a third of exports of clothing, while general clothing (not knitted) constitutes roughly 40 percent. Textile yarn and manmade fibers are the largest components of the textiles sector, at nearly 20 percent each.

Because it is highly labor-intensive, trade in textiles and clothing has remained subject to substantial trade barriers; indeed, with agriculture, it is the most restricted sector and remains outside the domain of the rules established by the WTO with regard to quantitative restrictions.[iii] By the end of 2004, however, the Agreement on Textiles and Clothing (ATC) is expected to be fully integrated into the WTO rules. This implies that quotas will need to be abolished, which is likely to cause important production and trade effects.

As far as exports of clothing are concerned, China accounts for the largest global share (see Table 9), with nearly 20 percent of the world market in clothing and accessories, 25 percent in household and furnishing textiles, and 15 percent in the case of sports and leisure wear. The country's accession to the WTO will probably lead to a further boost of exports in this area. Mexico's share in global trade of clothing has also grown rapidly, from a mere 0.5 percent in 1990 to 3.9 percent in 1999, which is largely thanks to the country's unrestricted access to the US and Canadian markets. Several least developed countries enjoy unrestricted market access, which is crucial with regard to the selection of production locations. Bangladesh may illustrate the importance of this factor, having enjoyed the largest increase in global export share other than Mexico. Of course, Bangladesh's low labor costs have also played an important role in this increase. Nevertheless, a number of industrialized countries, including Italy, the United States, and Germany, have been able to maintain relatively high export shares, although in all of these countries shares have actually declined in the second half of the 1990s. Consistent with this development, their TPI change rankings are at the bottom of the scale.

Table 9: Clothing and accessories

Country	Share in world exports 1999	TPI Current Index	Change in world export share	TPI Change Index
China	17.50%	2	0%	9
Italy	7.30%	1	–3%	49
Hong Kong	5.80%	12	–4%	50
USA	5.20%	34	5%	36
Germany	4.60%	7	–2%	59
Turkey	4.20%	6	5%	27
Mexico	3.90%	36	42%	4
France	3.40%	8	–1%	52
Korea	2.90%	3	–7%	29
United Kingdom	2.80%	9	–1%	40
India	2.57%	23	–1%	55
Thailand	2.33%	5	–5%	64
Belgium–Luxembourg	2.32%	14	1%	15
Bangladesh	2.19%	29	21%	3
Taiwan	2.12%	16	–5%	53
Portugal	2.05%	4	–3%	54
Netherlands	1.65%	13	–2%	22
Indonesia	1.46%	19	–7%	63
Dominican Republic	1.44%	37	4%	14
Tunisia	1.44%	17	2%	43

Notes: World trade in the sector is estimated at US$ 170 billion in 1999, with 64 exporting countries. Rankings range from 1 (strong performance) to 64 (poor performance).

Source: ITC

Table 10: Footwear

Country	Share in world exports 1999	TPI Current Index	Change in world export share	TPI Change Index
China	22.60%	6	5%	6
Italy	18.10%	1	–1%	29
Spain	6.10%	2	3%	14
Portugal	4.80%	3	–2%	39
Thailand	3.90%	5	–3%	21
Brazil	3.80%	23	–5%	16
Germany	3.80%	12	–1%	38
Vietnam	3.30%	9	48%	2
Indonesia	2.90%	21	–8%	30
France	2.70%	7	–1%	32
Belgium–Luxembourg	2.48%	14	11%	12
United Kingdom	2.39%	19	2%	37
Korea	2.07%	8	–11%	20
Taiwan	1.85%	4	–11%	26
USA	1.82%	18	0%	27
Romania	1.65%	15	15%	23
Netherlands	1.64%	13	3%	4
India	1.56%	24	–2%	42
Austria	1.54%	28	3%	35
Mexico	1.23%	27	18%	5

Notes: World trade in the sector is estimated at US$ 40 billion in 1999, with 45 exporting countries. Rankings range from 1 (strong performance) to 45 (poor performance).

Source: ITC

Leather and leather products and footwear

Exports in this area amounted to approximately US$ 100 billion in 2000, representing around 2 percent of total world trade. These exports are comprised of leather manufactures, raw hides and skins, fur skins, trunks and other carrier luggage, and footwear (footwear accounts for nearly 60 percent of total leather exports). According to the degree of processing, leather and leather products fall into three groups: raw leather, prepared leather (intermediate), and finished leather products. Raw leather is bound by the rules of the Agricultural Agreement of the WTO, as it belongs to the category of agricultural products (hides and skins). All other leather products are defined as industrial goods (manufactures).

Although a number of European countries—especially Italy, but also France, Germany, Portugal, and Spain—have been leading suppliers of manufactured leather, more recently there have been a number of serious new competitors, including Thailand, the Philippines, Brazil, and Indonesia. Sri Lanka, the Dominican Republic, Lithuania, and Paraguay have also shown remarkable increases in leather exports. As far as the shoe industry is concerned, China represents by far the largest exporter, accounting for almost 23 percent of global exports (Table 10). In terms of export growth, however, China is clearly outperformed by Vietnam, whose share has already risen to more than 3 percent, with sport shoes representing a particular subsegment. The runners-up in terms of export growth are Mexico and Romania, with the former benefiting greatly from its NAFTA membership. Nevertheless, a number of industrialized countries continue to enjoy high export shares, a fact that reflects the increased degree of sophistication in shoemaking that uses computer technology, and the speed and consistency associated with marketing techniques.

Conclusions

In this paper, we have looked at the sectoral trade performance of individual countries on the basis of disaggregate COMTRADE data. Specifically, we have focused on nine different sectors, encompassing almost three-quarters of global trade. The results show that the industrialized countries clearly dominate global trade in most areas, although in some sectors, notably electronic components but also clothing and footwear, emerging market economies already possess significant market shares. More importantly, however, a number of developing countries were found to show a considerable momentum in improving their trade performance. In fact, in virtually all sectors, exporters from developing countries outperformed industrialized countries on the change index—although admittedly the developing countries started from a relatively low base. Nevertheless, overall these findings confirm that many developing countries—led by Mexico and China—have become substantially more integrated over the last few years.

Trade can provide a powerful tool to help improve productivity and hence growth. This does not, however, necessarily mean that a country's performance with respect to merchandise trade is a good measure for its overall degree of competitiveness. Notwithstanding the substantial expansion of world trade over the last decades, improvements in standards of living continue to be driven primarily by domestic factors. Thus, this paper should be seen as an attempt to provide new insights into the competitive advantages of countries in specific *sectors*, complementing the *Report*'s country-by-country assessment of *national* competitiveness.

References

Frankel, Jeffrey A, and David Romer. "Does Trade Cause Growth?" *The American Economic Review* 89, 1999, pp 379–99.

Hyvärinen, Antero. "Implications of the introduction of the agreement of textiles and clothing (ATC) on the developing countries producing/exporting textiles and clothing," ITC working paper, 2000. (www.intracen.org/mds/sectors/textiles/welcome.htm).

International Monetary Fund. *World Economic Outlook*, May 2001 (Washington, DC: International Monetary Fund, 2001).

Krugman, Paul. "Competitiveness: A dangerous obsession," Foreign Affairs (1994).

Porter, Michael E. *On Competition* (Cambridge, Massachusetts: Harvard Business School Press, 1998).

Porter, Michael E, Jeffrey D Sachs, and Andrew M Warner. "Executive summary: Current competitiveness and growth competitiveness," in *The Global Competitiveness Report 2000* (Geneva: World Economic Forum and New York and Oxford: Oxford University Press, 2000), pp 14–17.

Sachs, Jeffrey D, and Andrew M Warner. "Economic reform and the process of global integration," *Brookings Papers on Economic Activity*: 1, 1995, pp 1–118.

Sakakibara, Mariko, and Michael E Porter. "Competing at home to win abroad: Evidence from Japanese industry," *The Review of Economics and Statistics*, Vol. 83 (2001), pp 310–322.

Tyson, Laura D'Andrea. *Who Is Bashing Whom?* (Washington, DC: Institute for International Economics, 1991).

Notes

[i] For details of the classification, see the full explanatory notes on the TPI on ITC's Web site www.intracen.org, select any country under *country approach* and click on *Trade Performance Index*.

[ii] This sector does not cover photographic cameras, electronic toys (such as TV and video games), scientific instruments, or electronic components.

[iii] The Multi-Fibre Agreement (MFA) signed in 1974 and extended five times introduced for the first time quota restrictions on fibers other than cotton. The MFA did not cover all textile and clothing products, and quota allocations were not fully utilized by exporting countries. Hence, the Agreement on Textiles and Clothing (ATC) was introduced in 1995, following arduous negotiations between the importing (restraining) and the developing countries at the Marrakech treaty. To avoid potentially serious problems for local industries, some developed countries negotiated special agreements with the supplier governments in developing countries in order to limit the quantities of their exports of cotton textiles. See Hyvärinen (2000) for more details.

137

Appendix 1: Indicators of the Trade Performance Index (G1–G7), Current Index (P1–P5), and Change Index (C1–C5)

	Indicators	What does it mean?	How is it calculated?	Ranking	Weight in the Ranking
G1	Value of exports	Importance of the sector considered	Exports in 1999	no	—
G2	Trend of exports	Development of exports	Growth of exports over the period 1995–1999 (based on the least-squares method)	yes	—
G3	Share in national exports	Importance of the sector in national exports	Exports in the group of products divided by total exports	no	—
G4	Share in national imports	Importance of the sector in national imports	Imports in the group of products divided by total imports	no	—
G5	Average annual change in per capita exports	Evolution in the outward lookingness of the economy	Percentage change in the ratio of exports to population	no	—
G6	Relative unit value	Standard of quality (or market segment) targeted by country exports	Unit value (value divided by quantity) of country relative to the world unit value	no	—
G7	Average annual change in relative unit value	Change in the quality standard (or market segment) targeted by country exports	Percent change of relative unit values	no	—
P1	Value of net exports	Importance of the trade balance in the sector considered	Exports less imports in 1999	yes	1
P2	Per capita exports	Extent to which the labor force produces for the world market	Exports divided by population	yes	1
P3	Share in world market	Success on the world market	Exports as percentage share of world imports	yes	1
	Product diversification, measured by:	Number and weight of relative contribution of exported products	See cells below		(1)
P4-a	Equivalent number of products	Number of export products of equal size that would lead to the observed concentration of exports	Inverse of the Herfindhal index	yes	0.5
P4-b	Product spread	Spread of export markets for products	Weighted standard error	yes	0.5
	Market diversification, measured by:	Number and weight of partner countries	See cells below		(1)
P5-a	Equivalent number of markets	Number of markets of equal size that would lead to the observed concentration of exports	Inverse of the Herfindhal index	yes	0.5
P5-b	Market spread	Spread of destination markets	Weighted standard error	yes	0.5
C1	Percentage annual change in world market share explained by:	Change in global performance	Change in the world market share	no	(1)
	Change in competitiveness	Gain (loss) in market share due to increased (worsened) competitiveness	Change in the exporting country's share in destination markets' imports, weighted by the initial share of partner countries' imports in world trade (weighted average of the variation in the country's position on elementary markets*)	yes	0.25
	Initial geographic specialization	Benefits associated with the initial specialization of domestic exporters on dynamic markets	Initial market share of the exporting country in partner countries weighted by the dynamics of their imports (weighted average of variations in the relative importance of export markets)	yes	0.25
	Initial product specialization	Benefits associated with the initial export specialization on products characterized by dynamic demand	Change in the share of elementary markets in world trade weighted by the difference between: the initial share of the exporting country in elementary markets*, and the initial market share of the exporting country in destination markets, all products	yes	0.25
	Adaptation to changes in world demand	Ability to adjust export supply to changes in world demand	Change in the share of the elementary markets* in world trade weighted by the change in the exporting country's market share in these elementary markets*	yes	0.25
C2	Trend of import coverage by exports	Development of sectoral surplus or deficit of exports over imports	Growth trend of the coverage ratio (exports divided by imports) over the period 1995–1999 (based on the least-squares method)	yes	1
C3	Matching with the dynamics of world demand	Similarity between the composition of national exports and product-specific dynamics of world demand	Spearman's rank correlation between the country's share of export products in national exports and the respective trends in world demand	yes	1
	Change in product diversification measured by:	Ability to develop new export products	See cells below		(1)
C4-a	Change in the equivalent number of products	Change in the number of export products of equal size that would lead to the observed concentration of exports	Variation in the inverse of the Herfindhal index	yes	0.5
C4-b	Change in the product spread	Change in the concentration of the export markets for products	Variation in the weighted standard error	yes	0.5
	Change in the diversification of markets measured by:	Ability to penetrate new markets	See cells below		(1)
C5-a	Change in the equivalent number of markets	Change in the number of markets of equal size that would lead to the observed concentration of exports	Variation in the inverse of the Herfindhal index	yes	0.5
C5-b	Change in market spread	Change in the concentration of the distribution of export markets	Variation in the weighted standard error	yes	0.5

Notes: All absolute values refer to 1999; growth rates to the period 1995–1999. World trade is calculated on the basis of some 100 reporting countries, which cover more than 90% of actual world trade. Coverage of nonreporting countries: The trade of nonreporting countries is reconstituted on the basis of partner country statistics (mirror statistics). This approach does not capture trade among nonreporting countries.
* An *elementary market* refers to one country's export of a specific product to a specific market.

Labor Markets in Europe: Performance, Reform, and Perception

PETER K. CORNELIUS, World Economic Forum
YONG ZHANG, World Economic Forum

Thanks to experiences with radical reforms, especially in the United Kingdom and the United States in the early 1980s, it is widely accepted today that structural policies play a key role in driving overall economic performance. With these reforms having greatly improved the functioning of goods, capital, and labor markets, both economies have enjoyed rapid economic growth over the last decade. In the United Kingdom, output expanded by an average of 3 percent per annum from 1993 through 2000; in the United States, annual output growth averaged 3.9 percent during this period. By contrast, average growth rates in the three largest countries in continental Europe—Germany, France, and Italy—have ranged from only 1.5 to 2 percent.[i] These low growth rates have coincided with a lack of structural reform.

Notwithstanding important macroeconomic factors, not least those associated with German reunification and monetary integration, few doubt that the profound lack of market flexibility has played a key role for the underperformance of the large continental European countries. Progress in reducing unemployment has thus remained slow in many member countries of the European Union (EU); with a significant economic growth gap vis-à-vis the United Kingdom and the United States having persisted until recently, public awareness of the need for more flexibility has risen appreciably in recent years. This has provided renewed impetus for structural reforms, notably regarding privatization, deregulation, labor market, tax reform, and social security reform. At the EU summit in Lisbon in March 2000, heads of state and government agreed on an ambitious plan for Europe "to become the most competitive and dynamic knowledge-based economy in the world, capable of sustainable economic growth with more and better jobs and greater social cohesion."[ii]

Arguably, the toughest challenge in the sphere of structural reform will remain the more rapid creation of employment opportunities. As far as the euro zone is concerned, 8.3 percent of the workforce were still unemployed in June 2001—a considerable improvement compared with the rate of unemployment in the mid-1990s.[iii] Even this improvement, however, is insufficient to reduce the aggregate level of unemployment back to that prevailing two decades ago. Although the recent decline in unemployment has benefited greatly from cyclical factors and wage moderation, there exists general agreement that sustained progress in reducing the number of jobless will require greater labor market flexibility. This view is consistent with most recent labor market developments, which suggest that the decline of unemployment is bottoming out in the wake of the recent decline in economic growth. More flexibility is all the more needed, as exchange rates in the common currency area, which in the past have served as shock absorbers, no longer exist (Soltwedel et al 2000). It is important to emphasize, however, that the need for greater labor market flexibility varies considerably across the euro zone. Although some countries—notably Ireland, the Netherlands, and, more recently, also Spain—have introduced important measures, others have continued to lag behind. As a result, unemployment rates in the common currency area show a considerable degree of dispersion (see Figure 1).

Following up on the analysis of Europe's labor markets published in the *Global Competitiveness Report 1999*,[iv] this paper aims at providing new insights regarding remaining labor market rigidities and hence impediments to job creation and economic growth in the euro zone. In doing so, the rest of the paper is structured as follows: First, we discuss recent developments in unemployment and job creation in the EU and more specifically in the countries of the euro zone. Second, we review the EU policy context aimed to bolster job growth in Europe. Third, we use the Executive Opinion Survey to examine cross-country variations with regard to the functioning of labor markets. Based on a simple index of labor market flexibility, reflecting, inter alia, the wage-setting process, hiring and firing practices, and the design of unemployment insurance schemes, we also look at the extent to which perceptions of business leaders have changed over the last five years. The final section summarizes and concludes.

Figure 1: Unemployment, GDP growth, and inflation in selected euro member countries, 1970–2000

Germany's unemployment, GDP growth, and inflation, 1970–2000

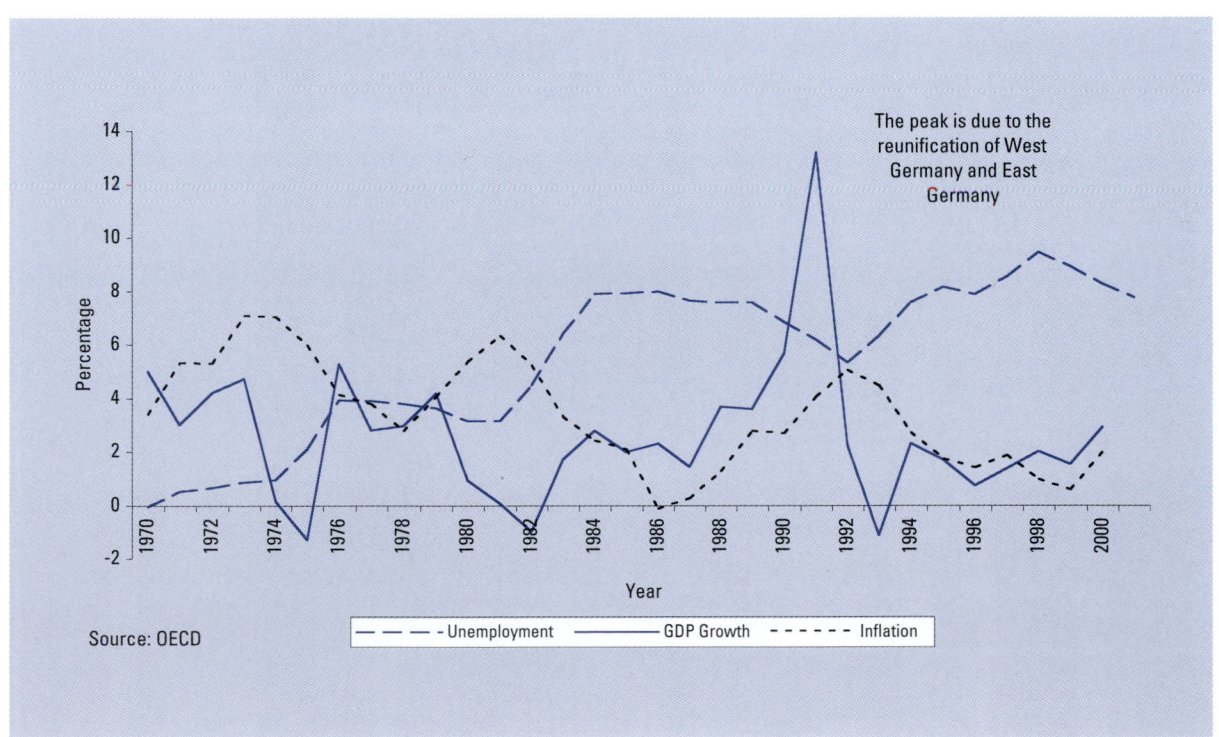

Source: OECD

Figure 1: Unemployment, GDP growth, and inflation in selected euro member countries, 1970–2000, *(cont'd.)*

France's unemployment, GDP growth, and inflation, 1970–2000

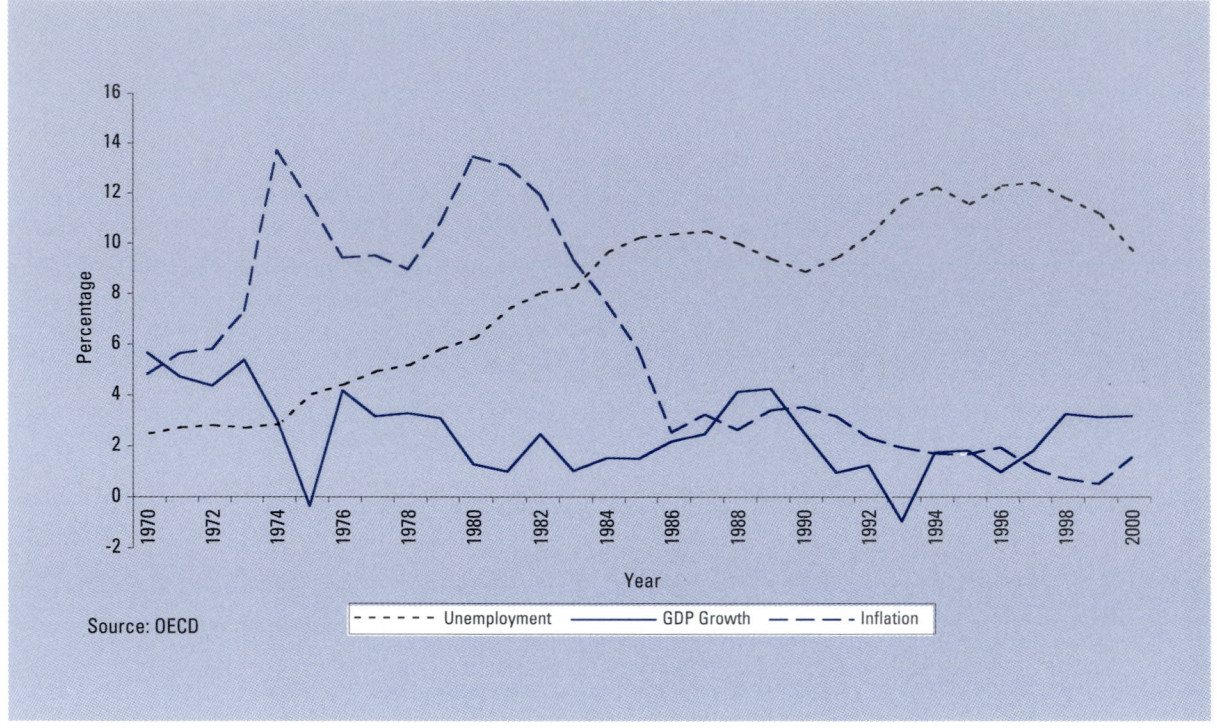

Italy's unemployment, GDP growth, and inflation, 1970–2000

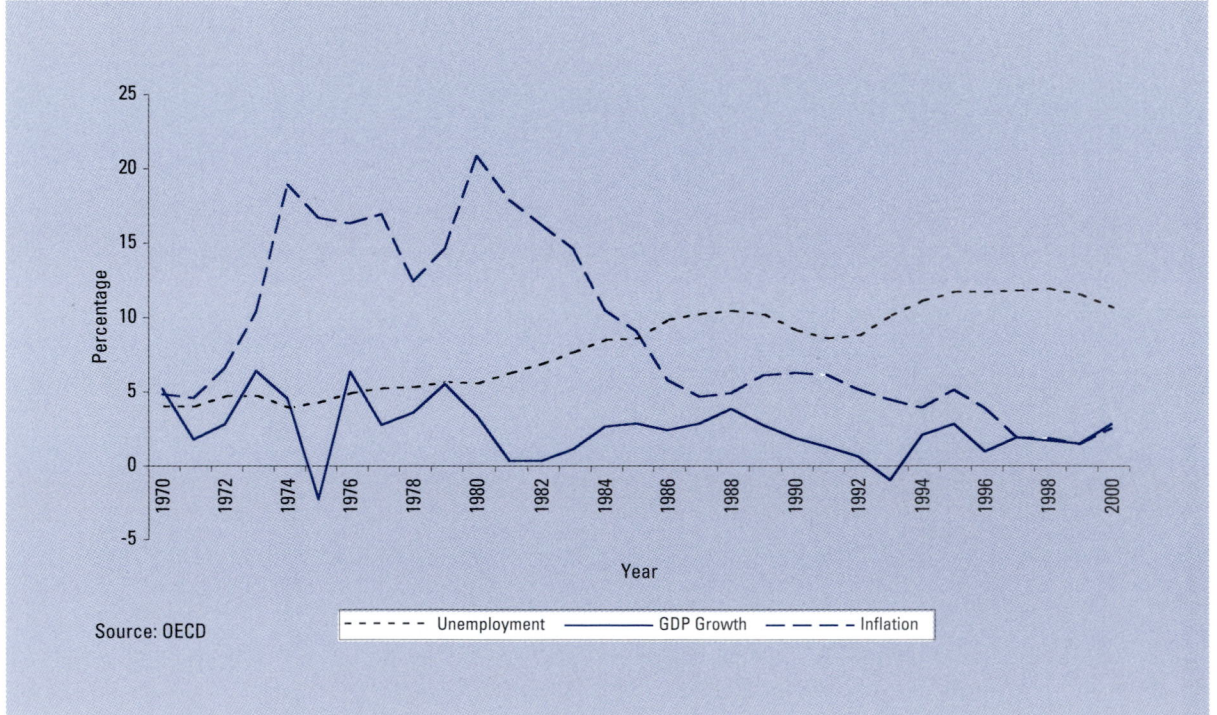

The Netherlands' unemployment, GDP growth, and inflation, 1970–2000

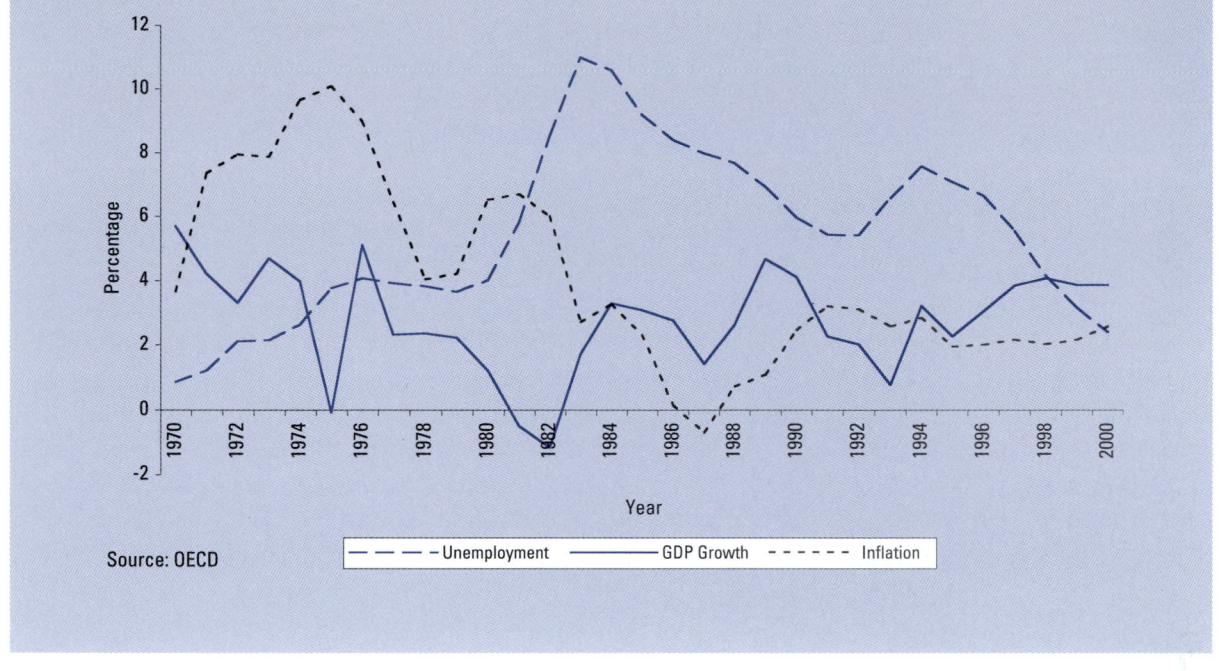

Source: OECD

Spain's unemployment, GDP growth, and inflation, 1970–2000

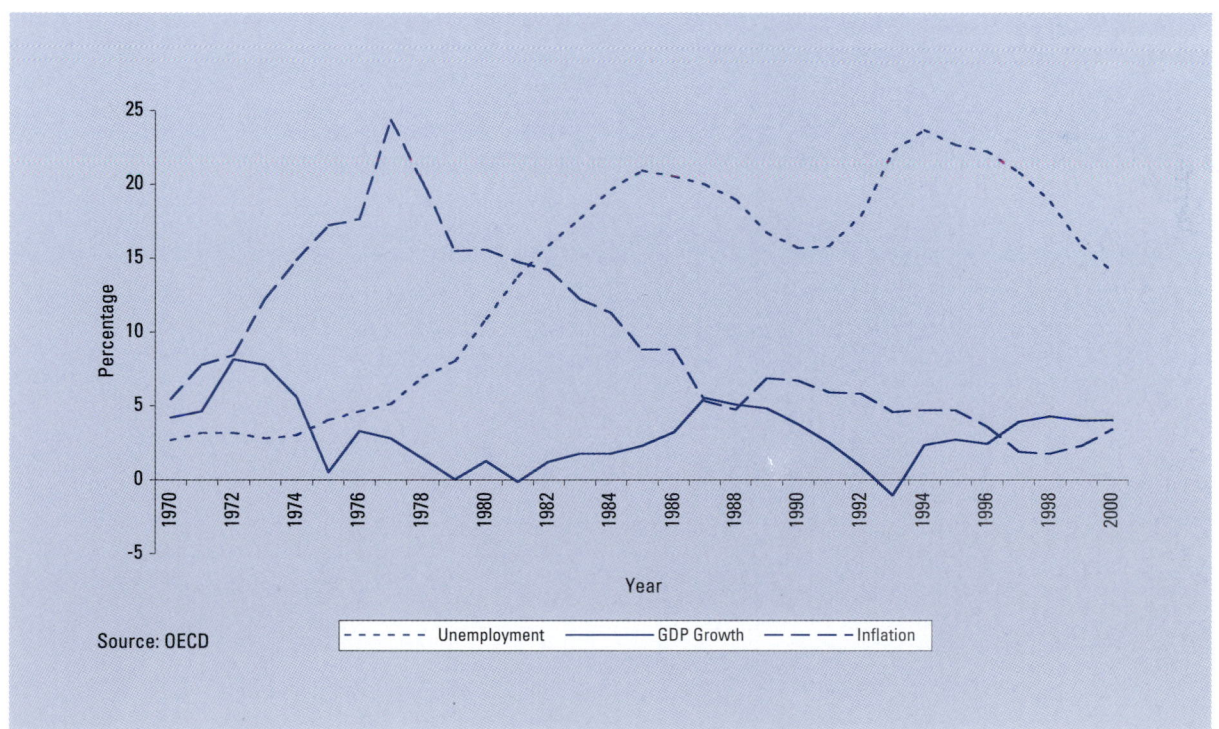

Source: OECD

Labor market developments in the euro zone

Despite certain improvements over the last few years, labor market performance in the euro zone has remained considerably weaker than in some other OECD countries. Although the average rate of unemployment has fallen to less than 8.5 percent from its peak of more than 11 percent in 1997, this has largely been due to cyclical factors, rather than to a reduction in the structural component of unemployment. According to OECD estimates, the non-accelerating inflation rate of unemployment (NAIRU)—that is, the rate of unemployment that is consistent with stable inflation[v]—has increased in about half the current EU member countries over the last decade. Germany, France, and Italy are the three largest economies among them.

By contrast, the NAIRU has fallen in the United States to a level that is now generally seen in the 4.5 to 5 percent range. Essentially, these divergences are consistent with a long-term trend that began in the 1970s when both the United States and Europe were hit by a sequence of averse supply shocks, namely the fall in (measured) productivity growth; the large deterioration in the terms of trade resulting from the steep oil price increases in 1973 and 1979; and the rise in real interest rates, especially at

the long end of the market. Although these shocks initially caused a large increase in unemployment in both the United States and Europe, the long-term labor market repercussions differed drastically due to marked differences in terms of how labor markets in the two economies operate. In the United States, real wage growth lagged behind labor productivity growth that was required to maintain full employment. In many European countries, however, the real cost of labor continued to increase in line with (or quicker than) labor productivity growth, with little growth in employment. High labor costs encouraged capital-intensive production, leading to a relatively faster rise in capital-to-labor ratios of actual employment, which in turn reduced labor demand. It also made many business activities unprofitable, reducing investment in these areas and leading to what has been described as "capital shortage." In short, both rapid labor productivity growth and flexible labor markets have contributed to the decline in the NAIRU in the United States (Blinder and Yellen 2001). By contrast, a combination of slower labor productivity growth and comparatively more rigid labor markets have pushed up the NAIRU in many EU member countries (see Figure 2).

Figure 2: Business sector employment, employment growth, and unemployment rate in selected OECD countries, 1970–2000

Business sector employment

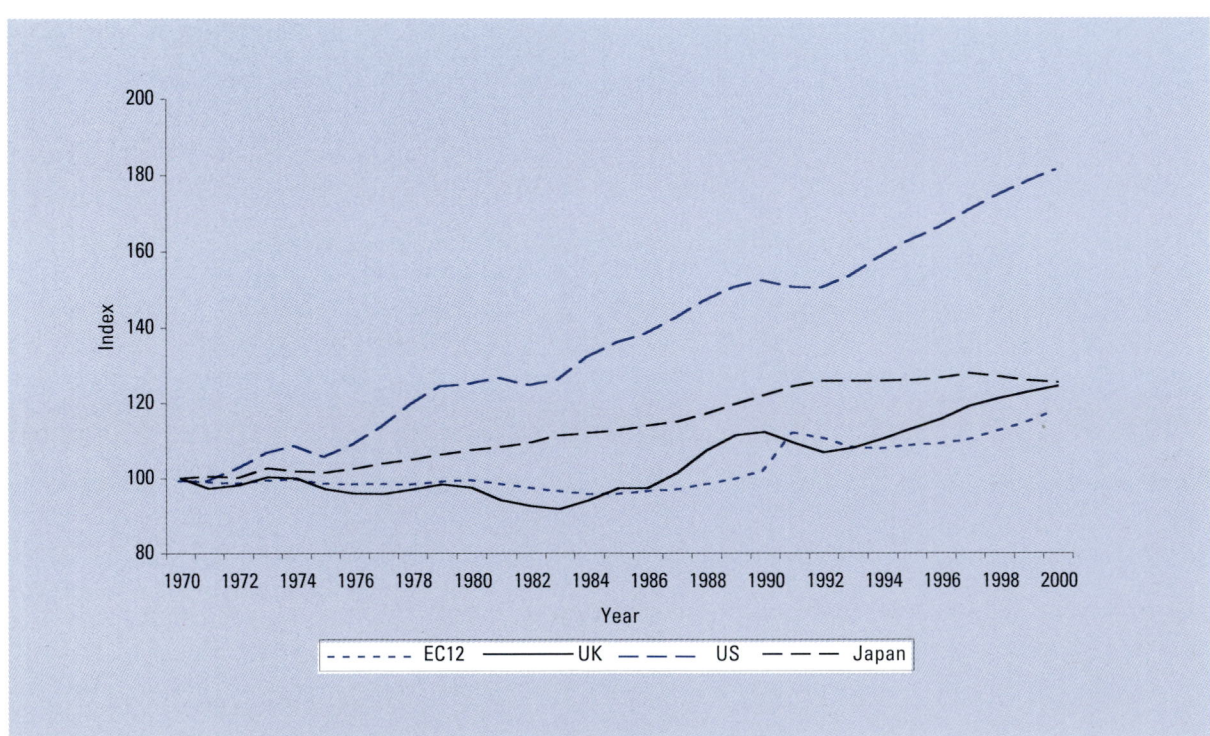

Employment growth

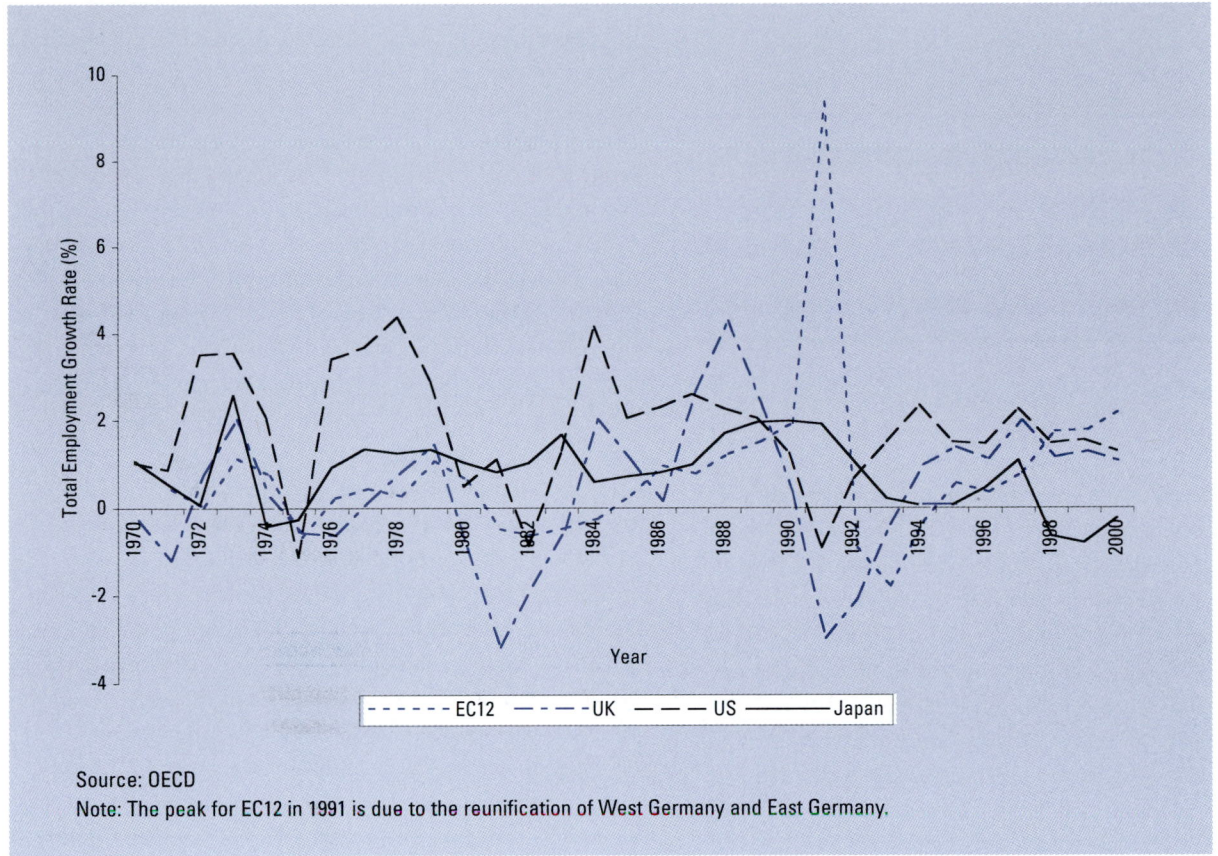

Source: OECD
Note: The peak for EC12 in 1991 is due to the reunification of West Germany and East Germany.

Unemployment rate

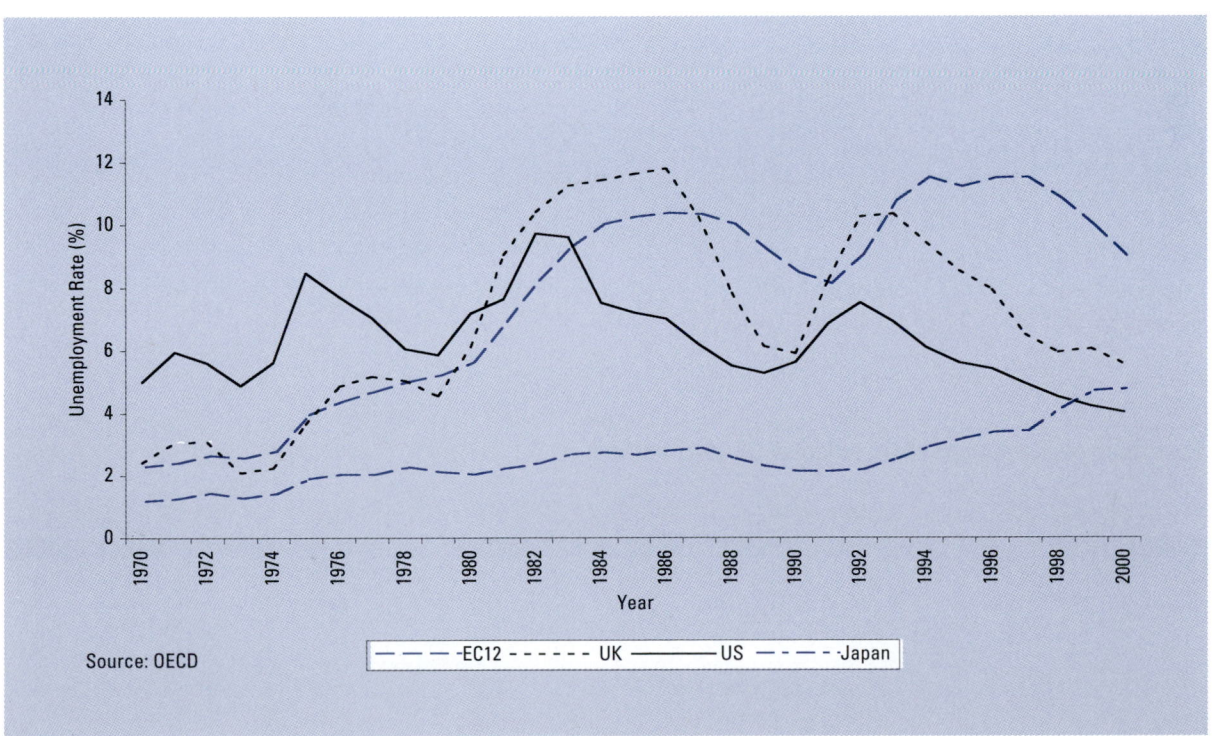

Source: OECD

Table 1: Recent labor market performance in selected countries of the euro zone

Country	Employment Growth 1996–99*	Change in Unemployment 1995–2000*	Rate of Unemployment April 2001**
France	5.3	–2.2	8.7
Germany	3.3	0.1	9.3
Ireland	23.9	–7.8	—
Italy	4.0	–1.4	9.9
Netherlands	12.4	–4.2	1.9
Spain	13.8	–8.7	13.1
Memorandum			
Japan	–0.2	1.6	4.8
United States	7.0	–1.6	4.4

Source: Eurostat, OECD, PWC
* in percentage points
** in percent of the workforce

Moreover, business sector employment in many euro zone economies has remained stagnant, and participation rates have continued to hover around 65 percent. At this rate, labor market participation has remained considerably lower than in United Kingdom and in some other OECD countries—especially among young and old age groups (see Table 2)—a gap the EU wants to narrow by the target rate of 70 percent it set at the Lisbon summit in 2000. The comparatively low degree of labor market participation suggests that the rate of unemployment actually underrepresents the magnitude of the jobless problem. In fact, the government training, employment, and early retirement schemes have kept the jobless rate artificially low, and many discouraged workers have simply dropped out of the labor force in response to low chances of finding employment (IMF 1999, p 88).

It is important to note, however, that labor market performance within the euro zone varies considerably, with the change of jobless rate ranging from a 0.1 percent increase in Germany to an 8.7 percent decrease in Spain in 1995–2000 (Table 1). These differences suggest the member countries' varying success in creating new jobs, arguably a superior concept to measure labor market performance (Garibaldi and Mauro 1999).[vi] Over the past 20 years, annual employment growth rates in the Netherlands and Spain, for example, averaged around 1.5 percent and 0.9 percent, respectively, whereas job creation in Germany amounted only to around 0.3 percent per year.[vii] In Italy, average employment growth was essentially flat over this period (see Figure 3). To be sure, these differences are huge: Had Italy created new jobs at the same speed as the Netherlands, there would exist around 6 million more jobs in Italy today.[viii] Had the entire euro zone created new jobs the way the Netherlands did from 1981 through 2000, there would now be around 22 million more jobs in the common currency area as a whole. This number is largely in line with the US experience, where employment growth during this period was slightly higher than it was in the Netherlands.

The picture of Europe's underperformance with regard to labor markets remains basically intact if changes in the working-age population are taken into account. Ireland and the Netherlands, where job creation has been more rapid than needed to keep pace with population growth, bringing a dramatic decline in unemployment, remain the most successful countries in the euro zone. This was particularly true in the 1990s when Ireland enjoyed, on average, a job creation rate of about 3.9 percent. In the Netherlands, too, employment growth accelerated at 2.2 percent per annum, whereas it remained sluggish in the core countries of the euro zone.

These different labor market developments are mirrored in considerable growth differentials, with Ireland having enjoyed a particularly strong GDP expansion of 8.3 percent per annum from 1993 through 2000, thus outperforming other members of the euro zone by a wide margin. By contrast, output growth in Germany, where employment growth has remained sluggish and unemployment high, averaged only 1.5 percent during this period. The same is true for France and Italy, both of which also have suffered from sagging job creations: The annual output growth rates in these two economies are only 1.9 percent and 1.7 percent, respectively.

Table 2: Labor force participation rate in selected OECD countries

COUNTRY	1990 15 to 24	1990 25 to 54	1990 55 to 64	1997 15 to 24	1997 25 to 54	1997 55 to 64	1998 15 to 24	1998 25 to 54	1998 55 to 64	1999 15 to 24	1999 25 to 54	1999 55 to 64	2000 15 to 24	2000 25 to 54	2000 55 to 64
Germany	59.8	78.0	41.6	51.1	84.3	45.2	51.1	84.7	44.8	51.2	84.9	44.7	52.5	86.5	44.7
France	36.4	84.1	38.1	28.0	86.0	36.7	28.0	86.2	36.1	28.4	86.2	37.4	29.5	86.2	37.2
Italy	46.8	72.8	32.5	38.0	72.4	28.6	38.4	73.4	29.0	38.1	73.9	28.9	38.1	74.2	28.6
Spain	54.9	70.3	40.0	46.6	75.3	37.8	46.4	75.6	38.8	47.4	76.2	38.7	48.2	77.4	40.7
Netherlands	59.6	76.0	30.9	63.1	81.8	32.7	66.1	82.3	33.8	67.7	83.0	36.3	72.2	83.6	38.6
Ireland	50.3	68.5	42.1	45.4	74.2	42.6	48.6	76.0	43.9	50.7	77.2	45.7	51.6	78.5	46.3
United Kingdom	78.0	83.9	53.0	70.5	83.3	51.7	69.5	83.3	51.0	69.2	83.8	52.1	69.7	84.1	52.8
United States	67.3	83.5	55.9	65.4	84.1	58.9	65.9	84.1	59.3	65.5	84.1	59.3	65.9	84.1	59.2
Japan	44.1	80.9	64.7	48.6	82.2	66.9	48.3	82.1	67.1	47.2	81.9	67.1	47.0	81.9	66.5
European Union	54.7	78.7	41.0	46.7	81.3	40.8	47.2	81.7	40.7	47.5	82.1	41.4	48.3	82.7	41.8

Source: OECD Employment Outlook, June 2001.

Figure 3: Average employment growth rates in selected OECD countries, 1981–2000

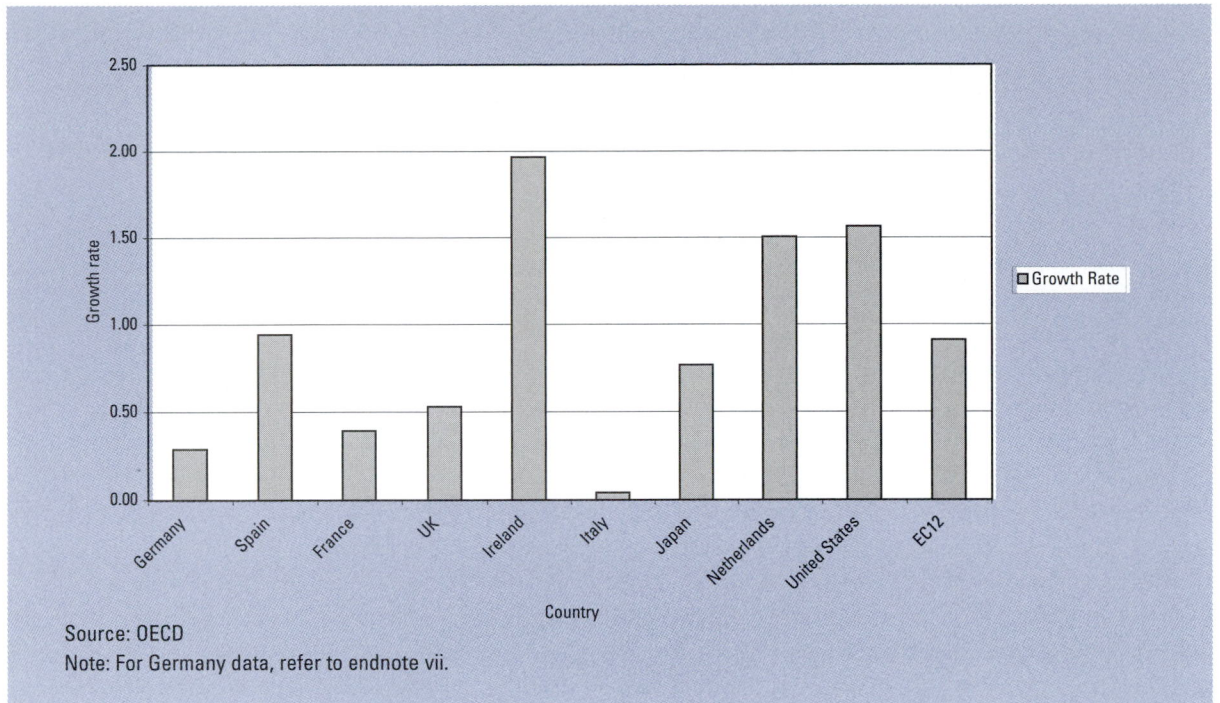

Source: OECD
Note: For Germany data, refer to endnote vii.

Finally, the composition of job creation by type of contract indicates that part-time jobs have proved increasingly popular, especially among women. Part-time employment has typically been associated with some crowding out of full-time jobs, yet also with some increase in the total number of jobs. With the notable exception of the Netherlands, where half the country's employment creation has been attributable to part-time contracts, it has remained difficult to find convincing evidence that a bigger share of part-time jobs has actually led to higher total job creation (Garibaldi and Mauro 1999).

As with part-time jobs, temporary work has also gained in importance. The most extreme example is Spain, where the percentage of temporary work now stands at around one-third of total employment. Presumably, Spain's very high share reflects the country's dismissal costs, which continue to be high by international standards despite considerable efforts in the recent past to reduce them.

In sum, although there exists a considerable degree of variation in Europe's labor market performance, overall progress in creating new jobs has remained slow. The recent decline in unemployment may therefore not be sustainable, given the recent slowdown in economic activity. Countries with rapid job creation have typically enjoyed higher economic growth, with positive repercussions on the labor market. Conversely, countries creating jobs at a slow pace have typically underperformed in terms of output expansion. Creating more jobs requires greater labor market flexibility. The following section therefore discusses recent reform efforts in Europe.

Labor market reform and the Lisbon agenda

In 1992, the OECD launched a major research project to analyze the causes of, and identify potential remedies for, the poor and deteriorating labor market performance that is especially prominent in large parts of the EU. Initial results were published in 1994 (OECD 1994). In total, over 60 detailed policy recommendations were produced, summarized in a list of 10 basic policy guidelines. Subsequently, the Ministerial Council mandated the OECD to follow up on the initial *Jobs Strategy* by designing detailed policy recommendations for individual countries and monitoring progress in implementing these recommendations.

Though recognizing the multidimensional character of the high and persistent level of unemployment in Europe, the OECD's policy recommendations acknowledged the key role of institutional arrangements affecting the operation of labor markets. Proposed labor market reforms focused on six broad areas, namely

1. reforming unemployment benefits (by reducing generosity, tightening work availability tests, and tightening eligibility);
2. reducing incentives for nonparticipation in the labor force (by reforming early retirement and invalidity schemes);
3. reducing taxation of labor, especially for low-income recipients;

4. liberalizing job protection legislation;
5. reforming the wage formation process (facilitating greater wage dispersion, decentralizing wage determination, and facilitating "opting out," including the curtailment of the widespread practice of extending administratively "key" negotiation results);
6. increasing work time flexibility, both in terms of daily hours and part-time work.

According to the follow-up work by the OECD (1997) on implementing the jobs strategy in individual countries, the need for specific reforms continues to vary considerably across Europe. Some countries have already made encouraging progress in reforming their systems of unemployment benefits in an effort to reduce disincentives for jobless people to find work. Others have implemented measures to make work time more flexible, while some countries have decentralized the wage determination process. By contrast, liberalizing the protection of jobs remains an important challenge for most European countries, and in a few cases there has even been some backtracking on reforms.[ix]

More recently, the sizable growth gap vis-à-vis the United States has provided renewed impetus for reforms in Europe, with the capital markets serving as an important catalyst for change (Mayer 2000). At the Lisbon summit in 2000, European heads of state and government agreed on an ambitious reform agenda that is driven primarily by the objective of fostering job creation and growth in a knowledge-based economy. The EU's program for a new economy aims to raise the EU employment rate to 70 percent of the working-age population by 2010.[x]

The Lisbon program includes eight areas of policy measures to meet the Council's strategic goal of ensuring that Europe becomes the most competitive and dynamic knowledge-based economy in the world. Specifically, the program aims to:

1. foster the development of information and communication technologies;
2. promote innovation and ensure attractive prospects for the best brains by providing a European research area;
3. promote small companies as the main engines of job creation;
4. introduce economic reforms to complete the single market and harmonize rules on competition;
5. improve the efficiency of financial markets and make more risk capital available;
6. improve economic coordination of macroeconomic policies;
7. build an active welfare state to ensure that the new economy does not aggravate unemployment, poverty, and social exclusion; and
8. promote employment and modernize social protection.

As far as labor market policies are concerned, the Lisbon program contains a number of specific measures that attach particular importance to establishing a pan-European labor market. In order to improve employability and reduce existing skill gaps, for example, the program envisages providing employment services with a Europe-wide database and learning opportunities, and promoting special measures enabling workers who are currently jobless to acquire necessary skills. Moreover, special importance is attached to lifelong learning. In this context, the program encourages agreements between the social partners in order to exploit the complementarities between lifelong learning and adaptability through flexible management of working time and job rotation, and suggests introducing a European award for particularly progressive firms.

With regard to particular sectors of the economy, the program aims to increase employment in services, including personal services, where there remain major shortages. Finally, the program emphasizes the importance of furthering all aspects of equal opportunities, including reducing occupational segregation, and making it easier to reconcile working life and family life, especially by setting a new benchmark for improved childcare provision.

The Stockholm European Council in 2001 reiterated the need for modernizing labor markets and encouraging labor mobility within the European space. However, apart from assessing "the feasibility of establishing a one-stop European mobility information site" and creating a high-level task force on skills and mobility ". . . to examine the characteristics and barriers within the European labor market, paying special attention to the need for ITC skills" (Stockholm European Council: Presidency Conclusions, http://ue.eu.int/newsroom/), few concrete measures were proposed. As a result, the Council's policy agenda has continued to fall short of the OECD recommendations.

Labor market rigidities not only restrain employment growth, but also cause labor markets to remain fragmented, an issue that has gained substantially in importance since the irrevocable fixing of the conversion rates in the common currency area at the beginning of 1999. With exchange rates no longer available as potential shock absorbers in the euro zone, it has become even more critical to have a clear picture of existing labor market impediments, even though their assessment is often aggravated by the complexity of the framework conditions and the degree of the *de facto* flexibility they sometimes provide. The IMF, in its May 2001 *World Economic Outlook* (2001, p 23), for example, urges Germany to implement ". . . legal changes . . . to allow employers and workers to reach wage agreements more in line with firm-level conditions," but also notes that the country does show ". . . signs of greater flexibility in *de facto* working conditions and wages." Similarly, with regard to France, the IMF welcomes the flexible way the 35-hour workweek initiative was actually introduced, which could have resulted in a major increase in labor costs.

In light of this, it appears important to examine not just the *de jure* structure of labor market regulations, but also the perception of those who are responsible for hiring people. Therefore, we now turn to the results of our Executive Survey and examine the evolution of views over time and the extent to which they continue to differ across the member states of the euro zone.

The functioning of labor markets in the view of the Survey respondents

Reflecting the views of more than 4,600 business leaders and entrepreneurs from 75 countries, the Executive Survey of the World Economic Forum includes a number of detailed questions on the functioning of labor markets. These concern the impact of minimum wages, unemployment insurance, social welfare, hiring and firing practices, labor-employer relations, union power, the wage-setting process, and pay-productivity relations, with answers to be given on a scale of 1 to 7. A higher score means more flexibility. Not all of the questions were asked each year, but most of them were similar over time. Box 1 presents the individual Survey questions; Table 3 provides detailed average scores for selected countries of the euro zone, plus the United Kingdom and the United States as comparator countries.

149

Box 1: Survey Questions on Labor Market Flexibility

The minimum wage set by law in your country
Raises the pay of low-wage workers/is too low to affect wages

Hiring and firing of workers is
Impeded by regulations/flexibly determined by employers

Your country's unemployment insurance program
Has substantially increased labor market rigidities/has preserved labor market flexibility (In the 2001–2002 Survey, the answers are phrased as follows: Offers excessive benefits and may have actually increased unemployment/offers a good trade-off between social protection and preserving work-incentives)

Your country's social welfare and unemployment program
Deters citizens from entering the workforce/strongly encourages and supports participation in the workforce

Employer-worker relations in your country are
Generally confrontational/generally cooperative

Union power in your country is
High/low (In the 2001 Survey, the answers are phrased in this way: Prevent productivity improvements/contribute to productivity improvements)

Wages in your country are
Set by a centralized bargaining process/up to each individual company

Pay in your country is
Not related to worker productivity/strongly related to productivity

Table 3: Average Survey responses to questions related to labor market flexibility

Country	Year	Minimum Wage	Hiring and Firing	Unemployment Insurance	Labor-employer Relations	Union Power	Social Welfare	Wage Setting	Pay-Productivity Relations
Germany	2001	2.4	2.1	—	5.3	4.1	2.6	2.4	4.1
	2000	3.2	2.0	2.5	5.3	2.6	—	2.4	4.1
	1999	3.8	2.4	2.6	5.3	1.7	2.6	—	—
	1998	3.0	2.3	2.8	5.1	2.8	2.5	—	—
	1997	3.4	2.3	2.7	5.2	2.9	—	—	—
France	2001	1.1	2.0	—	2.8	2.6	3.0	4.3	3.6
	2000	2.5	2.4	2.9	3.3	3.9	—	4.8	4.0
	1999	2.8	2.7	3.0	3.3	2.6	2.6	—	—
	1998	2.5	2.5	2.5	2.8	3.4	2.3	—	—
	1997	2.8	2.4	2.8	2.8	3.4	—	—	—
Italy	2001	3.2	2.3	—	4.4	4.4	3.8	3.2	4.2
	2000	3.8	2.1	3.9	4.3	2.5	—	3.0	3.6
	1999	3.7	2.4	3.7	4.2	2.5	2.5	—	—
	1998	—	—	—	—	—	—	—	—
	1997	2.6	2.2	3.1	3.4	2.8	—	—	—
Spain	2001	3.6	3.2	—	4.6	3.9	3.6	3.9	4.0
	2000	4.5	2.7	4.0	4.5	3.4	—	4.4	4.1
	1999	4.4	3.0	3.6	4.4	2.5	3.4	—	—
	1998	4.5	2.9	3.3	4.1	3.3	3.0	—	—
	1997	4.5	3.5	3.4	4.2	3.6	—	—	—
Netherlands	2001	1.9	2.5	—	6.1	5.2	3.6	3.6	4.1
	2000	2.7	2.8	3.7	5.9	4.1	—	3.3	3.8
	1999	3.4	2.9	3.4	5.7	1.9	3.1	—	—
	1998	3.7	3.5	4.0	6.0	4.4	4.0	—	—
	1997	3.5	3.2	3.9	5.9	4.5	—	—	—
Ireland	2001	1.9	3.3	—	4.7	4.3	3.9	2.8	4.3
	2000	3.9	2.7	4.2	5.2	3.7	—	2.1	4.1
	1999	5.0	3.3	3.7	5.2	2.2	3.7	—	—
	1998	5.2	4.2	3.8	5.6	5.0	3.5	—	—
	1997	5.1	3.7	3.4	5.2	4.2	—	—	—
UK	2001	1.9	3.9	—	5.4	4.6	4.6	6.2	5.4
	2000	4.0	3.4	4.9	5.5	5.2	—	6.1	5.1
	1999	5.1	5.1	4.8	5.1	3.5	4.4	—	—
	1998	5.0	5.5	4.5	5.4	5.0	5.0	—	—
	1997	4.7	4.9	4.6	5.2	4.7	—	—	—
USA	2001	2.1	5.0	—	5.0	3.6	5.0	6.0	5.4
	2000	3.4	4.6	5.2	5.1	4.8	—	6.0	5.3
	1999	5.0	4.9	4.9	5.0	2.9	4.8	—	—
	1998	4.5	5.3	5.0	5.0	4.1	4.7	—	—
	1997	4.5	5.1	4.9	5.1	4.2	—	—	—

Source: World Economic Forum Executive Survey.

In order to generate overall rankings for labor market flexibility, we employ a standard factor analysis (Harman 1976; Jackson 1991). In a first step, we generate the common factors to estimate the countries' scores. Then we standardize the scores into an index with a mean of 100 and a standard deviation of 10. Since there have been variations among questions (variables) asked each year and the wording of some of the questions has been subject to change, there exist differences concerning the variables used for generating common factors, leading to a potential bias for rank comparisons over time. However, the magnitude of the problem appears relatively small, as most questions were reasonably similar and directions of scores on measuring the labor market flexibility were the same (we adjusted the directions of a few questions where the high score meant less flexibility). Nevertheless, due to the potential sample bias and the lack of a common pool of people evaluating the reforms in different countries, the results need to be interpreted with caution.

Table 4 summarizes the results of our factor analysis for the 11 original euro zone economies as well as for the United Kingdom and the United States as comparator countries.[xi] According to the results, the three largest economies—Germany, France, and Italy—are perceived to suffer especially from a low degree of labor market flexibility. Based on this year's Survey, Germany and France come in last, and Italy now ranks 7th. For the preceding years, the factor analysis suggests slightly different rankings among the "Big-3," without altering the overall picture, however. A closer look at the individual variables reveals which factors are perceived to be particularly serious obstacles (see Table 3).

In all three countries, business people feel that laying off people is impeded by stringent regulations, and as a result, there exists considerable reluctance to hire new staff. In Germany, unemployment benefits are seen to be overly generous, discouraging people in finding a new job. Moreover, Germany shows the relatively lowest score with regard to the perceived degree of decentralization regarding the wage-setting process. This confirms that the wage growth solidarity principle—serving to benchmark real wage increases according to the economy's overall rate of labor productivity growth rather than productivity increases at the firm level—has remained largely untackled. Consistent with this view, workers' salaries in Germany are seen to be only partly related to productivity.

Table 4: Rank of labor market flexibility in selected OED countries

2001			2000			1999			1998			1997		
RANK	COUNTRY	SCORE	RANK	COUNTRY	SCORE	RANK	COUNTRY	SCORE	RANK	COUNTRY	SCORE	RANK	COUNTRY	SCORE
1	United States	122.4	1	United States	116.6	1	United States	115.9	1	United Kingdom	116.6	1	United Kingdom	113.3
2	United Kingdom	117.7	2	United Kingdom	114.1	2	United Kingdom	113.9	2	United States	112.9	2	United States	110.5
3	Luxembourg	101.1	3	Portugal	100.5	3	Portugal	103.1	3	Netherlands	104.4	3	Ireland	104.8
4	Ireland	96.1	4	Luxembourg	100.2	4	Ireland	100.9	4	Ireland	104.1	4	Netherlands	103.2
5	Spain	95.2	5	Spain	98.0	5	Spain	97.2	5	Portugal	103.2	5	Portugal	101.8
6	Finland	95.0	6	Netherlands	93.6	6	Luxembourg	97.1	6	Austria	96.9	6	Luxembourg	98.5
7	Austria	94.5	7	Ireland	93.4	7	Austria	94.3	7	Luxembourg	94.0	7	Spain	98.1
8	Netherlands	93.5	8	France	92.4	8	Netherlands	91.9	8	Spain	92.2	8	Austria	93.7
9	Italy	92.7	9	Austria	91.5	9	Italy	88.5	9	Belgium	86.1	9	France	87.1
10	Portugal	88.8	10	Finland	89.1	10	Finland	87.0	10	Finland	84.4	10	Germany	86.9
11	Belgium	88.7	11	Italy	87.8	11	France	86.2	11	Germany	84.1	11	Belgium	85.4
12	Germany	84.7	12	Belgium	84.7	12	Germany	85.4	12	France	82.3	12	Finland	84.0
13	France	84.4	13	Germany	83.1	13	Belgium	84.9				13	Italy	83.6

Note: This is just a partial list of the countries under study. There are no Executive Survey data for Italy in 1998.

In France and Italy, the pay-productivity relationship is also perceived to be relatively weak, although the wage-setting process is more decentralized, at least in France. In France, furthermore, unemployment benefits are perceived to deter the reintegration of the unemployed. While in Germany labor-employer relations are generally seen as fairly cooperative, French respondents to the Survey view the respective relation in their country as considerably more confrontational. Interestingly, the power of trade unions in Germany is perceived to be considerably stronger than in France. Trade union power is also perceived to be relatively strong in Italy, without a clear impact on the labor-employer relations.

It is interesting to note that the perceptions have not much changed over the five-year period under consideration. This is particularly true for the respondents' view on hiring and firing practices in the three countries, confirming the findings of numerous other studies on European labor markets (eg, Lindbeck 1996; Nickell 1997; Siebert 1997). In fact, a recent study conducted at the OECD (Nicoletti et al 2000) suggests that the (relative) stringency of employment protection in the three largest economies—and also in other EU countries—has hardly changed since the late 1980s—an even longer time span than we cover in this paper. Based on a factor analysis that distinguishes between regular and temporary contracts and takes into account three sets of factors,[xii] the study ranks 20 OECD member countries according to the stringency of their employment protection legislation (with the highest rank indicating the least stringent regime). For 1998, Germany, France, and Italy are ranked 14th, 16th, and 17th, respectively. In the late 1980s, their ranks were 16th, 11th, and 19th. By comparison, the United States and the United Kingdom have been top-ranked for both periods.

That perceptions do not seem to vary much over time applies to other labor market indicators as well. Essentially, there exist two possible explanations for this observation. First, labor market policies have actually remained largely unchanged. Alternatively, perceptions are subject to considerable inertia.

To be sure, several countries have introduced a number of important policy measures affecting the labor market. In France, for instance, a number of important tax measures have been introduced. By 2003, the corporate income tax rate in that country will have been reduced to 33.33 percent, and the bottom marginal rate of the personal income tax will be lowered to 7 percent. At the time, the 2001–2003 Tax Reduction Plan foresees to reduce the top marginal rate from 54 to 52.5 percent. Moreover, the local business tax was reformed by phasing out the wage bill from the tax base. Furthermore, firms implementing the 35-hour week have received an increased rebate on their social security contribution. Although all these measures serve to cushion the impact of the introduction of the 35-hour week, on balance it remains unclear how the supply of, and the demand for, labor is affected. In the view of the Survey respondents, the bottom line might not have changed much, notwithstanding important policy measures working in opposite directions.

151

A closer look at the empirical results suggests that perceptions do respond to changes in policies and reflect structural labor market conditions. Consider Finland, for instance. Back in 1997 this country was still perceived as the second worst performer in terms of the functioning of its labor market. Unemployment was still extremely high, mirroring the impact of the huge external shock the Finnish economy had suffered at the beginning of the decade in the context of the collapse of the former Soviet Union. However, in response to this massive shock, Finland embarked on an ambitious medium-term stabilization and reform program that included important labor market reforms. The results of this program became increasingly visible in the second half of the 1990s, as reflected in the perceptions of Survey respondents. Over the past five years, Finland's rank in terms of labor market flexibility has constantly improved, and according to our factor analysis it is seen today as belonging to the top-third among the countries of the euro zone. Note in this context that, according to this year's growth competitiveness rankings, Finland represents the most competitive economy in the world.

Another interesting case is Spain, where unemployment has fallen dramatically over the period under consideration. To be sure, Spain's decline in unemployment has not just been the result of strong economic growth, but to a considerable extent reflects also the impact of a major labor market reform program launched in 1997. Key features of this program have included the reduction of dismissal costs, which had been the highest in Europe, and the lowering of social security contributions for some categories of workers. With Spain having gradually moved up the ranking over the last five years, the country's experience suggests two things: First, labor market reforms do work—although a lot remains to be done. Second, possible inertia with regard to the Survey respondents' perceptions appears, if anything, to be limited—suggesting that reforms in many other countries have indeed remained halfhearted.

Spain's and Finland's labor markets continue to be perceived as less flexible than Ireland's, however. In fact, Ireland has enjoyed the strongest increase in employment over the last few years, even outperforming Spain. A particularly important factor in this regard has been Ireland's relatively low dismissal costs, which, unlike those in many other countries, have increased willingness of companies to hire new people. Although Ireland's exceptional growth over the last decade has led to a sharp increase in the demand for labor, there can be little doubt that more employment has contributed substantially to its phenomenal expansion of output.

The Netherlands, finally, where unemployment is particularly low, was perceived to possess the relatively most flexible labor market in the late-1990s, but more recently this perception has deteriorated in comparison with other members of the euro zone. Again, a closer look at Table 3 reveals that this deterioration has been due to two factors. First, overall regulations in the country are perceived to be more stringent now than they were a few years ago, despite the improving labor-employer relations associated with the decreasing power of unions. As far as hiring and firing practices are concerned, the average score slips gradually from 3.5 to 2.5. Second, regardless of any changes in labor market policies focusing on wage moderation in the Netherlands, several other countries have shown considerable improvements in the perception of the business community.

Even the most liberal economies in the euro zone, however, are consistently outperformed by the United Kingdom and the United States, according to the views of the Survey respondents. Their perceptions are largely in line with actual labor market developments in the two countries. As discussed above, both countries had already introduced bold reforms in the 1980s, which laid the foundation for rapid economic growth, fostered by a tremendous increase in new jobs and a fall in unemployment to 5.5 and 4.0 percent, respectively. Their experiences clearly suggest that a sustained improvement in labor market conditions in the euro zone will require substantive reforms in several areas. This concerns in particular the three largest economies (Germany, France, Italy), which account for about 75 percent of output of the entire euro zone. Policies aiming at restraining wage growth mainly through collective negotiations among social partners will remain insufficient. [xiii]

Conclusions

Examining recent labor market developments in the euro zone, this paper has raised doubts as to whether the recent decline in unemployment can be sustained in the absence of far-reaching structural reforms. Although labor market policies in the core economies of the euro zone have relied primarily on wage moderation, little has changed on the institutional side, which was emphasized in the 1997 study on implementing the OECD *Jobs Strategy*. Thus, there must remain serious concern that unemployment could rise again to double-digit numbers in the wake of weakening aggregate demand. In other countries, notably Ireland, the Netherlands, and Spain, however, structural reforms are more advanced, an important reason why these countries have enjoyed strong employment growth in recent years.

Different labor market regulations—leading to divergent labor market performances—are mirrored in our Executive Survey, which helps identify the key impediments that need to be removed if the structural unemployment is to fall on a pan–euro zone basis. Based on the experience in the more advanced countries, and consistent with the view of the surveyed business community, the three most demanding policies appear to be the following:

- reduce dismissal costs as a serious barrier to hiring new staff;
- decentralize the wage-setting process in order to allow wage settlements to reflect firm-level productivity growth better; and
- prevent unemployment benefits from discouraging unemployed workers to find new jobs.

There exist substantial variations regarding labor market flexibility and the need for reforms—both among the euro zone economies and vis-à-vis the United Kingdom and the United States, which began to implement far-reaching reforms in the 1980s and have enjoyed rapid output and employment growth. An additional challenge for the euro zone economies arises from their low degree of regional labor mobility, an issue that has been identified as particularly important by the recent Stockholm Council. In the absence of exchange rates in the common currency area, labor market reforms have become even more urgent. In some European countries, considerable efforts are already underway. Sustaining them and starting the process in others should be given high priority on the national and pan-European agendas.

References

Blinder, Alan and Janet Yellen. 2001. *The Fabulous Decade: Macroeconomic Lessons from the 1990s* (Washington, DC: The Century Foundation).

Garibaldi, Pietro, and Paolo Mauro. 1999. *Deconstructing Job Creation*, IMF Working Paper WP 99/109 (Washington, DC: International Monetary Fund).

Harman, Harry. 1976. *Modern Factor Analysis*, 3rd ed., (Chicago: University of Chicago Press).

International Monetary Fund. 1999. *World Economic Outlook*, May 1999 (Washington, DC: International Monetary Fund).

International Monetary Fund. 2001. *World Economic Outlook*, May 2001 (Washington, DC: International Monetary Fund).

Jackson, Edward. 1991. *A User's Guide to Principle Components* (New York: John Wiley & Sons).

Lindbeck, Assar. 1996. "The West European Employment Problem" *Weltwirtschaftliches Archiv* 132: 609–637.

Mayer, Thomas. 2000. Structural Reform in Euroland: Agenda, Progress, Effects, *The European Economics Analyst* (Goldman Sachs, 30th November).

Nicoletti, Guiseppe, Stefano Scarpetta, and Olivier Boylaud. 2000. *Summary Indicators of Product Market Regulation with an Extension to Employment Protection Legislation* Economics Department Working Papers No. 226 (Paris: OECD).

Nickell, Steven. 1997. "Unemployment and Labor Market rigidities: Europe versus North America," *Journal of Economic Perspectives* 11: 55–74.

OECD 1994. *The OECD Jobs Strategy—Evidence and Explanations. Part I: Labor Market Trends and Underlying forces of Change; Part II: The Adjustment Potential of the Labor Market*, (Paris: OECD).

OECD. 1995. Labor Force Statistics, 1973–1993, (Paris: OECD).

OECD. 1997. *Implementing the OECD Jobs Strategy. Lessons from Member Countries' Experience* (Paris: OECD).

OECD. 2000. OECD Economic Outlook, No. 68, December, (Paris: OECD).

OECD 2000. OECD Main Economic Indicators, December, (Paris: OECD).

OECD. 2001. OECD Economic Outlook, No. 69, June, (Paris: OECD).

OECD. 2001. OECD Main Economic Indicators, May, (Paris: OECD).

OECD 2001. OECD Employment Outlook, June, (Paris: OECD).

Oxford Economic Forecasting. 1996. *The New Oxford World Model: An Overview* (Oxford: Oxford University Press).

Siebert, Horst. 1997. "Labor Market Rigidities: At the Root of Unemployment in Europe," *Journal of Economic Perspectives* 11: 37–54.

Siebert, Horst. 1999. "How Competitive Is Europe's Labor?" in *The Global Competitiveness Report 1999* (Oxford: Oxford University Press), pp 86–93.

Soltwedel, Rüdiger, Dirk Dohse, and Christiane Krieger-Boden. 2000. "EMU Challenges to European Labor Markets," in *World Economic Outlook: Supporting Studies* (Washington, DC: International Monetary Fund), pp 184–210.

Notes

[i] OECD 2001, GDP volume, 1995 constant PPP.

[ii] The full text (Presidency Conclusions, Lisbon European Council, 23 and 24 March 2000) can be downloaded from http://europa.eu.int/comm/off/index_en.htm.

[iii] The euro zone comprises 12 countries: Austria, Belgium, Finland, France, Germany, Greece, Ireland, Italy, Luxembourg, the Netherlands, Portugal, and Spain.

[iv] See Siebert (1999).

[v] Unlike the cyclical component of unemployment (and abstracting from hysteresis effects), the NAIRU cannot be reduced by macroeconomic policy without causing wage growth—and thus inflation—to increase.

[vi] To begin with, measuring unemployment involves subtle distinctions between individuals who are in the labor force and those who are not. For example, in high-unemployment countries in particular, discouraged workers may have stopped looking for a job and remain uncounted, whereas others who claim to be looking for a job may be half-hearted about it. Second, for any given level of unemployment, faster job creation increases a country's output and raises the ratio of workers to pensioners, thus lowering the cost of the social safety net. Third, although stringent laws and labor arrangements can make it expensive to lay off workers and thus seem to have a positive effect on the jobless rate, they tend to have a sizable effect in holding down job creation. Finally, unemployment data tell us nothing about the kind of jobs in the workplace, or the terms under which workers hold them (permanent versus temporary jobs, full-time versus part-time).

[vii] For West Germany, the average annual employment rate in 1981 to 1990 is 0.5 percent. In 1991 to 2000, the rate is 0.029 percent for the reunified Germany.

[viii] Garibaldi and Mauro (1999) estimate that for a country the size of Italy, a 1 percentage point difference in employment growth amounts to a difference of some 200,000 jobs a year.

[ix] For information on detailed reforms and the key characteristics of the current labor market regimes in each individual country, refer to the Electronic Retrieval System for Employment Policies (ERSEP): http://www.ecotec.com/eeo/ersep/ersepen1.htm.

[x] At the European Council summit in Stockholm in March 2001, an intermediate target of 67 percent was set for 2005. The Stockholm summit also agreed on specific subtargets for a female employment rate of 57 percent by 2005, and for the 55- to 64-year-old age group of 50 percent by January 2010.

[xi] The rankings are based on a factor analysis that includes the OECD countries. The results are not materially different if one includes all 49 countries consistently covered by the Global Competitiveness Report from 1997 through 2001.

[xii] Three main factors are considered. The first factor includes different aspects of procedural inconveniences in cases of dismissal, but also the compensation in cases of unfair dismissal of a worker with 20 years of tenure. The latter factor also has a strong loading in the second factor that refers more specifically to the direct costs of dismissal, including severance payments in cases of no-fault dismissal and the costs of reinstatement in cases of unjustified dismissal. The third factor refers to the time involved in the dismissal procedure along two different dimensions: the notice period required for no-default dismissal, and also the trial period allowed before the standard rules of dismissal apply.

[xiii] Wage moderation based on collective negotiation, reduction of labor income tax, and corporate contributions to social welfare has characterized the major policy approaches, for instance, in the Netherlands and Germany.

CHAPTER 2.6

Perceptions of the Euro: An Update

PETER K. CORNELIUS, World Economic Forum

ANDREW M. WARNER, Center for International Development
at Harvard University

The 11 euro zone countries are getting ready for the introduction of bank notes and coins, the final step toward full monetary integration. This process of replacing the national monies will begin in January 2002, and by February the old currencies will lose their status as legal tender.[i] The question of whether the fixed exchange rates between the European currencies adopted at the start of the euro are appropriate and sustainable is receding into the background. Our evidence from last year suggested that these rates were widely accepted as appropriate by European executives very soon after the introduction of the euro.

The introduction of the euro in January 1999 was followed by a steady decline in the value of the euro relative to the US dollar. This decline has continued to puzzle many observers. Although the euro has regained some ground in recent months, the recovery has remained surprisingly moderate in light of the sharp decline in economic activity in the United States and the aggressive Fed easing, which has led to a reversal of interest rate differentials against Europe. The structure of portfolio equity flows has attracted attention in recent empirical studies as a possible explanation, but it has remained difficult to quantify the extent to which exchange rate movements are sensitive to such capital flows (IMF 2001, pp 74–75). There is causality in both directions, making it difficult to isolate the crucial factors.

This chapter discusses how expectations of currency stability are evolving in the euro zone based on the annual Executive Opinion Survey of the World Economic Forum. In last year's *Report*, we examined how the responses to the question "Does your exchange rate reflect economic fundamentals" had changed over the previous four years, from January 1997 through January 2000—a period that spanned the introduction of the euro in January 1999.[ii] The Survey responses indicated that European executives were generally unsure about the appropriate values of their currencies before the introduction of the euro. But after January 1999, opinion came around to the side of the euro's value in several key countries—especially France, Germany, Italy, and Spain. Only in Ireland was there deep division of opinion on whether the currency was properly valued. This support for the euro's value was probably partly the normal result of the resolution of uncertainty that had accumulated before January 1999, but may also represent a vote of confidence on the somewhat lower values that the euro achieved in the months and years after introduction. Our Survey indicated that European executives were expressing satisfaction with the level of the new currency, despite the initial doubts.

This year we focus on the immediate future, examining responses over the past four years to the question "Will your exchange rate be stable over the next two years?" The results are presented graphically in the 19 figures that accompany this article (Figures 2 through 20). The first eleven of these figures cover eleven of the twelve countries that have adopted the euro (excluding only Luxembourg). Next, for comparison, we include five major European countries: Denmark, Sweden, the United Kingdom, Norway and Switzerland. These are listed in Figures 13 through 17. Finally, we show Japan, the United States, and for a comparison with a country with high expectations of instability, Indonesia.

When we look at the responses from European countries, there are two issues: stability of the inter-European exchange rates and stability of the euro with respect to currencies in the rest of the world, primarily the US dollar and the yen.

On the first question, whether the fixed parities within Europe are still appropriate, we note that last year's Survey showed remarkable consensus. Even a full year after the introduction of the euro and even after the decline in the external value of the euro, the vast majority of executives in the euro countries responded with a 6 or a 7 to the question of whether their exchange rate was properly valued. A score of 7 was the maximum possible on our scale, representing a high degree of agreement with the statement that the exchange rate "properly reflected economic fundamentals." Therefore, the executives seemed to have few doubts that the euro was properly valued on either basis, within the euro area or outside the euro area.

What explains this high degree of consensus, especially given the voices before the introduction of the euro that suggested that the euro might become a straightjacket preventing relative price adjustment within the euro area? One explanation is that the problems that were anticipated at the introduction of the euro simply have not materialized. It has always been thought that flexible exchange rates and independent monetary policies were needed to enable countries to adjust to shocks when prices and wages were insufficiently flexible. What has happened is that countries within Europe have not been subjected to severe negative shocks that would have required country-specific interest rate cuts or depreciation.

One source of such shocks might have been the fact that different countries have different trading partners outside the euro area, and demand for exports from these trading partners could have been growing at different rates. However, in most euro countries, over 60 percent of trade is with other euro countries, so this source of divergence has been muted. Ireland, with only about 40 percent of its trade with euro countries, is different from other euro countries in this regard, but with growth around 8 percent per year, Ireland is not suffering from insufficient demand.

Growth rates have indeed differed in Europe since the introduction of the common currency, yet the evidence is that relative prices have adjusted in high-growth countries without the need for independent interest rate or exchange rate adjustments. Figure 1 shows that rates of inflation have tended to be higher in the high growth countries. This is evidence that relative prices within the euro area have been able to adjust in the required direction without nominal exchange rate changes. Therefore, one possible reading of our Survey results is that executives perceive that the adjustment has worked rather smoothly within the euro area. Severe negative shocks have not happened, and price levels have adjusted in the required way to differing real growth rates.

Figure 1: Growth and inflation in the euro zone, 1998–2000

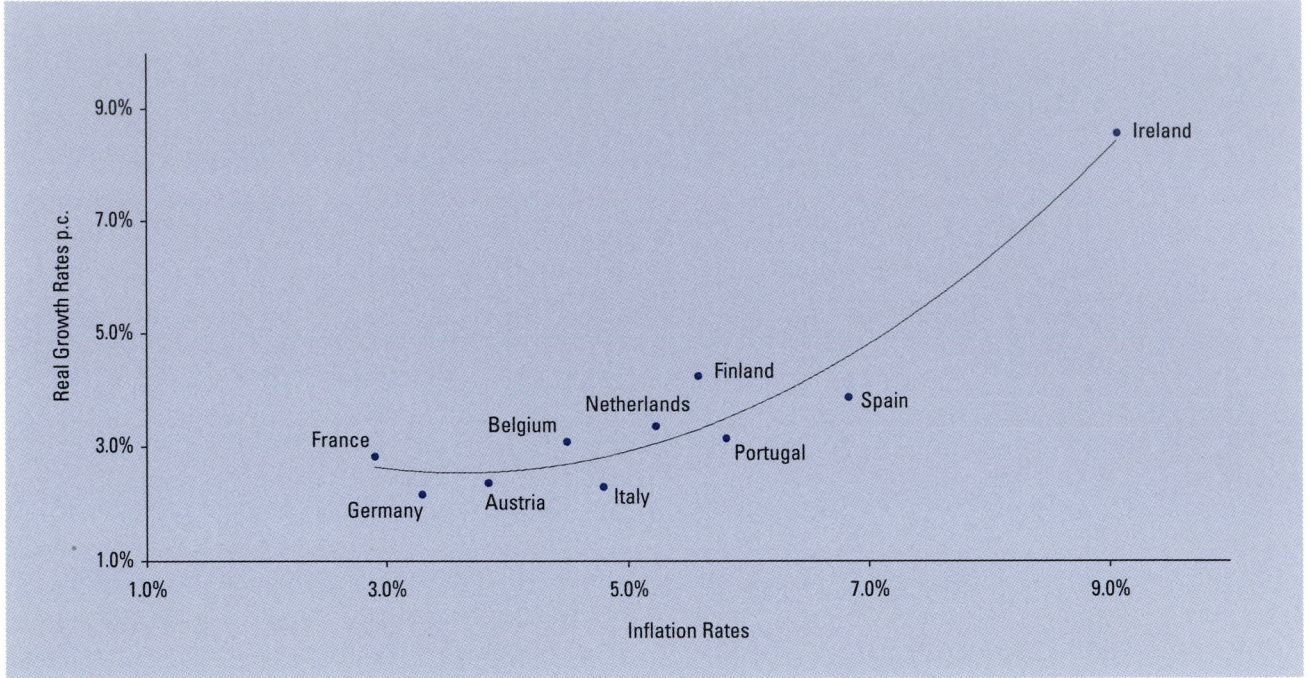

Given the evidence above about perceived stability of exchange rates within the euro zone, we would expect that the expectations recorded in Figures 2 through 12 mostly refer to expectations about changes in the value of the euro with respect to currencies outside the euro area.

When we look at the Figures for the euro countries (Figures 2 through 12) we see a high degree of expected stability—most of the respondents give their country high ratings, of close to 7 on the 1-to-7 scale—indicating high perceived stability. This contrasts sharply with the normal pattern for other countries not under a fixed exchange rate system like the euro. Note the United Kingdom (Figure 15), or for an extreme in this regard, Indonesia (Figure 20).

Nevertheless, despite the general perception of stability, we can also see that perceptions have started to shift in the other direction in some of the euro counties as of February 2001. Note for example France (Figure 5) or Germany (Figure 6). In each case the histogram has shifted slightly toward the left. This indicates that opinion within Europe regarding the euro during the past year has shifted from a high degree of perceived stability to somewhat less perceived stability.

In sum, there continues to be a high degree of confidence in the value of the euro on the part of business executives. There is evidence that prices are flexible enough within Europe and are adjusting upward in countries with higher than average growth. In this regard at least, flexible exchange rates have not been missed so far. This is one possible explanation for why executives in our Survey expect a high degree of future stability. There is some emerging evidence, however, that this confidence in the currency is beginning to soften in the euro area. We will continue to monitor the Survey results as a possible early-warning guide to emerging economic imbalances within the euro zone countries.

Figure 2: Austria

Will your exchange rate be stable over the next two years?

(1 = strongly disagree; 7 = strongly agree)

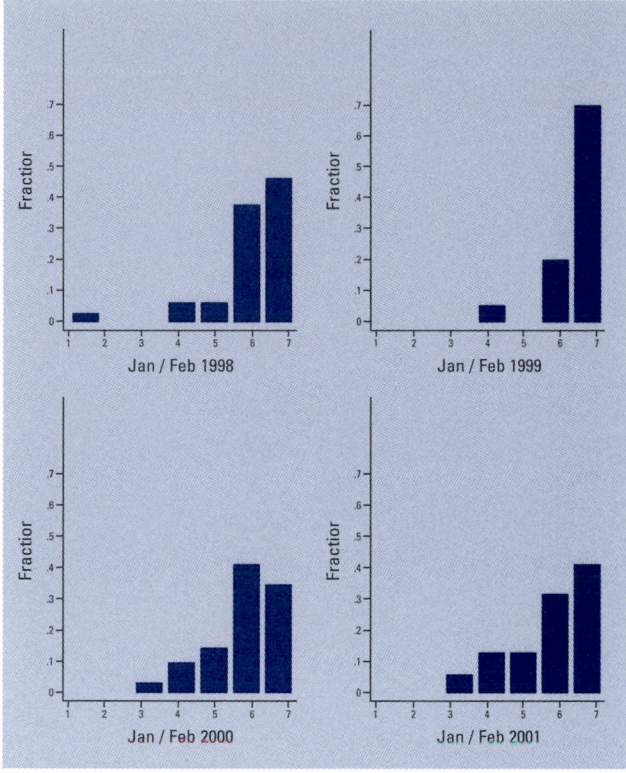

Figure 3: Belgium

Will your exchange rate be stable over the next two years?

(1 = strongly disagree; 7 = strongly agree)

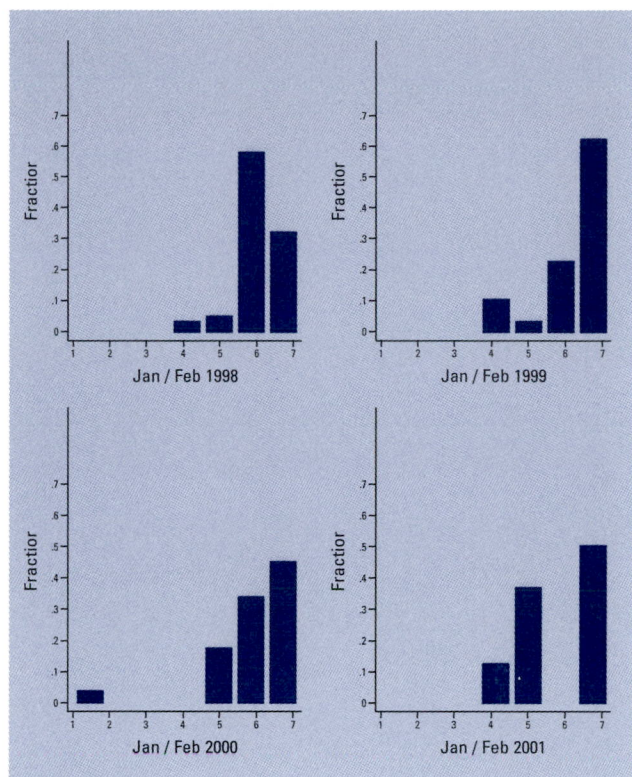

Figure 4: Finland

Will your exchange rate be stable over the next two years?

(1 = strongly disagree; 7 = strongly agree)

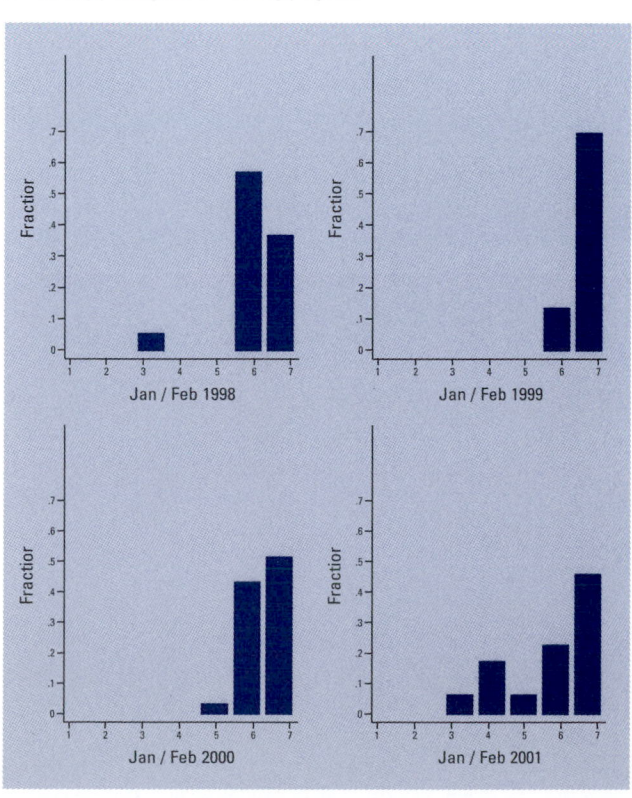

Figure 5: France

Will your exchange rate be stable over the next two years?

(1 = strongly disagree; 7 = strongly agree)

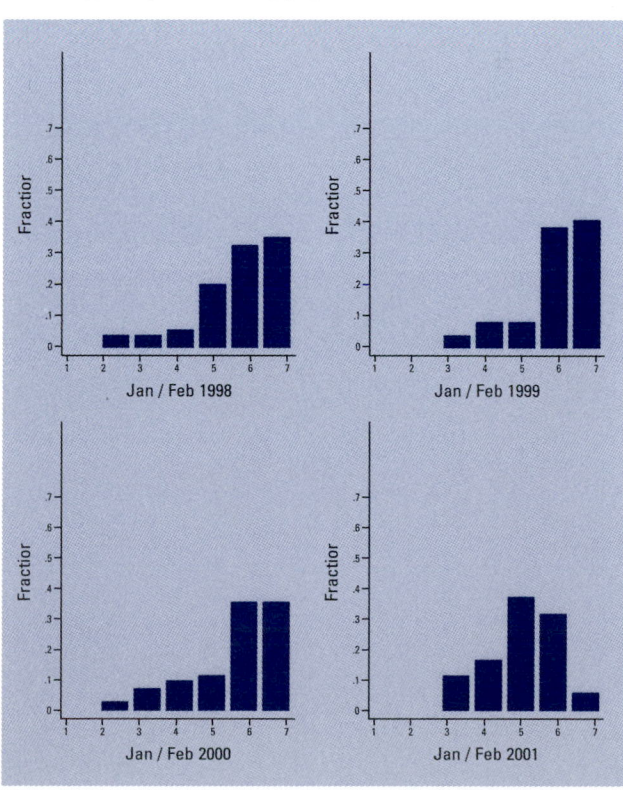

Figure 6: Germany
Will your exchange rate be stable over the next two years?
(1 = strongly disagree; 7 = strongly agree)

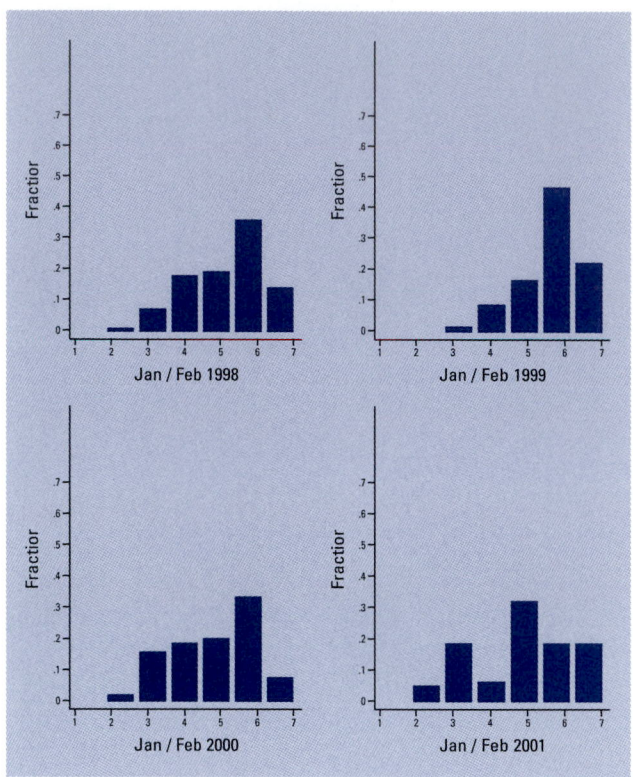

Figure 7: Greece
Will your exchange rate be stable over the next two years?
(1 = strongly disagree; 7 = strongly agree)

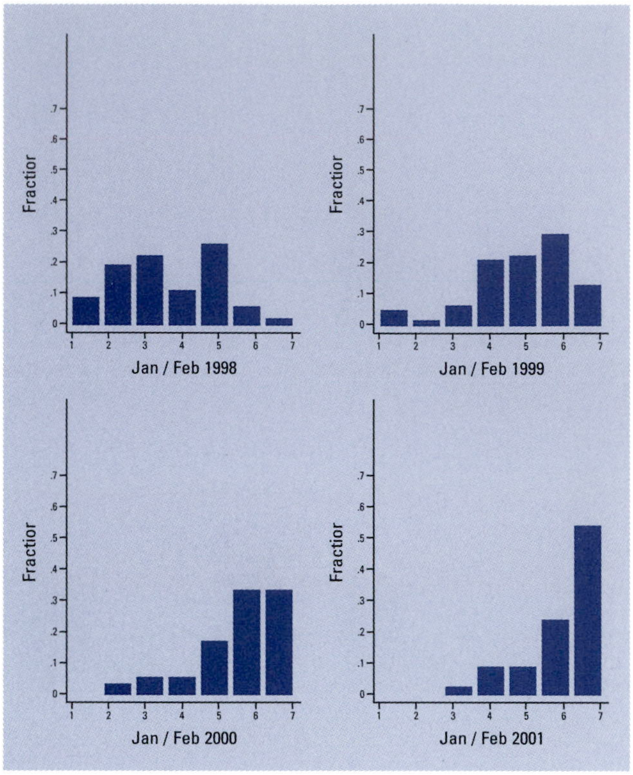

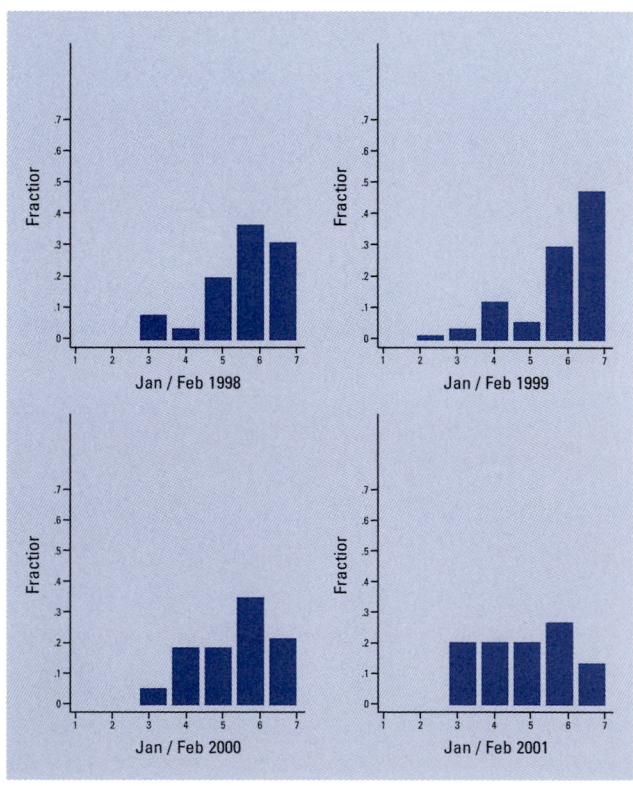

Figure 8: Ireland
Will your exchange rate be stable over the next two years?
(1 = strongly disagree; 7 = strongly agree)

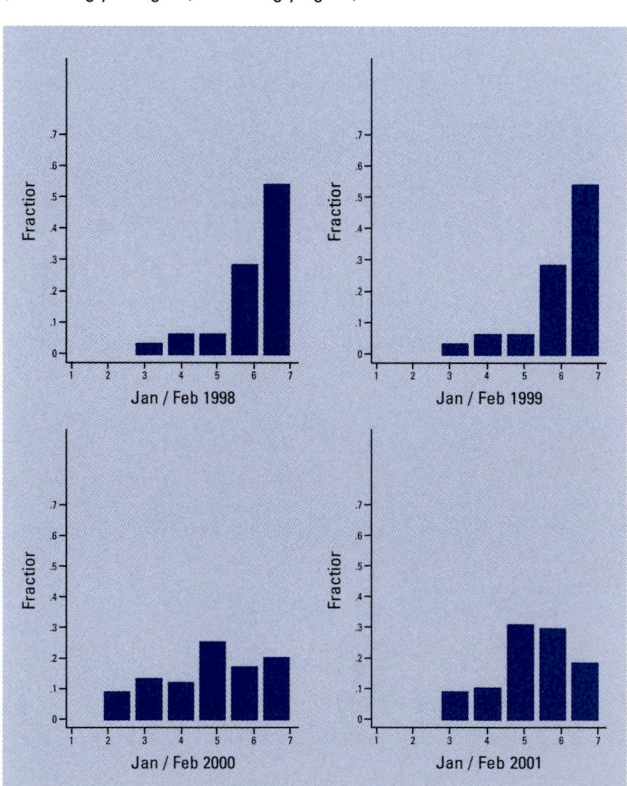

Figure 9: Italy
Will your exchange rate be stable over the next two years?
(1 = strongly disagree; 7 = strongly agree)

Figure 10: The Netherlands
Will your exchange rate be stable over the next two years?
(1 = strongly disagree; 7 = strongly agree)

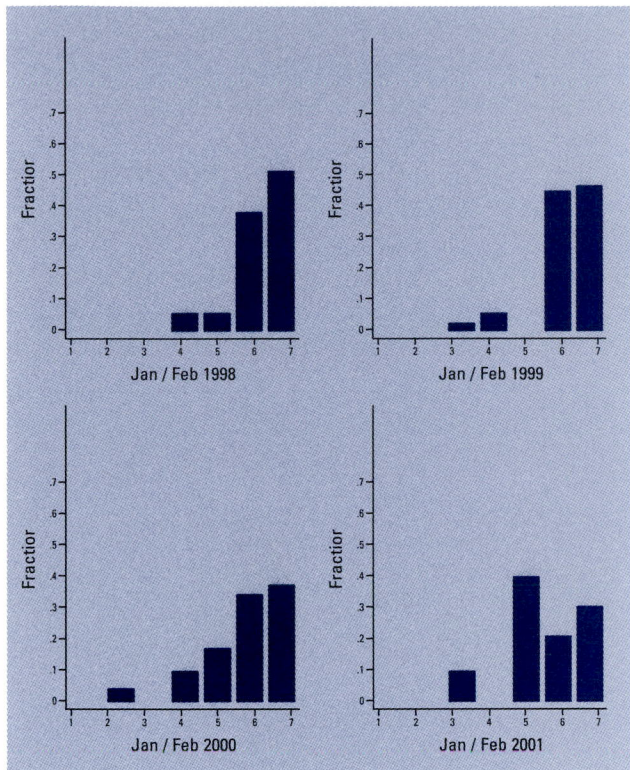

Figure 11: Portugal
Will your exchange rate be stable over the next two years?
(1 = strongly disagree; 7 = strongly agree)

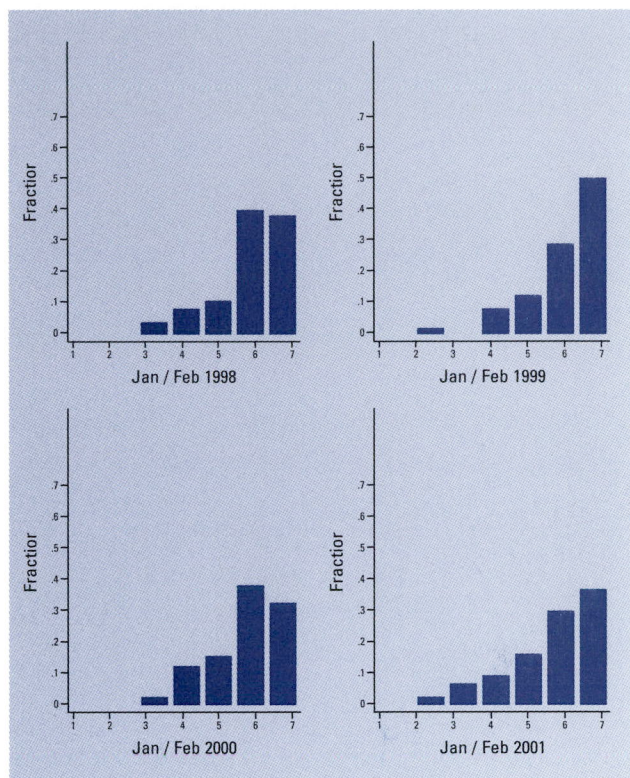

Figure 12: Spain
Will your exchange rate be stable over the next two years?
(1 = strongly disagree; 7 = strongly agree)

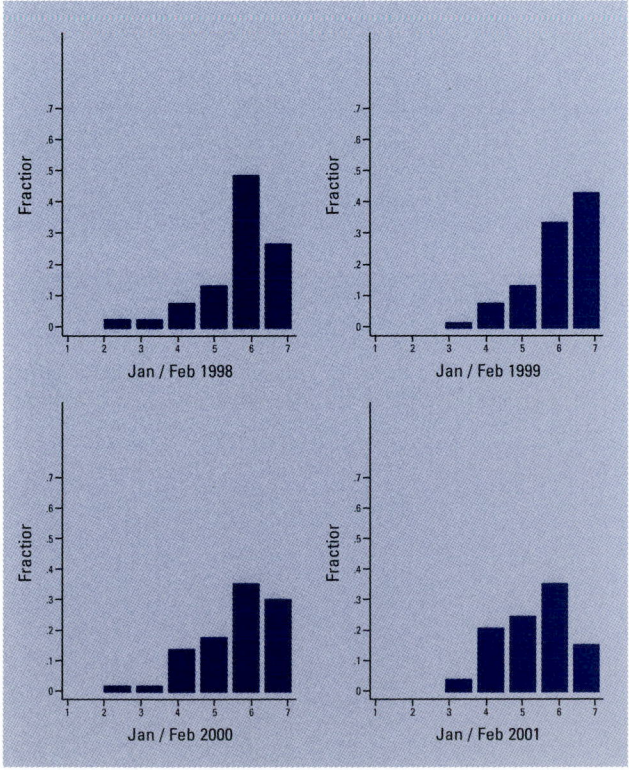

Figure 13: Denmark
Will your exchange rate be stable over the next two years?
(1 = strongly disagree; 7 = strongly agree)

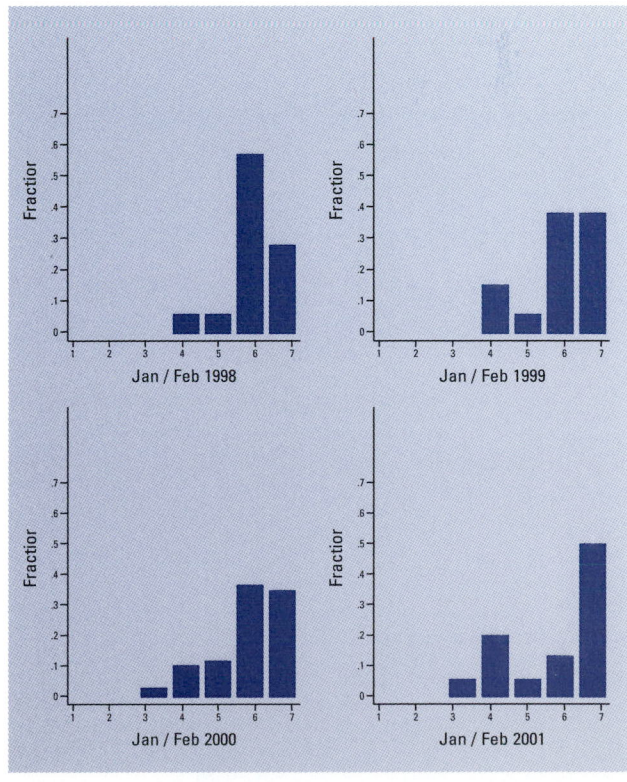

Figure 14: Sweden
Will your exchange rate be stable over the next two years?
(1 = strongly disagree; 7 = strongly agree)

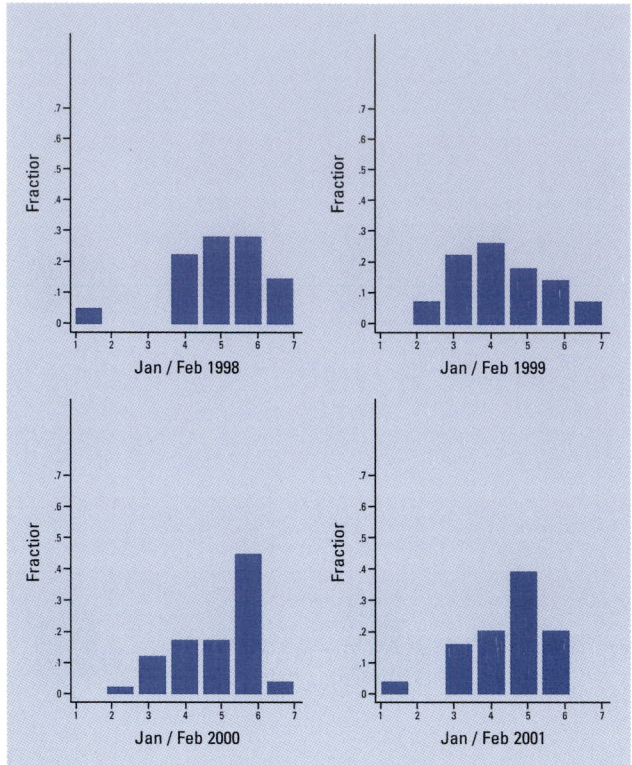

Figure 15: United Kingdom
Will your exchange rate be stable over the next two years?
(1 = strongly disagree; 7 = strongly agree)

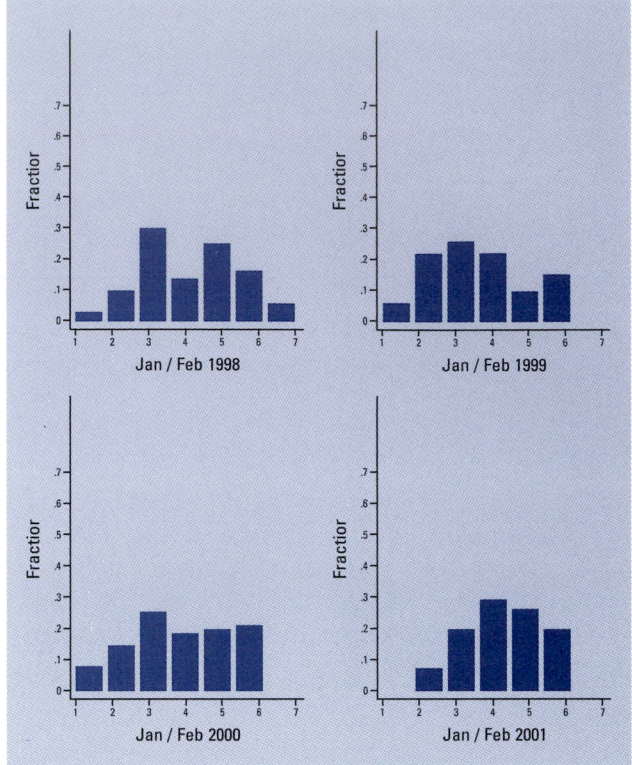

Figure 16: Norway
Will your exchange rate be stable over the next two years?
(1 = strongly disagree; 7 = strongly agree)

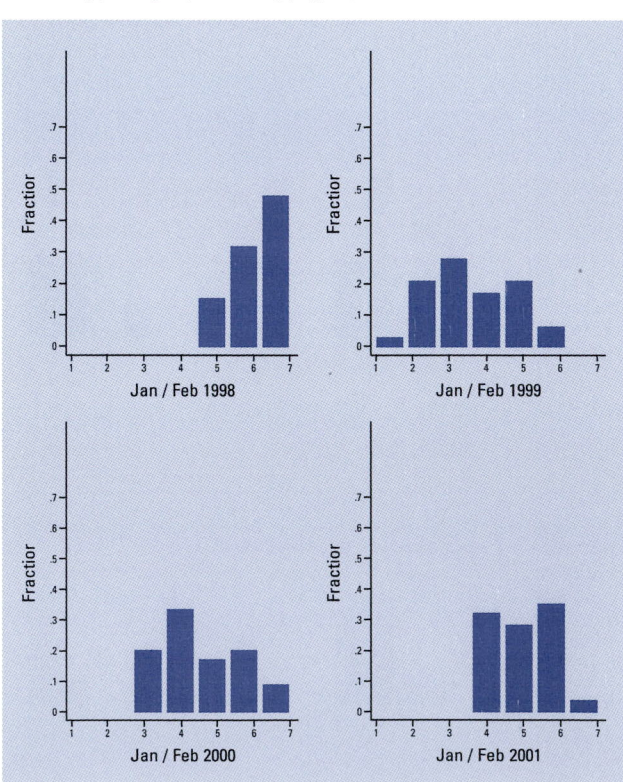

Figure 17: Switzerland
Will your exchange rate be stable over the next two years?
(1 = strongly disagree; 7 = strongly agree)

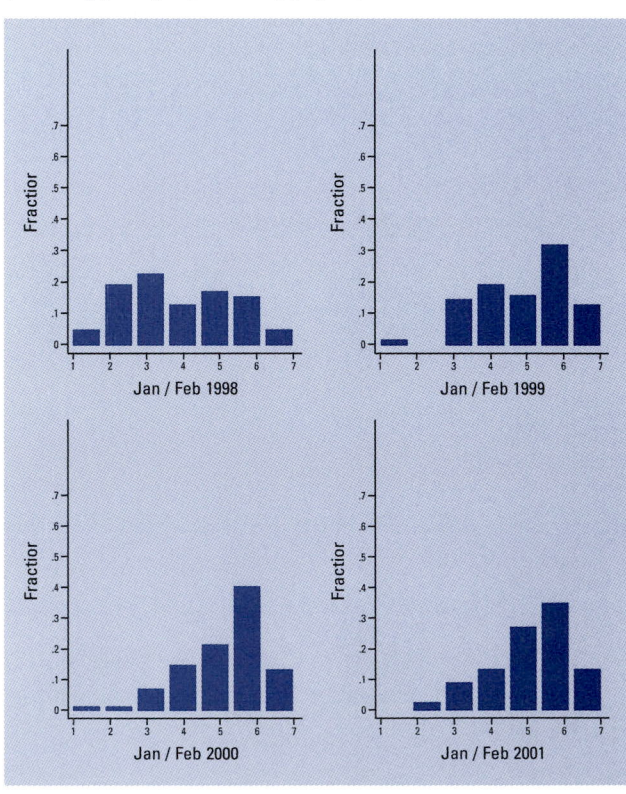

Figure 18: Japan
Will your exchange rate be stable over the next two years?
(1 = strongly disagree; 7 = strongly agree)

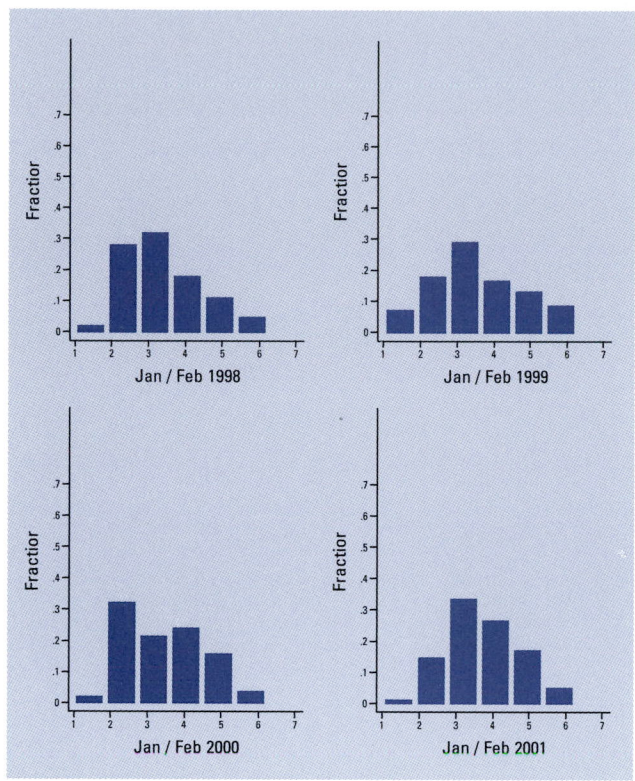

Figure 19: United States
Will your exchange rate be stable over the next two years?
(1 = strongly disagree; 7 = strongly agree)

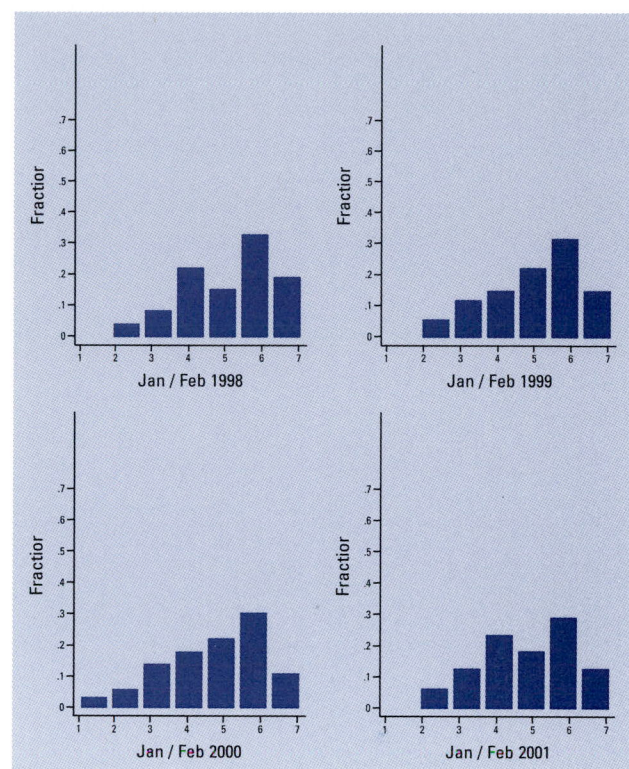

Figure 20: Indonesia
Will your exchange rate be stable over the next two years?
(1 = strongly disagree; 7 = strongly agree)

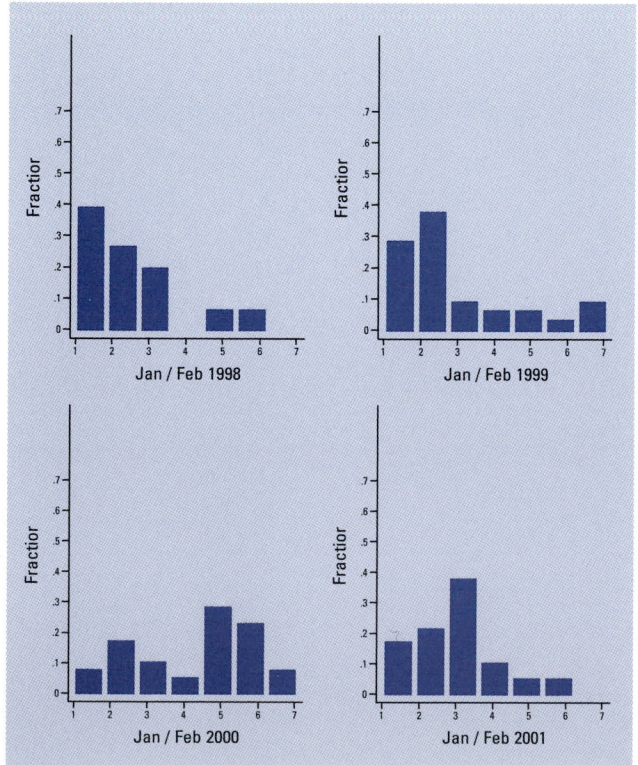

163

References

Cornelius, P., P. Malmgren, and A. M. Warner, "Assessing the Euro's Performance on the Basis of the Executive Opinion Surveys," *The Global Competitiveness Report 2000*, New York: Oxford University Press, 2000: 76–84.

International Monetary Fund, *World Economic Outlook*, Washington DC: International Monetary Fund, 2001.

Scacciavillani, F. and N. Sobczak, "Countdown to E-day: A Smooth Changeover to Euro Notes and Coins," *The European Economic Analyst*, March/April 2001, Goldman Sachs.

Notes

[i] People will, however, still be able to exchange old currencies for euros for an extended period. At commercial banks the changeover will continue until the end of June, and in some cases until December. Many national central banks have imposed no deadlines. For details see Scacciavillani and Sobszak (2001).

[ii] Cornelius et al (2000), pp 76–84.

The Executive Opinion Survey[i]

PETER K. CORNELIUS, World Economic Forum

JOHN W. MCARTHUR, Center for International Development
at Harvard University

The analysis in the *Global Competitiveness Report* hinges on both quantitative data published by major international institutions and qualitative data obtained through the World Economic Forum's annual Executive Opinion Survey. By capturing a broad array of intangible factors that cannot be found in official statistics but that nonetheless affect a country's ability to achieve sustained economic growth, the *Report's* international Survey provides a key instrument for assessing the macro- and microeconomic foundations of competitiveness. Such crucial underlying growth factors include hidden import and export barriers, quality of education, administrative red tape, corruption, and the nature of local supply networks. In many cases, the Survey provides unique insight into the gaps between economies' *de jure* regulatory frameworks and their *de facto* enforcement.

A central premise guides the logic of the Survey. We assume that there exists some underlying yet difficult-to-describe reality that could characterize, at some point in time, any particular growth-related factor in any particular economy. Although the nature of that reality will always be changing and, more often than not, will be tremendously complex, one can only begin to develop an understanding of it by recording the experiences of those who live and work within that economy. In its essence, the Executive Opinion Survey attempts to do just this. It is the business leaders and entrepreneurs whose success depends on fair and efficient economies who are best placed to assess their business environment on a global scale. These people on the ground best understand the nuances of their economy across a range of dimensions, so it is their experience that we aim to record as we compare the strengths and weaknesses of economies around the world.

Expanded thematic and geographic coverage

This year, our Survey has expanded significantly in terms of both the range of topics included and the number of countries covered. Within the Survey instrument itself, we continue to include well over 100 questions concerning the quality of government and public institutions, the macroeconomic environment, national technology levels, and domestic competition structures, as well as company operations and strategy. We also continue to include an entire section on the environment, an area that is tied inextricably to every country's standard of living. Many of the questions are carried over from previous years, and several have been tweaked in an attempt to distinguish more clearly the results across countries. Many other questions are new, reflecting ongoing updates in our research agenda, frequently as informed by past *Global Competitiveness Report* results. The largest number of new questions, nearly 40 in total, focuses on Information and

Communications Technology (ICT) and helps us assess the degree to which economies are "ICT-ready" in terms of both business practices and the public policy environment. These questions enable our ICT analysis to go well beyond the mere number of personal computers or Internet service providers in a country.[ii]

With regard to coverage, the Executive Opinion Survey this year includes 17 new economies on four continents. In Africa, we have included Nigeria; in Asia, we have added Bangladesh and Sri Lanka; in central and eastern Europe we now examine the three Baltic states (Estonia, Latvia, and Lithuania) as well as Romania and Slovenia. The largest group of new entrants are located, however, in the Western Hemisphere. Thanks in particular to the excellent cooperation of the Inter-American Development Bank, we have been able to include nine additional countries in this region, namely, the Dominican Republic, Guatemala, Honduras, Jamaica, Nicaragua, Panama, Paraguay, Trinidad and Tobago, and Uruguay.[iii] Overall, the *Global Competitiveness Report* now assesses 75 economies, representing 90 percent of world GDP and more than 80 percent of world population.[iv] With an increasing number of developing countries becoming more integrated into the world economy—and many still remaining isolated from the benefits of globalization—we are particularly pleased to have added so many countries to our analysis since most of them are classified as middle- and low-income economies. The broader the range of income levels included in our *Report*, the further we can develop our knowledge about the differing relative roles played by competitiveness factors at different stages of development.

We plan to continue expanding the list of countries covered in the *Report* in the years ahead. In principle, there is no reason why we should include fewer countries than those where CNN can be received on television (currently, this is more than 200). In practice, however, any expansion depends on the availability of reliable current data—both publicly available information (or "hard data") and Survey data—as the basis for a comparative assessment. With the Survey data, it is critical that a sufficient number of senior business leaders participate and that the sample remain unbiased with regard to any particular business group.

Methodology

In order to ensure that the Survey is sufficiently representative of each economy included, we continue to work closely with partner institutes in most countries. First, we asked each of our partner institutes to start with a comprehensive register of firms and then to choose a sample whose distribution across economic sectors of the economy is proportional to the distribution of the country's labor force across sectors, excluding agriculture

as much as possible. The employment distribution was taken from data in the most recent issue of the *Yearbook of Labour Statistics* of the International Labour Office. We then asked our partners to choose firms randomly within these broad sectors (for example, by selecting firms at regular intervals from an alphabetical list) and to pursue telephone or on-site interviews, following up for clarifications where necessary. The Survey respondents are typically a company's CEO or a member of its senior management. Their participation is purely voluntary.

It is important to note that the Executive Opinion Survey's main goal is not to form specific inferences about the population of firms in a country. For instance, the sample should not be used to estimate the average firm size in a country. We do, however, aim to construct a sample of firms that is adequately broad and representative to estimate non-firm information about an economy. The Survey helps to assess the economic environment within which firms operate by sampling the perspectives of a diversity of executives and managers across many business sectors and firm sizes. We aim, through the use of these various perspectives within each country, to paint as complete a picture as possible of the current economic conditions, particularly those related to growth and productivity.

The typical Executive Opinion Survey question asks the respondent to assess an issue by choosing a number between 1 and 7 that best reflects their perception of their business environment, with the value 1 representing one end of the spectrum and the value 7 representing the other end of the spectrum. A typical question is presented in Box 1. This question, like most others, is intentionally framed so that 7 represents the top standard in the world and 1 represents a bottom standard. Once completed, the Survey results are compiled and country-level means (for the most part) are calculated to create a country score on each question.

Box 1: Typical Executive Opinion Survey Question

Intellectual property protection in your country is:

Weak or non-existent	**1 2 3 4 5 6 7**	Equal to the world's most stringent

Circling 1.....means you agree wholeheartedly with the answer on the left-hand side

Circling 7.....means you agree wholeheartedly with the answer on the right-hand side

Circling 2.....means you largely agree with the left-hand side

Circling 3.....means you agree somewhat with left-hand side

Circling 4.....means your opinion is indifferent between the two answers

Circling 5.....means you agree somewhat with the right-hand side

Circling 6.....means you largely agree with the right-hand side

Table 1: Distribution of respondents by firm size and type

	# of firms responding	Surveys per million population	Distribution of Respondents by Firm Size (# employees in country)					Distribution of Respondents by Firm Type				
			<250	250–500	501–5000	5001–20000	>20000	Domestic[1]	Domestic/ Exporter[2]	MNC subsidiary[3]	State-owned[4]	Gov't organization
Argentina	30	0.81	29%	4%	32%	32%	4%	38%	21%	41%	—	—
Australia	27	1.41	9%	17%	43%	17%	13%	19%	42%	23%	—	15%
Austria	64	7.87	15%	21%	51%	13%	—	14%	45%	14%	16%	12%
Bangladesh	59	0.46	25%	20%	47%	5%	2%	18%	59%	23%	—	—
Belgium	15	1.46	17%	—	42%	8%	33%	8%	54%	31%	—	8%
Bolivia	141	17.30	76%	13%	10%	1%	—	50%	35%	10%	2%	2%
Brazil	40	0.24	13%	11%	34%	34%	8%	18%	20%	58%	5%	—
Bulgaria	122	15.25	50%	25%	25%	—	—	25%	50%	6%	11%	9%
Canada	40	1.30	8%	3%	55%	21%	13%	10%	59%	23%	8%	—
Chile	71	4.69	13%	7%	38%	22%	20%	54%	24%	19%	3%	—
China	146	0.12	25%	20%	41%	12%	2%	47%	17%	8%	19%	9%
Colombia	120	2.84	53%	12%	27%	7%	1%	50%	31%	12%	5%	1%
Costa Rica	61	15.25	69%	24%	7%	—	—	30%	38%	28%	3%	2%
Czech Republic	34	3.31	55%	10%	14%	17%	3%	32%	47%	18%	3%	—
Denmark	32	6.04	17%	10%	40%	27%	7%	13%	65%	16%	3%	3%
Dominican Republic	100	11.85	75%	13%	11%	—	—	70%	24%	3%	2%	1%
Ecuador	62	4.80	67%	23%	9%	2%	—	32%	53%	8%	5%	2%
Egypt	13	0.19	40%	—	40%	—	20%	9%	55%	18%	—	18%
El Salvador	45	7.35	66%	9%	25%	—	—	41%	41%	14%	—	5%
Estonia	61	44.56	92%	4%	4%	—	—	42%	23%	13%	7%	15%
Finland	18	3.48	17%	6%	28%	39%	11%	6%	76%	6%	12%	—
France	22	0.37	10%	19%	19%	19%	33%	14%	45%	36%	5%	—
Germany	44	0.53	12%	2%	39%	10%	37%	5%	68%	27%	—	—
Greece	42	4.00	21%	15%	56%	5%	3%	22%	62%	14%	—	3%
Guatemala	152	13.33	85%	9%	4%	1%	1%	53%	29%	7%	7%	3%
Honduras	155	23.48	80%	10%	10%	—	—	69%	21%	6%	3%	1%
Hong Kong SAR	51	7.50	34%	9%	38%	17%	2%	16%	35%	37%	10%	2%
Hungary	39	3.85	14%	24%	59%	3%	—	13%	21%	37%	8%	21%
Iceland	21	76.09	56%	25%	19%	—	—	19%	43%	5%	5%	29%
India	49	0.05	13%	10%	58%	15%	4%	21%	47%	30%	2%	—
Indonesia	25	0.11	13%	17%	42%	25%	4%	20%	48%	20%	8%	4%
Ireland	47	12.38	44%	12%	34%	10%	—	19%	38%	26%	11%	6%
Israel	24	4.14	29%	17%	33%	21%	—	21%	75%	4%	—	—
Italy	19	0.33	18%	—	41%	35%	6%	—	71%	29%	—	—
Jamaica	52	19.62	79%	10%	10%	—	—	65%	16%	12%	8%	—
Japan	73	0.58	11%	4%	34%	38%	12%	26%	58%	15%	1%	—
Jordan	81	16.07	63%	10%	21%	6%	—	11%	39%	8%	19%	24%
Korea	164	3.47	12%	11%	65%	11%	1%	33%	52%	10%	4%	1%
Latvia	29	12.19	41%	41%	14%	5%	—	28%	34%	10%	14%	14%
Lithuania	71	19.20	49%	14%	36%	—	—	22%	25%	10%	34%	7%
Malaysia	26	1.12	35%	17%	35%	13%	—	17%	33%	42%	4%	4%
Mauritius	16	13.49	50%	29%	21%	—	—	20%	60%	7%	—	13%
Mexico	83	0.85	19%	8%	36%	25%	12%	22%	40%	32%	2%	4%
Netherlands	11	0.69	20%	10%	10%	30%	30%	10%	40%	40%	10%	—
New Zealand	52	13.62	35%	25%	31%	8%	—	49%	31%	16%	4%	—
Nicaragua	153	30.00	83%	7%	10%	—	—	59%	21%	13%	5%	3%
Nigeria	71	0.64	42%	25%	25%	6%	2%	43%	34%	17%	—	6%
Norway	31	6.89	47%	13%	23%	17%	—	27%	53%	13%	7%	—
Panama	156	55.52	84%	9%	7%	—	—	72%	15%	7%	3%	2%
Paraguay	100	17.89	79%	13%	5%	2%	—	77%	15%	6%	—	1%
Peru	42	1.63	48%	23%	30%	—	—	43%	33%	19%	—	5%
Philippines	41	0.54	25%	20%	45%	10%	—	39%	34%	22%	—	5%
Poland	27	0.70	22%	30%	41%	—	7%	36%	32%	28%	4%	—
Portugal	45	4.50	31%	9%	37%	20%	3%	21%	54%	5%	15%	5%
Romania	51	2.28	31%	10%	47%	8%	4%	43%	18%	18%	22%	—
Russia	190	1.30	32%	24%	35%	8%	2%	48%	30%	3%	12%	7%
Singapore	67	16.68	53%	15%	32%	—	—	9%	27%	55%	3%	6%
Slovak Republic	5	0.93	75%	—	25%	—	—	20%	40%	20%	—	20%
Slovenia	77	38.69	45%	16%	36%	3%	—	40%	50%	3%	3%	4%
South Africa	75	1.72	30%	7%	25%	21%	16%	26%	40%	26%	9%	—
Spain	71	1.78	4%	4%	62%	23%	6%	29%	48%	20%	3%	—
Sri Lanka	92	4.78	58%	9%	18%	13%	2%	41%	33%	18%	8%	—
Sweden	27	3.03	22%	13%	48%	13%	4%	11%	37%	30%	7%	15%
Switzerland	47	6.47	27%	13%	47%	13%	—	7%	61%	30%	—	2%
Taiwan	33	1.49	10%	3%	37%	40%	10%	33%	40%	17%	7%	3%
Thailand	55	0.89	12%	14%	47%	14%	14%	20%	22%	11%	33%	15%
Trinidad and Tobago	50	38.46	80%	15%	5%	—	—	48%	40%	2%	8%	2%
Turkey	16	0.24	64%	14%	14%	7%	—	13%	31%	38%	13%	6%
Ukraine	101	2.01	72%	15%	4%	6%	2%	60%	18%	5%	8%	8%
United Kingdom	33	0.55	28%	16%	19%	31%	6%	6%	55%	39%	—	—
United States	81	0.29	29%	8%	22%	24%	18%	19%	70%	9%	3%	—
Uruguay	133	40.30	85%	8%	5%	1%	—	68%	19%	12%	2%	—
Venezuela	26	1.07	52%	24%	12%	12%	—	24%	36%	40%	—	—
Vietnam	39	0.50	64%	15%	18%	3%	—	26%	31%	18%	26%	—
Zimbabwe	17	1.40	24%	18%	29%	29%	—	25%	50%	25%	—	—
Total	**4601**											

[1] Domestically based, sells primarily in domestic market.

[2] Domestically based, sells both in domestic market and foreign market.

[3] Unit/subsidiary of a multinational operating in the country.

[4] Government or quasi-governmental enterprise.

Having conducted this process in the early months of 2001, as Table 1 shows, we received a total of 4,601 Survey responses, implying an average of around 60 Surveys per country. This ratio is basically in line with last year's Survey, although the number of responses increased appreciably in some countries. This year we received 100 or more Surveys from 15 countries. Only nine reached that level of response last year. At the same time, however, the response rate fell in a number of other countries. Presumably, the difficult economic situation played an important role in some of them, particularly Argentina and Turkey, since business executives simply did not have the time to participate in the Survey amidst their other pressing issues.

Key characteristics of the Survey respondents

Table 1 shows some important descriptive statistics concerning this year's Survey respondents. In a third of the countries, more than 70 firms completed the Survey while in two-thirds of the countries, the figure was greater than 40. Examining the sample in another way, in nearly three-quarters of the countries at least one firm completed the Survey per every one million inhabitants. The main exceptions are found in countries with huge populations—Brazil, China, India, Japan, Nigeria, the Philippines, and the United States.

Looking at the distribution of respondents by country, one sees that the industrialized economies in the sample tend to have fewer firms in relation to GDP than developing economies. This relationship is even more pronounced this year than in previous years, since this year the greatest increases in response rate were largely concentrated in Latin America and a number of transition economies. The sample's average firm in an industrialized economy thus "represents" a substantially larger part of national output than its average counterpart firm from a developing economy.

This observation does not suggest that large economies are underrepresented in our sample. It is, however, consistent with the fact that the largest companies in the world are concentrated in the industrialized countries. According to the most recent edition of the Global 500 list of the *Financial Times*, the largest emerging market–based company in terms of annual turnover remains Brazil's Petrobras, with around 25 billion US dollars. Korea's Samsung Electronics (21 billion US dollars) and Mexico's Telecom Carso Global (13 billion US dollars) are next largest. Although their turnovers are exceptional by emerging market standards, around a dozen companies in the United States alone have turnover of 50 billion US dollars or more.

One way to assess the representativeness and consistency of the Survey results is to examine the standard deviations among responses in each country. Figure 1 shows the responses to an Executive Survey question that asks about the commonness of "irregular extra payments or bribes" connected with annual tax collection. The thick bars indicate the average score in each country and the thin lines on the right side of each bar indicate the standard deviations. This graph tells us important information about the "average" perspective in a given country, and also provides useful insights into the diversity of perspectives within countries on any particular question. In some instances, the standard deviations are very small. Here for example, the standard deviation in Iceland is 0, implying that every respondent from that country answered with a value of 7 for this question. Yet there is also a fairly regular pattern in the standard deviations, with the typical value ranging from 1.0 to 1.5 for this and other questions.

Since average country responses form the heart of the Growth Competitiveness Index and the Current Competitiveness Index, another and perhaps more compelling way to test the consistency of our results is to compare the mean country responses to a Survey question with the mean responses after we randomly dropped half of the Surveys in each country. This is demonstrated in Figure 2. To create this graph, we asked the computer to drop one-half of its responses randomly from each country. We then recalculated mean country scores for the same question as above on corruption in tax collection and compared them with the results obtained using the full sample. If the results for the full sample and half sample were precisely the same, the collection of dots would form a perfectly straight line. The pattern on this graph, each dot representing a country's full-sample versus half-sample country average, is remarkably close to such a line, demonstrating a high degree of robustness in our country average approach. The results are similar when we perform the same test on different questions.

Looking more closely at Figure 2, one sees that Bangladesh and Iceland, the countries with the lowest and highest respective mean results on this question, have no change in their scores when half the sample is dropped. Belgium, Egypt, and Zimbabwe are moderate but not large outliers. This is not surprising, since those countries each had less than 18 responses in this year's Survey.

Figure 2 shows the results when the random drop test is applied to only one question. More importantly, when we perform the same test on the Growth Competitiveness Index's component institutions index, which is based entirely on Survey data, we see that full-sample versus half-sample variations on specific questions tend to cancel each other out once the questions are merged into the index. Figure 3 shows an even tighter relationship between the full and half samples than Figure 2. Here the simple correlation coefficient between the full- and

Figure 1: Country means and standard deviations for a typical Executive Opinion Survey question

"How commonly do firms in your industry give irregular payments or bribes connected with annual tax payments? (1 = common, 7 = never)"
Thick bars indicate scores; thin lines indicate standard deviations.

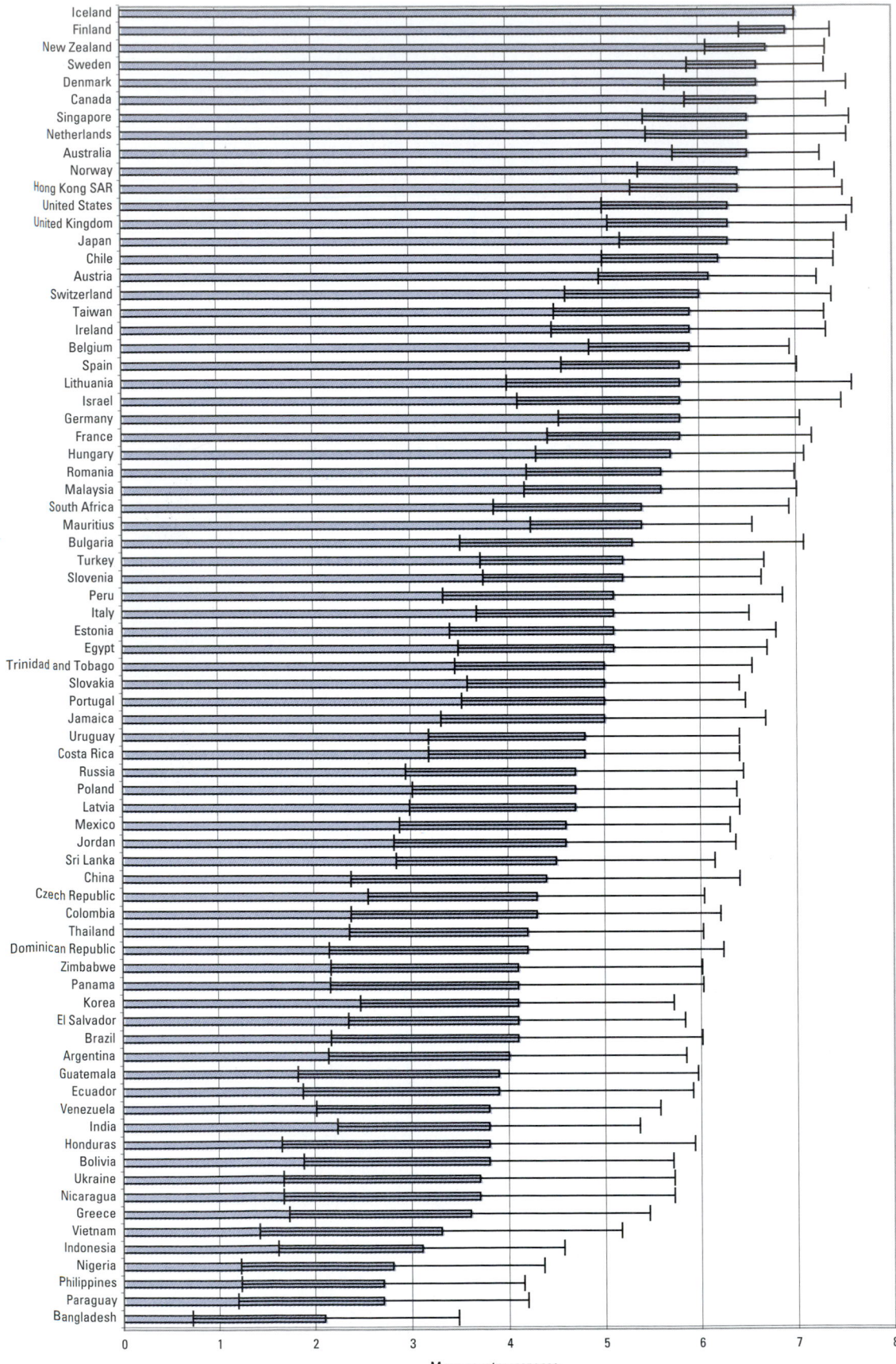

Mean country response

Figure 2: Robustness test of Survey data, part I: Results from random drop test on question regarding corruption in tax collection

"How commonly do firms in your industry give irregular payments or bribes connected with annual tax payments? (1 = common, 7 = never)"

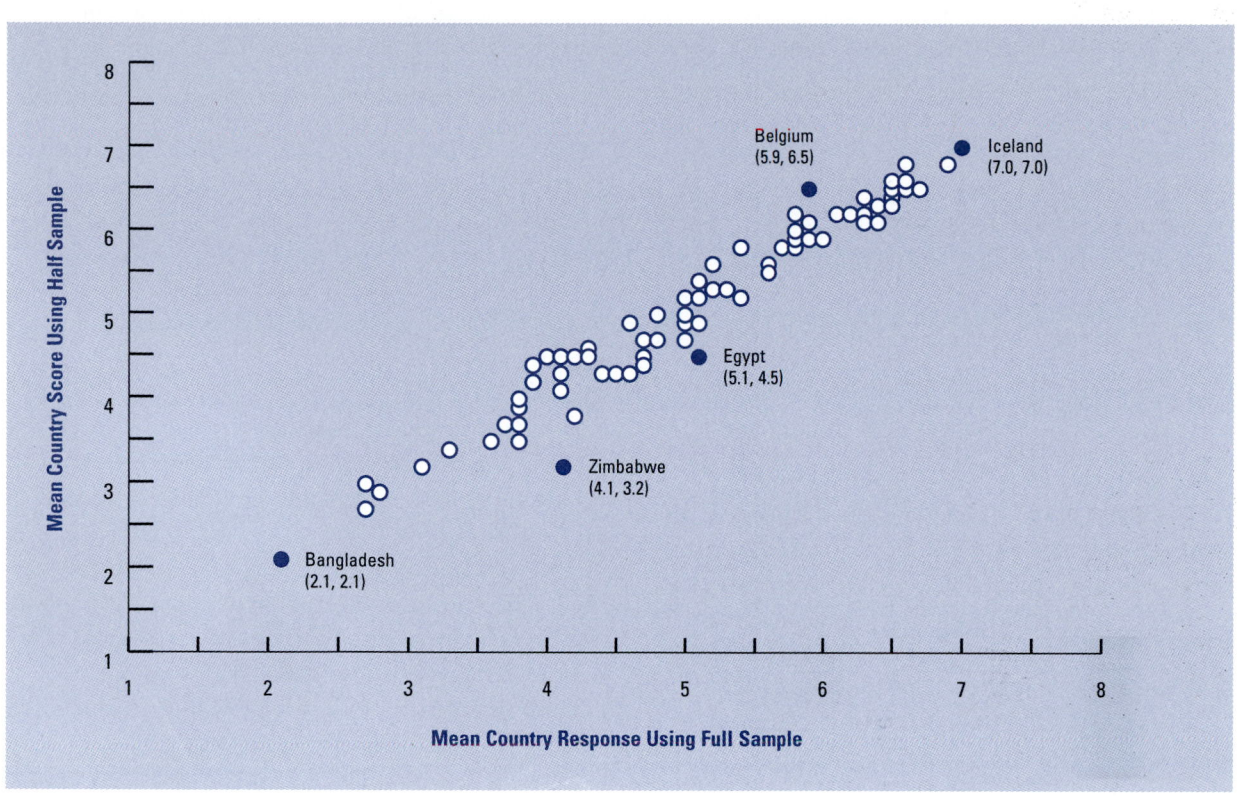

Figure 3: Robustness test of Survey data, part II: Results from random drop test on Growth Competitiveness institutions index

(1 = lowest possible score, 7 = highest possible score)

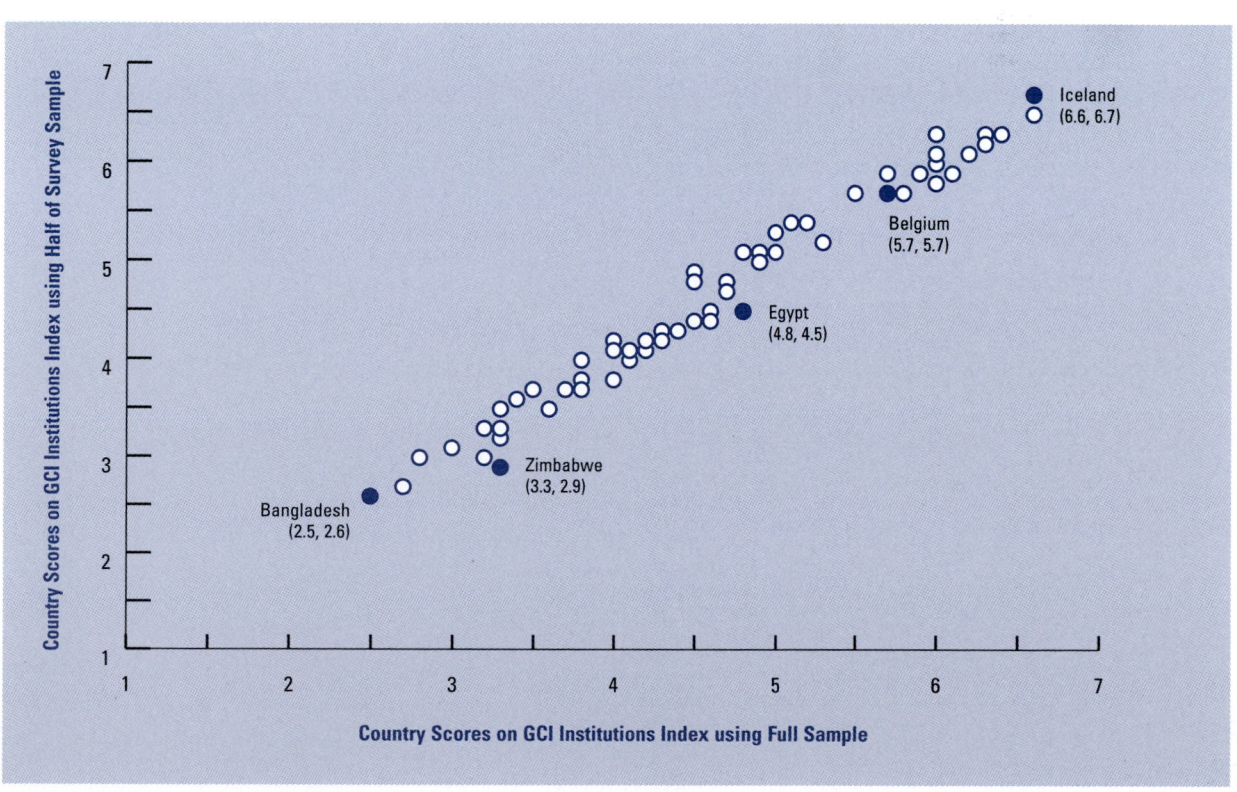

half-sample measures of institutional quality is near perfect, at 0.99. Note that the same countries that were outliers in Figure 2 show smaller full- versus half-sample discrepancies in Figure 3. The variation disappears for Belgium and is no greater than 0.4 in the worst case of Zimbabwe. This strongly suggests that the absolute number of Surveys completed in each country does not appear to be driving our results. Rather, the Executive Opinion Survey seems to be capturing important underlying information about the environments in which businesspeople live and work around the world.

Firm size

Table 1 also includes information about the cross-country size distribution of surveyed firms measured by number of employees. Not surprisingly, the average number of employees is relatively larger in industrialized countries, with France and Germany showing the relatively largest average size. Among middle-income and developing economies, South Africa and Chile have the largest representation of firms with more than 20,000 employees. This reflects in part the large number of natural resource and financial service firms responding from those economies. At the other end of the spectrum, many of the increases in this year's sample have come from the participation of smaller businesses. In the newly added countries of Central America, including Guatemala, Honduras, Nicaragua, and Panama, more than 80 percent of the respondents were from firms with fewer than 250 employees. The Bangladeshi and Nigerian samples, meanwhile, consist of a somewhat more uniform distributions across firm size, although each still has very few respondents with more than 5,000 firms—an unsurprising statistic given the developing nature of those two economies.

Looking at the transition economies, the distribution of firm size varies dramatically. In Estonia, one of the Survey's smallest countries in terms of population (roughly one and a half million), more than 90 percent of the respondents were from enterprises of fewer than 250 employees. More than 40 percent of the firms responding from Latvia are in the 250 to 500 employee range, and more than a third of those from Lithuania have between 500 and 5,000 employees. In Slovenia and Romania, two of the other new countries added this year, most of the sample was made of firms with between 250 and 5,000 employees.

Firm ownership and market orientation

Table 1 provides further information about the nature of ownership structure and market orientation of firms represented in our Survey. Most are privately owned, although some countries—such as China, Lithuania, Russia, Thailand, and Vietnam—all have a significant share of state-owned respondents. This is generally in line with those countries' history of command economies and public enterprise.

A large percentage of the firms included in our Survey are internationally oriented in their sales. As outlined above, we aim for a sample that is broadly representative of an economy, but as much as possible we also want to solicit the opinions of businesspeople with international perspectives. In a limited number of countries, including the Dominican Republic, Honduras, Jamaica, Nicaragua, Panama, and Uruguay, the majority of surveyed firms produce predominantly for the domestic market. But in most countries, as Table 1 shows, firms that are domestically based but sell both in domestic and in foreign markets dominate the Survey.

Notably, even among exporters the Survey respondents vary considerably with regard to degree of export orientation. In most developing economies, respondents report that the majority of their revenues come from local sales, with two-thirds or more of firms in these countries typically indicating that less than 30 percent of their revenues comes from exports.[v] The main exceptions are Bangladesh, Malaysia, and Vietnam, each of which had nearly half of their respondents indicate that more than 50 percent of their revenues were export-driven.

Among industrialized economy respondents, a much larger proportion of firms reported exports as a major source of revenues. Roughly two-thirds of the Finnish and Swiss firms participating indicated that exports account for more than half of their revenues. In other advanced economies, typically 40 percent or more of respondents indicated that exports generate at least 30 percent of revenues. The major exceptions here are Australia, Greece, Japan, and the United States, each of which had less than a quarter of respondents report that same level of exports as a share of revenues. This is in line with those countries' traditionally low levels of exports as a share of national output.

Regardless of a firm's degree of export orientation, the Survey records the manager's view regarding the country in which the firm operates, so locally based views may be described as "national." A priori, there might be a risk that these national views are overly optimistic or overly pessimistic. However, in order to provide insurance against such bias, the Survey also includes a substantial number of multinational firm executives working in countries of which they are not nationals. These businesspeople are asked to answer questions regarding the local economic environment, drawing upon their experience in their home country (and other countries as relevant). Perhaps not surprisingly, in countries that have been particularly successful in attracting foreign direct investment (FDI)—including Brazil, Malaysia, Singapore, and the Special Administrative Region (SAR) of Hong Kong—

subsidiaries of multinational firms account for the largest share of responses to the Survey. Theirs are the voices of global business, providing an important element of objectivity to the Survey and helping prevent domestically biased distortions.

Foreign direct investment

One sees another dimension of the Survey sample by considering firms' outwardly oriented FDI. Whereas many countries in our Survey are major recipients of FDI, many are also large providers. Table 2 indicates that the majority of respondents engage in no FDI at all, but that, particularly in the wealthier countries, large numbers of firms are foreign investors. Perhaps not surprisingly, the countries with high numbers of firms engaged in FDI include three of the world's wealthiest economies: Germany, Japan, and Switzerland. Approximately 90 percent of the German firms surveyed and 80 percent of those from the latter two countries are engaged in some form of FDI. Meanwhile, in other industrialized and relatively open economies such as Canada, Hong Kong SAR, Spain, the United Kingdom, and the United States, roughly two-thirds or more of the companies surveyed are involved with FDI. These are important data because they provide further support for the Survey's usefulness as a tool for cross-country comparison. In those economies where a large proportion of the respondents are directly engaged in international investment, the Executive Opinion Survey is drawing upon the experiences of business leaders with genuinely international experience. Such perspectives are invaluable when respondents participate in the Survey and are asked to assess aspects of their local economies on a global scale.

Other checks for Survey data robustness

Even though our Survey process makes great efforts to solicit the opinions of a broad array of perspectives in each country, it is still important to examine the possibility of perception bias among Survey respondents. Figures 2 and 3 demonstrated the stability of results even when half of the Survey results in each country are dropped at random, but there might still be some systematic bias that exists among respondents at the national level. For instance, the respondents in an economy might have similar pessimistic assessments of corruption if that issue has recently received a great deal of media attention due to a scandal or other event in the time leading up to our surveying period. Or perhaps a particular issue such as "brain drain" has received a great deal of recent public attention and thus become cemented in the minds of respondents as a major issue. As a first step, we try to correct for such biases by phrasing Survey questions as objectively as possible, so that the best situation in the world is at one end of the response spectrum and the worst situation at the other. This helps

Table 2: Firm engagement in foreign direct investment

Your company's foreign direct investment in other countries is:

country	non-existent	In 1-2 neighbouring countries	regional	global
Argentina	41%	14%	31%	14%
Australia	27%	23%	18%	32%
Austria	39%	10%	22%	29%
Bangladesh	83%	4%	6%	8%
Belgium	17%	8%	17%	58%
Bolivia	84%	7%	3%	7%
Brazil	55%	13%	3%	29%
Bulgaria	92%	4%	2%	2%
Canada	37%	8%	3%	53%
Chile	67%	17%	14%	3%
China	79%	8%	7%	7%
Colombia	72%	13%	7%	8%
Costa Rica	76%	7%	15%	2%
Czech Republic	74%	13%	—	13%
Denmark	27%	10%	17%	47%
Dominican Republic	89%	5%	2%	3%
Ecuador	82%	6%	6%	6%
Egypt	44%	22%	—	33%
El Salvador	47%	32%	13%	8%
Estonia	83%	13%	4%	—
Finland	13%	—	44%	44%
France	24%	14%	19%	43%
Germany	10%	7%	12%	71%
Greece	46%	10%	26%	18%
Guatemala	68%	14%	15%	3%
Honduras	86%	7%	4%	3%
Hong Kong SAR	30%	23%	30%	17%
Hungary	61%	14%	14%	11%
Iceland	50%	19%	19%	13%
India	63%	13%	4%	21%
Indonesia	65%	13%	9%	13%
Ireland	38%	21%	21%	21%
Israel	54%	4%	8%	33%
Italy	26%	5%	16%	53%
Jamaica	74%	2%	9%	15%
Japan	17%	6%	8%	69%
Jordan	57%	21%	9%	13%
Korea	48%	23%	12%	17%
Latvia	89%	5%	5%	—
Lithuania	91%	7%	—	1%
Malaysia	48%	22%	9%	22%
Mauritius	42%	25%	33%	—
Mexico	53%	14%	8%	25%
Netherlands	9%	18%	27%	45%
New Zealand	73%	10%	10%	8%
Nicaragua	75%	7%	13%	6%
Nigeria	65%	13%	5%	17%
Norway	38%	17%	21%	24%
Panama	79%	4%	9%	9%
Paraguay	92%	5%	—	4%
Peru	86%	8%	—	6%
Philippines	83%	6%	6%	6%
Poland	64%	12%	12%	12%
Portugal	29%	17%	14%	40%
Romania	98%	—	—	2%
Russia	95%	3%	1%	1%
Singapore	39%	11%	25%	25%
Slovak Republic	50%	25%	—	25%
Slovenia	60%	22%	6%	12%
South Africa	35%	18%	14%	32%
Spain	29%	24%	10%	37%
Sri Lanka	82%	8%	2%	8%
Sweden	43%	9%	26%	22%
Switzerland	20%	7%	11%	62%
Taiwan	20%	47%	17%	17%
Thailand	67%	14%	7%	12%
Trinidad and Tobago	64%	10%	13%	13%
Turkey	54%	15%	15%	15%
Ukraine	84%	9%	4%	4%
United Kingdom	28%	6%	9%	56%
United States	24%	4%	8%	64%
Uruguay	89%	7%	—	4%
Venezuela	63%	17%	13%	8%
Vietnam	86%	5%	5%	3%
Zimbabwe	53%	41%	—	6%

173

Figure 4: Hard versus Survey telephone data

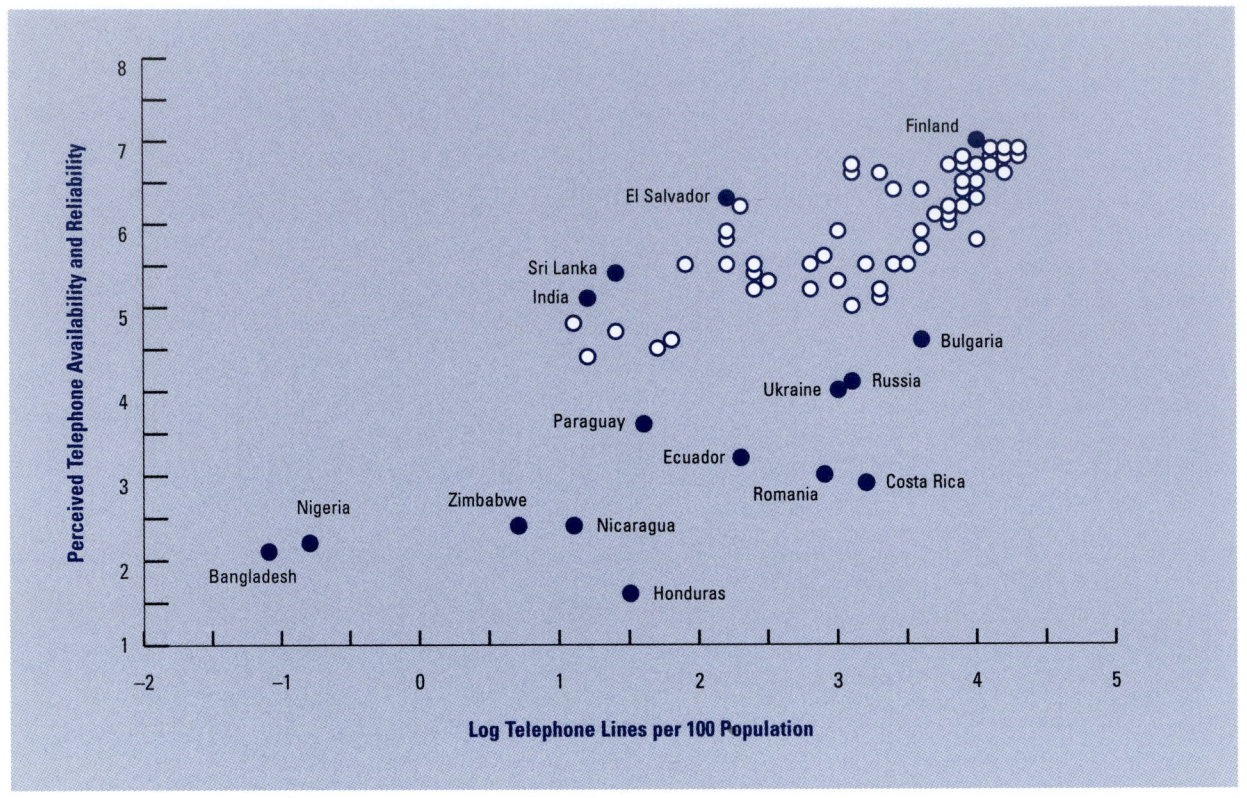

Figure 5: Hard versus Survey Internet data

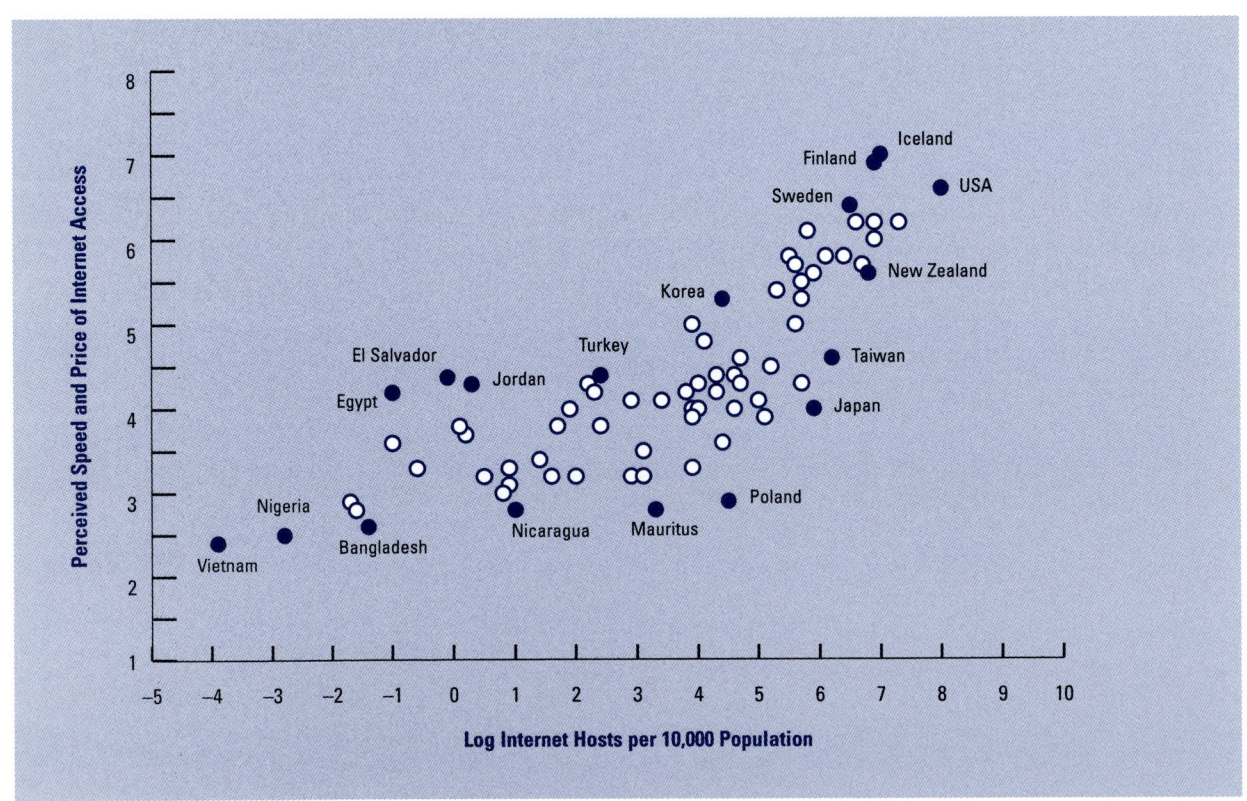

Figure 6: Telephone lines versus market competition in telecommunications

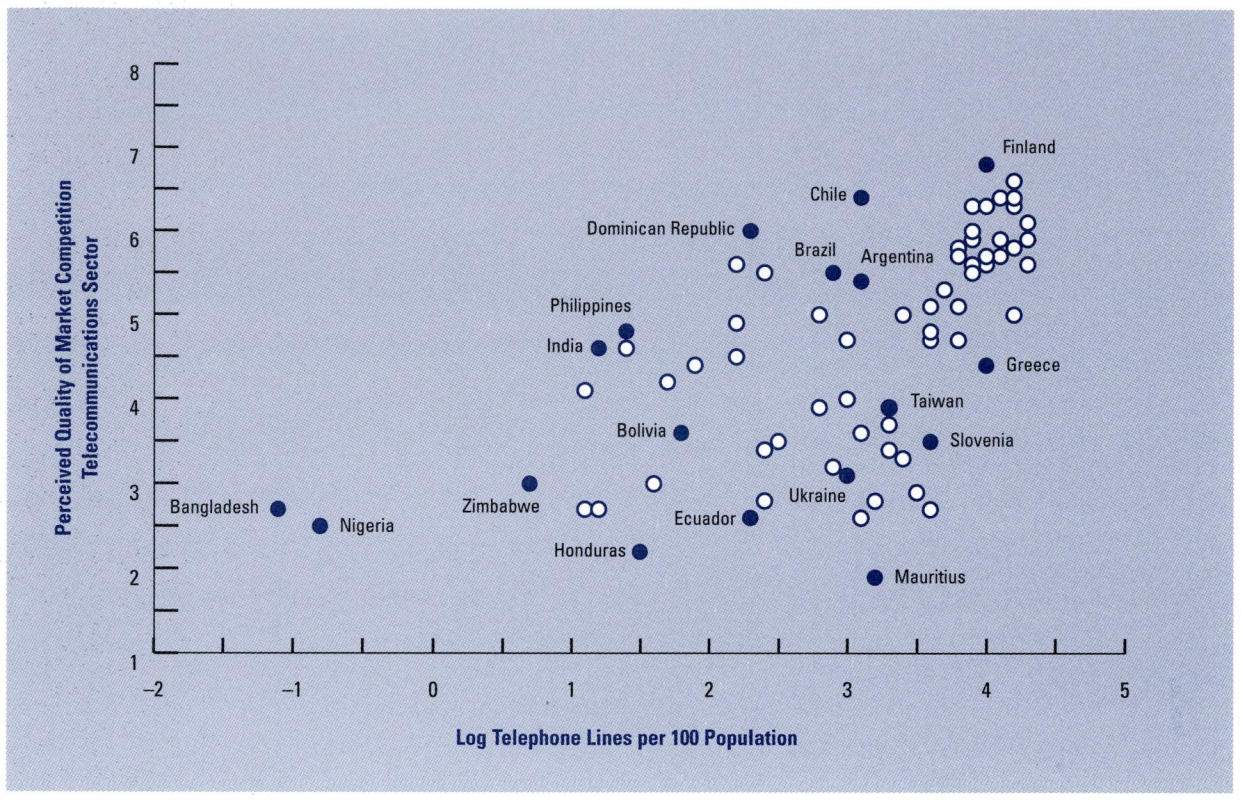

Figure 7: Internet hosts versus market competition among Internet Service Providers

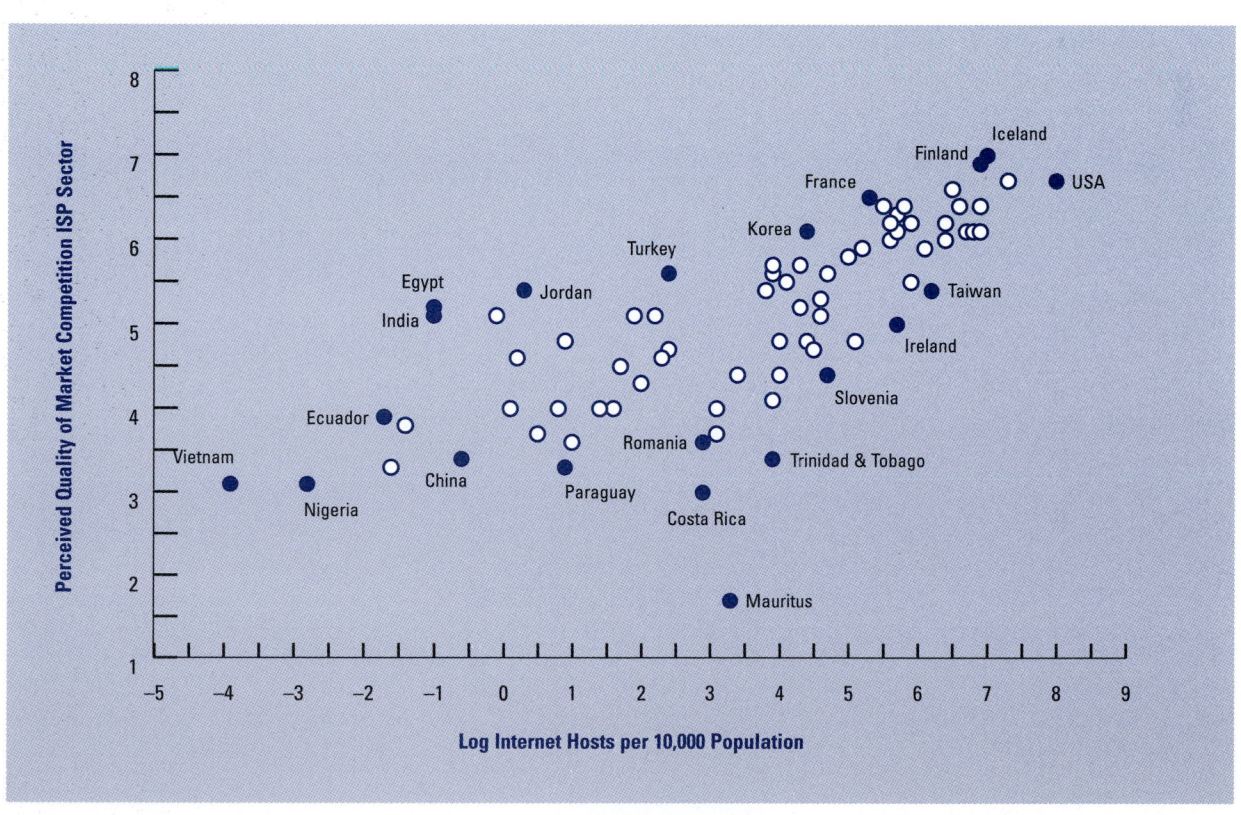

respondents to think of global reference points when assessing their own business environment on a particular dimension, instead of describing that same local dimension as abstractly "good" or "bad." Second, we test the Survey data for perception bias by comparing it with hard data.

For the most part, the Survey asks questions about issues for which there are either no hard measures possible or else no international data available, so thorough comparisons between qualitative and quantitative sources are difficult to perform. Yet in a few instances we can test for links between hard and soft data. Figure 4 plots the number of telephone lines per 100 people (in log form) on the horizontal axis and the Survey question that asks whether "new telephone lines for businesses are widely available and highly reliable" on the vertical axis. The graph shows a strong relationship between the two variables, with the main outliers in the lower right-hand quadrant being former Eastern bloc countries Bulgaria, Romania, Russia, and Ukraine along with Costa Rica, Ecuador, Honduras, Nicaragua, and Zimbabwe. The discrepancy in all these countries is most likely due to the Survey question's focus on reliability in addition to availability. Each of these economies has relatively extensive telephone infrastructures, but the quality of that infrastructure is questionable. Similar results are shown in Figure 5, which maps the very close link between the perceived speed of dial-up access and the (log) number of Internet hosts per 10,000 population. This relationship indicates a close connection between depth of the Internet service provider market and speed of Internet connection. Such links between hard and soft data also provide evidence that perception bias is not an overwhelming problem in our Survey.

However, it is not just the similarities between hard and Survey data that are interesting—differences also reveal some of the subtler information provided by the Survey. Compare the results of Figure 6 with those of Figure 7. These graphs map the number of telephone lines and Internet hosts, respectively, against the perceived level of market competition in the relevant national industries and whether there is sufficient competition to ensure high quality, infrequent interruptions, and low prices in each sector. Although the number of Internet hosts is quite closely linked to perceived level of competition, there is much more variation in the telecommunications sector, with a large disparity between numbers of telephone lines and level of market competition. This is exactly the type of information the Survey aims to elicit from respondents. The hard data tell us about certain infrastructural aspects of the telecommunications market. Yet of equal if not greater importance is the market structure and functioning of service provision. In Figure 6, for example, Chile and Ukraine have roughly the same number of telephone lines

per 100 population, but looking solely at this measure would provide a very weak reflection of the telecommunications industries in those two countries. The Survey data indicate that the level of market competition and quality of service provision is extremely high in Chile but quite low in Ukraine. This information forms a key distinction when assessing local ITC capacities and hence the prospects for overall growth competitiveness. It furthermore provides compelling evidence that the data produced by the Survey offer a crucial complement to existing hard data sources.

Summary

The Executive Opinion Survey aims to obtain accurate information about the economic environment in which firms operate. It aims to provide much richer information than is available through hard data sources by soliciting the opinions of senior managers with international perspectives. With the help of the Survey, we are able to develop a much more sophisticated understanding of the underlying dynamics of an economy. This is particularly relevant when assessing topics such as bureaucratic efficiency, quality of the legal system, quality of infrastructure, or the hidden costs within an economy.

The Survey is not immune from perception bias, but the evidence shows that, when we randomly drop half of our sample, the results are stable and thus not fundamentally driven by individual biases. Only when the samples are extremely small do we see significant changes in the results for single questions, and even then the deviations appear to be averaged out in the broader indexes. Nonetheless, in economies where small samples are an issue, we plan to broaden our coverage next year.

More complicated is the issue of nationwide biases, but the examples above do show that, when there is overlap, Survey results are fairly closely related to hard data. Moreover, when there is a discrepancy between the hard data and the Survey data, the evidence further suggests that the subtleties of the Survey questions are capturing information that is simply not available in the hard data.

The Executive Survey continues to provide a vital component of the analysis contained in the *Global Competitiveness Report*. Its results are central to both the Growth Competitiveness Index and the Current Competitiveness Index, as well as numerous other important research topics covered in this *Report* and elsewhere. It continues to offer a straightforward and effective means of assessing the currents both within and across economies.

Notes

[i] Many of the ideas in this chapter build on those presented in the same chapter within last year's *Global Competitiveness Report*. See "The Executive Opinion Survey" by Peter Cornelius and Andrew M. Warner, *The Global Competitiveness Report 2000*. New York and Oxford: Oxford University Press, 2000.

[ii] Several of the results from these questions are reported in this *Report*, but most will be presented in a supplementary and in-depth *IT-Readiness Report* currently under preparation.

[iii] A special Report on Latin America's competitiveness will be published shortly. While this report will examine issues of particular interest for the region, it will represent a companion study of the *Global Competitiveness Report*.

[iv] The reader should note that we have excluded Luxembourg from our competitiveness analysis this year since the number of Surveys produced by that country perennially number in the single digits and are thus too few to permit a consistent analysis.

[v] These figures come from Survey data not reported in the tables of this chapter.

Part 3

Country Profiles and Data Presentation

3.1: Country Profiles

How country profiles work

This section presents a two-page profile with selected data for each individual economy included in the *Global Competitiveness Report 2001–2002*.

❶ The left page lists key facts and results for each economy, including GDP per capita in 2000, GDP per capita growth from 1999 to 2000, and the number of US utility patents granted in 2000 per million population. Overall Growth Competitiveness Index (GCI) and Current Competitiveness Index (CCI) rankings (out of 75 countries except where noted otherwise) are also listed, along with results for the component indexes and subindexes.

❷ The right page of each profile forms a competitiveness balance sheet, providing detailed information on the relative strengths and weaknesses of each economy. The balance sheet is broken into two main sections, one on growth and one on current competitiveness, reflecting the two complementary perspectives on competitiveness presented in Chapter 1.1 and 1.2, respectively. It also includes a list of other noteworthy indicators of interest for readers researching the economic environment of a specific country.

To identify relative strengths and weaknesses, the absolute ranks or values of variables for each country are evaluated based on the country's level of development. The evaluation procedures by variable group (GCI variables, CCI variables, other variables) are described in more detail below.

❸ Growth Competitiveness

For variables included in the Growth Competitiveness Index (see Chapter 1.1 for more details), advantages and disadvantages are calculated based on an economy's rankings relative to other economies at similar levels of overall development. Specifically, advantages and disadvantages for specific variables were calculated as follows:

- For economies ranked in the top 26 on the overall GCI (ie, the technological core economies as defined in Chapter 1.1 plus Portugal and Spain), a variable is listed as an advantage if an economy ranks in the top 10 on it, and a disadvantage if the economy ranks 15 or more places lower on it than its overall GCI ranking.

- For the 27th through 38th ranked economies on the GCI (ie, the rest of the top half of the sample), a variable is listed as an advantage if an economy ranks in the top 15 on it and a disadvantage if the economy ranks 15 or more places lower on it than its overall GCI ranking.

- For the 39th through 54th place economies on the GCI, a variable is listed as an advantage if an economy ranks in the top 25 on it and a disadvantage if the economy places in the bottom 15 on it.

(cont'd.)

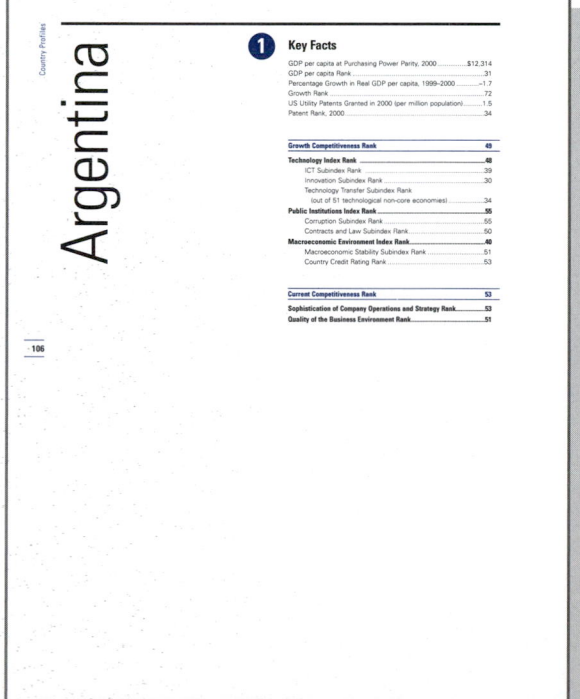

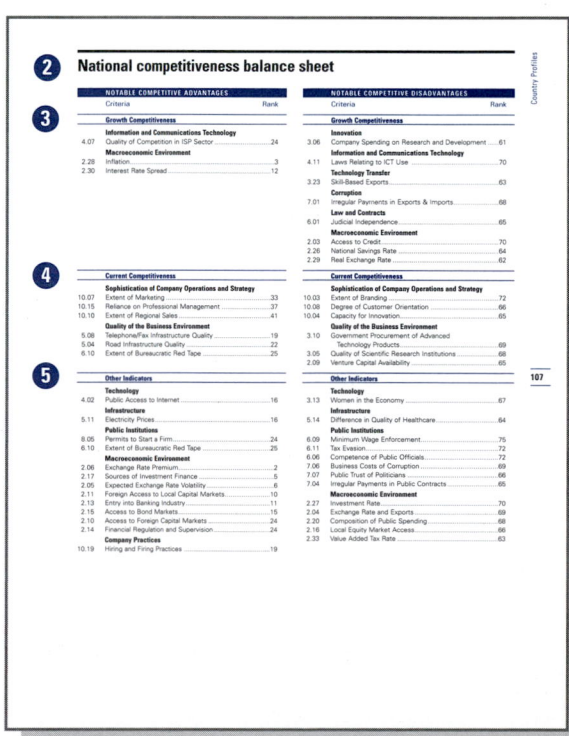

- For the economies ranked 55th through 75th on the GCI, a variable is listed as an advantage if an economy ranks in the top 45 on it and a disadvantage if the economy places in the bottom 10 on it.

The exception to this system is the variable "Potential for 'Catch-up' Growth." Rankings for this variable are simply the reverse ordering of GDP per capita, and are listed as a Growth Advantage if the reverse order GDP ranking is 10 or more places higher than an economy's overall Growth Competitiveness ranking.

❹ Current Competitiveness

For variables included in the Current Competitiveness Index (see Chapter 1.2 for more details), a different system was used to determine whether a criterion formed an advantage or disadvantage for an economy.

First, GDP per capita (PPP) in 2000 was regressed on each variable. Second, a predicted value and a standard error of the prediction for each country on each indicator was computed. Last, the difference between the actual value and the predicted value of an indicator for a country was calculated, and then divided by the standard error of the prediction. This creates a standardized measure of over- or underperformance in a variable given a country's GDP per capita.

This standardized measure indicates how far above or below the regression line a country lies from its predicted value based on the cross-section of countries in the *Report*'s sample. For each economy, indicators with the greatest positive distance values are listed as advantages, while those with the greatest (in absolute terms) negative distance values are listed as disadvantages.

We organize the variables by the subindex categories *Sophistication of Company Operations and Strategy* and *Quality of the Business Environment*.

A small number of variables are included in calculations for both the Growth Competitiveness Index and the Current Competitiveness Index. In instances where a variable qualifies as both a GCI and CCI advantage (or disadvantage), it is noted only under the GCI section and the next greatest advantage (or disadvantage) is listed under the CCI section.

❺ Other Indicators

Additional variables of interest to researchers are listed under *Other Indicators*. To identify advantages and disadvantages here, the same methodology was used as for variables of the Growth Competitiveness Index. Due to space constraints, only the highest ranked of the advantages and lowest ranked of the disadvantages are listed.

Argentina

Key Facts

GDP per capita at Purchasing Power Parity, 2000 ....$12,314
GDP per capita Rank 31
Percentage Growth in Real GDP per capita, 1999–2000 ....–1.7
Growth Rank 72
US Utility Patents Granted in 2000 (per million population)..........1.5
Patent Rank 34

Growth Competitiveness Rank	49

Technology Index Rank **48**
    ICT Subindex Rank 39
    Innovation Subindex Rank 30
    Technology Transfer Subindex Rank
        (out of 51 technological non-core economies) 34
Public Institutions Index Rank **55**
    Corruption Subindex Rank 55
    Contracts and Law Subindex Rank..50
Macroeconomic Environment Index Rank................................**40**
    Macroeconomic Stability Subindex Rank 51
    Country Credit Rating Rank 53

Current Competitiveness Rank	53

Sophistication of Company Operations and Strategy Rank...................**53**
Quality of the Business Environment Rank..**51**

National competitiveness balance sheet

NOTABLE COMPETITIVE ADVANTAGES

Criteria	Rank

Growth Competitiveness

Information and Communications Technology

4.07	Quality of Competition in ISP Sector	24

Macroeconomic Environment

2.28	Inflation	3
2.30	Interest Rate Spread	12

Current Competitiveness

Sophistication of Company Operations and Strategy

10.07	Extent of Marketing	33
10.15	Reliance on Professional Management	37
10.10	Extent of Regional Sales	41

Quality of the Business Environment

5.08	Telephone/Fax Infrastructure Quality	19
5.04	Road Infrastructure Quality	22
6.10	Extent of Bureaucratic Red Tape	25

Other Indicators

Technology

4.02	Public Access to Internet	16

Infrastructure

5.11	Electricity Prices	16

Public Institutions

8.05	Permits to Start a Firm	24

Macroeconomic Environment

2.06	Exchange Rate Premium	2
2.17	Sources of Investment Finance	5
2.05	Expected Exchange Rate Volatility	6
2.11	Foreign Access to Local Capital Markets	10
2.13	Entry into Banking Industry	11
2.15	Access to Bond Markets	15
2.10	Access to Foreign Capital Markets	24
2.14	Financial Regulation and Supervision	24

Company Practices

10.19	Hiring and Firing Practices	19

NOTABLE COMPETITIVE DISADVANTAGES

Criteria	Rank

Growth Competitiveness

Innovation

3.06	Company Spending on Research and Development	61

Information and Communications Technology

4.11	Laws Relating to ICT Use	70

Technology Transfer

3.23	Skill-Based Exports	63

Corruption

7.01	Irregular Payments in Exports & Imports	68

Law and Contracts

6.01	Judicial Independence	65

Macroeconomic Environment

2.03	Access to Credit	70
2.26	National Savings Rate	64
2.29	Real Exchange Rate	62

Current Competitiveness

Sophistication of Company Operations and Strategy

10.03	Extent of Branding	72
10.08	Degree of Customer Orientation	66
10.04	Capacity for Innovation	65

Quality of the Business Environment

3.10	Government Procurement of Advanced Technology Products	69
3.05	Quality of Scientific Research Institutions	68
2.09	Venture Capital Availability	65

Other Indicators

Technology

3.13	Women in the Economy	67

Infrastructure

5.14	Difference in Quality of Healthcare	64

Public Institutions

6.09	Minimum Wage Enforcement	75
6.11	Tax Evasion	72
6.06	Competence of Public Officials	72
7.06	Business Costs of Corruption	69
7.07	Public Trust of Politicians	66
7.04	Irregular Payments in Public Contracts	65

Macroeconomic Environment

2.27	Investment Rate	70
2.04	Exchange Rate and Exports	69
2.20	Composition of Public Spending	68
2.16	Local Equity Market Access	66
2.33	Value Added Tax Rate	63

Australia

186

Key Facts

GDP per capita at Purchasing Power Parity, 2000 ....$25,758
GDP per capita Rank 11
Percentage Growth in Real GDP per capita, 1999–2000 ....2.7
Growth Rank 51
US Utility Patents Granted in 2000 (per million population) 36.7
Patent Rank 20

Growth Competitiveness Rank	5

Technology Index Rank **5**
    ICT Subindex Rank 11
    Innovation Subindex Rank 5
Public Institutions Index Rank **8**
    Corruption Subindex Rank 8
    Contracts and Law Subindex Rank...11
Macroeconomic Environment Index Rank.................................**17**
    Macroeconomic Stability Subindex Rank 35
    Country Credit Rating Rank 20

Current Competitiveness Rank	9

Sophistication of Company Operations and Strategy Rank..................**24**
Quality of the Business Environment Rank...**7**

National competitiveness balance sheet

NOTABLE COMPETITIVE ADVANTAGES	
Criteria	**Rank**

Growth Competitiveness

Innovation

3.19	Tertiary Enrollment	3

Information and Communications Technology

4.17	Personal Computers	5
4.12	Legal Framework for ICT Development	7
4.15	Internet Hosts	7
4.03	Internet Access in Schools	9
4.14	Internet Users	10

Corruption

7.01	Irregular Payments in Exports & Imports	7
7.03	Irregular Payments in Tax Collection	8
7.02	Irregular Payments in Government Procurement	10

Law and Contracts

6.01	Judicial Independence	7
6.04	Favoritism in Decisions of Government Officials	8

Current Competitiveness (using GCR 2000 results)

Sophistication of Company Operations and Strategy

10.08	Degree of Customer Orientation	2
10.15	Reliance on Professional Management	5
10.13	Willingness to Delegate Authority	6

Quality of the Business Environment

5.04	Road Infrastructure Quality	2
2.09	Venture Capital Availability	2
8.07	Effectiveness of Anti-Trust Policy	2

Other Indicators

Technology

3.08	Tax Credits for Firm-Level Research and Development	6
3.07	Subsidies for Firm-Level Research and Development	8
3.05	Quality of Scientific Research Institutions	9

Public Institutions

6.09	Minimum Wage Enforcement	1
6.14	Informal Sector	4
6.04	Favoritism in Decisions of Government Officials	8
7.04	Irregular Payments in Public Contracts	8
7.05	Irregular Payments in Loan Applications	8
6.03	Intellectual Property Protection	10

Macroeconomic Environment

2.02	Soundness of Banks	2
2.04	Exchange Rate and Exports	2
2.14	Financial Regulation and Supervision	2
2.16	Local Equity Market Access	3
2.07	Financial Market Sophistication	6
2.20	Composition of Public Spending	8
2.15	Access to Bond Markets	10
2.17	Sources of Investment Finance	10

NOTABLE COMPETITIVE DISADVANTAGES	
Criteria	**Rank**

Growth Competitiveness

Innovation

3.02	Firm-Level Innovation	35
3.06	Company Spending on Research and Development	23
3.16	Utility Patents in 2000	20

Information and Communications Technology

4.09	Government Success in ICT Promotion	40
4.13	Cellular Telephones	25
4.08	Government Prioritization of ICT	24

Macroeconomic Environment

2.26	National Savings Rate	53
2.01	Recession Expectations	45
2.28	Inflation	44
2.03	Access to Credit	39
2.30	Interest Rate Spread	32
2.29	Real Exchange Rate	25
2.23	Country Credit Rating	20

Current Competitiveness (using GCR 2000 results)

Sophistication of Company Operations and Strategy

10.02	Value Chain Presence	40
10.09	Control of International Distribution	36
10.11	Breadth of International Markets	35

Quality of the Business Environment

8.01	Intensity of Local Competition	58
10.21	Cooperation in Labor-Employer Relations	50
9.09	Local Availability of Process Machinery	38

Other Indicators

Technology

3.12	Brain Drain	32
3.14	Minorities in the Economy	29
4.05	High Skilled IT Job Market	27

Infrastructure

5.13	Difference in Quality of Schools	29

Public Institutions

6.10	Extent of Bureaucratic Red Tape	49
8.05	Permits to Start a Firm	35

Macroeconomic Environment

2.32	Corporate Income Tax Rate	64
2.05	Expected Exchange Rate Volatility	59
2.06	Exchange Rate Premium	46
2.11	Foreign Access to Local Capital Markets	37
2.27	Investment Rate	32
2.13	Entry into Banking Industry	27

Company Practices

10.19	Hiring and Firing Practices	55
10.22	Union Contributions to Productivity	42
10.20	Employment Rules	27

187

Austria

Key Facts

GDP per capita at Purchasing Power Parity, 2000 .... $26,314
GDP per capita Rank 9
Percentage Growth in Real GDP per capita, 1999–2000 .... 2.8
Growth Rank 49
US Utility Patents Granted in 2000 (per million population) 62.1
Patent Rank 15

Growth Competitiveness Rank	18

Technology Index Rank **16**
    ICT Subindex Rank 13
    Innovation Subindex Rank 16
Public Institutions Index Rank **15**
    Corruption Subindex Rank 18
    Contracts and Law Subindex Rank.......................................9
Macroeconomic Environment Index Rank....................................**26**
    Macroeconomic Stability Subindex Rank 11
    Country Credit Rating Rank 8

Current Competitiveness Rank	13

Sophistication of Company Operations and Strategy Rank..................**11**
Quality of the Business Environment Rank..**13**

National competitiveness balance sheet

NOTABLE COMPETITIVE ADVANTAGES

Criteria		Rank

Growth Competitiveness

Innovation

3.02	Firm-Level Innovation	8

Information and Communications Technology

4.13	Cellular Telephones	3
4.11	Laws Relating to ICT Use	9

Law and Contracts

6.12	Organized Crime	6
6.02	Property Rights	10

Macroeconomic Environment

2.01	Recession Expectations	9

Current Competitiveness

Sophistication of Company Operations and Strategy

10.10	Extent of Regional Sales	6
10.01	Nature of Competitive Advantage	8
10.06	Production Process Sophistication	10

Quality of the Business Environment

5.12	Quality of Public Schools	3
11.06	Stringency of Environmental Regulations	4
10.21	Cooperation in Labor-Employer Relations	9

Other Indicators

Technology

3.07	Subsidies for Firm-Level Research and Development	4
4.04	Quality of Competition in Telecommunication Sector	7
4.05	High Skilled IT Job Market	8

Infrastructure

5.14	Difference in Quality of Healthcare	2
5.02	Tap Water Safety	3
5.13	Difference in Quality of Schools	3
5.04	Road Infrastructure Quality	4
5.03	Industrial Water Availability	6
5.10	Postal Efficiency	6
5.01	Overall Infrastructure Quality	7
5.15	Public Health Agencies	7
5.05	Railroad Infrastructure Development	8
5.09	Quality of Competition in Transportation Sector	9

Public Institutions

7.06	Business Costs of Corruption	6
6.03	Intellectual Property Protection	8

Macroeconomic Environment

1.09	Employment to Population Ratio, 2000	6
2.05	Expected Exchange Rate Volatility	7
2.18	Hidden Trade Barriers	7
2.22	Extent of Distortive Government Subsidies	7

NOTABLE COMPETITIVE DISADVANTAGES

Criteria		Rank

Growth Competitiveness

Macroeconomic Environment

2.26	National Savings Rate	41
2.30	Interest Rate Spread	36

Current Competitiveness

Sophistication of Company Operations and Strategy

10.14	Extent of Incentive Compensation	27
10.11	Breadth of International Markets	21
10.13	Willingness to Delegate Authority	18

Quality of the Business Environment

8.04	Administrative Burden for Start-Ups	47
5.06	Port Infrastructure Quality	29
2.07	Financial Market Sophistication	27

Other Indicators

Technology

3.13	Women in the Economy	45

Infrastructure

5.11	Electricity Prices	42

Public Institutions

8.06	Days to Start a Firm	45
8.05	Permits to Start a Firm	35
6.08	Burden of Regulation	33

Macroeconomic Environment

2.33	Value Added Tax Rate	57
2.17	Sources of Investment Finance	53
2.32	Corporate Income Tax Rate	48
2.13	Entry into Banking Industry	42
2.21	Social Transfer Recipients	41

Company Practices

10.19	Hiring and Firing Practices	58
10.20	Employment Rules	48
10.23	Pay and Productivity	38

189

Bangladesh

Key Facts

GDP per capita at Purchasing Power Parity, 2000 ....$1,561
GDP per capita Rank 74
Percentage Growth in Real GDP per capita, 1999–2000 ....3.2
Growth Rank 38
US Utility Patents Granted in 2000 (per million population)..........0.0
Patent Rank 65

Growth Competitiveness Rank	71

Technology Index Rank **74**
    ICT Subindex Rank 75
    Innovation Subindex Rank 75
    Technology Transfer Subindex Rank
       (out of 51 technological non-core economies) 26
Public Institutions Index Rank **75**
    Corruption Subindex Rank 75
    Contracts and Law Subindex Rank.......................................69
Macroeconomic Environment Index Rank..**48**
    Macroeconomic Stability Subindex Rank 55
    Country Credit Rating Rank 67

Current Competitiveness Rank	73

Sophistication of Company Operations and Strategy Rank...................**72**
Quality of the Business Environment Rank..**73**

190

National competitiveness balance sheet

NOTABLE COMPETITIVE ADVANTAGES	
Criteria	Rank

Growth Competitiveness

Technology Transfer

3.23	Skill-Based Exports	39

Macroeconomic Environment

	Potential for "Catch-up" Growth	2
2.01	Recession Expectations	36
2.29	Real Exchange Rate	44

Current Competitiveness

Sophistication of Company Operations and Strategy

10.08	Degree of Customer Orientation	44
10.11	Breadth of International Markets	54
10.06	Production Process Sophistication	55

Quality of the Business Environment

2.16	Local Equity Market Access	40
5.05	Railroad Infrastructure Development	47
9.01	Buyer Sophistication	57

Other Indicators

Technology

3.14	Minorities in the Economy	30

Macroeconomic Environment

1.08	Unemployment Rate, 2000	4
2.04	Exchange Rate and Exports	30
2.33	Value Added Tax Rate	32
1.09	Employment to Population Ratio, 2000	33
2.13	Entry into Banking Industry	39
2.11	Foreign Access to Local Capital Markets	41

NOTABLE COMPETITIVE DISADVANTAGES	
Criteria	Rank

Growth Competitiveness

Innovation

3.01	Technological Sophistication	73
3.19	Tertiary Enrollment	72
3.06	Company Spending on Research and Development	71
3.09	University/Industry Research Collaboration	71
3.16	Utility Patents in 2000	65

Information and Communications Technology

4.03	Internet Access in Schools	75
4.14	Internet Users	75
4.16	Telephone Lines	75
4.11	Laws Relating to ICT Use	74
4.13	Cellular Telephones	74
4.17	Personal Computers	74
4.15	Internet Hosts	71
4.09	Government Success in ICT Promotion	68

Technology Transfer

3.04	FDI and Technology Transfer	66

Corruption

7.01	Irregular Payments in Exports & Imports	75
7.02	Irregular Payments in Government Procurement	75
7.03	Irregular Payments in Tax Collection	75

Law and Contracts

6.12	Organized Crime	71
6.04	Favoritism in Decisions of Government Officials	68
6.02	Property Rights	67

Macroeconomic Environment

2.24	Government Surplus/Deficit	69

Current Competitiveness

Sophistication of Company Operations and Strategy

10.13	Willingness to Delegate Authority	75
10.14	Extent of Incentive Compensation	75
10.10	Extent of Regional Sales	73

Quality of the Business Environment

10.17	Efficacy of Corporate Boards	75
9.11	Local Availability of Information Technology Services	75
5.08	Telephone/Fax Infrastructure Quality	74

Other Indicators

Technology

3.13	Women in the Economy	75
4.02	Public Access to Internet	75

Infrastructure

5.02	Tap Water Safety	75
5.13	Difference in Quality of Schools	75

Public Institutions

7.04	Irregular Payments in Public Contracts	75
7.05	Irregular Payments in Loan Applications	75
7.06	Business Costs of Corruption	75

191

Belgium

Key Facts

GDP per capita at Purchasing Power Parity, 2000 ....$26,958
GDP per capita Rank 8
Percentage Growth in Real GDP per capita, 1999–2000 ....3.8
Growth Rank 28
US Utility Patents Granted in 2000 (per million population)........67.8
Patent Rank 13

Growth Competitiveness Rank	19

Technology Index Rank **13**
    ICT Subindex Rank 19
    Innovation Subindex Rank 8
Public Institutions Index Rank **22**
    Corruption Subindex Rank 23
    Contracts and Law Subindex Rank.......................................20
Macroeconomic Environment Index Rank..**24**
    Macroeconomic Stability Subindex Rank 13
    Country Credit Rating Rank 13

Current Competitiveness Rank	14

Sophistication of Company Operations and Strategy Rank...................**12**
Quality of the Business Environment Rank..**14**

192

National competitiveness balance sheet

NOTABLE COMPETITIVE ADVANTAGES

Criteria	Rank

Growth Competitiveness

Innovation

3.09	University/Industry Research Collaboration	5
3.19	Tertiary Enrollment	8
3.06	Company Spending on Research and Development	10

Information and Communications Technology

4.07	Quality of Competition in ISP Sector	10

Current Competitiveness

Sophistication of Company Operations and Strategy

10.10	Extent of Regional Sales	7
10.01	Nature of Competitive Advantage	10
10.12	Extent of Staff Training	12

Quality of the Business Environment

8.01	Intensity of Local Competition	3
9.05	Decentralization of Corporate Activity	4
6.10	Extent of Bureaucratic Red Tape	4

Other Indicators

Technology

3.12	Brain Drain	7
4.05	High Skilled IT Job Market	10

Infrastructure

5.10	Postal Efficiency	3
5.12	Quality of Public Schools	6
5.09	Quality of Competition in Transportation Sector	7
5.04	Road Infrastructure Quality	10
5.06	Port Infrastructure Quality	10

Public Institutions

6.13	Unreported Profits and Wages	1
6.10	Extent of Bureaucratic Red Tape	4

Macroeconomic Environment

2.10	Access to Foreign Capital Markets	3
2.11	Foreign Access to Local Capital Markets	3
2.12	Perceived Interest Rate Gap	6
2.13	Entry into Banking Industry	6
2.04	Exchange Rate and Exports	8
2.08	Ease of Access to Loans	8

NOTABLE COMPETITIVE DISADVANTAGES

Criteria	Rank

Growth Competitiveness

Information and Communications Technology

4.08	Government Prioritization of ICT	41

Macroeconomic Environment

2.03	Access to Credit	47

Current Competitiveness

Sophistication of Company Operations and Strategy

10.09	Control of International Distribution	24
10.03	Extent of Branding	20
10.07	Extent of Marketing	19

Quality of the Business Environment

3.11	Availability of Scientists and Engineers	48
3.10	Government Procurement of Advanced Technology Products	27
9.11	Local Availability of Information Technology Services	25

Other Indicators

Technology

3.14	Minorities in the Economy	50
4.10	Government On-line Services	35

Infrastructure

5.11	Electricity Prices	45

Public Institutions

8.06	Days to Start a Firm	70
8.05	Permits to Start a Firm	69
6.08	Burden of Regulation	57
6.11	Tax Evasion	45
6.06	Competence of Public Officials	38

Macroeconomic Environment

2.32	Corporate Income Tax Rate	68
2.33	Value Added Tax Rate	63
1.08	Unemployment Rate, 2000	47
1.09	Employment to Population Ratio, 2000	44
2.27	Investment Rate	40
2.17	Sources of Investment Finance	34

Company Practices

10.20	Employment Rules	64
10.19	Hiring and Firing Practices	54
10.23	Pay and Productivity	43

193

Bolivia

Key Facts

GDP per capita at Purchasing Power Parity, 2000 ....$2,408
GDP per capita Rank 70
Percentage Growth in Real GDP per capita, 1999–2000 ....0.2
Growth Rank 70
US Utility Patents Granted in 2000 (per million population).........0.2
Patent Rank 49

Growth Competitiveness Rank	67

Technology Index Rank **67**
    ICT Subindex Rank 65
    Innovation Subindex Rank 54
    Technology Transfer Subindex Rank
        (out of 51 technological non-core economies) 35
Public Institutions Index Rank **62**
    Corruption Subindex Rank 56
    Contracts and Law Subindex Rank..62
Macroeconomic Environment Index Rank...................................**70**
    Macroeconomic Stability Subindex Rank 73
    Country Credit Rating Rank 63

Current Competitiveness Rank	75

Sophistication of Company Operations and Strategy Rank..................**75**
Quality of the Business Environment Rank..**74**

National competitiveness balance sheet

NOTABLE COMPETITIVE ADVANTAGES		NOTABLE COMPETITIVE DISADVANTAGES	
Criteria	**Rank**	**Criteria**	**Rank**

Growth Competitiveness

Innovation

3.19 Tertiary Enrollment 43

Corruption

7.02 Irregular Payments in Government Procurement 33

Law and Contracts

6.12 Organized Crime 38

Macroeconomic Environment

Potential for "Catch-up" Growth 6

2.28 Inflation...45

Growth Competitiveness

Innovation

3.06 Company Spending on Research and Development 75
3.01 Technological Sophistication 74
3.09 University/Industry Research Collaboration 74
3.02 Firm-Level Innovation 73

Information and Communications Technology

4.12 Legal Framework for ICT Development.........................74
4.11 Laws Relating to ICT Use 73
4.08 Government Prioritization of ICT 72
4.09 Government Success in ICT Promotion.........................71
4.03 Internet Access in Schools 68

Law and Contracts

6.01 Judicial Independence.....................................74
6.04 Favoritism in Decisions of Government Officials...........71
6.02 Property Rights 66

Macroeconomic Environment

2.03 Access to Credit..74
2.01 Recession Expectations 73
2.30 Interest Rate Spread 73
2.26 National Savings Rate 70

Current Competitiveness

Sophistication of Company Operations and Strategy

10.03 Extent of Branding 60

Quality of the Business Environment

2.18 Hidden Trade Barriers.....................................57
5.08 Telephone/Fax Infrastructure Quality 62

Current Competitiveness

Sophistication of Company Operations and Strategy

10.08 Degree of Customer Orientation 75
10.07 Extent of Marketing 74
10.12 Extent of Staff Training...........................73

Quality of the Business Environment

9.01 Buyer Sophistication 75
3.10 Government Procurement of Advanced Technology Products.....................................74
9.02 Local Supplier Quantity 74

Other Indicators

Technology

4.02 Public Access to Internet 24

Public Institutions

7.05 Irregular Payments in Loan Applications.........................45

Macroeconomic Environment

2.32 Corporate Income Tax Rate...........................7
2.33 Value Added Tax Rate 26
2.05 Expected Exchange Rate Volatility 35
2.10 Access to Foreign Capital Markets 36
2.14 Financial Regulation and Supervision...........................43
2.31 Average Tariff Rate...........................44

Company Practices

10.19 Hiring and Firing Practices 28

Other Indicators

Technology

3.03 Firm-Level Technology Absorption...........................75
3.08 Tax Credits for Firm-Level Research and Development.....75
3.05 Quality of Scientific Research Institutions 73
4.06 IT Training and Education 72

Infrastructure

5.01 Overall Infrastructure Quality 75
5.06 Port Infrastructure Quality 75
5.12 Quality of Public Schools 74

Public Institutions

6.14 Informal Sector...........................75
6.03 Intellectual Property Protection...........................74
6.10 Extent of Bureaucratic Red Tape 74

Macroeconomic Environment

2.08 Ease of Access to Loans...........................72

Company Practices

10.13 Willingness to Delegate Authority 74
10.15 Reliance on Professional Management 74

195

Brazil

Key Facts

GDP per capita at Purchasing Power Parity, 2000 .... $7,389
GDP per capita Rank 44
Percentage Growth in Real GDP per capita, 1999–2000 .... 2.9
Growth Rank 44
US Utility Patents Granted in 2000 (per million population) 0.6
Patent Rank 43

Growth Competitiveness Rank	44

Technology Index Rank **49**
    ICT Subindex Rank 38
    Innovation Subindex Rank 49
    Technology Transfer Subindex Rank
       (out of 51 technological non-core economies) 30

Public Institutions Index Rank **47**
    Corruption Subindex Rank 49
    Contracts and Law Subindex Rank 45

Macroeconomic Environment Index Rank **33**
    Macroeconomic Stability Subindex Rank 31
    Country Credit Rating Rank 49

Current Competitiveness Rank	30

Sophistication of Company Operations and Strategy Rank **29**
Quality of the Business Environment Rank **32**

196

National competitiveness balance sheet

NOTABLE COMPETITIVE ADVANTAGES

Criteria	Rank

Growth Competitiveness

Information and Communications Technology
4.09 Government Success in ICT Promotion 18

Technology Transfer
3.04 FDI and Technology Transfer 10

Macroeconomic Environment
2.01 Recession Expectations 4
2.29 Real Exchange Rate 6
2.03 Access to Credit..7
Potential for "Catch-up" Growth 32

Current Competitiveness

Sophistication of Company Operations and Strategy
10.14 Extent of Incentive Compensation..................................21
10.15 Reliance on Professional Management 24
10.07 Extent of Marketing 25

Quality of the Business Environment
2.07 Financial Market Sophistication......................................12
9.11 Local Availability of Information Technology Services.....18
9.05 Decentralization of Corporate Activity............................19

Other Indicators

Technology
4.10 Government On-line Services 8
4.05 High Skilled IT Job Market 23
3.08 Tax Credits for Firm-Level Research and Development.....24
4.04 Quality of Competition in Telecommunication Sector.....25

Infrastructure
5.10 Postal Efficiency 15

Macroeconomic Environment
2.32 Corporate Income Tax Rate..2
2.22 Extent of Distortive Government Subsidies....................12
2.13 Entry into Banking Industry..15
2.04 Exchange Rate and Exports 19
2.17 Sources of Investment Finance 24

Company Practices
10.19 Hiring and Firing Practices 20

NOTABLE COMPETITIVE DISADVANTAGES

Criteria	Rank

Growth Competitiveness

Macroeconomic Environment
2.24 Government Surplus/Deficit..62

Current Competitiveness

Sophistication of Company Operations and Strategy
10.03 Extent of Branding 64

Quality of the Business Environment
2.18 Hidden Trade Barriers..65
5.06 Port Infrastructure Quality..58
5.12 Quality of Public Schools 58

Other Indicators

Infrastructure
5.14 Difference in Quality of Healthcare.................................74
5.13 Difference in Quality of Schools 65

Public Institutions
8.05 Permits to Start a Firm..67
6.08 Burden of Regulation 66

Macroeconomic Environment
2.31 Average Tariff Rate..68
2.12 Perceived Interest Rate Gap 67
2.21 Social Transfer Recipients 67

Company Practices
10.20 Employment Rules...62

197

Bulgaria

Key Facts

GDP per capita at Purchasing Power Parity, 2000 .... $5,469
GDP per capita Rank 54
Percentage Growth in Real GDP per capita, 1999–2000 .... 5.7
Growth Rank 12
US Utility Patents Granted in 2000 (per million population) 0.1
Patent Rank 56

Growth Competitiveness Rank	59

Technology Index Rank **50**
   ICT Subindex Rank 50
   Innovation Subindex Rank 39
   Technology Transfer Subindex Rank
     (out of 51 technological non-core economies) 24

Public Institutions Index Rank **51**
   Corruption Subindex Rank 34
   Contracts and Law Subindex Rank 64

Macroeconomic Environment Index Rank **69**
   Macroeconomic Stability Subindex Rank 59
   Country Credit Rating Rank 58

Current Competitiveness Rank	68

Sophistication of Company Operations and Strategy Rank **70**
Quality of the Business Environment Rank **65**

National competitiveness balance sheet

NOTABLE COMPETITIVE ADVANTAGES

Criteria		Rank

Growth Competitiveness

Innovation
3.19 Tertiary Enrollment 22

Information and Communications Technology
4.16 Telephone Lines 32

Technology Transfer
3.23 Skill-Based Exports 36

Corruption
7.03 Irregular Payments in Tax Collection 31
7.01 Irregular Payments in Exports & Imports 36
7.02 Irregular Payments in Government Procurement 39

Macroeconomic Environment
Potential for "Catch-up" Growth 22
2.24 Government Surplus/Deficit 33

Current Competitiveness

Sophistication of Company Operations and Strategy
10.03 Extent of Branding 35
10.05 Uniqueness of Product Designs 35
10.09 Control of International Distribution 38

Quality of the Business Environment
5.12 Quality of Public Schools 33
5.05 Railroad Infrastructure Quality 37
3.11 Availability of Scientists and Engineers 38

Other Indicators

Technology
3.13 Women in the Economy 20
4.02 Public Access to Internet 36

Infrastructure
5.13 Difference in Quality of Schools 34
5.14 Difference in Quality of Healthcare 41

Public Institutions
6.06 Competence of Public Officials 16
8.06 Days to Start a Firm 19
6.09 Minimum Wage Enforcement 27
7.04 Irregular Payments in Public Contracts 29
6.08 Burden of Regulation 37
7.05 Irregular Payments in Loan Applications 42

Macroeconomic Environment
2.21 Social Transfer Recipients 25
2.20 Composition of Public Spending 44

Company Practices
10.23 Pay and Productivity 24
10.20 Employment Rules 25
10.19 Hiring and Firing Practices 40

NOTABLE COMPETITIVE DISADVANTAGES

Criteria		Rank

Growth Competitiveness

Innovation
3.02 Firm-Level Innovation 75
3.06 Company Spending on Research and Development 69
3.09 University/Industry Research Collaboration 67

Information and Communications Technology
4.12 Legal Framework for ICT Development 66

Technology Transfer
3.04 FDI and Technology Transfer 72

Law and Contracts
6.02 Property Rights 73

Macroeconomic Environment
2.26 National Savings Rate 72

Current Competitiveness

Sophistication of Company Operations and Strategy
10.06 Production Process Sophistication 74
10.12 Extent of Staff Training 74
10.07 Extent of Marketing 71

Quality of the Business Environment
8.04 Administrative Burden for Start-Ups 75
2.16 Local Equity Market Access 74
5.07 Air Transport Infrastructure Quality 74

Other Indicators

Technology
3.14 Minorities in the Economy 73
4.05 High Skilled IT Job Market 73
3.03 Firm-Level Technology Absorption 72
3.12 Brain Drain 72
4.04 Quality of Competition in Telecommunication Sector 68

Infrastructure
5.15 Public Health Agencies 70

Public Institutions
8.05 Permits to Start a Firm 67

Macroeconomic Environment
2.07 Financial Market Sophistication 75
2.15 Access to Bond Markets 72
2.17 Sources of Investment Finance 72
2.19 Permits to Export 69
2.32 Corporate Income Tax Rate 69
1.08 Unemployment Rate, 2000 68
2.27 Investment Rate 67

Company Practices
10.13 Willingness to Delegate Authority 73
10.14 Extent of Incentive Compensation 73
10.15 Reliance on Professional Management 72

Canada

Key Facts

GDP per capita at Purchasing Power Parity, 2000 ....$27,783
GDP per capita Rank 6
Percentage Growth in Real GDP per capita, 1999–2000 ....3.7
Growth Rank 30
US Utility Patents Granted in 2000 (per million population) 111.2
Patent Rank 9

Growth Competitiveness Rank	3

Technology Index Rank 2
    ICT Subindex Rank 8
    Innovation Subindex Rank 1
Public Institutions Index Rank **11**
    Corruption Subindex Rank 6
    Contracts and Law Subindex Rank.......................................19
Macroeconomic Environment Index Rank............................**13**
    Macroeconomic Stability Subindex Rank 14
    Country Credit Rating Rank 9

CURRENT COMPETITIVENESS RANK	11

Sophistication of Company Operations and Strategy Rank..................14
Quality of the Business Environment Rank..11

National competitiveness balance sheet

NOTABLE COMPETITIVE ADVANTAGES

Criteria		Rank

Growth Competitiveness

Innovation

3.19	Tertiary Enrollment	1
3.09	University/Industry Research Collaboration	6
3.16	Utility Patents in 2000	9

Information and Communications Technology

4.03	Internet Access in Schools	3
4.14	Internet Users	5
4.07	Quality of Competition in ISP Sector	6
4.11	Laws Relating to ICT Use	6
4.12	Legal Framework for ICT Development	6
4.16	Telephone Lines	7
4.15	Internet Hosts	8
4.17	Personal Computers	10

Corruption

7.03	Irregular Payments in Tax Collection	6
7.01	Irregular Payments in Exports & Imports	8
7.02	Irregular Payments in Government Procurement	8

Law and Contracts

| 6.01 | Judicial Independence | 10 |

Macroeconomic Environment

| 2.24 | Government Surplus/Deficit | 4 |
| 2.30 | Interest Rate Spread | 4 |

Current Competitiveness

Sophistication of Company Operations and Strategy

10.14	Extent of Incentive Compensation	3
10.13	Willingness to Delegate Authority	8
10.15	Reliance on Professional Management	8

Quality of the Business Environment

3.10	Government Procurement of Advanced Technology Products	4
10.16	Quality of Management Schools	4
9.05	Decentralization of Corporate Activity	8

Other Indicators

Technology

| 3.08 | Tax Credits for Firm-Level Research and Development | 1 |
| 4.01 | Speed and Cost of Internet Access | 4 |

Infrastructure

| 5.11 | Electricity Prices | 5 |

Public Institutions

6.09	Minimum Wage Enforcement	5
7.05	Irregular Payments in Loan Applications	5
8.05	Permits to Start a Firm	5

Macroeconomic Environment

2.02	Soundness of Banks	1
2.19	Permits to Export	1
2.31	Average Tariff Rate	3
2.04	Exchange Rate and Exports	4

NOTABLE COMPETITIVE DISADVANTAGES

Criteria		Rank

Growth Competitiveness

Information and Communications Technology

| 4.13 | Cellular Telephones | 31 |
| 4.08 | Government Prioritization of ICT | 25 |

Law and Contracts

| 6.12 | Organized Crime | 29 |
| 6.04 | Favoritism in Decisions of Government Officials | 21 |

Macroeconomic Environment

2.01	Recession Expectations	41
2.26	National Savings Rate	38
2.03	Access to Credit	36
2.29	Real Exchange Rate	29
2.28	Inflation	26

Current Competitiveness

Sophistication of Company Operations and Strategy

10.01	Nature of Competitive Advantage	27
10.11	Breadth of International Markets	27
10.03	Extent of Branding	21

Quality of the Business Environment

10.21	Cooperation in Labor-Employer Relations	46
2.18	Hidden Trade Barriers	27
9.07	Extent of Product and Process Collaboration	25

Other Indicators

Public Institutions

| 6.10 | Extent of Bureaucratic Red Tape | 35 |

Macroeconomic Environment

2.32	Corporate Income Tax Rate	75
2.13	Entry into Banking Industry	56
2.11	Foreign Access to Local Capital Markets	54
2.27	Investment Rate	54
2.17	Sources of Investment Finance	47
2.05	Expected Exchange Rate Volatility	36
2.22	Extent of Distortive Government Subsidies	36
1.08	Unemployment Rate, 2000	30

Company Practices

| 10.22 | Union Contributions to Productivity | 33 |

201

Chile

Key Facts

GDP per capita at Purchasing Power Parity, 2000 .... $9,187
GDP per capita Rank 36
Percentage Growth in Real GDP per capita, 1999–2000 .... 4.0
Growth Rank 24
US Utility Patents Granted in 2000 (per million population) 1.0
Patent Rank 38

Growth Competitiveness Rank	27

Technology Index Rank **42**
    ICT Subindex Rank 32
    Innovation Subindex Rank 34
    Technology Transfer Subindex Rank
      (out of 51 technological non-core economies) 38

Public Institutions Index Rank **21**
    Corruption Subindex Rank 13
    Contracts and Law Subindex Rank 26

Macroeconomic Environment Index Rank **21**
    Macroeconomic Stability Subindex Rank 40
    Country Credit Rating Rank 26

Current Competitiveness Rank	29

Sophistication of Company Operations and Strategy Rank **30**
Quality of the Business Environment Rank **28**

National competitiveness balance sheet

NOTABLE COMPETITIVE ADVANTAGES

Criteria	Rank

Growth Competitiveness

Corruption

7.01	Irregular Payments in Exports & Imports	9
7.02	Irregular Payments in Government Procurement	13
7.03	Irregular Payments in Tax Collection	15

Law and Contracts

6.12	Organized Crime	10

Current Competitiveness

Sophistication of Company Operations and Strategy

10.11	Breadth of International Markets	19
10.06	Production Process Sophistication	25
10.07	Extent of Marketing	28

Quality of the Business Environment

8.02	Extent of Locally Based Competitors	6
2.18	Hidden Trade Barriers	13
8.07	Effectiveness of Anti-Trust Policy	19

Other Indicators

Technology

4.04	Quality of Competition in Telecommunication Sector	5
3.12	Brain Drain	11
4.10	Government On-line Services	14

Infrastructure

5.08	Telephone/Fax Infrastructure Quality	14

Public Institutions

6.11	Tax Evasion	7
6.14	Informal Sector	12
7.05	Irregular Payments in Loan Applications	13
6.09	Minimum Wage Enforcement	14

Macroeconomic Environment

2.32	Corporate Income Tax Rate	2
2.02	Soundness of Banks	15

Company Practices

10.19	Hiring and Firing Practices	14

NOTABLE COMPETITIVE DISADVANTAGES

Criteria	Rank

Growth Competitiveness

Information and Communications Technology

4.11	Laws Relating to ICT Use	44
4.16	Telephone Lines	42

Technology Transfer

3.23	Skill-Based Exports	65

Macroeconomic Environment

2.29	Real Exchange Rate	55
2.03	Access to Credit	45
2.30	Interest Rate Spread	42

Current Competitiveness

Sophistication of Company Operations and Strategy

10.14	Extent of Incentive Compensation	62
10.02	Value Chain Presence	48
10.01	Nature of Competitive Advantage	44

Quality of the Business Environment

5.12	Quality of Public Schools	57
5.05	Railroad Infrastructure Development	55
9.09	Local Availability of Process Machinery	47

Other Indicators

Technology

3.13	Women in the Economy	65
3.14	Minorities in the Economy	56
3.08	Tax Credits for Firm-Level Research and Development	53
3.10	Government Procurement of Advanced Technology Products	48
4.02	Public Access to Internet	44
3.05	Quality of Scientific Research Institutions	43

Infrastructure

5.13	Difference in Quality of Schools	62
5.14	Difference in Quality of Healthcare	60
5.01	Overall Infrastructure Quality	45
5.06	Port Infrastructure Quality	45

Public Institutions

6.06	Competence of Public Officials	66
8.06	Days to Start a Firm	54
6.07	Costs of Institutional Change	47

Macroeconomic Environment

1.09	Employment to Population Ratio, 2000	64
2.17	Sources of Investment Finance	51
2.10	Access to Foreign Capital Markets	48
2.16	Local Equity Market Access	47
2.33	Value Added Tax Rate	47
2.09	Venture Capital Availability	44
2.15	Access to Bond Markets	44
2.31	Average Tariff Rate	44

Company Practices

10.22	Union Contributions to Productivity	45
10.20	Employment Rules	43

203

China

Key Facts

GDP per capita at Purchasing Power Parity, 2000 ....$3,953
GDP per capita Rank 60
Percentage Growth in Real GDP per capita, 1999–2000 ....7.1
Growth Rank 7
US Utility Patents Granted in 2000 (per million population)..........0.1
Patent Rank 58

Growth Competitiveness Rank	39

Technology Index Rank **53**
    ICT Subindex Rank 56
    Innovation Subindex Rank 63
    Technology Transfer Subindex Rank
       (out of 51 technological non-core economies) 23

Public Institutions Index Rank **50**
    Corruption Subindex Rank 48
    Contracts and Law Subindex Rank..51

Macroeconomic Environment Index Rank..**6**
    Macroeconomic Stability Subindex Rank 15
    Country Credit Rating Rank 34

Current Competitiveness Rank	47

Sophistication of Company Operations and Strategy Rank.................**39**
Quality of the Business Environment Rank...**47**

204

National competitiveness balance sheet

NOTABLE COMPETITIVE ADVANTAGES	
Criteria	Rank

Growth Competitiveness

Information and Communications Technology
| 4.08 | Government Prioritization of ICT | 15 |
| 4.09 | Government Success in ICT Promotion | 15 |

Macroeconomic Environment
2.26	National Savings Rate	2
2.28	Inflation	5
	Potential for "Catch-up" Growth	16
2.01	Recession Expectations	17
2.30	Interest Rate Spread	18

Current Competitiveness

Sophistication of Company Operations and Strategy
10.04	Capacity for Innovation	20
10.03	Extent of Branding	25
10.09	Control of International Distribution	33

Quality of the Business Environment
9.09	Local Availability of Process Machinery	2
3.10	Government Procurement of Advanced Technology Products	12
9.05	Decentralization of Corporate Activity	16

Other Indicators

Technology
3.14	Minorities in the Economy	9
3.13	Women in the Economy	21
3.08	Tax Credits for Firm-Level Research and Development	22

Public Institutions
6.06	Competence of Public Officials	6
7.07	Public Trust of Politicians	18
8.06	Days to Start a Firm	19
8.04	Administrative Burden for Start-Ups	23

Macroeconomic Environment
1.09	Employment to Population Ratio, 2000	1
2.27	Investment Rate	2
2.32	Corporate Income Tax Rate	24

Company Practices
10.23	Pay and Productivity	11
10.22	Union Contributions to Productivity	14
10.20	Employment Rules	17
10.19	Hiring and Firing Practices	23

NOTABLE COMPETITIVE DISADVANTAGES	
Criteria	Rank

Growth Competitiveness

Innovation
| 3.19 | Tertiary Enrollment | 70 |

Information and Communications Technology
| 4.07 | Quality of Competition in ISP Sector | 69 |
| 4.15 | Internet Hosts | 68 |

Current Competitiveness

Sophistication of Company Operations and Strategy
10.07	Extent of Marketing	66
10.14	Extent of Incentive Compensation	65
10.13	Willingness to Delegate Authority	60

Quality of the Business Environment
10.17	Efficacy of Corporate Boards	67
2.07	Financial Market Sophistication	64
5.07	Air Transport Infrastructure Quality	61

Other Indicators

Technology
| 4.06 | IT Training and Education | 63 |
| 4.02 | Public Access to Internet | 62 |

Infrastructure
| 5.10 | Postal Efficiency | 64 |
| 5.01 | Overall Infrastructure Quality | 61 |

Public Institutions
| 6.09 | Minimum Wage Enforcement | 65 |
| 7.05 | Irregular Payments in Loan Applications | 64 |

Macroeconomic Environment
2.11	Foreign Access to Local Capital Markets	75
2.13	Entry into Banking Industry	74
2.06	Exchange Rate Premium	72
2.10	Access to Foreign Capital Markets	71
2.19	Permits to Export	71
2.31	Average Tariff Rate	71
2.02	Soundness of Banks	63
2.18	Hidden Trade Barriers	61

205

Colombia

Key Facts

GDP per capita at Purchasing Power Parity, 2000 ....$5,923
GDP per capita Rank 52
Percentage Growth in Real GDP per capita, 1999–2000 ....1.0
Growth Rank 66
US Utility Patents Granted in 2000 (per million population).........0.2
Patent Rank 51

Growth Competitiveness Rank	**65**

Technology Index Rank **56**
    ICT Subindex Rank 51
    Innovation Subindex Rank 57
    Technology Transfer Subindex Rank
      (out of 51 technological non-core economies) 39
Public Institutions Index Rank **57**
    Corruption Subindex Rank 40
    Contracts and Law Subindex Rank.......................................67
Macroeconomic Environment Index Rank..............................**66**
    Macroeconomic Stability Subindex Rank 70
    Country Credit Rating Rank 52

Current Competitiveness Rank	**56**

Sophistication of Company Operations and Strategy Rank.................**52**
Quality of the Business Environment Rank..**59**

National competitiveness balance sheet

NOTABLE COMPETITIVE ADVANTAGES

Criteria	Rank

Growth Competitiveness

Information and Communications Technology

4.11	Laws Relating to ICT Use	38
4.12	Legal Framework for ICT Development	42
4.03	Internet Access in Schools	43
4.08	Government Prioritization of ICT	44

Technology Transfer

3.04	FDI and Technology Transfer	44

Corruption

7.02	Irregular Payments in Government Procurement	37
7.01	Irregular Payments in Exports & Imports	39

Macroeconomic Environment

	Potential for "Catch-up" Growth	24

Current Competitiveness

Sophistication of Company Operations and Strategy

10.01	Nature of Competitive Advantage	36
10.03	Extent of Branding	36
10.10	Extent of Regional Sales	37

Quality of the Business Environment

8.02	Extent of Locally Based Competitors	19
10.16	Quality of Management Schools	29
10.17	Efficacy of Corporate Boards	33

Other Indicators

Technology

4.04	Quality of Competition in Telecommunication Sector	34
4.02	Public Access to Internet	37
4.10	Government On-line Services	37
3.13	Women in the Economy	42

Infrastructure

5.02	Tap Water Safety	40

Public Institutions

6.09	Minimum Wage Enforcement	21
6.13	Unreported Profits and Wages	31
6.08	Burden of Regulation	43
6.10	Extent of Bureaucratic Red Tape	43
6.06	Competence of Public Officials	45

Macroeconomic Environment

2.04	Exchange Rate and Exports	16
2.33	Value Added Tax Rate	37
2.17	Sources of Investment Finance	45
2.22	Extent of Distortive Government Subsidies	45

Company Practices

10.19	Hiring and Firing Practices	42

NOTABLE COMPETITIVE DISADVANTAGES

Criteria	Rank

Growth Competitiveness

Law and Contracts

6.12	Organized Crime	74

Macroeconomic Environment

2.26	National Savings Rate	69
2.30	Interest Rate Spread	67
2.03	Access to Credit	66
2.24	Government Surplus/Deficit	66

Current Competitiveness

Sophistication of Company Operations and Strategy

10.14	Extent of Incentive Compensation	68
3.06	Company Spending on Research and Development	63
10.07	Extent of Marketing	59

Quality of the Business Environment

5.06	Port Infrastructure Quality	71
5.04	Road Infrastructure Quality	68
8.04	Administrative Burden for Start-Ups	68

Other Indicators

Technology

3.14	Minorities in the Economy	68
4.05	High Skilled IT Job Market	66

Public Institutions

6.07	Costs of Institutional Change	69
7.07	Public Trust of Politicians	67

Macroeconomic Environment

2.27	Investment Rate	75
2.21	Social Transfer Recipients	70
2.20	Composition of Public Spending	66
1.08	Unemployment Rate, 2000	66

Company Practices

10.23	Pay and Productivity	70
10.22	Union Contributions to Productivity	67

207

Costa Rica

Key Facts

GDP per capita at Purchasing Power Parity, 2000 ....$9,236
GDP per capita Rank 34
Percentage Growth in Real GDP per capita, 1999–2000 ....2.2
Growth Rank 56
US Utility Patents Granted in 2000 (per million population)..........1.8
Patent Rank 32

Growth Competitiveness Rank	35

Technology Index Rank **32**	
ICT Subindex Rank 42	
Innovation Subindex Rank 32	
Technology Transfer Subindex Rank	
(out of 51 technological non-core economies) 5	
Public Institutions Index Rank **37**	
Corruption Subindex Rank 43	
Contracts and Law Subindex Rank........................35	
Macroeconomic Environment Index Rank............................**42**	
Macroeconomic Stability Subindex Rank 58	
Country Credit Rating Rank 47	

Current Competitiveness Rank	50

Sophistication of Company Operations and Strategy Rank.................**34**
Quality of the Business Environment Rank...**52**

National competitiveness balance sheet

NOTABLE COMPETITIVE ADVANTAGES

Criteria	Rank

Growth Competitiveness

Technology Transfer

3.04	FDI and Technology Transfer	6

Current Competitiveness

Sophistication of Company Operations and Strategy

10.01	Nature of Competitive Advantage	22
10.14	Extent of Incentive Compensation	26
10.12	Extent of Staff Training	31

Quality of the Business Environment

10.21	Cooperation in Labor-Employer Relations	12
10.16	Quality of Management Schools	17
6.01	Judicial Independence	30

Other Indicators

Public Institutions

6.09	Minimum Wage Enforcement	13

NOTABLE COMPETITIVE DISADVANTAGES

Criteria	Rank

Growth Competitiveness

Information and Communications Technology

4.07	Quality of Competition in ISP Sector	74
4.13	Cellular Telephones	57
4.12	Legal Framework for ICT Development	51

Macroeconomic Environment

2.26	National Savings Rate	71
2.28	Inflation	67
2.30	Interest Rate Spread	62
2.29	Real Exchange Rate	58

Current Competitiveness

Sophistication of Company Operations and Strategy

10.09	Control of International Distribution	63
10.08	Degree of Customer Orientation	60
10.11	Breadth of International Markets	46

Quality of the Business Environment

5.08	Telephone/Fax Infrastructure Quality	70
5.05	Railroad Infrastructure Development	69
5.06	Port Infrastructure Quality	67

Other Indicators

Technology

3.08	Tax Credits for Firm-Level Research and Development	66
4.04	Quality of Competition in Telecommunication Sector	66
3.07	Subsidies for Firm-Level Research and Development	61
4.01	Speed and Cost of Internet Access	61

Infrastructure

5.04	Road Infrastructure Quality	69
5.09	Quality of Competition in Transportation Sector	61
5.01	Overall Infrastructure Quality	57

Public Institutions

8.05	Permits to Start a Firm	64
6.13	Unreported Profits and Wages	61
8.04	Administrative Burden for Start-Ups	58
6.06	Competence of Public Officials	54
8.06	Days to Start a Firm	54

Macroeconomic Environment

2.08	Ease of Access to Loans	63
2.27	Investment Rate	63
2.15	Access to Bond Markets	62
1.09	Employment to Population Ratio, 2000	60
2.07	Financial Market Sophistication	58
2.09	Venture Capital Availability	58
2.12	Perceived Interest Rate Gap	57
2.16	Local Equity Market Access	55
2.22	Extent of Distortive Government Subsidies	54

Company Practices

10.20	Employment Rules	75
10.22	Union Contributions to Productivity	70

Czech Republic

Key Facts

GDP per capita at Purchasing Power Parity, 2000 ....$13,721
GDP per capita Rank 29
Percentage Growth in Real GDP per capita, 1999–2000 ....3.3
Growth Rank 36
US Utility Patents Granted in 2000 (per million population).........2.2
Patent Rank 30

Growth Competitiveness Rank	**37**

Technology Index Rank **20**	
ICT Subindex Rank 29	
Innovation Subindex Rank 38	
Technology Transfer Subindex Rank (out of 51 technological non-core economies) 3	
Public Institutions Index Rank **53**	
Corruption Subindex Rank 58	
Contracts and Law Subindex Rank....................................48	
Macroeconomic Environment Index Rank...............................**49**	
Macroeconomic Stability Subindex Rank 43	
Country Credit Rating Rank 30	

Current Competitiveness Rank	**35**

Sophistication of Company Operations and Strategy Rank.................**41**
Quality of the Business Environment Rank..**33**

National competitiveness balance sheet

NOTABLE COMPETITIVE ADVANTAGES		NOTABLE COMPETITIVE DISADVANTAGES	
Criteria	Rank	Criteria	Rank

Growth Competitiveness

Technology Transfer

3.04	FDI and Technology Transfer	5
3.23	Skill-Based Exports	8

Current Competitiveness

Sophistication of Company Operations and Strategy

3.06	Company Spending on Research and Development	27
10.05	Uniqueness of Product Designs	28
10.10	Extent of Regional Sales	34

Quality of the Business Environment

9.10	Local Availability of Specialized Research and Training Services	17
5.12	Quality of Public Schools	19
11.06	Stringency of Environmental Regulations	22

Other Indicators

Infrastructure

5.11	Electricity Prices	12
5.13	Difference in Quality of Schools	14
5.10	Postal Efficiency	15

Public Institutions

6.10	Extent of Bureaucratic Red Tape	13

Macroeconomic Environment

2.27	Investment Rate	9
2.31	Average Tariff Rate	13

Company Practices

10.20	Employment Rules	8
10.22	Union Contributions to Productivity	10

Growth Competitiveness

Information and Communications Technology

4.08	Government Prioritization of ICT	53

Corruption

7.02	Irregular Payments in Government Procurement	57
7.01	Irregular Payments in Exports & Imports	55

Law and Contracts

6.12	Organized Crime	52

Macroeconomic Environment

2.03	Access to Credit	58
2.24	Government Surplus/Deficit	55

Current Competitiveness

Sophistication of Company Operations and Strategy

10.13	Willingness to Delegate Authority	67
10.09	Control of International Distribution	66
10.06	Production Process Sophistication	58

Quality of the Business Environment

10.17	Efficacy of Corporate Boards	69
2.16	Local Equity Market Access	64
2.07	Financial Market Sophistication	61

Other Indicators

Infrastructure

5.06	Port Infrastructure Quality	56

Public Institutions

7.05	Irregular Payments in Loan Applications	68
7.04	Irregular Payments in Public Contracts	66
7.07	Public Trust of Politicians	58
6.13	Unreported Profits and Wages	56
6.11	Tax Evasion	55
8.06	Days to Start a Firm	54
6.06	Competence of Public Officials	52
6.09	Minimum Wage Enforcement	52

Macroeconomic Environment

2.02	Soundness of Banks	70
2.14	Financial Regulation and Supervision	65
2.33	Value Added Tax Rate	65
2.17	Sources of Investment Finance	60
2.13	Entry into Banking Industry	58
2.22	Extent of Distortive Government Subsidies	55
2.10	Access to Foreign Capital Markets	54

211

Denmark

Key Facts

GDP per capita at Purchasing Power Parity, 2000 ....$27,120
GDP per capita Rank 7
Percentage Growth in Real GDP per capita, 1999–2000 ....2.7
Growth Rank 50
US Utility Patents Granted in 2000 (per million population)........82.3
Patent Rank 10

Growth Competitiveness Rank	14

Technology Index Rank **12**
   ICT Subindex Rank 7
   Innovation Subindex Rank 15
Public Institutions Index Rank **3**
   Corruption Subindex Rank 3
   Contracts and Law Subindex Rank 2
Macroeconomic Environment Index Rank...**31**
   Macroeconomic Stability Subindex Rank 18
   Country Credit Rating Rank 10

Current Competitiveness Rank	8

Sophistication of Company Operations and Strategy Rank....................**9**
Quality of the Business Environment Rank..**10**

National competitiveness balance sheet

NOTABLE COMPETITIVE ADVANTAGES		NOTABLE COMPETITIVE DISADVANTAGES	
Criteria	Rank	Criteria	Rank

Growth Competitiveness

Innovation

3.16	Utility Patents in 2000	10

Information and Communications Technology

4.16	Telephone Lines	1
4.03	Internet Access in Schools	6
4.17	Personal Computers	6
4.14	Internet Users	9
4.15	Internet Hosts	10

Corruption

7.02	Irregular Payments in Government Procurement	3
7.03	Irregular Payments in Tax Collection	4
7.01	Irregular Payments in Exports & Imports	5

Law and Contracts

6.12	Organized Crime	2
6.04	Favoritism in Decisions of Government Officials	3
6.01	Judicial Independence	5
6.02	Property Rights	9

Macroeconomic Environment

2.24	Government Surplus/Deficit	7

Current Competitiveness

Sophistication of Company Operations and Strategy

10.12	Extent of Staff Training	2
10.13	Willingness to Delegate Authority	2
10.05	Uniqueness of Product Designs	3

Quality of the Business Environment

2.08	Ease of Access to Loans	3
11.06	Stringency of Environmental Regulations	3
10.21	Cooperation in Labor-Employer Relations	5

Other Indicators

Technology

4.02	Public Access to Internet	3

Infrastructure

5.10	Postal Efficiency	3
5.14	Difference in Quality of Healthcare	4

Public Institutions

7.05	Irregular Payments in Loan Applications	2
6.13	Unreported Profits and Wages	3
7.06	Business Costs of Corruption	3
6.14	Informal Sector	5
8.05	Permits to Start a Firm	5

Macroeconomic Environment

2.13	Entry into Banking Industry	1
2.19	Permits to Export	1
2.18	Hidden Trade Barriers	4

Growth Competitiveness

Macroeconomic Environment

2.30	Interest Rate Spread	36
2.01	Recession Expectations	33
2.28	Inflation	33
2.26	National Savings Rate	30

Current Competitiveness

Sophistication of Company Operations and Strategy

10.14	Extent of Incentive Compensation	33
3.06	Company Spending on Research and Development	13
10.06	Production Process Sophistication	12

Quality of the Business Environment

9.06	State of Cluster Development	36
8.01	Intensity of Local Competition	34
3.10	Government Procurement of Advanced Technology Products	23

Other Indicators

Technology

3.14	Minorities in the Economy	64
3.08	Tax Credits for Firm-Level Research and Development	41

Infrastructure

5.11	Electricity Prices	60

Public Institutions

6.08	Burden of Regulation	41

Macroeconomic Environment

2.33	Value Added Tax Rate	72
2.17	Sources of Investment Finance	46
2.32	Corporate Income Tax Rate	41
2.04	Exchange Rate and Exports	37
2.27	Investment Rate	37
1.09	Employment to Population Ratio, 2000	36
2.06	Exchange Rate Premium	31

213

Dominican Republic

Key Facts

GDP per capita at Purchasing Power Parity, 2000 ....$5,962
GDP per capita Rank 51
Percentage Growth in Real GDP per capita, 1999–2000 ....6.1
Growth Rank 10
US Utility Patents Granted in 2000 (per million population)..........0.4
Patent Rank 45

Growth Competitiveness Rank	50

Technology Index Rank **44**
ICT Subindex Rank 57
Innovation Subindex Rank 46
Technology Transfer Subindex Rank
(out of 51 technological non-core economies) 11
Public Institutions Index Rank **54**
Corruption Subindex Rank 47
Contracts and Law Subindex Rank.......................54
Macroeconomic Environment Index Rank............................**46**
Macroeconomic Stability Subindex Rank 66
Country Credit Rating Rank 60

Current Competitiveness Rank	59

Sophistication of Company Operations and Strategy Rank.................**59**
Quality of the Business Environment Rank..**58**

National competitiveness balance sheet

NOTABLE COMPETITIVE ADVANTAGES

Criteria	Rank

Growth Competitiveness
Technology Transfer
3.23	Skill-Based Exports	19
3.04	FDI and Technology Transfer	25

Current Competitiveness
Sophistication of Company Operations and Strategy
10.03	Extent of Branding	27
10.07	Extent of Marketing	36
10.14	Extent of Incentive Compensation	39

Quality of the Business Environment
5.08	Telephone/Fax Infrastructure Quality	28
5.07	Air Transport Infrastructure Quality	34
9.11	Local Availability of Information Technology Services	36

Other Indicators
Technology
4.04	Quality of Competition in Telecommunication Sector	11

Public Institutions
8.05	Permits to Start a Firm	24

Macroeconomic Environment
2.17	Sources of Investment Finance	7
2.32	Corporate Income Tax Rate	7
2.33	Value Added Tax Rate	11
2.27	Investment Rate	20

Company Practices
10.19	Hiring and Firing Practices	22

NOTABLE COMPETITIVE DISADVANTAGES

Criteria	Rank

Growth Competitiveness
Information and Communications Technology
4.14	Internet Users	71

Law and Contracts
6.04	Favoritism in Decisions of Government Officials	70

Macroeconomic Environment
2.30	Interest Rate Spread	72
2.01	Recession Expectations	69
2.29	Real Exchange Rate	65

Current Competitiveness
Sophistication of Company Operations and Strategy
10.15	Reliance on Professional Management	68
10.01	Nature of Competitive Advantage	67
10.10	Extent of Regional Sales	67

Quality of the Business Environment
2.18	Hidden Trade Barriers	71
9.04	Presence of Demanding Regulatory Standards	69
11.06	Stringency of Environmental Regulations	65

Other Indicators
Technology
3.05	Quality of Scientific Research Institutions	64
3.08	Tax Credits for Firm-Level Research and Development	64
3.11	Availability of Scientists and Engineers	64
4.02	Public Access to Internet	61

Infrastructure
5.11	Electricity Prices	74
5.05	Railroad Infrastructure Development	70
5.13	Difference in Quality of Schools	70
5.14	Difference in Quality of Healthcare	69
5.02	Tap Water Safety	68
5.03	Industrial Water Availability	67
5.12	Quality of Public Schools	65
5.15	Public Health Agencies	61

Public Institutions
6.05	Government Commitments	69
6.14	Informal Sector	68
6.03	Intellectual Property Protection	65
6.10	Extent of Bureaucratic Red Tape	61

Macroeconomic Environment
2.06	Exchange Rate Premium	74
2.09	Venture Capital Availability	68
2.31	Average Tariff Rate	64
2.12	Perceived Interest Rate Gap	63

Company Practices
10.20	Employment Rules	67

Ecuador

Key Facts

GDP per capita at Purchasing Power Parity, 2000 .... $3,068
GDP per capita Rank 66
Percentage Growth in Real GDP per capita, 1999–2000 .... 0.4
Growth Rank 69
US Utility Patents Granted in 2000 (per million population) 0.0
Patent Rank 65

Growth Competitiveness Rank	68

Technology Index Rank **69**
    ICT Subindex Rank 63
    Innovation Subindex Rank 59
    Technology Transfer Subindex Rank
      (out of 51 technological non-core economies) 48

Public Institutions Index Rank **68**
    Corruption Subindex Rank 63
    Contracts and Law Subindex Rank 73

Macroeconomic Environment Index Rank **62**
    Macroeconomic Stability Subindex Rank 52
    Country Credit Rating Rank 71

Current Competitiveness Rank	72

Sophistication of Company Operations and Strategy Rank **71**
Quality of the Business Environment Rank **72**

National competitiveness balance sheet

NOTABLE COMPETITIVE ADVANTAGES

Criteria	Rank

Growth Competitiveness

Macroeconomic Environment

2.29	Real Exchange Rate	7
	Potential for "Catch-up" Growth	10
2.24	Government Surplus/Deficit	16
2.26	National Savings Rate	20

Current Competitiveness

Sophistication of Company Operations and Strategy

10.04	Capacity for Innovation	51
10.05	Uniqueness of Product Designs	52
10.11	Breadth of International Markets	55

Quality of the Business Environment

10.21	Cooperation in Labor-Employer Relations	34
8.02	Extent of Locally Based Competitors	52
5.06	Port Infrastructure Quality	54

Other Indicators

Macroeconomic Environment

2.05	Expected Exchange Rate Volatility	3
2.32	Corporate Income Tax Rate	7
2.06	Exchange Rate Premium	9
2.10	Access to Foreign Capital Markets	15
2.33	Value Added Tax Rate	22
2.11	Foreign Access to Local Capital Markets	25
2.21	Social Transfer Recipients	26
1.08	Unemployment Rate, 2000	39

NOTABLE COMPETITIVE DISADVANTAGES

Criteria	Rank

Growth Competitiveness

Innovation

3.09	University/Industry Research Collaboration	73
3.01	Technological Sophistication	69
3.06	Company Spending on Research and Development	68
3.16	Utility Patents in 2000	65

Information and Communications Technology

4.15	Internet Hosts	73
4.12	Legal Framework for ICT Development	71
4.09	Government Success in ICT Promotion	70
4.08	Government Prioritization of ICT	67

Technology Transfer

3.23	Skill-Based Exports	66

Corruption

7.02	Irregular Payments in Government Procurement	66

Law and Contracts

6.04	Favoritism in Decisions of Government Officials	72
6.01	Judicial Independence	71
6.02	Property Rights	69

Macroeconomic Environment

2.03	Access to Credit	75
2.28	Inflation	75

Current Competitiveness

Sophistication of Company Operations and Strategy

10.08	Degree of Customer Orientation	74
10.12	Extent of Staff Training	71
10.15	Reliance on Professional Management	71

Quality of the Business Environment

9.01	Buyer Sophistication	74
9.04	Presence of Demanding Regulatory Standards	74
3.10	Government Procurement of Advanced Technology Products	73

Other Indicators

Technology

3.14	Minorities in the Economy	75

Infrastructure

5.14	Difference in Quality of Healthcare	73
5.15	Public Health Agencies	73

Macroeconomic Environment

2.02	Soundness of Banks	75
2.12	Perceived Interest Rate Gap	75
2.14	Financial Regulation and Supervision	75
2.15	Access to Bond Markets	75
2.17	Sources of Investment Finance	75
2.18	Hidden Trade Barriers	74

Company Practices

10.23	Pay and Productivity	75
10.22	Union Contributions to Productivity	74

Egypt

Key Facts

GDP per capita at Purchasing Power Parity, 2000 ....$3,602
GDP per capita Rank 64
Percentage Growth in Real GDP per capita, 1999–2000 ....3.2
Growth Rank 37
US Utility Patents Granted in 2000 (per million population).........0.1
Patent Rank 57

Growth Competitiveness Rank	51

Technology Index Rank **64**
    ICT Subindex Rank 61
    Innovation Subindex Rank 55
    Technology Transfer Subindex Rank
      (out of 51 technological non-core economies) 44
Public Institutions Index Rank **33**
    Corruption Subindex Rank 54
    Contracts and Law Subindex Rank........................24
Macroeconomic Environment Index Rank....................................**51**
    Macroeconomic Stability Subindex Rank 54
    Country Credit Rating Rank 43

Current Competitiveness Rank	45

Sophistication of Company Operations and Strategy Rank................36
Quality of the Business Environment Rank..46

National competitiveness balance sheet

NOTABLE COMPETITIVE ADVANTAGES		
Criteria		**Rank**

Growth Competitiveness

Information and Communications Technology

4.09	Government Success in ICT Promotion	6
4.08	Government Prioritization of ICT	14

Law and Contracts

6.12	Organized Crime	16
6.04	Favoritism in Decisions of Government Officials	25

Macroeconomic Environment

	Potential for "Catch-up" Growth	12
2.30	Interest Rate Spread	20

Current Competitiveness

Sophistication of Company Operations and Strategy

10.14	Extent of Incentive Compensation	22
10.02	Value Chain Presence	32
10.09	Control of International Distribution	32

Quality of the Business Environment

2.08	Ease of Access to Loans	16
6.01	Judicial Independence	27
6.03	Intellectual Property Protection	34

Other Indicators

Infrastructure

5.11	Electricity Prices	19
5.05	Railroad Infrastructure Development	24

Public Institutions

8.05	Permits to Start a Firm	5

Macroeconomic Environment

2.17	Sources of Investment Finance	6
2.11	Foreign Access to Local Capital Markets	12
2.33	Value Added Tax Rate	12
2.21	Social Transfer Recipients	21
2.19	Permits to Export	22

Company Practices

10.21	Cooperation in Labor-Employer Relations	19

NOTABLE COMPETITIVE DISADVANTAGES		
Criteria		**Rank**

Growth Competitiveness

Innovation

3.06	Company Spending on Research and Development	72
3.02	Firm-Level Innovation	61

Information and Communications Technology

4.15	Internet Hosts	69
4.13	Cellular Telephones	67
4.17	Personal Computers	64
4.03	Internet Access in Schools	62
4.14	Internet Users	61
4.16	Telephone Lines	61

Technology Transfer

3.23	Skill-Based Exports	67

Corruption

7.02	Irregular Payments in Government Procurement	63

Macroeconomic Environment

2.29	Real Exchange Rate	71
2.03	Access to Credit	67
2.01	Recession Expectations	64

Current Competitiveness

Sophistication of Company Operations and Strategy

10.01	Nature of Competitive Advantage	65
10.08	Degree of Customer Orientation	64

Quality of the Business Environment

6.10	Extent of Bureaucratic Red Tape	75
9.06	State of Cluster Development	75
9.03	Local Supplier Quality	73

Other Indicators

Technology

3.03	Firm-Level Technology Absorption	68
3.07	Subsidies for Firm-Level Research and Development	68
3.08	Tax Credits for Firm-Level Research and Development	63
4.10	Government On-line Services	63

Public Institutions

6.08	Burden of Regulation	68
6.09	Minimum Wage Enforcement	68

Macroeconomic Environment

2.31	Average Tariff Rate	73
2.05	Expected Exchange Rate Volatility	71
2.32	Corporate Income Tax Rate	69
1.09	Employment to Population Ratio, 2000	68
2.06	Exchange Rate Premium	65

219

El Salvador

Key Facts

GDP per capita at Purchasing Power Parity, 2000 ....$4,477
GDP per capita Rank 56
Percentage Growth in Real GDP per capita, 1999–2000 ....1.0
Growth Rank 65
US Utility Patents Granted in 2000 (per million population)..........0.0
Patent Rank 65

National competitiveness balance sheet

NOTABLE COMPETITIVE ADVANTAGES

Criteria	Rank

Growth Competitiveness

Information and Communications Technology

4.08	Government Prioritization of ICT	34
4.09	Government Success in ICT Promotion	37
4.07	Quality of Competition in ISP Sector	41

Technology Transfer

3.04	FDI and Technology Transfer	18

Corruption

7.02	Irregular Payments in Government Procurement	34

Macroeconomic Environment

	Potential for "Catch-up Growth"	20
2.28	Inflation	22
2.30	Interest Rate Spread	32
2.03	Access to Credit	43

Current Competitiveness

Sophistication of Company Operations and Strategy

10.14	Extent of Incentive Compensation	38
10.10	Extent of Regional Sales	40
10.13	Willingness to Delegate Authority	44

Quality of the Business Environment

10.21	Cooperation in Labor-Employer Relations	23
5.08	Telephone/Fax Infrastructure Quality	26
4.01	Speed and Cost of Internet Access	29

Other Indicators

Technology

4.04	Quality of Competition in Telecommunication Sector	21
3.13	Women in the Economy	28

Public Institutions

6.08	Burden of Regulation	13
8.06	Days to Start a Firm	19
6.07	Costs of Institutional Change	31
8.04	Administrative Burden for Start-Ups	34
6.13	Unreported Profits and Wages	35
8.05	Permits to Start a Firm	35

Macroeconomic Environment

2.05	Expected Exchange Rate Volatility	1
2.17	Sources of Investment Finance	1
2.06	Exchange Rate Premium	3
2.32	Corporate Income Tax Rate	7
2.19	Permits to Export	22
2.21	Social Transfer Recipients	22
2.33	Value Added Tax Rate	26
1.08	Unemployment Rate, 2000	29
2.10	Access to Foreign Capital Markets	33
2.20	Composition of Public Spending	34

Company Practices

10.19	Hiring and Firing Practices	30

NOTABLE COMPETITIVE DISADVANTAGES

Criteria	Rank

Growth Competitiveness

Innovation

3.09	University/Industry Research Collaboration	72
3.02	Firm-Level Innovation	68
3.16	Utility Patents in 2000	65

Information and Communications Technology

4.15	Internet Hosts	67

Law and Contracts

6.12	Organized Crime	75

Macroeconomic Environment

2.29	Real Exchange Rate	72
2.01	Recession Expectations	68
2.26	National Savings Rate	68

Current Competitiveness

Sophistication of Company Operations and Strategy

10.04	Capacity for Innovation	72
10.05	Uniqueness of Product Designs	70
10.15	Reliance on Professional Management	69

Quality of the Business Environment

3.05	Quality of Scientific Research Institutions	72
3.11	Availability of Scientists and Engineers	72
9.05	Decentralization of Corporate Activity	72

Other Indicators

Technology

3.08	Tax Credits for Firm-Level Research and Development	71

Infrastructure

5.05	Railroad Infrastructure Development	71
5.03	Industrial Water Availability	68
5.13	Difference in Quality of Schools	67

Public Institutions

6.14	Informal Sector	74
6.06	Competence of Public Officials	70

Macroeconomic Environment

2.27	Investment Rate	67

Company Practices

10.22	Union Contributions to Productivity	71
10.20	Employment Rules	68

221

Estonia

Key Facts

GDP per capita at Purchasing Power Parity, 2000 ....$9,178
GDP per capita Rank 37
Percentage Growth in Real GDP per capita, 1999–2000 ....7.6
Growth Rank 6
US Utility Patents Granted in 2000 (per million population)..........2.9
Patent Rank 28

Growth Competitiveness Rank	29

Technology Index Rank..8
    ICT Subindex Rank 20
    Innovation Subindex Rank 26
    Technology Transfer Subindex Rank
        (out of 51 technological non-core economies) 4
Public Institutions Index Rank 29
    Corruption Subindex Rank 29
    Contracts and Law Subindex Rank.......................................31
Macroeconomic Environment Index Rank...43
    Macroeconomic Stability Subindex Rank 36
    Country Credit Rating Rank 36

Current Competitiveness Rank	27

Sophistication of Company Operations and Strategy Rank...................32
Quality of the Business Environment Rank..26

National competitiveness balance sheet

NOTABLE COMPETITIVE ADVANTAGES

Criteria	Rank

Growth Competitiveness

Information and Communications Technology

4.08	Government Prioritization of ICT	3
4.09	Government Success in ICT Promotion	3
4.12	Legal Framework for ICT Development	12
4.03	Internet Access in Schools	13

Technology Transfer

3.23	Skill-Based Exports	9
3.04	FDI and Technology Transfer	11

Macroeconomic Environment

2.03	Access to Credit	12

Current Competitiveness

Sophistication of Company Operations and Strategy

10.15	Reliance on Professional Management	21
10.13	Willingness to Delegate Authority	22
10.08	Degree of Customer Orientation	26

Quality of the Business Environment

8.04	Administrative Burden for Start-Ups	5
2.18	Hidden Trade Barriers	12
4.11	Laws Relating to ICT Use	21

Other Indicators

Technology

4.10	Government On-line Services	5
4.02	Public Access to Internet	11
3.13	Women in the Economy	14

Public Institutions

6.08	Burden of Regulation	5
8.05	Permits to Start a Firm	5
6.07	Costs of Institutional Change	9
6.14	Informal Sector	9

Macroeconomic Environment

2.31	Average Tariff Rate	1
2.32	Corporate Income Tax Rate	1
2.05	Expected Exchange Rate Volatility	8
2.22	Extent of Distortive Government Subsidies	9
2.10	Access to Foreign Capital Markets	12
2.11	Foreign Access to Local Capital Markets	14

Company Practices

10.23	Pay and Productivity	7

NOTABLE COMPETITIVE DISADVANTAGES

Criteria	Rank

Growth Competitiveness

Law and Contracts

6.02	Property Rights	44

Macroeconomic Environment

2.29	Real Exchange Rate	53
2.26	National Savings Rate	52

Current Competitiveness

Sophistication of Company Operations and Strategy

10.03	Extent of Branding	61
10.09	Control of International Distribution	51
10.01	Nature of Competitive Advantage	50

Quality of the Business Environment

9.06	State of Cluster Development	63
9.09	Local Availability of Process Machinery	58
9.02	Local Supplier Quantity	56

Other Indicators

Technology

3.08	Tax Credits for Firm-Level Research and Development	52

Infrastructure

5.15	Public Health Agencies	45

Public Institutions

6.13	Unreported Profits and Wages	53

Macroeconomic Environment

2.17	Sources of Investment Finance	66
2.15	Access to Bond Markets	56
2.06	Exchange Rate Premium	52
2.33	Value Added Tax Rate	47
1.08	Unemployment Rate, 2000	45

Finland

Key Facts

GDP per capita at Purchasing Power Parity, 2000 ....$24,864
GDP per capita Rank 14
Percentage Growth in Real GDP per capita, 1999–2000 ....5.5
Growth Rank 14
US Utility Patents Granted in 2000 (per million population)......119.4
Patent Rank 8

Growth Competitiveness Rank	1
Technology Index Rank...**3**	
ICT Subindex Rank 1	
Innovation Subindex Rank 4	
Public Institutions Index Rank **1**	
Corruption Subindex Rank 2	
Contracts and Law Subindex Rank...1	
Macroeconomic Environment Index Rank....................................**10**	
Macroeconomic Stability Subindex Rank 3	
Country Credit Rating Rank 11	

Current Competitiveness Rank	1
Sophistication of Company Operations and Strategy Rank....................2	
Quality of the Business Environment Rank..1	

224

National competitiveness balance sheet

NOTABLE COMPETITIVE ADVANTAGES

Criteria	Rank

Growth Competitiveness

Innovation

3.09	University/Industry Research Collaboration	1
3.01	Technological Sophistication	3
3.19	Tertiary Enrollment	4
3.06	Company Spending on Research and Development	5
3.02	Firm-Level Innovation	7
3.16	Utility Patents in 2000	8

Information and Communications Technology

4.03	Internet Access in Schools	1
4.07	Quality of Competition in ISP Sector	1
4.11	Laws Relating to ICT Use	1
4.12	Legal Framework for ICT Development	1
4.08	Government Prioritization of ICT	2
4.09	Government Success in ICT Promotion	2
4.15	Internet Hosts	3
4.13	Cellular Telephones	5
4.14	Internet Users	7
4.17	Personal Computers	7

Corruption

7.01	Irregular Payments in Exports & Imports	2
7.02	Irregular Payments in Government Procurement	2
7.03	Irregular Payments in Tax Collection	2

Law and Contracts

6.04	Favoritism in Decisions of Government Officials	1
6.01	Judicial Independence	3
6.02	Property Rights	4
6.12	Organized Crime	5

Macroeconomic Environment

2.24	Government Surplus/Deficit	3
2.29	Real Exchange Rate	3
2.03	Access to Credit	5

Current Competitiveness

Sophistication of Company Operations and Strategy

10.04	Capacity for Innovation	1
10.05	Uniqueness of Product Designs	1
10.06	Production Process Sophistication	1

Quality of the Business Environment

9.06	State of Cluster Development	1
9.07	Extent of Product and Process Collaboration	1
2.22	Extent of Distortive Government Subsidies	2

Other Indicators

Infrastructure

5.13	Difference in Quality of Schools	1

Public Institutions

6.04	Favoritism in Decisions of Government Officials	1

Macroeconomic Environment

2.18	Hidden Trade Barriers	1
2.19	Permits to Export	1

NOTABLE COMPETITIVE DISADVANTAGES

Criteria	Rank

Growth Competitiveness

Macroeconomic Environment

2.30	Interest Rate Spread	36
2.28	Inflation	31

Current Competitiveness

Quality of the Business Environment

5.04	Road Infrastructure Quality	32

Other Indicators

Macroeconomic Environment

2.33	Value Added Tax Rate	65
2.27	Investment Rate	55
1.08	Unemployment Rate, 2000	43

Company Practices

10.20	Employment Rules	53
10.19	Hiring and Firing Practices	52

225

France

Key Facts

GDP per capita at Purchasing Power Parity, 2000 ....$24,032
GDP per capita Rank 16
Percentage Growth in Real GDP per capita, 1999–2000 ....2.8
Growth Rank 48
US Utility Patents Granted in 2000 (per million population)........64.4
Patent Rank 14

Growth Competitiveness Rank	20
Technology Index Rank	**17**
ICT Subindex Rank	21
Innovation Subindex Rank	12
Public Institutions Index Rank	**20**
Corruption Subindex Rank	24
Contracts and Law Subindex Rank	15
Macroeconomic Environment Index Rank	**22**
Macroeconomic Stability Subindex Rank	9
Country Credit Rating Rank	4

Current Competitiveness Rank	12
Sophistication of Company Operations and Strategy Rank	**10**
Quality of the Business Environment Rank	**12**

226

National competitiveness balance sheet

NOTABLE COMPETITIVE ADVANTAGES	
Criteria	Rank

Growth Competitiveness

Innovation

3.02	Firm-Level Innovation	3
3.06	Company Spending on Research and Development	9
3.01	Technological Sophistication	10
3.09	University/Industry Research Collaboration	10

Information and Communications Technology

4.07	Quality of Competition in ISP Sector	5
4.11	Laws Relating to ICT Use	5

Law and Contracts

6.12	Organized Crime	3

Macroeconomic Environment

2.01	Recession Expectations	3
2.29	Real Exchange Rate	9

Current Competitiveness (using GCR 2000 results)

Sophistication of Company Operations and Strategy

10.05	Uniqueness of Product Designs	4
10.02	Value Chain Presence	5
10.03	Extent of Branding	6

Quality of the Business Environment

5.04	Road Infrastructure Quality	1
10.16	Quality of Management Schools	3
4.01	Speed and Cost of Internet Access	4

Other Indicators

Technology

3.05	Quality of Scientific Research Institutions	4
3.10	Government Procurement of Advanced Technology Products	5

Infrastructure

5.05	Railroad Infrastructure Development	1
5.10	Postal Efficiency	1
5.12	Quality of Public Schools	2
5.01	Overall Infrastructure Quality	4
5.08	Telephone/Fax Infrastructure Quality	4
5.03	Industrial Water Availability	5
5.07	Air Transport Infrastructure Quality	5
5.06	Port Infrastructure Quality	6
5.11	Electricity Prices	6

Public Institutions

6.03	Intellectual Property Protection	1
6.09	Minimum Wage Enforcement	2
6.13	Unreported Profits and Wages	6

Macroeconomic Environment

2.15	Access to Bond Markets	1
2.21	Social Transfer Recipients	2
2.16	Local Equity Market Access	4

Company Practices

10.12	Extent of Staff Training	7

NOTABLE COMPETITIVE DISADVANTAGES	
Criteria	Rank

Growth Competitiveness

Macroeconomic Environment

2.26	National Savings Rate	35

Current Competitiveness (using GCR 2000 results)

Sophistication of Company Operations and Strategy

10.15	Reliance on Professional Management	34
10.08	Degree of Customer Orientation	25
3.06	Company Spending on Research and Development	17

Quality of the Business Environment

10.21	Cooperation in Labor-Employer Relations	75
8.04	Administrative Burden for Start-Ups	57
9.01	Buyer Sophistication	39

Other Indicators

Technology

3.14	Minorities in the Economy	49

Public Institutions

6.08	Burden of Regulation	60
6.07	Costs of Institutional Change	35
8.05	Permits to Start a Firm	35

Macroeconomic Environment

2.32	Corporate Income Tax Rate	74
2.33	Value Added Tax Rate	56
2.27	Investment Rate	50
1.09	Employment to Population Ratio, 2000	42
1.08	Unemployment Rate, 2000	41
2.10	Access to Foreign Capital Markets	38

Company Practices

10.19	Hiring and Firing Practices	74
10.20	Employment Rules	74
10.22	Union Contributions to Productivity	68
10.23	Pay and Productivity	52

Germany

Key Facts

GDP per capita at Purchasing Power Parity, 2000 ....$24,931
GDP per capita Rank 13
Percentage Growth in Real GDP per capita, 1999–2000 ....2.9
Growth Rank 43
US Utility Patents Granted in 2000 (per million population) 123.6
Patent Rank 7

Growth Competitiveness Rank	17

Technology Index Rank..**15**
    ICT Subindex Rank 15
    Innovation Subindex Rank 13
Public Institutions Index Rank **17**
    Corruption Subindex Rank 21
    Contracts and Law Subindex Rank..8
Macroeconomic Environment Index Rank......................................**19**
    Macroeconomic Stability Subindex Rank 16
    Country Credit Rating Rank 2

Current Competitiveness Rank	4

Sophistication of Company Operations and Strategy Rank....................**4**
Quality of the Business Environment Rank...**4**

National competitiveness balance sheet

NOTABLE COMPETITIVE ADVANTAGES

Criteria		Rank

Growth Competitiveness

Innovation

3.02	Firm-Level Innovation	4
3.06	Company Spending on Research and Development	4
3.01	Technological Sophistication	7
3.16	Utility Patents in 2000	7

Information and Communications Technology

| 4.07 | Quality of Competition in ISP Sector | 8 |
| 4.16 | Telephone Lines | 10 |

Law and Contracts

| 6.01 | Judicial Independence | 1 |
| 6.02 | Property Rights | 7 |

Macroeconomic Environment

| 2.01 | Recession Expectations | 7 |

Current Competitiveness

Sophistication of Company Operations and Strategy

10.11	Breadth of International Markets	1
10.05	Uniqueness of Product Designs	2
10.03	Extent of Branding	3

Quality of the Business Environment

9.03	Local Supplier Quality	1
9.02	Local Supplier Quantity	2
9.07	Extent of Product and Process Collaboration	3

Other Indicators

Technology

4.04	Quality of Competition in Telecommunication Sector	4
4.05	High Skilled IT Job Market	4
3.12	Brain Drain	6

Infrastructure

5.04	Road Infrastructure Quality	1
5.01	Overall Infrastructure Quality	3
5.06	Port Infrastructure Quality	4
5.02	Tap Water Safety	5
5.05	Railroad Infrastructure Development	5
5.07	Air Transport Infrastructure Quality	6
5.09	Quality of Competition in Transportation Sector	6
5.10	Postal Efficiency	6

Public Institutions

8.05	Permits to Start a Firm	5
6.03	Intellectual Property Protection	6
6.10	Extent of Bureaucratic Red Tape	6

Macroeconomic Environment

2.14	Financial Regulation and Supervision	1
2.19	Permits to Export	1
2.12	Perceived Interest Rate Gap	5
2.16	Local Equity Market Access	5
2.04	Exchange Rate and Exports	6
2.11	Foreign Access to Local Capital Markets	6

NOTABLE COMPETITIVE DISADVANTAGES

Criteria		Rank

Growth Competitiveness

Information and Communications Technology

| 4.08 | Government Prioritization of ICT | 35 |

Macroeconomic Environment

2.30	Interest Rate Spread	46
2.26	National Savings Rate	40
2.03	Access to Credit	33

Current Competitiveness

Sophistication of Company Operations and Strategy

| 10.08 | Degree of Customer Orientation | 15 |

Quality of the Business Environment

2.22	Extent of Distortive Government Subsidies	64
3.11	Availability of Scientists and Engineers	32
8.04	Administrative Burden for Start-Ups	27

Other Indicators

Technology

| 3.13 | Women in the Economy | 46 |
| 3.14 | Minorities in the Economy | 36 |

Infrastructure

| 5.11 | Electricity Prices | 38 |

Public Institutions

| 6.09 | Minimum Wage Enforcement | 39 |

Macroeconomic Environment

2.32	Corporate Income Tax Rate	69
1.08	Unemployment Rate, 2000	42
2.27	Investment Rate	40
2.21	Social Transfer Recipients	37
2.33	Value Added Tax Rate	37

Company Practices

10.19	Hiring and Firing Practices	72
10.20	Employment Rules	60
10.23	Pay and Productivity	41

229

Greece

Key Facts

GDP per capita at Purchasing Power Parity, 2000 ....$16,326
GDP per capita Rank 28
Percentage Growth in Real GDP per capita, 1999–2000 ....3.8
Growth Rank 29
US Utility Patents Granted in 2000 (per million population)..........1.7
Patent Rank 33

Growth Competitiveness Rank	36

Technology Index Rank..**38**
    ICT Subindex Rank 35
    Innovation Subindex Rank 25
    Technology Transfer Subindex Rank
      (out of 51 technological non-core economies) 31
Public Institutions Index Rank **40**
    Corruption Subindex Rank 44
    Contracts and Law Subindex Rank.......................................37
Macroeconomic Environment Index Rank....................................**32**
    Macroeconomic Stability Subindex Rank 25
    Country Credit Rating Rank 24

Current Competitiveness Rank	43

Sophistication of Company Operations and Strategy Rank.................**51**
Quality of the Business Environment Rank..**42**

230

National competitiveness balance sheet

NOTABLE COMPETITIVE ADVANTAGES	
Criteria	**Rank**

Growth Competitiveness

Macroeconomic Environment

2.03	Access to Credit	3

Current Competitiveness

Sophistication of Company Operations and Strategy

10.10	Extent of Regional Sales	32

Quality of the Business Environment

2.16	Local Equity Market Access	19
2.18	Hidden Trade Barriers	21
3.11	Availability of Scientists and Engineers	22

Other Indicators

Macroeconomic Environment

2.19	Permits to Export	1
2.05	Expected Exchange Rate Volatility	4
2.17	Sources of Investment Finance	14

NOTABLE COMPETITIVE DISADVANTAGES	
Criteria	**Rank**

Growth Competitiveness

Innovation

3.06	Company Spending on Research and Development	64

Information and Communications Technology

4.09	Government Success in ICT Promotion	59
4.12	Legal Framework for ICT Development	59
4.03	Internet Access in Schools	56
4.11	Laws Relating to ICT Use	55
4.08	Government Prioritization of ICT	54

Corruption

7.03	Irregular Payments in Tax Collection	69

Law and Contracts

6.04	Favoritism in Decisions of Government Officials	63

Current Competitiveness

Sophistication of Company Operations and Strategy

10.05	Uniqueness of Product Designs	63
10.13	Willingness to Delegate Authority	61
10.02	Value Chain Presence	52

Quality of the Business Environment

10.17	Efficacy of Corporate Boards	70
9.06	State of Cluster Development	68
10.16	Quality of Management Schools	64

Other Indicators

Technology

3.14	Minorities in the Economy	74
4.02	Public Access to Internet	66
3.03	Firm-Level Technology Absorption	65
3.13	Women in the Economy	63

Public Institutions

6.06	Competence of Public Officials	73
8.05	Permits to Start a Firm	64
8.04	Administrative Burden for Start-Ups	63
7.04	Irregular Payments in Public Contracts	61
6.08	Burden of Regulation	56
8.06	Days to Start a Firm	54

Macroeconomic Environment

2.32	Corporate Income Tax Rate	69
2.22	Extent of Distortive Government Subsidies	58
2.12	Perceived Interest Rate Gap	54

Company Practices

10.20	Employment Rules	69
10.19	Hiring and Firing Practices	65
10.15	Reliance on Professional Management	64
10.23	Pay and Productivity	63
10.21	Cooperation in Labor-Employer Relations	57
10.22	Union Contributions to Productivity	54

Guatemala

Key Facts

GDP per capita at Purchasing Power Parity, 2000 ....$3,784
GDP per capita Rank 61
Percentage Growth in Real GDP per capita, 1999–2000 ....0.9
Growth Rank 67
US Utility Patents Granted in 2000 (per million population)..........0.2
Patent Rank..53

Growth Competitiveness Rank	66

Technology Index Rank..**68**
    ICT Subindex Rank 66
    Innovation Subindex Rank 65
    Technology Transfer Subindex Rank
       (out of 51 technological non-core economies) 43
Public Institutions Index Rank **70**
    Corruption Subindex Rank 60
    Contracts and Law Subindex Rank.......................75
Macroeconomic Environment Index Rank................................**52**
    Macroeconomic Stability Subindex Rank 72
    Country Credit Rating Rank 61

Current Competitiveness Rank	69

Sophistication of Company Operations and Strategy Rank..................**69**
Quality of the Business Environment Rank..**69**

232

National competitiveness balance sheet

NOTABLE COMPETITIVE ADVANTAGES

Criteria	Rank

Growth Competitiveness

Macroeconomic Environment

	Potential for "Catch-up" Growth	15
2.24	Government Surplus/Deficit	42

Current Competitiveness

Sophistication of Company Operations and Strategy

10.03	Extent of Branding	47
10.01	Nature of Competitive Advantage	53
10.05	Uniqueness of Product Designs	54

Quality of the Business Environment

9.10	Local Availability of Specialized Research and Training Services	51
9.11	Local Availability of Information Technology Services	52
9.07	Extent of Product and Process Collaboration	53

Other Indicators

Public Institutions

8.06	Days to Start a Firm	19
8.05	Permits to Start a Firm	35

Macroeconomic Environment

2.32	Corporate Income Tax Rate	7
2.33	Value Added Tax Rate	12
1.08	Unemployment Rate, 2000	18
2.31	Average Tariff Rate	42

Company Practices

10.19	Hiring and Firing Practices	21

NOTABLE COMPETITIVE DISADVANTAGES

Criteria	Rank

Growth Competitiveness

Innovation

3.01	Technological Sophistication	67
3.02	Firm-Level Innovation	67

Information and Communications Technology

4.09	Government Success in ICT Promotion	72
4.08	Government Prioritization of ICT	71
4.11	Laws Relating to ICT Use	71
4.12	Legal Framework for ICT Development	70
4.03	Internet Access in Schools	69
4.14	Internet Users	66
4.17	Personal Computers	66

Law and Contracts

6.04	Favoritism in Decisions of Government Officials	74
6.12	Organized Crime	73
6.01	Judicial Independence	69
6.02	Property Rights	68

Macroeconomic Environment

2.26	National Savings Rate	74
2.03	Access to Credit	73
2.01	Recession Expectations	72

Current Competitiveness

Sophistication of Company Operations and Strategy

10.08	Degree of Customer Orientation	72
10.06	Production Process Sophistication	71
10.07	Extent of Marketing	68

Quality of the Business Environment

2.16	Local Equity Market Access	75
3.11	Availability of Scientists and Engineers	73
9.04	Presence of Demanding Regulatory Standards	73

Other Indicators

Technology

3.03	Firm-Level Technology Absorption	71
3.10	Government Procurement of Advanced Technology Products	71

Infrastructure

5.03	Industrial Water Availability	74
5.15	Public Health Agencies	74
5.12	Quality of Public Schools	72
5.13	Difference in Quality of Schools	71

Public Institutions

6.05	Government Commitments	75
6.04	Favoritism in Decisions of Government Officials	74
7.06	Business Costs of Corruption	74
6.14	Informal Sector	73
6.09	Minimum Wage Enforcement	72
7.07	Public Trust of Politicians	72
6.07	Costs of Institutional Change	71

Macroeconomic Environment

2.14	Financial Regulation and Supervision	73
2.02	Soundness of Banks	72

Company Practices

10.22	Union Contributions to Productivity	72

233

Honduras

Key Facts

GDP per capita at Purchasing Power Parity, 2000 ....$2,469
GDP per capita Rank 69
Percentage Growth in Real GDP per capita, 1999–2000 ....3.4
Growth Rank 32
US Utility Patents Granted in 2000 (per million population)..........0.2
Patent Rank 54

Growth Competitiveness Rank	70

Technology Index Rank...**70**
    ICT Subindex Rank 70
    Innovation Subindex Rank 66
    Technology Transfer Subindex Rank
        (out of 51 technological non-core economies) 37
Public Institutions Index Rank **72**
    Corruption Subindex Rank 67
    Contracts and Law Subindex Rank..74
Macroeconomic Environment Index Rank.....................................**72**
    Macroeconomic Stability Subindex Rank 65
    Country Credit Rating Rank 70

Current Competitiveness Rank	74

Sophistication of Company Operations and Strategy Rank..................**74**
Quality of the Business Environment Rank...**75**

234

National competitiveness balance sheet

NOTABLE COMPETITIVE ADVANTAGES	
Criteria	Rank

Growth Competitiveness

Technology Transfer

3.04	FDI and Technology Transfer	36

Macroeconomic Environment

	Potential for "Catch-up" Growth	7
2.26	National Savings Rate	15
2.24	Government Surplus/Deficit	40

Current Competitiveness

Sophistication of Company Operations and Strategy

10.14	Extent of Incentive Compensation	48

Quality of the Business Environment

5.04	Road Infrastructure Quality	36
10.21	Cooperation in Labor-Employer Relations	37

Other Indicators

Macroeconomic Environment

2.32	Corporate Income Tax Rate	7
2.27	Investment Rate	11
2.33	Value Added Tax Rate	22
2.04	Exchange Rate and Exports	29

NOTABLE COMPETITIVE DISADVANTAGES	
Criteria	Rank

Growth Competitiveness

Innovation

3.01	Technological Sophistication	75
3.06	Company Spending on Research and Development	73
3.09	University/Industry Research Collaboration	70

Information and Communications Technology

4.09	Government Success in ICT Promotion	73
4.03	Internet Access in Schools	72
4.15	Internet Hosts	72
4.07	Quality of Competition in ISP Sector	71
4.11	Laws Relating to ICT Use	69
4.12	Legal Framework for ICT Development	68
4.17	Personal Computers	68
4.08	Government Prioritization of ICT	66
4.16	Telephone Lines	66

Corruption

7.02	Irregular Payments in Government Procurement	68
7.03	Irregular Payments in Tax Collection	66

Law and Contracts

6.04	Favoritism in Decisions of Government Officials	73
6.01	Judicial Independence	72
6.12	Organized Crime	72
6.02	Property Rights	70

Macroeconomic Environment

2.03	Access to Credit	71
2.29	Real Exchange Rate	70
2.01	Recession Expectations	67
2.28	Inflation	66

Current Competitiveness

Sophistication of Company Operations and Strategy

10.08	Degree of Customer Orientation	73
10.15	Reliance on Professional Management	73
10.12	Extent of Staff Training	72

Quality of the Business Environment

5.08	Telephone/Fax Infrastructure Quality	75
9.04	Presence of Demanding Regulatory Standards	75
8.01	Intensity of Local Competition	73

Other Indicators

Technology

3.10	Government Procurement of Advanced Technology Products	75
3.03	Firm-Level Technology Absorption	74
3.05	Quality of Scientific Research Institutions	74
4.04	Quality of Competition in Telecommunication Sector	74
4.06	IT Training and Education	74

Infrastructure

5.09	Quality of Competition in Transportation Sector	74

Public Institutions

8.04	Administrative Burden for Start-Ups	74

235

Hong Kong SAR

Key Facts

GDP per capita at Purchasing Power Parity, 2000 ....$24,448
GDP per capita Rank 15
Percentage Growth in Real GDP per capita, 1999–2000 ....8.5
Growth Rank 3
US Utility Patents Granted in 2000 (per million population).........26.3
Patent Rank..24

Growth Competitiveness Rank	**13**

Technology Index Rank...**33**	
ICT Subindex Rank 10	
Innovation Subindex Rank 29	
Public Institutions Index Rank **10**	
Corruption Subindex Rank 12	
Contracts and Law Subindex Rank.......................................16	
Macroeconomic Environment Index Rank..................................**4**	
Macroeconomic Stability Subindex Rank 17	
Country Credit Rating Rank 25	

Current Competitiveness Rank	**18**

Sophistication of Company Operations and Strategy Rank..................**21**	
Quality of the Business Environment Rank...**16**	

National competitiveness balance sheet

NOTABLE COMPETITIVE ADVANTAGES	
Criteria	**Rank**

Growth Competitiveness

Information and Communications Technology

4.13	Cellular Telephones	2
4.07	Quality of Competition in ISP Sector	7
4.08	Government Prioritization of ICT	9
4.09	Government Success in ICT Promotion	10
4.12	Legal Framework for ICT Development	10

Technology Transfer

3.23	Skill-Based Exports	2

Corruption

7.03	Irregular Payments in Tax Collection	10

Law and Contracts

6.02	Property Rights	8

Macroeconomic Environment

2.28	Inflation	1
2.26	National Savings Rate	7
2.01	Recession Expectations	10

Current Competitiveness

Sophistication of Company Operations and Strategy

10.14	Extent of Incentive Compensation	6
10.02	Value Chain Presence	11
10.11	Breadth of International Markets	11

Quality of the Business Environment

8.04	Administrative Burden for Start-Ups	1
2.22	Extent of Distortive Government Subsidies	3
5.06	Port Infrastructure Quality	3

Other Indicators

Technology

3.13	Women in the Economy	1

Infrastructure

5.07	Air Transport Infrastructure Quality	2

Public Institutions

6.08	Burden of Regulation	1
8.05	Permits to Start a Firm	1
6.11	Tax Evasion	2

Macroeconomic Environment

2.19	Permits to Export	1
2.31	Average Tariff Rate	1
2.33	Value Added Tax Rate	1
2.05	Expected Exchange Rate Volatility	2
2.10	Access to Foreign Capital Markets	2
2.11	Foreign Access to Local Capital Markets	2

Company Practices

10.19	Hiring and Firing Practices	2
10.20	Employment Rules	2
10.23	Pay and Productivity	2

NOTABLE COMPETITIVE DISADVANTAGES	
Criteria	**Rank**

Growth Competitiveness

Innovation

3.19	Tertiary Enrollment	39
3.06	Company Spending on Research and Development	29

Macroeconomic Environment

2.29	Real Exchange Rate	67
2.30	Interest Rate Spread	32

Current Competitiveness

Sophistication of Company Operations and Strategy

10.05	Uniqueness of Product Designs	37
10.04	Capacity for Innovation	33
10.03	Extent of Branding	28

Quality of the Business Environment

9.09	Local Availability of Process Machinery	57
11.06	Stringency of Environmental Regulations	37
9.10	Local Availability of Specialized Research and Training Services	36

Other Indicators

Technology

3.08	Tax Credits for Firm-Level Research and Development	54
3.07	Subsidies for Firm-Level Research and Development	45
3.11	Availability of Scientists and Engineers	36
3.05	Quality of Scientific Research Institutions	31

Infrastructure

5.04	Road Infrastructure Quality	56
5.02	Tap Water Safety	39

Public Institutions

6.09	Minimum Wage Enforcement	62
6.10	Extent of Bureaucratic Red Tape	34

Macroeconomic Environment

2.04	Exchange Rate and Exports	51
2.17	Sources of Investment Finance	42
2.21	Social Transfer Recipients	33

Company Practices

10.15	Reliance on Professional Management	31

237

Hungary

Key Facts

GDP per capita at Purchasing Power Parity, 2000 ....$12,335
GDP per capita Rank 30
Percentage Growth in Real GDP per capita, 1999–2000 ....5.7
Growth Rank 11
US Utility Patents Granted in 2000 (per million population)..........3.6
Patent Rank 27

Growth Competitiveness Rank	28

Technology Index Rank..**21**

ICT Subindex Rank 30

Innovation Subindex Rank 35

Technology Transfer Subindex Rank
(out of 51 technological non-core economies) 2

Public Institutions Index Rank **26**

Corruption Subindex Rank 26

Contracts and Law Subindex Rank..29

Macroeconomic Environment Index Rank..**38**

Macroeconomic Stability Subindex Rank 22

Country Credit Rating Rank 31

Current Competitiveness Rank	26

Sophistication of Company Operations and Strategy Rank..................**33**

Quality of the Business Environment Rank..**25**

238

National competitiveness balance sheet

NOTABLE COMPETITIVE ADVANTAGES	
Criteria	Rank

Growth Competitiveness

Technology Transfer
3.04	FDI and Technology Transfer	3
3.23	Skill-Based Exports	6

Macroeconomic Environment
2.01	Recession Expectations	1
2.30	Interest Rate Spread	13

Current Competitiveness

Sophistication of Company Operations and Strategy
10.14	Extent of Incentive Compensation	24
3.06	Company Spending on Research and Development	26
10.15	Reliance on Professional Management	29

Quality of the Business Environment
2.22	Extent of Distortive Government Subsidies	4
5.12	Quality of Public Schools	15
2.18	Hidden Trade Barriers	17

Other Indicators

Technology
3.11	Availability of Scientists and Engineers	7

Macroeconomic Environment
2.32	Corporate Income Tax Rate	5

Company Practices
10.20	Employment Rules	13
10.23	Pay and Productivity	13
10.19	Hiring and Firing Practices	15

NOTABLE COMPETITIVE DISADVANTAGES	
Criteria	Rank

Growth Competitiveness

Innovation
3.02	Firm-Level Innovation	55
3.19	Tertiary Enrollment	44

Information and Communications Technology
4.12	Legal Framework for ICT Development	45

Law and Contracts
6.04	Favoritism in Decisions of Government Officials	43

Macroeconomic Environment
2.28	Inflation	63
2.24	Government Surplus/Deficit	46

Current Competitiveness

Sophistication of Company Operations and Strategy
10.03	Extent of Branding	54
10.02	Value Chain Presence	50
10.09	Control of International Distribution	50

Quality of the Business Environment
9.06	State of Cluster Development	65
5.06	Port Infrastructure Quality	62
5.07	Air Transport Infrastructure Quality	56

Other Indicators

Technology
3.14	Minorities in the Economy	58
4.01	Speed and Cost of Internet Access	43

Public Institutions
6.10	Extent of Bureaucratic Red Tape	50
6.05	Government Commitments	48
8.06	Days to Start a Firm	46
6.04	Favoritism in Decisions of Government Officials	43

Macroeconomic Environment
2.33	Value Added Tax Rate	72
2.21	Social Transfer Recipients	54
2.10	Access to Foreign Capital Markets	53
2.12	Perceived Interest Rate Gap	52
1.09	Employment to Population Ratio, 2000	51

239

Iceland

Key Facts

GDP per capita at Purchasing Power Parity, 2000 ....$29,167
GDP per capita Rank 3
Percentage Growth in Real GDP per capita, 1999–2000 ....2.7
Growth Rank 52
US Utility Patents Granted in 2000 (per million population) 61.6
Patent Rank 17

Growth Competitiveness Rank	16
Technology Index Rank..**19**	
ICT Subindex Rank 2	
Innovation Subindex Rank 24	
Public Institutions Index Rank **2**	
Corruption Subindex Rank 1	
Contracts and Law Subindex Rank...3	
Macroeconomic Environment Index Rank......................................**34**	
Macroeconomic Stability Subindex Rank 37	
Country Credit Rating Rank 23	

Current Competitiveness Rank	16
Sophistication of Company Operations and Strategy Rank.................**16**	
Quality of the Business Environment Rank...**15**	

National competitiveness balance sheet

NOTABLE COMPETITIVE ADVANTAGES	
Criteria	Rank

Growth Competitiveness

Innovation

3.01	Technological Sophistication	9

Information and Communications Technology

4.14	Internet Users	1
4.07	Quality of Competition in ISP Sector	2
4.15	Internet Hosts	2
4.09	Government Success in ICT Promotion	4
4.03	Internet Access in Schools	5
4.16	Telephone Lines	6
4.11	Laws Relating to ICT Use	8
4.12	Legal Framework for ICT Development	8
4.17	Personal Computers	9
4.08	Government Prioritization of ICT	10

Corruption

7.01	Irregular Payments in Exports & Imports	1
7.02	Irregular Payments in Government Procurement	1
7.03	Irregular Payments in Tax Collection	1

Law and Contracts

6.02	Property Rights	1
6.12	Organized Crime	1
6.04	Favoritism in Decisions of Government Officials	5

Macroeconomic Environment

2.24	Government Surplus/Deficit	9

Current Competitiveness

Sophistication of Company Operations and Strategy

10.08	Degree of Customer Orientation	5
10.09	Control of International Distribution	6
10.13	Willingness to Delegate Authority	7

Quality of the Business Environment

2.16	Local Equity Market Access	1
8.04	Administrative Burden for Start-Ups	4
3.11	Availability of Scientists and Engineers	6

Other Indicators

Technology

4.02	Public Access to Internet	1

Infrastructure

5.02	Tap Water Safety	1
5.10	Postal Efficiency	1
5.14	Difference in Quality of Healthcare	1

Public Institutions

7.04	Irregular Payments in Public Contracts	1
7.05	Irregular Payments in Loan Applications	1
7.06	Business Costs of Corruption	1
8.06	Days to Start a Firm	1

NOTABLE COMPETITIVE DISADVANTAGES	
Criteria	Rank

Growth Competitiveness

Macroeconomic Environment

2.26	National Savings Rate	67
2.30	Interest Rate Spread	57
2.28	Inflation	48
2.03	Access to Credit	32
2.29	Real Exchange Rate	31

Current Competitiveness

Sophistication of Company Operations and Strategy

10.14	Extent of Incentive Compensation	31
10.02	Value Chain Presence	27
10.01	Nature of Competitive Advantage	21

Quality of the Business Environment

9.08	Local Availability of Components and Parts	68
9.09	Local Availability of Process Machinery	60
3.05	Quality of Scientific Research Institutions	25

Other Indicators

Technology

3.08	Tax Credits for Firm-Level Research and Development	32

Public Institutions

6.09	Minimum Wage Enforcement	67

Macroeconomic Environment

2.33	Value Added Tax Rate	71
2.11	Foreign Access to Local Capital Markets	67
2.12	Perceived Interest Rate Gap	66
2.05	Expected Exchange Rate Volatility	46
2.22	Extent of Distortive Government Subsidies	44

India

Key Facts

National competitiveness balance sheet

NOTABLE COMPETITIVE ADVANTAGES	
Criteria	Rank

Growth Competitiveness

Innovation
3.01	Technological Sophistication	28
3.02	Firm-Level Innovation	34
3.09	University/Industry Research Collaboration	38
3.06	Company Spending on Research and Development	42

Information and Communications Technology
4.09	Government Success in ICT Promotion	11
4.08	Government Prioritization of ICT	13
4.12	Legal Framework for ICT Development	25
4.11	Laws Relating to ICT Use	27
4.07	Quality of Competition in ISP Sector	38

Technology Transfer
3.04	FDI and Technology Transfer	30

Law and Contracts
6.01	Judicial Independence	26
6.04	Favoritism in Decisions of Government Officials	36
6.12	Organized Crime	40
6.02	Property Rights	42

Macroeconomic Environment
2.03	Access to Credit	4
	Potential for "Catch-up" Growth	5
2.30	Interest Rate Spread	27
2.01	Recession Expectations	35
2.26	National Savings Rate	41
2.28	Inflation	41
2.29	Real Exchange Rate	42

Current Competitiveness

Sophistication of Company Operations and Strategy
10.07	Extent of Marketing	32
10.04	Capacity for Innovation	36
10.11	Breadth of International Markets	37

Quality of the Business Environment
3.11	Availability of Scientists and Engineers	4
9.11	Local Availability of Information Technology Services	11
3.05	Quality of Scientific Research Institutions	21

Other Indicators

Technology
3.08	Tax Credits for Firm-Level Research and Development	9
4.06	IT Training and Education	9
3.14	Minorities in the Economy	21

Infrastructure
5.05	Railroad Infrastructure Development	21

Macroeconomic Environment
2.06	Exchange Rate Premium	4
2.16	Local Equity Market Access	21
2.15	Access to Bond Markets	24

NOTABLE COMPETITIVE DISADVANTAGES	
Criteria	Rank

Growth Competitiveness

Innovation
3.19	Tertiary Enrollment	67

Information and Communications Technology
4.13	Cellular Telephones	73
4.17	Personal Computers	73
4.15	Internet Hosts	69
4.16	Telephone Lines	69
4.14	Internet Users	67

Corruption
7.02	Irregular Payments in Government Procurement	70

Macroeconomic Environment
2.24	Government Surplus/Deficit	72

Current Competitiveness

Quality of the Business Environment
5.04	Road Infrastructure Quality	73
2.22	Extent of Distortive Government Subsidies	68
10.21	Cooperation in Labor-Employer Relations	64

Other Indicators

Public Institutions
8.05	Permits to Start a Firm	72

Macroeconomic Environment
2.10	Access to Foreign Capital Markets	75
2.31	Average Tariff Rate	74
2.11	Foreign Access to Local Capital Markets	72

Company Practices
10.19	Hiring and Firing Practices	73

Indonesia

Key Facts

GDP per capita at Purchasing Power Parity, 2000 ....$3,014
GDP per capita Rank 67
Percentage Growth in Real GDP per capita, 1999–2000 ....3.4
Growth Rank 35
US Utility Patents Granted in 2000 (per million population)........0.03
Patent Rank 62

Growth Competitiveness Rank	64

Technology Index Rank..**61**
    ICT Subindex Rank 67
    Innovation Subindex Rank 64
    Technology Transfer Subindex Rank
        (out of 51 technological non-core economies) 21
Public Institutions Index Rank **66**
    Corruption Subindex Rank 72
    Contracts and Law Subindex Rank.......................................58
Macroeconomic Environment Index Rank...............................**41**
    Macroeconomic Stability Subindex Rank 39
    Country Credit Rating Rank 69

Current Competitiveness Rank	55

Sophistication of Company Operations and Strategy Rank..................**50**
Quality of the Business Environment Rank..**57**

244

National competitiveness balance sheet

NOTABLE COMPETITIVE ADVANTAGES

Criteria	Rank

Growth Competitiveness

Innovation
3.02 Firm-Level Innovation 22
3.09 University/Industry Research Collaboration 45

Technology Transfer
3.23 Skill-Based Exports 37
3.04 FDI and Technology Transfer 45

Macroeconomic Environment
2.29 Real Exchange Rate 1
     Potential for "Catch-up" Growth 9
2.26 National Savings Rate 32
2.28 Inflation 37
2.01 Recession Expectations 43
2.30 Interest Rate Spread 45

Current Competitiveness

Sophistication of Company Operations and Strategy
10.09 Control of International Distribution 34
10.11 Breadth of International Markets 34
10.08 Degree of Customer Orientation 41

Quality of the Business Environment
8.02 Extent of Locally Based Competitors 26
3.10 Government Procurement of Advanced
     Technology Products 36
9.03 Local Supplier Quality 43

Other Indicators

Technology
3.14 Minorities in the Economy 10
3.12 Brain Drain 13
4.05 High Skilled IT Job Market 41

Infrastructure
5.11 Electricity Prices 11
5.05 Railroad Infrastructure Development 45

Public Institutions
6.09 Minimum Wage Enforcement 33
6.13 Unreported Profits and Wages 36
8.04 Administrative Burden for Start-Ups 42

Macroeconomic Environment
2.04 Exchange Rate and Exports 1
2.33 Value Added Tax Rate 12
2.32 Corporate Income Tax Rate 24
2.27 Investment Rate 28
2.15 Access to Bond Markets 36
2.22 Extent of Distortive Government Subsidies 39

Company Practices
10.20 Employment Rules 31
10.12 Extent of Staff Training 41
10.13 Willingness to Delegate Authority 42

NOTABLE COMPETITIVE DISADVANTAGES

Criteria	Rank

Growth Competitiveness

Information and Communications Technology
4.16 Telephone Lines 71
4.13 Cellular Telephones 68
4.12 Legal Framework for ICT Development 67
4.11 Laws Relating to ICT Use 66
4.17 Personal Computers 66

Corruption
7.03 Irregular Payments in Tax Collection 71
7.01 Irregular Payments in Exports & Imports 70
7.02 Irregular Payments in Government Procurement 67

Macroeconomic Environment
2.03 Access to Credit 69

Current Competitiveness

Sophistication of Company Operations and Strategy
10.05 Uniqueness of Product Designs 66
10.15 Reliance on Professional Management 65
10.02 Value Chain Presence 59

Quality of the Business Environment
2.18 Hidden Trade Barriers 67
5.04 Road Infrastructure Quality 66
6.10 Extent of Bureaucratic Red Tape 59

Other Indicators

Technology
4.10 Government On-line Services 68

Infrastructure
5.02 Tap Water Safety 74

Public Institutions
6.07 Costs of Institutional Change 72
7.05 Irregular Payments in Loan Applications 71
7.04 Irregular Payments in Public Contracts 68

Macroeconomic Environment
2.02 Soundness of Banks 74
2.05 Expected Exchange Rate Volatility 73
2.14 Financial Regulation and Supervision 68

Company Practices
10.23 Pay and Productivity 67

245

Ireland

Key Facts

GDP per capita at Purchasing Power Parity, 2000 .... $29,080
GDP per capita Rank 4
Percentage Growth in Real GDP per capita, 1999–2000 .... 9.9
Growth Rank 1
US Utility Patents Granted in 2000 (per million population) 32.4
Patent Rank 21

Growth Competitiveness Rank	11

Technology Index Rank **28**
    ICT Subindex Rank 18
    Innovation Subindex Rank 23
Public Institutions Index Rank **18**
    Corruption Subindex Rank 19
    Contracts and Law Subindex Rank 14
Macroeconomic Environment Index Rank **2**
    Macroeconomic Stability Subindex Rank 12
    Country Credit Rating Rank 16

Current Competitiveness Rank	22

Sophistication of Company Operations and Strategy Rank **17**
Quality of the Business Environment Rank **22**

246

National competitiveness balance sheet

NOTABLE COMPETITIVE ADVANTAGES

Criteria	Rank

Growth Competitiveness

Information and Communications Technology
4.09 Government Success in ICT Promotion...........7
4.08 Government Prioritization of ICT......................8

Technology Transfer
3.04 FDI and Technology Transfer...........................2
3.23 Skill-Based Exports..4

Law and Contracts
6.04 Favoritism in Decisions of Government Officials...........10

Macroeconomic Environment
2.24 Government Surplus/Deficit............................2

Current Competitiveness

Sophistication of Company Operations and Strategy
10.14 Extent of Incentive Compensation..................5
10.10 Extent of Regional Sales 10
10.06 Production Process Sophistication.................14

Quality of the Business Environment
2.22 Extent of Distortive Government Subsidies.....5
5.12 Quality of Public Schools 9
9.06 State of Cluster Development 10

Other Indicators

Technology
3.07 Subsidies for Firm-Level Research and Development......3
4.05 High Skilled IT Job Market.............................5
3.08 Tax Credits for Firm-Level Research and Development.......7
4.06 IT Training and Education 10

Public Institutions
6.06 Competence of Public Officials......................5
8.05 Permits to Start a Firm.................................5
6.07 Costs of Institutional Change.........................8
6.08 Burden of Regulation 8
8.06 Days to Start a Firm 8

Macroeconomic Environment
2.19 Permits to Export 1
2.32 Corporate Income Tax Rate............................6
2.20 Composition of Public Spending 9
2.27 Investment Rate..9
2.02 Soundness of Banks 10
2.04 Exchange Rate and Exports 10

NOTABLE COMPETITIVE DISADVANTAGES

Criteria	Rank

Growth Competitiveness

Innovation
3.02 Firm-Level Innovation.....................................29

Information and Communications Technology
4.07 Quality of Competition in ISP Sector 42
4.16 Telephone Lines..26

Macroeconomic Environment
2.28 Inflation..50
2.30 Interest Rate Spread 32

Current Competitiveness

Sophistication of Company Operations and Strategy
10.09 Control of International Distribution 23
10.05 Uniqueness of Product Designs 22
10.01 Nature of Competitive Advantage.................20

Quality of the Business Environment
5.01 Overall Infrastructure Quality 43
5.06 Port Infrastructure Quality..............................42
4.01 Speed and Cost of Internet Access 35

Other Indicators

Technology
3.14 Minorities in the Economy 65
3.13 Women in the Economy 50
4.04 Quality of Competition in Telecommunication Sector.....40
4.02 Public Access to Internet 31

Infrastructure
5.04 Road Infrastructure Quality 61
5.09 Quality of Competition in Transportation Sector 60
5.05 Railroad Infrastructure Development 46
5.07 Air Transport Infrastructure Quality 38
5.11 Electricity Prices...37
5.14 Difference in Quality of Healthcare.................35
5.08 Telephone/Fax Infrastructure Quality 33

Macroeconomic Environment
2.33 Value Added Tax Rate 57
2.10 Access to Foreign Capital Markets 47
2.21 Social Transfer Recipients 44
2.06 Exchange Rate Premium...............................43
2.17 Sources of Investment Finance 37
2.16 Local Equity Market Access..........................31

Company Practices
10.19 Hiring and Firing Practices 48
10.20 Employment Rules.......................................35
10.21 Cooperation in Labor-Employer Relations 31
10.23 Pay and Productivity.....................................26

247

Israel

Key Facts

GDP per capita at Purchasing Power Parity, 2000 ....$19,577
GDP per capita Rank 22
Percentage Growth in Real GDP per capita, 1999–2000 ....4.0
Growth Rank 25
US Utility Patents Granted in 2000 (per million population) 135.0
Patent Rank 6

Growth Competitiveness Rank	24
Technology Index Rank...**26**	
ICT Subindex Rank 23	
Innovation Subindex Rank 18	
Public Institutions Index Rank **14**	
Corruption Subindex Rank 16	
Contracts and Law Subindex Rank 13	
Macroeconomic Environment Index Rank............................**61**	
Macroeconomic Stability Subindex Rank 44	
Country Credit Rating Rank 29	

Current Competitiveness Rank	17
Sophistication of Company Operations and Strategy Rank...................**18**	
Quality of the Business Environment Rank...**17**	

National competitiveness balance sheet

NOTABLE COMPETITIVE ADVANTAGES

Criteria		Rank

Growth Competitiveness

Innovation

3.01	Technological Sophistication	2
3.09	University/Industry Research Collaboration	4
3.16	Utility Patents in 2000	6
3.06	Company Spending on Research and Development	7

Information and Communications Technology

| 4.13 | Cellular Telephones | 8 |

Law and Contracts

| 6.12 | Organized Crime | 7 |
| 6.01 | Judicial Independence | 8 |

Macroeconomic Environment

| 2.28 | Inflation | 9 |

Current Competitiveness

Sophistication of Company Operations and Strategy

10.01	Nature of Competitive Advantage	4
10.04	Capacity for Innovation	6
10.02	Value Chain Presence	13

Quality of the Business Environment

2.09	Venture Capital Availability	2
9.11	Local Availability of Information Technology	3
3.05	Quality of Scientific Research Institutions	5

Other Indicators

Technology

3.07	Subsidies for Firm-Level Research and Development	2
3.11	Availability of Scientists and Engineers	2
3.08	Tax Credits for Firm-Level Research and Development	4
3.03	Firm-Level Technology Absorption	5
4.06	IT Training and Education	7

Public Institutions

8.06	Days to Start a Firm	4
8.05	Permits to Start a Firm	5
6.09	Minimum Wage Enforcement	6
7.06	Business Costs of Corruption	9
6.05	Government Commitments	10
8.04	Administrative Burden for Start-Ups	10

Macroeconomic Environment

2.17	Sources of Investment Finance	2
2.31	Average Tariff Rate	3
2.11	Foreign Access to Local Capital Markets	8

NOTABLE COMPETITIVE DISADVANTAGES

Criteria		Rank

Growth Competitiveness

Macroeconomic Environment

2.01	Recession Expectations	66
2.26	National Savings Rate	54
2.29	Real Exchange Rate	48
2.24	Government Surplus/Deficit	43

Current Competitiveness

Sophistication of Company Operations and Strategy

10.10	Extent of Regional Sales	75
10.08	Degree of Customer Orientation	39
10.09	Control of International Distribution	25

Quality of the Business Environment

5.05	Railroad Infrastructure Development	44
9.05	Decentralization of Corporate Activity	35
11.06	Stringency of Environmental Regulations	29

Other Indicators

Technology

| 3.13 | Women in the Economy | 44 |
| 3.14 | Minorities in the Economy | 44 |

Macroeconomic Environment

2.32	Corporate Income Tax Rate	64
2.27	Investment Rate	59
2.04	Exchange Rate and Exports	52
2.06	Exchange Rate Premium	50
2.13	Entry into Banking Industry	50
2.33	Value Added Tax Rate	41

Company Practices

| 10.22 | Union Contributions to Productivity | 49 |

Italy

Key Facts

GDP per capita at Purchasing Power Parity, 2000 ....$23,304
GDP per capita Rank 18
Percentage Growth in Real GDP per capita, 1999–2000 ....3.0
Growth Rank 41
US Utility Patents Granted in 2000 (per million population)........29.7
Patent Rank 22

Growth Competitiveness Rank	26

Technology Index Rank..**31**
    ICT Subindex Rank 27
    Innovation Subindex Rank 21
Public Institutions Index Rank **27**
    Corruption Subindex Rank 27
    Contracts and Law Subindex Rank........................32
Macroeconomic Environment Index Rank...**23**
    Macroeconomic Stability Subindex Rank 10
    Country Credit Rating Rank 18

Current Competitiveness Rank	24

Sophistication of Company Operations and Strategy Rank..................**13**
Quality of the Business Environment Rank..**24**

National competitiveness balance sheet

NOTABLE COMPETITIVE ADVANTAGES	
Criteria	Rank

Growth Competitiveness

Information and Communications Technology
4.13	Cellular Telephones	4

Macroeconomic Environment
2.03	Access to Credit	1
2.29	Real Exchange Rate	8

Current Competitiveness

Sophistication of Company Operations and Strategy
10.11	Breadth of International Markets	6
10.05	Uniqueness of Product Designs	8
10.03	Extent of Branding	8

Quality of the Business Environment
9.02	Local Supplier Quantity	3
9.06	State of Cluster Development	4
9.09	Local Availability of Process Machinery	4

Other Indicators

Macroeconomic Environment
2.15	Access to Bond Markets	3
2.16	Local Equity Market Access	9

NOTABLE COMPETITIVE DISADVANTAGES	
Criteria	Rank

Growth Competitiveness

Information and Communications Technology
4.08	Government Prioritization of ICT	49
4.03	Internet Access in Schools	48
4.09	Government Success in ICT Promotion	46

Law and Contracts
6.12	Organized Crime	47

Macroeconomic Environment
2.26	National Savings Rate	47

Current Competitiveness

Sophistication of Company Operations and Strategy
10.15	Reliance on Professional Management	45
10.13	Willingness to Delegate Authority	43
10.12	Extent of Staff Training	33

Quality of the Business Environment
5.01	Overall Infrastructure Quality	41
6.04	Favoritism in Decisions of Government Officials	40
2.09	Venture Capital Availability	30

Other Indicators

Technology
3.13	Women in the Economy	56
4.02	Public Access to Internet	45
3.14	Minorities in the Economy	42

Infrastructure
5.11	Electricity Prices	71

Public Institutions
8.06	Days to Start a Firm	75
6.08	Burden of Regulation	72
8.05	Permits to Start a Firm	72
8.04	Administrative Burden for Start-Ups	54
6.06	Competence of Public Officials	53
6.10	Extent of Bureaucratic Red Tape	53
6.11	Tax Evasion	48
6.09	Minimum Wage Enforcement	43

Macroeconomic Environment
2.32	Corporate Income Tax Rate	66
2.33	Value Added Tax Rate	57
1.09	Employment to Population Ratio, 2000	54
2.27	Investment Rate	52
2.20	Composition of Public Spending	49
1.08	Unemployment Rate, 2000	46
2.13	Entry into Banking Industry	43

Company Practices
10.20	Employment Rules	72
10.19	Hiring and Firing Practices	68
10.21	Cooperation in Labor-Employer Relations	47

Jamaica

Key Facts

GDP per capita at Purchasing Power Parity, 2000 ....$3,657
GDP per capita Rank 63
Percentage Growth in Real GDP per capita, 1999–2000 ....0.6
Growth Rank 68
US Utility Patents Granted in 2000 (per million population).........0.8
Patent Rank 40

Growth Competitiveness Rank	52

Technology Index Rank...**43**
    ICT Subindex Rank 47
    Innovation Subindex Rank 58
    Technology Transfer Subindex Rank
        (out of 51 technological non-core economies) 19
Public Institutions Index Rank **43**
    Corruption Subindex Rank 41
    Contracts and Law Subindex Rank..47
Macroeconomic Environment Index Rank...................................**71**
    Macroeconomic Stability Subindex Rank 67
    Country Credit Rating Rank 64

Current Competitiveness Rank	40

Sophistication of Company Operations and Strategy Rank..................**31**
Quality of the Business Environment Rank..**44**

252

National competitiveness balance sheet

NOTABLE COMPETITIVE ADVANTAGES

Criteria	Rank

Growth Competitiveness

Information and Communications Technology

4.08	Government Prioritization of ICT	22
4.09	Government Success in ICT Promotion	22

Macroeconomic Environment

	Potential for "Catch-up" Growth	13

Current Competitiveness

Sophistication of Company Operations and Strategy

10.03	Extent of Branding	14
10.05	Uniqueness of Product Designs	20
10.07	Extent of Marketing	30

Quality of the Business Environment

5.07	Air Transport Infrastructure Quality	22
5.06	Port Infrastructure Quality	24
6.01	Judicial Independence	33

Other Indicators

Technology

3.14	Minorities in the Economy	7
3.13	Women in the Economy	18

Public Institutions

8.05	Permits to Start a Firm	5
8.06	Days to Start a Firm	16

Macroeconomic Environment

2.27	Investment Rate	13

NOTABLE COMPETITIVE DISADVANTAGES

Criteria	Rank

Growth Competitiveness

Innovation

3.19	Tertiary Enrollment	66
3.09	University/Industry Research Collaboration	61

Law and Contracts

6.12	Organized Crime	62

Macroeconomic Environment

2.29	Real Exchange Rate	74
2.03	Access to Credit	64
2.30	Interest Rate Spread	63

Current Competitiveness

Sophistication of Company Operations and Strategy

10.10	Extent of Regional Sales	56

Quality of the Business Environment

2.08	Ease of Access to Loans	68
5.05	Local Availability of Components and Parts	67
8.02	Extent of Locally Based Competitors	61

Other Indicators

Technology

4.02	Public Access to Internet	67
3.12	Brain Drain	61

Macroeconomic Environment

2.17	Sources of Investment Finance	69
2.21	Social Transfer Recipients	66
1.08	Unemployment Rate, 2000	64
2.12	Perceived Interest Rate Gap	62
2.02	Soundness of Banks	61
2.06	Exchange Rate Premium	61

Company Practices

10.21	Cooperation in Labor-Employer Relations	63

Japan

Key Facts

GDP per capita at Purchasing Power Parity, 2000 ....$25,796
GDP per capita Rank 10
Percentage Growth in Real GDP per capita, 1999–2000 ....1.5
Growth Rank 61
US Utility Patents Granted in 2000 (per million population)......246.6
Patent Rank 2

Growth Competitiveness Rank	21

Technology Index Rank..**23**
    ICT Subindex Rank 24
    Innovation Subindex Rank 17
Public Institutions Index Rank **19**
    Corruption Subindex Rank 14
    Contracts and Law Subindex Rank........................23
Macroeconomic Environment Index Rank...........................**18**
    Macroeconomic Stability Subindex Rank 29
    Country Credit Rating Rank 12

Current Competitiveness Rank	15

Sophistication of Company Operations and Strategy Rank...................**8**
Quality of the Business Environment Rank..**18**

254

National competitiveness balance sheet

NOTABLE COMPETITIVE ADVANTAGES

Criteria		Rank

Growth Competitiveness

Innovation

3.06	Company Spending on Research and Development	2
3.16	Utility Patents in 2000	2
3.01	Technological Sophistication	5
3.02	Firm-Level Innovation	9

Information and Communications Technology

| 4.14 | Internet Users | 8 |
| 4.16 | Telephone Lines | 8 |

Corruption

| 7.01 | Irregular Payments in Exports & Imports | 10 |

Macroeconomic Environment

| 2.30 | Interest Rate Spread | 2 |
| 2.28 | Inflation | 4 |

Current Competitiveness

Sophistication of Company Operations and Strategy

10.03	Extent of Branding	2
10.09	Control of International Distribution	2
10.04	Capacity for Innovation	3

Quality of the Business Environment

9.09	Local Availability of Process Machinery	1
5.05	Railroad Infrastructure Quality	2
10.21	Cooperation in Labor-Employer Relations	4

Other Indicators

Technology

3.03	Firm-Level Technology Absorption	4
3.12	Brain Drain	4
3.10	Government Procurement of Advanced Technology Products	7
3.11	Availability of Scientists and Engineers	9

Infrastructure

| 5.14 | Difference in Quality of Healthcare | 10 |

Public Institutions

6.10	Extent of Bureaucratic Red Tape	1
6.06	Competence of Public Officials	2
6.14	Informal Sector	2
6.13	Unreported Profits and Wages	5
8.05	Permits to Start a Firm	5

Macroeconomic Environment

2.19	Permits to Export	1
2.33	Value Added Tax Rate	4
1.09	Employment to Population Ratio, 2000	7

Company Practices

| 10.22 | Union Contributions to Productivity | 3 |
| 10.12 | Extent of Staff Training | 9 |

NOTABLE COMPETITIVE DISADVANTAGES

Criteria		Rank

Growth Competitiveness

Information and Communications Technology

| 4.12 | Legal Framework for ICT Development | 47 |
| 4.09 | Government Success in ICT Promotion | 42 |

Macroeconomic Environment

2.24	Government Surplus/Deficit	67
2.01	Recession Expectations	58
2.29	Real Exchange Rate	51

Current Competitiveness

Sophistication of Company Operations and Strategy

10.14	Extent of Incentive Compensation	51
10.15	Reliance on Professional Management	26
10.13	Willingness to Delegate Authority	23

Quality of the Business Environment

10.17	Efficacy of Corporate Boards	71
4.01	Speed and Cost of Internet Access	47
2.18	Hidden Trade Barriers	46

Other Indicators

Technology

3.13	Women in the Economy	69
4.10	Government On-line Services	50
3.14	Minorities in the Economy	37

Infrastructure

| 5.11 | Electricity Prices | 70 |
| 5.04 | Road Infrastructure Quality | 52 |

Public Institutions

| 6.08 | Burden of Regulation | 47 |
| 7.07 | Public Trust of Politicians | 40 |

Macroeconomic Environment

2.13	Entry into Banking Industry	67
2.02	Soundness of Banks	66
2.22	Extent of Distortive Government Subsidies	65
2.05	Expected Exchange Rate Volatility	61
2.20	Composition of Public Spending	51
2.21	Social Transfer Recipients	50
2.14	Financial Regulation and Supervision	48
2.06	Exchange Rate Premium	42

Company Practices

| 10.19 | Hiring and Firing Practices | 41 |

255

Jordan

Key Facts

GDP per capita at Purchasing Power Parity, 2000 ....$4,079
GDP per capita Rank 58
Percentage Growth in Real GDP per capita, 1999–2000 ....1.1
Growth Rank 64
US Utility Patents Granted in 2000 (per million population)..........0.0
Patent Rank 65

Growth Competitiveness Rank	45

Technology Index Rank...**54**
    ICT Subindex Rank 52
    Innovation Subindex Rank 60
    Technology Transfer Subindex Rank
        (out of 51 technological non-core economies) 29

Public Institutions Index Rank **28**
    Corruption Subindex Rank 37
    Contracts and Law Subindex Rank.........................21

Macroeconomic Environment Index Rank....................................**54**
    Macroeconomic Stability Subindex Rank 46
    Country Credit Rating Rank 55

Current Competitiveness Rank	44

Sophistication of Company Operations and Strategy Rank..................**56**
Quality of the Business Environment Rank..**41**

National competitiveness balance sheet

NOTABLE COMPETITIVE ADVANTAGES

Criteria	Rank

Growth Competitiveness

Information and Communications Technology
4.08	Government Prioritization of ICT	7
4.09	Government Success in ICT Promotion	9

Law and Contracts
6.12	Organized Crime	14
6.01	Judicial Independence	23
6.02	Property Rights	24

Macroeconomic Environment
2.28	Inflation	6
2.30	Interest Rate Spread	8
2.26	National Savings Rate	14
	Potential for "Catch-up" Growth	18

Current Competitiveness

Sophistication of Company Operations and Strategy
10.09	Control of International Distribution	31
10.10	Extent of Regional Sales	42
10.06	Production Process Sophistication	48

Quality of the Business Environment
3.11	Availability of Scientists and Engineers	11
5.01	Overall Infrastructure Quality	24
6.03	Intellectual Property Protection	26

Other Indicators

Technology
3.14	Minorities in the Economy	6

Infrastructure
5.01	Overall Infrastructure Quality	24

Public Institutions
6.08	Burden of Regulation	16
7.07	Public Trust of Politicians	17
8.06	Days to Start a Firm	19
6.14	Informal Sector	20
6.05	Government Commitments	24

Macroeconomic Environment
2.20	Composition of Public Spending	11
2.05	Expected Exchange Rate Volatility	15

Company Practices
10.22	Union Contributions to Productivity	13
10.20	Employment Rules	22

NOTABLE COMPETITIVE DISADVANTAGES

Criteria	Rank

Growth Competitiveness

Innovation
3.16	Utility Patents in 2000	65

Information and Communications Technology
4.15	Internet Hosts	64
4.17	Personal Computers	61

Macroeconomic Environment
2.24	Government Surplus/Deficit	70
2.29	Real Exchange Rate	61

Current Competitiveness

Sophistication of Company Operations and Strategy
10.04	Capacity for Innovation	73
10.14	Extent of Incentive Compensation	71
10.05	Uniqueness of Product Designs	67

Quality of the Business Environment
9.09	Local Availability of Process Machinery	71
6.10	Extent of Bureaucratic Red Tape	69
8.02	Extent of Locally Based Competitors	65

Other Indicators

Technology
3.12	Brain Drain	63

Macroeconomic Environment
1.09	Employment to Population Ratio, 2000	72

257

Korea

Key Facts

GDP per capita at Purchasing Power Parity, 2000 ....$17,311
GDP per capita Rank 24
Percentage Growth in Real GDP per capita, 1999–2000 ....8.0
Growth Rank 4
US Utility Patents Granted in 2000 (per million population)........70.1
Patent Rank 12

Growth Competitiveness Rank	23

Technology Index Rank...**9**	
ICT Subindex Rank 22	
Innovation Subindex Rank 6	
Public Institutions Index Rank **44**	
Corruption Subindex Rank 51	
Contracts and Law Subindex Rank...........................43	
Macroeconomic Environment Index Rank............................**8**	
Macroeconomic Stability Subindex Rank 7	
Country Credit Rating Rank 28	

Current Competitiveness Rank	28

Sophistication of Company Operations and Strategy Rank...................**26**	
Quality of the Business Environment Rank..**30**	

National competitiveness balance sheet

NOTABLE COMPETITIVE ADVANTAGES	
Criteria	Rank

Growth Competitiveness

Innovation
3.19 Tertiary Enrollment 5

Information and Communications Technology
4.14 Internet Users 6
4.03 Internet Access in Schools 8

Macroeconomic Environment
2.30 Interest Rate Spread 1
2.26 National Savings Rate 10

Current Competitiveness

Sophistication of Company Operations and Strategy
3.06 Company Spending on Research and Development 18
10.09 Control of International Distribution 18
10.11 Breadth of International Markets 24

Quality of the Business Environment
9.06 State of Cluster Development 11
3.10 Government Procurement of Advanced
     Technology Products..................................15
5.05 Railroad Infrastructure Development 16

Other Indicators

Technology
4.02 Public Access to Internet 7

Macroeconomic Environment
2.27 Investment Rate...6

NOTABLE COMPETITIVE DISADVANTAGES	
Criteria	Rank

Growth Competitiveness

Innovation
3.02 Firm-Level Innovation 52

Corruption
7.03 Irregular Payments in Tax Collection.............................57
7.02 Irregular Payments in Government Procurement 51
7.01 Irregular Payments in Exports & Imports......................41

Law and Contracts
6.01 Judicial Independence....................................47
6.02 Property Rights 45
6.12 Organized Crime 44

Macroeconomic Environment
2.01 Recession Expectations 51
2.03 Access to Credit...50

Current Competitiveness

Sophistication of Company Operations and Strategy
10.15 Reliance on Professional Management 58
10.07 Extent of Marketing 38
10.13 Willingness to Delegate Authority 35

Quality of the Business Environment
10.21 Cooperation in Labor-Employer Relations 72
10.17 Efficacy of Corporate Boards 61
2.18 Hidden Trade Barriers...................................52

Other Indicators

Technology
3.13 Women in the Economy 74
3.14 Minorities in the Economy 67

Infrastructure
5.02 Tap Water Safety...55

Public Institutions
8.05 Permits to Start a Firm...................................72
7.05 Irregular Payments in Loan Applications........................66
6.05 Government Commitments 56
6.07 Costs of Institutional Change............................52
6.09 Minimum Wage Enforcement...........................51
7.07 Public Trust of Politicians 51
6.08 Burden of Regulation 50

Macroeconomic Environment
2.13 Entry into Banking Industry...............................73
2.21 Social Transfer Recipients 73
2.02 Soundness of Banks 67
2.06 Exchange Rate Premium.................................67
2.11 Foreign Access to Local Capital Markets......................65
2.32 Corporate Income Tax Rate..............................63
2.14 Financial Regulation and Supervision..........................61
2.10 Access to Foreign Capital Markets 58
2.31 Average Tariff Rate.......................................51

Latvia

Key Facts

GDP per capita at Purchasing Power Parity, 2000 ....$6,838
GDP per capita Rank 47
Percentage Growth in Real GDP per capita, 1999–2000 ....7.0
Growth Rank 8
US Utility Patents Granted in 2000 (per million population)..........0.4
Patent Rank 44

Growth Competitiveness Rank	47

| **Technology Index Rank**...**34** |
| ICT Subindex Rank ....36 |
| Innovation Subindex Rank ....36 |
| Technology Transfer Subindex Rank |
| (out of 51 technological non-core economies) ....17 |
| **Public Institutions Index Rank** ....**48** |
| Corruption Subindex Rank ....39 |
| Contracts and Law Subindex Rank.......................53 |
| **Macroeconomic Environment Index Rank**..........................**59** |
| Macroeconomic Stability Subindex Rank ....45 |
| Country Credit Rating Rank ....44 |

Current Competitiveness Rank	42

Sophistication of Company Operations and Strategy Rank.................**35**
Quality of the Business Environment Rank...**43**

National competitiveness balance sheet

NOTABLE COMPETITIVE ADVANTAGES	
Criteria	Rank

Growth Competitiveness

Macroeconomic Environment

2.03	Access to Credit	8
2.01	Recession Expectations	20
2.28	Inflation	24
	Potential for "Catch-up" Growth	29

Current Competitiveness

Sophistication of Company Operations and Strategy

10.05	Uniqueness of Product Designs	23
10.08	Degree of Customer Orientation	29
10.06	Production Process Sophistication	33

Quality of the Business Environment

9.07	Extent of Product and Process Collaboration	26
5.06	Port Infrastructure Quality	28
11.06	Stringency of Environmental Regulations	30

Other Indicators

Technology

3.13	Women in the Economy	12
3.14	Minorities in the Economy	13

Public Institutions

8.06	Days to Start a Firm	10
6.06	Competence of Public Officials	22
6.08	Burden of Regulation	23
8.05	Permits to Start a Firm	24

Macroeconomic Environment

2.31	Average Tariff Rate	3
2.32	Corporate Income Tax Rate	7
2.05	Expected Exchange Rate Volatility	13
2.27	Investment Rate	21
2.17	Sources of Investment Finance	23

Company Practices

10.23	Pay and Productivity	12
10.20	Employment Rules	19

NOTABLE COMPETITIVE DISADVANTAGES	
Criteria	Rank

Growth Competitiveness

Macroeconomic Environment

2.29	Real Exchange Rate	66

Current Competitiveness

Sophistication of Company Operations and Strategy

10.07	Extent of Marketing	55
10.09	Control of International Distribution	52
10.04	Capacity for Innovation	49

Quality of the Business Environment

6.10	Extent of Bureaucratic Red Tape	68
2.16	Local Equity Market Access	57
4.11	Laws Relating to ICT Use	57

Other Indicators

Public Institutions

6.05	Government Commitments	62

Lithuania

Key Facts

GDP per capita at Purchasing Power Parity, 2000 .... $6,999
GDP per capita Rank 45
Percentage Growth in Real GDP per capita, 1999–2000 .... 3.0
Growth Rank 39
US Utility Patents Granted in 2000 (per million population) 0.0
Patent Rank 65

Growth Competitiveness Rank	**43**

Technology Index Rank	**41**
ICT Subindex Rank	43
Innovation Subindex Rank	48
Technology Transfer Subindex Rank (out of 51 technological non-core economies)	22
Public Institutions Index Rank	**34**
Corruption Subindex Rank ....:	17
Contracts and Law Subindex Rank	59
Macroeconomic Environment Index Rank	**56**
Macroeconomic Stability Subindex Rank	53
Country Credit Rating Rank	48

Current Competitiveness Rank	**49**

Sophistication of Company Operations and Strategy Rank	**47**
Quality of the Business Environment Rank	**48**

National competitiveness balance sheet

NOTABLE COMPETITIVE ADVANTAGES

Criteria	Rank

Growth Competitiveness

Corruption

7.02	Irregular Payments in Government Procurement	15
7.01	Irregular Payments in Exports & Imports	17
7.03	Irregular Payments in Tax Collection	24

Macroeconomic Environment

2.28	Inflation	7
	Potential for "Catch-up" Growth	31

Current Competitiveness

Sophistication of Company Operations and Strategy

10.02	Value Chain Presence	26
10.05	Uniqueness of Product Designs	29
10.04	Capacity for Innovation	34

Quality of the Business Environment

3.11	Availability of Scientists and Engineers	23
9.04	Presence of Demanding Regulatory Standards	31
11.06	Stringency of Environmental Regulations	33

Other Indicators

Technology

3.14	Minorities in the Economy	23
4.10	Government On-line Services	23

Infrastructure

5.13	Difference in Quality of Schools	23

Public Institutions

6.06	Competence of Public Officials	9
6.09	Minimum Wage Enforcement	9
7.04	Irregular Payments in Public Contracts	16
7.05	Irregular Payments in Loan Applications	18
8.06	Days to Start a Firm	19

Macroeconomic Environment

2.31	Average Tariff Rate	9
2.32	Corporate Income Tax Rate	21

Company Practices

10.23	Pay and Productivity	17

NOTABLE COMPETITIVE DISADVANTAGES

Criteria	Rank

Growth Competitiveness

Innovation

3.02	Firm-Level Innovation	69
3.16	Utility Patents in 2000	65

Information and Communications Technology

4.08	Government Prioritization of ICT	61
4.12	Legal Framework for ICT Development	61

Law and Contracts

6.12	Organized Crime	66
6.01	Judicial Independence	64

Macroeconomic Environment

2.29	Real Exchange Rate	73

Current Competitiveness

Sophistication of Company Operations and Strategy

10.01	Nature of Competitive Advantage	66
10.14	Extent of Incentive Compensation	66
10.07	Extent of Marketing	63

Quality of the Business Environment

8.02	Extent of Locally Based Competitors	66
6.03	Intellectual Property Protection	62
8.04	Administrative Burden for Start-Ups	61

Other Indicators

Technology

4.04	Quality of Competition in Telecommunication Sector	64
4.05	High Skilled IT Job Market	62

Public Institutions

6.05	Government Commitments	67
8.05	Permits to Start a Firm	64
6.08	Burden of Regulation	63

Macroeconomic Environment

2.19	Permits to Export	71
2.04	Exchange Rate and Exports	66
2.21	Social Transfer Recipients	64
2.20	Composition of Public Spending	62
2.22	Extent of Distortive Government Subsidies	61

Company Practices

10.19	Hiring and Firing Practices	62
10.21	Cooperation in Labor-Employer Relations	61

263

Malaysia

Key Facts

GDP per capita at Purchasing Power Parity, 2000 ....$8,924

GDP per capita Rank 39

Percentage Growth in Real GDP per capita, 1999–2000 ....6.5

Growth Rank 9

US Utility Patents Granted in 2000 (per million population)..........1.8

Patent Rank 31

Growth Competitiveness Rank	**30**

Technology Index Rank...**22**

    ICT Subindex Rank 33

    Innovation Subindex Rank 50

    Technology Transfer Subindex Rank

        (out of 51 technological non-core economies) 1

Public Institutions Index Rank **39**

    Corruption Subindex Rank 36

    Contracts and Law Subindex Rank...........................42

Macroeconomic Environment Index Rank..**20**

    Macroeconomic Stability Subindex Rank 24

    Country Credit Rating Rank 33

Current Competitiveness Rank	**37**

Sophistication of Company Operations and Strategy Rank.................**37**

Quality of the Business Environment Rank..**38**

National competitiveness balance sheet

NOTABLE COMPETITIVE ADVANTAGES	
Criteria	**Rank**

NOTABLE COMPETITIVE DISADVANTAGES	
Criteria	**Rank**

Growth Competitiveness

Innovation
3.02 Firm-Level Innovation 14

Information and Communications Technology
4.08 Government Prioritization of ICT 11

Technology Transfer
3.23 Skill-Based Exports 3
3.04 FDI and Technology Transfer 4

Macroeconomic Environment
2.26 National Savings Rate 4
2.28 Inflation...13

Current Competitiveness

Sophistication of Company Operations and Strategy
10.12 Extent of Staff Training.......................................24
10.11 Breadth of International Markets 26
10.06 Production Process Sophistication....................27

Quality of the Business Environment
5.06 Port Infrastructure Quality................................15
5.01 Overall Infrastructure Quality 20
4.11 Laws Relating to ICT Use 22

Other Indicators

Technology
3.08 Tax Credits for Firm-Level Research and Development.......8
3.07 Subsidies for Firm-Level Research and Development....15

Infrastructure
5.11 Electricity Prices...13
5.04 Road Infrastructure Quality 15

Public Institutions
6.10 Extent of Bureaucratic Red Tape 8
6.11 Tax Evasion...15

Macroeconomic Environment
2.19 Permits to Export 1
1.08 Unemployment Rate, 2000 8
2.33 Value Added Tax Rate 12
2.20 Composition of Public Spending 15

Company Practices
10.20 Employment Rules 7
10.21 Cooperation in Labor-Employer Relations 10
10.22 Union Contributions to Productivity 15

Growth Competitiveness

Innovation
3.19 Tertiary Enrollment 60

Information and Communications Technology
4.07 Quality of Competition in ISP Sector 53
4.16 Telephone Lines 45

Law and Contracts
6.01 Judicial Independence...51
6.04 Favoritism in Decisions of Government Officials............50

Macroeconomic Environment
2.24 Government Surplus/Deficit................................65

Current Competitiveness

Sophistication of Company Operations and Strategy
10.03 Extent of Branding 74
10.05 Uniqueness of Product Designs 73
10.01 Nature of Competitive Advantage......................69

Quality of the Business Environment
9.10 Local Availability of Specialized Research
and Training Services 74
9.07 Extent of Product and Process Collaboration 69
9.11 Local Availability of Information Technology Services.....67

Other Indicators

Technology
3.11 Availability of Scientists and Engineers...........................60
4.10 Government On-line Services 49
3.05 Quality of Scientific Research Institutions 48
3.03 Firm-Level Technology Absorption 47
3.12 Brain Drain...45

Public Institutions
6.09 Minimum Wage Enforcement.............................70
6.06 Competence of Public Officials...........................65
7.04 Irregular Payments in Public Contracts 57
8.06 Days to Start a Firm 54
6.04 Favoritism in Decisions of Government Officials............50
7.06 Business Costs of Corruption 50
6.03 Intellectual Property Protection......................45

Macroeconomic Environment
2.13 Entry into Banking Industry..............................75
2.10 Access to Foreign Capital Markets 66
2.11 Foreign Access to Local Capital Markets.......................66
2.21 Social Transfer Recipients 58
2.31 Average Tariff Rate 56
2.17 Sources of Investment Finance 55
2.15 Access to Bond Markets.....................................49
2.02 Soundness of Banks 48

Company Practices
10.14 Extent of Incentive Compensation...................50
10.19 Hiring and Firing Practices 46

265

Mauritius

Key Facts

GDP per capita at Purchasing Power Parity, 2000 ....$9,512
GDP per capita Rank 33
Percentage Growth in Real GDP per capita, 1999–2000 ....2.3
Growth Rank 54
US Utility Patents Granted in 2000 (per million population)..........0.0
Patent Rank 65

Growth Competitiveness Rank	32

Technology Index Rank..**37**
    ICT Subindex Rank 41
    Innovation Subindex Rank 73
    Technology Transfer Subindex Rank
        (out of 51 technological non-core economies) 10
Public Institutions Index Rank **32**
    Corruption Subindex Rank 42
    Contracts and Law Subindex Rank.......................................28
Macroeconomic Environment Index Rank..................................**30**
    Macroeconomic Stability Subindex Rank 41
    Country Credit Rating Rank 37

Current Competitiveness Rank	52

Sophistication of Company Operations and Strategy Rank..................**49**
Quality of the Business Environment Rank...**50**

National competitiveness balance sheet

NOTABLE COMPETITIVE ADVANTAGES

Criteria		Rank

Growth Competitiveness

Information and Communications Technology

4.08	Government Prioritization of ICT	12

Technology Transfer

3.23	Skill-Based Exports	13

Macroeconomic Environment

2.01	Recession Expectations	2

Current Competitiveness

Sophistication of Company Operations and Strategy

10.06	Production Process Sophistication	26
10.02	Value Chain Presence	28
10.09	Control of International Distribution	35

Quality of the Business Environment

2.18	Hidden Trade Barriers	22
5.06	Port Infrastructure Quality	25
6.01	Judicial Independence	28

Other Indicators

Public Institutions

6.09	Minimum Wage Enforcement	12
6.11	Tax Evasion	14

Macroeconomic Environment

2.27	Investment Rate	4
2.33	Value Added Tax Rate	12
2.06	Exchange Rate Premium	15

Company Practices

10.21	Cooperation in Labor-Employer Relations	15

NOTABLE COMPETITIVE DISADVANTAGES

Criteria		Rank

Growth Competitiveness

Innovation

3.19	Tertiary Enrollment	70
3.06	Company Spending on Research and Development	66
3.16	Utility Patents in 2000	65
3.01	Technological Sophistication	61
3.09	University/Industry Research Collaboration	48
3.02	Firm-Level Innovation	47

Information and Communications Technology

4.07	Quality of Competition in ISP Sector	75
4.03	Internet Access in Schools	58
4.13	Cellular Telephones	49

Technology Transfer

3.04	FDI and Technology Transfer	49

Corruption

7.01	Irregular Payments in Exports & Imports	56
7.02	Irregular Payments in Government Procurement	52

Macroeconomic Environment

2.24	Government Surplus/Deficit	68
2.30	Interest Rate Spread	61
2.28	Inflation	49

Current Competitiveness

Sophistication of Company Operations and Strategy

10.11	Breadth of International Markets	68
10.04	Capacity for Innovation	63
10.15	Reliance on Professional Management	62

Quality of the Business Environment

9.05	Decentralization of Corporate Activity	73
10.17	Efficacy of Corporate Boards	73
9.07	Extent of Product and Process Collaboration	71

Other Indicators

Technology

4.04	Quality of Competition in Telecommunication Sector	75
4.01	Speed and Cost of Internet Access	72
3.11	Availability of Scientists and Engineers	65
4.10	Government On-line Services	65
4.06	IT Training and Education	64
3.13	Women in the Economy	62

Infrastructure

5.05	Railroad Infrastructure Development	75
5.11	Electricity Prices	64

Macroeconomic Environment

2.13	Entry into Banking Industry	66
2.31	Average Tariff Rate	63

Company Practices

10.23	Pay and Productivity	74
10.19	Hiring and Firing Practices	71

Mexico

Key Facts

GDP per capita at Purchasing Power Parity, 2000 .... $8,914
GDP per capita Rank 40
Percentage Growth in Real GDP per capita, 1999–2000 .... 5.3
Growth Rank 15
US Utility Patents Granted in 2000 (per million population) 0.8
Patent Rank 39

Growth Competitiveness Rank	42

Technology Index Rank **36**
    ICT Subindex Rank 46
    Innovation Subindex Rank 52
    Technology Transfer Subindex Rank
        (out of 51 technological non-core economies) 9
Public Institutions Index Rank **56**
    Corruption Subindex Rank 52
    Contracts and Law Subindex Rank 55
Macroeconomic Environment Index Rank **36**
    Macroeconomic Stability Subindex Rank 57
    Country Credit Rating Rank 35

Current Competitiveness Rank	51

Sophistication of Company Operations and Strategy Rank............**46**
Quality of the Business Environment Rank..**53**

National competitiveness balance sheet

NOTABLE COMPETITIVE ADVANTAGES

Criteria	Rank

Growth Competitiveness

Technology Transfer

3.04 FDI and Technology Transfer..15
3.23 Skill-Based Exports..17

Macroeconomic Environment

Potential for "Catch-up" Growth 36

Current Competitiveness

Sophistication of Company Operations and Strategy

10.10 Extent of Regional Sales 18
10.07 Extent of Marketing 39
10.06 Production Process Sophistication...................................45

Quality of the Business Environment

5.04 Road Infrastructure Quality 25
8.02 Extent of Locally Based Competitors............................33
2.18 Hidden Trade Barriers...36

Other Indicators

Public Institutions

6.09 Minimum Wage Enforcement...24

Macroeconomic Environment

1.08 Unemployment Rate, 2000 3
2.31 Average Tariff Rate 3
2.06 Exchange Rate Premium..12
2.19 Permits to Export 22

NOTABLE COMPETITIVE DISADVANTAGES

Criteria	Rank

Growth Competitiveness

Information and Communications Technology

4.12 Legal Framework for ICT Development..........................62

Law and Contracts

6.12 Organized Crime 64

Macroeconomic Environment

2.29 Real Exchange Rate 68
2.30 Interest Rate Spread 64
2.28 Inflation...61

Current Competitiveness

Sophistication of Company Operations and Strategy

10.02 Value Chain Presence..70
10.05 Uniqueness of Product Designs 64
10.04 Capacity for Innovation...54

Quality of the Business Environment

8.04 Administrative Burden for Start-Ups 69
2.08 Ease of Access to Loans..64
2.09 Venture Capital Availability 63

Other Indicators

Technology

3.11 Availability of Scientists and Engineers..........................62
3.14 Minorities in the Economy 62
3.05 Quality of Scientific Research Institutions 61

Infrastructure

5.10 Postal Efficiency...71
5.02 Tap Water Safety 70
5.13 Difference in Quality of Schools 68
5.14 Difference in Quality of Healthcare................................67
5.03 Industrial Water Availability 64

Public Institutions

8.05 Permits to Start a Firm...72
6.08 Burden of Regulation 71
6.11 Tax Evasion..70
8.06 Days to Start a Firm 70
6.14 Informal Sector..67

Macroeconomic Environment

2.04 Exchange Rate and Exports 73
2.02 Soundness of Banks 69
2.12 Perceived Interest Rate Gap 69

269

Netherlands

Key Facts

GDP per capita at Purchasing Power Parity, 2000 ....$25,598
GDP per capita Rank 12
Percentage Growth in Real GDP per capita, 1999–2000 ....3.6
Growth Rank 31
US Utility Patents Granted in 2000 (per million population)........78.1
Patent Rank 11

Growth Competitiveness Rank	8

Technology Index Rank...**14**
    ICT Subindex Rank 9
    Innovation Subindex Rank 14
Public Institutions Index Rank **5**
    Corruption Subindex Rank 9
    Contracts and Law Subindex Rank..........................4
Macroeconomic Environment Index Rank...................................**9**
    Macroeconomic Stability Subindex Rank 4
    Country Credit Rating Rank 3

Current Competitiveness Rank	3

Sophistication of Company Operations and Strategy Rank...................**3**
Quality of the Business Environment Rank..**3**

National competitiveness balance sheet

NOTABLE COMPETITIVE ADVANTAGES	
Criteria	**Rank**

Growth Competitiveness

Innovation

3.01	Technological Sophistication	8
3.06	Company Spending on Research and Development	8
3.09	University/Industry Research Collaboration	9

Information and Communications Technology

4.15	Internet Hosts	4
4.12	Legal Framework for ICT Development	5
4.17	Personal Computers	8
4.07	Quality of Competition in ISP Sector	9
4.16	Telephone Lines	9
4.11	Laws Relating to ICT Use	10
4.13	Cellular Telephones	10

Corruption

7.01	Irregular Payments in Exports & Imports	6
7.02	Irregular Payments in Government Procurement	9
7.03	Irregular Payments in Tax Collection	9

Law and Contracts

6.01	Judicial Independence	2
6.02	Property Rights	2
6.04	Favoritism in Decisions of Government Officials	7
6.12	Organized Crime	

Macroeconomic Environment

2.30	Interest Rate Spread	6
2.01	Recession Expectations	8

Current Competitiveness

Sophistication of Company Operations and Strategy

10.07	Extent of Marketing	2
10.09	Control of International Distribution	3
10.02	Value Chain Presence	4

Quality of the Business Environment

11.06	Stringency of Environmental Regulations	1
9.03	Local Supplier Quality	3
10.21	Cooperation in Labor-Employer Relations	3

Other Indicators

Technology

4.05	High Skilled IT Job Market	1

Infrastructure

5.09	Quality of Competition in Transportation Sector	1
5.15	Public Health Agencies	1

Macroeconomic Environment

2.19	Permits to Export	1

Company Practices

10.12	Extent of Staff Training	1

NOTABLE COMPETITIVE DISADVANTAGES	
Criteria	**Rank**

Growth Competitiveness

Information and Communications Technology

4.09	Government Success in ICT Promotion	24

Current Competitiveness

Quality of the Business Environment

3.11	Availability of Scientists and Engineers	28
9.06	State of Cluster Development	23
9.11	Local Availability of Information Technology Services	17

Other Indicators

Technology

3.13	Women in the Economy	51
3.14	Minorities in the Economy	43

Macroeconomic Environment

2.33	Value Added Tax Rate	53
2.32	Corporate Income Tax Rate	50
2.27	Investment Rate	34

Company Practices

10.19	Hiring and Firing Practices	64
10.23	Pay and Productivity	40
10.20	Employment Rules	39

271

New Zealand

Key Facts

GDP per capita at Purchasing Power Parity, 2000 ....$20,010
GDP per capita Rank 21
Percentage Growth in Real GDP per capita, 1999–2000 ....2.6
Growth Rank 53
US Utility Patents Granted in 2000 (per million population)........28.0
Patent Rank 23

Growth Competitiveness Rank	10

Technology Index Rank..**11**
    ICT Subindex Rank 17
    Innovation Subindex Rank 10
Public Institutions Index Rank **4**
    Corruption Subindex Rank 4
    Contracts and Law Subindex Rank...........................5
Macroeconomic Environment Index Rank...................................**14**
    Macroeconomic Stability Subindex Rank 23
    Country Credit Rating Rank 21

Current Competitiveness Rank	20

Sophistication of Company Operations and Strategy Rank..................**19**
Quality of the Business Environment Rank..**20**

National competitiveness balance sheet

NOTABLE COMPETITIVE ADVANTAGES

Criteria	Rank

Growth Competitiveness

Innovation

3.19	Tertiary Enrollment	6

Information and Communications Technology

4.15	Internet Hosts	6

Corruption

7.01	Irregular Payments in Exports & Imports	3
7.03	Irregular Payments in Tax Collection	3
7.02	Irregular Payments in Government Procurement	7

Law and Contracts

6.01	Judicial Independence	9
6.12	Organized Crime	9
8.07	Effectiveness of Anti-Trust Policy	13

Current Competitiveness

Sophistication of Company Operations and Strategy

10.15	Reliance on Professional Management	6
10.13	Willingness to Delegate Authority	13
10.14	Extent of Incentive Compensation	19

Quality of the Business Environment

6.04	Favoritism in Decisions of Government Officials	2
2.18	Hidden Trade Barriers	3
11.06	Stringency of Environmental Regulations	16

Other Indicators

Infrastructure

5.10	Postal Efficiency	6
5.11	Electricity Prices	7
5.02	Tap Water Safety	8
5.03	Industrial Water Availability	10

Public Institutions

6.11	Tax Evasion	3
6.09	Minimum Wage Enforcement	4
7.05	Irregular Payments in Loan Applications	4
8.06	Days to Start a Firm	4
7.04	Irregular Payments in Public Contracts	5
8.05	Permits to Start a Firm	5
6.13	Unreported Profits and Wages	7
6.14	Informal Sector	7
7.06	Business Costs of Corruption	8
8.04	Administrative Burden for Start-Ups	8

Macroeconomic Environment

2.21	Social Transfer Recipients	4
2.04	Exchange Rate and Exports	5
2.22	Extent of Distortive Government Subsidies	6
2.02	Soundness of Banks	7
2.13	Entry into Banking Industry	7
2.10	Access to Foreign Capital Markets	10

NOTABLE COMPETITIVE DISADVANTAGES

Criteria	Rank

Growth Competitiveness

Innovation

3.02	Firm-Level Innovation	43
3.06	Company Spending on Research and Development	28
3.09	University/Industry Research Collaboration	25

Information and Communications Technology

4.08	Government Prioritization of ICT	40
4.09	Government Success in ICT Promotion	38
4.13	Cellular Telephones	27

Macroeconomic Environment

2.26	National Savings Rate	62
2.01	Recession Expectations	26

Current Competitiveness

Sophistication of Company Operations and Strategy

10.02	Value Chain Presence	31
10.01	Nature of Competitive Advantage	28
10.12	Extent of Staff Training	21

Quality of the Business Environment

3.11	Availability of Scientists and Engineers	49
8.02	Extent of Locally Based Competitors	47
9.06	State of Cluster Development	41

Other Indicators

Technology

3.08	Tax Credits for Firm-Level Research and Development	62
3.12	Brain Drain	47
4.05	High Skilled IT Job Market	46
3.07	Subsidies for Firm-Level Research and Development	41
3.14	Minorities in the Economy	38
3.10	Government Procurement of Advanced Technology Products	30
4.04	Quality of Competition in Telecommunication Sector	27

Infrastructure

5.05	Railroad Infrastructure Development	32
5.13	Difference in Quality of Schools	28

Public Institutions

6.07	Costs of Institutional Change	46
6.05	Government Commitments	32

Macroeconomic Environment

2.05	Expected Exchange Rate Volatility	58
2.27	Investment Rate	47
2.32	Corporate Income Tax Rate	46
2.17	Sources of Investment Finance	41
2.11	Foreign Access to Local Capital Markets	31

Company Practices

10.19	Hiring and Firing Practices	56
10.20	Employment Rules	32
10.22	Union Contributions to Productivity	31

273

Nicaragua

Key Facts

GDP per capita at Purchasing Power Parity, 2000 ....$2,396
GDP per capita Rank 72
Percentage Growth in Real GDP per capita, 1999–2000 ....3.0
Growth Rank 40
US Utility Patents Granted in 2000 (per million population) 0.0
Patent Rank 65

Growth Competitiveness Rank	73

Technology Index Rank..**71**
    ICT Subindex Rank 71
    Innovation Subindex Rank 68
    Technology Transfer Subindex Rank
        (out of 51 technological non-core economies) 41

Public Institutions Index Rank **67**
    Corruption Subindex Rank 65
    Contracts and Law Subindex Rank..68

Macroeconomic Environment Index Rank..**74**
    Macroeconomic Stability Subindex Rank 74
    Country Credit Rating Rank 74

Current Competitiveness Rank	71

Sophistication of Company Operations and Strategy Rank..................**73**
Quality of the Business Environment Rank..**70**

274

National competitiveness balance sheet

NOTABLE COMPETITIVE ADVANTAGES

Criteria	Rank

Growth Competitiveness

Macroeconomic Environment

	Potential for "Catch-up" Growth	4
2.29	Real Exchange Rate	30

Current Competitiveness

Sophistication of Company Operations and Strategy

10.01	Nature of Competitive Advantage	57
10.13	Willingness to Delegate Authority	57
10.03	Extent of Branding	58

Quality of the Business Environment

10.21	Cooperation in Labor-Employer Relations	43
10.16	Quality of Management Schools	47
2.09	Venture Capital Availability	57

Other Indicators

Infrastructure

5.02	Tap Water Safety	44

Public Institutions

8.05	Permits to Start a Firm	35
6.06	Competence of Public Officials	37
6.13	Unreported Profits and Wages	41

Macroeconomic Environment

2.27	Investment Rate	1
2.32	Corporate Income Tax Rate	7
2.33	Value Added Tax Rate	32
2.10	Access to Foreign Capital Markets	42

Company Practices

10.19	Hiring and Firing Practices	9

NOTABLE COMPETITIVE DISADVANTAGES

Criteria	Rank

Growth Competitiveness

Innovation

3.01	Technological Sophistication	70
3.06	Company Spending on Research and Development	67
3.02	Firm-Level Innovation	66
3.09	University/Industry Research Collaboration	66
3.16	Utility Patents in 2000	65

Information and Communications Technology

4.13	Cellular Telephones	72
4.16	Telephone Lines	72
4.03	Internet Access in Schools	70
4.17	Personal Computers	70
4.12	Legal Framework for ICT Development	69
4.11	Laws Relating to ICT Use	68
4.14	Internet Users	68
4.07	Quality of Competition in ISP Sector	67
4.09	Government Success in ICT Promotion	66

Technology Transfer

3.04	FDI and Technology Transfer	69

Corruption

7.03	Irregular Payments in Tax Collection	67
7.01	Irregular Payments in Exports & Imports	66

Law and Contracts

6.02	Property Rights	72
6.01	Judicial Independence	70
6.04	Favoritism in Decisions of Government Officials	66

Macroeconomic Environment

2.26	National Savings Rate	75
2.24	Government Surplus/Deficit	74
2.01	Recession Expectations	70
2.03	Access to Credit	68

Current Competitiveness

Sophistication of Company Operations and Strategy

10.06	Production Process Sophistication	75
10.09	Control of International Distribution	74
10.07	Extent of Marketing	72

Quality of the Business Environment

5.06	Port Infrastructure Quality	74
5.08	Telephone/Fax Infrastructure Quality	72
9.04	Presence of Demanding Regulatory Standards	72

Other Indicators

Infrastructure

5.09	Quality of Competition in Transportation Sector	75
5.11	Electricity Prices	75
5.12	Quality of Public Schools	75
5.01	Overall Infrastructure Quality	73

Public Institutions

7.06	Business Costs of Corruption	73

Macroeconomic Environment

2.14	Financial Regulation and Supervision	74
2.02	Soundness of Banks	73

275

Nigeria

Key Facts

GDP per capita at Purchasing Power Parity, 2000 .... $871
GDP per capita Rank 75
Percentage Growth in Real GDP per capita, 1999–2000 .... 0.0
Growth Rank 71
US Utility Patents Granted in 2000 (per million population) 0.02
Patent Rank 64

Growth Competitiveness Rank	74

Technology Index Rank **75**
    ICT Subindex Rank 74
    Innovation Subindex Rank 74
    Technology Transfer Subindex Rank
      (out of 51 technological non-core economies) 50

Public Institutions Index Rank **73**
    Corruption Subindex Rank 74
    Contracts and Law Subindex Rank 65

Macroeconomic Environment Index Rank **55**
    Macroeconomic Stability Subindex Rank 21
    Country Credit Rating Rank 72

Current Competitiveness Rank	67

Sophistication of Company Operations and Strategy Rank **61**
Quality of the Business Environment Rank **68**

276

National competitiveness balance sheet

NOTABLE COMPETITIVE ADVANTAGES

Criteria	Rank

Growth Competitiveness

Innovation

3.02	Firm-Level Innovation	21
3.06	Company Spending on Research and Development	45

Technology Transfer

3.04	FDI and Technology Transfer	42

Macroeconomic Environment

	Potential for "Catch-up" Growth	1
2.26	National Savings Rate	7
2.30	Interest Rate Spread	15
2.29	Real Exchange Rate	18
2.01	Recession Expectations	22
2.24	Government Surplus/Deficit	24
2.03	Access to Credit	44

Current Competitiveness

Sophistication of Company Operations and Strategy

10.15	Reliance on Professional Management	42
10.03	Extent of Branding	44
10.08	Degree of Customer Orientation	52

Quality of the Business Environment

2.16	Local Equity Market Access	24
9.06	State of Cluster Development	31
9.05	Decentralization of Corporate Activity	34

Other Indicators

Infrastructure

5.11	Electricity Prices	14

Public Institutions

8.05	Permits to Start a Firm	5

Macroeconomic Environment

2.33	Value Added Tax Rate	4
2.13	Entry into Banking Industry	9

Company Practices

10.19	Hiring and Firing Practices	5
10.20	Employment Rules	6
10.22	Union Contributions to Productivity	9

NOTABLE COMPETITIVE DISADVANTAGES

Criteria	Rank

Growth Competitiveness

Innovation

3.19	Tertiary Enrollment	74
3.01	Technological Sophistication	66

Information and Communications Technology

4.13	Cellular Telephones	75
4.14	Internet Users	74
4.15	Internet Hosts	74
4.16	Telephone Lines	74
4.03	Internet Access in Schools	73
4.07	Quality of Competition in ISP Sector	72
4.17	Personal Computers	71

Technology Transfer

3.23	Skill-Based Exports	71

Corruption

7.02	Irregular Payments in Government Procurement	74
7.03	Irregular Payments in Tax Collection	72
7.01	Irregular Payments in Exports & Imports	71

Law and Contracts

6.04	Favoritism in Decisions of Government Officials	69
6.12	Organized Crime	69

Current Competitiveness

Sophistication of Company Operations and Strategy

10.06	Production Process Sophistication	70
10.11	Breadth of International Markets	69

Quality of the Business Environment

5.08	Telephone/Fax Infrastructure Quality	73
10.21	Cooperation in Labor-Employer Relations	73

Other Indicators

Technology

4.01	Speed and Cost of Internet Access	74
4.02	Public Access to Internet	74
4.04	Quality of Competition in Telecommunication Sector	73

Infrastructure

5.03	Industrial Water Availability	75

Public Institutions

7.04	Irregular Payments in Public Contracts	74
6.11	Tax Evasion	73

Macroeconomic Environment

2.21	Social Transfer Recipients	75
2.31	Average Tariff Rate	75

277

Norway

Key Facts

GDP per capita at Purchasing Power Parity, 2000 ....$29,500
GDP per capita Rank 2
Percentage Growth in Real GDP per capita, 1999–2000 ....1.7
Growth Rank 60
US Utility Patents Granted in 2000 (per million population) 55.1
Patent Rank 18

Growth Competitiveness Rank	6

Technology Index Rank...**7**
    ICT Subindex Rank 6
    Innovation Subindex Rank 7
Public Institutions Index Rank **16**
    Corruption Subindex Rank 15
    Contracts and Law Subindex Rank.......................................18
Macroeconomic Environment Index Rank..**5**
    Macroeconomic Stability Subindex Rank 2
    Country Credit Rating Rank 7

Current Competitiveness Rank	19

Sophistication of Company Operations and Strategy Rank..................**23**
Quality of the Business Environment Rank...**19**

National competitiveness balance sheet

NOTABLE COMPETITIVE ADVANTAGES

Criteria	Rank

Growth Competitiveness

Innovation

3.19	Tertiary Enrollment	7

Information and Communications Technology

4.16	Telephone Lines	2
4.14	Internet Users	3
4.17	Personal Computers	3
4.15	Internet Hosts	5
4.11	Laws Relating to ICT Use	7
4.13	Cellular Telephones	7

Macroeconomic Environment

2.24	Government Surplus/Deficit	1
2.26	National Savings Rate	3
2.30	Interest Rate Spread	3

Current Competitiveness

Quality of the Business Environment

10.17	Efficacy of Corporate Boards	4
2.08	Ease of Access to Loans	5
10.21	Cooperation in Labor-Employer Relations	8

Other Indicators

Technology

3.12	Brain Drain	3
4.02	Public Access to Internet	4
4.10	Government On-line Services	4
4.05	High Skilled IT Job Market	7

Infrastructure

5.11	Electricity Prices	3
5.14	Difference in Quality of Healthcare	5
5.10	Postal Efficiency	6
5.15	Public Health Agencies	6

Public Institutions

6.13	Unreported Profits and Wages	4
8.06	Days to Start a Firm	4
6.10	Extent of Bureaucratic Red Tape	5

Macroeconomic Environment

2.19	Permits to Export	1
2.15	Access to Bond Markets	4
2.09	Venture Capital Availability	7

Company Practices

10.22	Union Contributions to Productivity	7

NOTABLE COMPETITIVE DISADVANTAGES

Criteria	Rank

Growth Competitiveness

Innovation

3.06	Company Spending on Research and Development	21
3.09	University/Industry Research Collaboration	21

Information and Communications Technology

4.09	Government Success in ICT Promotion	33
4.08	Government Prioritization of ICT	31
4.12	Legal Framework for ICT Development	21

Macroeconomic Environment

2.28	Inflation	32
2.03	Access to Credit	23

Current Competitiveness

Sophistication of Company Operations and Strategy

10.14	Extent of Incentive Compensation	36
10.11	Breadth of International Markets	29
10.09	Control of International Distribution	27

Quality of the Business Environment

5.04	Road Infrastructure Quality	53
9.02	Local Supplier Quantity	38
9.03	Local Supplier Quality	20

Other Indicators

Technology

3.14	Minorities in the Economy	61

Infrastructure

5.05	Railroad Infrastructure Development	39

Public Institutions

6.09	Minimum Wage Enforcement	57
6.08	Burden of Regulation	51
8.05	Permits to Start a Firm	35
6.11	Tax Evasion	31

Macroeconomic Environment

2.33	Value Added Tax Rate	70
2.06	Exchange Rate Premium	56
2.27	Investment Rate	48
2.04	Exchange Rate and Exports	45
2.22	Extent of Distortive Government Subsidies	41
2.11	Foreign Access to Local Capital Markets	40
2.10	Access to Foreign Capital Markets	37
2.20	Composition of Public Spending	32
2.13	Entry into Banking Industry	31

Company Practices

10.19	Hiring and Firing Practices	70
10.20	Employment Rules	63
10.23	Pay and Productivity	50

Panama

Key Facts

GDP per capita at Purchasing Power Parity, 2000 ....$6,169
GDP per capita Rank 50
Percentage Growth in Real GDP per capita, 1999–2000 ....2.9
Growth Rank 45
US Utility Patents Granted in 2000 (per million population)..........0.7
Patent Rank ....42˚

Growth Competitiveness Rank	53

Technology Index Rank...**57**	
ICT Subindex Rank 49	
Innovation Subindex Rank 37	
Technology Transfer Subindex Rank	
(out of 51 technological non-core economies) 47	
Public Institutions Index Rank **59**	
Corruption Subindex Rank 57	
Contracts and Law Subindex Rank........................57	
Macroeconomic Environment Index Rank............................**44**	
Macroeconomic Stability Subindex Rank 49	
Country Credit Rating Rank 46	

Current Competitiveness Rank	48

Sophistication of Company Operations and Strategy Rank..................**40**
Quality of the Business Environment Rank...**49**

National competitiveness balance sheet

NOTABLE COMPETITIVE ADVANTAGES

Criteria	Rank

Growth Competitiveness

Macroeconomic Environment

2.28	Inflation	12
2.30	Interest Rate Spread	14
	Potential for "Catch-up" Growth	26

Current Competitiveness

Sophistication of Company Operations and Strategy

10.01	Nature of Competitive Advantage	24
10.02	Value Chain Presence	25
10.07	Extent of Marketing	31

Quality of the Business Environment

5.07	Air Transport Infrastructure Quality	26
5.06	Port Infrastructure Quality	27
2.07	Financial Market Sophistication	30

Other Indicators

Technology

3.13	Women in the Economy	22

Public Institutions

8.06	Days to Start a Firm	19
6.08	Burden of Regulation	25

Macroeconomic Environment

1.09	Employment to Population Ratio, 2000	4
2.33	Value Added Tax Rate	4
2.13	Entry into Banking Industry	16
2.12	Perceived Interest Rate Gap	18
2.27	Investment Rate	22
2.32	Corporate Income Tax Rate	24
2.05	Expected Exchange Rate Volatility	25

NOTABLE COMPETITIVE DISADVANTAGES

Criteria	Rank

Growth Competitiveness

Technology Transfer

3.23	Skill-Based Exports	72

Law and Contracts

6.04	Favoritism in Decisions of Government Officials	65

Macroeconomic Environment

2.01	Recession Expectations	71
2.03	Access to Credit	61

Current Competitiveness

Sophistication of Company Operations and Strategy

10.15	Reliance on Professional Management	66
10.05	Uniqueness of Product Designs	61
10.10	Extent of Regional Sales	57

Quality of the Business Environment

6.10	Extent of Bureaucratic Red Tape	73
5.12	Quality of Public Schools	61
5.05	Railroad Infrastructure Development	60

Other Indicators

Technology

3.10	Government Procurement of Advanced Technology Products	63
3.11	Availability of Scientists and Engineers	63

Infrastructure

5.11	Electricity Prices	73
5.09	Quality of Competition in Transportation Sector	68

Public Institutions

6.07	Costs of Institutional Change	67
7.06	Business Costs of Corruption	66
6.05	Government Commitments	61

Macroeconomic Environment

2.04	Exchange Rate and Exports	61
2.31	Average Tariff Rate	61

Company Practices

10.20	Employment Rules	73
10.22	Union Contributions to Productivity	63

Paraguay

Key Facts

GDP per capita at Purchasing Power Parity, 2000 ....$4,396
GDP per capita Rank 57
Percentage Growth in Real GDP per capita, 1999–2000 ....–1.7
Growth Rank 73
US Utility Patents Granted in 2000 (per million population)..........0.0
Patent Rank 65

Growth Competitiveness Rank	72

Technology Index Rank..**73**
    ICT Subindex Rank 64
    Innovation Subindex Rank 72
    Technology Transfer Subindex Rank
        (out of 51 technological non-core economies) 51
Public Institutions Index Rank **74**
    Corruption Subindex Rank 73
    Contracts and Law Subindex Rank..72
Macroeconomic Environment Index Rank................................**65**
    Macroeconomic Stability Subindex Rank 68
    Country Credit Rating Rank 62

Current Competitiveness Rank	70

Sophistication of Company Operations and Strategy Rank..................**68**
Quality of the Business Environment Rank..**71**

National competitiveness balance sheet

NOTABLE COMPETITIVE ADVANTAGES

Criteria	Rank

Growth Competitiveness

Information and Communications Technology

4.13	Cellular Telephones	37

Macroeconomic Environment

	Potential for "Catch-up" Growth	19
2.29	Real Exchange Rate	39

Current Competitiveness

Sophistication of Company Operations and Strategy

10.04	Capacity for Innovation	41
10.01	Nature of Competitive Advantage	45

Quality of the Business Environment

9.09	Local Availability of Process Machinery	35
2.08	Ease of Access to Loans	46
2.09	Venture Capital Availability	46

Other Indicators

Infrastructure

5.10	Postal Efficiency	28

Public Institutions

8.06	Days to Start a Firm	19

Macroeconomic Environment

2.33	Value Added Tax Rate	12
2.32	Corporate Income Tax Rate	24
2.12	Perceived Interest Rate Gap	27
2.06	Exchange Rate Premium	29
2.27	Investment Rate	33

Company Practices

10.20	Employment Rules	30
10.19	Hiring and Firing Practices	32

NOTABLE COMPETITIVE DISADVANTAGES

Criteria	Rank

Growth Competitiveness

Innovation

3.02	Firm-Level Innovation	74
3.01	Technological Sophistication	68
3.09	University/Industry Research Collaboration	68
3.16	Utility Patents in 2000	65

Information and Communications Technology

4.08	Government Prioritization of ICT	73
4.12	Legal Framework for ICT Development	73
4.07	Quality of Competition in ISP Sector	70
4.14	Internet Users	70
4.09	Government Success in ICT Promotion	69

Technology Transfer

3.04	FDI and Technology Transfer	74
3.23	Skill-Based Exports	70

Corruption

7.01	Irregular Payments in Exports & Imports	74
7.02	Irregular Payments in Government Procurement	73
7.03	Irregular Payments in Tax Collection	73

Law and Contracts

6.02	Property Rights	74
6.01	Judicial Independence	67

Macroeconomic Environment

2.01	Recession Expectations	74

Current Competitiveness

Sophistication of Company Operations and Strategy

10.15	Reliance on Professional Management	75
10.14	Extent of Incentive Compensation	69
10.08	Degree of Customer Orientation	68

Quality of the Business Environment

3.05	Quality of Scientific Research Institutions	75
9.02	Local Supplier Quantity	75
8.01	Intensity of Local Competition	74

Other Indicators

Technology

3.11	Availability of Scientists and Engineers	74

Infrastructure

5.15	Public Health Agencies	75

Public Institutions

6.09	Minimum Wage Enforcement	74

Macroeconomic Environment

2.18	Hidden Trade Barriers	75
2.19	Permits to Export	75
2.05	Expected Exchange Rate Volatility	74
2.11	Foreign Access to Local Capital Markets	74
2.20	Composition of Public Spending	74
2.21	Social Transfer Recipients	74

Peru

Key Facts

GDP per capita at Purchasing Power Parity, 2000 ....$4,797
GDP per capita Rank 55
Percentage Growth in Real GDP per capita, 1999–2000 ....1.7
Growth Rank 59
US Utility Patents Granted in 2000 (per million population).........0.1
Patent Rank 59

Growth Competitiveness Rank	55

Technology Index Rank..**62**
    ICT Subindex Rank 58
    Innovation Subindex Rank 51
    Technology Transfer Subindex Rank
        (out of 51 technological non-core economies) 42
Public Institutions Index Rank **45**
    Corruption Subindex Rank 30
    Contracts and Law Subindex Rank.........................60
Macroeconomic Environment Index Rank...................................**58**
    Macroeconomic Stability Subindex Rank 62
    Country Credit Rating Rank 55

Current Competitiveness Rank	63

Sophistication of Company Operations and Strategy Rank..................**65**
Quality of the Business Environment Rank...**62**

National competitiveness balance sheet

NOTABLE COMPETITIVE ADVANTAGES

Criteria	Rank

Growth Competitiveness

Innovation
3.02 Firm-Level Innovation 33
3.19 Tertiary Enrollment 41

Technology Transfer
3.04 FDI and Technology Transfer 28

Corruption
7.02 Irregular Payments in Government Procurement 30
7.01 Irregular Payments in Exports & Imports 33
7.03 Irregular Payments in Tax Collection 35

Macroeconomic Environment
Potential for "Catch-up" Growth 21
2.28 Inflation 38
2.29 Real Exchange Rate 43

Current Competitiveness

Sophistication of Company Operations and Strategy
10.01 Nature of Competitive Advantage 41
10.09 Control of International Distribution 45
10.08 Degree of Customer Orientation 56

Quality of the Business Environment
2.22 Extent of Distortive Government Subsidies 22
6.10 Extent of Bureaucratic Red Tape 27
2.18 Hidden Trade Barriers 32

Other Indicators

Technology
4.02 Public Access to Internet 13

Public Institutions
6.08 Burden of Regulation 21
7.05 Irregular Payments in Loan Applications 32
8.05 Permits to Start a Firm 35

Macroeconomic Environment
2.06 Exchange Rate Premium 1
2.21 Social Transfer Recipients 8
2.11 Foreign Access to Local Capital Markets 15
2.10 Access to Foreign Capital Markets 22
2.19 Permits to Export 22
2.32 Corporate Income Tax Rate 24
2.13 Entry into Banking Industry 26
2.17 Sources of Investment Finance 26
2.05 Expected Exchange Rate Volatility 27
1.08 Unemployment Rate, 2000 28
2.14 Financial Regulation and Supervision 35

Company Practices
10.19 Hiring and Firing Practices 3
10.20 Employment Rules 11
10.21 Cooperation in Labor-Employer Relations 32
10.22 Union Contributions to Productivity 36

NOTABLE COMPETITIVE DISADVANTAGES

Criteria	Rank

Growth Competitiveness

Innovation
3.06 Company Spending on Research and Development 70
3.09 University/Industry Research Collaboration 69

Technology Transfer
3.23 Skill-Based Exports 68

Law and Contracts
6.01 Judicial Independence 73

Macroeconomic Environment
2.03 Access to Credit 72
2.30 Interest Rate Spread 68

Current Competitiveness

Sophistication of Company Operations and Strategy
10.05 Uniqueness of Product Designs 71
10.04 Capacity for Innovation 67
10.10 Extent of Regional Sales 66

Quality of the Business Environment
3.10 Government Procurement of Advanced
     Technology Products 72
8.04 Administrative Burden for Start-Ups 71
8.02 Extent of Locally Based Competitors 68

Other Indicators

Technology
3.07 Subsidies for Firm-Level Research and Development 73
3.08 Tax Credits for Firm-Level Research and Development 72
3.12 Brain Drain 66

Infrastructure
5.13 Difference in Quality of Schools 74
5.14 Difference in Quality of Healthcare 71
5.06 Port Infrastructure Quality 66
5.12 Quality of Public Schools 66

Public Institutions
7.07 Public Trust of Politicians 74
6.07 Costs of Institutional Change 68
6.09 Minimum Wage Enforcement 66

Macroeconomic Environment
2.12 Perceived Interest Rate Gap 72
2.09 Venture Capital Availability 69
1.09 Employment to Population Ratio, 2000 67

285

Philippines

Key Facts

GDP per capita at Purchasing Power Parity, 2000 ....$3,956
GDP per capita Rank 59
Percentage Growth in Real GDP per capita, 1999–2000 ....1.9
Growth Rank 58
US Utility Patents Granted in 2000 (per million population)........0.03
Patent Rank 63

Growth Competitiveness Rank	48

Technology Index Rank..**40**
    ICT Subindex Rank 55
    Innovation Subindex Rank 45
    Technology Transfer Subindex Rank
       (out of 51 technological non-core economies) 7
Public Institutions Index Rank **64**
    Corruption Subindex Rank 69
    Contracts and Law Subindex Rank...........................56
Macroeconomic Environment Index Rank.................................**28**
    Macroeconomic Stability Subindex Rank 38
    Country Credit Rating Rank 51

Current Competitiveness Rank	54

Sophistication of Company Operations and Strategy Rank..................**45**
Quality of the Business Environment Rank..**54**

National competitiveness balance sheet

NOTABLE COMPETITIVE ADVANTAGES		
	Criteria	Rank

Growth Competitiveness

Innovation
3.02 Firm-Level Innovation 15

Technology Transfer
3.23 Skill-Based Exports 10
3.04 FDI and Technology Transfer..19

Macroeconomic Environment
2.30 Interest Rate Spread 8
2.26 National Savings Rate 11
     Potential for "Catch-up" Growth 17
2.01 Recession Expectations 23

Current Competitiveness

Sophistication of Company Operations and Strategy
10.14 Extent of Incentive Compensation..................................30
10.07 Extent of Marketing 35
10.12 Extent of Staff Training...40

Quality of the Business Environment
10.16 Quality of Management Schools....................................23
4.11 Laws Relating to ICT Use 33
9.01 Buyer Sophistication 36

Other Indicators

Technology
3.13 Women in the Economy 9

Public Institutions
8.06 Days to Start a Firm 19
8.05 Permits to Start a Firm...24

Macroeconomic Environment
2.04 Exchange Rate and Exports 7
2.33 Value Added Tax Rate 12
2.17 Sources of Investment Finance 21
2.19 Permits to Export 22

NOTABLE COMPETITIVE DISADVANTAGES		
	Criteria	Rank

Growth Competitiveness

Innovation
3.16 Utility Patents in 2000...63

Information and Communications Technology
4.16 Telephone Lines 68

Corruption
7.03 Irregular Payments in Tax Collection 74
7.01 Irregular Payments in Exports & Imports........................67

Macroeconomic Environment
2.24 Government Surplus/Deficit..61

Current Competitiveness

Sophistication of Company Operations and Strategy
10.03 Extent of Branding 67
10.11 Breadth of International Markets 59
10.02 Value Chain Presence..51

Quality of the Business Environment
5.04 Road Infrastructure Quality 74
5.06 Port Infrastructure Quality 70
5.01 Overall Infrastructure Quality 68

Other Indicators

Technology
3.12 Brain Drain...71
4.05 High Skilled IT Job Market 70
4.02 Public Access to Internet 63

Infrastructure
5.11 Electricity Prices 72
5.10 Postal Efficiency 69
5.02 Tap Water Safety...66
5.03 Industrial Water Availability..66
5.14 Difference in Quality of Healthcare................................66
5.05 Railroad Infrastructure Development 63
5.12 Quality of Public Schools 63
5.13 Difference in Quality of Schools 63
5.07 Air Transport Infrastructure Quality 61

Public Institutions
6.11 Tax Evasion...75
7.04 Irregular Payments in Public Contracts 69
6.07 Costs of Institutional Change.......................................66
6.13 Unreported Profits and Wages......................................66
7.06 Business Costs of Corruption 65
6.03 Intellectual Property Protection....................................61

Macroeconomic Environment
2.18 Hidden Trade Barriers..66
2.06 Exchange Rate Premium...62

Poland

Key Facts

GDP per capita at Purchasing Power Parity, 2000 ....$8,971
GDP per capita Rank 38
Percentage Growth in Real GDP per capita, 1999–2000 ....4.0
Growth Rank 26
US Utility Patents Granted in 2000 (per million population) 0.3
Patent Rank 47

Growth Competitiveness Rank	41

Technology Index Rank..**35**
    ICT Subindex Rank 37
    Innovation Subindex Rank 43
    Technology Transfer Subindex Rank
        (out of 51 technological non-core economies) 15

Public Institutions Index Rank **41**
    Corruption Subindex Rank 45
    Contracts and Law Subindex Rank......................................38

Macroeconomic Environment Index Rank................................**50**
    Macroeconomic Stability Subindex Rank 48
    Country Credit Rating Rank 32

Current Competitiveness Rank	41

Sophistication of Company Operations and Strategy Rank..................**55**
Quality of the Business Environment Rank..**40**

National competitiveness balance sheet

NOTABLE COMPETITIVE ADVANTAGES

Criteria	Rank

Growth Competitiveness

Technology Transfer

3.04	FDI and Technology Transfer	8

Macroeconomic Environment

2.03	Access to Credit	15

Current Competitiveness (using GCR 2000 results)

Sophistication of Company Operations and Strategy

10.14	Extent of Incentive Compensation	25
10.05	Uniqueness of Product Designs	38
10.07	Extent of Marketing	39

Quality of the Business Environment

6.10	Extent of Bureaucratic Red Tape	1
2.08	Ease of Access to Loans	9
4.01	Speed and Cost of Internet Access	16

Other Indicators

Technology

3.14	Minorities in the Economy	3

Infrastructure

5.11	Electricity Prices	17

Public Institutions

8.05	Permits to Start a Firm	5
8.04	Administrative Burden for Start-Ups	18
8.06	Days to Start a Firm	19
6.09	Minimum Wage Enforcement	25

Macroeconomic Environment

2.15	Access to Bond Markets	18
2.27	Investment Rate	19
2.19	Permits to Export	22
2.13	Entry into Banking Industry	23

Company Practices

10.23	Pay and Productivity	23

NOTABLE COMPETITIVE DISADVANTAGES

Criteria	Rank

Growth Competitiveness

Information and Communications Technology

4.08	Government Prioritization of ICT	68
4.12	Legal Framework for ICT Development	64
4.09	Government Success in ICT Promotion	61

Macroeconomic Environment

2.28	Inflation	64

Current Competitiveness (using GCR 2000 results)

Sophistication of Company Operations and Strategy

10.02	Value Chain Presence	70
10.11	Breadth of International Markets	69
10.01	Nature of Competitive Advantage	67

Quality of the Business Environment

5.04	Road Infrastructure Quality	75
5.07	Air Transport Infrastructure Quality	68
9.01	Buyer Sophistication	64

Other Indicators

Technology

4.01	Speed and Cost of Internet Access	69

Macroeconomic Environment

2.10	Access to Foreign Capital Markets	69
2.04	Exchange Rate and Exports	67
2.22	Extent of Distortive Government Subsidies	66
2.33	Value Added Tax Rate	65
1.08	Unemployment Rate, 2000	62

Company Practices

10.22	Union Contributions to Productivity	66
10.21	Cooperation in Labor-Employer Relations	65
10.19	Hiring and Firing Practices	63

Portugal

Key Facts

GDP per capita at Purchasing Power Parity, 2000 ....$16,882
GDP per capita Rank 27
Percentage Growth in Real GDP per capita, 1999–2000 ....3.0
Growth Rank 42
US Utility Patents Granted in 2000 (per million population).........1.1
Patent Rank...37

Growth Competitiveness Rank	25

Technology Index Rank..**25**
    ICT Subindex Rank 25
    Innovation Subindex Rank 31
    Technology Transfer Subindex Rank
       (out of 51 technological non-core economies) 13
Public Institutions Index Rank **25**
    Corruption Subindex Rank 28
    Contracts and Law Subindex Rank..25
Macroeconomic Environment Index Rank...................................**35**
    Macroeconomic Stability Subindex Rank 33
    Country Credit Rating Rank 19

Current Competitiveness Rank	31

Sophistication of Company Operations and Strategy Rank.................**38**
Quality of the Business Environment Rank..**29**

National competitiveness balance sheet

NOTABLE COMPETITIVE ADVANTAGES

Criteria	Rank

Growth Competitiveness

Information and Communications Technology

4.14	Internet Users	2

Current Competitiveness

Quality of the Business Environment

2.08	Ease of Access to Loans	18
2.18	Hidden Trade Barriers	24
2.16	Local Equity Market Access	25

Other Indicators

Macroeconomic Environment

2.15	Access to Bond Markets	5
2.27	Investment Rate	7

NOTABLE COMPETITIVE DISADVANTAGES

Criteria	Rank

Growth Competitiveness

Innovation

3.02	Firm-Level Innovation	60
3.06	Company Spending on Research and Development	51
3.01	Technological Sophistication	46

Macroeconomic Environment

2.26	National Savings Rate	55
2.01	Recession Expectations	47

Current Competitiveness

Sophistication of Company Operations and Strategy

10.13	Willingness to Delegate Authority	58
10.02	Value Chain Presence	53
10.12	Extent of Staff Training	47

Quality of the Business Environment

10.17	Efficacy of Corporate Boards	53
3.05	Quality of Scientific Research Institutions	42
9.03	Local Supplier Quality	42

Other Indicators

Technology

3.14	Minorities in the Economy	60
3.03	Firm-Level Technology Absorption	59
3.11	Availability of Scientists and Engineers	50

Infrastructure

5.11	Electricity Prices	62
5.06	Port Infrastructure Quality	44
5.14	Difference in Quality of Healthcare	44
5.05	Railroad Infrastructure Development	41

Public Institutions

6.06	Competence of Public Officials	62
6.13	Unreported Profits and Wages	60
6.08	Burden of Regulation	58
8.06	Days to Start a Firm	54
6.11	Tax Evasion	46
6.14	Informal Sector	42

Macroeconomic Environment

2.20	Composition of Public Spending	60
2.22	Extent of Distortive Government Subsidies	51
2.06	Exchange Rate Premium	44
2.32	Corporate Income Tax Rate	41
2.33	Value Added Tax Rate	41

Company Practices

10.19	Hiring and Firing Practices	61
10.23	Pay and Productivity	60
10.20	Employment Rules	55
10.22	Union Contributions to Productivity	51
10.15	Reliance on Professional Management	50
10.21	Cooperation in Labor-Employer Relations	40

Romania

Key Facts

GDP per capita at Purchasing Power Parity, 2000 ....$6,309
GDP per capita Rank 49
Percentage Growth in Real GDP per capita, 1999–2000 ....2.3
Growth Rank 55
US Utility Patents Granted in 2000 (per million population)..........0.2
Patent Rank 52

Growth Competitiveness Rank	56

Technology Index Rank...**47**
    ICT Subindex Rank 59
    Innovation Subindex Rank 53
    Technology Transfer Subindex Rank
      (out of 51 technological non-core economies) 12
Public Institutions Index Rank **52**
    Corruption Subindex Rank 64
    Contracts and Law Subindex Rank.........................39
Macroeconomic Environment Index Rank....................................**67**
    Macroeconomic Stability Subindex Rank 56
    Country Credit Rating Rank 66

Current Competitiveness Rank	61

Sophistication of Company Operations and Strategy Rank..................**63**
Quality of the Business Environment Rank..**61**

292

National competitiveness balance sheet

NOTABLE COMPETITIVE ADVANTAGES		NOTABLE COMPETITIVE DISADVANTAGES	
Criteria	Rank	Criteria	Rank
Growth Competitiveness		**Growth Competitiveness**	
Innovation		**Innovation**	
3.02 Firm-Level Innovation	2	3.09 University/Industry Research Collaboration	75
Information and Communications Technology		3.06 Company Spending on Research and Development	74
4.14 Internet Users	43	3.01 Technological Sophistication	72
Technology Transfer		**Information and Communications Technology**	
3.04 FDI and Technology Transfer	12	4.08 Government Prioritization of ICT	75
3.23 Skill-Based Exports	30	4.09 Government Success in ICT Promotion	75
Corruption		4.11 Laws Relating to ICT Use	75
7.03 Irregular Payments in Tax Collection	28	4.12 Legal Framework for ICT Development	75
Law and Contracts		4.03 Internet Access in Schools	74
6.12 Organized Crime	25	4.07 Quality of Competition in ISP Sector	66
6.04 Favoritism in Decisions of Government Officials	27	**Corruption**	
Macroeconomic Environment		7.01 Irregular Payments in Exports & Imports	72
2.01 Recession Expectations	13	7.02 Irregular Payments in Government Procurement	71
2.03 Access to Credit	13	**Macroeconomic Environment**	
Potential for "Catch-up" Growth	27	2.28 Inflation	72
		2.30 Interest Rate Spread	66
Current Competitiveness		**Current Competitiveness**	
Sophistication of Company Operations and Strategy		**Sophistication of Company Operations and Strategy**	
10.08 Degree of Customer Orientation	19	10.09 Control of International Distribution	75
10.15 Reliance on Professional Management	19	10.10 Extent of Regional Sales	74
10.03 Extent of Branding	33	10.14 Extent of Incentive Compensation	74
Quality of the Business Environment		**Quality of the Business Environment**	
3.11 Availability of Scientists and Engineers	1	2.09 Venture Capital Availability	75
10.17 Efficacy of Corporate Boards	12	8.01 Intensity of Local Competition	75
5.12 Quality of Public Schools	28	9.11 Local Availability of Information Technology Services	74
Other Indicators		**Other Indicators**	
Technology		**Technology**	
3.14 Minorities in the Economy	2	3.07 Subsidies for Firm-Level Research and Development	75
3.13 Women in the Economy	6	3.08 Tax Credits for Firm-Level Research and Development	75
Public Institutions		4.05 High Skilled IT Job Market	75
6.09 Minimum Wage Enforcement	8	4.06 IT Training and Education	75
8.06 Days to Start a Firm	8	4.10 Government On-line Services	74
6.07 Costs of Institutional Change	23	4.02 Public Access to Internet	71
Macroeconomic Environment		**Infrastructure**	
2.13 Entry into Banking Industry	5	5.04 Road Infrastructure Quality	75
2.21 Social Transfer Recipients	5	5.10 Postal Efficiency	75
2.06 Exchange Rate Premium	6	**Public Institutions**	
2.11 Foreign Access to Local Capital Markets	7	6.13 Unreported Profits and Wages	75
2.05 Expected Exchange Rate Volatility	17	6.08 Burden of Regulation	73
2.19 Permits to Export	22	6.14 Informal Sector	71
Company Practices		**Macroeconomic Environment**	
10.19 Hiring and Firing Practices	1	2.08 Ease of Access to Loans	75
10.20 Employment Rules	1	2.22 Extent of Distortive Government Subsidies	75
10.22 Union Contributions to Productivity	21	2.17 Sources of Investment Finance	74
10.23 Pay and Productivity	27	2.07 Financial Market Sophistication	71

293

Russian Federation

Key Facts

GDP per capita at Purchasing Power Parity, 2000 ....$8,213
GDP per capita Rank 43
Percentage Growth in Real GDP per capita, 1999–2000 ....7.7
Growth Rank 5
US Utility Patents Granted in 2000 (per million population).........1.3
Patent Rank 35

Growth Competitiveness Rank	63

Technology Index Rank..**60**
    ICT Subindex Rank 54
    Innovation Subindex Rank 28
    Technology Transfer Subindex Rank
      (out of 51 technological non-core economies) 49

Public Institutions Index Rank **61**
    Corruption Subindex Rank 53
    Contracts and Law Subindex Rank............................66

Macroeconomic Environment Index Rank...................................**57**
    Macroeconomic Stability Subindex Rank 30
    Country Credit Rating Rank 68

Current Competitiveness Rank	58

Sophistication of Company Operations and Strategy Rank..................**54**
Quality of the Business Environment Rank..**56**

National competitiveness balance sheet

NOTABLE COMPETITIVE ADVANTAGES

Criteria	Rank

Growth Competitiveness

Innovation
3.19	Tertiary Enrollment	19
3.16	Utility Patents in 2000	35
3.06	Company Spending on Research and Development	36

Information and Communications Technology
4.16	Telephone Lines	43

Corruption
7.03	Irregular Payments in Tax Collection	44

Law and Contracts
6.04	Favoritism in Decisions of Government Officials	29

Macroeconomic Environment
2.26	National Savings Rate	4
2.24	Government Surplus/Deficit	6
2.29	Real Exchange Rate	10
2.03	Access to Credit	31
	Potential for "Catch-up" Growth	33
2.01	Recession Expectations	40

Current Competitiveness

Sophistication of Company Operations and Strategy
10.05	Uniqueness of Product Designs	18
10.02	Value Chain Presence	24
10.04	Capacity for Innovation	24

Quality of the Business Environment
9.09	Local Availability of Process Machinery	9
9.10	Local Availability of Specialized Research and Training Services	16
9.07	Extent of Product and Process Collaboration	17

Other Indicators

Technology
3.08	Tax Credits for Firm-Level Research and Development	29
3.11	Availability of Scientists and Engineers	31
3.05	Quality of Scientific Research Institutions	33
3.14	Minorities in the Economy	33
3.07	Subsidies for Firm-Level Research and Development	34

Infrastructure
5.11	Electricity Prices	15
5.05	Railroad Infrastructure Development	17

Public Institutions
6.06	Competence of Public Officials	8
8.06	Days to Start a Firm	18
6.08	Burden of Regulation	27
6.04	Favoritism in Decisions of Government Officials	29

Macroeconomic Environment
1.09	Employment to Population Ratio, 2000	10

Company Practices
10.19	Hiring and Firing Practices	10
10.23	Pay and Productivity	14

NOTABLE COMPETITIVE DISADVANTAGES

Criteria	Rank

Growth Competitiveness

Innovation
3.02	Firm-Level Innovation	70

Information and Communications Technology
4.11	Laws Relating to ICT Use	72
4.12	Legal Framework for ICT Development	72
4.03	Internet Access in Schools	66
4.13	Cellular Telephones	66

Technology Transfer
3.04	FDI and Technology Transfer	73

Law and Contracts
6.02	Property Rights	75
6.12	Organized Crime	68

Macroeconomic Environment
2.28	Inflation	70
2.30	Interest Rate Spread	70

Current Competitiveness

Sophistication of Company Operations and Strategy
10.07	Extent of Marketing	73
10.12	Extent of Staff Training	70
10.06	Production Process Sophistication	63

Quality of the Business Environment
6.03	Intellectual Property Protection	73
2.07	Financial Market Sophistication	69
2.18	Hidden Trade Barriers	68

Other Indicators

Technology
4.02	Public Access to Internet	70
4.06	IT Training and Education	66

Infrastructure
5.02	Tap Water Safety	69

Public Institutions
6.13	Unreported Profits and Wages	70
6.11	Tax Evasion	69

Macroeconomic Environment
2.11	Foreign Access to Local Capital Markets	71
2.14	Financial Regulation and Supervision	71
2.15	Access to Bond Markets	71
2.10	Access to Foreign Capital Markets	70
2.21	Social Transfer Recipients	68
2.31	Average Tariff Rate	66

Company Practices
10.14	Extent of Incentive Compensation	67

295

Singapore

Key Facts

GDP per capita at Purchasing Power Parity, 2000 ....$23,000
GDP per capita Rank 20
Percentage Growth in Real GDP per capita, 1999–2000 ....8.5
Growth Rank 2
US Utility Patents Granted in 2000 (per million population)........54.3
Patent Rank 19

Growth Competitiveness Rank	4

Technology Index Rank...**18**
    ICT Subindex Rank 4
    Innovation Subindex Rank 19
Public Institutions Index Rank **6**
    Corruption Subindex Rank 5
    Contracts and Law Subindex Rank...7
Macroeconomic Environment Index Rank..**1**
    Macroeconomic Stability Subindex Rank 1
    Country Credit Rating Rank 15

Current Competitiveness Rank	10

Sophistication of Company Operations and Strategy Rank.................**15**
Quality of the Business Environment Rank..**9**

296

National competitiveness balance sheet

NOTABLE COMPETITIVE ADVANTAGES

Criteria	Rank

Growth Competitiveness

Innovation

3.09	University/Industry Research Collaboration	3
3.02	Firm-Level Innovation	5

Information and Communications Technology

4.08	Government Prioritization of ICT	1
4.09	Government Success in ICT Promotion	1
4.03	Internet Access in Schools	2
4.11	Laws Relating to ICT Use	2
4.12	Legal Framework for ICT Development	2
4.17	Personal Computers	4
4.13	Cellular Telephones	9

Technology Transfer

3.04	FDI and Technology Transfer	1
3.23	Skill-Based Exports	1

Corruption

7.01	Irregular Payments in Exports & Imports	4
7.02	Irregular Payments in Government Procurement	6
7.03	Irregular Payments in Tax Collection	7

Law and Contracts

6.04	Favoritism in Decisions of Government Officials	4
6.12	Organized Crime	4
6.02	Property Rights	6

Macroeconomic Environment

2.26	National Savings Rate	1
2.24	Government Surplus/Deficit	5
2.03	Access to Credit	9

Current Competitiveness

Sophistication of Company Operations and Strategy

10.14	Extent of Incentive Compensation	7
10.12	Extent of Staff Training	10
3.06	Company Spending on Research and Development	11

Quality of the Business Environment

2.22	Extent of Distortive Government Subsidies	1
3.10	Government Procurement of Advanced Technology Products	1
10.21	Cooperation in Labor-Employer Relations	1

Other Indicators

Technology

3.07	Subsidies for Firm-Level Research and Development	1

Infrastructure

5.06	Port Infrastructure Quality	1
5.07	Air Transport Infrastructure Quality	1

Public Institutions

6.06	Competence of Public Officials	1
6.11	Tax Evasion	1
6.14	Informal Sector	1
8.05	Permits to Start a Firm	1

NOTABLE COMPETITIVE DISADVANTAGES

Criteria	Rank

Growth Competitiveness

Innovation

3.19	Tertiary Enrollment	28
3.16	Utility Patents in 2000	19

Information and Communications Technology

4.07	Quality of Competition in ISP Sector	21
4.16	Telephone Lines	20

Law and Contracts

6.01	Judicial Independence	22

Macroeconomic Environment

2.29	Real Exchange Rate	40
2.30	Interest Rate Spread	25
2.01	Recession Expectations	24

Current Competitiveness

Sophistication of Company Operations and Strategy

10.05	Uniqueness of Product Designs	34
10.04	Capacity for Innovation	26
10.03	Extent of Branding	23

Quality of the Business Environment

8.02	Extent of Locally Based Competitors	45
9.09	Local Availability of Process Machinery	41
9.07	Extent of Product and Process Collaboration	32

Other Indicators

Infrastructure

5.11	Electricity Prices	49
5.04	Road Infrastructure Quality	40

Public Institutions

6.09	Minimum Wage Enforcement	49

Macroeconomic Environment

2.13	Entry into Banking Industry	63
2.04	Exchange Rate and Exports	42
2.21	Social Transfer Recipients	38
2.11	Foreign Access to Local Capital Markets	35

Slovak Republic

Key Facts

GDP per capita at Purchasing Power Parity, 2000 ....$11,035
GDP per capita Rank 32
Percentage Growth in Real GDP per capita, 1999–2000 ....2.1
Growth Rank 57
US Utility Patents Granted in 2000 (per million population)..........0.7
Patent Rank 41

Growth Competitiveness Rank	40

Technology Index Rank...**29**
    ICT Subindex Rank 31
    Innovation Subindex Rank 44
    Technology Transfer Subindex Rank
      (out of 51 technological non-core economies) 6
Public Institutions Index Rank **38**
    Corruption Subindex Rank 33
    Contracts and Law Subindex Rank.......................46
Macroeconomic Environment Index Rank...................................**64**
    Macroeconomic Stability Subindex Rank 47
    Country Credit Rating Rank 45

Current Competitiveness Rank	39

Sophistication of Company Operations and Strategy Rank.................**57**
Quality of the Business Environment Rank..**36**

National competitiveness balance sheet

NOTABLE COMPETITIVE ADVANTAGES

Criteria	Rank

Growth Competitiveness

Innovation
3.09 University/Industry Research Collaboration 22

Information and Communications Technology
4.12 Legal Framework for ICT Development..........................22

Technology Transfer
3.23 Skill-Based Exports...12
3.04 FDI and Technology Transfer.................................14

Macroeconomic Environment
2.26 National Savings Rate 21
2.01 Recession Expectations 25

Current Competitiveness

Sophistication of Company Operations and Strategy
10.14 Extent of Incentive Compensation...........................32
10.15 Reliance on Professional Management 34

Quality of the Business Environment
3.11 Availability of Scientists and Engineers....................3
5.12 Quality of Public Schools 5
9.04 Presence of Demanding Regulatory Standards 20

Other Indicators

Technology
3.13 Women in the Economy 2
3.14 Minorities in the Economy 17

Infrastructure
5.03 Industrial Water Availability 1
5.13 Difference in Quality of Schools 4
5.02 Tap Water Safety...15
5.14 Difference in Quality of Healthcare........................16
5.11 Electricity Prices...18
5.08 Telephone/Fax Infrastructure Quality 23

Public Institutions
8.06 Days to Start a Firm 19

Macroeconomic Environment
2.19 Permits to Export 1
2.27 Investment Rate...5
2.17 Sources of Investment Finance 12
2.31 Average Tariff Rate..15
2.20 Composition of Public Spending 16
2.04 Exchange Rate and Exports 21
2.32 Corporate Income Tax Rate..................................21
2.21 Social Transfer Recipients 23
2.12 Perceived Interest Rate Gap 25

NOTABLE COMPETITIVE DISADVANTAGES

Criteria	Rank

Growth Competitiveness

Innovation
3.02 Firm-Level Innovation......................................64

Law and Contracts
6.12 Organized Crime 61

Macroeconomic Environment
2.28 Inflation..68

Current Competitiveness

Sophistication of Company Operations and Strategy
10.11 Breadth of International Markets 71
10.08 Degree of Customer Orientation 70
10.12 Extent of Staff Training..................................64

Quality of the Business Environment
5.07 Air Transport Infrastructure Quality 75
8.04 Administrative Burden for Start-Ups 72
2.16 Local Equity Market Access.................................71

Other Indicators

Public Institutions
6.10 Extent of Bureaucratic Red Tape 71
6.06 Competence of Public Officials.............................69
6.13 Unreported Profits and Wages...............................69
6.07 Costs of Institutional Change..............................63

Macroeconomic Environment
2.33 Value Added Tax Rate 68
1.08 Unemployment Rate, 2000....................................67
2.15 Access to Bond Markets.....................................66
2.07 Financial Market Sophistication............................62

Company Practices
10.22 Union Contributions to Productivity 75
10.21 Cooperation in Labor-Employer Relations 70
10.13 Willingness to Delegate Authority 65

299

Slovenia

Key Facts

GDP per capita at Purchasing Power Parity, 2000 ....$17,127
GDP per capita Rank 26
Percentage Growth in Real GDP per capita, 1999–2000 ....5.0
Growth Rank 17
US Utility Patents Granted in 2000 (per million population)..........8.0
Patent Rank 25

Growth Competitiveness Rank	31

Technology Index Rank..**30**
    ICT Subindex Rank 28
    Innovation Subindex Rank 27
    Technology Transfer Subindex Rank
        (out of 51 technological non-core economies) 14
Public Institutions Index Rank **30**
    Corruption Subindex Rank 31
    Contracts and Law Subindex Rank..36
Macroeconomic Environment Index Rank.....................................**39**
    Macroeconomic Stability Subindex Rank 32
    Country Credit Rating Rank 27

Current Competitiveness Rank	32

Sophistication of Company Operations and Strategy Rank.................**28**
Quality of the Business Environment Rank..**35**

National competitiveness balance sheet

NOTABLE COMPETITIVE ADVANTAGES

Criteria	Rank

Growth Competitiveness

Technology Transfer
3.23 Skill-Based Exports..7

Macroeconomic Environment
2.03 Access to Credit...14
2.29 Real Exchange Rate 15

Current Competitiveness

Sophistication of Company Operations and Strategy
10.09 Control of International Distribution 21
10.04 Capacity for Innovation..25
10.10 Extent of Regional Sales 31

Quality of the Business Environment
6.10 Extent of Bureaucratic Red Tape 20
5.12 Quality of Public Schools 21
2.18 Hidden Trade Barriers..28

Other Indicators

Technology
3.14 Minorities in the Economy 15

Infrastructure
5.13 Difference in Quality of Schools 10

Public Institutions
6.06 Competence of Public Officials..12

Macroeconomic Environment
2.32 Corporate Income Tax Rate..7
2.27 Investment Rate..12

NOTABLE COMPETITIVE DISADVANTAGES

Criteria	Rank

Growth Competitiveness

Innovation
3.02 Firm-Level Innovation..58

Information and Communications Technology
4.08 Government Prioritization of ICT.....................................58
4.07 Quality of Competition in ISP Sector 54

Technology Transfer
3.04 FDI and Technology Transfer...68

Macroeconomic Environment
2.28 Inflation...58

Current Competitiveness

Sophistication of Company Operations and Strategy
10.14 Extent of Incentive Compensation..................................52
10.07 Extent of Marketing 50
10.06 Production Process Sophistication....................................37

Quality of the Business Environment
9.06 State of Cluster Development 69
2.07 Financial Market Sophistication.......................................51
2.09 Venture Capital Availability 41

Other Indicators

Technology
4.04 Quality of Competition in Telecommunication Sector.....55
3.03 Firm-Level Technology Absorption 48

Infrastructure
5.07 Air Transport Infrastructure Quality 51

Public Institutions
6.13 Unreported Profits and Wages.......................................59
8.06 Days to Start a Firm 54
7.05 Irregular Payments in Loan Applications.........................47

Macroeconomic Environment
2.11 Foreign Access to Local Capital Markets.......................69
2.10 Access to Foreign Capital Markets 59
2.13 Entry into Banking Industry..59
2.17 Sources of Investment Finance 56
2.33 Value Added Tax Rate 53
2.16 Local Equity Market Access...52
2.31 Average Tariff Rate...52
2.04 Exchange Rate and Exports 50
2.15 Access to Bond Markets..48
2.12 Perceived Interest Rate Gap 47
1.09 Employment to Population Ratio, 2000 46

Company Practices
10.19 Hiring and Firing Practices 66
10.20 Employment Rules..57
10.21 Cooperation in Labor-Employer Relations.......................55
10.15 Reliance on Professional Management 47

South Africa

Key Facts

GDP per capita at Purchasing Power Parity, 2000 ....$9,189
GDP per capita Rank 35
Percentage Growth in Real GDP per capita, 1999–2000 ....1.1
Growth Rank 63
US Utility Patents Granted in 2000 (per million population)..........2.5
Patent Rank 29

Growth Competitiveness Rank	34

Technology Index Rank..**46**
    ICT Subindex Rank 40
    Innovation Subindex Rank 40
    Technology Transfer Subindex Rank
       (out of 51 technological non-core economies) 28

Public Institutions Index Rank **35**
    Corruption Subindex Rank 32
    Contracts and Law Subindex Rank..40

Macroeconomic Environment Index Rank................................**27**
    Macroeconomic Stability Subindex Rank 28
    Country Credit Rating Rank 40

Current Competitiveness Rank	25

Sophistication of Company Operations and Strategy Rank.................**25**
Quality of the Business Environment Rank..**27**

302

National competitiveness balance sheet

NOTABLE COMPETITIVE ADVANTAGES	
Criteria	**Rank**

Growth Competitiveness

Macroeconomic Environment

2.29	Real Exchange Rate	2

Current Competitiveness

Sophistication of Company Operations and Strategy

10.14	Extent of Incentive Compensation	14
10.07	Extent of Marketing	20
3.06	Company Spending on Research and Development	22

Quality of the Business Environment

5.04	Road Infrastructure Quality	3
2.07	Financial Market Sophistication	16
6.01	Judicial Independence	20

Other Indicators

Infrastructure

5.11	Electricity Prices	1

Macroeconomic Environment

2.21	Social Transfer Recipients	1
2.04	Exchange Rate and Exports	3
2.16	Local Equity Market Access	7

NOTABLE COMPETITIVE DISADVANTAGES	
Criteria	**Rank**

Growth Competitiveness

Innovation

3.19	Tertiary Enrollment	53

Information and Communications Technology

4.16	Telephone Lines	53
4.03	Internet Access in Schools	49

Law and Contracts

6.12	Organized Crime	70

Macroeconomic Environment

2.26	National Savings Rate	59
2.28	Inflation	51

Current Competitiveness

Sophistication of Company Operations and Strategy

10.08	Degree of Customer Orientation	63

Quality of the Business Environment

10.21	Cooperation in Labor-Employer Relations	71
3.11	Availability of Scientists and Engineers	67
5.12	Quality of Public Schools	53

Other Indicators

Technology

3.13	Women in the Economy	68
4.04	Quality of Competition in Telecommunication Sector	65
3.12	Brain Drain	64
4.02	Public Access to Internet	57

Infrastructure

5.14	Difference in Quality of Healthcare	70
5.13	Difference in Quality of Schools	64
5.15	Public Health Agencies	63
5.08	Telephone/Fax Infrastructure Quality	55

Public Institutions

6.06	Competence of Public Officials	71

Macroeconomic Environment

1.08	Unemployment Rate, 2000	71
1.09	Employment to Population Ratio, 2000	71
2.27	Investment Rate	71
2.05	Expected Exchange Rate Volatility	70
2.10	Access to Foreign Capital Markets	65
2.31	Average Tariff Rate	61

Company Practices

10.19	Hiring and Firing Practices	69
10.23	Pay and Productivity	62
10.20	Employment Rules	59
10.22	Union Contributions to Productivity	53

303

Spain

Key Facts

National competitiveness balance sheet

NOTABLE COMPETITIVE ADVANTAGES

Criteria	Rank

Growth Competitiveness

Innovation
3.19 Tertiary Enrollment 10

Information and Communications Technology
4.08 Government Prioritization of ICT 6

Macroeconomic Environment
2.29 Real Exchange Rate 5
2.03 Access to Credit..6
2.30 Interest Rate Spread 7

Current Competitiveness

Sophistication of Company Operations and Strategy
10.14 Extent of Incentive Compensation...................................13
10.03 Extent of Branding 15
10.07 Extent of Marketing 16

Quality of the Business Environment
8.02 Extent of Locally Based Competitors..............................3
10.16 Quality of Management Schools.....................................5
9.02 Local Supplier Quantity 10

Other Indicators

Infrastructure
5.04 Road Infrastructure Quality 7

Public Institutions
6.08 Burden of Regulation 6
7.07 Public Trust of Politicians 9

Macroeconomic Environment
2.17 Sources of Investment Finance 4
2.20 Composition of Public Spending 6

NOTABLE COMPETITIVE DISADVANTAGES

Criteria	Rank

Growth Competitiveness

Innovation
3.02 Firm-Level Innovation...40

Technology Transfer
3.04 FDI and Technology Transfer...39

Current Competitiveness

Sophistication of Company Operations and Strategy
10.09 Control of International Distribution 29
10.13 Willingness to Delegate Authority 25
3.06 Company Spending on Research and Development 24

Quality of the Business Environment
8.04 Administrative Burden for Start-Ups 39
9.06 State of Cluster Development 38
4.01 Speed and Cost of Internet Access 24

Other Indicators

Technology
3.14 Minorities in the Economy 71
3.13 Women in the Economy 53

Infrastructure
5.11 Electricity Prices...40

Public Institutions
8.05 Permits to Start a Firm...55
8.06 Days to Start a Firm 54

Macroeconomic Environment
1.08 Unemployment Rate, 2000..61
1.09 Employment to Population Ratio, 2000 57
2.32 Corporate Income Tax Rate..50
2.19 Permits to Export 46
2.16 Local Equity Market Access...38
2.33 Value Added Tax Rate 37

Company Practices
10.19 Hiring and Firing Practices 49
10.20 Employment Rules...44
10.23 Pay and Productivity..42
10.21 Cooperation in Labor-Employer Relations 38

Sri Lanka

Key Facts

GDP per capita at Purchasing Power Parity, 2000 ....$3,512
GDP per capita Rank 65
Percentage Growth in Real GDP per capita, 1999–2000 ....4.9
Growth Rank 18
US Utility Patents Granted in 2000 (per million population)..........0.1
Patent Rank 61

Growth Competitiveness Rank	61

Technology Index Rank..**59**
    ICT Subindex Rank 69
    Innovation Subindex Rank 69
    Technology Transfer Subindex Rank
        (out of 51 technological non-core economies) 18

Public Institutions Index Rank **58**
    Corruption Subindex Rank 62
    Contracts and Law Subindex Rank..52

Macroeconomic Environment Index Rank................................**60**
    Macroeconomic Stability Subindex Rank 61
    Country Credit Rating Rank 59

Current Competitiveness Rank	57

Sophistication of Company Operations and Strategy Rank.................**58**

Quality of the Business Environment Rank...............................**55**

National competitiveness balance sheet

NOTABLE COMPETITIVE ADVANTAGES

Criteria	Rank

Growth Competitiveness

Technology Transfer
3.23   Skill-Based Exports 21

Law and Contracts
6.01   Judicial Independence....................................43

Macroeconomic Environment
      Potential for "Catch-up" Growth 11
2.30   Interest Rate Spread 41
2.26   National Savings Rate 43

Current Competitiveness

Sophistication of Company Operations and Strategy
10.11   Breadth of International Markets 40
10.08   Degree of Customer Orientation 48
10.12   Extent of Staff Training...................................52

Quality of the Business Environment
8.04   Administrative Burden for Start-Ups 24
2.09   Venture Capital Availability 36
2.08   Ease of Access to Loans...............................40

Other Indicators

Technology
3.14   Minorities in the Economy 22
3.13   Women in the Economy 38
4.04   Quality of Competition in Telecommunication Sector.....42

Infrastructure
5.14   Difference in Quality of Healthcare.................38

Public Institutions
8.05   Permits to Start a Firm......................................1
6.08   Burden of Regulation 11
8.06   Days to Start a Firm 19
7.04   Irregular Payments in Public Contracts..........36
6.10   Extent of Bureaucratic Red Tape 37
6.14   Informal Sector..44

Macroeconomic Environment
2.19   Permits to Export 1
2.27   Investment Rate..8
2.04   Exchange Rate and Exports 11
2.33   Value Added Tax Rate 24
2.22   Extent of Distortive Government Subsidies....30
1.08   Unemployment Rate, 2000.............................33
2.02   Soundness of Banks 35
2.13   Entry into Banking Industry............................35
2.17   Sources of Investment Finance 35

Company Practices
10.20   Employment Rules...33

NOTABLE COMPETITIVE DISADVANTAGES

Criteria	Rank

Growth Competitiveness

Innovation
3.19   Tertiary Enrollment 73

Information and Communications Technology
4.17   Personal Computers.......................................72
4.16   Telephone Lines 67
4.15   Internet Hosts 66

Macroeconomic Environment
2.24   Government Surplus/Deficit............................71

Current Competitiveness

Sophistication of Company Operations and Strategy
10.02   Value Chain Presence....................................60
10.05   Uniqueness of Product Designs 58
10.09   Control of International Distribution 56

Quality of the Business Environment
5.04   Road Infrastructure Quality 72
10.21   Cooperation in Labor-Employer Relations......67
9.08   Local Availability of Components and Parts....66

Other Indicators

Technology
4.05   High Skilled IT Job Market..............................71
4.10   Government On-line Services 71
3.12   Brain Drain..68

Macroeconomic Environment
2.05   Expected Exchange Rate Volatility.................72
2.10   Access to Foreign Capital Markets 72

307

Sweden

Key Facts

GDP per capita at Purchasing Power Parity, 2000 ....$23,884
GDP per capita Rank 17
Percentage Growth in Real GDP per capita, 1999–2000 ....3.4
Growth Rank 33
US Utility Patents Granted in 2000 (per million population)......177.2
Patent Rank 5

Growth Competitiveness Rank	9

Technology Index Rank..**6**
    ICT Subindex Rank 3
    Innovation Subindex Rank 9
Public Institutions Index Rank **7**
    Corruption Subindex Rank 7
    Contracts and Law Subindex Rank.......................10
Macroeconomic Environment Index Rank............................**29**
    Macroeconomic Stability Subindex Rank 5
    Country Credit Rating Rank 14

Current Competitiveness Rank	6

Sophistication of Company Operations and Strategy Rank...................**6**
Quality of the Business Environment Rank...**6**

308

National competitiveness balance sheet

NOTABLE COMPETITIVE ADVANTAGES

Criteria	Rank

Growth Competitiveness

Innovation

3.09	University/Industry Research Collaboration	2
3.01	Technological Sophistication	4
3.16	Utility Patents in 2000	5
3.06	Company Spending on Research and Development	6

Information and Communications Technology

4.17	Personal Computers	1
4.11	Laws Relating to ICT Use	3
4.03	Internet Access in Schools	4
4.07	Quality of Competition in ISP Sector	4
4.08	Government Prioritization of ICT	4
4.12	Legal Framework for ICT Development	4
4.14	Internet Users	4
4.16	Telephone Lines	5
4.13	Cellular Telephones	6
4.09	Government Success in ICT Promotion	8
4.15	Internet Hosts	9

Corruption

7.02	Irregular Payments in Government Procurement	5
7.03	Irregular Payments in Tax Collection	5

Law and Contracts

6.01	Judicial Independence	6
6.04	Favoritism in Decisions of Government Officials	9

Macroeconomic Environment

2.29	Real Exchange Rate	4
2.24	Government Surplus/Deficit	7
2.28	Inflation	8

Current Competitiveness

Sophistication of Company Operations and Strategy

10.13	Willingness to Delegate Authority	1
10.12	Extent of Staff Training	3
10.05	Uniqueness of Product Designs	4

Quality of the Business Environment

2.08	Ease of Access to Loans	1
2.09	Venture Capital Availability	3
11.06	Stringency of Environmental Regulations	5

Other Indicators

Technology

4.04	Quality of Competition in Telecommunication Sector	2
4.01	Speed and Cost of Internet Access	3
4.06	IT Training and Education	4

Infrastructure

5.08	Telephone/Fax Infrastructure Quality	2
5.11	Electricity Prices	2

Public Institutions

6.06	Competence of Public Officials	3
7.04	Irregular Payments in Public Contracts	3

NOTABLE COMPETITIVE DISADVANTAGES

Criteria	Rank

Growth Competitiveness

Macroeconomic Environment

2.01	Recession Expectations	39
2.26	National Savings Rate	39

Current Competitiveness

Quality of the Business Environment

8.02	Extent of Locally Based Competitors	53
9.09	Local Availability of Process Machinery	24
5.12	Quality of Public Schools	23

Other Indicators

Technology

3.14	Minorities in the Economy	55

Macroeconomic Environment

2.33	Value Added Tax Rate	72
2.27	Investment Rate	64
2.17	Sources of Investment Finance	58

Company Practices

10.19	Hiring and Firing Practices	67
10.20	Employment Rules	46

309

Switzerland

Key Facts

GDP per capita at Purchasing Power Parity, 2000 ....$28,518
GDP per capita Rank 5
Percentage Growth in Real GDP per capita, 1999–2000 ....2.8
Growth Rank 47
US Utility Patents Granted in 2000 (per million population)......182.1
Patent Rank 4

Growth Competitiveness Rank	15

Technology Index Rank...**24**
    ICT Subindex Rank 12
    Innovation Subindex Rank 22
Public Institutions Index Rank **13**
    Corruption Subindex Rank 20
    Contracts and Law Subindex Rank.........6
Macroeconomic Environment Index Rank.............................**3**
    Macroeconomic Stability Subindex Rank 6
    Country Credit Rating Rank 1

Current Competitiveness Rank	5

Sophistication of Company Operations and Strategy Rank...................**5**
Quality of the Business Environment Rank..**5**

National competitiveness balance sheet

NOTABLE COMPETITIVE ADVANTAGES

Criteria	Rank

Growth Competitiveness

Innovation

3.06	Company Spending on Research and Development	1
3.16	Utility Patents in 2000	4
3.01	Technological Sophistication	6
3.09	University/Industry Research Collaboration	8
3.02	Firm-Level Innovation	10

Information and Communications Technology

4.17	Personal Computers	2
4.16	Telephone Lines	3

Law and Contracts

6.02	Property Rights	3
6.01	Judicial Independence	4
6.12	Organized Crime	8

Macroeconomic Environment

2.01	Recession Expectations	5
2.30	Interest Rate Spread	5
2.26	National Savings Rate	6

Current Competitiveness

Sophistication of Company Operations and Strategy

10.01	Nature of Competitive Advantage	1
10.03	Extent of Branding	1
10.02	Value Chain Presence	2

Quality of the Business Environment

10.21	Cooperation in Labor-Employer Relations	2
2.07	Financial Market Sophistication	3
5.05	Railroad Infrastructure Development	3

Other Indicators

Technology

3.05	Quality of Scientific Research Institutions	3

Infrastructure

5.01	Overall Infrastructure Quality	1
5.12	Quality of Public Schools	1
5.15	Public Health Agencies	4

Public Institutions

6.05	Government Commitments	1
6.03	Intellectual Property Protection	2
7.07	Public Trust of Politicians	2
6.10	Extent of Bureaucratic Red Tape	3

Macroeconomic Environment

2.12	Perceived Interest Rate Gap	1
2.19	Permits to Export	1
1.08	Unemployment Rate, 2000	2
2.14	Financial Regulation and Supervision	3
2.31	Average Tariff Rate	3

NOTABLE COMPETITIVE DISADVANTAGES

Criteria	Rank

Growth Competitiveness

Innovation

3.19	Tertiary Enrollment	33

Information and Communications Technology

4.08	Government Prioritization of ICT	38

Macroeconomic Environment

2.03	Access to Credit	35
2.24	Government Surplus/Deficit	32

Current Competitiveness

Sophistication of Company Operations and Strategy

10.10	Extent of Regional Sales	13
10.15	Reliance on Professional Management	12
10.07	Extent of Marketing	7

Quality of the Business Environment

5.06	Port Infrastructure Quality	22
8.07	Effectiveness of Anti-Trust Policy	22
4.11	Laws Relating to ICT Use	18

Other Indicators

Technology

3.13	Women in the Economy	49
3.07	Subsidies for Firm-Level Research and Development	37
3.14	Minorities in the Economy	35

Infrastructure

5.11	Electricity Prices	56

Public Institutions

6.09	Minimum Wage Enforcement	54

Macroeconomic Environment

2.17	Sources of Investment Finance	61
2.27	Investment Rate	46
2.04	Exchange Rate and Exports	44
2.32	Corporate Income Tax Rate	41

Taiwan

Key Facts

GDP per capita at Purchasing Power Parity, 2000 ....$17,223
GDP per capita Rank 25
Percentage Growth in Real GDP per capita, 1999–2000 ....4.8
Growth Rank 19
US Utility Patents Granted in 2000 (per million population)......210.3
Patent Rank 3

Growth Competitiveness Rank	7

Technology Index Rank..**4**
    ICT Subindex Rank 16
    Innovation Subindex Rank 3
Public Institutions Index Rank **24**
    Corruption Subindex Rank 22
    Contracts and Law Subindex Rank..30
Macroeconomic Environment Index Rank..**15**
    Macroeconomic Stability Subindex Rank 27
    Country Credit Rating Rank 22

Current Competitiveness Rank	21

Sophistication of Company Operations and Strategy Rank.................**20**
Quality of the Business Environment Rank..**21**

National competitiveness balance sheet

NOTABLE COMPETITIVE ADVANTAGES

Criteria	Rank

Growth Competitiveness

Innovation

3.16	Utility Patents in 2000	3

Information and Communications Technology

4.13	Cellular Telephones	1
4.08	Government Prioritization of ICT	5
4.09	Government Success in ICT Promotion	5
4.03	Internet Access in Schools	10

Macroeconomic Environment

2.03	Access to Credit	2
2.28	Inflation	10

Current Competitiveness

Sophistication of Company Operations and Strategy

10.08	Degree of Customer Orientation	10
10.01	Nature of Competitive Advantage	16
10.06	Production Process Sophistication	19

Quality of the Business Environment

9.06	State of Cluster Development	2
3.10	Government Procurement of Advanced Technology Products	3
9.07	Extent of Product and Process Collaboration	5

Other Indicators

Technology

3.08	Tax Credits for Firm-Level Research and Development	3
3.07	Subsidies for Firm-Level Research and Development	7
3.03	Firm-Level Technology Absorption	8
3.12	Brain Drain	9

Public Institutions

8.05	Permits to Start a Firm	5
6.09	Minimum Wage Enforcement	10

Macroeconomic Environment

2.33	Value Added Tax Rate	4
1.08	Unemployment Rate, 2000	6
2.32	Corporate Income Tax Rate	7
2.22	Extent of Distortive Government Subsidies	8
2.20	Composition of Public Spending	10

Company Practices

10.23	Pay and Productivity	6

NOTABLE COMPETITIVE DISADVANTAGES

Criteria	Rank

Growth Competitiveness

Information and Communications Technology

4.12	Legal Framework for ICT Development	35
4.07	Quality of Competition in ISP Sector	32
4.11	Laws Relating to ICT Use	32
4.17	Personal Computers	23

Corruption

7.02	Irregular Payments in Government Procurement	24

Law and Contracts

6.01	Judicial Independence	40
6.12	Organized Crime	37
6.02	Property Rights	27
6.04	Favoritism in Decisions of Government Officials	23

Macroeconomic Environment

2.24	Government Surplus/Deficit	63
2.01	Recession Expectations	59
2.29	Real Exchange Rate	33
2.26	National Savings Rate	25

Current Competitiveness

Sophistication of Company Operations and Strategy

10.03	Extent of Branding	32
10.04	Capacity for Innovation	27
10.05	Uniqueness of Product Designs	25

Quality of the Business Environment

5.04	Road Infrastructure Quality	64
2.07	Financial Market Sophistication	28
4.01	Speed and Cost of Internet Access	25

Other Indicators

Infrastructure

5.03	Industrial Water Availability	52
5.02	Tap Water Safety	45
5.15	Public Health Agencies	39

Public Institutions

6.05	Government Commitments	66
6.07	Costs of Institutional Change	43
6.14	Informal Sector	35

Macroeconomic Environment

2.11	Foreign Access to Local Capital Markets	70
2.02	Soundness of Banks	53
2.10	Access to Foreign Capital Markets	49
2.13	Entry into Banking Industry	48
2.21	Social Transfer Recipients	45
2.14	Financial Regulation and Supervision	41
2.05	Expected Exchange Rate Volatility	38

Company Practices

10.20	Employment Rules	45

313

Thailand

Key Facts

GDP per capita at Purchasing Power Parity, 2000 .... $6,469
GDP per capita Rank 48
Percentage Growth in Real GDP per capita, 1999–2000 .... 3.4
Growth Rank 34
US Utility Patents Granted in 2000 (per million population) 0.2
Patent Rank 50

Growth Competitiveness Rank	33

Technology Index Rank **39**
    ICT Subindex Rank 53
    Innovation Subindex Rank 47
    Technology Transfer Subindex Rank
        (out of 51 technological non-core economies) 8

Public Institutions Index Rank **42**
    Corruption Subindex Rank 59
    Contracts and Law Subindex Rank 34

Macroeconomic Environment Index Rank **16**
    Macroeconomic Stability Subindex Rank 34
    Country Credit Rating Rank 41

Current Competitiveness Rank	38

Sophistication of Company Operations and Strategy Rank.................**42**
Quality of the Business Environment Rank..**39**

314

National competitiveness balance sheet

NOTABLE COMPETITIVE ADVANTAGES

Criteria	Rank

Growth Competitiveness

Technology Transfer
3.23 Skill-Based Exports...11

Macroeconomic Environment
2.28 Inflation...14
2.29 Real Exchange Rate 14
     Potential for "Catch-up" Growth 28

Current Competitiveness

Sophistication of Company Operations and Strategy
10.08 Degree of Customer Orientation 25
10.11 Breadth of International Markets 28
10.10 Extent of Regional Sales 38

Quality of the Business Environment
5.04 Road Infrastructure Quality 12
8.04 Administrative Burden for Start-Ups 17
5.01 Overall Infrastructure Quality 30

Other Indicators

Technology
3.13 Women in the Economy 13

Public Institutions
8.05 Permits to Start a Firm.....................................5

Macroeconomic Environment
1.09 Employment to Population Ratio, 2000 3
2.17 Sources of Investment Finance 8
2.33 Value Added Tax Rate 8
2.04 Exchange Rate and Exports 9
1.08 Unemployment Rate, 2000.............................10
2.20 Composition of Public Spending 12

Company Practices
10.20 Employment Rules 14

NOTABLE COMPETITIVE DISADVANTAGES

Criteria	Rank

Growth Competitiveness

Innovation
3.02 Firm-Level Innovation......................................62
3.16 Utility Patents in 2000...................................50
3.19 Tertiary Enrollment 49

Information and Communications Technology
4.12 Legal Framework for ICT Development...........60
4.13 Cellular Telephones 60
4.16 Telephone Lines 60
4.17 Personal Computers.......................................55
4.14 Internet Users 54
4.15 Internet Hosts 52
4.07 Quality of Competition in ISP Sector 50
4.11 Laws Relating to ICT Use 49

Corruption
7.01 Irregular Payments in Exports & Imports........60
7.02 Irregular Payments in Government Procurement 54
7.03 Irregular Payments in Tax Collection 53

Macroeconomic Environment
2.03 Access to Credit...63
2.01 Recession Expectations 49

Current Competitiveness

Sophistication of Company Operations and Strategy
10.03 Extent of Branding 63
10.04 Capacity for Innovation..................................62
10.05 Uniqueness of Product Designs 62

Quality of the Business Environment
6.10 Extent of Bureaucratic Red Tape 72
9.11 Local Availability of Information Technology Services.....68
9.10 Local Availability of Specialized Research
     and Training Services 54

Other Indicators

Technology
3.11 Availability of Scientists and Engineers...........54
4.10 Government On-line Services 52

Infrastructure
5.13 Difference in Quality of Schools 50

Public Institutions
6.13 Unreported Profits and Wages.......................64
7.04 Irregular Payments in Public Contracts 52
7.05 Irregular Payments in Loan Applications........52

Macroeconomic Environment
2.13 Entry into Banking Industry............................72
2.12 Perceived Interest Rate Gap 68
2.02 Soundness of Banks 65
2.10 Access to Foreign Capital Markets 62
2.11 Foreign Access to Local Capital Markets........61
2.21 Social Transfer Recipients 56
2.14 Financial Regulation and Supervision..............54

315

Trinidad and Tobago

Key Facts

GDP per capita at Purchasing Power Parity, 2000 ....$8,771
GDP per capita Rank 42
Percentage Growth in Real GDP per capita, 1999–2000 ....5.1
Growth Rank 16
US Utility Patents Granted in 2000 (per million population)..........0.0
Patent Rank 65

Growth Competitiveness Rank	38
Technology Index Rank...**52**	
ICT Subindex Rank 44	
Innovation Subindex Rank 67	
Technology Transfer Subindex Rank (out of 51 technological non-core economies) 33	
Public Institutions Index Rank **36**	
Corruption Subindex Rank 35	
Contracts and Law Subindex Rank..41	
Macroeconomic Environment Index Rank.............................**25**	
Macroeconomic Stability Subindex Rank 20	
Country Credit Rating Rank 38	

Current Competitiveness Rank	34
Sophistication of Company Operations and Strategy Rank..................**27**	
Quality of the Business Environment Rank..**37**	

National competitiveness balance sheet

NOTABLE COMPETITIVE ADVANTAGES

Criteria	Rank

Growth Competitiveness

Macroeconomic Environment

2.01	Recession Expectations	6
2.26	National Savings Rate	9
2.03	Access to Credit	10
2.24	Government Surplus/Deficit	14

Current Competitiveness

Sophistication of Company Operations and Strategy

10.10	Extent of Regional Sales	15
10.09	Control of International Distribution	17
10.02	Value Chain Presence	22

Quality of the Business Environment

5.01	Overall Infrastructure Quality	23
5.07	Air Transport Infrastructure Quality	24
9.01	Buyer Sophistication	25

Other Indicators

Public Institutions

8.05	Permits to Start a Firm	5
6.07	Costs of Institutional Change	7
6.08	Burden of Regulation	10

Macroeconomic Environment

2.05	Expected Exchange Rate Volatility	10

Company Practices

10.19	Hiring and Firing Practices	12

NOTABLE COMPETITIVE DISADVANTAGES

Criteria	Rank

Growth Competitiveness

Innovation

3.16	Utility Patents in 2000	65
3.19	Tertiary Enrollment	65

Information and Communications Technology

4.07	Quality of Competition in ISP Sector	68
4.08	Government Prioritization of ICT	57

Technology Transfer

3.23	Skill-Based Exports	59

Law and Contracts

6.04	Favoritism in Decisions of Government Officials	57

Macroeconomic Environment

2.30	Interest Rate Spread	53

Current Competitiveness

Sophistication of Company Operations and Strategy

10.14	Extent of Incentive Compensation	42

Quality of the Business Environment

11.06	Stringency of Environmental Regulations	64
8.07	Effectiveness of Anti-Trust Policy	63
9.04	Presence of Demanding Regulatory Structures	61

Other Indicators

Technology

4.10	Government On-line Services	72
4.04	Quality of Competition in Telecommunication Sector	71
3.05	Quality of Scientific Research Institutions	59

Infrastructure

5.08	Telephone/Fax Infrastructure Quality	58

Public Institutions

6.04	Favoritism in Decisions of Government Officials	57

Macroeconomic Environment

2.13	Entry into Banking Industry	69
2.11	Foreign Access to Local Capital Markets	64
2.21	Social Transfer Recipients	59
1.08	Unemployment Rate, 2000	53

Company Practices

10.21	Cooperation in Labor-Employer Relations	58

Turkey

Key Facts

GDP per capita at Purchasing Power Parity, 2000 ....$6,870
GDP per capita Rank 46
Percentage Growth in Real GDP per capita, 1999–2000 ....5.5
Growth Rank 13
US Utility Patents Granted in 2000 (per million population)..........0.1
Patent Rank 60

Growth Competitiveness Rank	**54**

Technology Index Rank..**51**
ICT Subindex Rank 45
Innovation Subindex Rank 56
Technology Transfer Subindex Rank
(out of 51 technological non-core economies) 25
Public Institutions Index Rank **46**
Corruption Subindex Rank 50
Contracts and Law Subindex Rank.......................................44
Macroeconomic Environment Index Rank....................................**68**
Macroeconomic Stability Subindex Rank 71
Country Credit Rating Rank 49

Current Competitiveness Rank	**33**

Sophistication of Company Operations and Strategy Rank..................**44**
Quality of the Business Environment Rank..**31**

National competitiveness balance sheet

NOTABLE COMPETITIVE ADVANTAGES	
Criteria	Rank

Growth Competitiveness

Macroeconomic Environment
Potential for "Catch-up" Growth 30

Current Competitiveness (using GCR 2000 results)

Sophistication of Company Operations and Strategy

10.12	Extent of Staff Training	24
10.06	Production Process Sophistication	26
10.11	Breadth of International Markets	30

Quality of the Business Environment

5.07	Air Transport Infrastructure Quality	15
9.03	Local Supplier Quality	16
8.07	Effectiveness of Anti-Trust Policy	20

Other Indicators

Technology

3.14	Minorities in the Economy	4

Macroeconomic Environment

2.11	Foreign Access to Local Capital Markets	9
2.06	Exchange Rate Premium	13
2.19	Permits to Export	22
2.32	Corporate Income Tax Rate	24

Company Practices

10.20	Employment Rules	15
10.19	Hiring and Firing Practices	17

NOTABLE COMPETITIVE DISADVANTAGES	
Criteria	Rank

Growth Competitiveness

Innovation

3.02	Firm-Level Innovation	71

Information and Communications Technology

4.08	Government Prioritization of ICT	69
4.09	Government Success in ICT Promotion	62

Corruption

7.02	Irregular Payments in Government Procurement	62

Macroeconomic Environment

2.28	Inflation	73
2.24	Government Surplus/Deficit	72
2.30	Interest Rate Spread	69
2.01	Recession Expectations	61

Current Competitiveness (using GCR 2000 results)

Sophistication of Company Operations and Strategy

10.04	Capacity for Innovation	71
3.06	Company Spending on Research and Development	65
10.09	Control of International Distribution	57

Quality of the Business Environment

9.07	Extent of Product and Process Collaboration	74
9.01	Buyer Sophistication	65
9.10	Local Availability of Specialized Research and Training Services	62

Other Indicators

Technology

3.05	Quality of Scientific Research Institutions	65

Infrastructure

5.11	Electricity Prices	69

Public Institutions

6.11	Tax Evasion	74
6.13	Unreported Profits and Wages	72
6.08	Burden of Regulation	69
6.06	Competence of Public Officials	67
6.10	Extent of Bureaucratic Red Tape	63
6.14	Informal Sector	63

Macroeconomic Environment

2.09	Venture Capital Availability	72
2.02	Soundness of Banks	71
2.14	Financial Regulation and Supervision	64
1.09	Employment to Population Ratio, 2000	63
2.21	Social Transfer Recipients	61

Ukraine

Key Facts

National competitiveness balance sheet

NOTABLE COMPETITIVE ADVANTAGES	
Criteria	**Rank**

Growth Competitiveness

Innovation

3.19	Tertiary Enrollment	21

Macroeconomic Environment

2.24	Government Surplus/Deficit	10
	Potential for "Catch-up" Growth	14
2.26	National Savings Rate	27
2.29	Real Exchange Rate	41

Current Competitiveness

Sophistication of Company Operations and Strategy

10.04	Capacity for Innovation	29
10.13	Willingness to Delegate Authority	33
10.08	Degree of Customer Orientation	35

Quality of the Business Environment

5.05	Railroad Infrastructure Development	14
9.10	Local Availability of Specialized Research and Training Services	14
9.04	Presence of Demanding Regulatory Standards	34

Other Indicators

Technology

3.14	Minorities in the Economy	1
3.08	Tax Credits for Firm-Level Research and Development	23

Public Institutions

8.06	Days to Start a Firm	10

Macroeconomic Environment

2.21	Social Transfer Recipients	13
1.08	Unemployment Rate, 2000	21
2.32	Corporate Income Tax Rate	24

Company Practices

10.20	Employment Rules	5
10.19	Hiring and Firing Practices	8
10.23	Pay and Productivity	8

NOTABLE COMPETITIVE DISADVANTAGES	
Criteria	**Rank**

Growth Competitiveness

Innovation

3.02	Firm-Level Innovation	72

Information and Communications Technology

4.08	Government Prioritization of ICT	70
4.13	Cellular Telephones	69
4.14	Internet Users	69
4.03	Internet Access in Schools	67
4.09	Government Success in ICT Promotion	67

Technology Transfer

3.04	FDI and Technology Transfer	75

Corruption

7.01	Irregular Payments in Exports & Imports	69
7.02	Irregular Payments in Government Procurement	69
7.03	Irregular Payments in Tax Collection	68

Law and Contracts

6.02	Property Rights	71
6.01	Judicial Independence	68
6.04	Favoritism in Decisions of Government Officials	67

Macroeconomic Environment

2.30	Interest Rate Spread	74
2.28	Inflation	71

Current Competitiveness

Sophistication of Company Operations and Strategy

10.06	Production Process Sophistication	72
10.07	Extent of Marketing	70
10.12	Extent of Staff Training	69

Quality of the Business Environment

8.04	Administrative Burden for Start-Ups	73
2.16	Local Equity Market Access	72
2.22	Extent of Distortive Government Subsidies	71

Other Indicators

Infrastructure

5.02	Tap Water Safety	71

Public Institutions

6.05	Government Commitments	74
6.13	Unreported Profits and Wages	74
7.05	Irregular Payments in Loan Applications	74

Macroeconomic Environment

2.06	Exchange Rate Premium	73
2.17	Sources of Investment Finance	73

321

United Kingdom

Key Facts

GDP per capita at Purchasing Power Parity, 2000 ....$23,197
GDP per capita Rank 19
Percentage Growth in Real GDP per capita, 1999–2000 ....2.9
Growth Rank 46
US Utility Patents Granted in 2000 (per million population)........61.6
Patent Rank 16

Growth Competitiveness Rank	**12**
Technology Index Rank..**10**	
ICT Subindex Rank 14	
Innovation Subindex Rank 11	
Public Institutions Index Rank..**9**	
Corruption Subindex Rank 10	
Contracts and Law Subindex Rank.........................12	
Macroeconomic Environment Index Rank............................**12**	
Macroeconomic Stability Subindex Rank 26	
Country Credit Rating Rank 6	

Current Competitiveness Rank	**7**
Sophistication of Company Operations and Strategy Rank....................7	
Quality of the Business Environment Rank...............................8	

National competitiveness balance sheet

NOTABLE COMPETITIVE ADVANTAGES	
Criteria	Rank

Growth Competitiveness

Innovation
3.02	Firm-Level Innovation	6
3.19	Tertiary Enrollment	9

Information and Communications Technology
4.12	Legal Framework for ICT Development	9

Corruption
7.02	Irregular Payments in Government Procurement	4

Law and Contracts
6.04	Favoritism in Decisions of Government Officials	6

Macroeconomic Environment
2.30	Interest Rate Spread	8

Current Competitiveness

Sophistication of Company Operations and Strategy
10.14	Extent of Incentive Compensation	2
10.02	Value Chain Presence	5
10.03	Extent of Branding	6

Quality of the Business Environment
2.07	Financial Market Sophistication	2
9.10	Local Availability of Specialized Research and Training Services	3
9.02	Local Supplier Quantity	6

Other Indicators

Technology
4.05	High Skilled IT Job Market	6

Infrastructure
5.10	Postal Efficiency	6

Public Institutions
8.05	Permits to Start a Firm	1
8.06	Days to Start a Firm	2
6.04	Favoritism in Decisions of Government Officials	6

Macroeconomic Environment
2.19	Permits to Export	1
2.02	Soundness of Banks	3
2.11	Foreign Access to Local Capital Markets	5
2.14	Financial Regulation and Supervision	5
2.18	Hidden Trade Barriers	5

Company Practices
10.15	Reliance on Professional Management	5
10.23	Pay and Productivity	5

NOTABLE COMPETITIVE DISADVANTAGES	
Criteria	Rank

Growth Competitiveness

Macroeconomic Environment
2.26	National Savings Rate	60
2.29	Real Exchange Rate	49
2.03	Access to Credit	27

Current Competitiveness

Quality of the Business Environment
3.11	Availability of Scientists and Engineers	37
3.10	Government Procurement of Advanced Technology Products	32
5.12	Quality of Public Schools	30

Other Indicators

Infrastructure
5.13	Difference in Quality of Schools	40
5.11	Electricity Prices	32
5.05	Railroad Infrastructure Development	28

Macroeconomic Environment
2.04	Exchange Rate and Exports	72
2.27	Investment Rate	62
2.17	Sources of Investment Finance	59
2.06	Exchange Rate Premium	55
2.33	Value Added Tax Rate	46
2.05	Expected Exchange Rate Volatility	43

Company Practices
10.19	Hiring and Firing Practices	29

323

United States

Key Facts

GDP per capita at Purchasing Power Parity, 2000 ....$33,886
GDP per capita Rank 1
Percentage Growth in Real GDP per capita, 1999–2000 ....4.2
Growth Rank 22
US Utility Patents Granted in 2000 (per million population)......308.7
Patent Rank 1

Growth Competitiveness Rank	2

Technology Index Rank...1
    ICT Subindex Rank 5
    Innovation Subindex Rank 2
Public Institutions Index Rank 12
    Corruption Subindex Rank 11
    Contracts and Law Subindex Rank.......................................17
Macroeconomic Environment Index Rank................................7
    Macroeconomic Stability Subindex Rank 42
    Country Credit Rating Rank 5

Current Competitiveness Rank	2

Sophistication of Company Operations and Strategy Rank...................1
Quality of the Business Environment Rank...2

National competitiveness balance sheet

NOTABLE COMPETITIVE ADVANTAGES

Criteria	Rank

Growth Competitiveness

Innovation

3.01	Technological Sophistication	1
3.02	Firm-Level Innovation	1
3.16	Utility Patents in 2000	1
3.19	Tertiary Enrollment	2
3.06	Company Spending on Research and Development	3
3.09	University/Industry Research Collaboration	7

Information and Communications Technology

4.15	Internet Hosts	1
4.07	Quality of Competition in ISP Sector	3
4.12	Legal Framework for ICT Development	3
4.11	Laws Relating to ICT Use	4
4.16	Telephone Lines	4
4.03	Internet Access in Schools	7

Law and Contracts

6.02	Property Rights	5

Current Competitiveness

Sophistication of Company Operations and Strategy

10.14	Extent of Incentive Compensation	1
10.02	Value Chain Presence	1
10.09	Control of International Distribution	4

Quality of the Business Environment

9.02	Local Supplier Quantity	1
9.06	State of Cluster Development	3
9.09	Local Availability of Process Machinery	3

Other Indicators

Technology

3.05	Quality of Scientific Research Institutions	1
3.12	Brain Drain	1
3.03	Firm-Level Technology Absorption	2
4.01	Speed and Cost of Internet Access	2
4.05	High Skilled IT Job Market	2
4.04	Quality of Competition in Telecommunication Sector	3
4.06	IT Training and Education	3

Infrastructure

5.09	Quality of Competition in Transportation Sector	2

Public Institutions

6.03	Intellectual Property Protection	3
6.09	Minimum Wage Enforcement	3
8.04	Administrative Burden for Start-Ups	3

Macroeconomic Environment

2.07	Financial Market Sophistication	1
2.09	Venture Capital Availability	1
2.19	Permits to Export	1
2.33	Value Added Tax Rate	1

NOTABLE COMPETITIVE DISADVANTAGES

Criteria	Rank

Growth Competitiveness

Information and Communications Technology

4.13	Cellular Telephones	29
4.08	Government Prioritization of ICT	21
4.09	Government Success in ICT Promotion	17

Law and Contracts

6.12	Organized Crime	21
6.04	Favoritism in Decisions of Government Officials	17

Macroeconomic Environment

2.26	National Savings Rate	65
2.29	Real Exchange Rate	60
2.01	Recession Expectations	56
2.03	Access to Credit	51
2.28	Inflation	34

Current Competitiveness

Sophistication of Company Operations and Strategy

10.10	Extent of Regional Sales	12
10.06	Production Process Sophistication	4
10.12	Extent of Staff Training	4

Quality of the Business Environment

5.12	Quality of Public Schools	26
2.18	Hidden Trade Barriers	19
11.06	Stringency of Environmental Regulations	12

Other Indicators

Technology

3.14	Minorities in the Economy	25

Infrastructure

5.13	Difference in Quality of Schools	42
5.14	Difference in Quality of Healthcare	27

Public Institutions

6.06	Competence of Public Officials	41

Macroeconomic Environment

2.04	Exchange Rate and Exports	64
2.27	Investment Rate	59
2.32	Corporate Income Tax Rate	50
2.17	Sources of Investment Finance	40
2.05	Expected Exchange Rate Volatility	32
2.15	Access to Bond Markets	31
2.06	Exchange Rate Premium	30

Company Practices

10.22	Union Contributions to Productivity	43

325

Uruguay

Key Facts

GDP per capita at Purchasing Power Parity, 2000 .... $8,904
GDP per capita Rank 41
Percentage Growth in Real GDP per capita, 1999–2000 .... –1.7
Growth Rank 74
US Utility Patents Granted in 2000 (per million population) 0.3
Patent Rank 48

Growth Competitiveness Rank	46

Technology Index Rank **45**
    ICT Subindex Rank 34
    Innovation Subindex Rank 41
    Technology Transfer Subindex Rank
       (out of 51 technological non-core economies) 36
Public Institutions Index Rank **31**
    Corruption Subindex Rank 38
    Contracts and Law Subindex Rank............................ 27
Macroeconomic Environment Index Rank....................................**63**
    Macroeconomic Stability Subindex Rank 69
    Country Credit Rating Rank 39

Current Competitiveness Rank	46

Sophistication of Company Operations and Strategy Rank.................**48**
Quality of the Business Environment Rank...............................**45**

National competitiveness balance sheet

NOTABLE COMPETITIVE ADVANTAGES	
Criteria	Rank

Growth Competitiveness

Information and Communications Technology
4.15 Internet Hosts 25

Law and Contracts
6.01 Judicial Independence.....................................25
6.02 Property Rights 25

Macroeconomic Environment
Potential for "Catch-up" Growth 35

Current Competitiveness

Sophistication of Company Operations and Strategy
10.01 Nature of Competitive Advantage....................................26
10.10 Extent of Regional Sales 27
10.03 Extent of Branding 30

Quality of the Business Environment
5.08 Telephone/Fax Infrastructure Quality 20
6.03 Intellectual Property Protection.....................................29
6.04 Favoritism in Decisions of Government Office...............30

Other Indicators

Infrastructure
5.02 Tap Water Safety...13
5.03 Industrial Water Availability 20
5.15 Public Health Agencies 21
5.04 Road Infrastructure Quality 24

Public Institutions
8.06 Days to Start a Firm 19
6.05 Government Commitments 22
8.05 Permits to Start a Firm...............................24

Macroeconomic Environment
2.06 Exchange Rate Premium...............................8
2.32 Corporate Income Tax Rate...........................24
2.10 Access to Foreign Capital Markets 25

NOTABLE COMPETITIVE DISADVANTAGES	
Criteria	Rank

Growth Competitiveness

Innovation
3.02 Firm-Level Innovation......................................63

Technology Transfer
3.04 FDI and Technology Transfer............................63

Macroeconomic Environment
2.30 Interest Rate Spread 75
2.26 National Savings Rate 73
2.29 Real Exchange Rate 69
2.01 Recession Expectations 62

Current Competitiveness

Sophistication of Company Operations and Strategy
10.13 Willingness to Delegate Authority 66
10.15 Reliance on Professional Management 63
10.12 Extent of Staff Training.....................................56

Quality of the Business Environment
8.07 Effectiveness of Anti-Trust Policy 72
10.21 Cooperation in Labor-Employer Relations 69
2.16 Local Equity Market Access...........................68

Other Indicators

Technology
3.03 Firm-Level Technology Absorption...................................62
3.12 Brain Drain...62
3.13 Women in the Economy 61

Infrastructure
5.11 Electricity Prices...68
5.05 Railroad Infrastructure Development 62

Macroeconomic Environment
2.27 Investment Rate..74
2.04 Exchange Rate and Exports 70
2.33 Value Added Tax Rate 68
2.15 Access to Bond Markets.............................63

Company Practices
10.20 Employment Rules...71
10.22 Union Contributions to Productivity 61

327

Venezuela

Key Facts

GDP per capita at Purchasing Power Parity, 2000 ....$5,677
GDP per capita Rank 53
Percentage Growth in Real GDP per capita, 1999–2000 ....1.2
Growth Rank 62
US Utility Patents Granted in 2000 (per million population)..........1.1
Patent Rank 36

Growth Competitiveness Rank	62

Technology Index Rank...**55**
    ICT Subindex Rank 48
    Innovation Subindex Rank 42
    Technology Transfer Subindex Rank
        (out of 51 technological non-core economies) 46
Public Institutions Index Rank **65**
    Corruption Subindex Rank 61
    Contracts and Law Subindex Rank....................................71
Macroeconomic Environment Index Rank....................................**53**
    Macroeconomic Stability Subindex Rank 63
    Country Credit Rating Rank 57

Current Competitiveness Rank	66

Sophistication of Company Operations and Strategy Rank...................**67**
Quality of the Business Environment Rank..**66**

National competitiveness balance sheet

NOTABLE COMPETITIVE ADVANTAGES

Criteria	Rank

Growth Competitiveness

Innovation
3.16	Utility Patents in 2000	36
3.19	Tertiary Enrollment	39

Information and Communications Technology
4.13	Cellular Telephones	35
4.07	Quality of Competition in ISP Sector	39
4.11	Laws Relating to ICT Use	41
4.14	Internet Users	42
4.17	Personal Computers	45

Technology Transfer
3.04	FDI and Technology Transfer	24

Macroeconomic Environment
	Potential for "Catch-up" Growth	23
2.26	National Savings Rate	25
2.24	Government Surplus/Deficit	38

Current Competitiveness

Sophistication of Company Operations and Strategy
10.07	Extent of Marketing	43

Quality of the Business Environment
5.04	Road Infrastructure Quality	33
10.16	Quality of Management Schools	40
5.08	Telephone/Fax Infrastructure	44

Other Indicators

Technology
3.13	Women in the Economy	24
3.14	Minorities in the Economy	26
4.04	Quality of Competition in Telecommunication Sector	26
3.03	Firm-Level Technology Absorption	42
3.11	Availability of Scientists and Engineers	42

Infrastructure
5.09	Quality of Competition in Transportation Sector	41

Public Institutions
6.13	Unreported Profits and Wages	34
6.09	Minimum Wage Enforcement	36

Macroeconomic Environment
2.10	Access to Foreign Capital Markets	8
2.21	Social Transfer Recipients	17
2.06	Exchange Rate Premium	26
2.11	Foreign Access to Local Capital Markets	28
2.33	Value Added Tax Rate	31
2.13	Entry into Banking Industry	32

Company Practices
10.19	Hiring and Firing Practices	37

NOTABLE COMPETITIVE DISADVANTAGES

Criteria	Rank

Growth Competitiveness

Technology Transfer
3.23	Skill-Based Exports	69

Law and Contracts
6.01	Judicial Independence	75
6.12	Organized Crime	67

Macroeconomic Environment
2.29	Real Exchange Rate	75
2.28	Inflation	69

Current Competitiveness

Sophistication of Company Operations and Strategy
10.05	Uniqueness of Product Designs	74
10.08	Degree of Customer Orientation	69
10.12	Extent of Staff Training	67

Quality of the Business Environment
10.21	Cooperation in Labor-Employer Relations	74
8.02	Extent of Locally Based Competitors	72
5.12	Quality of Public Schools	69

Other Indicators

Technology
3.07	Subsidies for Firm-Level Research and Development	70

Infrastructure
5.14	Difference in Quality of Healthcare	75
5.13	Difference in Quality of Schools	73
5.10	Postal Efficiency	71

Public Institutions
6.06	Competence of Public Officials	74
6.07	Costs of Institutional Change	74

Macroeconomic Environment
2.04	Exchange Rate and Exports	75
2.12	Perceived Interest Rate Gap	73
2.27	Investment Rate	73
2.17	Sources of Investment Finance	71
2.20	Composition of Public Spending	71

Company Practices
10.23	Pay and Productivity	73

329

Vietnam

Key Facts

GDP per capita at Purchasing Power Parity, 2000 ....\$1,974
GDP per capita Rank 73
Percentage Growth in Real GDP per capita, 1999–2000 ....4.0
Growth Rank 27
US Utility Patents Granted in 2000 (per million population)..........0.0
Patent Rank 65

Growth Competitiveness Rank	60

Technology Index Rank..**65**
    ICT Subindex Rank 73
    Innovation Subindex Rank 70
    Technology Transfer Subindex Rank
        (out of 51 technological non-core economies) 16
Public Institutions Index Rank **63**
    Corruption Subindex Rank 71
    Contracts and Law Subindex Rank........................49
Macroeconomic Environment Index Rank................................**37**
    Macroeconomic Stability Subindex Rank 19
    Country Credit Rating Rank 64

Current Competitiveness Rank	62

Sophistication of Company Operations and Strategy Rank..................**64**
Quality of the Business Environment Rank..**64**

National competitiveness balance sheet

NOTABLE COMPETITIVE ADVANTAGES	
Criteria	Rank

Growth Competitiveness

Innovation

3.02	Firm-Level Innovation	32
3.06	Company Spending on Research and Development	39
3.09	University/Industry Research Collaboration	43

Technology Transfer

3.04	FDI and Technology Transfer	23
3.23	Skill-Based Exports	33

Macroeconomic Environment

2.28	Inflation	2
	Potential for "Catch-up" Growth	3
2.26	National Savings Rate	12
2.01	Recession Expectations	32
2.29	Real Exchange Rate	34
2.30	Interest Rate Spread	39

Current Competitiveness

Sophistication of Company Operations and Strategy

10.08	Degree of Customer Orientation	32
10.02	Value Chain Presence	33
10.05	Uniqueness of Product Designs	43

Quality of the Business Environment

8.02	Extent of Locally Based Competitors	13
9.01	Buyer Sophistication	27
9.05	Decentralization of Corporate Activity	28

Other Indicators

Technology

3.03	Firm-Level Technology Absorption	23

Public Institutions

7.07	Public Trust of Politicians	15
8.06	Days to Start a Firm	19
8.04	Administrative Burden for Start-Ups	22
6.06	Competence of Public Officials	25
6.14	Informal Sector	25
6.07	Costs of Institutional Change	30

Macroeconomic Environment

2.33	Value Added Tax Rate	12
2.27	Investment Rate	14
1.09	Employment to Population Ratio, 2000	15
2.22	Extent of Distortive Government Subsidies	25
1.08	Unemployment Rate, 2000	27

Company Practices

10.23	Pay and Productivity	3
10.22	Union Contributions to Productivity	12
10.21	Cooperation in Labor-Employer Relations	18
10.19	Hiring and Firing Practices	27

NOTABLE COMPETITIVE DISADVANTAGES	
Criteria	Rank

Growth Competitiveness

Innovation

3.01	Technological Sophistication	71
3.19	Tertiary Enrollment	68
3.16	Utility Patents in 2000	65

Information and Communications Technology

4.15	Internet Hosts	75
4.07	Quality of Competition in ISP Sector	73
4.14	Internet Users	73
4.13	Cellular Telephones	71
4.16	Telephone Lines	70
4.17	Personal Computers	69
4.11	Laws Relating to ICT Use	67

Corruption

7.01	Irregular Payments in Exports & Imports	73
7.03	Irregular Payments in Tax Collection	70

Current Competitiveness

Sophistication of Company Operations and Strategy

10.07	Extent of Marketing	75

Quality of the Business Environment

4.01	Speed and Cost of Internet Access	75
6.03	Intellectual Property Protection	75
9.11	Local Availability of Information Technology Services	73

Other Indicators

Infrastructure

5.02	Tap Water Safety	72
5.03	Industrial Water Availability	72
5.09	Quality of Competition in Transportation Sector	72

Public Institutions

6.08	Burden of Regulation	74
7.05	Irregular Payments in Loan Applications	72

Macroeconomic Environment

2.11	Foreign Access to Local Capital Markets	73
2.18	Hidden Trade Barriers	73
2.07	Financial Market Sophistication	72
2.31	Average Tariff Rate	72

Company Practices

10.13	Willingness to Delegate Authority	70

331

Zimbabwe

Key Facts

GDP per capita at Purchasing Power Parity, 2000 ....$2,697
GDP per capita Rank 68
Percentage Growth in Real GDP per capita, 1999–2000 ....–8.1
Growth Rank 75
US Utility Patents Granted in 2000 (per million population)..........0.0
Patent Rank 65

Growth Competitiveness Rank	75

Technology Index Rank..**72**
    ICT Subindex Rank 72
    Innovation Subindex Rank 71
    Technology Transfer Subindex Rank
      (out of 51 technological non-core economies) 40
Public Institutions Index Rank **69**
    Corruption Subindex Rank 68
    Contracts and Law Subindex Rank........................63
Macroeconomic Environment Index Rank................................**75**
    Macroeconomic Stability Subindex Rank 75
    Country Credit Rating Rank 75

Current Competitiveness Rank	65

Sophistication of Company Operations and Strategy Rank..................**60**
Quality of the Business Environment Rank..**67**

National competitiveness balance sheet

<table>
<tr><td colspan="2">NOTABLE COMPETITIVE ADVANTAGES</td></tr>
<tr><td>Criteria</td><td>Rank</td></tr>
</table>

Growth Competitiveness

Macroeconomic Environment

| | Potential for "Catch-up" Growth | 8 |
| 2.29 | Real Exchange Rate | 32 |

Current Competitiveness

Sophistication of Company Operations and Strategy

10.14	Extent of Incentive Compensation	23
10.15	Reliance on Professional Management	28
10.12	Extent of Staff Training	34

Quality of the Business Environment

5.04	Road Infrastructure Quality	11
2.16	Local Equity Market Access	26
5.05	Railroad Infrastructure Quality	33

Other Indicators

Technology

| 3.14 | Minorities in the Economy | 14 |

Public Institutions

| 6.13 | Unreported Profits and Wages | 25 |

Macroeconomic Environment

| 2.19 | Permits to Export | 1 |
| 2.13 | Entry into Banking Industry | 22 |

Company Practices

| 10.22 | Union Contributions to Productivity | 20 |

<table>
<tr><td colspan="2">NOTABLE COMPETITIVE DISADVANTAGES</td></tr>
<tr><td>Criteria</td><td>Rank</td></tr>
</table>

Growth Competitiveness

Innovation

| 3.19 | Tertiary Enrollment | 68 |
| 3.16 | Utility Patents in 2000 | 65 |

Information and Communications Technology

4.08	Government Prioritization of ICT	74
4.09	Government Success in ICT Promotion	74
4.16	Telephone Lines	73
4.14	Internet Users	72
4.03	Internet Access in Schools	71
4.13	Cellular Telephones	70

Technology Transfer

| 3.04 | FDI and Technology Transfer | 67 |

Corruption

| 7.02 | Irregular Payments in Government Procurement | 72 |

Law and Contracts

| 6.04 | Favoritism in Decisions of Government Officials | 75 |
| 6.01 | Judicial Independence | 66 |

Macroeconomic Environment

2.01	Recession Expectations	75
2.24	Government Surplus/Deficit	75
2.28	Inflation	74
2.30	Interest Rate Spread	71

Current Competitiveness

Sophistication of Company Operations and Strategy

10.02	Value Chain Presence	75
10.03	Extent of Branding	73
10.09	Control of International Distribution	69

Quality of the Business Environment

3.11	Availability of Scientists and Engineers	75
2.22	Extent of Distortive Government Subsidies	74
5.08	Telephone/Fax Infrastructure Quality	71

Other Indicators

Technology

| 3.12 | Brain Drain | 75 |

Public Institutions

6.04	Favoritism in Decisions of Government Officials	75
6.06	Competence of Public Officials	75
6.07	Costs of Institutional Change	75
6.08	Burden of Regulation	75
7.07	Public Trust of Politicians	75

Macroeconomic Environment

2.05	Expected Exchange Rate Volatility	75
2.06	Exchange Rate Premium	75
2.20	Composition of Public Spending	75

333

3.2: Data Tables

How data pages work

The following pages provide detailed data for all 75 economies included in the *Global Competitiveness Report 2001–2002*. The data are organized into eleven categories:

I	Aggregate country performance indicators
II	Macroeconomic environment
III	Technological innovation and diffusion
IV	Information and communications technology
V	General infrastructure
VI	Public institutions: contracts and law
VII	Public institutions: corruption
VIII	Domestic competition
IX	Cluster development
X	Company operations and strategy
XI	Environmental policy

Two types of variables are presented in these tables: (1) average country responses to questions included in the World Economic Forum's Executive Opinion Survey, conducted in the early months of 2001; and (2) "hard data" obtained from a variety of sources.

❶ Survey data

Data yielded from the Executive Opinion Survey are presented with blue-colored bar graphs. In sections containing both hard and Survey data, the Survey data are presented first. For each Survey variable, the original question is included in the description at the top of the page, with minor abbreviations made in some instances due to space constraints. As outlined in Chapter 2.7 of this *Report*, in most cases questions asked for responses on a scale of 1 to 7, where an answer of 1 corresponds to one end of a spectrum of responses and an answer of 7 corresponds to the other end. We report the average response for each country. Variable 2.01, for example, asks about respondents' recession expectations at the time of the Survey, with higher scores corresponding to a lower perceived likelihood of recession. The score noted for Hungary is 6.3, indicating the arithmetic mean of responses to this question from executives in Hungary and a low average expectation of recession.

❷ A dotted line on the graph indicates the mean country score across the sample of 75 economies.

❸ We report country responses rounded to a single decimal point, but use the exact figures to determine rankings and for graphs. In the case of variable 2.01, for example, France's average score was 6.045, Brazil's was 6.000, and Switzerland's was 5.957. These economies are therefore ranked third through fifth respectively, even though they are all listed with the same rounded score of 6.0.

When questions ask for specific data instead of degree of agreement with a statement, we report the median instead of the average response. An example is variable 8.05, which asks, "Approximately how many permits would you need to start a new firm?" Average responses for this type of questions are biased by outliers—a problem resolved by using the median measure. In these cases ties are true, so shared rankings are indicated accordingly. In question 8.05, for example, the median response was "2 permits" in four countries: Hong Kong SAR, Singapore, Sri Lanka, and the United Kingdom. All four countries are thus ranked as tied for first.

(cont'd.)

335

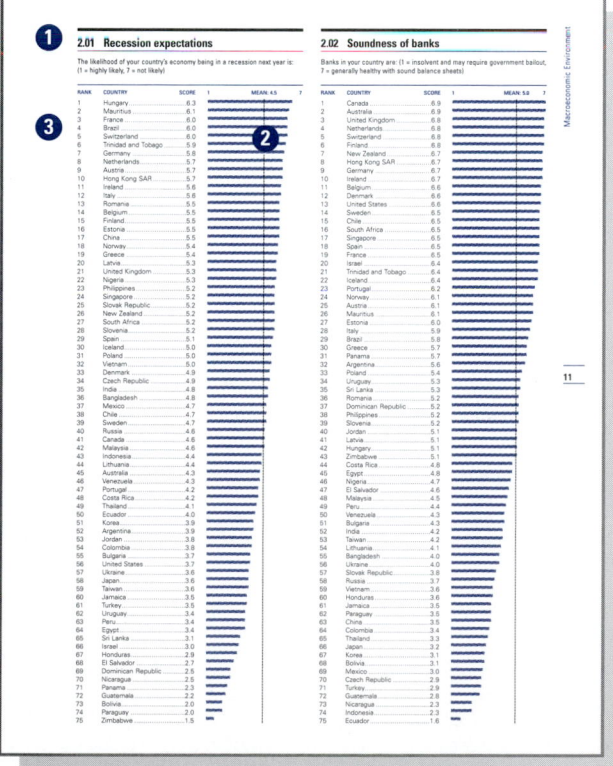

Hard data

Data originating not from the Executive Opinion Survey but from other publicly available sources are presented in gray-shaded bar graphs and are followed on each page with a brief reference to the source from which they were obtained. More detailed citation information can be found in the Technical Notes and Sources section at the end of this *Report*. Here again, true ties are indicated by shared rankings where relevant.

The reader should note that many of these variables, although presented as "hard data," still depend to a great extent on surveying techniques. Indeed, several labor market statistics, as well as GDP itself, rely heavily on surveying methodologies.

General notes

In many cases, for both the Survey data and hard data the rankings reflect what is desirable for a country's competitiveness, but this is not always the case. There is broad agreement, for instance, that less organized crime is better for an economy (see variable 6.12); it is not clear, however, that it is better if firms typically finance investment through external rather than internal sources (see variable 2.17). In cases such as the latter, the data are in a certain order for consistency in presentation, but the order should not be interpreted as a clear indicator of competitiveness.

Readers should further note that many of the data in these tables are presented for information only, and are not used in any of the indexes constructed in this *Report*.

Index of tables

(cont'd.)

Section XI: Environmental Policy

Section I: Aggregate Country Performance Indicators

1.01 Total GDP, 2000

Gross Domestic Product in billions of US dollars, 2000

RANK	COUNTRY		HARD DATA
1	United States	9962.65	
2	Japan	4759.52	
3	Germany	1878.11	
4	United Kingdom	1416.68	
5	France	1289.10	
6	China	1079.84	
7	Italy	1076.90	
8	Canada	699.47	
9	Brazil	588.13	
10	Mexico	574.48	
11	Spain	560.08	
12	India	474.19	
13	Korea	457.46	
14	Australia	381.92	
15	Netherlands	370.08	
16	Taiwan	310.22	
17	Argentina	285.04	
18	Russian Federation	246.74	
19	Switzerland	242.03	
20	Sweden	228.39	
21	Belgium	227.07	
22	Turkey	202.58	
23	Austria	190.35	
24	Hong Kong SAR	163.22	
25	Denmark	162.34	
26	Poland	160.86	
27	Norway	159.40	
28	Indonesia	153.71	
29	South Africa	125.71	
30	Finland	121.98	
31	Thailand	121.93	
32	Venezuela	120.49	
33	Greece	113.29	
34	Israel	110.33	
35	Portugal	105.06	
36	Egypt	96.05	
37	Ireland	94.60	
38	Singapore	92.25	
39	Malaysia	89.32	
40	Colombia	82.51	
41	Philippines	75.19	
42	Chile	70.02	
43	Peru	52.25	
44	New Zealand	50.18	
45	Czech Republic	49.81	
46	Hungary	49.70	
47	Bangladesh	48.77	
48	Nigeria	40.57	
49	Romania	37.85	
50	Ukraine	30.35	
51	Vietnam	30.06	
52	Slovak Republic	20.88	
53	Uruguay	20.18	
54	Dominican Republic	19.80	
55	Guatemala	18.58	
56	Slovenia	18.30	
57	Sri Lanka	16.66	
58	Costa Rica	16.28	
59	El Salvador	13.06	
60	Ecuador	12.82	
61	Bulgaria	12.06	
62	Lithuania	11.13	
63	Panama	9.91	
64	Jamaica	8.58	
65	Iceland	8.51	
66	Bolivia	8.44	
67	Jordan	8.35	
68	Trinidad and Tobago	7.47	
69	Paraguay	7.32	
70	Zimbabwe	7.19	
71	Latvia	6.83	
72	Honduras	5.86	
73	Estonia	5.09	
74	Mauritius	4.30	
75	Nicaragua	2.44	

SOURCE: IMF *World Economic Outlook Database, May 2001*

1.02 Total population, 2000

Population in millions, 2000

RANK	COUNTRY		HARD DATA
1	China	1261.8	
2	India	1014.0	
3	United States	275.6	
4	Indonesia	224.8	
5	Brazil	169.5	
6	Russian Federation	146.0	
7	Bangladesh	128.8	
8	Japan	126.9	
9	Nigeria	111.6	
10	Mexico	97.4	
11	Germany	82.8	
12	Vietnam	77.5	
13	Philippines	76.5	
14	Egypt	68.5	
15	Turkey	65.7	
16	Thailand	61.9	
17	United Kingdom	59.5	
18	France	59.3	
19	Italy	57.6	
20	Ukraine	50.3	
21	Korea	47.3	
22	South Africa	43.7	
23	Colombia	42.3	
24	Spain	40.0	
25	Poland	38.6	
26	Argentina	37.0	
27	Canada	30.8	
28	Peru	25.7	
29	Venezuela	24.2	
30	Malaysia	23.3	
31	Romania	22.4	
32	Taiwan	22.2	
33	Sri Lanka	19.2	
34	Australia	19.2	
35	Netherlands	15.9	
36	Chile	15.2	
37	Ecuador	12.9	
38	Zimbabwe	12.1	
39	Guatemala	11.4	
40	Greece	10.5	
41	Czech Republic	10.3	
42	Belgium	10.2	
43	Hungary	10.1	
44	Portugal	10.0	
45	Sweden	8.9	
46	Dominican Republic	8.4	
47	Bolivia	8.2	
48	Austria	8.1	
49	Bulgaria	8.0	
50	Switzerland	7.3	
51	Hong Kong SAR	6.8	
52	Honduras	6.6	
53	El Salvador	6.1	
54	Israel	5.8	
55	Paraguay	5.6	
56	Slovak Republic	5.4	
57	Denmark	5.3	
58	Finland	5.2	
59	Nicaragua	5.1	
60	Jordan	5.0	
61	Norway	4.5	
62	Singapore	4.0	
63	Costa Rica	4.0	
64	New Zealand	3.8	
65	Ireland	3.8	
66	Lithuania	3.7	
67	Uruguay	3.3	
68	Panama	2.8	
69	Jamaica	2.7	
70	Latvia	2.4	
71	Slovenia	2.0	
72	Estonia	1.4	
73	Trinidad and Tobago	1.3	
74	Mauritius	1.2	
75	Iceland	0.3	

SOURCES: Economist Intelligence Unit and National Sources

341

1.03 GDP per capita (PPP), 2000

Gross Domestic Product per capita in US dollars, measured at Purchasing Power Parity, 2000

RANK	COUNTRY		HARD DATA
1	United States	33,886	
2	Norway	29,500	
3	Iceland	29,167	
4	Ireland	29,080	
5	Switzerland	28,518	
6	Canada	27,783	
7	Denmark	27,120	
8	Belgium	26,958	
9	Austria	26,314	
10	Japan	25,796	
11	Australia	25,758	
12	Netherlands	25,598	
13	Germany	24,931	
14	Finland	24,864	
15	Hong Kong SAR	24,448	
16	France	24,032	
17	Sweden	23,884	
18	Italy	23,304	
19	United Kingdom	23,197	
20	Singapore	23,000	
21	New Zealand	20,010	
22	Israel	19,577	
23	Spain	19,202	
24	Korea	17,311	
25	Taiwan	17,223	
26	Slovenia	17,127	
27	Portugal	16,882	
28	Greece	16,326	
29	Czech Republic	13,721	
30	Hungary	12,335	
31	Argentina	12,314	
32	Slovak Republic	11,035	
33	Mauritius	9,512	
34	Costa Rica	9,236	
35	South Africa	9,189	
36	Chile	9,187	
37	Estonia	9,178	
38	Poland	8,971	
39	Malaysia	8,924	
40	Mexico	8,914	
41	Uruguay	8,904	
42	Trinidad and Tobago	8,771	
43	Russian Federation	8,213	
44	Brazil	7,389	
45	Lithuania	6,999	
46	Turkey	6,870	
47	Latvia	6,838	
48	Thailand	6,469	
49	Romania	6,309	
50	Panama	6,169	
51	Dominican Republic	5,962	
52	Colombia	5,923	
53	Venezuela	5,677	
54	Bulgaria	5,469	
55	Peru	4,797	
56	El Salvador	4,477	
57	Paraguay	4,396	
58	Jordan	4,079	
59	Philippines	3,956	
60	China	3,953	
61	Guatemala	3,784	
62	Ukraine	3,693	
63	Jamaica	3,657	
64	Egypt	3,602	
65	Sri Lanka	3,512	
66	Ecuador	3,068	
67	Indonesia	3,014	
68	Zimbabwe	2,697	
69	Honduras	2,469	
70	Bolivia	2,408	
71	India	2,403	
72	Nicaragua	2,396	
73	Vietnam	1,974	
74	Bangladesh	1,561	
75	Nigeria	871	

SOURCES: World Bank, *World Development Indicators 2001*, IMF *World Economic Outlook Database, May 2001*, US Bureau of Economic Analysis, and authors' calculations

1.04 Real growth in GDP per capita, 1999 to 2000

Real growth in GDP per capita from 1999 to 2000

RANK	COUNTRY		HARD DATA
1	Ireland	9.9	
2	Singapore	8.5	
3	Hong Kong SAR	8.5	
4	Korea	8.0	
5	Russian Federation	7.7	
6	Estonia	7.6	
7	China	7.1	
8	Latvia	7.0	
9	Malaysia	6.5	
10	Dominican Republic	6.1	
11	Hungary	5.7	
12	Bulgaria	5.7	
13	Turkey	5.5	
14	Finland	5.5	
15	Mexico	5.3	
16	Trinidad and Tobago	5.1	
17	Slovenia	5.0	
18	Sri Lanka	4.9	
19	Taiwan	4.8	
20	India	4.7	
21	Ukraine	4.6	
22	United States	4.2	
23	Spain	4.1	
24	Chile	4.0	
25	Israel	4.0	
26	Poland	4.0	
27	Vietnam	4.0	
28	Belgium	3.8	
29	Greece	3.8	
30	Canada	3.7	
31	Netherlands	3.6	
32	Honduras	3.4	
33	Sweden	3.4	
34	Thailand	3.4	
35	Indonesia	3.4	
36	Czech Republic	3.3	
37	Egypt	3.2	
38	Bangladesh	3.2	
39	Lithuania	3.0	
40	Nicaragua	3.0	
41	Italy	3.0	
42	Portugal	3.0	
43	Germany	2.9	
44	Brazil	2.9	
45	Panama	2.9	
46	United Kingdom	2.9	
47	Switzerland	2.8	
48	France	2.8	
49	Austria	2.8	
50	Denmark	2.7	
51	Australia	2.7	
52	Iceland	2.7	
53	New Zealand	2.6	
54	Mauritius	2.3	
55	Romania	2.3	
56	Costa Rica	2.2	
57	Slovak Republic	2.1	
58	Philippines	1.9	
59	Peru	1.7	
60	Norway	1.7	
61	Japan	1.5	
62	Venezuela	1.2	
63	South Africa	1.1	
64	Jordan	1.1	
65	El Salvador	1.0	
66	Colombia	1.0	
67	Guatemala	0.9	
68	Jamaica	0.6	
69	Ecuador	0.4	
70	Bolivia	0.2	
71	Nigeria	0.0	
72	Argentina	−1.7	
73	Paraguay	−1.7	
74	Uruguay	−1.7	
75	Zimbabwe	−8.1	

SOURCE: IMF *World Economic Outlook Database, May 2001*, and authors' calculations

1.05 GDP per capita relative to the United States, 2000

GDP per capita (PPP) as a proportion of US GDP per capita in 2000

RANK	COUNTRY	HARD DATA
1	United States	1.00
2	Norway	0.87
3	Iceland	0.86
4	Ireland	0.86
5	Switzerland	0.84
6	Canada	0.82
7	Denmark	0.80
8	Belgium	0.80
9	Austria	0.78
10	Japan	0.76
11	Australia	0.76
12	Netherlands	0.76
13	Germany	0.74
14	Finland	0.73
15	Hong Kong SAR	0.72
16	France	0.71
17	Sweden	0.70
18	Italy	0.69
19	United Kingdom	0.68
20	Singapore	0.68
21	New Zealand	0.59
22	Israel	0.58
23	Spain	0.57
24	Korea	0.51
25	Taiwan	0.51
26	Slovenia	0.51
27	Portugal	0.50
28	Greece	0.48
29	Czech Republic	0.40
30	Hungary	0.36
31	Argentina	0.36
32	Slovak Republic	0.33
33	Mauritius	0.28
34	Costa Rica	0.27
35	South Africa	0.27
36	Chile	0.27
37	Estonia	0.27
38	Poland	0.26
39	Malaysia	0.26
40	Mexico	0.26
41	Uruguay	0.26
42	Trinidad and Tobago	0.26
43	Russian Federation	0.24
44	Brazil	0.22
45	Lithuania	0.21
46	Turkey	0.20
47	Latvia	0.20
48	Thailand	0.19
49	Romania	0.19
50	Panama	0.18
51	Dominican Republic	0.18
52	Colombia	0.17
53	Venezuela	0.17
54	Bulgaria	0.16
55	Peru	0.14
56	El Salvador	0.13
57	Paraguay	0.13
58	Jordan	0.12
59	Philippines	0.12
60	China	0.12
61	Guatemala	0.11
62	Ukraine	0.11
63	Jamaica	0.11
64	Egypt	0.11
65	Sri Lanka	0.10
66	Ecuador	0.09
67	Indonesia	0.09
68	Zimbabwe	0.08
69	Honduras	0.07
70	Bolivia	0.07
71	India	0.07
72	Nicaragua	0.07
73	Vietnam	0.06
74	Bangladesh	0.05
75	Nigeria	0.03

SOURCES: World Bank, *World Development Indicators 2001*, IMF *World Economic Outlook Database, May 2001*, US Bureau of Economic Analysis, and authors' calculations

1.06 GDP per capita relative to the United States, 1992

GDP per capita (PPP) as a proportion of US GDP per capita in 1992 (1995 for transition economies)

RANK	COUNTRY	HARD DATA
1	United States	1.00
2	Switzerland	0.99
3	Japan	0.87
4	Norway	0.86
5	Belgium	0.85
6	Iceland	0.85
7	Denmark	0.83
8	Canada	0.82
9	Austria	0.82
10	Germany	0.80
11	France	0.77
12	Hong Kong SAR	0.77
13	Netherlands	0.76
14	Italy	0.76
15	Sweden	0.75
16	Australia	0.73
17	Finland	0.69
18	United Kingdom	0.69
19	Israel	0.59
20	Singapore	0.58
21	New Zealand	0.58
22	Ireland	0.56
23	Spain	0.56
24	Portugal	0.50
25	Greece	0.48
26	Slovenia	0.47
27	Czech Republic	0.44
28	Korea	0.43
29	Taiwan	0.40
30	Argentina	0.39
31	Hungary	0.34
32	South Africa	0.32
33	Slovak Republic	0.31
34	Uruguay	0.28
35	Mexico	0.28
36	Russian Federation	0.26
37	Mauritius	0.25
38	Trinidad and Tobago	0.25
39	Chile	0.24
40	Poland	0.24
41	Venezuela	0.24
42	Costa Rica	0.24
43	Estonia	0.23
44	Romania	0.23
45	Malaysia	0.23
46	Brazil	0.23
47	Turkey	0.21
48	Colombia	0.21
49	Bulgaria	0.20
50	Lithuania	0.20
51	Panama	0.19
52	Thailand	0.19
53	Latvia	0.18
54	Paraguay	0.17
55	Dominican Republic	0.15
56	Jordan	0.15
57	Jamaica	0.15
58	Peru	0.14
59	Ukraine	0.14
60	El Salvador	0.13
61	Philippines	0.13
62	Guatemala	0.12
63	Ecuador	0.12
64	Egypt	0.10
65	Nicaragua	0.09
66	Zimbabwe	0.09
67	Indonesia	0.09
68	Sri Lanka	0.09
69	Honduras	0.09
70	Bolivia	0.08
71	China	0.07
72	India	0.06
73	Vietnam	0.05
74	Bangladesh	0.04
75	Nigeria	0.03

SOURCES: World Bank, *World Development Indicators 2001*, and authors' calculations

1.07 Change in GDP per capita relative to United States, 1992 to 2000

Average annual percentage change in ratio of GDP per capita (PPP) relative to US GDP per capita from 1992 to 2000 (1995 to 2000 for transition economies)

RANK	COUNTRY	HARD DATA
1	China	6.03
2	Ireland	5.25
3	Vietnam	3.11
4	Taiwan	3.05
5	Estonia	3.03
6	Latvia	2.42
7	Korea	2.28
8	Dominican Republic	2.04
9	Singapore	1.99
10	India	1.87
11	Poland	1.86
12	Costa Rica	1.75
13	Malaysia	1.66
14	Sri Lanka	1.53
15	Slovenia	1.53
16	Hungary	1.37
17	Chile	1.35
18	Mauritius	1.23
19	Slovak Republic	1.14
20	Finland	0.74
21	Lithuania	0.67
22	Peru	0.55
23	Bangladesh	0.51
24	Australia	0.47
25	New Zealand	0.30
26	Trinidad and Tobago	0.25
27	Iceland	0.21
28	Egypt	0.21
29	Thailand	0.21
30	Spain	0.14
31	Norway	0.08
32	Portugal	0.07
33	Greece	0.02
34	United States	0.00
35	Canada	−0.04
36	United Kingdom	−0.06
37	Netherlands	−0.06
38	El Salvador	−0.09
39	Israel	−0.20
40	Denmark	−0.48
41	Panama	−0.53
42	Brazil	−0.54
43	Turkey	−0.55
44	Indonesia	−0.58
45	Austria	−0.70
46	Sweden	−0.71
47	Mexico	−0.76
48	Hong Kong SAR	−0.84
49	Belgium	−0.85
50	Uruguay	−0.93
51	Argentina	−0.94
52	France	−1.08
53	Russian Federation	−1.08
54	Germany	−1.08
55	Bolivia	−1.10
56	Guatemala	−1.13
57	Italy	−1.18
58	Philippines	−1.55
59	Czech Republic	−1.69
60	Japan	−1.73
61	Colombia	−2.01
62	Zimbabwe	−2.06
63	Switzerland	−2.07
64	South Africa	−2.09
65	Honduras	−2.54
66	Jordan	−2.61
67	Nigeria	−2.95
68	Ecuador	−3.25
69	Paraguay	−3.27
70	Nicaragua	−3.67
71	Jamaica	−3.75
72	Ukraine	−4.33
73	Venezuela	−4.37
74	Romania	−4.42
75	Bulgaria	−4.45

SOURCES: IMF *World Economic Outlook Database, May 2001,* US Bureau of Economic Analysis, and authors' calculations

1.08 Unemployment rate, 2000

Recorded official unemployment rate as a percentage of total labor force in 2000

RANK	COUNTRY	HARD DATA
1	Iceland	1.3
2	Switzerland	2.0
3	Mexico	2.2
4	Bangladesh	2.4
5	Netherlands	2.6
6	Taiwan	3.0
7	Singapore	3.1
8	Malaysia	3.1
9	Norway	3.5
10	Thailand	3.6
11	Austria	3.7
12	Portugal	4.0
13	United States	4.0
14	Korea	4.1
15	Ireland	4.1
16	Sweden	4.7
17	Japan	4.7
18	Guatemala	4.9
19	Hong Kong SAR	5.1
20	Costa Rica	5.2
21	Ukraine	5.3
22	Denmark	5.4
23	United Kingdom	5.6
24	New Zealand	6.0
25	Australia	6.3
26	Hungary	6.4
27	Vietnam	6.4
28	Peru	6.5
29	El Salvador	6.6
30	Canada	6.8
31	China	7.0
32	Brazil	7.1
33	Sri Lanka	7.7
34	Latvia	7.8
35	Mauritius	8.0
36	Turkey	8.3
37	Israel	8.8
38	Czech Republic	9.0
39	Ecuador	9.0
40	Chile	9.2
41	France	9.5
42	Germany	9.6
43	Finland	9.8
44	Russian Federation	9.8
45	Estonia	10.1
46	Italy	10.5
47	Belgium	10.9
48	Philippines	11.1
49	Romania	11.1
50	Greece	11.3
51	Lithuania	11.5
52	Egypt	11.8
53	Trinidad and Tobago	12.1
54	Slovenia	12.2
55	Indonesia	13.0
55	Panama	13.0
57	Uruguay	13.5
58	Jordan	13.7
59	Dominican Republic	13.8
60	Venezuela	13.9
61	Spain	14.1
62	Poland	14.4
63	Argentina	14.6
64	Jamaica	15.8
65	Paraguay	16.0
66	Colombia	16.5
67	Slovakia	17.8
68	Bulgaria	18.1
69	Nicaragua	22.0
70	Honduras	28.0
71	South Africa	29.5
	Bolivia	N/A
	India	N/A
	Nigeria	N/A
	Zimbabwe	N/A

SOURCES: Economist Intelligence Unit and national sources

1.09 Employment to population ratio, 2000

Ratio of recorded employed persons to population, 2000

RANK	COUNTRY	HARD DATA
1	China	56.4
2	Iceland	56.3
3	Thailand	53.6
4	Panama	52.6
5	Singapore	52.1
6	Austria	50.9
7	Japan	50.8
8	Norway	50.7
9	Hong Kong SAR	49.6
10	Russian Federation	49.5
11	Switzerland	49.4
12	United States	49.1
13	Portugal	49.0
14	United Kingdom	48.9
15	Vietnam	48.8
16	Canada	48.5
17	Australia	47.3
18	Sweden	46.8
19	Germany	46.8
20	New Zealand	46.6
21	Netherlands	46.6
22	Czech Republic	46.3
23	Finland	45.1
24	Ireland	45.0
25	Korea	44.5
26	Estonia	44.2
27	Latvia	43.6
28	Taiwan	43.0
29	Brazil	42.6
30	Mauritius	42.4
31	Romania	42.4
32	Ukraine	42.2
33	Bangladesh	42.0
34	Israel	41.6
35	Mexico	41.5
36	Denmark	41.4
37	Lithuania	41.0
38	Jamaica	40.8
39	India	40.5
40	Trinidad and Tobago	40.2
41	Malaysia	40.1
42	France	40.0
43	Indonesia	40.0
44	Belgium	39.7
45	Poland	39.6
46	Slovenia	39.5
47	Bulgaria	38.9
48	Slovak Republic	38.9
49	Colombia	38.9
50	Uruguay	38.8
51	Hungary	37.8
52	Guatemala	37.7
53	Greece	37.6
54	Italy	37.1
55	Dominican Republic	36.7
56	El Salvador	36.6
57	Spain	36.5
58	Philippines	36.3
59	Argentina	33.9
60	Costa Rica	33.2
61	Venezuela	31.9
62	Sri Lanka	31.7
63	Turkey	30.7
64	Chile	30.2
65	Paraguay	30.1
66	Nicaragua	29.2
67	Peru	28.5
68	Egypt	25.7
69	Honduras	25.3
70	Ecuador	23.7
71	South Africa	21.2
72	Jordan	18.1
	Zimbabwe	N/A
	Bolivia	N/A
	Nigeria	N/A

SOURCES: Economist Intelligence Unit and national sources

Section II: Macroeconomic Environment

2.01 Recession expectations

The likelihood of your country's economy being in a recession next year is:
(1 = highly likely, 7 = not likely) [Question asked in February–April 2001.]

RANK	COUNTRY	SCORE
1	Hungary	6.3
2	Mauritius	6.1
3	France	6.0
4	Brazil	6.0
5	Switzerland	6.0
6	Trinidad and Tobago	5.9
7	Germany	5.8
8	Netherlands	5.7
9	Austria	5.7
10	Hong Kong SAR	5.7
11	Ireland	5.6
12	Italy	5.6
13	Romania	5.5
14	Belgium	5.5
15	Finland	5.5
16	Estonia	5.5
17	China	5.5
18	Norway	5.4
19	Greece	5.4
20	Latvia	5.3
21	United Kingdom	5.3
22	Nigeria	5.3
23	Philippines	5.2
24	Singapore	5.2
25	Slovak Republic	5.2
26	New Zealand	5.2
27	South Africa	5.2
28	Slovenia	5.2
29	Spain	5.1
30	Iceland	5.0
31	Poland	5.0
32	Vietnam	5.0
33	Denmark	4.9
34	Czech Republic	4.9
35	India	4.8
36	Bangladesh	4.8
37	Mexico	4.7
38	Chile	4.7
39	Sweden	4.7
40	Russian Federation	4.6
41	Canada	4.6
42	Malaysia	4.6
43	Indonesia	4.4
44	Lithuania	4.4
45	Australia	4.3
46	Venezuela	4.3
47	Portugal	4.2
48	Costa Rica	4.2
49	Thailand	4.1
50	Ecuador	4.0
51	Korea	3.9
52	Argentina	3.9
53	Jordan	3.8
54	Colombia	3.8
55	Bulgaria	3.7
56	United States	3.7
57	Ukraine	3.6
58	Japan	3.6
59	Taiwan	3.6
60	Jamaica	3.5
61	Turkey	3.5
62	Uruguay	3.4
63	Peru	3.4
64	Egypt	3.4
65	Sri Lanka	3.1
66	Israel	3.0
67	Honduras	2.9
68	El Salvador	2.7
69	Dominican Republic	2.5
70	Nicaragua	2.5
71	Panama	2.3
72	Guatemala	2.2
73	Bolivia	2.0
74	Paraguay	2.0
75	Zimbabwe	1.5

MEAN: 4.5

2.02 Soundness of banks

Banks in your country are: (1 = insolvent and may require government bailout,
7 = generally healthy with sound balance sheets)

RANK	COUNTRY	SCORE
1	Canada	6.9
2	Australia	6.9
3	United Kingdom	6.8
4	Netherlands	6.8
5	Switzerland	6.8
6	Finland	6.8
7	New Zealand	6.7
8	Hong Kong SAR	6.7
9	Germany	6.7
10	Ireland	6.7
11	Belgium	6.6
12	Denmark	6.6
13	United States	6.6
14	Sweden	6.5
15	Chile	6.5
16	South Africa	6.5
17	Singapore	6.5
18	Spain	6.5
19	France	6.5
20	Israel	6.4
21	Trinidad and Tobago	6.4
22	Iceland	6.4
23	Portugal	6.2
24	Norway	6.1
25	Austria	6.1
26	Mauritius	6.1
27	Estonia	6.0
28	Italy	5.9
29	Brazil	5.8
30	Greece	5.7
31	Panama	5.7
32	Argentina	5.6
33	Poland	5.4
34	Uruguay	5.3
35	Sri Lanka	5.3
36	Romania	5.2
37	Dominican Republic	5.2
38	Philippines	5.2
39	Slovenia	5.2
40	Jordan	5.1
41	Latvia	5.1
42	Hungary	5.1
43	Zimbabwe	5.1
44	Costa Rica	4.8
45	Egypt	4.8
46	Nigeria	4.7
47	El Salvador	4.6
48	Malaysia	4.5
49	Peru	4.4
50	Venezuela	4.3
51	Bulgaria	4.3
52	India	4.2
53	Taiwan	4.2
54	Lithuania	4.1
55	Bangladesh	4.0
56	Ukraine	4.0
57	Slovak Republic	3.8
58	Russian Federation	3.7
59	Vietnam	3.6
60	Honduras	3.6
61	Jamaica	3.5
62	Paraguay	3.5
63	China	3.5
64	Colombia	3.4
65	Thailand	3.3
66	Japan	3.2
67	Korea	3.1
68	Bolivia	3.1
69	Mexico	3.0
70	Czech Republic	2.9
71	Turkey	2.9
72	Guatemala	2.8
73	Nicaragua	2.3
74	Indonesia	2.3
75	Ecuador	1.6

MEAN: 5.0

2.03 Access to credit

During the past year, obtaining credit for your company has become: (1 = more difficult, 7 = easier) [Question asked in February–April 2001.]

RANK	COUNTRY	SCORE
1	Italy	5.7
2	Taiwan	5.2
3	Greece	5.1
4	India	5.1
5	Finland	5.1
6	Spain	5.0
7	Brazil	4.9
8	Latvia	4.9
9	Singapore	4.9
10	Trinidad and Tobago	4.9
11	Netherlands	4.8
12	Estonia	4.8
13	Romania	4.8
14	Slovenia	4.8
15	Poland	4.8
16	New Zealand	4.8
17	Hong Kong SAR	4.7
18	Ireland	4.7
19	Sweden	4.7
20	Denmark	4.7
21	Austria	4.6
22	Portugal	4.6
23	Norway	4.6
24	France	4.6
25	Hungary	4.6
26	South Africa	4.5
27	United Kingdom	4.5
28	Japan	4.5
29	Mauritius	4.4
30	Slovak Republic	4.4
31	Russian Federation	4.3
32	Iceland	4.3
33	Germany	4.3
34	Israel	4.3
35	Switzerland	4.3
36	Canada	4.3
37	Dominican Republic	4.2
38	Lithuania	4.2
39	Australia	4.2
40	Uruguay	4.2
41	Jordan	4.1
42	Malaysia	4.1
43	El Salvador	4.1
44	Nigeria	4.1
45	Chile	4.1
46	Vietnam	4.1
47	Belgium	4.1
48	Costa Rica	4.1
49	Bangladesh	4.0
50	Korea	4.0
51	United States	4.0
52	Turkey	3.9
53	Zimbabwe	3.9
54	Venezuela	3.9
55	Sri Lanka	3.8
56	Mexico	3.7
57	Philippines	3.6
58	Czech Republic	3.6
59	China	3.6
60	Bulgaria	3.5
61	Panama	3.4
62	Ukraine	3.4
63	Thailand	3.4
64	Jamaica	3.4
65	Paraguay	3.3
66	Colombia	3.2
67	Egypt	3.1
68	Nicaragua	2.9
69	Indonesia	2.9
70	Argentina	2.8
71	Honduras	2.6
72	Peru	2.5
73	Guatemala	2.4
74	Bolivia	1.9
75	Ecuador	1.8

MEAN: 4.1

2.04 Exchange rate and exports

The official exchange rate in your country is: (1 = highly appreciated and bad for exports, 7 = highly depreciated and good for exports)

RANK	COUNTRY	SCORE
1	Indonesia	6.4
2	Australia	6.3
3	South Africa	6.0
4	Canada	5.7
5	New Zealand	5.6
6	Germany	5.6
7	Philippines	5.3
8	Belgium	5.2
9	Thailand	5.2
10	Ireland	5.2
11	Sri Lanka	5.1
12	Finland	5.1
13	Iceland	5.0
14	Austria	5.0
15	Sweden	5.0
16	Colombia	4.9
17	Trinidad and Tobago	4.8
18	Italy	4.8
19	Brazil	4.8
20	France	4.8
21	Slovak Republic	4.8
22	Estonia	4.8
23	Nigeria	4.7
24	Czech Republic	4.7
25	Netherlands	4.6
26	Spain	4.6
27	Hungary	4.5
28	Jamaica	4.5
29	Honduras	4.5
30	Bangladesh	4.5
31	Chile	4.4
32	Japan	4.4
33	Taiwan	4.4
34	Malaysia	4.4
35	Mauritius	4.4
36	Korea	4.4
37	Denmark	4.4
38	India	4.4
39	Portugal	4.3
40	Romania	4.3
41	Costa Rica	4.2
42	Singapore	4.2
43	Jordan	4.2
44	Switzerland	4.2
45	Norway	4.2
46	Dominican Republic	4.1
47	Greece	4.0
48	China	3.9
49	Vietnam	3.9
50	Slovenia	3.8
51	Hong Kong SAR	3.7
52	Israel	3.7
53	Bolivia	3.7
54	Guatemala	3.6
55	Egypt	3.6
56	Bulgaria	3.6
57	Russian Federation	3.5
58	Latvia	3.4
59	Ukraine	3.4
60	Turkey	3.4
61	Panama	3.4
62	Nicaragua	3.4
63	El Salvador	3.4
64	United States	3.2
65	Peru	3.2
66	Lithuania	3.0
67	Poland	2.9
68	Paraguay	2.8
69	Argentina	2.8
70	Uruguay	2.8
71	Ecuador	2.8
72	United Kingdom	2.7
73	Mexico	2.5
74	Zimbabwe	2.4
75	Venezuela	1.6

MEAN: 4.2

2.05 Expected exchange rate volatility

Over the next two years, your country's exchange rate will be:
(1 = very volatile, 7 = very stable) [Question asked in February–April 2001.]

RANK	COUNTRY	SCORE	1 MEAN: 4.6 7
1	El Salvador	6.6	
2	Hong Kong SAR	6.3	
3	Ecuador	6.3	
4	Greece	6.2	
5	Denmark	6.1	
6	Argentina	6.0	
7	Austria	5.9	
8	Estonia	5.9	
9	Finland	5.9	
10	Trinidad and Tobago	5.8	
11	Singapore	5.7	
12	Portugal	5.7	
13	Latvia	5.7	
14	Netherlands	5.6	
15	Jordan	5.5	
16	Belgium	5.5	
17	Romania	5.4	
18	Ireland	5.4	
19	Spain	5.4	
20	Switzerland	5.2	
21	Costa Rica	5.2	
22	France	5.1	
23	Hungary	5.1	
24	Norway	5.1	
25	Panama	5.0	
26	Malaysia	5.0	
27	Peru	5.0	
28	Czech Republic	5.0	
29	Israel	5.0	
30	Germany	5.0	
31	Uruguay	4.9	
32	United States	4.9	
33	Slovenia	4.8	
34	Slovak Republic	4.8	
35	Bolivia	4.7	
36	Canada	4.7	
37	Italy	4.7	
38	Taiwan	4.7	
39	Brazil	4.6	
40	China	4.5	
41	Sweden	4.5	
42	Chile	4.4	
43	United Kingdom	4.4	
44	Thailand	4.4	
45	Venezuela	4.4	
46	Iceland	4.4	
47	Mexico	4.3	
48	India	4.3	
49	Bulgaria	4.2	
50	Korea	4.2	
51	Philippines	4.2	
52	Poland	4.1	
53	Mauritius	4.1	
54	Turkey	3.9	
55	Colombia	3.9	
56	Jamaica	3.9	
57	Lithuania	3.8	
58	New Zealand	3.8	
59	Australia	3.7	
60	Dominican Republic	3.7	
61	Japan	3.6	
62	Nicaragua	3.6	
63	Guatemala	3.5	
64	Nigeria	3.5	
65	Russian Federation	3.5	
66	Bangladesh	3.3	
67	Honduras	3.2	
68	Vietnam	3.1	
69	Ukraine	3.0	
70	South Africa	2.9	
71	Egypt	2.8	
72	Sri Lanka	2.8	
73	Indonesia	2.5	
74	Paraguay	2.5	
75	Zimbabwe	1.3	

2.06 Exchange rate premium

To obtain foreign currency, your firm must pay a premium over the official exchange rate of (1 = 0%, 2 = 1–10%, 3 = 11–20%, . . . , 8 = 61–70%, 9 = greater than 70%)

RANK	COUNTRY	PREMIUM	1 MEAN: 1.5 9
1	Peru	1.03	
2	Argentina	1.03	
3	El Salvador	1.07	
4	India	1.11	
5	Hong Kong SAR	1.14	
6	Romania	1.14	
7	Iceland	1.17	
8	Uruguay	1.18	
9	Ecuador	1.19	
10	Sweden	1.22	
11	New Zealand	1.24	
12	Mexico	1.24	
13	Turkey	1.25	
14	Belgium	1.25	
15	Mauritius	1.27	
16	Canada	1.27	
17	Austria	1.27	
18	Malaysia	1.28	
19	Switzerland	1.29	
20	Singapore	1.29	
21	Hungary	1.30	
22	Germany	1.31	
23	Taiwan	1.31	
24	Finland	1.31	
25	South Africa	1.32	
26	Venezuela	1.33	
27	Italy	1.33	
28	France	1.33	
29	Paraguay	1.34	
30	United States	1.36	
31	Denmark	1.36	
32	Netherlands	1.36	
33	Poland	1.38	
34	Greece	1.38	
35	Spain	1.39	
36	Slovak Republic	1.40	
37	Trinidad and Tobago	1.40	
38	Chile	1.44	
39	Costa Rica	1.44	
40	Brazil	1.45	
41	Czech Republic	1.45	
42	Japan	1.45	
43	Ireland	1.45	
44	Portugal	1.46	
45	Slovenia	1.47	
46	Australia	1.48	
47	Latvia	1.48	
48	Bolivia	1.48	
49	Indonesia	1.50	
50	Israel	1.50	
51	Lithuania	1.51	
52	Estonia	1.54	
53	Thailand	1.56	
54	Bangladesh	1.57	
55	United Kingdom	1.57	
56	Norway	1.57	
57	Sri Lanka	1.58	
58	Colombia	1.59	
59	Panama	1.62	
60	Jordan	1.67	
61	Jamaica	1.67	
62	Philippines	1.71	
63	Bulgaria	1.72	
64	Russian Federation	1.76	
65	Egypt	1.82	
66	Guatemala	1.84	
67	Korea	1.85	
68	Vietnam	1.86	
69	Nicaragua	1.98	
70	Honduras	2.03	
71	Nigeria	2.10	
72	China	2.14	
73	Ukraine	2.19	
74	Dominican Republic	2.41	
75	Zimbabwe	4.50	

2.07 Financial market sophistication

The level of financial market sophistication in your country is:
(1 = lower than international norms, 7 = higher than international norms)

RANK	COUNTRY	SCORE
1	United States	6.8
2	United Kingdom	6.8
3	Switzerland	6.7
4	Hong Kong SAR	6.4
5	Netherlands	6.3
6	Australia	6.0
7	Germany	6.0
8	Canada	6.0
9	Finland	5.9
10	Sweden	5.9
11	Singapore	5.7
12	Brazil	5.7
13	France	5.6
14	Israel	5.6
15	Denmark	5.6
16	South Africa	5.5
17	Ireland	5.5
18	Spain	5.3
19	Belgium	5.2
20	New Zealand	5.2
21	Iceland	5.0
22	Norway	5.0
23	Italy	4.9
24	Portugal	4.8
25	Chile	4.8
26	Japan	4.7
27	Austria	4.6
28	Taiwan	4.6
29	Hungary	4.5
30	Panama	4.4
31	Argentina	4.4
32	Estonia	4.4
33	Trinidad and Tobago	4.2
34	Mexico	4.1
35	Turkey	4.1
36	India	4.0
37	Poland	4.0
38	Zimbabwe	3.9
39	Uruguay	3.9
40	Philippines	3.9
41	Malaysia	3.9
42	Latvia	3.9
43	Greece	3.8
44	Jamaica	3.8
45	Dominican Republic	3.8
46	Korea	3.8
47	Thailand	3.6
48	El Salvador	3.6
49	Colombia	3.5
50	Peru	3.5
51	Slovenia	3.4
52	Jordan	3.4
53	Nigeria	3.3
54	Egypt	3.3
55	Indonesia	3.2
56	Sri Lanka	3.2
57	Venezuela	3.2
58	Costa Rica	3.1
59	Mauritius	3.1
60	Lithuania	3.0
61	Czech Republic	2.9
62	Slovak Republic	2.8
63	Paraguay	2.7
64	China	2.7
65	Ecuador	2.6
66	Guatemala	2.6
67	Nicaragua	2.6
68	Ukraine	2.4
69	Russian Federation	2.4
70	Bolivia	2.3
71	Romania	2.3
72	Vietnam	2.2
73	Honduras	2.1
74	Bangladesh	2.1
75	Bulgaria	2.0

MEAN: 4.2

2.08 Ease of access to loans

How easy is it to obtain a loan in your country with only a good business plan and no collateral? (1 = impossible, 7 = easy)

RANK	COUNTRY	SCORE
1	Sweden	5.3
2	Finland	5.2
3	Denmark	5.0
4	Netherlands	4.9
5	Norway	4.9
6	United States	4.9
7	Switzerland	4.8
8	Belgium	4.6
9	Iceland	4.6
10	Singapore	4.5
11	United Kingdom	4.5
12	France	4.3
13	Germany	4.3
14	Australia	4.2
15	Hong Kong SAR	4.2
16	Egypt	4.2
17	Canada	4.2
18	Portugal	4.1
19	Ireland	4.1
20	Israel	4.0
21	Austria	4.0
22	Taiwan	3.7
23	New Zealand	3.7
24	Spain	3.5
25	India	3.5
26	Mauritius	3.4
27	Poland	3.4
28	Japan	3.4
29	Brazil	3.3
30	Italy	3.3
31	South Africa	3.3
32	Panama	3.2
33	Lithuania	3.2
34	Trinidad and Tobago	3.2
35	Estonia	3.2
36	Hungary	3.1
37	Turkey	3.1
38	Korea	3.1
39	Chile	3.0
40	Sri Lanka	3.0
41	Malaysia	3.0
42	Slovenia	2.9
43	Czech Republic	2.8
44	Slovak Republic	2.8
45	Greece	2.8
46	Paraguay	2.8
47	Philippines	2.8
48	Indonesia	2.7
49	Uruguay	2.7
50	Latvia	2.7
51	Thailand	2.6
52	Dominican Republic	2.6
53	Jordan	2.5
54	Colombia	2.4
55	El Salvador	2.4
56	Argentina	2.4
57	Zimbabwe	2.4
58	Venezuela	2.3
59	Peru	2.2
60	China	2.2
61	Nicaragua	2.2
62	Nigeria	2.1
63	Costa Rica	2.1
64	Mexico	2.0
65	Russian Federation	2.0
66	Bulgaria	2.0
67	Ukraine	2.0
68	Jamaica	1.9
69	Vietnam	1.9
70	Guatemala	1.9
71	Honduras	1.9
72	Bolivia	1.8
73	Ecuador	1.8
74	Bangladesh	1.7
75	Romania	1.5

MEAN: 3.2

2.09 Venture capital availability

Entrepreneurs with innovative but risky projects can generally find venture capital in your country. (1 = not true, 7 = true)

RANK	COUNTRY	SCORE
1	United States	5.8
2	Israel	5.7
3	Sweden	5.6
4	Finland	5.5
5	Netherlands	5.5
6	Denmark	5.1
7	Norway	5.1
8	Canada	5.0
9	United Kingdom	4.9
10	Germany	4.9
11	Switzerland	4.7
12	France	4.7
13	Taiwan	4.6
14	Singapore	4.5
15	Iceland	4.5
16	Hong Kong SAR	4.5
17	Ireland	4.5
18	Belgium	4.4
19	Australia	4.2
20	Korea	4.1
21	Austria	4.1
22	New Zealand	4.0
23	Spain	3.9
24	Portugal	3.9
25	Trinidad and Tobago	3.8
26	India	3.8
27	Brazil	3.7
28	Hungary	3.6
29	South Africa	3.5
30	Italy	3.5
31	Japan	3.5
32	Estonia	3.5
33	Panama	3.2
34	Egypt	3.2
35	Czech Republic	3.2
36	Sri Lanka	3.1
37	Poland	3.0
38	Jamaica	3.0
39	Malaysia	3.0
40	Greece	3.0
41	Slovenia	2.9
42	Lithuania	2.9
43	Jordan	2.9
44	Chile	2.9
45	Zimbabwe	2.9
46	Paraguay	2.9
47	Latvia	2.9
48	Slovak Republic	2.8
49	China	2.8
50	Philippines	2.7
51	Thailand	2.7
52	Uruguay	2.7
53	Bulgaria	2.6
54	Ukraine	2.6
55	Vietnam	2.6
56	Mauritius	2.6
57	Nicaragua	2.5
58	Costa Rica	2.5
59	Russian Federation	2.4
60	Colombia	2.4
61	El Salvador	2.4
62	Indonesia	2.3
63	Mexico	2.3
64	Nigeria	2.3
65	Argentina	2.2
66	Guatemala	2.2
67	Bangladesh	2.2
68	Dominican Republic	2.1
69	Peru	2.0
70	Venezuela	2.0
71	Ecuador	2.0
72	Turkey	2.0
73	Honduras	2.0
74	Bolivia	1.7
75	Romania	1.3

MEAN: 3.4

2.10 Access to foreign capital markets

Citizens of your country who wish to invest in stocks and bonds and open bank accounts in other country: (1 = are prohibited from doing so, 7 = are free to do so)

RANK	COUNTRY	SCORE
1	Finland	7.0
2	Hong Kong SAR	6.9
3	Belgium	6.9
4	Netherlands	6.9
5	Iceland	6.9
6	Switzerland	6.9
7	United Kingdom	6.8
8	Venezuela	6.8
9	Germany	6.8
10	New Zealand	6.8
11	United States	6.7
12	Estonia	6.7
13	Denmark	6.7
14	Australia	6.6
15	Ecuador	6.6
16	Mauritius	6.6
17	Austria	6.6
18	Singapore	6.6
19	Costa Rica	6.5
20	Japan	6.5
21	Israel	6.5
22	Peru	6.5
23	Portugal	6.4
24	Argentina	6.4
25	Uruguay	6.4
26	Canada	6.4
27	Italy	6.4
28	Spain	6.4
29	Egypt	6.3
30	Jordan	6.3
31	Turkey	6.3
32	Sweden	6.3
33	El Salvador	6.3
34	Jamaica	6.3
35	Philippines	6.2
36	Bolivia	6.2
37	Norway	6.2
38	France	6.2
39	Trinidad and Tobago	6.1
40	Mexico	6.1
41	Dominican Republic	6.1
42	Nicaragua	6.1
43	Greece	6.0
44	Honduras	6.0
45	Nigeria	6.0
46	Panama	6.0
47	Ireland	6.0
48	Chile	6.0
49	Taiwan	6.0
50	Lithuania	5.9
51	Latvia	5.8
52	Indonesia	5.6
53	Hungary	5.6
54	Czech Republic	5.4
55	Colombia	5.3
56	Slovak Republic	5.0
57	Guatemala	5.0
58	Korea	4.9
59	Slovenia	4.9
60	Brazil	4.7
61	Bulgaria	4.7
62	Thailand	4.6
63	Ukraine	4.5
64	Paraguay	4.4
65	South Africa	4.3
66	Malaysia	4.3
67	Romania	4.2
68	Vietnam	3.9
69	Poland	3.9
70	Russian Federation	3.7
71	China	3.4
72	Sri Lanka	3.4
73	Bangladesh	2.8
74	Zimbabwe	2.6
75	India	1.9

MEAN: 5.7

2.11 Foreign access to local capital markets

Foreign investors: (1 = are prohibited from investing in stocks and bonds in your country, 7 = are free to invest in stocks and bonds)

RANK	COUNTRY	SCORE
1	Finland	7.0
2	Hong Kong SAR	7.0
3	Belgium	6.9
4	Netherlands	6.9
5	United Kingdom	6.9
6	Germany	6.9
7	Romania	6.8
8	Israel	6.8
9	Turkey	6.8
10	Argentina	6.8
11	Switzerland	6.8
12	Egypt	6.8
13	France	6.7
14	Estonia	6.7
15	Peru	6.7
16	Denmark	6.7
17	United States	6.7
18	South Africa	6.6
19	Greece	6.6
20	Costa Rica	6.6
21	Austria	6.6
22	Spain	6.6
23	Sweden	6.6
24	Ireland	6.5
25	Ecuador	6.5
26	Italy	6.5
27	Japan	6.5
28	Venezuela	6.4
29	Portugal	6.4
30	Uruguay	6.4
31	New Zealand	6.4
32	Slovak Republic	6.4
33	Nigeria	6.4
34	Hungary	6.4
35	Singapore	6.4
36	Mexico	6.4
37	Australia	6.3
38	Chile	6.3
39	Brazil	6.3
40	Norway	6.3
41	Bangladesh	6.3
42	Poland	6.2
43	Honduras	6.2
44	Latvia	6.2
45	Indonesia	6.2
46	Jamaica	6.2
47	Bolivia	6.1
48	Colombia	6.1
49	Jordan	6.1
50	Ukraine	6.1
51	Czech Republic	6.1
52	El Salvador	6.0
53	Dominican Republic	6.0
54	Canada	6.0
55	Mauritius	5.9
56	Nicaragua	5.9
57	Philippines	5.9
58	Sri Lanka	5.9
59	Panama	5.9
60	Lithuania	5.9
61	Thailand	5.8
62	Guatemala	5.7
63	Bulgaria	5.7
64	Trinidad and Tobago	5.7
65	Korea	5.6
66	Malaysia	5.6
67	Iceland	5.5
68	Zimbabwe	5.4
69	Slovenia	5.2
70	Taiwan	5.2
71	Russian Federation	5.1
72	India	5.0
73	Vietnam	4.9
74	Paraguay	4.4
75	China	4.2

MEAN: 6.2

2.12 Perceived interest rate gap

The gap between interest rates for bank loans and interest rates for deposits is: (1 = greater than international norms, 7 = smaller than international norms)

RANK	COUNTRY	SCORE
1	Switzerland	5.3
2	Netherlands	5.0
3	Finland	4.9
4	United States	4.9
5	Germany	4.7
6	Belgium	4.7
7	Canada	4.7
8	Singapore	4.6
9	France	4.5
10	United Kingdom	4.5
11	Taiwan	4.4
12	Austria	4.4
13	Spain	4.4
14	Sweden	4.3
15	Denmark	4.2
16	New Zealand	4.2
17	Chile	4.1
18	Panama	4.1
19	Japan	4.1
20	Norway	4.1
21	Australia	4.0
22	Israel	4.0
23	Portugal	3.9
24	Ireland	3.8
25	Slovak Republic	3.8
26	Hong Kong SAR	3.8
27	Paraguay	3.7
28	Egypt	3.7
29	Romania	3.6
30	China	3.6
31	Malaysia	3.5
32	Italy	3.4
33	Latvia	3.3
34	Trinidad and Tobago	3.3
35	Korea	3.3
36	Estonia	3.3
37	South Africa	3.3
38	Honduras	3.2
39	Czech Republic	3.2
40	El Salvador	3.1
41	Russian Federation	3.1
42	Uruguay	3.1
43	Vietnam	3.1
44	Mauritius	3.1
45	Jordan	3.0
46	Poland	3.0
47	Slovenia	3.0
48	Lithuania	3.0
49	Sri Lanka	2.9
50	Bulgaria	2.9
51	India	2.9
52	Hungary	2.8
53	Nicaragua	2.8
54	Greece	2.7
55	Turkey	2.7
56	Nigeria	2.6
57	Costa Rica	2.6
58	Philippines	2.5
59	Indonesia	2.5
60	Argentina	2.5
61	Guatemala	2.5
62	Jamaica	2.5
63	Dominican Republic	2.5
64	Colombia	2.4
65	Bangladesh	2.4
66	Iceland	2.3
67	Brazil	2.3
68	Thailand	2.3
69	Mexico	2.2
70	Ukraine	2.1
71	Bolivia	2.1
72	Peru	1.9
73	Venezuela	1.8
74	Zimbabwe	1.7
75	Ecuador	1.6

MEAN: 3.3

2.13 Entry into banking industry

The entry of new banks into the domestic banking industry is: (1 = very difficult and rarely allowed, 7 = easy and subject only to reasonable regulations)

RANK	COUNTRY	SCORE
1	Denmark	5.9
2	Netherlands	5.9
3	Finland	5.9
4	Iceland	5.9
5	Romania	5.8
6	Belgium	5.8
7	New Zealand	5.7
8	United States	5.6
9	Nigeria	5.5
10	United Kingdom	5.5
11	Argentina	5.4
12	Hong Kong SAR	5.4
13	Portugal	5.4
14	Germany	5.3
15	Brazil	5.3
16	Panama	5.2
17	Greece	5.2
18	Switzerland	5.2
19	Ireland	5.2
20	Hungary	5.1
21	South Africa	5.1
22	Zimbabwe	5.1
23	Poland	5.0
24	France	5.0
25	Estonia	5.0
26	Peru	5.0
27	Australia	4.9
28	Sweden	4.9
29	India	4.8
30	Uruguay	4.8
31	Norway	4.7
32	Venezuela	4.7
33	Costa Rica	4.7
34	Spain	4.7
35	Sri Lanka	4.6
36	Chile	4.6
37	Jordan	4.5
38	Mexico	4.5
39	Bangladesh	4.5
40	Egypt	4.5
41	Dominican Republic	4.5
42	Austria	4.4
43	Italy	4.4
44	Jamaica	4.4
45	Philippines	4.4
46	Guatemala	4.4
47	Colombia	4.4
48	Taiwan	4.3
49	Nicaragua	4.3
50	Israel	4.3
51	Slovak Republic	4.2
52	Bulgaria	4.1
53	Lithuania	4.1
54	Latvia	4.1
55	Turkey	4.1
56	Canada	4.1
57	Bolivia	4.0
58	Czech Republic	3.9
59	Slovenia	3.9
60	Honduras	3.8
61	El Salvador	3.8
62	Indonesia	3.8
63	Singapore	3.7
64	Vietnam	3.7
65	Russian Federation	3.6
66	Mauritius	3.6
67	Japan	3.5
68	Paraguay	3.5
69	Trinidad and Tobago	3.4
70	Ukraine	3.4
71	Ecuador	3.3
72	Thailand	3.3
73	Korea	2.9
74	China	2.4
75	Malaysia	2.2

MEAN: 4.5

2.14 Financial regulation and supervision

Regulations and supervision of financial institutions are: (1 = inadequate for financial stability, 7 = among the world's most stringent)

RANK	COUNTRY	SCORE
1	Germany	6.6
2	Australia	6.5
3	Switzerland	6.5
4	United States	6.4
5	United Kingdom	6.4
6	Netherlands	6.4
7	Canada	6.3
8	Singapore	6.3
9	Denmark	6.3
10	Hong Kong SAR	6.2
11	Finland	6.1
12	Spain	6.0
13	Ireland	5.9
14	Iceland	5.9
15	Sweden	5.9
16	France	5.9
17	Belgium	5.9
18	Israel	5.8
19	Chile	5.7
20	South Africa	5.7
21	Austria	5.7
22	Norway	5.6
23	New Zealand	5.6
24	Argentina	5.5
25	Italy	5.5
26	Portugal	5.5
27	Trinidad and Tobago	5.4
28	Brazil	5.3
29	Uruguay	5.2
30	Poland	5.1
31	Hungary	5.1
32	Panama	4.9
33	Malaysia	4.8
34	Latvia	4.8
35	Peru	4.8
36	Costa Rica	4.8
37	Jordan	4.7
38	Estonia	4.7
39	India	4.7
40	Slovenia	4.6
41	Taiwan	4.6
42	Greece	4.5
43	Bolivia	4.5
44	Mauritius	4.4
45	El Salvador	4.4
46	Nigeria	4.4
47	Dominican Republic	4.4
48	Japan	4.4
49	Philippines	4.3
50	Jamaica	4.3
51	Slovak Republic	4.2
52	Egypt	4.1
53	Colombia	4.1
54	Thailand	4.1
55	Mexico	3.9
56	Venezuela	3.8
57	Sri Lanka	3.8
58	Lithuania	3.8
59	Bulgaria	3.8
60	China	3.7
61	Korea	3.7
62	Zimbabwe	3.6
63	Ukraine	3.6
64	Turkey	3.6
65	Czech Republic	3.5
66	Paraguay	3.3
67	Bangladesh	3.2
68	Indonesia	3.1
69	Vietnam	3.0
70	Romania	2.9
71	Russian Federation	2.8
72	Honduras	2.7
73	Guatemala	2.7
74	Nicaragua	2.6
75	Ecuador	1.8

MEAN: 4.7

2.15 Access to bond markets

Your company could borrow on the international bond market if necessary.
(1 = not true, 7 = true)

RANK	COUNTRY	SCORE
1	France	6.4
2	Finland	6.3
3	Italy	6.2
4	Norway	6.2
5	Portugal	6.2
6	Germany	6.0
7	Denmark	6.0
8	Switzerland	6.0
9	Netherlands	5.8
10	Australia	5.8
11	Sweden	5.8
12	Iceland	5.7
13	Canada	5.7
14	Belgium	5.7
15	Argentina	5.6
16	New Zealand	5.3
17	Japan	5.3
18	Poland	5.3
19	Greece	5.3
20	Ireland	5.2
21	United Kingdom	5.1
22	Taiwan	5.1
23	Hong Kong SAR	5.1
24	India	5.0
25	Hungary	4.9
26	Mexico	4.9
27	Singapore	4.9
28	Spain	4.9
29	Austria	4.9
30	Brazil	4.8
31	United States	4.6
32	Lithuania	4.6
33	Israel	4.6
34	South Africa	4.5
35	Turkey	4.4
36	Indonesia	4.2
37	Latvia	4.2
38	Korea	4.2
39	Czech Republic	4.1
40	Philippines	4.1
41	Thailand	3.8
42	Jamaica	3.8
43	Peru	3.7
44	Chile	3.6
45	Zimbabwe	3.6
46	Nigeria	3.5
47	Egypt	3.5
48	Slovenia	3.4
49	Malaysia	3.4
50	Trinidad and Tobago	3.4
51	Romania	3.2
52	Panama	3.2
53	Colombia	3.1
54	Paraguay	3.0
55	Jordan	3.0
56	Estonia	2.9
57	China	2.9
58	Mauritius	2.9
59	Venezuela	2.8
60	Dominican Republic	2.8
61	El Salvador	2.8
62	Costa Rica	2.6
63	Uruguay	2.6
64	Nicaragua	2.5
65	Sri Lanka	2.4
66	Slovak Republic	2.4
67	Guatemala	2.3
68	Ukraine	2.2
69	Bolivia	2.2
70	Vietnam	2.2
71	Russian Federation	2.1
72	Bulgaria	2.0
73	Honduras	2.0
74	Bangladesh	1.8
75	Ecuador	1.7

MEAN: 4.1

2.16 Local equity market access

Raising money by issuing shares on the local stock market is:
(1 = nearly impossible, 7 = quite possible for a good company)

RANK	COUNTRY	SCORE
1	Iceland	6.7
2	Netherlands	6.6
3	Australia	6.6
4	France	6.5
5	Germany	6.5
6	Switzerland	6.4
7	South Africa	6.4
8	Canada	6.4
9	Italy	6.4
10	Finland	6.4
11	Israel	6.3
12	Hong Kong SAR	6.3
13	United Kingdom	6.3
14	New Zealand	6.3
15	Sweden	6.3
16	United States	6.3
17	Denmark	6.2
18	Taiwan	6.2
19	Greece	6.1
20	Singapore	6.1
21	India	6.1
22	Japan	6.1
23	Norway	6.0
24	Nigeria	5.9
25	Portugal	5.9
26	Zimbabwe	5.8
27	Egypt	5.8
28	Poland	5.7
29	Austria	5.7
30	Malaysia	5.7
31	Ireland	5.6
32	Belgium	5.6
33	Turkey	5.6
34	Brazil	5.5
35	Trinidad and Tobago	5.4
36	Philippines	5.4
37	Hungary	5.4
38	Spain	5.3
39	Estonia	5.3
40	Bangladesh	5.2
41	Mauritius	5.2
42	Thailand	5.2
43	Jordan	5.2
44	Korea	5.1
45	Sri Lanka	5.1
46	Jamaica	5.0
47	Chile	4.9
48	Mexico	4.8
49	Indonesia	4.6
50	Vietnam	4.3
51	Lithuania	4.1
52	Slovenia	4.1
53	China	4.1
54	Panama	4.1
55	Costa Rica	3.8
56	Dominican Republic	3.8
57	Latvia	3.7
58	Russian Federation	3.7
59	El Salvador	3.7
60	Colombia	3.6
61	Romania	3.4
62	Peru	3.4
63	Paraguay	3.4
64	Czech Republic	3.3
65	Nicaragua	3.2
66	Argentina	3.2
67	Venezuela	3.2
68	Uruguay	3.2
69	Bolivia	3.0
70	Honduras	2.8
71	Slovak Republic	2.8
72	Ukraine	2.8
73	Ecuador	2.6
74	Bulgaria	2.5
75	Guatemala	2.3

MEAN: 5.0

2.17 Sources of investment finance

When financing investments, your company typically: (1 = relies on its own retained earnings, 7 = raises funds from banks or the bond markets)

RANK	COUNTRY	SCORE
1	El Salvador	4.8
2	Israel	4.7
3	Iceland	4.6
4	Spain	4.5
5	Argentina	4.4
6	Egypt	4.3
7	Dominican Republic	4.2
8	Thailand	4.1
9	Finland	4.1
10	Australia	4.1
11	Portugal	4.1
12	Slovak Republic	4.0
13	Korea	4.0
14	Greece	4.0
15	Germany	3.9
16	Singapore	3.9
17	Netherlands	3.9
18	Italy	3.9
19	Taiwan	3.9
20	Costa Rica	3.9
21	Philippines	3.8
22	Hungary	3.8
23	Latvia	3.8
24	Brazil	3.8
25	Norway	3.8
26	Peru	3.8
27	Poland	3.7
28	Panama	3.7
29	Japan	3.7
30	Mauritius	3.7
31	France	3.7
32	Trinidad and Tobago	3.7
33	China	3.7
34	Belgium	3.7
35	Sri Lanka	3.7
36	India	3.7
37	Ireland	3.7
38	Paraguay	3.6
39	Vietnam	3.6
40	United States	3.6
41	New Zealand	3.6
42	Hong Kong SAR	3.6
43	Indonesia	3.5
44	Lithuania	3.4
45	Colombia	3.4
46	Denmark	3.4
47	Canada	3.4
48	South Africa	3.4
49	Mexico	3.4
50	Uruguay	3.4
51	Chile	3.4
52	Jordan	3.4
53	Austria	3.3
54	Turkey	3.3
55	Malaysia	3.3
56	Slovenia	3.3
57	Nigeria	3.3
58	Sweden	3.2
59	United Kingdom	3.2
60	Czech Republic	3.1
61	Switzerland	3.1
62	Bolivia	3.1
63	Honduras	3.1
64	Bangladesh	3.1
65	Russian Federation	3.1
66	Estonia	3.1
67	Nicaragua	3.0
68	Zimbabwe	3.0
69	Jamaica	3.0
70	Guatemala	2.9
71	Venezuela	2.9
72	Bulgaria	2.7
73	Ukraine	2.7
74	Romania	2.5
75	Ecuador	2.5

MEAN: 3.6

2.18 Hidden trade barriers

In your country, hidden import barriers other than published tariffs and quotas are: (1 = an important problem, 7 = not an important problem)

RANK	COUNTRY	SCORE
1	Finland	6.8
2	Netherlands	6.5
3	New Zealand	6.4
4	Denmark	6.4
5	United Kingdom	6.4
6	Hong Kong SAR	6.4
7	Austria	6.3
8	Sweden	6.3
9	Singapore	6.3
10	Germany	6.1
11	France	6.0
12	Estonia	6.0
13	Chile	6.0
14	Iceland	6.0
15	Switzerland	5.9
16	Belgium	5.9
17	Hungary	5.9
18	Ireland	5.9
19	United States	5.9
20	Australia	5.8
21	Greece	5.8
22	Mauritius	5.7
23	Norway	5.7
24	Portugal	5.6
25	Italy	5.6
26	Spain	5.6
27	Canada	5.5
28	Slovenia	5.4
29	Czech Republic	5.4
30	Taiwan	5.3
31	Israel	5.1
32	Peru	5.1
33	Malaysia	5.0
34	Slovak Republic	5.0
35	South Africa	5.0
36	Mexico	4.8
37	Uruguay	4.7
38	Poland	4.7
39	Trinidad and Tobago	4.7
40	Argentina	4.7
41	Thailand	4.4
42	Jamaica	4.4
43	El Salvador	4.4
44	Turkey	4.4
45	Romania	4.3
46	Japan	4.3
47	Jordan	4.2
48	India	4.2
49	Latvia	4.2
50	Zimbabwe	4.1
51	Lithuania	4.1
52	Korea	4.1
53	Costa Rica	4.1
54	Panama	4.0
55	Colombia	3.9
56	Venezuela	3.9
57	Bolivia	3.9
58	Sri Lanka	3.8
59	Bangladesh	3.8
60	Egypt	3.7
61	China	3.6
62	Bulgaria	3.6
63	Guatemala	3.5
64	Ukraine	3.4
65	Brazil	3.4
66	Philippines	3.4
67	Indonesia	3.3
68	Russian Federation	3.3
69	Nicaragua	3.3
70	Honduras	3.0
71	Dominican Republic	3.0
72	Nigeria	2.9
73	Vietnam	2.9
74	Ecuador	2.9
75	Paraguay	2.5

MEAN: 4.8

2.19 Permits to export

Approximately how many permits does your company require to export goods? (median response given for each country)

RANK	COUNTRY	# OF PERMITS
1	Canada	1.0
1	Denmark	1.0
1	Finland	1.0
1	Germany	1.0
1	Greece	1.0
1	Hong Kong SAR	1.0
1	Ireland	1.0
1	Japan	1.0
1	Malaysia	1.0
1	Netherlands	1.0
1	Norway	1.0
1	Singapore	1.0
1	Slovak Republic	1.0
1	Sri Lanka	1.0
1	Switzerland	1.0
1	United Kingdom	1.0
1	United States	1.0
1	Zimbabwe	1.0
19	Belgium	1.5
19	France	1.5
19	Sweden	1.5
22	Australia	2.0
22	Austria	2.0
22	Chile	2.0
22	Egypt	2.0
22	El Salvador	2.0
22	Estonia	2.0
22	Hungary	2.0
22	Iceland	2.0
22	Israel	2.0
22	Italy	2.0
22	Mauritius	2.0
22	Mexico	2.0
22	New Zealand	2.0
22	Peru	2.0
22	Philippines	2.0
22	Poland	2.0
22	Portugal	2.0
22	Romania	2.0
22	Slovenia	2.0
22	South Africa	2.0
22	Taiwan	2.0
22	Turkey	2.0
44	Argentina	2.5
44	Jordan	2.5
46	Bangladesh	3.0
46	Bolivia	3.0
46	Brazil	3.0
46	Costa Rica	3.0
46	Czech Republic	3.0
46	India	3.0
46	Indonesia	3.0
46	Jamaica	3.0
46	Korea	3.0
46	Nigeria	3.0
46	Spain	3.0
46	Thailand	3.0
46	Trinidad and Tobago	3.0
46	Venezuela	3.0
60	Colombia	4.0
60	Dominican Republic	4.0
60	Ecuador	4.0
60	Guatemala	4.0
60	Latvia	4.0
60	Nicaragua	4.0
60	Panama	4.0
60	Russian Federation	4.0
60	Uruguay	4.0
69	Bulgaria	4.5
69	Vietnam	4.5
71	China	5.0
71	Honduras	5.0
71	Lithuania	5.0
71	Ukraine	5.0
75	Paraguay	6.0

MEAN: 2.5

2.20 Composition of public spending

The composition of government spending in your country: (1 = is wasteful, 7 = provides necessary goods and services not provided by the market)

RANK	COUNTRY	SCORE
1	Singapore	5.9
2	Finland	5.6
3	Hong Kong SAR	5.5
4	Iceland	5.3
5	Switzerland	5.2
6	Spain	5.1
7	Netherlands	5.0
8	Australia	4.8
9	Ireland	4.5
10	Taiwan	4.3
11	Jordan	4.3
12	Thailand	4.3
13	United States	4.2
14	Denmark	4.2
15	Malaysia	4.2
16	Slovak Republic	4.2
17	Austria	4.2
18	United Kingdom	4.2
19	Mauritius	4.1
20	Germany	4.1
21	Trinidad and Tobago	4.1
22	New Zealand	4.1
23	Belgium	4.1
24	Hungary	4.1
25	France	4.0
26	Canada	3.9
27	Egypt	3.9
28	Chile	3.9
29	Sweden	3.9
30	South Africa	3.8
31	Israel	3.7
32	Norway	3.7
33	Estonia	3.6
34	El Salvador	3.5
35	Korea	3.3
36	China	3.3
37	Mexico	3.3
38	Slovenia	3.3
39	Poland	3.2
40	Latvia	3.2
41	India	3.2
42	Panama	3.2
43	Czech Republic	3.2
44	Bulgaria	3.2
45	Jamaica	3.2
46	Vietnam	3.1
47	Indonesia	3.1
48	Greece	3.0
49	Italy	3.0
50	Uruguay	2.9
51	Japan	2.9
52	Costa Rica	2.9
53	Philippines	2.8
54	Turkey	2.8
55	Peru	2.8
56	Bangladesh	2.7
57	Nigeria	2.7
58	Dominican Republic	2.7
59	Brazil	2.7
60	Portugal	2.7
61	Sri Lanka	2.6
62	Lithuania	2.6
63	Bolivia	2.5
64	Romania	2.5
65	Russian Federation	2.5
66	Colombia	2.3
67	Nicaragua	2.3
68	Argentina	2.2
69	Honduras	2.2
70	Guatemala	2.2
71	Venezuela	2.2
72	Ukraine	2.1
73	Ecuador	2.0
74	Paraguay	1.7
75	Zimbabwe	1.4

MEAN: 3.5

2.21 Social transfer recipients

Government social transfers go primarily to: (1 = poor people, 7 = rich people)

RANK	COUNTRY	SCORE	MEAN: 3.1
1	South Africa	2.0	
2	France	2.2	
3	Finland	2.2	
4	New Zealand	2.3	
5	Romania	2.3	
6	Iceland	2.3	
7	Netherlands	2.4	
8	Peru	2.4	
9	Denmark	2.5	
10	Canada	2.5	
11	Italy	2.6	
12	Australia	2.6	
13	Ukraine	2.6	
14	Israel	2.7	
15	United Kingdom	2.7	
16	Czech Republic	2.7	
17	Venezuela	2.7	
18	Chile	2.7	
19	Costa Rica	2.7	
20	United States	2.7	
21	Egypt	2.8	
22	El Salvador	2.8	
23	Slovak Republic	2.8	
24	Norway	2.8	
25	Bulgaria	2.8	
26	Ecuador	2.8	
27	Dominican Republic	2.8	
28	Sweden	2.9	
29	Mexico	2.9	
30	Belgium	2.9	
31	Estonia	2.9	
32	Mauritius	2.9	
33	Hong Kong SAR	2.9	
34	Switzerland	2.9	
35	Spain	2.9	
36	Portugal	2.9	
37	Germany	2.9	
38	Singapore	2.9	
39	Jordan	2.9	
40	Greece	3.0	
41	Austria	3.0	
42	Uruguay	3.0	
43	Slovenia	3.1	
44	Ireland	3.1	
45	Taiwan	3.2	
46	Sri Lanka	3.2	
47	India	3.2	
48	Guatemala	3.3	
49	Poland	3.3	
50	Japan	3.3	
51	Panama	3.3	
52	Latvia	3.4	
53	Bolivia	3.4	
54	Hungary	3.4	
55	Argentina	3.4	
56	Thailand	3.5	
57	China	3.5	
58	Malaysia	3.5	
59	Trinidad and Tobago	3.5	
60	Philippines	3.5	
61	Turkey	3.5	
62	Vietnam	3.5	
63	Indonesia	3.5	
64	Lithuania	3.5	
65	Honduras	3.5	
66	Jamaica	3.6	
67	Brazil	3.6	
68	Russian Federation	3.7	
69	Zimbabwe	3.8	
70	Colombia	3.8	
71	Bangladesh	4.1	
72	Nicaragua	4.1	
73	Korea	4.2	
74	Paraguay	4.6	
75	Nigeria	4.9	

2.22 Extent of distortive government subsidies

Government subsidies to business in your country: (1 = keep uncompetitive industries alive artificially, 7 = improve the productivity of industries)

RANK	COUNTRY	SCORE	MEAN: 3.6
1	Singapore	6.1	
2	Finland	5.6	
3	Hong Kong SAR	5.2	
4	Hungary	5.0	
5	Ireland	4.5	
6	New Zealand	4.4	
7	Austria	4.4	
8	Taiwan	4.3	
9	Estonia	4.2	
10	United Kingdom	4.2	
11	Italy	4.2	
12	Brazil	4.2	
13	Netherlands	4.2	
14	Australia	4.2	
15	Spain	4.1	
16	Switzerland	4.1	
17	Chile	4.1	
18	Sweden	4.0	
19	Thailand	3.9	
20	Denmark	3.9	
21	South Africa	3.9	
22	Peru	3.9	
23	France	3.8	
24	United States	3.8	
25	Vietnam	3.8	
26	Belgium	3.8	
27	Israel	3.8	
28	Jordan	3.8	
29	Latvia	3.8	
30	Sri Lanka	3.8	
31	Trinidad and Tobago	3.7	
32	Mexico	3.7	
33	Korea	3.7	
34	China	3.6	
35	Slovak Republic	3.6	
36	Canada	3.6	
37	Argentina	3.5	
38	Mauritius	3.5	
39	Indonesia	3.4	
40	El Salvador	3.4	
41	Norway	3.4	
42	Slovenia	3.4	
43	Malaysia	3.4	
44	Iceland	3.4	
45	Colombia	3.4	
46	Panama	3.4	
47	Jamaica	3.3	
48	Philippines	3.3	
49	Uruguay	3.3	
50	Egypt	3.3	
51	Portugal	3.2	
52	Russian Federation	3.2	
53	Turkey	3.2	
54	Costa Rica	3.2	
55	Czech Republic	3.1	
56	Nicaragua	3.1	
57	Nigeria	3.1	
58	Greece	3.1	
59	Bulgaria	3.1	
60	Dominican Republic	3.0	
61	Lithuania	2.9	
62	Bolivia	2.9	
63	Bangladesh	2.9	
64	Germany	2.9	
65	Japan	2.8	
66	Poland	2.8	
67	Paraguay	2.7	
68	India	2.7	
69	Venezuela	2.6	
70	Guatemala	2.5	
71	Ukraine	2.4	
72	Honduras	2.4	
73	Ecuador	2.4	
74	Zimbabwe	2.0	
75	Romania	1.9	

2.23 Country credit rating, March 2001

Institutional Investor country credit rating (scale of 1 to 100), March 2001

RANK	COUNTRY	HARD DATA
1	Switzerland	95.1
2	Germany	94.0
3	Netherlands	93.4
4	France	92.9
5	United States	92.7
6	United Kingdom	92.3
7	Norway	90.8
8	Austria	89.5
9	Canada	88.2
10	Denmark	88.1
11	Finland	87.5
12	Japan	87.2
13	Belgium	86.9
14	Sweden	86.5
15	Singapore	85.8
16	Ireland	85.7
17	Spain	84.5
18	Italy	84.2
19	Portugal	81.5
20	Australia	79.0
21	New Zealand	76.9
22	Taiwan	76.1
23	Iceland	73.3
24	Greece	71.2
25	Hong Kong SAR	67.0
26	Chile	65.7
27	Slovenia	64.0
28	Korea	62.4
29	Israel	62.1
30	Czech Republic	60.7
31	Hungary	60.2
32	Poland	59.3
33	Malaysia	58.9
34	China	58.6
35	Mexico	57.3
36	Estonia	53.2
37	Mauritius	52.2
38	Trinidad and Tobago	51.2
39	Uruguay	51.0
40	South Africa	50.6
41	Thailand	50.2
42	India	47.7
43	Egypt	47.5
44	Latvia	45.8
45	Slovak Republic	45.5
46	Panama	45.4
47	Costa Rica	44.4
48	Lithuania	44.0
49	Brazil	43.7
49	Turkey	43.7
51	Philippines	43.1
52	Colombia	40.5
53	Argentina	39.8
54	El Salvador	38.7
55	Jordan	38.5
55	Peru	38.5
57	Venezuela	35.8
58	Bulgaria	35.0
59	Sri Lanka	34.6
60	Dominican Republic	34.3
61	Guatemala	32.6
62	Paraguay	30.0
63	Bolivia	29.0
64	Jamaica	28.5
64	Vietnam	28.5
66	Romania	28.3
67	Bangladesh	27.4
68	Russian Federation	27.0
69	Indonesia	25.1
70	Honduras	23.9
71	Ecuador	19.6
72	Nigeria	18.0
73	Ukraine	17.2
74	Nicaragua	16.3
75	Zimbabwe	16.2

SOURCE: *Institutional Investor Online*

2.24 Government surplus/deficit, 2000

General government fiscal surplus/deficit as a percentage of GDP, 2000

RANK	COUNTRY	HARD DATA
1	Norway	14.9
2	Ireland	4.7
3	Finland	4.5
4	Canada	3.4
5	Singapore	3.4
6	Russian Federation	3.1
7	Denmark	2.9
7	Sweden	2.9
9	Iceland	2.8
10	Ukraine	2.2
11	United Kingdom	2.1
12	Netherlands	2.0
12	United States	2.0
14	Trinidad and Tobago	1.8
15	Australia	1.6
16	Ecuador	1.5
17	Korea	1.0
18	New Zealand	0.3
19	Chile	0.1
20	Belgium	0.0
21	Hong Kong SAR	–0.3
21	Spain	–0.3
23	Estonia	–0.7
24	Greece	–0.8
24	Nigeria	–0.8
26	Dominican Republic	–1.0
27	Jamaica	–1.0
28	Austria	–1.1
28	Germany	–1.1
28	Mexico	–1.1
28	Panama	–1.1
32	Switzerland	–1.2
33	Bulgaria	–1.3
34	France	–1.3
35	Portugal	–1.4
35	Slovenia	–1.4
37	Italy	–1.5
38	South Africa	–1.9
38	Venezuela	–1.9
40	Honduras	–2.0
41	Thailand	–2.2
42	Guatemala	–2.4
43	Israel	–2.5
44	China	–2.7
45	Lithuania	–2.8
46	Costa Rica	–2.9
46	Hungary	–2.9
48	El Salvador	–3.0
48	Peru	–3.0
50	Indonesia	–3.3
50	Latvia	–3.3
50	Poland	–3.3
53	Paraguay	–3.4
54	Argentina	–3.6
55	Bolivia	–3.7
55	Czech Republic	–3.7
55	Romania	–3.7
58	Egypt	–3.8
58	Slovak Republic	–3.8
58	Uruguay	–3.8
61	Philippines	–4.1
62	Brazil	–4.3
63	Taiwan	–4.7
64	Vietnam	–4.8
65	Malaysia	–5.8
66	Colombia	–6.4
67	Japan	–7.1
68	Mauritius	–7.3
69	Bangladesh	–7.7
70	Jordan	–7.9
71	Sri Lanka	–9.4
72	India	–10.1
72	Turkey	–10.1
74	Nicaragua	–13.5
75	Zimbabwe	–30.4

SOURCES: IMF Country Reports, Economist Intelligence Unit, and national sources

2.25 Government expenditure, 2000

General government expenditure as a percentage of GDP, 2000

RANK	COUNTRY	HARD DATA
1	Guatemala	12.8
2	Dominican Republic	14.9
3	Thailand	17.4
4	China	17.8
5	El Salvador	18.6
6	Bangladesh	18.9
7	Hong Kong SAR	19.1
8	Philippines	19.3
9	Venezuela	21.4
10	Indonesia	22.2
11	Costa Rica	22.3
12	Mexico	23.4
13	Argentina	24.1
14	Vietnam	24.9
15	Mauritius	25.3
16	Korea	25.4
17	Chile	26.4
18	Ecuador	26.5
18	Peru	26.5
20	Singapore	26.6
20	South Africa	26.6
20	Sri Lanka	26.6
23	Trinidad and Tobago	27.4
24	Malaysia	27.6
25	Brazil	27.7
26	Paraguay	28.1
27	Ireland	28.9
27	United States	28.9
29	Bolivia	29.3
30	Panama	29.8
31	Colombia	30.9
32	Egypt	31.5
33	India	31.8
33	Nigeria	31.8
35	Lithuania	32.3
36	Australia	32.8
37	Taiwan	33.0
38	Honduras	33.3
39	Jordan	33.9
40	New Zealand	34.2
41	Jamaica	34.8
42	Ukraine	35.0
42	Uruguay	35.0
44	Russian Federation	36.0
45	Turkey	36.6
46	Romania	37.1
47	Nicaragua	37.6
48	Switzerland	37.7
49	United Kingdom	39.1
50	Japan	39.3
51	Estonia	39.6
52	Spain	40.6
53	Latvia	40.9
54	Iceland	41.0
55	Bulgaria	41.1
56	Norway	41.4
57	Poland	42.7
58	Canada	42.9
59	Greece	43.3
60	Czech Republic	43.6
60	Slovenia	43.6
62	Hungary	44.1
63	Netherlands	45.2
64	Finland	45.3
65	Portugal	46.6
66	Slovak Republic	46.7
67	Germany	47.6
68	Italy	48.1
69	Belgium	49.6
70	Zimbabwe	49.9
71	Israel	50.6
72	Austria	51.8
73	France	52.6
74	Denmark	53.7
75	Sweden	54.9

SOURCES: IMF Country Reports, Economist Intelligence Unit, and national sources

2.26 National savings rate, 2000

National savings rate as a percentage of GDP, 2000

RANK	COUNTRY	HARD DATA
1	Singapore	58.3
2	China	39.2
3	Norway	36.3
4	Malaysia	36.1
4	Russian Federation	36.1
6	Switzerland	33.9
7	Hong Kong SAR	32.9
7	Nigeria	32.9
9	Trinidad and Tobago	32.0
10	Korea	31.0
11	Philippines	29.6
12	Vietnam	29.0
13	Japan	28.5
14	Jordan	28.1
15	Finland	27.8
15	Honduras	27.8
17	Hungary	27.3
17	Thailand	27.3
19	Mauritius	27.0
20	Ecuador	26.8
21	Netherlands	26.6
21	Slovak Republic	26.6
23	Ireland	26.3
24	Belgium	26.2
25	Taiwan	25.8
25	Venezuela	25.8
27	Czech Republic	25.4
27	Ukraine	25.4
29	Slovenia	24.6
30	Denmark	24.2
31	Egypt	23.1
32	Indonesia	22.9
33	Spain	22.8
34	Jamaica	22.7
35	France	22.3
35	Latvia	22.3
37	Chile	22.0
38	Canada	21.8
39	Sweden	21.6
40	Germany	21.5
41	Austria	21.2
41	India	21.2
43	Sri Lanka	20.9
44	Brazil	20.8
45	Mexico	20.4
46	Dominican Republic	20.3
47	Italy	20.1
48	Panama	19.8
49	Greece	19.7
49	Poland	19.7
51	Turkey	18.8
52	Estonia	18.6
53	Australia	18.4
54	Israel	18.2
55	Portugal	18.1
56	Lithuania	17.7
57	Peru	17.6
58	Paraguay	17.0
59	South Africa	16.5
60	United Kingdom	16.1
61	Romania	15.6
62	New Zealand	15.0
63	Bangladesh	14.5
64	Argentina	14.3
65	United States	14.0
65	Zimbabwe	14.0
67	Iceland	13.7
68	El Salvador	13.1
69	Colombia	12.8
70	Bolivia	12.6
71	Costa Rica	11.8
72	Bulgaria	10.7
73	Uruguay	10.5
74	Guatemala	9.3
75	Nicaragua	5.8

SOURCES: Economist Intelligence Unit and IMF Country Reports

2.27 Investment rate, 2000

Gross fixed investment as a percentage of GDP, 2000

RANK	COUNTRY	HARD DATA
1	Nicaragua	36.7
2	China	36.3
3	Singapore	32.8
4	Mauritius	30.2
5	Slovak Republic	30.0
6	Korea	28.6
7	Portugal	28.2
8	Sri Lanka	27.3
9	Czech Republic	27.2
9	Ireland	27.2
11	Honduras	27.1
12	Slovenia	27.0
13	Jamaica	26.6
14	Vietnam	26.2
15	Japan	26.1
16	Hong Kong SAR	25.8
17	Malaysia	25.7
18	Spain	25.5
19	Poland	25.4
20	Dominican Republic	25.2
21	Latvia	25.0
22	Panama	24.9
23	Estonia	24.7
23	Greece	24.7
25	Hungary	24.6
25	Nigeria	24.6
27	Trinidad and Tobago	24.3
28	Iceland	23.8
28	Indonesia	23.8
30	Austria	23.7
31	Taiwan	23.3
32	Australia	22.9
33	Paraguay	22.4
34	Chile	22.3
34	Netherlands	22.3
36	Lithuania	22.2
37	Denmark	21.9
37	India	21.9
39	Turkey	21.7
40	Belgium	21.4
40	Germany	21.4
42	Jordan	21.1
43	Egypt	21.0
44	Mexico	20.8
44	Ukraine	20.8
46	Switzerland	20.7
47	New Zealand	20.0
48	Norway	19.8
48	Peru	19.8
50	France	19.7
50	Thailand	19.7
52	Italy	19.6
53	Brazil	19.4
54	Canada	19.3
55	Finland	19.0
56	Romania	18.5
57	Bolivia	18.4
58	Russian Federation	18.3
59	Israel	17.8
59	Philippines	17.8
59	United States	17.8
62	United Kingdom	17.7
63	Costa Rica	17.2
64	Guatemala	17.1
64	Sweden	17.1
67	Bangladesh	16.2
67	Bulgaria	16.2
67	Ecuador	16.2
67	El Salvador	16.2
70	Argentina	16.0
71	South Africa	15.7
72	Zimbabwe	15.2
73	Venezuela	14.5
74	Uruguay	13.0
75	Colombia	11.8

SOURCE: Economist Intelligence Unit

2.28 Inflation, 2000

Percentage change in Consumer Price Index, 2000

RANK	COUNTRY	HARD DATA
1	Hong Kong SAR	–3.7
2	Vietnam	–1.7
3	Argentina	–0.7
4	Japan	–0.6
5	China	0.4
6	Jordan	0.7
7	Lithuania	1.0
8	Sweden	1.0
9	Israel	1.1
10	Taiwan	1.3
11	Singapore	1.4
12	Panama	1.4
13	Malaysia	1.5
14	Thailand	1.6
15	Switzerland	1.6
16	France	1.8
17	Austria	2.0
18	Germany	2.1
19	United Kingdom	2.1
20	Korea	2.2
21	Netherlands	2.3
22	El Salvador	2.5
23	Italy	2.6
24	Latvia	2.7
24	New Zealand	2.7
26	Canada	2.7
27	Portugal	2.8
28	Egypt	2.8
29	Greece	2.9
30	Belgium	2.9
31	Finland	3.0
32	Norway	3.0
33	Denmark	3.1
34	United States	3.4
35	Spain	3.4
36	Trinidad and Tobago	3.5
37	Indonesia	3.8
38	Peru	3.8
39	Chile	3.8
40	Czech Republic	3.9
41	Estonia	4.0
41	India	4.0
43	Philippines	4.3
44	Australia	4.5
45	Bolivia	4.6
46	Bangladesh	4.7
47	Uruguay	4.8
48	Iceland	5.0
49	Mauritius	5.3
50	Ireland	5.3
51	South Africa	5.4
52	Sri Lanka	6.2
53	Nigeria	6.9
54	Brazil	7.0
54	Guatemala	7.0
56	Jamaica	7.7
57	Dominican Republic	7.7
58	Slovenia	8.9
59	Paraguay	9.0
60	Colombia	9.2
61	Mexico	9.5
62	Nicaragua	9.7
63	Hungary	9.8
64	Poland	10.1
65	Bulgaria	10.4
66	Honduras	10.5
67	Costa Rica	11.5
68	Slovak Republic	12.0
69	Venezuela	16.2
70	Russian Federation	20.8
71	Ukraine	28.2
72	Romania	45.7
73	Turkey	54.9
74	Zimbabwe	55.9
75	Ecuador	96.2

SOURCES: IMF *World Economic Outlook Database, May 2001*, IMF *International Financial Statistics, June 2001*, and Economist Intelligence Unit

2.29 Real exchange rate

2000 period average real exchange rate relative to the United States (1990 to 1995 average = 100, 1995 = 100 for transition economies). Values greater (less) than 100 indicate depreciation (appreciation) relative to the United States.

RANK	COUNTRY	HARD DATA
1	Indonesia	177.2
2	South Africa	155.7
3	Finland	151.0
4	Sweden	149.1
5	Spain	148.1
6	Brazil	143.0
7	Ecuador	142.9
8	Italy	142.7
9	France	142.6
10	Russian Federation	142.4
11	Belgium	141.6
12	Austria	140.9
13	Germany	140.7
14	Thailand	138.7
15	Slovenia	138.2
16	Norway	137.4
17	Netherlands	136.9
18	Nigeria	136.9
19	Ireland	136.8
20	New Zealand	136.0
21	Malaysia	135.6
22	Switzerland	135.3
23	Denmark	135.1
24	Portugal	133.7
25	Australia	131.5
26	Greece	129.1
27	Korea	128.9
28	Hungary	126.1
29	Canada	125.9
30	Nicaragua	125.1
31	Iceland	123.5
32	Zimbabwe	122.4
33	Taiwan	122.3
34	Vietnam	121.1
35	Mauritius	120.2
36	Slovak Republic	118.9
37	Czech Republic	118.5
38	Philippines	118.1
39	Paraguay	117.5
40	Singapore	116.4
41	Ukraine	114.8
42	India	113.8
43	Peru	113.8
44	Bangladesh	111.5
45	Panama	111.4
46	Poland	111.2
47	Bolivia	108.2
48	Israel	107.3
49	United Kingdom	107.1
50	Trinidad and Tobago	106.7
51	Japan	106.5
52	Sri Lanka	106.0
53	Estonia	105.7
54	Bulgaria	103.6
55	Chile	102.9
56	Turkey	102.1
57	China	101.9
58	Costa Rica	101.0
59	Romania	101.0
60	United States	100.0
61	Jordan	99.3
62	Argentina	96.4
63	Colombia	95.9
64	Guatemala	93.8
65	Dominican Republic	93.2
66	Latvia	92.6
67	Hong Kong SAR	91.7
68	Mexico	89.1
69	Uruguay	86.4
70	Honduras	84.8
71	Egypt	84.7
72	El Salvador	79.8
73	Lithuania	77.9
74	Jamaica	74.7
75	Venezuela	58.8

SOURCE: IMF *International Financial Statistics, June 2001*

2.30 Interest rate spread, 2000

Average interest rate spread in 2000: Difference between typical lending and deposit rates

RANK	COUNTRY	HARD DATA
1	Korea	0.6
2	Japan	1.3
3	Norway	1.5
4	Canada	1.6
5	Switzerland	1.8
6	Netherlands	1.9
7	Spain	2.2
8	Jordan	2.6
8	Philippines	2.6
8	United Kingdom	2.6
11	United States	2.7
12	Argentina	2.8
13	Hungary	3.0
14	Panama	3.1
15	Nigeria	3.2
16	Taiwan	3.4
17	Malaysia	3.4
18	China	3.6
18	Sweden	3.6
20	Czech Republic	3.7
20	Egypt	3.7
22	New Zealand	3.8
23	Estonia	3.9
24	Portugal	3.9
25	France	4.1
25	Singapore	4.1
27	India	4.3
28	Israel	4.3
29	Belgium	4.4
30	Italy	4.5
30	Thailand	4.5
32	Australia	4.7
32	El Salvador	4.7
32	Hong Kong SAR	4.7
32	Ireland	4.7
36	Austria	5.0
36	Denmark	5.0
36	Finland	5.0
39	South Africa	5.3
39	Vietnam	5.3
41	Sri Lanka	5.5
42	Chile	5.6
43	Slovenia	5.7
44	Poland	5.8
45	Indonesia	6.0
46	Germany	6.2
46	Greece	6.2
48	Slovak Republic	6.5
49	Bangladesh	7.3
50	Latvia	7.5
51	Lithuania	8.2
52	Bulgaria	8.4
53	Trinidad and Tobago	8.5
54	Ecuador	8.9
54	Venezuela	8.9
56	Brazil	9.6
57	Iceland	9.7
58	Guatemala	10.7
59	Honduras	10.9
60	Paraguay	11.1
61	Mauritius	11.2
62	Costa Rica	11.5
63	Jamaica	11.8
64	Mexico	11.9
65	Nicaragua	12.0
66	Romania	13.5
67	Colombia	14.3
68	Peru	14.6
69	Turkey	15.0
70	Russian Federation	17.9
71	Zimbabwe	18.0
72	Dominican Republic	22.5
73	Bolivia	23.6
74	Ukraine	28.8
75	Uruguay	37.0

SOURCES: IMF *International Financial Statistics, June 2001* and Economist Intelligence Unit

2.31 Average tariff rate (%), 2001

Average tariff rate (%), 2001

RANK	COUNTRY	HARD DATA
1	Estonia	0.0
1	Hong Kong SAR	0.0
3	Canada	1.0
3	Israel	1.0
3	Latvia	1.0
3	Mexico	1.0
3	Singapore	1.0
3	Switzerland	1.0
9	Lithuania	1.1
10	Iceland	1.3
11	Norway	2.0
11	United States	2.0
13	Czech Republic	2.2
13	Japan	2.2
15	Slovak Republic	2.4
16	Australia	3.0
17	Taiwan	3.1
18	Austria	3.5
18	Belgium	3.5
18	Denmark	3.5
18	Finland	3.5
18	France	3.5
18	Germany	3.5
18	Greece	3.5
18	Ireland	3.5
18	Italy	3.5
18	Netherlands	3.5
18	New Zealand	3.5
18	Portugal	3.5
18	Spain	3.5
18	Sweden	3.5
18	United Kingdom	3.5
33	Hungary	3.6
34	Uruguay	3.6
35	Poland	3.7
35	Thailand	3.7
37	El Salvador	3.9
38	Jamaica	4.3
39	Honduras	5.6
40	Romania	5.8
41	Turkey	6.0
42	Guatemala	6.2
43	Costa Rica	6.6
44	Bolivia	6.7
44	Chile	6.7
46	Sri Lanka	7.4
47	Argentina	7.5
47	Ukraine	7.5
49	Colombia	7.9
50	Philippines	8.3
51	Korea	8.6
52	Slovenia	8.8
53	Indonesia	8.9
54	Trinidad and Tobago	9.1
55	Peru	9.2
56	Malaysia	9.5
57	Jordan	9.6
57	Paraguay	9.6
59	Nicaragua	9.7
60	Venezuela	11.8
61	South Africa	12.0
61	Panama	12.0
63	Mauritius	12.4
64	Dominican Republic	12.8
65	Ecuador	13.0
66	Bulgaria	13.9
66	Russian Federation	13.9
68	Brazil	14.0
69	Bangladesh	15.6
70	Zimbabwe	15.8
71	China	17.0
72	Vietnam	17.5
73	Egypt	18.9
74	India	27.2
75	Nigeria	29.0

SOURCE: G P O'Driscoll Jr, K Holmes, and M Kirkpatrick, *2001 Index of Economic Freedom* (Heritage Foundation and Dow Jones and Company)

2.32 Corporate income tax rate, 2001

Top corporate tax rate (%), 2001

RANK	COUNTRY	HARD DATA
1	Estonia	0.0
2	Brazil	15.0
2	Chile	15.0
4	Hong Kong SAR	16.0
5	Hungary	18.0
6	Ireland	24.0
7	Bolivia	25.0
7	Dominican Republic	25.0
7	Ecuador	25.0
7	El Salvador	25.0
7	Guatemala	25.0
7	Honduras	25.0
7	Latvia	25.0
7	Nicaragua	25.0
7	Slovenia	25.0
7	Taiwan	25.0
17	Singapore	25.5
18	Malaysia	28.0
18	Norway	28.0
18	Sweden	28.0
21	Finland	29.0
21	Lithuania	29.0
21	Slovak Republic	29.0
24	China	30.0
24	Costa Rica	30.0
24	Iceland	30.0
24	Indonesia	30.0
24	Japan	30.0
24	Nigeria	30.0
24	Panama	30.0
24	Paraguay	30.0
24	Peru	30.0
24	South Africa	30.0
24	Thailand	30.0
24	Turkey	30.0
24	Ukraine	30.0
24	United Kingdom	30.0
24	Uruguay	30.0
39	Czech Republic	31.0
41	Denmark	32.0
41	Philippines	32.0
41	Poland	32.0
41	Portugal	32.0
41	Switzerland	32.0
41	Vietnam	32.0
46	New Zealand	33.0
47	Jamaica	33.3
48	Austria	34.0
48	Venezuela	34.0
50	Argentina	35.0
50	Colombia	35.0
50	India	35.0
50	Jordan	35.0
50	Mauritius	35.0
50	Mexico	35.0
50	Netherlands	35.0
50	Russian Federation	35.0
50	Spain	35.0
50	Sri Lanka	35.0
50	Trinidad and Tobago	35.0
50	United States	35.0
50	Zimbabwe	35.0
63	Korea	35.5
64	Australia	36.0
64	Israel	36.0
66	Italy	37.0
67	Romania	38.0
68	Belgium	39.0
69	Bangladesh	40.0
69	Bulgaria	40.0
69	Egypt	40.0
69	Germany	40.0
69	Greece	40.0
74	France	41.7
75	Canada	46.1

SOURCE: G P O'Driscoll Jr, K Holmes, and M Kirkpatrick, *2001 Index of Economic Freedom* (Heritage Foundation and Dow Jones and Company)

2.33 Value added tax rate

Representative value added tax (%), 2001

RANK	COUNTRY	HARD DATA
1	Hong Kong SAR	0.0
1	United States	0.0
3	Singapore	3.0
4	Japan	5.0
4	Nigeria	5.0
4	Panama	5.0
4	Taiwan	5.0
8	Canada	7.0
8	Thailand	7.0
10	Switzerland	7.6
11	Dominican Republic	8.0
12	Australia	10.0
12	Egypt	10.0
12	Guatemala	10.0
12	Indonesia	10.0
12	Korea	10.0
12	Malaysia	10.0
12	Mauritius	10.0
12	Paraguay	10.0
12	Philippines	10.0
12	Vietnam	10.0
22	Ecuador	12.0
22	Honduras	12.0
24	New Zealand	12.5
24	Sri Lanka	12.5
26	Bolivia	13.0
26	Costa Rica	13.0
26	El Salvador	13.0
26	Jordan	13.0
30	South Africa	14.0
31	Venezuela	14.5
32	Bangladesh	15.0
32	Jamaica	15.0
32	Mexico	15.0
32	Nicaragua	15.0
32	Trinidad and Tobago	15.0
37	Colombia	16.0
37	Germany	16.0
37	India	16.0
37	Spain	16.0
41	Brazil	17.0
41	China	17.0
41	Israel	17.0
41	Portugal	17.0
41	Turkey	17.0
46	United Kingdom	17.5
47	Chile	18.0
47	Estonia	18.0
47	Greece	18.0
47	Latvia	18.0
47	Lithuania	18.0
47	Peru	18.0
53	Netherlands	19.0
53	Romania	19.0
53	Slovenia	19.0
56	France	19.6
57	Austria	20.0
57	Bulgaria	20.0
57	Ireland	20.0
57	Italy	20.0
57	Russian Federation	20.0
57	Ukraine	20.0
63	Argentina	21.0
63	Belgium	21.0
65	Czech Republic	22.0
65	Finland	22.0
65	Poland	22.0
68	Slovak Republic	23.0
68	Uruguay	23.0
70	Norway	24.0
71	Iceland	24.5
72	Denmark	25.0
72	Hungary	25.0
72	Sweden	25.0
72	Zimbabwe	25.0

363

SOURCE: G P O'Driscoll Jr, K Holmes, and M Kirkpatrick, *2001 Index of Economic Freedom* (Heritage Foundation and Dow Jones and Company)

Section III: Technological Innovation and Diffusion

3.01 Technological sophistication

Your country's position in technology: (1 = generally lags behind most countries, 7 = is among the world's leaders)

RANK	COUNTRY	SCORE
1	United States	6.8
2	Israel	6.6
3	Finland	6.6
4	Sweden	6.6
5	Japan	6.4
6	Switzerland	6.4
7	Germany	6.3
8	Netherlands	6.3
9	Iceland	6.1
10	France	6.0
11	United Kingdom	6.0
12	Canada	5.9
13	Singapore	5.9
14	Ireland	5.8
15	Denmark	5.8
16	Australia	5.7
17	Austria	5.7
18	Belgium	5.6
19	Taiwan	5.5
20	Norway	5.5
21	Hong Kong SAR	5.0
22	Korea	4.9
23	New Zealand	4.8
24	Czech Republic	4.7
25	Chile	4.6
26	Spain	4.6
27	Hungary	4.5
28	India	4.5
29	South Africa	4.5
30	Estonia	4.3
31	Italy	4.3
32	Slovak Republic	4.2
33	Trinidad and Tobago	4.2
34	Costa Rica	4.1
35	Slovenia	4.1
36	Brazil	4.1
37	Poland	3.9
38	Malaysia	3.8
39	Jamaica	3.8
40	Thailand	3.8
41	Latvia	3.8
42	China	3.7
43	Jordan	3.7
44	Argentina	3.6
45	Uruguay	3.6
46	Portugal	3.6
47	Venezuela	3.5
48	Mexico	3.5
49	Lithuania	3.4
50	Philippines	3.4
51	Dominican Republic	3.4
52	Greece	3.4
53	Indonesia	3.3
54	Panama	3.3
55	Turkey	3.3
56	Russian Federation	3.2
57	Sri Lanka	3.2
58	Egypt	3.2
59	Zimbabwe	3.1
60	Ukraine	3.0
61	Mauritius	2.9
62	Colombia	2.9
63	Peru	2.8
64	El Salvador	2.7
65	Bulgaria	2.6
66	Nigeria	2.4
67	Guatemala	2.4
68	Paraguay	2.4
69	Ecuador	2.2
70	Nicaragua	2.2
71	Vietnam	2.1
72	Romania	2.0
73	Bangladesh	2.0
74	Bolivia	1.8
75	Honduras	1.8

MEAN: 4.2

3.02 Firm-level innovation

In your business, continuous innovation plays a major role in generating revenue. (1 = not true, 7 = true)

RANK	COUNTRY	SCORE
1	United States	6.4
2	Romania	6.3
3	France	6.2
4	Germany	6.2
5	Singapore	6.2
6	United Kingdom	6.2
7	Finland	6.1
8	Austria	6.1
9	Japan	6.0
10	Switzerland	6.0
11	Canada	6.0
12	Belgium	5.9
13	Sweden	5.8
14	Malaysia	5.8
15	Philippines	5.8
16	Norway	5.7
17	Netherlands	5.7
18	Czech Republic	5.7
19	Taiwan	5.7
20	Denmark	5.7
21	Nigeria	5.7
22	Indonesia	5.6
23	Chile	5.6
24	Hong Kong SAR	5.6
25	Iceland	5.6
26	South Africa	5.5
27	Poland	5.5
28	Brazil	5.5
29	Ireland	5.5
30	Argentina	5.5
31	Costa Rica	5.5
32	Vietnam	5.4
33	Peru	5.4
34	India	5.4
35	Australia	5.4
36	Mexico	5.4
37	Israel	5.3
38	Trinidad and Tobago	5.3
39	Italy	5.3
40	Spain	5.3
41	China	5.3
42	Estonia	5.3
43	New Zealand	5.3
44	Dominican Republic	5.2
45	Panama	5.2
46	Venezuela	5.2
47	Mauritius	5.2
48	Latvia	5.2
49	Sri Lanka	5.2
50	Greece	5.1
51	Jamaica	5.1
52	Korea	5.1
53	Bangladesh	5.1
54	Honduras	5.0
55	Hungary	5.0
56	Jordan	5.0
57	Zimbabwe	5.0
58	Slovenia	4.9
59	Colombia	4.9
60	Portugal	4.9
61	Egypt	4.8
62	Thailand	4.8
63	Uruguay	4.8
64	Slovak Republic	4.8
65	Ecuador	4.8
66	Nicaragua	4.7
67	Guatemala	4.7
68	El Salvador	4.7
69	Lithuania	4.6
70	Russian Federation	4.5
71	Turkey	4.5
72	Ukraine	4.5
73	Bolivia	4.2
74	Paraguay	4.0
75	Bulgaria	3.5

MEAN: 5.3

3.03 Firm-level technology absorption

Companies in your country are: (1 = not interested in absorbing new technology, 7 = aggressive in absorbing new technology)

RANK	COUNTRY	SCORE
1	Finland	6.6
2	United States	6.5
3	Iceland	6.5
4	Japan	6.4
5	Israel	6.3
6	Sweden	6.3
7	Switzerland	6.2
8	Taiwan	6.1
9	Singapore	6.1
10	Netherlands	6.0
11	Canada	6.0
12	Germany	5.9
13	Australia	5.8
14	Denmark	5.8
15	Ireland	5.8
16	United Kingdom	5.8
17	France	5.7
18	Austria	5.6
19	Norway	5.6
20	Belgium	5.6
21	Hong Kong SAR	5.5
22	Italy	5.5
23	Vietnam	5.5
24	New Zealand	5.5
25	Estonia	5.5
26	Spain	5.5
27	Korea	5.4
28	Brazil	5.4
29	South Africa	5.4
30	Costa Rica	5.2
31	India	5.2
32	Chile	5.1
33	Hungary	5.1
34	Romania	5.0
35	Poland	5.0
36	Czech Republic	5.0
37	Latvia	5.0
38	Thailand	4.9
39	Trinidad and Tobago	4.9
40	Turkey	4.9
41	Jamaica	4.9
42	Venezuela	4.9
43	Philippines	4.9
44	Lithuania	4.9
45	Nigeria	4.8
46	China	4.8
47	Malaysia	4.8
48	Slovenia	4.8
49	Peru	4.8
50	Jordan	4.8
51	Panama	4.7
52	Dominican Republic	4.7
53	Indonesia	4.6
54	Slovak Republic	4.6
55	Russian Federation	4.6
56	Mauritius	4.6
57	Ukraine	4.5
58	Argentina	4.5
59	Portugal	4.5
60	Mexico	4.5
61	Colombia	4.5
62	Uruguay	4.4
63	El Salvador	4.4
64	Sri Lanka	4.3
65	Greece	4.3
66	Zimbabwe	4.2
67	Bangladesh	4.1
68	Egypt	3.9
69	Nicaragua	3.9
70	Ecuador	3.8
71	Guatemala	3.7
72	Bulgaria	3.7
73	Paraguay	3.5
74	Honduras	3.3
75	Bolivia	3.0

MEAN: 5.0

3.04 FDI and technology transfer

Foreign direct investment in your country: (1 = brings little new technology, 7 = is an important source of new technology)

RANK	COUNTRY	SCORE
1	Singapore	6.3
2	Ireland	6.3
3	Hungary	6.2
4	Malaysia	6.1
5	Czech Republic	6.0
6	Costa Rica	5.9
7	Belgium	5.8
8	Poland	5.8
9	United Kingdom	5.8
10	Brazil	5.7
11	Estonia	5.7
12	Romania	5.7
13	Hong Kong SAR	5.6
14	Slovak Republic	5.6
15	Mexico	5.6
16	Israel	5.6
17	Netherlands	5.5
18	El Salvador	5.5
19	Philippines	5.5
20	Canada	5.5
21	Australia	5.5
22	Chile	5.4
23	Vietnam	5.4
24	Venezuela	5.4
25	Dominican Republic	5.4
26	Egypt	5.3
27	Thailand	5.3
28	Peru	5.3
29	Portugal	5.3
30	India	5.3
31	Panama	5.3
32	Jamaica	5.3
33	Argentina	5.2
34	Latvia	5.2
35	Trinidad and Tobago	5.2
36	Honduras	5.2
37	New Zealand	5.2
38	Taiwan	5.2
39	Spain	5.1
40	South Africa	5.1
41	Austria	5.1
42	Nigeria	5.1
43	Denmark	5.1
44	Colombia	5.0
45	Indonesia	5.0
46	Korea	4.9
47	Germany	4.9
48	Greece	4.9
49	Mauritius	4.9
50	Jordan	4.8
51	France	4.8
52	Norway	4.8
53	China	4.8
54	Lithuania	4.7
55	Sweden	4.7
56	Italy	4.6
57	Guatemala	4.6
58	Iceland	4.6
59	Turkey	4.6
60	Sri Lanka	4.6
61	Switzerland	4.5
62	Ecuador	4.5
63	Uruguay	4.5
64	Japan	4.5
65	Bolivia	4.4
66	Bangladesh	4.4
67	Zimbabwe	4.4
68	Slovenia	4.2
69	Nicaragua	4.2
70	United States	4.2
71	Finland	4.1
72	Bulgaria	4.1
73	Russian Federation	4.0
74	Paraguay	3.9
75	Ukraine	3.6

MEAN: 5.1

3.05 Quality of scientific research institutions

Scientific research institutions in your country, such as university and government laboratories, are: (1 = nonexistent, 7 = the best in their fields)

RANK	COUNTRY	SCORE
1	United States	6.7
2	Finland	6.3
3	Switzerland	6.3
4	France	6.2
5	Israel	6.2
6	Netherlands	6.2
7	United Kingdom	6.1
8	Sweden	6.0
9	Australia	5.9
10	Germany	5.9
11	Belgium	5.8
12	Japan	5.7
13	Canada	5.7
14	New Zealand	5.6
15	Singapore	5.6
16	Austria	5.6
17	Ireland	5.6
18	Norway	5.4
19	Taiwan	5.4
20	Denmark	5.3
21	India	5.2
22	Estonia	5.2
23	Hungary	5.2
24	South Africa	5.1
25	Iceland	5.1
26	Czech Republic	5.0
27	Korea	4.9
28	Slovenia	4.8
29	Spain	4.8
30	Ukraine	4.8
31	Hong Kong SAR	4.8
32	Costa Rica	4.8
33	Russian Federation	4.7
34	Lithuania	4.7
35	Italy	4.6
36	China	4.5
37	Jamaica	4.5
38	Poland	4.5
39	Jordan	4.5
40	Slovak Republic	4.4
41	Brazil	4.4
42	Portugal	4.4
43	Chile	4.3
44	Latvia	4.3
45	Egypt	4.3
46	Mauritius	4.3
47	Thailand	4.2
48	Malaysia	4.2
49	Greece	4.1
50	Philippines	4.0
51	Nigeria	4.0
52	Sri Lanka	4.0
53	Bulgaria	4.0
54	Vietnam	4.0
55	Venezuela	4.0
56	Zimbabwe	3.9
57	Panama	3.9
58	Uruguay	3.9
59	Trinidad and Tobago	3.9
60	Indonesia	3.7
61	Mexico	3.7
62	Colombia	3.7
63	Peru	3.6
64	Dominican Republic	3.5
65	Turkey	3.5
66	Guatemala	3.4
67	Bangladesh	3.4
68	Argentina	3.4
69	Romania	3.2
70	Ecuador	3.1
71	Nicaragua	3.0
72	El Salvador	2.9
73	Bolivia	2.8
74	Honduras	2.6
75	Paraguay	2.5

MEAN: 4.6

3.06 Company spending on research and development

Companies' spending on research and development in your country: (1 = is nonexistent, 7 = is heavy relative to international peers)

RANK	COUNTRY	SCORE
1	Switzerland	6.1
2	Japan	6.0
3	United States	6.0
4	Germany	5.9
5	Finland	5.8
6	Sweden	5.8
7	Israel	5.7
8	Netherlands	5.6
9	France	5.5
10	Belgium	5.3
11	Singapore	5.2
12	United Kingdom	5.1
13	Denmark	4.9
14	Ireland	4.8
15	Canada	4.8
16	Austria	4.7
17	Iceland	4.5
18	Korea	4.5
19	Italy	4.5
20	Taiwan	4.5
21	Norway	4.4
22	South Africa	4.4
23	Australia	4.2
24	Spain	4.2
25	Slovenia	4.1
26	Hungary	4.1
27	Czech Republic	4.0
28	New Zealand	4.0
29	Hong Kong SAR	4.0
30	Poland	3.9
31	Costa Rica	3.8
32	Brazil	3.8
33	Malaysia	3.7
34	China	3.7
35	Estonia	3.7
36	Russian Federation	3.7
37	Chile	3.7
38	Philippines	3.7
39	Vietnam	3.6
40	Trinidad and Tobago	3.6
41	Slovak Republic	3.6
42	India	3.5
43	Panama	3.5
44	Jamaica	3.5
45	Nigeria	3.4
46	Latvia	3.4
47	Thailand	3.4
48	Lithuania	3.3
49	Ukraine	3.3
50	Indonesia	3.3
51	Portugal	3.3
52	Dominican Republic	3.2
53	Uruguay	3.2
54	Mexico	3.2
55	Jordan	3.1
56	Sri Lanka	3.1
57	Zimbabwe	3.1
58	Turkey	3.0
60	Guatemala	3.0
59	Paraguay	3.0
61	Argentina	2.9
62	Venezuela	2.9
63	Colombia	2.9
64	Greece	2.8
65	El Salvador	2.8
66	Mauritius	2.8
67	Nicaragua	2.7
68	Ecuador	2.7
69	Bulgaria	2.7
70	Peru	2.6
71	Bangladesh	2.6
72	Egypt	2.5
73	Honduras	2.5
74	Romania	2.3
75	Bolivia	2.3

MEAN: 3.9

3.07 Subsidies for firm-level research and development

Direct government subsidies for firms conducting research and development in your country: (1 = never occur, 7 = are widespread and large)

RANK	COUNTRY	SCORE
1	Singapore	5.4
2	Israel	5.3
3	Ireland	5.0
4	Austria	4.8
5	Netherlands	4.7
6	Finland	4.6
7	Taiwan	4.6
8	Australia	4.5
9	Germany	4.5
10	Canada	4.4
11	France	4.4
12	Belgium	4.4
13	Portugal	4.3
14	Spain	4.2
15	Malaysia	4.2
16	Norway	4.2
17	Italy	4.2
18	Hungary	4.2
19	United States	4.1
20	Korea	4.1
21	Greece	4.1
22	Sweden	4.0
23	United Kingdom	3.9
24	Iceland	3.9
25	Slovenia	3.9
26	Ukraine	3.8
27	Slovak Republic	3.8
28	Japan	3.8
29	India	3.7
30	Denmark	3.6
31	China	3.6
32	Czech Republic	3.6
33	Estonia	3.6
34	Russian Federation	3.5
35	Brazil	3.5
36	Poland	3.3
37	Switzerland	3.2
38	Turkey	3.2
39	South Africa	3.1
40	Chile	3.1
41	New Zealand	3.1
42	Latvia	3.0
43	Panama	2.9
44	Thailand	2.9
45	Hong Kong SAR	2.8
46	Trinidad and Tobago	2.8
47	Sri Lanka	2.8
48	Uruguay	2.8
49	Jordan	2.7
50	Vietnam	2.7
51	Paraguay	2.7
52	Indonesia	2.7
53	Mexico	2.6
54	Philippines	2.6
55	Bulgaria	2.6
56	Dominican Republic	2.5
57	Jamaica	2.5
58	Mauritius	2.5
59	Colombia	2.4
60	Lithuania	2.4
61	Costa Rica	2.4
62	Argentina	2.3
63	Nigeria	2.3
64	Zimbabwe	2.3
65	El Salvador	2.2
66	Nicaragua	2.2
67	Guatemala	2.2
68	Egypt	2.2
69	Honduras	2.1
70	Venezuela	2.0
71	Bangladesh	1.8
72	Bolivia	1.7
73	Peru	1.7
74	Ecuador	1.7
75	Romania	1.2

MEAN: 3.3

3.08 Tax credits for firm-level research and development

Government tax credits for firms conducting research and development in your country: (1 = never occur, 7 = are widespread and large)

RANK	COUNTRY	SCORE
1	Canada	5.7
2	Singapore	5.6
3	Taiwan	5.4
4	Israel	5.3
5	United States	4.9
6	Australia	4.9
7	Ireland	4.8
8	Malaysia	4.7
9	India	4.7
10	France	4.5
11	Korea	4.4
12	Netherlands	4.4
13	Spain	4.4
14	Belgium	4.2
15	United Kingdom	4.1
16	Hungary	4.1
17	Portugal	4.0
18	Japan	4.0
19	Austria	4.0
20	Germany	3.9
21	Finland	3.8
22	China	3.6
23	Ukraine	3.5
24	Brazil	3.5
25	Switzerland	3.4
26	Thailand	3.4
27	Italy	3.4
28	Norway	3.4
29	Russian Federation	3.2
30	Slovenia	3.2
31	Panama	3.1
32	Iceland	3.1
33	Vietnam	3.1
34	Jordan	3.1
35	Greece	3.0
36	South Africa	3.0
37	Philippines	3.0
38	Zimbabwe	3.0
39	Nigeria	2.9
40	Sweden	2.9
41	Denmark	2.9
42	Turkey	2.9
43	Mexico	2.8
44	Czech Republic	2.8
45	Sri Lanka	2.8
46	Lithuania	2.8
47	Slovak Republic	2.8
48	Latvia	2.8
49	Uruguay	2.8
50	Poland	2.8
51	Mauritius	2.8
52	Estonia	2.7
53	Chile	2.7
54	Hong Kong SAR	2.7
55	Colombia	2.6
56	Trinidad and Tobago	2.6
57	Paraguay	2.6
58	Jamaica	2.5
59	Argentina	2.5
60	Bulgaria	2.5
61	Venezuela	2.5
62	New Zealand	2.3
63	Egypt	2.3
64	Dominican Republic	2.3
65	Indonesia	2.3
66	Costa Rica	2.2
67	Honduras	2.2
68	Nicaragua	2.2
69	Bangladesh	2.1
70	Guatemala	2.1
71	El Salvador	1.9
72	Peru	1.7
73	Ecuador	1.7
74	Bolivia	1.6
75	Romania	1.2

MEAN: 3.2

3.09 University/industry research collaboration

In its R&D activity, business collaboration with local universities is:
(1 = minimal or nonexistent, 7 = intensive and ongoing)

RANK	COUNTRY	SCORE
1	Finland	6.1
2	Sweden	5.7
3	Singapore	5.6
4	Israel	5.5
5	Belgium	5.4
6	Canada	5.3
7	United States	5.3
8	Switzerland	5.3
9	Netherlands	5.2
10	France	5.1
11	Ireland	5.1
12	Germany	5.1
13	Austria	5.1
14	Australia	5.1
15	Taiwan	5.1
16	Denmark	5.0
17	United Kingdom	4.9
18	Iceland	4.9
19	Hungary	4.8
20	Korea	4.6
21	Norway	4.6
22	Slovak Republic	4.6
23	South Africa	4.6
24	Hong Kong SAR	4.6
25	New Zealand	4.4
26	Japan	4.4
27	Italy	4.2
28	China	4.2
29	Brazil	4.2
30	Spain	4.2
31	Estonia	4.1
32	Czech Republic	4.1
33	Thailand	3.9
34	Greece	3.9
35	Poland	3.8
36	Slovenia	3.8
37	Portugal	3.8
38	India	3.7
39	Chile	3.7
40	Latvia	3.7
41	Costa Rica	3.7
42	Malaysia	3.6
43	Vietnam	3.5
44	Panama	3.5
45	Indonesia	3.4
46	Zimbabwe	3.4
47	Trinidad and Tobago	3.4
48	Mauritius	3.4
49	Turkey	3.4
50	Jordan	3.3
51	Uruguay	3.3
52	Russian Federation	3.3
53	Ukraine	3.3
54	Lithuania	3.3
55	Philippines	3.3
56	Egypt	3.3
57	Mexico	3.2
58	Colombia	3.2
59	Argentina	3.1
60	Dominican Republic	3.1
61	Jamaica	3.1
62	Sri Lanka	3.0
63	Nigeria	3.0
64	Guatemala	3.0
65	Venezuela	2.9
66	Nicaragua	2.8
67	Bulgaria	2.8
68	Paraguay	2.7
69	Peru	2.5
70	Honduras	2.4
71	Bangladesh	2.4
72	El Salvador	2.4
73	Ecuador	2.3
74	Bolivia	2.2
75	Romania	1.6

MEAN: 3.9

3.10 Government procurement of advanced technology products

Government decisions on the procurement of advanced technology products are based on: (1 = price alone, 7 = technology and encouraging innovation)

RANK	COUNTRY	SCORE
1	Singapore	5.7
2	Finland	5.3
3	Taiwan	5.1
4	Canada	4.9
5	France	4.9
6	Switzerland	4.8
7	Japan	4.8
8	Sweden	4.7
9	Iceland	4.7
10	Germany	4.6
11	Netherlands	4.6
12	China	4.6
13	United States	4.6
14	Spain	4.6
15	Korea	4.6
16	Israel	4.5
17	Estonia	4.5
18	Hong Kong SAR	4.4
19	Ireland	4.4
20	Malaysia	4.4
21	Australia	4.4
22	Austria	4.3
23	Denmark	4.3
24	Norway	4.3
25	Italy	4.2
26	Slovak Republic	4.2
27	Belgium	4.2
28	Slovenia	4.2
29	Czech Republic	4.1
30	New Zealand	4.1
31	Portugal	4.1
32	United Kingdom	4.1
33	Thailand	4.0
34	Vietnam	4.0
35	Hungary	4.0
36	Indonesia	4.0
37	Latvia	4.0
38	Trinidad and Tobago	4.0
39	South Africa	3.9
40	Ukraine	3.9
41	Poland	3.9
42	Jordan	3.9
43	Brazil	3.9
44	Jamaica	3.9
45	India	3.8
46	Costa Rica	3.8
47	Uruguay	3.8
48	Chile	3.8
49	Nigeria	3.7
50	Mexico	3.7
51	Egypt	3.6
52	Turkey	3.6
53	Russian Federation	3.6
54	Bulgaria	3.5
55	Greece	3.5
56	Sri Lanka	3.5
57	Lithuania	3.4
58	Philippines	3.4
59	Dominican Republic	3.4
60	Mauritius	3.4
61	Colombia	3.4
62	Zimbabwe	3.3
63	Panama	3.3
64	Romania	3.3
65	El Salvador	3.1
66	Venezuela	3.1
67	Nicaragua	3.1
68	Bangladesh	3.0
69	Argentina	2.9
70	Paraguay	2.7
71	Guatemala	2.7
72	Peru	2.7
73	Ecuador	2.6
74	Bolivia	2.4
75	Honduras	2.4

MEAN: 3.9

3.11 Availability of scientists and engineers

Scientists and engineers in your country are: (1 = nonexistent or rare, 7 = widely available)

RANK	COUNTRY	SCORE
		MEAN: 5.1
1	Romania	6.5
2	Israel	6.4
3	Slovak Republic	6.4
4	India	6.4
5	Finland	6.4
6	Iceland	6.2
7	Hungary	6.2
8	United States	6.2
9	Japan	6.1
10	France	6.0
11	Jordan	6.0
12	Sweden	6.0
13	Canada	5.9
14	Singapore	5.9
15	Taiwan	5.8
16	Switzerland	5.8
17	Czech Republic	5.8
18	Austria	5.8
19	Ireland	5.8
20	Denmark	5.7
21	Norway	5.7
22	Greece	5.7
23	Lithuania	5.7
24	Australia	5.7
25	Ukraine	5.6
26	Spain	5.6
27	Egypt	5.6
28	Netherlands	5.6
29	Chile	5.5
30	Estonia	5.5
31	Russian Federation	5.5
32	Germany	5.5
33	Italy	5.4
34	Poland	5.3
35	Korea	5.3
36	Hong Kong SAR	5.3
37	United Kingdom	5.3
38	Bulgaria	5.3
39	Slovenia	5.2
40	Uruguay	5.2
41	Costa Rica	5.1
42	Venezuela	5.0
43	Trinidad and Tobago	5.0
44	Brazil	5.0
45	Argentina	4.9
46	Sri Lanka	4.9
47	Peru	4.9
48	Belgium	4.9
49	New Zealand	4.8
50	Portugal	4.8
51	Nigeria	4.7
52	Indonesia	4.7
53	Philippines	4.6
54	Thailand	4.6
55	Latvia	4.6
56	Turkey	4.6
57	Jamaica	4.5
58	Bangladesh	4.5
59	China	4.4
60	Malaysia	4.4
61	Colombia	4.4
62	Mexico	4.3
63	Panama	4.3
64	Dominican Republic	4.3
65	Mauritius	4.3
66	Vietnam	4.1
67	South Africa	4.1
68	Ecuador	3.7
69	Bolivia	3.6
70	Nicaragua	3.6
71	Honduras	3.5
72	El Salvador	3.5
73	Guatemala	3.4
74	Paraguay	3.2
75	Zimbabwe	2.9

3.12 Brain drain

Scientists and engineers in your country: (1 = normally leave to pursue opportunities elsewhere, 7 = almost always remain in the country)

RANK	COUNTRY	SCORE
		MEAN: 4.0
1	United States	6.6
2	Finland	6.1
3	Norway	5.6
4	Japan	5.6
5	Netherlands	5.5
6	Germany	5.4
7	Belgium	5.4
8	France	5.3
9	Taiwan	5.3
10	Austria	5.2
11	Chile	5.2
12	Singapore	5.2
13	Indonesia	5.2
14	Iceland	5.1
15	Denmark	5.1
16	Czech Republic	5.1
17	Thailand	5.0
18	Switzerland	5.0
19	United Kingdom	4.8
20	Spain	4.8
21	Costa Rica	4.8
22	Sweden	4.8
23	Israel	4.8
24	Ireland	4.6
25	Hong Kong SAR	4.6
26	Canada	4.6
27	Brazil	4.6
28	Greece	4.5
29	Estonia	4.4
30	Portugal	4.4
31	Slovenia	4.2
32	Australia	4.2
33	Italy	4.1
34	Korea	4.1
35	Turkey	4.0
36	Egypt	4.0
37	Hungary	4.0
38	Panama	4.0
39	Poland	3.9
40	Mexico	3.9
41	Russian Federation	3.9
42	China	3.8
43	Mauritius	3.8
44	Trinidad and Tobago	3.8
45	Malaysia	3.8
46	Dominican Republic	3.5
47	New Zealand	3.5
48	Guatemala	3.4
49	Slovak Republic	3.4
50	Honduras	3.4
51	Venezuela	3.4
52	Lithuania	3.3
53	El Salvador	3.3
54	Argentina	3.3
55	Romania	3.3
56	Vietnam	3.3
57	Latvia	3.3
58	Colombia	3.1
59	Ukraine	3.1
60	Paraguay	3.1
61	Jamaica	3.1
62	Uruguay	3.0
63	Jordan	2.9
64	South Africa	2.9
65	India	2.9
66	Peru	2.8
67	Nicaragua	2.8
68	Sri Lanka	2.7
69	Ecuador	2.7
70	Bolivia	2.6
71	Philippines	2.5
72	Bulgaria	2.5
73	Nigeria	2.5
74	Bangladesh	2.4
75	Zimbabwe	2.1

3.13 Women in the economy

Women's participation in the economy is: (1 = limited and usually takes place in less important jobs, 7 = equal to that of men)

RANK	COUNTRY	SCORE
1	Hong Kong SAR	6.3
2	Slovak Republic	6.2
3	Finland	6.1
4	Singapore	6.1
5	Denmark	5.8
6	Romania	5.7
7	Iceland	5.6
8	Sweden	5.6
9	Philippines	5.6
10	Canada	5.6
11	United States	5.4
12	Latvia	5.4
13	Thailand	5.3
14	Estonia	5.3
15	United Kingdom	5.3
16	Hungary	5.2
17	New Zealand	5.2
18	Jamaica	5.1
19	Taiwan	5.1
20	Bulgaria	5.1
21	China	5.1
22	Panama	5.1
23	Norway	5.1
24	Venezuela	5.0
25	Australia	5.0
26	Portugal	5.0
27	Malaysia	4.9
28	El Salvador	4.9
29	France	4.9
30	Turkey	4.8
31	Egypt	4.8
32	Costa Rica	4.7
33	Belgium	4.7
34	Dominican Republic	4.7
35	Slovenia	4.7
36	Vietnam	4.7
37	Trinidad and Tobago	4.7
38	Sri Lanka	4.6
39	Czech Republic	4.6
40	Lithuania	4.6
41	Poland	4.6
42	Colombia	4.5
43	Ukraine	4.4
44	Israel	4.4
45	Austria	4.4
46	Germany	4.4
47	Nicaragua	4.3
48	Nigeria	4.3
49	Switzerland	4.2
50	Ireland	4.2
51	Netherlands	4.2
52	Jordan	4.2
53	Spain	4.1
54	Peru	4.1
55	Indonesia	4.1
56	Italy	4.0
57	Russian Federation	4.0
58	Brazil	3.9
59	Honduras	3.9
60	Mexico	3.9
61	Uruguay	3.9
62	Mauritius	3.8
63	Greece	3.8
64	Guatemala	3.8
65	Chile	3.6
66	India	3.6
67	Argentina	3.6
68	South Africa	3.6
69	Japan	3.6
70	Ecuador	3.5
71	Bolivia	3.4
72	Zimbabwe	3.3
73	Paraguay	3.2
74	Korea	3.2
75	Bangladesh	2.6

MEAN: 4.6

3.14 Minorities in the economy

Minority groups' participation in the economy is: (1 = limited and usually takes place in less important jobs, 7 = equal to that of other groups)

RANK	COUNTRY	SCORE
1	Ukraine	6.0
2	Romania	5.7
3	Poland	5.7
4	Turkey	5.6
5	Iceland	5.6
6	Jordan	5.5
7	Jamaica	5.5
8	Singapore	5.5
9	China	5.5
10	Indonesia	5.4
11	Hong Kong SAR	5.4
12	Canada	5.3
13	Latvia	5.2
14	Zimbabwe	5.1
15	Slovenia	5.0
16	United Kingdom	5.0
17	Slovak Republic	5.0
18	Trinidad and Tobago	5.0
19	Mauritius	4.9
20	Estonia	4.9
21	India	4.9
22	Sri Lanka	4.9
23	Lithuania	4.9
24	Taiwan	4.8
25	United States	4.8
26	Venezuela	4.8
27	Finland	4.8
28	South Africa	4.8
29	Australia	4.7
30	Bangladesh	4.7
31	Malaysia	4.6
32	Austria	4.6
33	Russian Federation	4.5
34	Thailand	4.5
35	Switzerland	4.5
36	Germany	4.5
37	Japan	4.2
38	New Zealand	4.2
39	Nigeria	4.2
40	Costa Rica	4.2
41	Egypt	4.1
42	Italy	4.1
43	Netherlands	4.1
44	Israel	4.1
45	El Salvador	4.0
46	Panama	4.0
47	Czech Republic	3.9
48	Argentina	3.9
49	France	3.9
50	Belgium	3.8
51	Peru	3.8
52	Philippines	3.8
53	Vietnam	3.8
54	Dominican Republic	3.8
55	Sweden	3.7
56	Chile	3.7
57	Brazil	3.7
58	Hungary	3.7
59	Uruguay	3.6
60	Portugal	3.6
61	Norway	3.5
62	Mexico	3.5
63	Nicaragua	3.5
64	Denmark	3.5
65	Ireland	3.4
66	Honduras	3.3
67	Korea	3.2
68	Colombia	3.1
69	Paraguay	3.1
70	Guatemala	3.1
71	Spain	3.1
72	Bolivia	3.0
73	Bulgaria	3.0
74	Greece	2.9
75	Ecuador	2.7

MEAN: 4.3

371

3.15 Research and development spending

Overall research and development spending as a percentage of gross national income in 1997 or most recent year available

RANK	COUNTRY	HARD DATA
1	Sweden	3.76
2	Korea, Rep.	2.82
3	Japan	2.80
4	Finland	2.78
5	United States	2.63
6	Switzerland	2.60
7	Germany	2.41
8	Israel	2.35
9	France	2.25
10	Italy	2.21
11	Netherlands	2.08
12	Denmark	1.95
12	United Kingdom	1.95
14	Taiwan	1.85
15	Australia	1.80
16	Canada	1.66
17	Ireland	1.61
18	Belgium	1.60
19	Norway	1.58
20	Iceland	1.55
21	Austria	1.53
22	Slovenia	1.46
23	Czech Republic	1.20
24	Singapore	1.13
25	Slovak Republic	1.05
26	New Zealand	1.04
27	Spain	0.90
28	Russian Federationn Federation	0.88
29	Brazil	0.81
30	Poland	0.77
31	India	0.73
32	Romania	0.72
33	Lithuania	0.70
33	South Africa	0.70
35	Chile	0.68
35	Hungary	0.68
37	China	0.66
38	Portugal	0.62
39	Bulgaria	0.57
39	Estonia	0.57
41	Bolivia	0.50
42	Venezuela, RB	0.49
43	Greece	0.47
44	Turkey	0.45
45	Latvia	0.43
46	Mauritius	0.40
47	Argentina	0.38
48	Mexico	0.33
49	Malaysia	0.24
50	Egypt, Arab Rep.	0.22
50	Philippines	0.22
52	Costa Rica	0.21
53	Thailand	0.13
54	Indonesia	0.07
55	Bangladesh	0.03
56	Ecuador	0.02
	Colombia	N/A
	Dominican Republic	N/A
	El Salvador	N/A
	Guatemala	N/A
	Honduras	N/A
	Hong Kong SAR	N/A
	Jamaica	N/A
	Jordan	N/A
	Nicaragua	N/A
	Nigeria	N/A
	Panama	N/A
	Paraguay	N/A
	Peru	N/A
	Sri Lanka	N/A
	Trinidad and Tobago	N/A
	Ukraine	N/A
	Uruguay	N/A
	Vietnam	N/A
	Zimbabwe	N/A

SOURCES: World Development Indicators 2001 and national sources

3.16 Utility patents in 2000

US utility patents (ie, patents for invention) granted per million population, 2000

RANK	COUNTRY	HARD DATA
1	United States	308.7
2	Japan	246.6
3	Taiwan	210.3
4	Switzerland	182.1
5	Sweden	177.2
6	Israel	135.0
7	Germany	123.6
8	Finland	119.4
9	Canada	111.2
10	Denmark	82.3
11	Netherlands	78.1
12	Korea	70.1
13	Belgium	67.8
14	France	64.4
15	Austria	62.1
16	United Kingdom	61.6
17	Iceland	61.6
18	Norway	55.1
19	Singapore	54.3
20	Australia	36.7
21	Ireland	32.4
22	Italy	29.7
23	New Zealand	28.0
24	Hong Kong SAR	26.3
25	Slovenia	8.0
26	Spain	6.8
27	Hungary	3.6
28	Estonia	2.9
29	South Africa	2.5
30	Czech Republic	2.2
31	Malaysia	1.8
32	Costa Rica	1.8
33	Greece	1.7
34	Argentina	1.5
35	Russian Federation	1.3
36	Venezuela	1.1
37	Portugal	1.1
38	Chile	1.0
39	Mexico	0.8
40	Jamaica	0.8
41	Slovak Republic	0.7
42	Panama	0.7
43	Brazil	0.6
44	Latvia	0.4
45	Dominican Republic	0.4
46	Ukraine	0.3
47	Poland	0.3
48	Uruguay	0.3
49	Bolivia	0.2
50	Thailand	0.2
51	Colombia	0.2
52	Romania	0.2
53	Guatemala	0.2
54	Honduras	0.2
55	India	0.1
56	Bulgaria	0.1
57	Egypt	0.1
58	China	0.1
59	Peru	0.1
60	Turkey	0.1
61	Sri Lanka	0.1
62	Indonesia	0.03
63	Philippines	0.03
64	Nigeria	0.02
65	Bangladesh	0.00
65	Ecuador	0.00
65	El Salvador	0.00
65	Jordan	0.00
65	Lithuania	0.00
65	Mauritius	0.00
65	Nicaragua	0.00
65	Paraguay	0.00
65	Trinidad and Tobago	0.00
65	Zimbabwe	0.00

SOURCE: US Patent and Trademark Office, March 2001

3.17 Utility patents in 1980s

Average number of US utility patents granted per million population, 1980 to 1989

RANK	COUNTRY	HARD DATA
1	Switzerland	189.7
2	United States	165.9
3	Japan	101.3
4	Sweden	94.4
5	Germany	85.1
6	Netherlands	52.0
7	Canada	50.4
8	United Kingdom	43.3
9	France	43.0
10	Israel	42.2
11	Austria	40.4
12	Finland	37.1
13	Denmark	31.8
14	Belgium	26.5
15	Norway	22.7
16	Australia	21.5
17	Italy	16.5
18	New Zealand	15.2
19	Taiwan	12.8
20	Hungary	10.4
21	Iceland	9.0
22	Ireland	8.8
23	Hong Kong SAR	5.4
24	South Africa	3.0
25	Bulgaria	2.4
26	Singapore	2.4
27	Spain	2.2
28	Korea	1.3
29	Venezuela	0.9
30	Greece	0.7
31	Trinidad and Tobago	0.7
32	Argentina	0.6
33	Costa Rica	0.6
34	Poland	0.5
35	Mexico	0.5
36	Panama	0.5
37	Portugal	0.4
38	Jamaica	0.3
39	Chile	0.3
40	Romania	0.2
41	Brazil	0.2
42	Uruguay	0.2
43	Mauritius	0.2
44	Colombia	0.1
45	Zimbabwe	0.1
46	Malaysia	0.1
47	Bolivia	0.1
48	Dominican Republic	0.1
49	Guatemala	0.1
50	Paraguay	0.1
51	Philippines	0.1
52	Ecuador	0.1
53	Peru	0.1
54	El Salvador	0.1
55	Turkey	0.05
56	Honduras	0.04
57	Egypt	0.04
58	Jordan	0.04
59	Thailand	0.04
60	India	0.01
61	China	0.01
62	Sri Lanka	0.01
63	Indonesia	0.01
64	Nigeria	0.01
65	Bangladesh	0.00
66	Nicaragua	0.00
66	Vietnam	0.00
	Czech Republic	N/A
	Estonia	N/A
	Latvia	N/A
	Lithuania	N/A
	Russian Federation	N/A
	Slovak Republic	N/A
	Slovenia	N/A
	Ukraine	N/A

SOURCE: US Patent and Trademark Office, March 2001

3.18 Secondary enrollment

Net secondary school enrollment in 1997 or most recent year available

RANK	COUNTRY	HARD DATA
1	Sweden	98.9
2	Japan	98.6
3	Korea	97.4
3	Norway	97.4
5	France	94.8
6	Finland	93.1
7	United Kingdom	91.5
8	Canada	91.1
9	Netherlands	90.7
10	New Zealand	90.3
11	United States	90.0
12	Australia	88.9
13	Germany	88.4
14	Austria	88.2
15	Belgium	88.0
16	Denmark	87.7
17	Czech Republic	87.1
17	Iceland	87.1
19	Greece	86.5
20	Hungary	86.0
21	Ireland	85.8
22	Poland	84.5
23	Switzerland	83.5
24	Estonia	83.4
25	Lithuania	80.5
26	Latvia	78.6
27	Portugal	77.7
28	Bulgaria	74.2
29	Romania	73.1
30	Hong Kong SAR	69.0
31	Egypt	67.5
32	Trinidad & Tob	65.0
33	Jamaica	63.8
34	Philippines	58.8
35	Chile	58.3
36	South Africa	57.6
37	Peru	55.2
38	Turkey	51.3
39	Mexico	51.2
40	Panama	50.8
41	Colombia	45.6
42	Indonesia	42.3
43	Jordan	41.4
44	Costa Rica	40.4
45	Paraguay	37.9
46	Bolivia	29.4
47	Venezuela	22.3
48	Dom Republic	22.2
49	El Salvador	22.0
50	Honduras	20.5
51	Brazil	19.5
52	Bangladesh	18.0
	Argentina	N/A
	China	N/A
	Ecuador	N/A
	Guatemala	N/A
	India	N/A
	Israel	N/A
	Italy	N/A
	Malaysia	N/A
	Mauritius	N/A
	Nicaragua	N/A
	Nigeria	N/A
	Russian Federation	N/A
	Singapore	N/A
	Slovak Republic	N/A
	Slovenia	N/A
	Spain	N/A
	Sri Lanka	N/A
	Taiwan	N/A
	Thailand	N/A
	Ukraine	N/A
	Uruguay	N/A
	Vietnam	N/A
	Zimbabwe	N/A

SOURCE: World Bank World Development Indicators 2001

3.19 Tertiary enrollment

Gross tertiary enrollment rate in 1997 or most recent year available

RANK	COUNTRY		HARD DATA
1	Canada	87.8	
2	United States	80.9	
3	Australia	79.8	
4	Finland	74.1	
5	Korea	67.7	
6	New Zealand	62.6	
7	Norway	62.0	
8	Belgium	56.3	
9	United Kingdom	52.3	
10	Spain	51.4	
11	France	51.0	
12	Sweden	50.3	
13	Austria	48.3	
14	Denmark	48.2	
15	Netherlands	47.3	
16	Germany	47.2	
17	Italy	46.9	
18	Greece	46.8	
19	Russian Federation	42.8	
20	Estonia	41.8	
21	Ukraine	41.7	
22	Bulgaria	41.2	
23	Ireland	41.0	
24	Israel	40.9	
25	Japan	40.5	
26	Argentina	39.0	
27	Portugal	38.8	
28	Singapore	38.5	
29	Iceland	37.5	
30	Slovenia	36.1	
31	Latvia	33.3	
32	Costa Rica	33.0	
33	Switzerland	32.6	
34	Chile	31.5	
34	Panama	31.5	
36	Lithuania	31.4	
37	Uruguay	29.5	
38	Philippines	29.0	
39	Hong Kong SAR	26.0	
39	Venezuela	26.0	
41	Peru	25.8	
42	Poland	24.7	
43	Bolivia	24.0	
44	Hungary	23.6	
45	Czech Republic	23.5	
46	Ecuador	23.0	
47	Dominican Republic	22.9	
48	Romania	22.5	
49	Slovak Republic	22.1	
49	Thailand	22.1	
51	Turkey	21.0	
52	Egypt	20.2	
53	South Africa	18.9	
54	Jordan	17.9	
55	El Salvador	17.8	
56	Colombia	16.7	
57	Mexico	16.0	
58	Brazil	14.5	
59	Nicaragua	11.8	
60	Malaysia	11.7	
61	Indonesia	11.3	
62	Paraguay	10.3	
63	Honduras	10.0	
64	Guatemala	8.5	
65	Trinidad and Tobago	8.2	
66	Jamaica	7.8	
67	India	6.9	
68	Vietnam	6.9	
68	Zimbabwe	6.6	
70	China	6.1	
70	Mauritius	6.1	
72	Bangladesh	6.0	
73	Sri Lanka	5.1	
74	Nigeria	4.3	
	Taiwan	N/A	

SOURCES: World Bank *World Development Indicators 2001*, The Task Force on Higher Education and Society *Higher Education in Developing Countries* (2000)

3.20 Years of schooling

Average total years of schooling among population aged 15 and above, 1999

RANK	COUNTRY		HARD DATA
1	United States	12.0	
2	Norway	11.8	
3	New Zealand	11.7	
4	Canada	11.6	
5	Sweden	11.4	
6	Australia	10.9	
7	Korea	10.8	
8	Switzerland	10.5	
9	Germany	10.2	
10	Finland	10.0	
11	Poland	9.8	
12	Denmark	9.7	
13	Israel	9.6	
14	Japan	9.5	
15	United Kingdom	9.4	
16	Hong Kong SAR	9.4	
17	Netherlands	9.4	
18	Ireland	9.4	
19	Belgium	9.3	
20	Hungary	9.1	
21	Iceland	8.8	
22	Argentina	8.8	
23	Taiwan	8.8	
24	Greece	8.7	
25	Panama	8.6	
26	Austria	8.4	
27	Philippines	8.2	
28	France	7.9	
29	Trinidad & Tob	7.8	
30	Peru	7.6	
31	Uruguay	7.6	
32	Chile	7.5	
33	Spain	7.3	
34	Mexico	7.2	
35	Italy	7.2	
36	Singapore	7.0	
37	Jordan	6.9	
38	Sri Lanka	6.9	
39	Malaysia	6.8	
40	Venezuela	6.6	
41	Thailand	6.5	
42	Ecuador	6.4	
43	China	6.4	
44	Paraguay	6.2	
45	South Africa	6.1	
46	Costa Rica	6.0	
47	Mauritius	6.0	
48	Portugal	5.9	
49	Bolivia	5.6	
50	Egypt	5.5	
51	Zimbabwe	5.4	
52	Turkey	5.3	
53	Colombia	5.3	
54	Jamaica	5.3	
55	El Salvador	5.2	
56	India	5.1	
57	Indonesia	5.0	
58	Dom Republic	4.9	
59	Brazil	4.9	
60	Honduras	4.8	
61	Nicaragua	4.6	
62	Guatemala	3.5	
63	Bangladesh	2.6	
	Bulgaria	N/A	
	Czech Republic	N/A	
	Estonia	N/A	
	Latvia	N/A	
	Lithuania	N/A	
	Nigeria	N/A	
	Romania	N/A	
	Russian Federation	N/A	
	Slovak Republic	N/A	
	Slovenia	N/A	
	Ukraine	N/A	
	Vietnam	N/A	

SOURCE: Barro and Lee (2000) calculations based on census and survey information compiled by UNESCO and other sources

3.21 Mathematics achievement

Average eighth-grade mathematics achievement scale score (out of 800), 1999

RANK	COUNTRY	HARD DATA
1	Singapore	604
2	Korea	587
3	Taiwan	585
4	Hong Kong SAR	582
5	Japan	579
6	Belgium	558
7	Netherlands	540
8	Slovak Republic	534
9	Hungary	532
10	Canada	531
11	Slovenia	530
12	Russian Federation	526
13	Australia	525
14	Czech Republic	520
14	Finland	520
16	Malaysia	519
17	Bulgaria	511
18	Latvia	505
19	United States	502
20	England	496
21	New Zealand	491
22	Lithuania	482
23	Italy	479
24	Romania	472
25	Thailand	467
26	Israel	466
27	Turkey	429
28	Jordan	428
29	Indonesia	403
30	Chile	392
31	Philippines	345
32	South Africa	275
	Argentina	N/A
	Austria	N/A
	Bangladesh	N/A
	Bolivia	N/A
	Brazil	N/A
	China	N/A
	Colombia	N/A
	Costa Rica	N/A
	Denmark	N/A
	Dominican Republic	N/A
	Ecuador	N/A
	Egypt	N/A
	El Salvador	N/A
	Estonia	N/A
	France	N/A
	Germany	N/A
	Greece	N/A
	Guatemala	N/A
	Honduras	N/A
	Iceland	N/A
	India	N/A
	Ireland	N/A
	Jamaica	N/A
	Mauritius	N/A
	Mexico	N/A
	Nicaragua	N/A
	Nigeria	N/A
	Norway	N/A
	Panama	N/A
	Paraguay	N/A
	Peru	N/A
	Poland	N/A
	Portugal	N/A
	Spain	N/A
	Sri Lanka	N/A
	Sweden	N/A
	Switzerland	N/A
	Trinidad & Tobago	N/A
	Ukraine	N/A
	Uruguay	N/A
	Venezuela	N/A
	Vietnam	N/A
	Zimbabwe	N/A

SOURCE: Third International Mathematics and Science Study *International Mathematics Report*

3.22 Science achievement

Average eighth-grade science achievement scale score (out of 800), 1999

RANK	COUNTRY	HARD DATA
1	Taiwan	569
2	Singapore	568
3	Hungary	552
4	Japan	550
5	Korea	549
6	Netherlands	545
7	Australia	540
8	Czech Republic	539
9	England	538
10	Belgium	535
10	Finland	535
10	Slovak Republic	535
13	Canada	533
13	Slovenia	533
15	Hong Kong SAR	530
16	Russian Federation	529
17	Bulgaria	518
18	United States	515
19	New Zealand	510
20	Latvia	503
21	Italy	493
22	Malaysia	492
23	Lithuania	488
24	Thailand	482
25	Romania	472
26	Israel	468
27	Jordan	450
28	Indonesia	435
29	Turkey	433
30	Chile	420
31	Philippines	345
32	South Africa	243
	Argentina	N/A
	Austria	N/A
	Bangladesh	N/A
	Bolivia	N/A
	Brazil	N/A
	China	N/A
	Colombia	N/A
	Costa Rica	N/A
	Denmark	N/A
	Dominican Republic	N/A
	Ecuador	N/A
	Egypt	N/A
	El Salvador	N/A
	Estonia	N/A
	France	N/A
	Germany	N/A
	Greece	N/A
	Guatemala	N/A
	Honduras	N/A
	Iceland	N/A
	India	N/A
	Ireland	N/A
	Jamaica	N/A
	Mauritius	N/A
	Mexico	N/A
	Nicaragua	N/A
	Nigeria	N/A
	Norway	N/A
	Panama	N/A
	Paraguay	N/A
	Peru	N/A
	Poland	N/A
	Portugal	N/A
	Spain	N/A
	Sri Lanka	N/A
	Sweden	N/A
	Switzerland	N/A
	Trinidad & Tobago	N/A
	Ukraine	N/A
	Uruguay	N/A
	Venezuela	N/A
	Vietnam	N/A
	Zimbabwe	N/A

SOURCE: Third International Mathematics and Science Study *International Science Report*

3.23 Skill-based exports

Average skill-based manufactured exports as a percentage of GDP,
1997 to 1999. (See Technical Notes section for full description.)

RANK	COUNTRY	HARD DATA
1	Singapore	100.8
2	Hong Kong SAR	92.9
3	Malaysia	66.7
4	Ireland	42.8
5	Belgium	33.9
6	Hungary	32.8
7	Slovenia	29.0
8	Czech Republic	28.6
9	Estonia	28.2
10	Philippines	27.2
11	Thailand	27.0
12	Slovak Republic	26.4
13	Mauritius	26.0
14	Korea	25.2
15	Netherlands	24.6
16	Sweden	21.7
17	Mexico	21.7
18	Costa Rica	20.4
19	Dominican Republic	19.9
20	Switzerland	19.8
21	Sri Lanka	18.5
22	Canada	18.2
23	Germany	16.7
24	Finland	16.7
25	Austria	16.6
26	Portugal	15.2
27	Denmark	14.1
28	China	13.9
29	Italy	13.7
30	Romania	13.3
31	United Kingdom	12.8
32	France	12.2
33	Vietnam	12.1
34	Israel	11.3
35	Spain	11.2
36	Bulgaria	11.1
37	Indonesia	10.4
38	Latvia	10.2
39	Bangladesh	9.2
40	Poland	9.0
41	Turkey	8.1
42	Jamaica	8.1
43	Japan	8.1
44	Norway	5.4
45	United States	5.1
46	South Africa	3.7
47	Jordan	3.5
48	India	3.4
49	New Zealand	3.3
50	Greece	3.2
51	Bolivia	2.9
52	Zimbabwe	2.8
53	El Salvador	2.6
54	Uruguay	2.6
55	Nicaragua	2.4
56	Australia	2.2
57	Brazil	2.1
58	Russian Federation	2.0
59	Trinidad and Tobago	1.9
60	Guatemala	1.9
61	Colombia	1.8
62	Iceland	1.7
63	Argentina	1.7
64	Honduras	1.5
65	Chile	1.2
66	Ecuador	1.2
67	Egypt	1.2
68	Peru	1.1
69	Venezuela	0.9
70	Paraguay	0.6
71	Nigeria	0.5
72	Panama	0.5
	Lithuania	N/A
	Taiwan	N/A
	Ukraine	N/A

SOURCES: UN COMTRADE Database 1995–1999, Statistics Canada, World Trade Analyzer, 1980–1996, and authors' calculations

4.01 Speed and cost of Internet access

Lease-line or dial-up access to the Internet in your country is: (1 = slow and expensive, 7 = as fast and cheap as anywhere in the world)

RANK	COUNTRY	SCORE
1	Finland	6.9
2	United States	6.6
3	Sweden	6.4
4	Canada	6.2
5	Iceland	6.2
6	Netherlands	6.2
7	Hong Kong SAR	6.1
8	Norway	6.0
9	Singapore	5.8
10	Germany	5.8
11	Austria	5.8
12	Denmark	5.8
13	Australia	5.7
14	United Kingdom	5.7
15	New Zealand	5.6
16	Switzerland	5.6
17	Israel	5.5
18	France	5.4
19	Korea	5.3
20	Belgium	5.3
21	Chile	5.0
22	Estonia	5.0
23	Portugal	4.8
24	Spain	4.6
25	Taiwan	4.6
26	Italy	4.5
27	Turkey	4.4
28	Greece	4.4
29	El Salvador	4.4
30	Slovak Republic	4.4
31	Dominican Republic	4.3
32	Panama	4.3
33	Slovenia	4.3
34	Jordan	4.3
35	Ireland	4.3
36	South Africa	4.2
37	Thailand	4.2
38	Egypt	4.2
39	Argentina	4.2
40	Czech Republic	4.1
41	Romania	4.1
42	Malaysia	4.1
43	Hungary	4.0
44	Mexico	4.0
45	Brazil	4.0
46	Venezuela	4.0
47	Japan	4.0
48	Uruguay	3.9
49	Trinidad and Tobago	3.9
50	Sri Lanka	3.8
51	Jamaica	3.8
52	Colombia	3.8
53	Indonesia	3.7
54	India	3.6
55	Latvia	3.6
56	Bulgaria	3.5
57	Peru	3.4
58	China	3.3
59	Philippines	3.3
60	Lithuania	3.3
61	Costa Rica	3.2
62	Guatemala	3.2
63	Russian Federation	3.2
64	Bolivia	3.2
65	Ukraine	3.2
66	Paraguay	3.1
67	Zimbabwe	3.0
68	Ecuador	2.9
69	Poland	2.9
70	Nicaragua	2.8
71	Honduras	2.8
72	Mauritius	2.8
73	Bangladesh	2.6
74	Nigeria	2.5
75	Vietnam	2.4

MEAN: 4.3

4.02 Public access to Internet

Public access to the Internet through libraries, post offices, etc is: (1 = very limited, 7 = pervasive—most people have frequent access)

RANK	COUNTRY	SCORE
1	Iceland	6.4
2	Finland	6.3
3	Denmark	6.0
4	Norway	5.8
5	Sweden	5.8
6	Singapore	5.7
7	Korea	5.5
8	Canada	5.4
9	Netherlands	5.4
10	United States	5.4
11	Estonia	5.3
12	Australia	5.3
13	Peru	5.2
14	New Zealand	5.2
15	United Kingdom	5.0
16	Argentina	4.9
17	Belgium	4.8
18	Hong Kong SAR	4.8
19	Switzerland	4.7
20	Austria	4.7
21	Germany	4.7
22	Taiwan	4.4
23	Costa Rica	4.2
24	Bolivia	4.2
25	Spain	4.1
26	Japan	4.1
27	Czech Republic	4.0
28	Portugal	4.0
29	India	4.0
30	Turkey	3.9
31	Ireland	3.9
32	Israel	3.9
33	France	3.9
34	Hungary	3.7
35	Slovenia	3.7
36	Bulgaria	3.7
37	Colombia	3.6
38	Paraguay	3.6
39	Panama	3.6
40	Uruguay	3.5
41	El Salvador	3.5
42	Jordan	3.5
43	Malaysia	3.4
44	Chile	3.4
45	Italy	3.4
46	Indonesia	3.4
47	Thailand	3.4
48	Slovak Republic	3.4
49	Latvia	3.3
50	Trinidad and Tobago	3.3
51	Ecuador	3.3
52	Lithuania	3.3
53	Egypt	3.2
54	Venezuela	3.1
55	Poland	3.1
56	Brazil	3.1
57	South Africa	3.1
58	Mexico	3.0
59	Mauritius	2.9
60	Guatemala	2.9
61	Dominican Republic	2.9
62	China	2.8
63	Philippines	2.8
64	Sri Lanka	2.8
65	Nicaragua	2.8
66	Greece	2.7
67	Jamaica	2.7
68	Ukraine	2.6
69	Vietnam	2.6
70	Russian Federation	2.6
71	Romania	2.4
72	Honduras	2.3
73	Zimbabwe	2.2
74	Nigeria	2.2
75	Bangladesh	1.8

MEAN: 3.9

4.03 Internet access in schools

Internet access in schools is: (1 = very limited, 7 = pervasive—most children have frequent access/widely used)

RANK	COUNTRY	SCORE
1	Finland	6.6
2	Singapore	6.1
3	Canada	6.1
4	Sweden	6.0
5	Iceland	6.0
6	Denmark	5.9
7	United States	5.7
8	Korea	5.6
9	Australia	5.6
10	Taiwan	5.5
11	United Kingdom	5.5
12	New Zealand	5.4
13	Estonia	5.3
14	Norway	5.3
15	Hong Kong SAR	5.3
16	Netherlands	5.1
17	Hungary	5.1
18	Austria	5.0
19	Czech Republic	4.9
20	Slovenia	4.8
21	Switzerland	4.8
22	Germany	4.7
23	Belgium	4.7
24	Ireland	4.5
25	Chile	4.4
26	Portugal	4.4
27	Slovak Republic	4.4
28	Israel	4.3
29	France	4.2
30	Latvia	3.9
31	Spain	3.9
32	Japan	3.7
33	Thailand	3.6
34	Poland	3.6
35	Costa Rica	3.5
36	Argentina	3.4
37	Brazil	3.3
38	Uruguay	3.3
39	China	3.2
40	Mexico	3.1
41	Turkey	3.1
42	Malaysia	3.0
43	Colombia	3.0
44	Trinidad and Tobago	3.0
45	Philippines	3.0
46	India	2.9
47	Lithuania	2.9
48	Italy	2.9
49	South Africa	2.9
50	Peru	2.9
51	Jamaica	2.8
52	Bulgaria	2.8
53	Jordan	2.8
54	Indonesia	2.8
55	Panama	2.7
56	Greece	2.7
57	Dominican Republic	2.5
58	Mauritius	2.5
59	Ecuador	2.5
60	El Salvador	2.5
61	Venezuela	2.3
62	Egypt	2.3
63	Sri Lanka	2.2
64	Paraguay	2.2
65	Vietnam	2.1
66	Russian Federation	2.1
67	Ukraine	2.1
68	Bolivia	2.1
69	Guatemala	2.0
70	Nicaragua	2.0
71	Zimbabwe	1.9
72	Honduras	1.9
73	Nigeria	1.8
74	Romania	1.7
75	Bangladesh	1.5

MEAN: 3.7

4.04 Quality of competition in telecommunications sector

Is competition in your country's telecommunications sector sufficient to ensure high quality, infrequent interruptions, and low prices? (1 = no, 7 = yes, equal to world's best)

RANK	COUNTRY	SCORE
1	Finland	6.8
2	Sweden	6.6
3	United States	6.4
4	Germany	6.4
5	Chile	6.4
6	Hong Kong SAR	6.4
7	Austria	6.3
8	Canada	6.3
9	United Kingdom	6.3
10	Norway	6.1
11	Dominican Republic	6.0
12	Singapore	6.0
13	Italy	5.9
14	France	5.9
15	Switzerland	5.9
16	Korea	5.8
17	Iceland	5.8
18	Netherlands	5.7
19	Portugal	5.7
20	Taiwan	5.7
21	El Salvador	5.6
22	Australia	5.6
23	Denmark	5.6
24	Belgium	5.6
25	Brazil	5.5
26	Venezuela	5.5
27	New Zealand	5.5
28	Argentina	5.4
29	Spain	5.3
30	Israel	5.1
31	Estonia	5.1
32	Slovak Republic	5.0
33	Japan	5.0
34	Colombia	5.0
35	Jordan	4.9
36	Philippines	4.8
37	Hungary	4.8
38	Malaysia	4.7
39	Czech Republic	4.7
40	Ireland	4.7
41	India	4.6
42	Sri Lanka	4.6
43	Egypt	4.5
44	Thailand	4.5
45	Greece	4.4
46	Peru	4.4
47	Guatemala	4.2
48	Indonesia	4.1
49	Jamaica	4.0
50	Uruguay	3.9
51	Panama	3.9
52	Turkey	3.7
53	Bolivia	3.6
54	Russian Federation	3.6
55	Slovenia	3.5
56	Mexico	3.5
57	Poland	3.4
58	China	3.4
59	Latvia	3.3
60	Romania	3.2
61	Ukraine	3.1
62	Zimbabwe	3.0
63	Paraguay	3.0
64	Lithuania	2.9
65	South Africa	2.8
66	Costa Rica	2.8
67	Vietnam	2.7
68	Bulgaria	2.7
69	Bangladesh	2.7
70	Nicaragua	2.7
71	Trinidad and Tobago	2.6
72	Ecuador	2.6
73	Nigeria	2.5
74	Honduras	2.2
75	Mauritius	1.9

MEAN: 4.6

379

4.05 High-skilled IT job market

Highly skilled information technology workers in your industry: (1 = must leave the country to find good jobs, 7 = have their pick of well-paid, desirable jobs within the country)

RANK	COUNTRY	SCORE
1	Netherlands	6.7
2	United States	6.7
3	Finland	6.6
4	Germany	6.5
5	Ireland	6.4
6	United Kingdom	6.3
7	Norway	6.3
8	Austria	6.2
9	Singapore	6.2
10	Belgium	6.1
11	Denmark	6.1
12	Sweden	6.1
13	Iceland	6.1
14	Israel	6.1
15	Switzerland	6.1
16	Spain	6.0
17	Japan	5.9
18	Italy	5.9
19	Hong Kong SAR	5.8
20	Taiwan	5.8
21	France	5.7
22	Canada	5.6
23	Brazil	5.4
24	Portugal	5.4
25	Chile	5.3
26	Poland	5.3
27	Australia	5.3
28	Costa Rica	5.3
29	Czech Republic	5.2
30	Greece	5.2
31	Estonia	5.2
32	Turkey	5.1
33	Slovenia	4.9
34	Thailand	4.9
35	Malaysia	4.9
36	Hungary	4.8
37	Egypt	4.8
38	Korea	4.8
39	Slovak Republic	4.8
40	South Africa	4.6
41	Indonesia	4.5
42	China	4.5
43	India	4.4
44	Dominican Republic	4.4
45	Panama	4.3
46	New Zealand	4.3
47	Mexico	4.2
48	Mauritius	4.2
49	Honduras	4.2
50	Argentina	4.1
51	Trinidad and Tobago	4.1
52	Latvia	4.1
53	Jamaica	4.1
54	Vietnam	4.0
55	El Salvador	3.9
56	Venezuela	3.9
57	Guatemala	3.8
58	Uruguay	3.8
59	Nigeria	3.7
60	Jordan	3.7
61	Russian Federation	3.7
62	Lithuania	3.6
63	Zimbabwe	3.6
64	Peru	3.5
65	Paraguay	3.3
66	Colombia	3.3
67	Bolivia	3.2
68	Nicaragua	3.2
69	Ecuador	3.2
70	Philippines	3.2
71	Sri Lanka	3.2
72	Ukraine	2.7
73	Bulgaria	2.5
74	Bangladesh	2.3
75	Romania	2.2

MEAN: 4.7

4.06 IT training and education

Your country's IT training and educational programs: (1 = lag far behind most countries, 7 = are among the world's best)

RANK	COUNTRY	SCORE
1	Finland	6.3
2	Netherlands	6.3
3	United States	6.2
4	Sweden	6.2
5	Singapore	6.1
6	Iceland	6.0
7	Israel	6.0
8	Canada	5.7
9	India	5.6
10	Ireland	5.6
11	Taiwan	5.5
12	United Kingdom	5.5
13	France	5.4
14	Switzerland	5.4
15	Denmark	5.4
16	Austria	5.3
17	Norway	5.2
18	Estonia	5.1
19	Germany	5.1
20	Australia	5.1
21	Hong Kong SAR	5.1
22	Belgium	5.1
23	Hungary	5.0
24	Spain	5.0
25	New Zealand	4.9
26	Costa Rica	4.8
27	Czech Republic	4.8
28	Korea	4.7
29	Chile	4.5
30	Slovenia	4.5
31	Italy	4.4
32	Philippines	4.4
33	Japan	4.4
34	Uruguay	4.4
35	Portugal	4.3
36	Thailand	4.3
37	Jordan	4.2
38	Malaysia	4.2
39	Latvia	4.2
40	Brazil	4.1
41	Jamaica	4.1
42	Greece	4.1
43	Trinidad and Tobago	4.0
44	South Africa	4.0
45	Slovak Republic	4.0
46	Poland	3.9
47	Sri Lanka	3.9
48	Dominican Republic	3.9
49	Argentina	3.8
50	Zimbabwe	3.8
51	Egypt	3.8
52	Bulgaria	3.7
53	Venezuela	3.7
54	Turkey	3.7
55	Indonesia	3.6
56	Panama	3.6
57	Peru	3.6
58	Mexico	3.6
59	Ukraine	3.6
60	Lithuania	3.5
61	El Salvador	3.5
62	Colombia	3.5
63	China	3.4
64	Mauritius	3.3
65	Paraguay	3.2
66	Russian Federation	3.1
67	Guatemala	3.1
68	Nicaragua	3.0
69	Nigeria	2.9
70	Vietnam	2.9
71	Ecuador	2.8
72	Bolivia	2.6
73	Bangladesh	2.5
74	Honduras	2.5
75	Romania	2.0

MEAN: 4.3

4.07 Quality of competition in ISP sector

Is competition among your country's Internet Service Providers sufficient to ensure high quality, infrequent interruptions and low prices? (1 = no, 7 = yes, equal to world's best)

RANK	COUNTRY	SCORE
1	Finland	6.9
2	Iceland	6.7
3	United States	6.7
4	Sweden	6.6
5	France	6.5
6	Canada	6.4
7	Hong Kong SAR	6.4
8	Germany	6.4
9	Netherlands	6.4
10	Belgium	6.3
11	Switzerland	6.2
12	United Kingdom	6.2
13	Austria	6.2
14	New Zealand	6.1
15	Norway	6.1
16	Israel	6.1
17	Korea	6.1
18	Australia	6.1
19	Denmark	6.0
20	Estonia	6.0
21	Singapore	5.9
22	Italy	5.9
23	Czech Republic	5.8
24	Argentina	5.7
25	Chile	5.7
26	Brazil	5.6
27	Spain	5.6
28	Turkey	5.6
29	Portugal	5.5
30	Japan	5.5
31	Jordan	5.4
32	Taiwan	5.4
33	South Africa	5.4
34	Hungary	5.3
35	Slovak Republic	5.2
36	Egypt	5.2
37	Dominican Republic	5.1
38	India	5.1
39	Venezuela	5.1
40	Greece	5.1
41	El Salvador	5.1
42	Ireland	5.0
43	Panama	4.8
44	Latvia	4.8
45	Philippines	4.8
46	Uruguay	4.8
47	Poland	4.7
48	Colombia	4.7
49	Indonesia	4.6
50	Thailand	4.6
51	Jamaica	4.5
52	Mexico	4.4
53	Malaysia	4.4
54	Slovenia	4.4
55	Ukraine	4.3
56	Lithuania	4.1
57	Sri Lanka	4.0
58	Guatemala	4.0
59	Bulgaria	4.0
60	Peru	4.0
61	Zimbabwe	4.0
62	Ecuador	3.9
63	Bangladesh	3.8
64	Bolivia	3.7
65	Russian Federation	3.7
66	Romania	3.6
67	Nicaragua	3.6
68	Trinidad and Tobago	3.4
69	China	3.4
70	Paraguay	3.3
71	Honduras	3.3
72	Nigeria	3.1
73	Vietnam	3.1
74	Costa Rica	3.0
75	Mauritius	1.7

MEAN: 5.0

4.08 Government prioritization of ICT

Information and communications technologies are an overall government priority. (1 = strongly disagree, 7 = strongly agree)

RANK	COUNTRY	SCORE
1	Singapore	6.4
2	Finland	6.3
3	Estonia	5.8
4	Sweden	5.8
5	Taiwan	5.7
6	Spain	5.6
7	Jordan	5.6
8	Ireland	5.6
9	Hong Kong SAR	5.6
10	Iceland	5.5
11	Malaysia	5.4
12	Mauritius	5.4
13	India	5.3
14	Egypt	5.3
15	China	5.3
16	Netherlands	5.3
17	Austria	5.3
18	United Kingdom	5.2
19	Chile	5.2
20	Denmark	5.2
21	United States	5.2
22	Jamaica	5.1
23	Japan	5.1
24	Australia	5.1
25	Canada	5.1
26	Portugal	5.0
27	Brazil	5.0
28	France	5.0
29	Korea	5.0
30	Hungary	4.9
31	Norway	4.9
32	Costa Rica	4.9
33	Uruguay	4.9
34	El Salvador	4.8
35	Germany	4.8
36	Latvia	4.7
37	Israel	4.7
38	Switzerland	4.7
39	Mexico	4.7
40	New Zealand	4.7
41	Belgium	4.6
42	South Africa	4.6
43	Thailand	4.6
44	Colombia	4.5
45	Dominican Republic	4.4
46	Slovak Republic	4.4
47	Venezuela	4.3
48	Philippines	4.3
49	Italy	4.3
50	Russian Federation	4.3
51	Panama	4.3
52	Sri Lanka	4.3
53	Czech Republic	4.3
54	Greece	4.2
55	Argentina	4.2
56	Bulgaria	4.0
57	Trinidad and Tobago	4.0
58	Slovenia	4.0
59	Peru	4.0
60	Vietnam	3.9
61	Lithuania	3.9
62	Indonesia	3.8
63	Nigeria	3.8
64	Bangladesh	3.7
65	Nicaragua	3.7
66	Honduras	3.7
67	Ecuador	3.5
68	Poland	3.4
69	Turkey	3.4
70	Ukraine	3.4
71	Guatemala	3.3
72	Bolivia	3.2
73	Paraguay	3.2
74	Zimbabwe	2.7
75	Romania	2.1

MEAN: 4.6

4.09 Government success in ICT promotion

Government programs promoting the use of ICT are: (1 = not very successful, 7 = highly successful)

RANK	COUNTRY	SCORE	MEAN: 4.0
1	Singapore	6.0	
2	Finland	5.9	
3	Estonia	5.4	
4	Iceland	5.3	
5	Taiwan	5.3	
6	Egypt	5.3	
7	Ireland	5.3	
8	Sweden	5.2	
9	Jordan	5.1	
10	Hong Kong SAR	4.9	
11	India	4.9	
12	Korea	4.8	
13	Austria	4.7	
14	Canada	4.7	
15	China	4.5	
16	Denmark	4.5	
17	United States	4.5	
18	Brazil	4.5	
19	Germany	4.5	
20	Mauritius	4.4	
21	Spain	4.4	
22	Jamaica	4.4	
23	Switzerland	4.4	
24	Netherlands	4.4	
25	United Kingdom	4.4	
26	Portugal	4.3	
27	Israel	4.3	
28	Hungary	4.3	
29	Belgium	4.3	
30	France	4.2	
31	Malaysia	4.2	
32	Slovak Republic	4.2	
33	Norway	4.2	
34	Chile	4.1	
35	Latvia	4.0	
36	Uruguay	4.0	
37	El Salvador	4.0	
38	New Zealand	4.0	
39	South Africa	4.0	
40	Australia	3.9	
41	Costa Rica	3.9	
42	Japan	3.9	
43	Slovenia	3.9	
44	Thailand	3.9	
45	Mexico	3.8	
46	Italy	3.8	
47	Vietnam	3.8	
48	Trinidad and Tobago	3.8	
49	Philippines	3.7	
50	Venezuela	3.7	
51	Czech Republic	3.7	
52	Dominican Republic	3.6	
53	Argentina	3.6	
54	Sri Lanka	3.6	
55	Colombia	3.5	
56	Nigeria	3.5	
57	Panama	3.5	
58	Bulgaria	3.4	
59	Greece	3.3	
60	Lithuania	3.3	
61	Poland	3.3	
62	Turkey	3.3	
63	Indonesia	3.2	
64	Peru	3.2	
65	Russian Federation	3.1	
66	Nicaragua	3.1	
67	Ukraine	3.1	
68	Bangladesh	2.8	
69	Paraguay	2.8	
70	Ecuador	2.7	
71	Bolivia	2.7	
72	Guatemala	2.6	
73	Honduras	2.6	
74	Zimbabwe	2.2	
75	Romania	1.7	

4.10 Government on-line services

On-line government services—eg, downloadable permit applications, tax payments—in your country are: (1 = not available, 7 = commonly available)

RANK	COUNTRY	SCORE	MEAN: 3.8
1	Singapore	6.4	
2	Iceland	6.2	
3	Finland	5.8	
4	Norway	5.8	
5	Estonia	5.8	
6	Hong Kong SAR	5.7	
7	Sweden	5.7	
8	Brazil	5.6	
9	Canada	5.6	
10	Denmark	5.6	
11	United Kingdom	5.5	
12	United States	5.4	
13	Taiwan	5.4	
14	Chile	5.3	
15	Australia	5.3	
16	Netherlands	5.2	
17	Ireland	5.1	
18	Austria	5.1	
19	Spain	5.0	
20	New Zealand	5.0	
21	Portugal	4.8	
22	France	4.7	
23	Lithuania	4.5	
24	Korea	4.5	
25	Italy	4.5	
26	Czech Republic	4.5	
27	Hungary	4.4	
28	Switzerland	4.2	
29	Poland	4.1	
30	Argentina	4.1	
31	Germany	4.0	
32	Israel	3.9	
33	Mexico	3.9	
34	India	3.9	
35	Belgium	3.7	
36	Slovenia	3.7	
37	Colombia	3.6	
38	South Africa	3.6	
39	Peru	3.6	
40	China	3.5	
41	Ukraine	3.5	
42	Panama	3.5	
43	Uruguay	3.4	
44	Slovak Republic	3.4	
45	Dominican Republic	3.3	
46	El Salvador	3.3	
47	Jamaica	3.3	
48	Latvia	3.3	
49	Malaysia	3.3	
50	Japan	3.2	
51	Turkey	3.2	
52	Thailand	3.2	
53	Costa Rica	3.2	
54	Greece	3.0	
55	Guatemala	3.0	
56	Bulgaria	3.0	
57	Ecuador	2.9	
58	Jordan	2.7	
59	Russian Federation	2.6	
60	Philippines	2.3	
61	Nicaragua	2.3	
62	Nigeria	2.2	
63	Egypt	2.2	
64	Vietnam	2.2	
65	Mauritius	2.1	
66	Paraguay	2.1	
67	Bolivia	2.1	
68	Indonesia	2.0	
69	Honduras	2.0	
70	Venezuela	2.0	
71	Sri Lanka	1.9	
72	Trinidad and Tobago	1.5	
73	Bangladesh	1.5	
74	Romania	1.2	
75	Zimbabwe	1.2	

4.11 Laws relating to ICT use

Laws relating to electronic commerce, digital signatures, and consumer protection are: (1 = nonexistent, 7 = well developed and enforced)

RANK	COUNTRY	SCORE
1	Finland	6.2
2	Singapore	5.8
3	Sweden	5.7
4	United States	5.6
5	France	5.5
6	Canada	5.5
7	Norway	5.5
8	Iceland	5.5
9	Austria	5.5
10	Netherlands	5.5
11	United Kingdom	5.4
12	Denmark	5.4
13	Australia	5.3
14	Ireland	5.3
15	Hong Kong SAR	5.2
16	Germany	5.2
17	Belgium	5.2
18	Switzerland	5.0
19	New Zealand	4.9
20	Israel	4.9
21	Estonia	4.8
22	Malaysia	4.8
23	Spain	4.6
24	Italy	4.5
25	Korea	4.5
26	Czech Republic	4.4
27	India	4.4
28	Portugal	4.3
29	Slovenia	4.2
30	Japan	4.2
31	Mauritius	4.1
32	Taiwan	4.1
33	Philippines	4.1
34	South Africa	4.1
35	Uruguay	4.0
36	Poland	3.9
37	Jordan	3.8
38	Colombia	3.8
39	Brazil	3.8
40	Hungary	3.8
41	Venezuela	3.7
42	Panama	3.7
43	Trinidad and Tobago	3.7
44	Chile	3.6
45	Jamaica	3.6
46	Peru	3.4
47	Costa Rica	3.4
48	Lithuania	3.4
49	Thailand	3.3
50	El Salvador	3.2
51	Slovak Republic	3.2
52	Dominican Republic	3.2
53	China	3.2
54	Mexico	3.1
55	Greece	3.1
56	Egypt	3.1
57	Latvia	3.0
58	Bulgaria	3.0
59	Ukraine	3.0
60	Turkey	2.9
61	Zimbabwe	2.9
62	Sri Lanka	2.8
63	Paraguay	2.7
64	Ecuador	2.7
65	Nigeria	2.7
66	Indonesia	2.7
67	Vietnam	2.6
68	Nicaragua	2.6
69	Honduras	2.5
70	Argentina	2.5
71	Guatemala	2.5
72	Russian Federation	2.4
73	Bolivia	2.1
74	Bangladesh	2.1
75	Romania	1.9

MEAN: 3.9

4.12 Legal framework for ICT development

The legal framework in your country supports the development of IT businesses. (1 = no, strongly impedes, 7 = yes, significantly promotes)

RANK	COUNTRY	SCORE
1	Finland	6.2
2	Singapore	6.2
3	United States	6.2
4	Sweden	5.7
5	Netherlands	5.6
6	Canada	5.6
7	Australia	5.5
8	Iceland	5.5
9	United Kingdom	5.5
10	Hong Kong SAR	5.4
11	Austria	5.4
12	Estonia	5.3
13	Ireland	5.3
14	New Zealand	5.3
15	Denmark	5.3
16	Malaysia	5.3
17	France	5.1
18	Switzerland	5.1
19	Germany	5.1
20	Israel	5.0
21	Norway	5.0
22	Slovak Republic	5.0
23	Korea	5.0
24	Spain	4.9
25	India	4.9
26	Italy	4.8
27	Portugal	4.7
28	Brazil	4.7
29	Belgium	4.7
30	South Africa	4.7
31	Jordan	4.7
32	Philippines	4.5
33	Czech Republic	4.4
34	Trinidad and Tobago	4.4
35	Taiwan	4.4
36	Uruguay	4.4
37	Egypt	4.3
38	Slovenia	4.3
39	Chile	4.3
40	Dominican Republic	4.3
41	Jamaica	4.3
42	Colombia	4.3
43	Mauritius	4.3
44	Turkey	4.3
45	Hungary	4.2
46	China	4.2
47	Japan	4.2
48	Panama	4.1
49	Argentina	4.1
50	Nigeria	4.1
51	Costa Rica	4.0
52	Latvia	4.0
53	Peru	4.0
54	Zimbabwe	4.0
55	El Salvador	4.0
56	Venezuela	4.0
57	Ukraine	3.9
58	Vietnam	3.9
59	Greece	3.9
60	Thailand	3.8
61	Lithuania	3.8
62	Mexico	3.8
63	Sri Lanka	3.7
64	Poland	3.7
65	Bangladesh	3.7
66	Bulgaria	3.6
67	Indonesia	3.6
68	Honduras	3.5
69	Nicaragua	3.4
70	Guatemala	3.4
71	Ecuador	3.3
72	Russian Federation	3.3
73	Paraguay	3.2
74	Bolivia	3.1
75	Romania	3.1

MEAN: 4.5

383

4.13 Cellular telephones

Cellular mobile subscribers per 100 inhabitants, 2000

RANK	COUNTRY	HARD DATA
1	Taiwan	80.3
2	Hong Kong SAR	80.2
3	Austria	78.6
4	Italy	73.7
5	Finland	72.6
6	Sweden	71.4
7	Norway	70.3
8	Israel	70.2
9	Singapore	68.4
10	Netherlands	67.1
11	Iceland	67.0
12	United Kingdom	67.0
13	Ireland	66.8
14	Portugal	66.5
15	Switzerland	64.5
16	Denmark	61.0
17	Spain	60.9
18	Germany	58.6
19	Korea	56.7
20	Greece	55.9
21	Belgium	54.9
22	Slovenia	54.7
23	Japan	52.6
24	France	49.4
25	Australia	44.6
26	Czech Republic	42.4
27	New Zealand	40.3
28	Estonia	38.7
29	United States	36.5
30	Hungary	29.3
31	Canada	28.5
32	Turkey	24.6
33	Slovak Republic	23.9
34	Chile	22.4
35	Venezuela	21.8
36	Malaysia	21.3
37	Paraguay	19.6
38	Poland	17.4
39	Latvia	16.9
40	Argentina	16.3
41	Jamaica	14.2
42	Mexico	14.2
43	Lithuania	14.2
44	Brazil	13.6
45	Uruguay	13.2
46	South Africa	12.0
47	Romania	11.2
48	Trinidad and Tobago	10.3
49	Mauritius	10.2
50	Bulgaria	9.0
51	Panama	8.3
52	Philippines	8.2
53	China	6.6
54	El Salvador	6.2
55	Jordan	5.8
56	Colombia	5.3
57	Costa Rica	5.2
58	Bolivia	5.2
59	Dominican Republic	5.0
60	Thailand	4.4
61	Peru	4.0
62	Ecuador	3.8
63	Guatemala	3.1
64	Honduras	2.4
65	Sri Lanka	2.4
66	Russian Federation	2.2
67	Egypt	2.1
68	Indonesia	1.7
69	Ukraine	1.6
70	Zimbabwe	1.5
71	Vietnam	1.0
72	Nicaragua	0.9
73	India	0.4
74	Bangladesh	0.1
75	Nigeria	0.03

SOURCE: International Telecommunications Union, July 2001

4.14 Internet users

Internet users per 10,000 inhabitants, 2000

RANK	COUNTRY	HARD DATA
1	Iceland	5,978.7
2	Portugal	5,950.1
3	Norway	4,905.2
4	Sweden	4,558.3
5	Canada	4,130.1
6	Korea	4,025.4
7	Finland	3,723.0
8	Japan	3,709.5
9	Denmark	3,658.5
10	Australia	3,497.4
11	United States	3,465.8
12	Hong Kong SAR	3,359.0
13	Singapore	2,986.8
14	Switzerland	2,978.6
15	Germany	2,920.6
16	Taiwan	2,812.6
17	United Kingdom	2,576.7
18	Austria	2,557.5
19	Estonia	2,547.3
20	Netherlands	2,381.5
21	New Zealand	2,166.7
22	Ireland	2,101.9
23	Belgium	1,968.3
24	Israel	1,754.5
25	Malaysia	1,590.0
26	France	1,445.6
27	Spain	1,327.0
28	Slovenia	1,257.0
29	Slovak Republic	1,202.6
30	Chile	1,155.3
31	Uruguay	1,108.8
32	Italy	1,047.2
33	Czech Republic	976.2
34	Greece	939.4
35	Mauritius	733.6
36	Poland	722.3
37	Hungary	699.1
38	Argentina	675.1
39	Latvia	630.3
40	Costa Rica	621.4
41	South Africa	549.4
42	Venezuela	393.1
43	Romania	358.3
44	Trinidad and Tobago	330.3
45	Turkey	304.4
46	Brazil	293.9
47	Bulgaria	283.4
48	Lithuania	278.5
49	Mexico	274.3
50	Philippines	261.4
51	Jamaica	234.4
52	Russian Federation	211.0
53	Colombia	207.5
54	Thailand	198.0
55	Jordan	190.9
56	China	173.7
57	Panama	159.8
58	Peru	158.5
59	Ecuador	142.3
60	Bolivia	95.8
61	Egypt	70.9
62	Indonesia	68.4
63	El Salvador	65.0
64	Sri Lanka	64.2
65	Honduras	61.7
66	Guatemala	58.6
67	India	49.4
68	Nicaragua	40.5
69	Ukraine	39.5
70	Paraguay	37.3
71	Dominican Republic	29.9
72	Zimbabwe	17.4
73	Vietnam	12.7
74	Nigeria	9.2
75	Bangladesh	3.9

SOURCE: International Telecommunications Union, July 2001

4.15 Internet hosts

Internet hosts per 10,000 inhabitants, 2000

RANK	COUNTRY		HARD DATA
1	United States	2,928.3	
2	Iceland	1,420.0	
3	Finland	1,022.5	
4	Netherlands	1,017.5	
5	Norway	1,009.3	
6	New Zealand	900.9	
7	Australia	843.5	
8	Canada	768.8	
9	Sweden	670.8	
10	Denmark	626.6	
11	Austria	588.5	
12	Taiwan	492.3	
13	Singapore	437.6	
14	Switzerland	366.4	
15	Japan	365.7	
16	Hong Kong SAR	336.9	
17	Ireland	296.4	
18	Belgium	295.4	
19	Israel	287.5	
20	Estonia	284.3	
21	United Kingdom	280.8	
22	Germany	248.3	
23	France	190.9	
24	Italy	178.0	
25	Uruguay	162.0	
26	Czech Republic	155.5	
27	Spain	112.2	
28	Slovenia	110.1	
29	Greece	103.9	
30	Hungary	102.1	
31	Poland	87.7	
32	Korea	84.1	
33	Latvia	83.7	
34	Argentina	73.0	
35	Slovak Republic	70.2	
36	Portugal	62.0	
37	Mexico	56.6	
38	Panama	52.8	
39	Brazil	51.5	
40	Trinidad and Tobago	51.0	
41	Chile	49.1	
42	Lithuania	48.1	
43	South Africa	43.0	
44	Malaysia	29.3	
45	Mauritius	27.6	
46	Bulgaria	22.4	
47	Russian Federation	22.2	
48	Romania	18.6	
49	Costa Rica	18.3	
50	Colombia	11.1	
51	Turkey	10.6	
52	Thailand	10.5	
53	Dominican Republic	9.4	
54	Ukraine	7.1	
55	Venezuela	6.7	
56	Jamaica	5.7	
57	Guatemala	4.9	
58	Peru	4.2	
59	Nicaragua	2.8	
60	Philippines	2.5	
61	Paraguay	2.4	
62	Zimbabwe	2.3	
63	Bolivia	1.6	
64	Jordan	1.4	
65	Indonesia	1.3	
66	Sri Lanka	1.1	
67	El Salvador	0.9	
68	China	0.6	
69	Egypt	0.4	
69	India	0.4	
71	Bangladesh	0.3	
72	Honduras	0.2	
73	Ecuador	0.2	
74	Nigeria	0.1	
75	Vietnam	0.02	

SOURCE: International Telecommunications Union, July 2001

4.16 Telephone lines

Main telephone lines per 100 inhabitants, 2000

RANK	COUNTRY		HARD DATA
1	Denmark	75.3	
2	Norway	72.9	
3	Switzerland	72.0	
4	United States	70.0	
5	Sweden	68.2	
6	Iceland	67.7	
7	Canada	67.7	
8	Japan	65.3	
9	Netherlands	60.7	
10	Germany	60.1	
11	France	58.0	
12	Hong Kong SAR	57.8	
13	Taiwan	56.8	
14	United Kingdom	56.7	
15	Finland	54.7	
16	Greece	53.2	
17	Australia	52.4	
18	Belgium	49.9	
19	New Zealand	49.6	
20	Singapore	48.5	
21	Italy	47.4	
22	Austria	47.4	
23	Korea	46.4	
24	Israel	46.3	
25	Portugal	43.1	
26	Ireland	42.6	
27	Spain	42.1	
28	Slovenia	37.8	
29	Czech Republic	37.8	
30	Hungary	37.1	
31	Estonia	36.3	
32	Bulgaria	35.0	
33	Lithuania	32.1	
34	Slovak Republic	31.4	
35	Latvia	30.0	
36	Poland	28.2	
37	Turkey	28.0	
38	Uruguay	27.8	
39	Costa Rica	24.9	
40	Mauritius	23.7	
41	Trinidad and Tobago	23.1	
42	Chile	22.1	
43	Russian Federation	21.8	
44	Argentina	21.3	
45	Malaysia	19.9	
46	Ukraine	19.9	
47	Jamaica	19.9	
48	Brazil	18.2	
49	Romania	17.5	
50	Colombia	16.9	
51	Panama	16.4	
52	Mexico	12.5	
53	South Africa	11.4	
54	China	11.1	
55	Venezuela	10.8	
56	Ecuador	10.0	
57	Dominican Republic	9.8	
58	Jordan	9.3	
59	El Salvador	9.1	
60	Thailand	8.7	
61	Egypt	8.6	
62	Peru	6.4	
63	Bolivia	6.2	
64	Guatemala	5.7	
65	Paraguay	5.0	
66	Honduras	4.6	
67	Sri Lanka	4.1	
68	Philippines	3.9	
69	India	3.2	
70	Vietnam	3.2	
71	Indonesia	3.1	
72	Nicaragua	3.0	
73	Zimbabwe	2.1	
74	Nigeria	0.4	
75	Bangladesh	0.3	

SOURCE: International Telecommunications Union, July 2001

4.17 Personal computers

Personal computers per 100 Inhabitants, 2000

RANK	COUNTRY		HARD DATA
1	Sweden	50.7	
2	Switzerland	50.3	
3	Norway	49.1	
4	Singapore	48.3	
5	Australia	46.5	
6	Denmark	43.2	
7	Finland	39.6	
8	Netherlands	39.5	
9	Iceland	39.2	
10	Canada	39.0	
11	Ireland	36.5	
12	New Zealand	36.0	
13	Hong Kong SAR	34.7	
14	Belgium	34.5	
15	United States	33.8	
16	Germany	33.6	
17	United Kingdom	33.5	
18	Japan	31.5	
19	France	30.5	
20	Austria	27.7	
21	Israel	25.4	
22	Slovenia	25.1	
23	Taiwan	22.5	
24	Italy	20.9	
25	Korea	19.0	
26	Spain	14.3	
27	Estonia	13.5	
28	Czech Republic	12.2	
29	Slovak Republic	10.9	
30	Portugal	10.5	
31	Costa Rica	10.2	
32	Uruguay	10.0	
33	Malaysia	9.5	
34	Mauritius	9.4	
35	Chile	8.6	
36	Hungary	8.5	
37	Latvia	8.2	
38	Greece	7.1	
39	Poland	6.9	
40	South Africa	6.2	
41	Lithuania	6.0	
42	Trinidad and Tobago	5.4	
43	Argentina	5.1	
44	Mexico	5.1	
45	Venezuela	4.6	
46	Brazil	4.4	
47	Jamaica	4.3	
48	Russian Federation	4.3	
49	Turkey	3.8	
50	Peru	3.6	
51	Colombia	3.4	
52	Panama	3.2	
53	Romania	2.7	
54	Bulgaria	2.7	
55	Thailand	2.4	
56	Ecuador	2.0	
57	Philippines	1.9	
58	El Salvador	1.6	
59	China	1.6	
60	Ukraine	1.6	
61	Jordan	1.4	
62	Zimbabwe	1.3	
63	Bolivia	1.2	
64	Egypt	1.2	
65	Paraguay	1.1	
66	Guatemala	1.0	
66	Indonesia	1.0	
68	Honduras	1.0	
69	Vietnam	0.9	
70	Nicaragua	0.8	
71	Nigeria	0.6	
72	Sri Lanka	0.6	
73	India	0.5	
74	Bangladesh	0.1	
	Dominican Republic	N/A	

SOURCE: International Telecommunications Union, July 2001

5.01 Overall infrastructure quality

General infrastructure in your country is: (1 = poorly developed and inefficient, 7 = among the best in the world)

RANK	COUNTRY	SCORE
1	Switzerland	6.9
2	Singapore	6.8
3	Germany	6.8
4	France	6.8
5	Finland	6.8
6	Denmark	6.7
7	Austria	6.6
8	Hong Kong SAR	6.6
9	United States	6.6
10	Iceland	6.5
11	Sweden	6.5
12	Canada	6.4
13	Netherlands	6.2
14	Australia	6.1
15	Japan	6.0
16	Belgium	6.0
17	New Zealand	5.7
18	United Kingdom	5.6
19	Norway	5.5
20	Malaysia	5.4
21	Spain	5.1
22	South Africa	5.1
23	Trinidad and Tobago	5.1
24	Jordan	5.0
25	Taiwan	4.9
26	Slovak Republic	4.8
27	Korea	4.8
28	Israel	4.8
29	Mauritius	4.7
30	Thailand	4.6
31	Czech Republic	4.5
32	Portugal	4.4
33	Romania	4.2
34	Estonia	4.2
35	Egypt	4.2
36	Hungary	4.1
37	Slovenia	4.0
38	Latvia	4.0
39	Poland	4.0
40	Uruguay	3.9
41	Italy	3.9
42	Brazil	3.8
43	Ireland	3.7
44	Turkey	3.7
45	Chile	3.7
46	Argentina	3.6
47	Lithuania	3.6
48	Jamaica	3.6
49	Greece	3.5
50	Ukraine	3.4
51	Dominican Republic	3.4
52	Panama	3.4
53	Venezuela	3.3
54	Mexico	3.3
55	Zimbabwe	3.3
56	Peru	3.2
57	Costa Rica	3.0
58	Bulgaria	3.0
59	Indonesia	3.0
60	El Salvador	3.0
61	China	2.9
62	Sri Lanka	2.9
63	Guatemala	2.7
64	Colombia	2.7
65	Russian Federation	2.6
66	India	2.6
67	Paraguay	2.4
68	Philippines	2.4
69	Honduras	2.3
70	Ecuador	2.3
71	Vietnam	2.2
72	Nigeria	2.1
73	Nicaragua	2.1
74	Bangladesh	2.0
75	Bolivia	1.7

MEAN: 4.3

5.02 Tap water safety

Tap water in your city is: (1 = unsafe and inaccessible for drinking, 7 = safe and easily accessible for drinking)

RANK	COUNTRY	SCORE
1	Iceland	7.0
2	Netherlands	7.0
3	Austria	7.0
4	Sweden	7.0
5	Germany	7.0
6	Finland	6.9
7	Switzerland	6.9
8	New Zealand	6.9
9	France	6.9
10	Denmark	6.9
11	Belgium	6.9
12	Spain	6.9
13	Uruguay	6.8
14	Singapore	6.8
15	Slovak Republic	6.8
16	Australia	6.8
17	Norway	6.7
18	Japan	6.7
19	United Kingdom	6.7
20	Hungary	6.6
21	United States	6.6
22	Chile	6.5
23	Greece	6.5
24	Canada	6.5
25	Ireland	6.4
26	Italy	6.4
27	Slovenia	6.3
28	Costa Rica	6.3
29	Portugal	6.3
30	South Africa	6.2
31	Argentina	6.2
32	Panama	6.1
33	Mauritius	6.1
34	Jamaica	5.9
35	Israel	5.9
36	Czech Republic	5.9
37	Zimbabwe	5.8
38	Egypt	5.7
39	Hong Kong SAR	5.7
40	Colombia	5.4
41	Estonia	5.4
42	Romania	5.4
43	Malaysia	5.2
44	Nicaragua	5.2
45	Taiwan	5.1
46	Trinidad and Tobago	5.1
47	Bulgaria	5.0
48	Thailand	5.0
49	Bolivia	5.0
50	Brazil	4.9
51	Ecuador	4.6
52	China	4.6
53	Jordan	4.5
54	Lithuania	4.5
55	Korea	4.3
56	Paraguay	4.2
57	Poland	4.2
58	Latvia	4.1
59	Turkey	4.1
60	Sri Lanka	3.9
61	Peru	3.7
62	Guatemala	3.7
63	Venezuela	3.7
64	El Salvador	3.6
65	Honduras	3.5
66	Philippines	3.4
67	India	3.4
68	Dominican Republic	3.4
69	Russian Federation	3.4
70	Mexico	3.4
71	Ukraine	3.3
72	Vietnam	3.3
73	Nigeria	2.9
74	Indonesia	2.2
75	Bangladesh	2.0

MEAN: 5.4

388

5.03 Industrial water availability

Water for industrial purposes is: (1 = not available, 7 = readily available)

RANK	COUNTRY	SCORE
1	Slovak Republic	7.0
2	Iceland	7.0
3	Netherlands	7.0
4	Finland	6.9
5	France	6.9
6	Austria	6.9
7	Sweden	6.9
8	Germany	6.9
9	Switzerland	6.8
10	New Zealand	6.8
11	Norway	6.8
12	United Kingdom	6.8
13	Singapore	6.7
14	Canada	6.7
15	Japan	6.7
16	Denmark	6.7
17	United States	6.7
18	Australia	6.7
19	Belgium	6.6
20	Uruguay	6.6
21	Spain	6.5
22	Ireland	6.5
23	Hong Kong SAR	6.4
24	Italy	6.4
25	Hungary	6.3
26	South Africa	6.3
27	Malaysia	6.2
28	Slovenia	6.1
29	Israel	6.1
30	Argentina	6.1
31	Portugal	6.1
32	Czech Republic	6.1
33	Chile	6.1
34	Costa Rica	6.1
35	Egypt	6.0
36	Jamaica	5.9
37	Greece	5.9
38	Lithuania	5.8
39	Brazil	5.8
40	Estonia	5.8
41	Zimbabwe	5.8
42	Panama	5.7
43	Poland	5.7
44	Latvia	5.7
45	Mauritius	5.6
46	Colombia	5.6
47	Trinidad and Tobago	5.5
48	Korea	5.5
49	Thailand	5.4
50	Venezuela	5.3
51	Turkey	5.3
52	Taiwan	5.2
53	Russian Federation	5.2
54	Romania	5.0
55	China	5.0
56	Bolivia	4.9
57	Jordan	4.8
58	Sri Lanka	4.8
59	Ecuador	4.8
60	Indonesia	4.7
61	India	4.6
62	Bulgaria	4.6
63	Peru	4.6
64	Mexico	4.6
65	Ukraine	4.5
66	Philippines	4.4
67	Dominican Republic	4.4
68	El Salvador	4.3
69	Nicaragua	4.3
70	Bangladesh	4.1
71	Honduras	4.1
72	Vietnam	3.9
73	Paraguay	3.9
74	Guatemala	3.5
75	Nigeria	2.9

MEAN: 5.7

5.04 Road infrastructure quality

Accounting for road quality outside of major cities, the typical driving speed between cities is (1 = 10km/hr, 7 = 150 km/hr)

RANK	COUNTRY	SCORE
1	Germany	6.1
2	France	5.7
3	South Africa	5.7
4	Austria	5.6
5	United States	5.5
6	Canada	5.5
7	Spain	5.5
8	Netherlands	5.5
9	Switzerland	5.4
10	Belgium	5.4
11	Zimbabwe	5.4
12	Thailand	5.3
13	Denmark	5.3
14	Australia	5.3
15	Malaysia	5.2
16	Czech Republic	5.2
17	United Kingdom	5.1
18	Portugal	5.1
19	Sweden	5.1
20	New Zealand	5.1
21	Iceland	5.0
22	Argentina	5.0
23	Estonia	5.0
24	Uruguay	5.0
25	Mexico	5.0
26	Turkey	4.9
27	Egypt	4.9
28	Lithuania	4.9
29	Jordan	4.9
30	Italy	4.9
31	Greece	4.8
32	Finland	4.8
33	Venezuela	4.8
34	Slovak Republic	4.8
35	Trinidad and Tobago	4.8
36	Honduras	4.8
37	Israel	4.8
38	Hungary	4.7
39	Slovenia	4.7
40	Singapore	4.7
41	Ukraine	4.6
42	Chile	4.6
43	Dominican Republic	4.6
44	Russian Federation	4.6
45	Poland	4.5
46	Panama	4.5
47	Korea	4.4
48	China	4.4
49	Latvia	4.4
50	Nigeria	4.4
51	Brazil	4.4
52	Japan	4.3
53	Norway	4.3
54	Peru	4.3
55	Nicaragua	4.3
56	Hong Kong SAR	4.3
57	Ecuador	4.2
58	Bulgaria	4.2
59	El Salvador	4.1
60	Jamaica	4.1
61	Ireland	4.1
62	Mauritius	4.0
63	Guatemala	3.9
64	Taiwan	3.9
65	Paraguay	3.9
66	Indonesia	3.9
67	Bolivia	3.9
68	Colombia	3.7
69	Costa Rica	3.7
70	Bangladesh	3.7
71	Vietnam	3.6
72	Sri Lanka	3.6
73	India	3.6
74	Philippines	3.5
75	Romania	3.4

MEAN: 4.7

5.05 Railroad infrastructure development

Railroads in your country are: (1 = underdeveloped, 7 = as extensive and efficient as the world's best)

RANK	COUNTRY	SCORE
1	France	7.0
2	Japan	6.9
3	Switzerland	6.7
4	Hong Kong SAR	6.4
5	Germany	6.2
6	Finland	6.1
7	Denmark	6.0
8	Austria	6.0
9	Sweden	5.9
10	Canada	5.6
11	Belgium	5.6
12	Netherlands	5.5
13	Spain	5.4
14	Ukraine	5.4
15	Singapore	5.4
16	Korea	5.2
17	Russian Federation	5.2
18	Taiwan	5.2
19	Czech Republic	5.0
20	Australia	4.9
21	India	4.9
22	Italy	4.8
23	United States	4.7
24	Egypt	4.5
25	South Africa	4.5
26	Hungary	4.3
27	Romania	4.3
28	United Kingdom	4.3
29	Malaysia	4.2
30	Latvia	4.1
31	Poland	4.1
32	New Zealand	4.1
33	Zimbabwe	4.0
34	China	3.9
35	Lithuania	3.9
36	Slovak Republic	3.8
37	Bulgaria	3.8
38	Thailand	3.8
39	Norway	3.6
40	Slovenia	3.6
41	Portugal	3.6
42	Estonia	3.6
43	Argentina	3.5
44	Israel	3.3
45	Indonesia	3.2
46	Ireland	2.9
47	Bangladesh	2.8
48	Greece	2.8
49	Mexico	2.7
50	Sri Lanka	2.7
51	Brazil	2.5
52	Turkey	2.3
53	Colombia	2.1
54	Vietnam	2.1
55	Chile	2.0
56	Paraguay	2.0
57	Bolivia	1.9
58	Peru	1.9
59	Jordan	1.8
60	Panama	1.7
61	Nigeria	1.7
62	Uruguay	1.6
63	Philippines	1.5
64	Venezuela	1.5
65	Nicaragua	1.5
66	Guatemala	1.4
67	Jamaica	1.4
68	Honduras	1.4
69	Costa Rica	1.4
70	Dominican Republic	1.3
71	El Salvador	1.2
72	Ecuador	1.2
73	Trinidad and Tobago	1.1
74	Iceland	1.1
75	Mauritius	1.0

MEAN: 3.6

5.06 Port infrastructure quality

Port facilities and inland waterways in your country are: (1 = underdeveloped, 7 = as developed as the world's best)

RANK	COUNTRY	SCORE
1	Singapore	6.9
2	Netherlands	6.7
3	Hong Kong SAR	6.7
4	Germany	6.5
5	Finland	6.5
6	France	6.3
7	Canada	6.2
8	Sweden	6.2
9	Denmark	6.2
10	Belgium	6.2
11	Japan	6.1
12	United States	6.1
13	Iceland	6.1
14	Norway	5.8
15	Malaysia	5.7
16	New Zealand	5.5
17	United Kingdom	5.5
18	Australia	5.4
19	South Africa	5.3
20	Spain	5.3
21	Estonia	5.3
22	Switzerland	5.2
23	Israel	5.1
24	Jamaica	5.1
25	Mauritius	5.1
26	Taiwan	5.1
27	Panama	5.0
28	Latvia	4.9
29	Austria	4.8
30	Trinidad and Tobago	4.7
31	Korea	4.7
32	Slovenia	4.6
33	Romania	4.6
34	Italy	4.5
35	Egypt	4.4
36	Thailand	4.4
37	Ukraine	4.3
38	Argentina	4.3
39	Uruguay	4.3
40	Greece	4.3
41	Lithuania	4.2
42	Ireland	4.2
43	Slovak Republic	4.2
44	Portugal	4.1
45	Chile	4.1
46	Russian Federation	4.0
47	Jordan	3.9
48	Sri Lanka	3.8
49	Turkey	3.8
50	Bulgaria	3.7
51	China	3.7
52	Poland	3.6
53	Honduras	3.6
54	Ecuador	3.6
55	Mexico	3.3
56	Czech Republic	3.3
57	India	3.3
58	Brazil	3.2
59	Indonesia	3.1
60	Dominican Republic	3.0
61	El Salvador	3.0
62	Hungary	3.0
63	Nigeria	2.9
64	Venezuela	2.9
65	Guatemala	2.8
66	Peru	2.8
67	Costa Rica	2.8
68	Zimbabwe	2.7
69	Vietnam	2.5
70	Philippines	2.5
71	Colombia	2.5
72	Bangladesh	2.5
73	Paraguay	2.4
74	Nicaragua	2.2
75	Bolivia	1.8

MEAN: 4.4

5.07 Air transport infrastructure quality

Air transport in your country is: (1 = infrequent and inefficient,
7 = as extensive and efficient as the world's best)

RANK	COUNTRY	SCORE
1	Singapore	7.0
2	Hong Kong SAR	6.8
3	Netherlands	6.7
4	United States	6.7
5	France	6.6
6	Germany	6.6
7	Switzerland	6.5
8	Finland	6.4
9	Denmark	6.3
10	Australia	6.3
11	Canada	6.3
12	Sweden	6.2
13	United Kingdom	6.2
14	New Zealand	6.2
15	Norway	6.1
16	Austria	6.1
17	South Africa	5.9
18	Iceland	5.9
19	Chile	5.8
20	Israel	5.8
21	Belgium	5.8
22	Jamaica	5.8
23	Malaysia	5.7
24	Trinidad and Tobago	5.7
25	Taiwan	5.7
26	Panama	5.6
27	Mauritius	5.6
28	Japan	5.6
29	Spain	5.5
30	Thailand	5.5
31	Italy	5.4
32	Brazil	5.4
33	Turkey	5.2
34	Dominican Republic	5.2
35	Jordan	5.2
36	Korea	5.0
37	Romania	5.0
38	Ireland	5.0
39	Portugal	5.0
40	Estonia	5.0
41	El Salvador	5.0
42	Greece	5.0
43	Latvia	4.8
44	Mexico	4.8
45	Venezuela	4.7
46	Czech Republic	4.7
47	India	4.7
48	Colombia	4.6
49	Argentina	4.6
50	Egypt	4.6
51	Slovenia	4.5
52	Poland	4.5
53	Costa Rica	4.5
54	Ukraine	4.4
55	Uruguay	4.3
56	Hungary	4.3
57	Lithuania	4.2
58	Indonesia	4.0
59	Sri Lanka	4.0
60	Guatemala	3.9
61	Philippines	3.8
62	China	3.7
63	Ecuador	3.7
64	Russian Federation	3.6
65	Peru	3.6
66	Nicaragua	3.5
67	Paraguay	3.4
68	Nigeria	3.4
69	Vietnam	3.2
70	Honduras	3.1
71	Zimbabwe	3.1
72	Bolivia	3.0
73	Bangladesh	3.0
74	Bulgaria	2.6
75	Slovak Republic	1.6

MEAN: 5.0

5.08 Telephone/fax infrastructure quality

New telephone lines for your business are: (1 = scarce and difficult to obtain,
7 = widely available and highly reliable)

RANK	COUNTRY	SCORE
1	Finland	7.0
2	Sweden	6.9
3	Hong Kong SAR	6.9
4	France	6.9
5	Switzerland	6.9
6	Iceland	6.9
7	Germany	6.8
8	Singapore	6.8
9	Denmark	6.8
10	Norway	6.8
11	Japan	6.8
12	United Kingdom	6.7
13	Netherlands	6.7
14	Chile	6.7
15	Israel	6.7
16	Austria	6.7
17	United States	6.6
18	Canada	6.6
19	Argentina	6.6
20	Uruguay	6.6
21	Australia	6.5
22	New Zealand	6.5
23	Slovak Republic	6.4
24	Hungary	6.4
25	Belgium	6.4
26	El Salvador	6.3
27	Taiwan	6.3
28	Dominican Republic	6.2
29	Portugal	6.2
30	Italy	6.2
31	Spain	6.1
32	Korea	6.1
33	Ireland	6.0
34	Thailand	5.9
35	Czech Republic	5.9
36	Malaysia	5.9
37	Estonia	5.9
38	Jordan	5.8
39	Greece	5.8
40	Slovenia	5.7
41	Brazil	5.6
42	Lithuania	5.5
43	Panama	5.5
44	Venezuela	5.5
45	Latvia	5.5
46	Mauritius	5.5
47	Peru	5.5
48	Egypt	5.5
49	China	5.4
50	Sri Lanka	5.4
51	Mexico	5.3
52	Jamaica	5.3
53	Colombia	5.2
54	Turkey	5.2
55	South Africa	5.2
56	Poland	5.1
57	India	5.1
58	Trinidad and Tobago	5.0
59	Indonesia	4.8
60	Philippines	4.7
61	Bulgaria	4.6
62	Bolivia	4.6
63	Guatemala	4.5
64	Vietnam	4.4
65	Russian Federation	4.1
66	Ukraine	4.0
67	Paraguay	3.6
68	Ecuador	3.2
69	Romania	3.0
70	Costa Rica	2.9
71	Zimbabwe	2.4
72	Nicaragua	2.4
73	Nigeria	2.2
74	Bangladesh	2.1
75	Honduras	1.6

MEAN: 5.5

5.09 Quality of competition in transportation sector

Is competition in your country's transportation sector sufficient to ensure high quality, infrequent interruptions, and low prices? (1 = no, 7 = yes, equal to world's best)

RANK	COUNTRY	SCORE
1	Netherlands	6.5
2	United States	6.5
3	Finland	6.5
4	Hong Kong SAR	6.3
5	Sweden	6.1
6	Germany	6.1
7	Belgium	6.0
8	Singapore	5.9
9	Austria	5.8
10	Switzerland	5.7
11	New Zealand	5.7
12	Australia	5.6
13	Canada	5.5
14	France	5.5
15	Denmark	5.5
16	Norway	5.4
17	Spain	5.4
18	Japan	5.4
19	Taiwan	5.3
20	United Kingdom	5.2
21	Czech Republic	5.1
22	Chile	5.1
23	Iceland	5.1
24	Israel	5.0
25	Estonia	5.0
26	Korea	5.0
27	Trinidad and Tobago	4.9
28	Portugal	4.9
29	Jordan	4.9
30	Hungary	4.8
31	Slovak Republic	4.8
32	Slovenia	4.7
33	Brazil	4.7
34	Poland	4.7
35	Argentina	4.6
36	Italy	4.5
37	Latvia	4.4
38	Lithuania	4.4
39	Uruguay	4.4
40	Malaysia	4.4
41	Venezuela	4.3
42	Thailand	4.2
43	South Africa	4.2
44	Mauritius	4.1
45	Zimbabwe	4.1
46	Colombia	4.0
47	Dominican Republic	3.9
48	Turkey	3.9
49	Jamaica	3.9
50	Philippines	3.9
51	India	3.8
52	Egypt	3.8
53	Greece	3.7
54	Peru	3.7
55	Mexico	3.7
56	Ukraine	3.7
57	Indonesia	3.7
58	Romania	3.6
59	China	3.6
60	Ireland	3.6
61	Costa Rica	3.5
62	Bulgaria	3.4
63	El Salvador	3.4
64	Sri Lanka	3.3
65	Russian Federation	3.3
66	Guatemala	3.2
67	Nigeria	3.1
68	Panama	3.1
69	Bangladesh	3.0
70	Bolivia	2.8
71	Paraguay	2.7
72	Vietnam	2.7
73	Ecuador	2.7
74	Honduras	2.5
75	Nicaragua	2.1

MEAN: 4.4

5.10 Postal efficiency

How many days do you normally wait for the delivery of a cross-ocean airmail letter to your country? (median response listed for each country)

RANK	COUNTRY	DAYS
1	France	3.0
1	Iceland	3.0
3	Belgium	3.5
3	Denmark	3.5
3	Finland	3.5
6	Austria	4.0
6	Germany	4.0
6	Hong Kong SAR	4.0
6	Netherlands	4.0
6	New Zealand	4.0
6	Norway	4.0
6	Sweden	4.0
6	Switzerland	4.0
6	United Kingdom	4.0
15	Australia	5.0
15	Brazil	5.0
15	Czech Republic	5.0
15	Ireland	5.0
15	Israel	5.0
15	Japan	5.0
15	Portugal	5.0
15	Singapore	5.0
15	Spain	5.0
15	United States	5.0
25	Italy	6.0
25	Slovenia	6.0
27	Latvia	6.5
28	Argentina	7.0
28	Canada	7.0
28	Chile	7.0
28	Egypt	7.0
28	Estonia	7.0
28	Greece	7.0
28	Hungary	7.0
28	Korea	7.0
28	Malaysia	7.0
28	Paraguay	7.0
28	Taiwan	7.0
28	Thailand	7.0
28	Uruguay	7.0
41	Lithuania	7.5
42	Trinidad and Tobago	8.0
42	Turkey	8.0
44	Poland	8.5
45	Panama	9.5
46	Bolivia	10.0
46	Bulgaria	10.0
46	Costa Rica	10.0
46	India	10.0
46	Indonesia	10.0
46	Jordan	10.0
46	Mauritius	10.0
46	Peru	10.0
46	Slovak Republic	10.0
46	South Africa	10.0
46	Sri Lanka	10.0
46	Ukraine	10.0
46	Vietnam	10.0
59	Colombia	11.0
59	Dominican Republic	11.0
59	Guatemala	11.0
59	Jamaica	11.0
63	Bangladesh	11.5
64	China	12.0
64	El Salvador	12.0
64	Russian Federation	12.0
64	Zimbabwe	12.0
68	Honduras	13.5
69	Nigeria	14.0
69	Philippines	14.0
71	Ecuador	15.0
71	Mexico	15.0
71	Nicaragua	15.0
71	Venezuela	15.0
75	Romania	20.0

MEAN: 8.1

5.11 Electricity prices

The price of electricity per kilowatt-hour in your country compared with international standards is: (1 = much higher, 7 = among the world's lowest)

RANK	COUNTRY	SCORE		MEAN: 4.1	
1	South Africa	6.2			
2	Sweden	6.0			
3	Norway	6.0			
4	Finland	5.8			
5	Canada	5.7			
6	France	5.6			
7	New Zealand	5.6			
8	United States	5.6			
9	Iceland	5.5			
10	Australia	5.2			
11	Indonesia	5.1			
12	Czech Republic	4.9			
13	Malaysia	4.8			
14	Nigeria	4.7			
15	Russian Federation	4.7			
16	Argentina	4.6			
17	Poland	4.6			
18	Slovak Republic	4.6			
19	Egypt	4.6			
20	Estonia	4.5			
21	Korea	4.5			
22	Thailand	4.5			
23	Netherlands	4.5			
24	Hong Kong SAR	4.5			
25	Chile	4.4			
26	Taiwan	4.4			
27	Latvia	4.4			
28	Hungary	4.3			
29	Brazil	4.3			
30	Slovenia	4.3			
31	Ukraine	4.3			
32	United Kingdom	4.2			
33	Trinidad and Tobago	4.2			
34	Romania	4.1			
35	Jordan	4.1			
36	Israel	4.1			
37	Ireland	4.1			
38	Germany	4.0			
39	Greece	4.0			
40	Spain	4.0			
41	Mexico	3.9			
42	Austria	3.9			
43	China	3.9			
44	Lithuania	3.8			
45	Belgium	3.8			
46	Bulgaria	3.8			
47	Costa Rica	3.8			
48	Colombia	3.7			
49	Singapore	3.7			
50	Bangladesh	3.7			
51	Paraguay	3.6			
52	Honduras	3.5			
53	Ecuador	3.5			
54	El Salvador	3.5			
55	Peru	3.5			
56	Switzerland	3.4			
57	Zimbabwe	3.4			
58	Jamaica	3.4			
59	Bolivia	3.4			
60	Denmark	3.3			
61	Sri Lanka	3.3			
62	Portugal	3.3			
63	Venezuela	3.3			
64	Mauritius	3.3			
65	Vietnam	3.2			
66	Guatemala	3.2			
67	India	3.1			
68	Uruguay	3.0			
69	Turkey	3.0			
70	Japan	2.9			
71	Italy	2.6			
72	Philippines	2.6			
73	Panama	2.4			
74	Dominican Republic	2.1			
75	Nicaragua	2.0			

5.12 Quality of public schools

Public (free) schools in your country are (1 = of poor quality, 7 = equal to the best in the world)

RANK	COUNTRY	SCORE		MEAN: 4.2	
1	Switzerland	6.7			
2	France	6.6			
3	Austria	6.6			
4	Finland	6.6			
5	Slovak Republic	6.6			
6	Belgium	6.4			
7	Singapore	6.4			
8	Netherlands	6.4			
9	Ireland	6.3			
10	Germany	6.1			
11	Iceland	6.0			
12	Canada	5.8			
13	Denmark	5.8			
14	Japan	5.8			
15	Hungary	5.8			
16	Taiwan	5.8			
17	New Zealand	5.7			
18	Norway	5.7			
19	Czech Republic	5.7			
20	Israel	5.6			
21	Slovenia	5.5			
22	Australia	5.5			
23	Sweden	5.4			
24	Estonia	5.4			
25	Hong Kong SAR	5.3			
26	United States	5.2			
27	Spain	5.1			
28	Romania	5.0			
29	Italy	5.0			
30	United Kingdom	4.9			
31	Poland	4.7			
32	Trinidad and Tobago	4.6			
33	Bulgaria	4.6			
34	Costa Rica	4.4			
35	Latvia	4.4			
36	Korea	4.4			
37	Russian Federation	4.4			
38	Uruguay	4.3			
39	Lithuania	4.3			
40	Portugal	4.3			
41	Malaysia	4.2			
42	Thailand	3.9			
43	Jamaica	3.9			
44	Mauritius	3.8			
45	Jordan	3.7			
46	Ukraine	3.7			
47	Sri Lanka	3.7			
48	Greece	3.6			
49	China	3.3			
50	Vietnam	3.3			
51	Egypt	3.2			
52	Turkey	3.1			
53	South Africa	3.1			
54	Zimbabwe	3.1			
55	Argentina	3.0			
56	Colombia	2.9			
57	Chile	2.7			
58	Brazil	2.7			
59	Indonesia	2.7			
60	Mexico	2.6			
61	Panama	2.6			
62	India	2.3			
63	Philippines	2.3			
64	El Salvador	2.3			
65	Dominican Republic	2.3			
66	Peru	2.2			
67	Paraguay	2.2			
68	Nigeria	1.9			
69	Venezuela	1.9			
70	Honduras	1.9			
71	Ecuador	1.9			
72	Guatemala	1.8			
73	Bangladesh	1.8			
74	Bolivia	1.7			
75	Nicaragua	1.7			

5.13 Difference in quality of schools

The difference in the quality of schools available to rich and poor children in your country is: (1 = large, 7 = small)

RANK	COUNTRY	SCORE
1	Finland	6.8
2	Iceland	6.7
3	Austria	6.6
4	Slovak Republic	6.4
5	Switzerland	6.4
6	Netherlands	6.4
7	Denmark	6.3
8	Norway	6.3
9	Germany	6.2
10	Slovenia	6.1
11	Belgium	6.1
12	Taiwan	5.8
13	Singapore	5.6
14	Czech Republic	5.6
15	Japan	5.5
16	France	5.3
17	Sweden	5.3
18	Israel	5.3
19	Canada	5.2
20	Estonia	4.8
21	Ireland	4.8
22	Italy	4.7
23	Lithuania	4.7
24	Hong Kong SAR	4.6
25	Hungary	4.6
26	Poland	4.5
27	Trinidad and Tobago	4.5
28	New Zealand	4.5
29	Australia	4.3
30	Korea	4.3
31	Portugal	4.1
32	Spain	4.1
33	Latvia	4.0
34	Bulgaria	3.9
35	Jamaica	3.8
36	Malaysia	3.6
37	Romania	3.6
38	Russian Federation	3.5
39	Mauritius	3.5
40	United Kingdom	3.5
41	Greece	3.3
42	United States	3.2
43	Uruguay	3.1
44	China	3.1
45	Vietnam	2.9
46	Sri Lanka	2.9
47	Jordan	2.8
48	Costa Rica	2.8
49	Ukraine	2.6
50	Thailand	2.5
51	Argentina	2.4
52	Paraguay	2.2
53	Indonesia	2.1
54	Egypt	2.1
55	Panama	2.1
56	Ecuador	2.0
57	Colombia	1.9
58	India	1.9
59	Honduras	1.9
60	Turkey	1.9
61	Bolivia	1.8
62	Chile	1.8
63	Philippines	1.8
64	South Africa	1.8
65	Brazil	1.8
66	Zimbabwe	1.8
67	El Salvador	1.8
68	Mexico	1.7
69	Nigeria	1.7
70	Dominican Republic	1.7
71	Guatemala	1.7
72	Nicaragua	1.6
73	Venezuela	1.6
74	Peru	1.6
75	Bangladesh	1.5

MEAN: 3.7

5.14 Difference in quality of healthcare

The difference in the quality of healthcare available to rich and poor people in your country is: (1 = large, 7 = small)

RANK	COUNTRY	SCORE
1	Iceland	6.9
2	Austria	6.2
3	Finland	6.2
4	Denmark	5.9
5	Norway	5.8
6	Netherlands	5.8
7	Switzerland	5.8
8	Sweden	5.8
9	France	5.8
10	Japan	5.7
11	Belgium	5.6
12	Singapore	5.6
13	Taiwan	5.5
14	Germany	5.5
15	Canada	5.4
16	Slovak Republic	5.2
17	Australia	5.2
18	Spain	4.8
19	Slovenia	4.8
20	Czech Republic	4.5
21	Hong Kong SAR	4.3
22	Israel	4.1
23	New Zealand	4.1
24	Costa Rica	3.8
25	United Kingdom	3.7
26	Estonia	3.7
27	United States	3.6
28	Italy	3.6
29	Malaysia	3.5
30	Korea	3.3
31	China	3.2
32	Hungary	2.9
33	Jordan	2.9
34	Uruguay	2.9
35	Ireland	2.8
36	Jamaica	2.8
37	Trinidad and Tobago	2.8
38	Sri Lanka	2.7
39	Latvia	2.6
40	Mauritius	2.6
41	Bulgaria	2.5
42	Lithuania	2.5
43	Thailand	2.5
44	Portugal	2.5
45	Paraguay	2.4
46	Poland	2.3
47	Greece	2.3
48	Egypt	2.3
49	Vietnam	2.2
50	Colombia	2.2
51	Panama	2.0
52	Romania	2.0
53	Turkey	2.0
54	Bolivia	1.9
55	Russian Federation	1.9
56	Honduras	1.9
57	Ukraine	1.9
58	India	1.9
59	El Salvador	1.8
60	Chile	1.8
61	Guatemala	1.8
62	Indonesia	1.8
63	Nigeria	1.8
64	Argentina	1.8
65	Zimbabwe	1.8
66	Philippines	1.8
67	Mexico	1.7
68	Nicaragua	1.7
69	Dominican Republic	1.7
70	South Africa	1.7
71	Peru	1.6
72	Bangladesh	1.5
73	Ecuador	1.5
74	Brazil	1.5
75	Venezuela	1.3

MEAN: 3.3

5.15 Public health agencies

Public health agencies in your country are able to deal with public outbreaks
of disease: (1 = barely at all, 7 = very effectively)

RANK	COUNTRY	SCORE
1	Netherlands	6.9
2	Iceland	6.9
3	Finland	6.8
4	Switzerland	6.7
5	Denmark	6.6
6	Norway	6.6
7	Austria	6.6
8	Sweden	6.6
9	Germany	6.6
10	France	6.5
11	Singapore	6.5
12	Australia	6.5
13	United States	6.5
14	Canada	6.4
15	New Zealand	6.3
16	Japan	6.3
17	United Kingdom	6.3
18	Spain	6.3
19	Hungary	6.2
20	Czech Republic	6.2
21	Uruguay	6.2
22	Ireland	6.2
23	Israel	6.1
24	Hong Kong SAR	6.1
25	Belgium	6.1
26	Romania	6.1
27	Slovenia	6.0
28	Italy	6.0
29	Costa Rica	5.8
30	Mauritius	5.8
31	Slovak Republic	5.8
32	Jordan	5.7
33	Chile	5.5
34	Portugal	5.4
35	Greece	5.4
36	Thailand	5.4
37	Egypt	5.3
38	China	5.3
39	Taiwan	5.3
40	Peru	5.2
41	Mexico	5.1
42	Jamaica	5.0
43	Poland	4.9
44	Malaysia	4.9
45	Estonia	4.8
46	Korea	4.7
47	Turkey	4.7
48	Sri Lanka	4.7
49	Panama	4.6
50	Argentina	4.5
51	Brazil	4.5
52	Honduras	4.5
53	Russian Federation	4.3
54	Indonesia	4.2
55	Trinidad and Tobago	4.2
56	Latvia	4.1
57	El Salvador	4.0
58	Lithuania	4.0
59	Ukraine	4.0
60	Philippines	4.0
61	Dominican Republic	3.9
62	Colombia	3.8
63	South Africa	3.8
64	India	3.8
65	Vietnam	3.8
66	Bolivia	3.7
67	Bangladesh	3.6
68	Venezuela	3.5
69	Zimbabwe	3.5
70	Bulgaria	3.4
71	Nigeria	3.4
72	Nicaragua	3.3
73	Ecuador	3.2
74	Guatemala	3.0
75	Paraguay	2.7

MEAN: 5.2

Section VI: Public Institutions—Contracts and Law

6.01 Judicial independence

The judiciary in your country is independent and not subject to interference by the government and/or parties to disputes. (1 = not true, 7 = true)

RANK	COUNTRY	SCORE	MEAN: 4.4
1	Germany	6.7	
2	Netherlands	6.6	
3	Finland	6.6	
4	Switzerland	6.5	
5	Denmark	6.5	
6	Sweden	6.5	
7	Australia	6.4	
8	Israel	6.4	
9	New Zealand	6.4	
10	Canada	6.4	
11	United Kingdom	6.3	
12	Austria	6.3	
13	Norway	6.2	
14	United States	6.1	
15	Ireland	6.1	
16	Iceland	6.1	
17	Hong Kong SAR	5.9	
18	Belgium	5.9	
19	Japan	5.8	
20	South Africa	5.7	
21	France	5.7	
22	Singapore	5.7	
23	Jordan	5.5	
24	Hungary	5.3	
25	Uruguay	5.3	
26	India	5.3	
27	Egypt	5.2	
28	Mauritius	5.1	
29	Portugal	5.1	
30	Costa Rica	5.1	
31	Estonia	5.1	
32	Poland	5.0	
33	Jamaica	5.0	
34	Spain	5.0	
35	Greece	4.7	
36	Thailand	4.7	
37	Italy	4.5	
38	Slovenia	4.4	
39	Chile	4.3	
40	Taiwan	4.2	
41	Trinidad and Tobago	4.2	
42	Brazil	4.1	
43	Sri Lanka	4.1	
44	Czech Republic	4.0	
45	Slovak Republic	4.0	
46	Turkey	3.9	
47	Korea	3.8	
48	Philippines	3.7	
49	Vietnam	3.7	
50	Dominican Republic	3.6	
51	Malaysia	3.6	
52	Mexico	3.5	
53	El Salvador	3.5	
54	Colombia	3.3	
55	Latvia	3.3	
56	Romania	3.3	
57	Nigeria	3.3	
58	Panama	3.1	
59	China	3.1	
60	Bangladesh	3.0	
61	Bulgaria	3.0	
62	Russian Federation	2.9	
63	Indonesia	2.8	
64	Lithuania	2.8	
65	Argentina	2.7	
66	Zimbabwe	2.6	
67	Paraguay	2.3	
68	Ukraine	2.3	
69	Guatemala	2.2	
70	Nicaragua	2.2	
71	Ecuador	2.1	
72	Honduras	2.1	
73	Peru	2.0	
74	Bolivia	2.0	
75	Venezuela	1.7	

6.02 Property rights

Financial assets and wealth are: (1 = poorly delineated and not protected by law, 7 = clearly delineated and protected by law)

RANK	COUNTRY	SCORE	MEAN: 5.0
1	Iceland	6.6	
2	Netherlands	6.5	
3	Switzerland	6.5	
4	Finland	6.5	
5	United States	6.5	
6	Singapore	6.5	
7	Germany	6.5	
8	Hong Kong SAR	6.4	
9	Denmark	6.4	
10	Austria	6.4	
11	France	6.4	
12	United Kingdom	6.3	
13	Israel	6.3	
14	Canada	6.2	
15	Italy	6.2	
16	Australia	6.2	
17	Japan	6.1	
18	Ireland	6.1	
19	Norway	5.9	
20	Belgium	5.9	
21	New Zealand	5.9	
22	Spain	5.9	
23	Sweden	5.9	
24	Jordan	5.8	
25	Uruguay	5.6	
26	Chile	5.6	
27	Taiwan	5.6	
28	Egypt	5.6	
29	Mauritius	5.4	
30	South Africa	5.3	
31	Portugal	5.3	
32	Hungary	5.3	
33	Malaysia	5.2	
34	Slovak Republic	5.2	
35	Costa Rica	5.2	
36	Argentina	5.1	
37	Thailand	5.0	
38	Greece	5.0	
39	Brazil	5.0	
40	Jamaica	4.9	
41	Trinidad and Tobago	4.9	
42	India	4.9	
43	Slovenia	4.8	
44	Estonia	4.8	
45	Korea	4.7	
46	Panama	4.6	
47	Poland	4.6	
48	Mexico	4.6	
49	Romania	4.5	
50	Czech Republic	4.4	
51	El Salvador	4.3	
52	Latvia	4.3	
53	Philippines	4.3	
54	Colombia	4.3	
55	Lithuania	4.2	
56	Sri Lanka	4.2	
57	Turkey	4.2	
58	Vietnam	4.2	
59	Dominican Republic	4.2	
60	China	4.1	
61	Peru	4.1	
62	Zimbabwe	3.9	
63	Indonesia	3.8	
64	Venezuela	3.8	
65	Nigeria	3.8	
66	Bolivia	3.8	
67	Bangladesh	3.7	
68	Guatemala	3.4	
69	Ecuador	3.3	
70	Honduras	3.3	
71	Ukraine	3.2	
72	Nicaragua	3.2	
73	Bulgaria	3.2	
74	Paraguay	2.9	
75	Russian Federation	2.4	

6.03 Intellectual property protection

Intellectual property protection in your country is: (1 = weak or nonexistent, 7 = equal to the world's most stringent)

RANK	COUNTRY	SCORE
1	France	6.6
2	Switzerland	6.5
3	United States	6.5
4	Netherlands	6.5
5	Finland	6.4
6	Germany	6.3
7	Denmark	6.3
8	Austria	6.2
9	United Kingdom	6.1
10	Australia	6.0
11	Sweden	5.8
12	Canada	5.8
13	Italy	5.7
14	Iceland	5.6
15	Singapore	5.6
16	Belgium	5.5
17	Japan	5.5
18	Norway	5.3
19	Spain	5.3
20	New Zealand	5.3
21	Ireland	5.2
22	Israel	4.9
23	Portugal	4.9
24	Hong Kong SAR	4.8
25	Taiwan	4.6
26	Jordan	4.6
27	South Africa	4.5
28	Czech Republic	4.4
29	Uruguay	4.3
30	Hungary	4.3
31	Slovenia	4.2
32	Trinidad and Tobago	4.2
33	Chile	4.2
34	Egypt	4.1
35	Brazil	4.1
36	Estonia	4.0
37	Korea	4.0
38	Greece	3.9
39	Mauritius	3.9
40	Slovak Republic	3.8
41	Poland	3.8
42	Costa Rica	3.7
43	Thailand	3.6
44	Mexico	3.6
45	Malaysia	3.5
46	Romania	3.5
47	Jamaica	3.5
48	Panama	3.4
49	El Salvador	3.4
50	Latvia	3.3
51	Argentina	3.2
52	Sri Lanka	3.1
53	Turkey	3.1
54	Venezuela	3.0
55	Bulgaria	3.0
56	Peru	3.0
57	Colombia	3.0
58	India	3.0
59	Zimbabwe	2.9
60	China	2.9
61	Philippines	2.9
62	Lithuania	2.9
63	Indonesia	2.9
64	Ecuador	2.8
65	Dominican Republic	2.7
66	Nigeria	2.5
67	Ukraine	2.4
68	Honduras	2.4
69	Paraguay	2.4
70	Guatemala	2.3
71	Nicaragua	2.2
72	Bangladesh	2.2
73	Russian Federation	2.1
74	Bolivia	2.0
75	Vietnam	1.5

MEAN: 4.1

6.04 Favoritism in decisions of government officials

When deciding upon policies and contracts, government officials: (1 = usually favor well-connected firms and individuals, 7 = are neutral among firms and individuals)

RANK	COUNTRY	SCORE
1	Finland	5.7
2	New Zealand	5.6
3	Denmark	5.3
4	Singapore	5.1
5	Iceland	5.1
6	United Kingdom	5.0
7	Netherlands	5.0
8	Australia	5.0
9	Sweden	5.0
10	Ireland	4.9
11	Hong Kong SAR	4.5
12	Switzerland	4.5
13	Spain	4.4
14	Austria	4.4
15	Norway	4.4
16	Germany	4.3
17	United States	4.2
18	Belgium	4.1
19	France	4.1
20	Israel	4.1
21	Canada	4.1
22	Chile	4.0
23	Taiwan	3.9
24	Japan	3.9
25	Egypt	3.8
26	Jordan	3.8
27	Romania	3.7
28	Portugal	3.7
29	Russian Federation	3.7
30	Uruguay	3.6
31	Thailand	3.5
32	Slovenia	3.5
33	Mauritius	3.4
34	China	3.4
35	Korea	3.4
36	India	3.4
37	Costa Rica	3.3
38	Lithuania	3.3
39	Estonia	3.3
40	Italy	3.3
41	Mexico	3.2
42	Slovak Republic	3.2
43	Hungary	3.2
44	Poland	3.1
45	South Africa	3.1
46	Turkey	3.1
47	Brazil	3.0
48	Czech Republic	3.0
49	Vietnam	3.0
50	Malaysia	3.0
51	Peru	2.9
52	Latvia	2.9
53	El Salvador	2.8
54	Bulgaria	2.8
55	Philippines	2.7
56	Sri Lanka	2.7
57	Trinidad and Tobago	2.7
58	Argentina	2.7
59	Indonesia	2.6
60	Jamaica	2.6
61	Venezuela	2.6
62	Paraguay	2.6
63	Greece	2.5
64	Colombia	2.3
65	Panama	2.3
66	Nicaragua	2.2
67	Ukraine	2.1
68	Bangladesh	2.1
69	Nigeria	2.0
70	Dominican Republic	1.9
71	Bolivia	1.9
72	Ecuador	1.9
73	Honduras	1.8
74	Guatemala	1.7
75	Zimbabwe	1.9

MEAN: 3.4

6.05 Government commitments

New governments honor the contractual commitments and obligations of previous regimes (1 = not true, 7 = true)

RANK	COUNTRY	SCORE
1	Switzerland	6.7
2	Finland	6.5
3	Iceland	6.5
4	Netherlands	6.5
5	Singapore	6.3
6	Denmark	6.3
7	Germany	6.3
8	Hong Kong SAR	6.3
9	United States	6.2
10	Israel	6.1
11	United Kingdom	6.1
12	Belgium	6.0
13	Sweden	6.0
14	Australia	5.9
15	France	5.9
16	Ireland	5.9
17	Canada	5.8
18	Austria	5.7
19	Norway	5.6
20	South Africa	5.6
21	Mauritius	5.4
22	Uruguay	5.4
23	Portugal	5.4
24	Jordan	5.4
25	Japan	5.4
26	Chile	5.3
27	Poland	5.2
28	Turkey	5.1
29	China	5.1
30	India	5.1
31	Czech Republic	5.1
32	New Zealand	5.1
33	Argentina	5.0
34	Spain	5.0
35	Italy	4.9
36	Mexico	4.9
37	Egypt	4.9
38	Thailand	4.9
39	Philippines	4.8
40	Trinidad and Tobago	4.8
41	Estonia	4.8
42	Jamaica	4.6
43	Malaysia	4.6
44	Greece	4.6
45	Slovenia	4.5
46	Costa Rica	4.5
47	Bulgaria	4.3
48	Hungary	4.2
49	Brazil	4.2
50	Bangladesh	4.1
51	Sri Lanka	4.1
52	Zimbabwe	4.1
53	El Salvador	4.0
54	Russian Federation	4.0
55	Slovak Republic	4.0
56	Korea	4.0
57	Peru	3.9
58	Venezuela	3.9
59	Colombia	3.9
60	Indonesia	3.8
61	Panama	3.7
62	Latvia	3.7
63	Nigeria	3.7
64	Vietnam	3.7
65	Honduras	3.6
66	Taiwan	3.6
67	Lithuania	3.5
68	Ecuador	3.3
69	Dominican Republic	3.2
70	Romania	3.2
71	Nicaragua	3.2
72	Bolivia	2.9
73	Paraguay	2.9
74	Ukraine	2.5
75	Guatemala	2.2

MEAN: 4.8

6.06 Competence of public officials

The competence of personnel in the public sector is (1 = lower than the private sector, 7 = higher than the private sector)

RANK	COUNTRY	SCORE
1	Singapore	4.7
2	Japan	3.8
3	Sweden	3.7
4	Hong Kong SAR	3.6
5	Ireland	3.6
6	China	3.5
7	France	3.5
8	Russian Federation	3.4
9	Lithuania	3.4
10	Canada	3.4
11	Taiwan	3.4
12	Slovenia	3.4
13	Denmark	3.3
14	Iceland	3.3
15	Finland	3.3
16	Bulgaria	3.3
17	New Zealand	3.3
18	Austria	3.2
19	Australia	3.2
20	Spain	3.2
21	Germany	3.1
22	Latvia	3.1
23	United Kingdom	3.1
24	Netherlands	3.1
25	Vietnam	3.1
26	Ukraine	3.1
27	Korea	3.0
28	Switzerland	3.0
29	Norway	3.0
30	Jamaica	3.0
31	Israel	3.0
32	Trinidad and Tobago	3.0
33	Estonia	3.0
34	India	2.9
35	Paraguay	2.9
36	Hungary	2.8
37	Nicaragua	2.8
38	Belgium	2.8
39	Jordan	2.7
40	Poland	2.7
41	United States	2.7
42	Mauritius	2.6
43	Honduras	2.6
44	Thailand	2.6
45	Colombia	2.6
46	Romania	2.6
47	Mexico	2.6
48	Indonesia	2.6
49	Panama	2.4
50	Brazil	2.4
51	Uruguay	2.4
52	Czech Republic	2.3
53	Italy	2.3
54	Costa Rica	2.3
55	Sri Lanka	2.3
56	Egypt	2.3
57	Dominican Republic	2.3
58	Philippines	2.2
59	Ecuador	2.2
60	Peru	2.2
61	Nigeria	2.2
62	Portugal	2.2
63	Guatemala	2.1
64	Bolivia	2.1
65	Malaysia	2.1
66	Chile	2.1
67	Turkey	2.1
68	Bangladesh	2.0
69	Slovak Republic	2.0
70	El Salvador	2.0
71	South Africa	1.9
72	Argentina	1.9
73	Greece	1.8
74	Venezuela	1.7
75	Zimbabwe	1.6

MEAN: 2.8

6.07 Costs of institutional change

Legal or political changes over the past five years have: (1 = severely undermined your firm's planning capacity, 7 = had no effect)

RANK	COUNTRY	SCORE
1	Finland	6.6
2	Netherlands	6.4
3	Singapore	6.3
4	United States	5.9
5	Hong Kong SAR	5.9
6	Iceland	5.8
7	Trinidad and Tobago	5.7
8	Ireland	5.6
9	Estonia	5.6
10	Denmark	5.6
11	Canada	5.5
12	Switzerland	5.5
13	Germany	5.5
14	Sweden	5.4
15	Belgium	5.4
16	Austria	5.3
17	Japan	5.2
18	Czech Republic	5.2
19	United Kingdom	5.2
20	Norway	5.2
21	Spain	5.2
22	Australia	5.1
23	Romania	5.1
24	Mauritius	5.1
25	Slovenia	5.1
26	India	5.0
27	Malaysia	5.0
28	Hungary	4.9
29	Poland	4.9
30	Vietnam	4.9
31	El Salvador	4.8
32	Israel	4.8
33	South Africa	4.7
34	Portugal	4.7
35	France	4.7
36	Jamaica	4.6
37	Uruguay	4.6
38	Brazil	4.6
39	Italy	4.6
40	China	4.6
41	Jordan	4.5
42	Costa Rica	4.5
43	Taiwan	4.5
44	Thailand	4.5
45	Greece	4.4
46	New Zealand	4.3
47	Chile	4.3
48	Honduras	4.2
49	Bulgaria	4.2
50	Mexico	4.2
51	Egypt	4.2
52	Korea	4.0
53	Dominican Republic	3.8
54	Nicaragua	3.7
55	Lithuania	3.7
56	Russian Federation	3.7
57	Bangladesh	3.7
58	Sri Lanka	3.6
59	Latvia	3.6
60	Turkey	3.6
61	Bolivia	3.5
62	Argentina	3.5
63	Slovak Republic	3.4
64	Nigeria	3.4
65	Ukraine	3.3
66	Philippines	3.3
67	Panama	3.3
68	Peru	3.1
69	Colombia	3.1
70	Paraguay	3.1
71	Guatemala	2.9
72	Indonesia	2.7
73	Ecuador	2.5
74	Venezuela	2.4
75	Zimbabwe	1.9

MEAN: 4.5

6.08 Burden of regulation

Administrative regulations in your country are: (1 = burdensome, 7 = not burdensome)

RANK	COUNTRY	SCORE
1	Hong Kong SAR	5.9
2	Singapore	5.6
3	Iceland	5.5
4	Finland	5.3
5	Estonia	4.8
6	Spain	4.7
7	Switzerland	4.6
8	Ireland	4.5
9	Netherlands	4.4
10	Trinidad and Tobago	4.4
11	Sri Lanka	4.1
12	Sweden	4.0
13	El Salvador	4.0
14	United States	4.0
15	United Kingdom	3.9
16	Jordan	3.8
17	Mauritius	3.8
18	New Zealand	3.7
19	Canada	3.7
20	Hungary	3.7
21	Peru	3.6
22	Australia	3.6
23	Latvia	3.5
24	Czech Republic	3.4
25	Panama	3.4
26	Israel	3.4
27	Russian Federation	3.4
28	Germany	3.4
29	Chile	3.3
30	Poland	3.3
31	Taiwan	3.3
32	Uruguay	3.3
33	Austria	3.2
34	South Africa	3.2
35	Dominican Republic	3.2
36	Slovenia	3.2
37	Bulgaria	3.2
38	Malaysia	3.1
39	Costa Rica	3.1
40	Thailand	3.1
41	Denmark	3.1
42	Jamaica	3.0
43	Colombia	3.0
44	Philippines	3.0
45	Slovak Republic	3.0
46	Honduras	3.0
47	Japan	3.0
48	China	3.0
49	Nicaragua	2.9
50	Korea	2.9
51	Norway	2.9
52	Guatemala	2.9
53	Argentina	2.9
54	Paraguay	2.9
55	India	2.9
56	Greece	2.8
57	Belgium	2.8
58	Portugal	2.8
59	Indonesia	2.8
60	France	2.7
61	Bolivia	2.7
62	Ecuador	2.7
63	Lithuania	2.6
64	Nigeria	2.6
65	Venezuela	2.5
66	Brazil	2.5
67	Ukraine	2.5
68	Egypt	2.5
69	Turkey	2.4
70	Bangladesh	2.4
71	Mexico	2.4
72	Italy	2.4
73	Romania	2.3
74	Vietnam	2.2
75	Zimbabwe	2.1

MEAN: 3.3

400

6.09 Minimum wage enforcement

The minimum wage set by law in your country is: (1 = never enforced, 7 = strongly enforced)

RANK	COUNTRY	SCORE
1	Australia	6.5
2	France	6.5
3	United States	6.3
4	New Zealand	6.2
5	Canada	6.2
6	Israel	6.1
7	Denmark	6.0
8	Romania	6.0
9	Lithuania	6.0
10	Taiwan	5.9
11	Belgium	5.9
12	Mauritius	5.9
13	Costa Rica	5.9
14	Chile	5.8
15	Spain	5.7
16	Netherlands	5.7
17	Slovenia	5.6
18	Finland	5.6
19	Hungary	5.6
20	Japan	5.5
21	Colombia	5.5
22	United Kingdom	5.5
23	Ireland	5.5
24	Mexico	5.4
25	Poland	5.4
26	Estonia	5.4
27	Bulgaria	5.4
28	Greece	5.3
29	Dominican Republic	5.3
30	Austria	5.3
31	Ukraine	5.3
32	Zimbabwe	5.2
33	Indonesia	5.2
34	Jamaica	5.2
35	Honduras	5.2
36	Venezuela	5.2
37	Thailand	5.2
38	Brazil	5.1
39	Germany	5.1
40	Portugal	5.1
41	Sweden	5.0
42	Trinidad and Tobago	5.0
43	Italy	5.0
44	Philippines	5.0
45	Panama	5.0
46	South Africa	4.9
47	Turkey	4.9
48	El Salvador	4.9
49	Singapore	4.9
50	Uruguay	4.8
51	Korea	4.8
52	Czech Republic	4.7
53	Russian Federation	4.7
54	Switzerland	4.7
55	Bolivia	4.6
56	Latvia	4.5
57	Norway	4.5
58	Ecuador	4.5
59	Jordan	4.5
60	Slovak Republic	4.4
61	Sri Lanka	4.4
62	Hong Kong SAR	4.3
63	Vietnam	4.3
64	India	4.2
65	China	4.2
66	Peru	4.2
67	Iceland	4.1
68	Egypt	4.0
69	Nigeria	3.9
70	Malaysia	3.9
71	Nicaragua	3.9
72	Guatemala	3.6
73	Bangladesh	3.5
74	Paraguay	3.4
75	Argentina	3.1

MEAN: 5.1

6.10 Extent of bureaucratic red tape

How much time does your company's senior management spend working with government agencies/regulations? (1 = less than 10% of its time, 2 = 10–20%, 3 = 21–30%, . . . , 8 = 71–80%)

RANK	COUNTRY	SCORE
1	Japan	1.4
2	Netherlands	1.4
3	Switzerland	1.4
4	Belgium	1.5
5	Norway	1.5
6	Germany	1.6
7	Finland	1.6
8	Malaysia	1.6
9	Iceland	1.6
10	Sweden	1.7
11	Denmark	1.7
12	United States	1.7
13	Czech Republic	1.8
14	France	1.8
15	Singapore	1.8
16	United Kingdom	1.8
17	Ireland	1.8
18	Chile	1.8
19	Spain	1.8
20	Slovenia	1.9
21	New Zealand	1.9
22	Israel	1.9
23	Trinidad and Tobago	1.9
24	Korea	1.9
25	Argentina	2.0
26	Mauritius	2.0
27	Peru	2.0
28	Romania	2.0
29	Lithuania	2.0
30	Austria	2.0
31	India	2.0
32	Brazil	2.1
33	Taiwan	2.1
34	Hong Kong SAR	2.1
35	Canada	2.1
36	Portugal	2.1
37	Sri Lanka	2.1
38	Estonia	2.1
39	Poland	2.1
40	Zimbabwe	2.2
41	Vietnam	2.2
42	Jamaica	2.3
43	Colombia	2.3
44	Philippines	2.3
45	South Africa	2.4
46	Uruguay	2.4
47	Greece	2.4
48	Mexico	2.5
49	Australia	2.5
50	Hungary	2.5
51	Venezuela	2.5
52	Costa Rica	2.5
53	Italy	2.6
54	Nigeria	2.6
55	Bulgaria	2.6
56	Bangladesh	2.7
57	El Salvador	2.8
58	China	2.8
59	Indonesia	2.9
60	Ecuador	2.9
61	Dominican Republic	2.9
62	Nicaragua	2.9
63	Turkey	2.9
64	Russian Federation	3.0
65	Paraguay	3.0
66	Honduras	3.0
67	Ukraine	3.1
68	Latvia	3.1
69	Jordan	3.2
70	Guatemala	3.2
71	Slovak Republic	3.2
72	Thailand	3.4
73	Panama	3.4
74	Bolivia	3.5
75	Egypt	3.9

MEAN: 2.3

6.11 Tax evasion

Tax evasion in your country is: (1 = rampant, 7 = minimal)

RANK	COUNTRY	SCORE
1	Singapore	6.3
2	Hong Kong SAR	6.1
3	New Zealand	5.5
4	Switzerland	5.5
5	United States	5.4
6	United Kingdom	5.4
7	Chile	5.3
8	Canada	5.2
9	Finland	5.1
10	Netherlands	4.8
11	Australia	4.7
12	Japan	4.7
13	Spain	4.7
14	Mauritius	4.6
15	Malaysia	4.6
16	Iceland	4.5
17	Austria	4.2
18	Ireland	4.1
19	Taiwan	4.0
20	France	4.0
21	Slovenia	3.9
22	Germany	3.8
23	Israel	3.7
24	Sweden	3.7
25	Estonia	3.6
26	Denmark	3.6
27	Trinidad and Tobago	3.6
28	Uruguay	3.6
29	Jordan	3.6
30	Hungary	3.4
31	Norway	3.4
32	Vietnam	3.4
33	Latvia	3.3
34	Romania	3.3
35	Korea	3.3
36	El Salvador	3.3
37	Egypt	3.1
38	Thailand	3.1
39	Poland	3.0
40	South Africa	3.0
41	Costa Rica	3.0
42	China	3.0
43	Panama	3.0
44	Lithuania	3.0
45	Belgium	2.9
46	Portugal	2.8
47	Dominican Republic	2.8
48	Italy	2.8
49	Nicaragua	2.8
50	India	2.7
51	Greece	2.7
52	Ecuador	2.7
53	Peru	2.6
54	Slovak Republic	2.6
55	Czech Republic	2.6
56	Jamaica	2.6
57	Bulgaria	2.5
58	Colombia	2.4
59	Brazil	2.4
60	Sri Lanka	2.4
61	Zimbabwe	2.4
62	Paraguay	2.4
63	Indonesia	2.3
64	Honduras	2.3
65	Venezuela	2.3
66	Bolivia	2.2
67	Guatemala	2.2
68	Bangladesh	2.2
69	Russian Federation	2.1
70	Mexico	2.0
71	Ukraine	2.0
72	Argentina	2.0
73	Nigeria	2.0
74	Turkey	2.0
75	Philippines	1.9

MEAN: 3.4

6.12 Organized crime

In your country, organized crime such as racketeering and extortion: (1 = imposes significant costs on businesses, 7 = does not impose significant costs on businesses)

RANK	COUNTRY	SCORE
1	Iceland	6.8
2	Denmark	6.7
3	France	6.6
4	Singapore	6.6
5	Finland	6.6
6	Austria	6.5
7	Israel	6.4
8	Switzerland	6.4
9	New Zealand	6.3
10	Chile	6.2
11	Sweden	6.2
12	Netherlands	6.2
13	Portugal	6.1
14	Jordan	6.0
15	Germany	6.0
16	Egypt	6.0
17	Norway	6.0
18	Australia	5.9
19	United Kingdom	5.8
20	Hong Kong SAR	5.8
21	United States	5.7
22	Belgium	5.7
23	Ireland	5.7
24	Spain	5.7
25	Romania	5.7
26	Mauritius	5.6
27	Greece	5.5
28	Uruguay	5.5
29	Canada	5.3
30	Slovenia	5.3
31	Japan	5.1
32	Estonia	5.0
33	Hungary	5.0
34	Thailand	4.9
35	Trinidad and Tobago	4.9
36	Turkey	4.8
37	Taiwan	4.8
38	Bolivia	4.7
39	Dominican Republic	4.7
40	India	4.7
41	Malaysia	4.6
42	Argentina	4.5
43	Poland	4.5
44	Korea	4.5
45	Costa Rica	4.4
46	China	4.3
47	Italy	4.3
48	Vietnam	4.2
49	Nicaragua	4.1
50	Indonesia	4.1
51	Latvia	4.0
52	Czech Republic	4.0
53	Brazil	3.7
54	Ukraine	3.7
55	Panama	3.6
56	Sri Lanka	3.6
57	Peru	3.6
58	Zimbabwe	3.6
59	Ecuador	3.4
60	Philippines	3.4
61	Slovak Republic	3.4
62	Jamaica	3.1
63	Paraguay	3.1
64	Mexico	3.0
65	Bulgaria	3.0
66	Lithuania	3.0
67	Venezuela	3.0
68	Russian Federation	3.0
69	Nigeria	2.9
70	South Africa	2.5
71	Bangladesh	2.4
72	Honduras	2.4
73	Guatemala	1.9
74	Colombia	1.9
75	El Salvador	1.8

MEAN: 4.7

6.13 Unreported profits and wages

What amount of profits and wages does a company in your industry typically "keep off the books"? (1 = less than 5%, 2 = 5–10%, 3 = 11–20%, 4 = 21–30%, . . . , 9 = 71–80%, 10 = more than 80%)

RANK	COUNTRY	SCORE		MEAN: 2.1	
			1		10
1	Belgium	1.0			
2	Finland	1.0			
3	Denmark	1.1			
4	Norway	1.1			
5	Japan	1.1			
6	France	1.2			
7	New Zealand	1.2			
8	Iceland	1.2			
9	Sweden	1.2			
10	Singapore	1.2			
11	United States	1.2			
12	Ireland	1.3			
13	Australia	1.3			
14	Switzerland	1.3			
15	Spain	1.3			
16	Canada	1.4			
17	Netherlands	1.4			
18	United Kingdom	1.4			
19	Hong Kong SAR	1.4			
20	Chile	1.4			
21	Austria	1.4			
22	Germany	1.5			
23	South Africa	1.6			
24	Taiwan	1.6			
25	Zimbabwe	1.6			
26	Israel	1.6			
27	Malaysia	1.7			
28	Italy	1.9			
29	Mauritius	1.9			
30	Korea	2.0			
31	Colombia	2.0			
32	India	2.0			
33	Mexico	2.0			
34	Venezuela	2.0			
35	El Salvador	2.0			
36	Indonesia	2.1			
37	Trinidad and Tobago	2.1			
38	Lithuania	2.2			
39	Egypt	2.2			
40	Hungary	2.2			
41	Nicaragua	2.3			
42	Peru	2.3			
43	Poland	2.4			
44	China	2.4			
45	Argentina	2.4			
46	Panama	2.5			
47	Sri Lanka	2.5			
48	Jordan	2.5			
49	Jamaica	2.5			
50	Honduras	2.5			
51	Greece	2.5			
52	Uruguay	2.5			
53	Estonia	2.6			
54	Bulgaria	2.6			
55	Dominican Republic	2.6			
56	Czech Republic	2.6			
57	Brazil	2.6			
58	Latvia	2.6			
59	Slovenia	2.6			
60	Portugal	2.6			
61	Costa Rica	2.6			
62	Paraguay	2.7			
63	Guatemala	2.7			
64	Thailand	2.7			
65	Vietnam	2.7			
66	Philippines	3.0			
67	Bolivia	3.0			
68	Ecuador	3.2			
69	Slovak Republic	3.2			
70	Russian Federation	3.2			
71	Nigeria	3.4			
72	Turkey	3.4			
73	Bangladesh	3.8			
74	Ukraine	4.2			
75	Romania	4.2			

6.14 Informal sector

What percentage of businesses in your country would you guess are unofficial or not registered? (1 = less than 5%, 2 = 6–10%, 3 = 11–20%, 4 = 21–30%, . . . , 8 = 61–70%, 9 = more than 70%)

RANK	COUNTRY	SCORE		MEAN: 3.2	
			1		9
1	Singapore	1.2			
2	Japan	1.3			
3	Finland	1.4			
4	Australia	1.4			
5	Denmark	1.4			
6	Canada	1.5			
7	New Zealand	1.5			
8	Switzerland	1.5			
9	Estonia	1.6			
10	United States	1.6			
11	Netherlands	1.7			
12	Chile	1.7			
13	Norway	1.8			
14	Iceland	1.8			
15	France	1.8			
16	United Kingdom	1.8			
17	Ireland	1.9			
18	Germany	1.9			
19	Hong Kong SAR	1.9			
20	Jordan	2.0			
21	Mauritius	2.0			
22	Slovenia	2.0			
23	Austria	2.0			
24	Malaysia	2.1			
25	Vietnam	2.1			
26	Israel	2.1			
27	Lithuania	2.2			
28	Sweden	2.2			
29	Korea	2.2			
30	Belgium	2.4			
31	Spain	2.4			
32	Italy	2.5			
33	Trinidad and Tobago	2.5			
34	Czech Republic	2.6			
35	Taiwan	2.7			
36	Poland	2.8			
37	Slovak Republic	2.8			
38	Hungary	2.9			
39	China	3.0			
40	Latvia	3.1			
41	Greece	3.1			
42	Portugal	3.2			
43	Egypt	3.5			
44	Sri Lanka	3.6			
45	Uruguay	3.6			
46	Indonesia	3.6			
47	Thailand	3.7			
48	Costa Rica	3.7			
49	India	3.8			
50	South Africa	3.8			
51	Colombia	3.9			
52	Argentina	4.1			
53	Russian Federation	4.2			
54	Panama	4.3			
55	Philippines	4.3			
56	Bulgaria	4.4			
57	Ukraine	4.4			
58	Jamaica	4.5			
59	Brazil	4.5			
60	Bangladesh	4.6			
61	Nigeria	4.6			
62	Venezuela	4.7			
63	Turkey	4.8			
64	Zimbabwe	4.8			
65	Peru	4.8			
66	Paraguay	4.8			
67	Mexico	4.8			
68	Dominican Republic	5.0			
69	Nicaragua	5.2			
70	Honduras	5.3			
71	Romania	5.6			
72	Ecuador	5.9			
73	Guatemala	5.9			
74	El Salvador	6.0			
75	Bolivia	6.6			

Section VII: Public Institutions—Corruption

7.01 Irregular payments in exports & imports

How commonly do firms in your industry give irregular extra payments or bribes connected with import and export permits? (1 = common, 7 = never)

RANK	COUNTRY	SCORE	MEAN: 4.8
1	Iceland	7.0	
2	Finland	6.7	
3	New Zealand	6.6	
4	Singapore	6.5	
5	Denmark	6.5	
6	Netherlands	6.5	
7	Australia	6.4	
8	Canada	6.4	
9	Chile	6.4	
10	Japan	6.4	
11	Israel	6.4	
12	Sweden	6.3	
13	United States	6.3	
14	United Kingdom	6.3	
15	Hong Kong SAR	6.3	
16	Norway	6.3	
17	Lithuania	6.1	
18	Germany	6.1	
19	Taiwan	6.1	
20	Austria	6.0	
21	Ireland	5.9	
22	Belgium	5.8	
23	Switzerland	5.8	
24	Italy	5.7	
25	Portugal	5.6	
26	Hungary	5.6	
27	France	5.4	
28	Spain	5.4	
29	Slovak Republic	5.4	
30	Estonia	5.4	
31	Slovenia	5.3	
32	Greece	5.2	
33	Peru	5.1	
34	South Africa	5.1	
35	Trinidad and Tobago	5.0	
36	Bulgaria	4.9	
37	Jordan	4.9	
38	China	4.8	
39	Colombia	4.6	
40	Brazil	4.4	
41	Korea	4.4	
42	Uruguay	4.4	
43	Malaysia	4.3	
44	Mexico	4.3	
45	Jamaica	4.2	
46	Latvia	4.2	
47	Dominican Republic	4.2	
48	Costa Rica	4.1	
49	Poland	4.0	
50	Turkey	4.0	
51	El Salvador	4.0	
52	Egypt	3.9	
53	Ecuador	3.9	
54	Panama	3.9	
55	Czech Republic	3.9	
56	Mauritius	3.9	
57	Russian Federation	3.8	
58	India	3.8	
59	Zimbabwe	3.7	
60	Thailand	3.7	
61	Guatemala	3.7	
62	Bolivia	3.6	
63	Sri Lanka	3.6	
64	Honduras	3.5	
65	Venezuela	3.5	
66	Nicaragua	3.4	
67	Philippines	3.4	
68	Argentina	3.4	
69	Ukraine	3.1	
70	Indonesia	3.0	
71	Nigeria	3.0	
72	Romania	2.9	
73	Vietnam	2.9	
74	Paraguay	2.8	
75	Bangladesh	2.4	

7.02 Irregular payments in government procurement

How commonly do firms in your industry give irregular extra payments or bribes when getting connected to public utilities? (1 = common, 7 = never)

RANK	COUNTRY	SCORE	MEAN: 5.2
1	Iceland	6.9	
2	Finland	6.9	
3	Denmark	6.7	
4	United Kingdom	6.7	
5	Sweden	6.6	
6	Singapore	6.6	
7	New Zealand	6.6	
8	Canada	6.6	
9	Netherlands	6.5	
10	Australia	6.5	
11	United States	6.5	
12	Hong Kong SAR	6.5	
13	Chile	6.4	
14	Israel	6.3	
15	Lithuania	6.3	
16	Norway	6.2	
17	Ireland	6.2	
18	Japan	6.2	
19	Switzerland	6.2	
20	Austria	6.1	
21	France	6.0	
22	Germany	6.0	
23	Belgium	6.0	
24	Taiwan	6.0	
25	Spain	5.9	
26	Italy	5.8	
27	Hungary	5.8	
28	Estonia	5.8	
29	Portugal	5.7	
30	Peru	5.7	
31	Argentina	5.5	
32	Trinidad and Tobago	5.4	
33	Bolivia	5.4	
34	El Salvador	5.3	
35	Slovenia	5.3	
36	Latvia	5.3	
37	Colombia	5.3	
38	Uruguay	5.2	
39	Bulgaria	5.1	
40	South Africa	5.1	
41	Dominican Republic	5.1	
42	Malaysia	5.0	
43	Slovak Republic	5.0	
44	Costa Rica	5.0	
45	Greece	5.0	
46	Jamaica	4.9	
47	Jordan	4.9	
48	Venezuela	4.8	
49	Brazil	4.8	
50	Guatemala	4.8	
51	Korea	4.8	
52	Mauritius	4.8	
53	Panama	4.7	
54	Thailand	4.7	
55	Poland	4.7	
56	Russian Federation	4.6	
57	Czech Republic	4.5	
58	Philippines	4.5	
59	Mexico	4.3	
60	China	4.2	
61	Nicaragua	4.1	
62	Turkey	4.1	
63	Egypt	4.1	
64	Sri Lanka	4.1	
65	Vietnam	4.0	
66	Ecuador	3.9	
67	Indonesia	3.9	
68	Honduras	3.7	
69	Ukraine	3.6	
70	India	3.4	
71	Romania	3.0	
72	Zimbabwe	2.9	
73	Paraguay	2.8	
74	Nigeria	2.3	
75	Bangladesh	1.8	

7.03 Irregular payments in tax collection

How commonly do firms in your industry give irregular extra payments or bribes connected with annual tax payments? (1 = common, 7 = never)

RANK	COUNTRY	SCORE
1	Iceland	7.0
2	Finland	6.9
3	New Zealand	6.7
4	Denmark	6.6
5	Sweden	6.6
6	Canada	6.6
7	Singapore	6.5
8	Australia	6.5
9	Netherlands	6.5
10	Hong Kong SAR	6.4
11	Norway	6.4
12	Japan	6.3
13	United Kingdom	6.3
14	United States	6.3
15	Chile	6.2
16	Austria	6.1
17	Switzerland	6.0
18	Ireland	5.9
19	Belgium	5.9
20	Taiwan	5.9
21	Germany	5.8
22	Israel	5.8
23	Spain	5.8
24	Lithuania	5.8
25	France	5.8
26	Hungary	5.7
27	Malaysia	5.6
28	Romania	5.6
29	South Africa	5.4
30	Mauritius	5.4
31	Bulgaria	5.3
32	Slovenia	5.2
33	Turkey	5.2
34	Italy	5.1
35	Peru	5.1
36	Egypt	5.1
37	Estonia	5.1
38	Slovak Republic	5.0
39	Portugal	5.0
40	Trinidad and Tobago	5.0
41	Jamaica	5.0
42	Uruguay	4.8
43	Costa Rica	4.8
44	Russian Federation	4.7
45	Poland	4.7
46	Latvia	4.7
47	Jordan	4.6
48	Mexico	4.6
49	Sri Lanka	4.5
50	China	4.4
51	Czech Republic	4.3
52	Colombia	4.3
53	Thailand	4.2
54	Dominican Republic	4.2
55	Panama	4.1
56	El Salvador	4.1
57	Korea	4.1
58	Zimbabwe	4.1
59	Brazil	4.1
60	Argentina	4.0
61	Ecuador	3.9
62	Guatemala	3.9
63	Venezuela	3.8
64	Bolivia	3.8
65	India	3.8
66	Honduras	3.8
67	Nicaragua	3.7
68	Ukraine	3.7
69	Greece	3.6
70	Vietnam	3.3
71	Indonesia	3.1
72	Nigeria	2.8
73	Paraguay	2.7
74	Philippines	2.7
75	Bangladesh	2.1

MEAN: 5.0

7.04 Irregular payments in public contracts

How commonly do firms in your industry give irregular extra payments or bribes connected with public contracts/investment projects? (1 = common, 7 = never)

RANK	COUNTRY	SCORE
1	Iceland	7.0
2	Finland	6.6
3	Sweden	6.4
4	Singapore	6.4
5	New Zealand	6.3
6	Denmark	6.3
7	United Kingdom	6.2
8	Australia	6.2
9	Hong Kong SAR	6.1
10	Canada	6.1
11	Norway	6.0
12	United States	6.0
13	Israel	5.9
14	Belgium	5.8
15	Netherlands	5.8
16	Lithuania	5.7
17	Japan	5.6
18	Taiwan	5.6
19	Switzerland	5.6
20	Austria	5.6
21	Ireland	5.5
22	Germany	5.4
23	Chile	5.3
24	Italy	5.1
25	France	5.0
26	Spain	4.9
27	Jordan	4.8
28	Hungary	4.8
29	Bulgaria	4.4
30	South Africa	4.4
31	Egypt	4.4
32	Uruguay	4.4
33	Estonia	4.4
34	Jamaica	4.4
35	Portugal	4.3
36	Sri Lanka	4.3
37	Peru	4.2
38	Trinidad and Tobago	4.2
39	Costa Rica	4.2
40	Romania	4.1
41	Slovenia	4.1
42	Mexico	4.1
43	Slovak Republic	4.0
44	Brazil	4.0
45	Korea	4.0
46	China	3.9
47	Dominican Republic	3.9
48	Russian Federation	3.8
49	Latvia	3.8
50	Turkey	3.8
51	El Salvador	3.7
52	Thailand	3.7
53	Colombia	3.7
54	Poland	3.6
55	Vietnam	3.5
56	Venezuela	3.5
57	Malaysia	3.5
58	Panama	3.4
59	Mauritius	3.4
60	India	3.4
61	Greece	3.3
62	Ecuador	3.2
63	Nicaragua	3.2
64	Honduras	3.2
65	Argentina	3.1
66	Czech Republic	3.1
67	Guatemala	3.1
68	Indonesia	3.0
69	Philippines	3.0
70	Ukraine	2.9
71	Bolivia	2.8
72	Paraguay	2.6
73	Zimbabwe	2.5
74	Nigeria	2.3
75	Bangladesh	2.1

MEAN: 4.4

7.05 Irregular payments in loan applications

How commonly do firms in your industry give irregular extra payments or bribes connected with loan applications? (1 = common, 7 = never)

RANK	COUNTRY	SCORE
1	Iceland	7.0
2	Denmark	6.7
3	Finland	6.7
4	New Zealand	6.6
5	Canada	6.6
6	Sweden	6.4
7	United Kingdom	6.4
8	Australia	6.4
9	Singapore	6.4
10	Netherlands	6.4
11	Norway	6.3
12	United States	6.3
13	Chile	6.2
14	Belgium	6.2
15	Hong Kong SAR	6.1
16	Austria	6.1
17	Japan	6.0
18	Lithuania	6.0
19	Ireland	6.0
20	Israel	5.9
21	Switzerland	5.9
22	France	5.9
23	Spain	5.9
24	Germany	5.8
25	Taiwan	5.7
26	Mauritius	5.6
27	Portugal	5.5
28	Italy	5.4
29	Jamaica	5.4
30	Trinidad and Tobago	5.3
31	South Africa	5.3
32	Peru	5.2
33	Hungary	5.2
34	Estonia	5.1
35	Slovak Republic	5.0
36	Malaysia	5.0
37	Greece	4.9
38	Romania	4.9
39	Dominican Republic	4.9
40	Jordan	4.9
41	Egypt	4.9
42	Bulgaria	4.9
43	Brazil	4.9
44	Mexico	4.9
45	Bolivia	4.8
46	Costa Rica	4.8
47	Slovenia	4.7
48	Poland	4.7
49	Colombia	4.7
50	Panama	4.7
51	Ecuador	4.7
52	Thailand	4.6
53	Uruguay	4.6
54	Sri Lanka	4.6
55	El Salvador	4.6
56	Philippines	4.6
57	Latvia	4.5
58	Turkey	4.5
59	Venezuela	4.4
60	Guatemala	4.4
61	India	4.3
62	Argentina	4.2
63	Honduras	4.2
64	China	4.1
65	Russian Federation	4.1
66	Korea	4.0
67	Zimbabwe	4.0
68	Czech Republic	3.9
69	Nicaragua	3.9
70	Nigeria	3.7
71	Indonesia	3.7
72	Vietnam	3.6
73	Paraguay	3.3
74	Ukraine	3.1
75	Bangladesh	2.3

MEAN: 5.1

7.06 Business costs of corruption

Do unfair or corrupt activities of other firms impose costs on your firm? (1 = impose large costs, 7 = impose no costs/not relevant)

RANK	COUNTRY	SCORE
1	Iceland	6.9
2	Finland	6.6
3	Denmark	6.4
4	Sweden	6.4
5	Singapore	6.3
6	Austria	6.2
7	France	6.2
8	New Zealand	6.1
9	Israel	6.1
10	United Kingdom	6.0
11	Norway	5.9
12	Hong Kong SAR	5.9
13	Japan	5.7
14	Italy	5.7
15	Switzerland	5.7
16	Taiwan	5.6
17	Germany	5.6
18	United States	5.6
19	Canada	5.6
20	Netherlands	5.5
21	Australia	5.5
22	Belgium	5.5
23	Hungary	5.3
24	Ireland	5.3
25	Spain	5.3
26	Trinidad and Tobago	5.3
27	Estonia	5.2
28	Czech Republic	5.1
29	Slovak Republic	5.0
30	Mauritius	4.9
31	Chile	4.9
32	Poland	4.9
33	Portugal	4.8
34	South Africa	4.8
35	Slovenia	4.8
36	Latvia	4.7
37	Jamaica	4.7
38	Uruguay	4.7
39	Thailand	4.6
40	India	4.6
41	Costa Rica	4.5
42	Jordan	4.5
43	Korea	4.5
44	Lithuania	4.5
45	Mexico	4.5
46	Bulgaria	4.3
47	Turkey	4.3
48	Greece	4.3
49	Peru	4.2
50	Malaysia	4.1
51	Colombia	4.1
52	Brazil	4.1
53	El Salvador	4.1
54	Indonesia	4.0
55	Dominican Republic	3.9
56	China	3.9
57	Sri Lanka	3.8
58	Egypt	3.8
59	Vietnam	3.7
60	Honduras	3.6
61	Venezuela	3.6
62	Romania	3.6
63	Russian Federation	3.6
64	Bolivia	3.6
65	Philippines	3.5
66	Panama	3.5
67	Zimbabwe	3.5
68	Ecuador	3.3
69	Argentina	3.3
70	Ukraine	3.2
71	Nigeria	3.1
72	Paraguay	3.1
73	Nicaragua	3.1
74	Guatemala	3.1
75	Bangladesh	2.9

MEAN: 4.7

7.07 Public trust of politicians

Public trust in the honesty of politicians is: (1 = very low, 7 = very high)

RANK	COUNTRY	SCORE
1	Singapore	6.4
2	Switzerland	5.6
3	Finland	5.4
4	Netherlands	5.4
5	Iceland	5.2
6	Denmark	5.2
7	Sweden	4.5
8	Norway	4.4
9	Spain	4.4
10	Hong Kong SAR	4.2
11	Germany	4.2
12	Canada	4.1
13	United Kingdom	4.1
14	Austria	4.0
15	Vietnam	3.8
16	Australia	3.8
17	Jordan	3.8
18	China	3.8
19	Israel	3.8
20	Belgium	3.8
21	United States	3.8
22	France	3.7
23	New Zealand	3.6
24	Italy	3.4
25	Egypt	3.3
26	Uruguay	3.2
27	Ireland	3.2
28	Portugal	3.2
29	Taiwan	3.2
30	Romania	3.1
31	Costa Rica	3.0
32	Slovenia	3.0
33	Chile	2.9
34	South Africa	2.9
35	Estonia	2.8
36	Slovak Republic	2.8
37	Thailand	2.8
38	Malaysia	2.8
39	Mauritius	2.6
40	Japan	2.6
41	Hungary	2.6
42	Trinidad and Tobago	2.5
43	Mexico	2.5
44	Greece	2.5
45	Poland	2.4
46	Latvia	2.3
47	Bulgaria	2.3
48	Brazil	2.2
49	India	2.1
50	Paraguay	2.1
51	Korea	2.1
52	Philippines	2.1
53	Indonesia	2.0
54	Jamaica	2.0
55	Panama	2.0
56	Sri Lanka	2.0
57	Lithuania	1.9
58	Czech Republic	1.9
59	Turkey	1.9
60	Dominican Republic	1.8
61	Russian Federation	1.8
62	Nigeria	1.8
63	El Salvador	1.7
64	Venezuela	1.7
65	Nicaragua	1.6
66	Argentina	1.6
67	Colombia	1.6
68	Ukraine	1.6
69	Bangladesh	1.6
70	Honduras	1.5
71	Bolivia	1.5
72	Guatemala	1.4
73	Ecuador	1.4
74	Peru	1.3
75	Zimbabwe	1.2

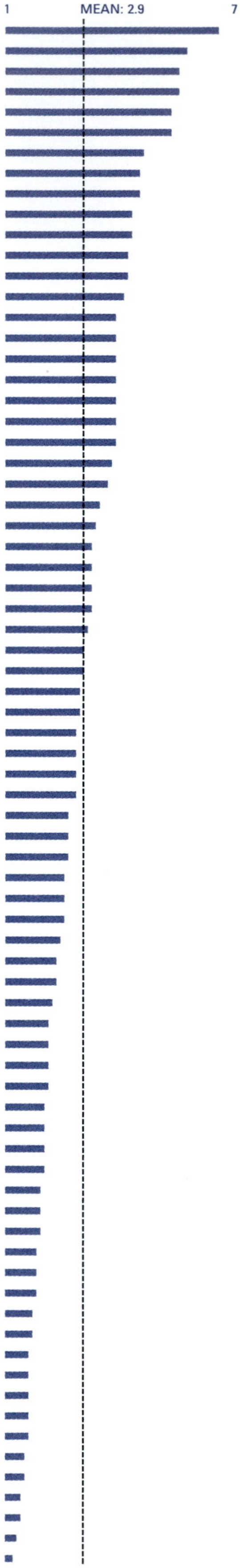

Chart: 1 — MEAN: 2.9 — 7

8.01 Intensity of local competition

In most industries, competition in the local market is: (1 = limited and price-cutting is rare, 7 = intense and market leadership changes over time)

RANK	COUNTRY	SCORE
1	United States	6.5
2	Germany	6.3
3	Belgium	6.2
4	Netherlands	6.2
5	France	6.1
6	United Kingdom	6.1
7	Finland	6.1
8	Hong Kong SAR	5.9
9	Chile	5.9
10	New Zealand	5.8
11	Sweden	5.8
12	Austria	5.8
13	Canada	5.7
14	Spain	5.7
15	India	5.6
16	Estonia	5.6
17	Israel	5.6
18	Ireland	5.6
19	Australia	5.6
20	Czech Republic	5.5
21	China	5.5
22	Norway	5.5
23	Japan	5.4
24	Switzerland	5.4
25	Egypt	5.4
26	South Africa	5.4
27	Singapore	5.4
28	Hungary	5.3
29	Iceland	5.3
30	Taiwan	5.3
31	Vietnam	5.3
32	Portugal	5.3
33	Turkey	5.3
34	Denmark	5.3
35	Italy	5.3
36	Peru	5.2
37	Brazil	5.2
38	Slovak Republic	5.2
39	Costa Rica	5.2
40	Poland	5.2
41	Greece	5.2
42	Indonesia	5.2
43	Nigeria	5.2
44	Argentina	5.1
45	Latvia	5.1
46	Sri Lanka	5.1
47	Dominican Republic	5.0
48	Trinidad and Tobago	5.0
49	Slovenia	5.0
50	Lithuania	5.0
51	El Salvador	5.0
52	Mexico	5.0
53	Thailand	5.0
54	Panama	5.0
55	Philippines	4.9
56	Korea	4.9
57	Uruguay	4.9
58	Jamaica	4.9
59	Colombia	4.7
60	Jordan	4.7
61	Malaysia	4.6
62	Mauritius	4.6
63	Bangladesh	4.5
64	Ukraine	4.5
65	Venezuela	4.3
66	Nicaragua	4.2
67	Russian Federation	4.2
68	Guatemala	4.2
69	Bulgaria	4.1
70	Bolivia	4.0
71	Zimbabwe	3.9
72	Ecuador	3.9
73	Honduras	3.4
74	Paraguay	3.4
75	Romania	3.3

MEAN: 5.1

8.02 Extent of locally based competitors

Competition in the local market comes primarily from: (1 = imports, 7 = local firms or local subsidiaries of multinationals)

RANK	COUNTRY	SCORE
1	United States	5.8
2	France	5.6
3	Spain	5.6
4	Hong Kong SAR	5.6
5	Finland	5.5
6	Chile	5.4
7	United Kingdom	5.4
8	Taiwan	5.3
9	India	5.3
10	Belgium	5.3
11	Germany	5.2
12	China	5.2
13	Vietnam	5.2
14	Brazil	5.2
15	Turkey	5.0
16	Netherlands	5.0
17	Switzerland	5.0
18	Thailand	4.9
19	Colombia	4.9
20	Italy	4.9
21	Austria	4.9
22	Norway	4.9
23	Canada	4.9
24	Korea	4.8
25	Denmark	4.8
26	Indonesia	4.8
27	Poland	4.7
28	Greece	4.7
29	South Africa	4.7
30	Japan	4.7
31	Trinidad and Tobago	4.7
32	Malaysia	4.7
33	Mexico	4.7
34	Argentina	4.7
35	Australia	4.7
36	Estonia	4.6
37	Portugal	4.6
38	Philippines	4.6
39	Iceland	4.6
40	Israel	4.5
41	Panama	4.4
42	Russian Federation	4.4
43	Ukraine	4.4
44	Slovenia	4.4
45	Singapore	4.4
46	Costa Rica	4.3
47	New Zealand	4.3
48	Ireland	4.3
49	Hungary	4.2
50	Zimbabwe	4.2
51	Czech Republic	4.2
52	Ecuador	4.2
53	Sweden	4.2
54	El Salvador	4.0
55	Egypt	4.0
56	Latvia	4.0
57	Slovak Republic	4.0
58	Uruguay	3.9
59	Guatemala	3.9
60	Dominican Republic	3.7
61	Jamaica	3.7
62	Nicaragua	3.6
63	Sri Lanka	3.6
64	Nigeria	3.6
65	Jordan	3.6
66	Lithuania	3.6
67	Bangladesh	3.4
68	Peru	3.3
69	Mauritius	3.3
70	Paraguay	3.3
71	Honduras	3.2
72	Venezuela	3.1
73	Bulgaria	3.0
74	Romania	3.0
75	Bolivia	3.0

MEAN: 4.4

8.03 Entry into local markets

Entry of new competitors: (1 = almost never occurs in the local market, 7 = is common in the local market)

RANK	COUNTRY	SCORE
		MEAN: 5.2
1	Hong Kong SAR	6.1
2	Belgium	5.9
3	Israel	5.9
4	Germany	5.9
5	Slovak Republic	5.8
6	Finland	5.8
7	United Kingdom	5.8
8	United States	5.7
9	Chile	5.7
10	Nigeria	5.7
11	Czech Republic	5.7
12	France	5.6
13	Netherlands	5.6
14	Brazil	5.6
15	Singapore	5.6
16	Vietnam	5.6
17	Taiwan	5.6
18	Estonia	5.6
19	China	5.6
20	Portugal	5.5
21	Jordan	5.5
22	Bangladesh	5.5
23	Austria	5.5
24	Egypt	5.5
25	New Zealand	5.5
26	Trinidad and Tobago	5.5
27	Hungary	5.4
28	Poland	5.4
29	Spain	5.4
30	Turkey	5.4
31	Dominican Republic	5.4
32	India	5.4
33	Switzerland	5.4
34	Lithuania	5.4
35	Sri Lanka	5.4
36	Sweden	5.4
37	El Salvador	5.4
38	Philippines	5.3
39	Ireland	5.3
40	Canada	5.3
41	Latvia	5.3
42	Malaysia	5.3
43	Denmark	5.2
44	Greece	5.2
45	Iceland	5.2
46	Slovenia	5.2
47	Indonesia	5.2
48	Panama	5.2
49	South Africa	5.1
50	Thailand	5.1
51	Italy	5.1
52	Costa Rica	5.1
53	Jamaica	5.1
54	Argentina	5.1
55	Peru	5.0
56	Uruguay	5.0
57	Australia	5.0
58	Mexico	5.0
59	Romania	5.0
60	Korea	4.9
61	Japan	4.9
62	Colombia	4.9
63	Venezuela	4.8
64	Ukraine	4.8
65	Russian Federation	4.7
66	Guatemala	4.7
67	Bulgaria	4.7
68	Norway	4.6
69	Nicaragua	4.6
70	Mauritius	4.6
71	Honduras	4.5
72	Bolivia	4.3
73	Ecuador	4.2
74	Zimbabwe	4.1
75	Paraguay	3.9

8.04 Administrative burden for startups

Starting a new business in your country is generally: (1 = extremely difficult and time consuming, 7 = easy)

RANK	COUNTRY	SCORE
		MEAN: 4.5
1	Hong Kong SAR	6.4
2	Finland	6.3
3	United States	6.0
4	Iceland	6.0
5	Estonia	5.8
6	Singapore	5.8
7	Sweden	5.7
8	New Zealand	5.7
9	United Kingdom	5.6
10	Israel	5.6
11	Switzerland	5.6
12	Netherlands	5.5
13	Taiwan	5.5
14	Canada	5.5
15	Australia	5.4
16	Hungary	5.4
17	Thailand	5.4
18	Poland	5.2
19	Ireland	5.1
20	Norway	5.1
21	Trinidad and Tobago	5.0
22	Vietnam	4.9
23	China	4.9
24	Sri Lanka	4.9
25	Denmark	4.9
26	Belgium	4.8
27	Germany	4.8
28	Malaysia	4.8
29	Jordan	4.8
30	India	4.6
31	South Africa	4.5
32	Japan	4.5
33	Egypt	4.5
34	El Salvador	4.5
35	Slovenia	4.4
36	Brazil	4.4
37	Jamaica	4.4
38	Zimbabwe	4.4
39	Spain	4.4
40	Portugal	4.4
41	Chile	4.4
42	Indonesia	4.4
43	Philippines	4.4
44	Czech Republic	4.3
45	Panama	4.3
46	Dominican Republic	4.3
47	Austria	4.3
48	Mauritius	4.3
49	Korea	4.2
50	Turkey	4.1
51	France	4.1
52	Nigeria	4.1
53	Guatemala	4.1
54	Italy	4.1
55	Uruguay	4.0
56	Latvia	4.0
57	Argentina	3.9
58	Costa Rica	3.8
59	Venezuela	3.8
60	Bangladesh	3.7
61	Lithuania	3.5
62	Nicaragua	3.5
63	Greece	3.5
64	Russian Federation	3.4
65	Paraguay	3.4
66	Ecuador	3.4
67	Bolivia	3.3
68	Colombia	3.3
69	Mexico	3.2
70	Romania	3.2
71	Peru	3.1
72	Slovak Republic	2.8
73	Ukraine	2.7
74	Honduras	2.7
75	Bulgaria	2.5

8.05 Permits to start a firm

Approximately how many permits would you need to start a new firm? (median response listed for each country)

RANK	COUNTRY	MEDIAN # OF PERMITS
		MEAN: 4.8
1	Hong Kong SAR	2.0
1	Singapore	2.0
1	Sri Lanka	2.0
1	United Kingdom	2.0
5	Canada	3.0
5	Denmark	3.0
5	Egypt	3.0
5	Estonia	3.0
5	Finland	3.0
5	Germany	3.0
5	Iceland	3.0
5	Ireland	3.0
5	Israel	3.0
5	Jamaica	3.0
5	Japan	3.0
5	Netherlands	3.0
5	New Zealand	3.0
5	Nigeria	3.0
5	Poland	3.0
5	Switzerland	3.0
5	Taiwan	3.0
5	Thailand	3.0
5	Trinidad and Tobago	3.0
24	Argentina	4.0
24	Czech Republic	4.0
24	Dominican Republic	4.0
24	Latvia	4.0
24	Mauritius	4.0
24	Philippines	4.0
24	South Africa	4.0
24	United States	4.0
24	Uruguay	4.0
33	Jordan	4.5
33	Zimbabwe	4.5
35	Australia	5.0
35	Austria	5.0
35	Chile	5.0
35	El Salvador	5.0
35	France	5.0
35	Guatemala	5.0
35	Hungary	5.0
35	Malaysia	5.0
35	Nicaragua	5.0
35	Norway	5.0
35	Panama	5.0
35	Paraguay	5.0
35	Peru	5.0
35	Portugal	5.0
35	Romania	5.0
35	Slovak Republic	5.0
35	Slovenia	5.0
35	Sweden	5.0
35	Turkey	5.0
35	Vietnam	5.0
55	Indonesia	5.5
55	Spain	5.5
57	Bangladesh	6.0
57	Bolivia	6.0
57	China	6.0
57	Colombia	6.0
57	Ecuador	6.0
57	Honduras	6.0
57	Russian Federation	6.0
64	Costa Rica	6.5
64	Greece	6.5
64	Lithuania	6.5
67	Brazil	7.0
67	Bulgaria	7.0
69	Belgium	8.0
69	Ukraine	8.0
69	Venezuela	9.0
72	India	10.0
72	Italy	10.0
72	Korea	10.0
72	Mexico	10.0

8.06 Days to start a firm

Considering license and permit requirements, what is the typical number of days required to start a new firm in your country? (median response listed for each country)

RANK	COUNTRY	MEDIAN # OF DAYS
		MEAN: 40.2
1	Iceland	5
2	United Kingdom	7
3	Hong Kong SAR	9
4	Israel	10
4	Netherlands	10
4	New Zealand	10
4	Norway	10
8	Ireland	15
8	Romania	15
10	Latvia	20
10	Ukraine	20
12	Singapore	21
13	Canada	22
14	Finland	23
15	Switzerland	24
16	Jamaica	25
16	Sweden	25
18	Russian Federation	26
19	Australia	30
19	Bulgaria	30
19	China	30
19	Denmark	30
19	El Salvador	30
19	Estonia	30
19	France	30
19	Germany	30
19	Guatemala	30
19	Japan	30
19	Jordan	30
19	Korea	30
19	Lithuania	30
19	Panama	30
19	Paraguay	30
19	Philippines	30
19	Poland	30
19	Slovak Republic	30
19	Sri Lanka	30
19	Taiwan	30
19	Thailand	30
19	United States	30
19	Uruguay	30
19	Vietnam	30
43	Nigeria	31
44	Trinidad and Tobago	33
45	Austria	35
46	Argentina	45
46	Colombia	45
46	Hungary	45
46	Indonesia	45
46	South Africa	45
46	Turkey	45
52	Nicaragua	48
53	Dominican Republic	55
54	Bolivia	60
54	Brazil	60
54	Chile	60
54	Costa Rica	60
54	Czech Republic	60
54	Ecuador	60
54	Egypt	60
54	Greece	60
54	Malaysia	60
54	Mauritius	60
54	Peru	60
54	Portugal	60
54	Slovenia	60
54	Spain	60
54	Venezuela	60
69	Honduras	75
70	Bangladesh	90
70	Belgium	90
70	India	90
70	Mexico	90
70	Zimbabwe	90
75	Italy	105

8.07   Effectiveness of anti-trust policy

Anti-monopoly policy in your country: (1 = is lax and not effective at promoting competition, 7 = effectively promotes competition)

RANK	COUNTRY	SCORE
1	Finland	6.6
2	Germany	6.2
3	Netherlands	6.2
4	United States	6.0
5	United Kingdom	5.8
6	France	5.8
7	Belgium	5.8
8	Denmark	5.7
9	Australia	5.7
10	Israel	5.7
11	Iceland	5.6
12	Canada	5.6
13	New Zealand	5.5
14	Sweden	5.5
15	Norway	5.3
16	Taiwan	5.2
17	Spain	5.2
18	Italy	5.2
19	Chile	5.1
20	Singapore	5.1
21	Ireland	5.0
22	Switzerland	5.0
23	Japan	5.0
24	Austria	4.9
25	South Africa	4.8
26	Hungary	4.8
27	Korea	4.7
28	Brazil	4.7
29	Poland	4.6
30	Portugal	4.5
31	Hong Kong SAR	4.5
32	Estonia	4.2
33	Slovenia	4.2
34	India	4.1
35	Turkey	4.1
36	Greece	4.1
37	Panama	4.0
38	Mexico	4.0
39	Thailand	3.9
40	Jamaica	3.9
41	Jordan	3.8
42	Latvia	3.8
43	Argentina	3.8
44	Sri Lanka	3.8
45	Venezuela	3.8
46	Peru	3.8
47	Slovak Republic	3.8
48	Philippines	3.8
49	Czech Republic	3.7
50	Costa Rica	3.7
51	Romania	3.7
52	China	3.7
53	Mauritius	3.6
54	Indonesia	3.6
55	Colombia	3.5
56	Lithuania	3.4
57	Egypt	3.4
58	Dominican Republic	3.4
59	Ukraine	3.3
60	Zimbabwe	3.3
61	Bulgaria	3.3
62	Malaysia	3.2
63	Trinidad and Tobago	3.2
64	Paraguay	3.1
65	El Salvador	3.1
66	Russian Federation	3.1
67	Nigeria	3.0
68	Nicaragua	3.0
69	Bangladesh	2.9
70	Vietnam	2.9
71	Bolivia	2.8
72	Uruguay	2.8
73	Guatemala	2.5
74	Ecuador	2.5
75	Honduras	2.1

MEAN: 4.2

413

9.01 Buyer sophistication

Buyers in your country are: (1 = unsophisticated and choose based on the lowest price, 7 = knowledgeable and demanding and buy innovative products)

MEAN: 4.3

RANK	COUNTRY	SCORE
1	Switzerland	6.1
2	Finland	6.1
3	United States	5.9
4	Hong Kong SAR	5.8
5	France	5.8
6	Sweden	5.8
7	United Kingdom	5.7
8	Iceland	5.7
9	Canada	5.7
10	Germany	5.6
11	Netherlands	5.5
12	Australia	5.5
13	Japan	5.5
14	Denmark	5.5
15	Singapore	5.5
16	Ireland	5.4
17	Italy	5.4
18	Norway	5.4
19	Belgium	5.4
20	New Zealand	5.3
21	Taiwan	5.2
22	Israel	5.2
23	Spain	5.1
24	Austria	5.1
25	Trinidad and Tobago	4.9
26	Korea	4.8
27	Vietnam	4.7
28	Portugal	4.6
29	Czech Republic	4.6
30	Poland	4.6
31	Brazil	4.5
32	Malaysia	4.5
33	South Africa	4.5
34	Estonia	4.4
35	Jamaica	4.4
36	Philippines	4.4
37	Mauritius	4.4
38	Slovenia	4.3
39	India	4.3
40	Costa Rica	4.3
41	Argentina	4.3
42	Slovak Republic	4.2
43	Thailand	4.1
44	Chile	4.0
45	Greece	3.9
46	Sri Lanka	3.9
47	Latvia	3.9
48	Hungary	3.8
49	China	3.8
50	Nigeria	3.7
51	Russian Federation	3.7
52	Romania	3.6
53	Turkey	3.6
54	Uruguay	3.6
55	Panama	3.6
56	Jordan	3.6
57	Bangladesh	3.6
58	Mexico	3.6
59	Indonesia	3.6
60	Venezuela	3.5
61	Zimbabwe	3.5
62	Lithuania	3.4
63	Egypt	3.3
64	Colombia	3.3
65	El Salvador	3.2
66	Bulgaria	3.1
67	Dominican Republic	3.0
68	Peru	2.9
69	Ukraine	2.9
70	Paraguay	2.9
71	Nicaragua	2.8
72	Guatemala	2.6
73	Honduras	2.4
74	Ecuador	2.3
75	Bolivia	2.1

9.02 Local supplier quantity

Local suppliers in your country are: (1 = largely nonexistent, 7 = numerous and include the most important materials, components, equipment, and services)

MEAN: 5.1

RANK	COUNTRY	SCORE
1	United States	6.5
2	Germany	6.5
3	Italy	6.4
4	France	6.4
5	Japan	6.3
6	United Kingdom	6.1
7	Switzerland	6.0
8	Netherlands	6.0
9	Belgium	5.9
10	Spain	5.9
11	Finland	5.8
12	Austria	5.8
13	Sweden	5.7
14	Israel	5.6
15	India	5.6
16	South Africa	5.5
17	Australia	5.5
18	Denmark	5.5
19	Brazil	5.5
20	Canada	5.5
21	Hong Kong SAR	5.5
22	Slovak Republic	5.4
23	Iceland	5.3
24	Singapore	5.3
25	Ireland	5.3
26	Turkey	5.3
27	Taiwan	5.3
28	Czech Republic	5.2
29	Chile	5.2
30	Hungary	5.2
31	Portugal	5.2
32	New Zealand	5.1
33	Panama	5.1
34	Malaysia	5.1
35	Vietnam	5.1
36	Korea	5.1
37	Poland	5.0
38	Norway	5.0
39	Dominican Republic	5.0
40	Lithuania	5.0
41	Nigeria	5.0
42	China	4.9
43	Trinidad and Tobago	4.9
44	Thailand	4.9
45	Indonesia	4.9
46	Latvia	4.8
47	Argentina	4.8
48	Greece	4.8
49	Russian Federation	4.8
50	Colombia	4.8
51	Slovenia	4.7
52	Jamaica	4.7
53	Ukraine	4.7
54	Romania	4.6
55	Costa Rica	4.6
56	Estonia	4.6
57	Philippines	4.6
58	Mauritius	4.6
59	Jordan	4.6
60	Peru	4.6
61	Mexico	4.6
62	El Salvador	4.6
63	Sri Lanka	4.6
64	Uruguay	4.5
65	Egypt	4.5
66	Venezuela	4.4
67	Guatemala	4.4
68	Bulgaria	4.4
69	Zimbabwe	4.2
70	Nicaragua	4.2
71	Bangladesh	4.1
72	Ecuador	4.1
73	Honduras	3.9
74	Bolivia	3.7
75	Paraguay	3.4

9.03 Local supplier quality

Local suppliers in your country are: (1 = inefficient and have little technological capability, 7 = internationally competitive and assist in new product and process development)

RANK	COUNTRY	SCORE
1	Germany	6.5
2	United States	6.4
3	Netherlands	6.4
4	France	6.2
5	Switzerland	6.1
6	Belgium	6.0
7	Japan	6.0
8	Denmark	6.0
9	United Kingdom	5.9
10	Sweden	5.9
11	Austria	5.9
12	Italy	5.8
13	Finland	5.8
14	Spain	5.7
15	Canada	5.6
16	Australia	5.6
17	Iceland	5.6
18	Hong Kong SAR	5.5
19	Singapore	5.3
20	Norway	5.3
21	New Zealand	5.3
22	Taiwan	5.3
23	Israel	5.2
24	Ireland	5.2
25	Chile	5.0
26	South Africa	5.0
27	Brazil	4.9
28	Hungary	4.9
29	Czech Republic	4.9
30	Korea	4.8
31	Slovak Republic	4.8
32	Turkey	4.8
33	Latvia	4.8
34	Estonia	4.7
35	Trinidad and Tobago	4.7
36	Slovenia	4.6
37	Panama	4.6
38	Lithuania	4.6
39	Dominican Republic	4.5
40	Thailand	4.5
41	Poland	4.5
42	Portugal	4.5
43	Indonesia	4.4
44	Costa Rica	4.4
45	Colombia	4.4
46	Malaysia	4.3
47	Vietnam	4.3
48	Romania	4.3
49	India	4.3
50	Mauritius	4.3
51	Greece	4.2
52	Mexico	4.2
53	Jamaica	4.2
54	Uruguay	4.2
55	Sri Lanka	4.1
56	El Salvador	4.0
57	Philippines	4.0
58	Argentina	4.0
59	Guatemala	4.0
60	Jordan	3.9
61	Russian Federation	3.9
62	China	3.9
63	Ukraine	3.9
64	Peru	3.9
65	Zimbabwe	3.6
66	Nicaragua	3.6
67	Paraguay	3.6
68	Venezuela	3.5
69	Bulgaria	3.5
70	Bangladesh	3.4
71	Nigeria	3.4
72	Ecuador	3.3
73	Egypt	3.3
74	Bolivia	3.2
75	Honduras	3.2

MEAN: 4.7

9.04 Presence of demanding regulatory standards

Regulatory standards—eg, for products, energy, safety, environment—in your country are: (1 = lax or nonexistent, 7 = among the world's most stringent)

RANK	COUNTRY	SCORE
1	Germany	6.7
2	Austria	6.5
3	Finland	6.5
4	Netherlands	6.4
5	Switzerland	6.4
6	United States	6.3
7	Sweden	6.3
8	Australia	6.3
9	Denmark	6.3
10	France	6.2
11	United Kingdom	6.2
12	Canada	6.2
13	Iceland	6.1
14	Japan	6.1
15	Norway	6.1
16	Singapore	6.0
17	New Zealand	5.9
18	Belgium	5.8
19	Italy	5.7
20	Slovak Republic	5.6
21	Ireland	5.5
22	Israel	5.5
23	Taiwan	5.3
24	Hungary	5.3
25	Hong Kong SAR	5.3
26	Czech Republic	5.2
27	Spain	5.1
28	Portugal	5.0
29	Slovenia	5.0
30	South Africa	4.9
31	Lithuania	4.9
32	Poland	4.9
33	Korea	4.8
34	Ukraine	4.7
35	Chile	4.7
36	Estonia	4.7
37	Brazil	4.6
38	Latvia	4.6
39	Malaysia	4.5
40	Jordan	4.4
41	Thailand	4.4
42	Russian Federation	4.3
43	Uruguay	4.2
44	Jamaica	4.2
45	Mauritius	4.2
46	India	4.2
47	Greece	4.1
48	Colombia	4.1
49	Mexico	4.0
50	Zimbabwe	4.0
51	Bulgaria	3.9
52	Turkey	3.9
53	Costa Rica	3.9
54	Egypt	3.9
55	Philippines	3.8
56	China	3.8
57	Sri Lanka	3.7
58	Panama	3.7
59	Indonesia	3.7
60	Argentina	3.7
61	Trinidad and Tobago	3.7
62	Peru	3.5
63	Romania	3.5
64	Venezuela	3.4
65	Paraguay	3.2
66	Vietnam	3.2
67	El Salvador	3.2
68	Nigeria	3.0
69	Dominican Republic	2.9
70	Bolivia	2.8
71	Bangladesh	2.8
72	Nicaragua	2.7
73	Guatemala	2.7
74	Ecuador	2.7
75	Honduras	2.3

MEAN: 4.6

9.05 Decentralization of corporate activity

Corporate activity in your country is: (1 = dominated by a few business groups, 7 = spread among many firms)

RANK	COUNTRY	SCORE	1 — MEAN: 4.1 — 7
1	United States	6.3	
2	Germany	6.2	
3	Netherlands	6.1	
4	Belgium	5.8	
5	Finland	5.8	
6	Denmark	5.7	
7	United Kingdom	5.7	
8	Canada	5.7	
9	France	5.6	
10	Switzerland	5.3	
11	Austria	5.3	
12	Japan	5.3	
13	Australia	5.2	
14	Taiwan	5.1	
15	Singapore	5.1	
16	China	5.1	
17	Slovak Republic	5.0	
18	Sweden	5.0	
19	Brazil	5.0	
20	India	4.9	
21	Poland	4.8	
22	Ireland	4.8	
23	Hungary	4.8	
24	Norway	4.6	
25	Spain	4.6	
26	New Zealand	4.6	
27	Iceland	4.5	
28	Vietnam	4.5	
29	Italy	4.4	
30	Slovenia	4.3	
31	Romania	4.3	
32	Trinidad and Tobago	4.3	
33	Latvia	4.1	
34	Nigeria	4.1	
35	Israel	4.1	
36	Estonia	4.1	
37	Panama	4.1	
38	Hong Kong SAR	4.0	
39	Czech Republic	4.0	
40	Thailand	4.0	
41	Greece	4.0	
42	Bulgaria	3.9	
43	Jamaica	3.9	
44	Malaysia	3.9	
45	Korea	3.8	
46	Portugal	3.8	
47	South Africa	3.7	
48	Uruguay	3.7	
49	Jordan	3.7	
50	Chile	3.6	
51	Dominican Republic	3.6	
52	Costa Rica	3.5	
53	Sri Lanka	3.5	
54	Indonesia	3.5	
55	Egypt	3.4	
56	Zimbabwe	3.2	
57	Ukraine	3.2	
58	Russian Federation	3.2	
59	Lithuania	3.1	
60	Turkey	3.1	
61	Philippines	3.1	
62	Paraguay	3.1	
63	Mexico	3.1	
64	Argentina	2.9	
65	Peru	2.9	
66	Colombia	2.9	
67	Guatemala	2.7	
68	Venezuela	2.6	
69	Nicaragua	2.6	
70	Bolivia	2.5	
71	Bangladesh	2.4	
72	El Salvador	2.3	
73	Mauritius	2.2	
74	Ecuador	2.2	
75	Honduras	2.1	

9.06 State of cluster development

How common are clusters in your country? (1 = clusters are limited and shallow, 7 = clusters are common and deep)

RANK	COUNTRY	SCORE	1 — MEAN: 3.5 — 7
1	Finland	5.7	
2	Taiwan	5.4	
3	United States	5.3	
4	Italy	5.0	
5	United Kingdom	4.7	
6	Sweden	4.7	
7	Germany	4.7	
8	Japan	4.6	
9	Singapore	4.6	
10	Ireland	4.6	
11	Korea	4.5	
12	Canada	4.4	
13	Austria	4.4	
14	Switzerland	4.2	
15	Hong Kong SAR	4.2	
16	Ukraine	4.1	
17	Turkey	4.1	
18	Belgium	4.0	
19	Romania	4.0	
20	Iceland	3.9	
21	Norway	3.9	
22	France	3.8	
23	Netherlands	3.8	
24	India	3.8	
25	Israel	3.7	
26	Thailand	3.7	
27	Trinidad and Tobago	3.7	
28	Portugal	3.7	
29	Mexico	3.6	
30	South Africa	3.6	
31	Nigeria	3.6	
32	Brazil	3.6	
33	Malaysia	3.5	
34	Poland	3.5	
35	Panama	3.5	
36	Denmark	3.5	
37	Russian Federation	3.4	
38	Spain	3.3	
39	China	3.3	
40	Indonesia	3.3	
41	New Zealand	3.2	
42	Chile	3.2	
43	Mauritius	3.2	
44	Philippines	3.2	
45	Dominican Republic	3.1	
46	Lithuania	3.1	
47	Peru	3.0	
48	Argentina	3.0	
49	Slovak Republic	3.0	
50	Australia	3.0	
51	Sri Lanka	3.0	
52	Guatemala	2.9	
53	Colombia	2.9	
54	Czech Republic	2.9	
55	Latvia	2.9	
56	Jamaica	2.8	
57	Honduras	2.8	
58	Vietnam	2.8	
59	Uruguay	2.8	
60	Bangladesh	2.8	
61	Venezuela	2.7	
62	Paraguay	2.7	
63	Estonia	2.7	
64	Jordan	2.7	
65	Hungary	2.6	
66	Costa Rica	2.5	
67	Nicaragua	2.5	
68	Greece	2.5	
69	Slovenia	2.4	
70	El Salvador	2.4	
71	Ecuador	2.3	
72	Bolivia	2.3	
73	Bulgaria	2.3	
74	Zimbabwe	2.2	
75	Egypt	2.2	

9.07 Extent of product and process collaboration

Product and process development in your country are conducted: (1 = within companies or with foreign suppliers, 7 = in collaboration with local suppliers, customers, and research institutions)

RANK	COUNTRY	SCORE
1	Finland	5.9
2	United States	5.5
3	Germany	5.4
4	Japan	5.3
5	Taiwan	5.1
6	United Kingdom	5.0
7	Austria	4.9
8	Netherlands	4.8
9	Italy	4.8
10	Switzerland	4.8
11	France	4.8
12	Iceland	4.8
13	Israel	4.7
14	Sweden	4.6
15	Denmark	4.6
16	New Zealand	4.5
17	Russian Federation	4.5
18	South Africa	4.5
19	Belgium	4.5
20	Norway	4.5
21	Australia	4.5
22	Spain	4.4
23	Brazil	4.3
24	Jamaica	4.3
25	Canada	4.3
26	Latvia	4.3
27	Korea	4.3
28	Slovak Republic	4.2
29	China	4.2
30	Czech Republic	4.2
31	Hong Kong SAR	4.2
32	Singapore	4.1
33	Ukraine	4.1
34	Estonia	4.1
35	Ireland	4.1
36	Poland	4.0
37	Chile	3.9
38	Portugal	3.9
39	Trinidad and Tobago	3.9
40	Dominican Republic	3.9
41	India	3.9
42	Hungary	3.9
43	Slovenia	3.8
44	Panama	3.7
45	Uruguay	3.7
46	Bulgaria	3.7
47	Costa Rica	3.7
48	Thailand	3.6
49	Philippines	3.6
50	Lithuania	3.6
51	Vietnam	3.6
52	Egypt	3.6
53	Guatemala	3.6
54	El Salvador	3.6
55	Nigeria	3.5
56	Colombia	3.5
57	Peru	3.5
58	Paraguay	3.4
59	Mexico	3.4
60	Greece	3.4
61	Indonesia	3.4
62	Argentina	3.3
63	Sri Lanka	3.2
64	Honduras	3.2
65	Venezuela	3.2
66	Zimbabwe	3.2
67	Jordan	3.2
68	Ecuador	3.1
69	Malaysia	3.0
70	Nicaragua	3.0
71	Mauritius	2.9
72	Bolivia	2.9
73	Romania	2.9
74	Turkey	2.8
75	Bangladesh	2.6

MEAN: 4.0

9.08 Local availability of components and parts

In your industry, components and parts are: (1 = almost always imported, 7 = almost always sourced locally)

RANK	COUNTRY	SCORE
1	Italy	5.6
2	Japan	5.5
3	China	5.4
4	India	5.3
5	United States	5.3
6	Romania	5.1
7	Brazil	5.1
8	France	5.1
9	Taiwan	5.1
10	Germany	4.8
11	Netherlands	4.8
12	Finland	4.8
13	Spain	4.7
14	Russian Federation	4.7
15	United Kingdom	4.7
16	Slovak Republic	4.6
17	Austria	4.5
18	Czech Republic	4.5
19	Sweden	4.5
20	Poland	4.3
21	Belgium	4.3
22	Canada	4.2
23	Hungary	4.1
24	South Africa	4.1
25	Ireland	4.0
26	Ukraine	4.0
27	Egypt	4.0
28	Korea	4.0
29	Switzerland	3.9
30	Norway	3.9
31	Australia	3.9
32	Denmark	3.9
33	Uruguay	3.9
34	Portugal	3.9
35	New Zealand	3.9
36	Bulgaria	3.9
37	Thailand	3.8
38	Singapore	3.8
39	Panama	3.8
40	Colombia	3.8
41	Argentina	3.7
42	Indonesia	3.6
43	Israel	3.6
44	Peru	3.6
45	Lithuania	3.6
46	Slovenia	3.5
47	Mexico	3.5
48	Malaysia	3.5
49	Turkey	3.5
50	Chile	3.5
51	Costa Rica	3.4
52	Estonia	3.3
53	Zimbabwe	3.2
54	Latvia	3.2
55	Trinidad and Tobago	3.1
56	Dominican Republic	3.1
57	Paraguay	3.1
58	Guatemala	3.0
59	Honduras	3.0
60	Greece	3.0
61	Vietnam	2.9
62	Hong Kong SAR	2.9
63	Venezuela	2.9
64	El Salvador	2.9
65	Philippines	2.7
66	Sri Lanka	2.7
67	Jamaica	2.7
68	Iceland	2.7
69	Jordan	2.6
70	Ecuador	2.5
71	Bolivia	2.5
72	Bangladesh	2.4
73	Nicaragua	2.4
74	Nigeria	2.4
75	Mauritius	2.0

MEAN: 3.8

9.09 Local availability of process machinery

In your industry, process machinery is: (1 = almost always imported,
7 = almost always sourced locally)

RANK	COUNTRY	SCORE
1	Japan	5.8
2	China	5.3
3	United States	5.2
4	Italy	5.1
5	Germany	4.9
6	Finland	4.8
7	Switzerland	4.6
8	India	4.5
9	Russian Federation	4.2
10	Romania	4.2
11	Netherlands	4.2
12	France	4.2
13	United Kingdom	4.1
14	Taiwan	4.1
15	Austria	4.1
16	Spain	4.0
17	Brazil	4.0
18	Poland	3.8
19	Ukraine	3.8
20	Korea	3.8
21	Slovak Republic	3.8
22	Czech Republic	3.8
23	Belgium	3.7
24	Sweden	3.5
25	Denmark	3.4
26	Canada	3.4
27	Bulgaria	3.3
28	South Africa	3.3
29	Uruguay	3.2
30	Norway	3.2
31	Panama	3.1
32	New Zealand	3.1
33	Lithuania	3.1
34	Israel	3.0
35	Paraguay	3.0
36	Slovenia	3.0
37	Turkey	2.9
38	Australia	2.9
39	Indonesia	2.9
40	Ireland	2.8
41	Singapore	2.8
42	Portugal	2.7
43	Thailand	2.7
44	Egypt	2.7
45	Costa Rica	2.7
46	Guatemala	2.6
47	Chile	2.5
48	Trinidad and Tobago	2.5
49	Hungary	2.5
50	Mexico	2.5
51	Colombia	2.5
52	Jamaica	2.4
53	Latvia	2.4
54	Argentina	2.4
55	Greece	2.3
56	Vietnam	2.3
57	Hong Kong SAR	2.3
58	Estonia	2.3
59	Dominican Republic	2.3
60	Iceland	2.3
61	Philippines	2.3
62	Sri Lanka	2.3
63	Honduras	2.2
64	Zimbabwe	2.1
65	Peru	2.1
66	Malaysia	2.1
67	Nicaragua	2.1
68	Venezuela	2.0
69	Ecuador	2.0
70	Bolivia	2.0
71	Jordan	2.0
72	El Salvador	1.9
73	Nigeria	1.9
74	Bangladesh	1.6
75	Mauritius	1.5

MEAN: 3.1

9.10 Local availability of specialized research and training services

In your industry, specialized research and training services are: (1 = not available in the country, 7 = available from world-class local institutions)

RANK	COUNTRY	SCORE
1	United States	6.5
2	Finland	6.1
3	United Kingdom	6.0
4	France	6.0
5	Germany	6.0
6	Switzerland	5.9
7	Israel	5.9
8	Sweden	5.7
9	Japan	5.7
10	Australia	5.7
11	Netherlands	5.6
12	Austria	5.6
13	Denmark	5.4
14	Ukraine	5.4
15	Spain	5.3
16	Russian Federation	5.3
17	Czech Republic	5.2
18	Taiwan	5.2
19	Canada	5.2
20	Belgium	5.2
21	Brazil	5.1
22	Ireland	5.1
23	Iceland	5.1
24	Norway	5.0
25	South Africa	5.0
26	Slovak Republic	5.0
27	Chile	5.0
28	Hungary	5.0
29	Poland	5.0
30	Italy	4.9
31	Estonia	4.9
32	Singapore	4.8
33	New Zealand	4.8
34	India	4.6
35	Lithuania	4.5
36	Hong Kong SAR	4.5
37	Latvia	4.5
38	Korea	4.5
39	Costa Rica	4.5
40	Panama	4.4
41	Portugal	4.4
42	Uruguay	4.4
43	Slovenia	4.3
44	Trinidad and Tobago	4.2
45	China	4.2
46	Nigeria	4.1
47	Dominican Republic	4.1
48	Jordan	4.1
49	Mexico	4.0
50	Argentina	4.0
51	Guatemala	4.0
52	Bulgaria	3.9
53	Jamaica	3.9
54	Thailand	3.9
55	Egypt	3.9
56	Greece	3.9
57	Philippines	3.8
58	El Salvador	3.8
59	Paraguay	3.8
60	Venezuela	3.8
61	Indonesia	3.7
62	Turkey	3.7
63	Colombia	3.7
64	Peru	3.6
65	Nicaragua	3.6
66	Vietnam	3.5
67	Sri Lanka	3.4
68	Romania	3.4
69	Honduras	3.4
70	Zimbabwe	3.3
71	Mauritius	3.3
72	Bolivia	3.2
73	Ecuador	3.1
74	Malaysia	3.1
75	Bangladesh	2.6

MEAN: 4.5

9.11 Local availability of information technology services

In your industry, specialized IT services are: (1 = not available in the country, 7 = available from world-class local institutions)

RANK	COUNTRY	SCORE
1	United States	6.6
2	Finland	6.4
3	Israel	6.2
4	Sweden	6.1
5	Germany	6.1
6	Australia	6.0
7	United Kingdom	6.0
8	Switzerland	6.0
9	Denmark	5.9
10	France	5.9
11	India	5.8
12	Austria	5.7
13	Ireland	5.7
14	Japan	5.7
15	Spain	5.7
16	Canada	5.6
17	Netherlands	5.6
18	Brazil	5.6
19	Iceland	5.5
20	Slovak Republic	5.5
21	Czech Republic	5.5
22	South Africa	5.4
23	Estonia	5.4
24	Taiwan	5.3
25	Belgium	5.3
26	Norway	5.3
27	Singapore	5.2
28	New Zealand	5.2
29	Hungary	5.1
30	Chile	5.1
31	Hong Kong SAR	5.1
32	Costa Rica	5.1
33	Italy	5.1
34	Latvia	5.0
35	Poland	5.0
36	Dominican Republic	4.9
37	Uruguay	4.9
38	Argentina	4.9
39	Panama	4.8
40	Peru	4.7
41	Portugal	4.7
42	Korea	4.7
43	Philippines	4.6
44	Lithuania	4.6
45	Slovenia	4.5
46	Jordan	4.5
47	Trinidad and Tobago	4.5
48	Mexico	4.5
49	Colombia	4.4
50	Russian Federation	4.4
51	El Salvador	4.3
52	Guatemala	4.3
53	China	4.3
54	Bulgaria	4.3
55	Nigeria	4.2
56	Greece	4.2
57	Ecuador	4.2
58	Jamaica	4.2
59	Ukraine	4.2
60	Turkey	4.2
61	Sri Lanka	4.2
62	Honduras	4.1
63	Egypt	4.1
64	Indonesia	4.0
65	Venezuela	4.0
66	Nicaragua	4.0
67	Malaysia	3.9
68	Thailand	3.9
69	Bolivia	3.8
70	Paraguay	3.7
71	Mauritius	3.7
72	Zimbabwe	3.5
73	Vietnam	3.4
74	Romania	2.9
75	Bangladesh	2.8

MEAN: 4.9

10.01 Nature of competitive advantage

Competitive advantage of your nation's companies in international markets is due to: (1 = low cost labor or natural resources, 7 = unique products and processes)

RANK	COUNTRY	SCORE
1	Switzerland	6.3
2	Germany	6.3
3	United States	6.2
4	Israel	6.2
5	Japan	6.2
6	Denmark	6.2
7	Finland	6.0
8	Austria	5.9
9	Netherlands	5.9
10	Belgium	5.8
11	Sweden	5.8
12	France	5.8
13	United Kingdom	5.7
14	Italy	5.6
15	Singapore	5.4
16	Taiwan	5.2
17	Hong Kong SAR	5.0
18	Norway	4.9
19	Spain	4.7
20	Ireland	4.6
21	Iceland	4.5
22	Costa Rica	4.5
23	Korea	4.4
24	Panama	4.3
25	Australia	4.1
26	Uruguay	4.1
27	Canada	4.1
28	New Zealand	4.0
29	Trinidad and Tobago	4.0
30	Jamaica	3.9
31	Slovenia	3.7
32	Argentina	3.5
33	South Africa	3.4
34	Portugal	3.4
35	Brazil	3.3
36	Colombia	3.3
37	Hungary	3.3
38	Mauritius	3.3
39	Greece	3.2
40	China	3.2
41	Peru	3.2
42	Philippines	3.2
43	Poland	3.1
44	Chile	3.1
45	Paraguay	3.1
46	Turkey	3.0
47	Latvia	3.0
48	Czech Republic	3.0
49	Mexico	2.9
50	Estonia	2.9
51	India	2.8
52	El Salvador	2.8
53	Guatemala	2.8
54	Thailand	2.7
55	Russian Federation	2.7
56	Sri Lanka	2.7
57	Nicaragua	2.7
58	Zimbabwe	2.6
59	Vietnam	2.6
60	Nigeria	2.6
61	Indonesia	2.6
62	Bulgaria	2.6
63	Venezuela	2.5
64	Jordan	2.5
65	Egypt	2.5
66	Lithuania	2.5
67	Dominican Republic	2.4
68	Slovak Republic	2.4
69	Malaysia	2.4
70	Bolivia	2.3
71	Honduras	2.3
72	Ukraine	2.3
73	Romania	2.2
74	Ecuador	2.2
75	Bangladesh	1.7

MEAN: 3.8

10.02 Value chain presence

Exporting companies in your country: (1 = are involved primarily in production, 7 = conduct not just in production but also product development, distribution, and marketing)

RANK	COUNTRY	SCORE
1	United States	6.4
2	Switzerland	6.4
3	Finland	6.3
4	Netherlands	6.3
5	United Kingdom	6.1
6	France	6.0
7	Denmark	6.0
8	Sweden	5.9
9	Germany	5.8
10	Italy	5.7
11	Hong Kong SAR	5.7
12	Japan	5.7
13	Israel	5.7
14	Austria	5.4
15	Singapore	5.4
16	Belgium	5.2
17	Taiwan	5.2
18	Spain	5.0
19	Ireland	4.8
20	Canada	4.8
21	Norway	4.7
22	Trinidad and Tobago	4.6
23	Korea	4.5
24	Russian Federation	4.4
25	Panama	4.4
26	Lithuania	4.4
27	Iceland	4.3
28	Mauritius	4.2
29	Australia	4.2
30	Slovenia	4.2
31	New Zealand	4.1
32	Egypt	4.0
33	Vietnam	4.0
34	China	3.9
35	Estonia	3.9
36	South Africa	3.8
37	Costa Rica	3.7
38	India	3.7
39	Brazil	3.7
40	Slovak Republic	3.6
41	Jamaica	3.6
42	Uruguay	3.6
43	Thailand	3.6
44	Latvia	3.6
45	Colombia	3.5
46	Czech Republic	3.5
47	Jordan	3.5
48	Chile	3.4
49	Ukraine	3.4
50	Hungary	3.4
51	Philippines	3.1
52	Greece	3.1
53	Portugal	3.1
54	Argentina	3.1
55	Dominican Republic	3.1
56	Poland	3.0
57	Ecuador	3.0
58	Nigeria	3.0
59	Indonesia	3.0
60	Sri Lanka	3.0
61	Peru	3.0
62	Paraguay	3.0
63	El Salvador	3.0
64	Bulgaria	3.0
65	Turkey	2.9
66	Guatemala	2.9
67	Malaysia	2.9
68	Bolivia	2.8
69	Nicaragua	2.8
70	Mexico	2.8
71	Honduras	2.8
72	Romania	2.7
73	Venezuela	2.7
74	Bangladesh	2.6
75	Zimbabwe	2.5

MEAN: 4.1

10.03 Extent of branding

Companies that sell internationally: (1 = sell commodities or market under foreign brands, 7 = have developed their own international brands)

RANK	COUNTRY	SCORE	MEAN: 4.2
1	Switzerland	6.4	
2	Japan	6.4	
3	Germany	6.3	
4	Finland	6.3	
5	United States	6.2	
6	United Kingdom	6.2	
7	France	6.1	
8	Italy	6.1	
9	Sweden	6.0	
10	Netherlands	5.9	
11	Denmark	5.9	
12	Austria	5.4	
13	Iceland	5.4	
14	Jamaica	5.4	
15	Spain	5.3	
16	Ireland	5.2	
17	Israel	5.1	
18	New Zealand	5.1	
19	Norway	4.9	
20	Belgium	4.8	
21	Canada	4.7	
22	Korea	4.6	
23	Singapore	4.5	
24	Russian Federation	4.4	
25	China	4.3	
26	South Africa	4.3	
27	Dominican Republic	4.2	
28	Hong Kong SAR	4.2	
29	Trinidad and Tobago	4.2	
30	Uruguay	4.1	
31	Slovenia	4.1	
32	Taiwan	4.1	
33	Romania	4.0	
34	Australia	4.0	
35	Bulgaria	4.0	
36	Colombia	4.0	
37	Jordan	3.9	
38	Chile	3.9	
39	Costa Rica	3.9	
40	Lithuania	3.9	
41	Czech Republic	3.8	
42	Panama	3.8	
43	Latvia	3.7	
44	Nigeria	3.7	
45	Vietnam	3.7	
46	Egypt	3.7	
47	Guatemala	3.7	
48	Portugal	3.6	
49	India	3.6	
50	Poland	3.5	
51	Venezuela	3.5	
52	Indonesia	3.5	
53	Mexico	3.5	
54	Hungary	3.5	
55	Sri Lanka	3.5	
56	Greece	3.5	
57	Paraguay	3.4	
58	Nicaragua	3.4	
59	Peru	3.4	
60	Bolivia	3.4	
61	Estonia	3.4	
62	Mauritius	3.4	
63	Thailand	3.3	
64	Brazil	3.3	
65	Ukraine	3.3	
66	El Salvador	3.2	
67	Philippines	3.2	
68	Turkey	3.2	
69	Ecuador	3.1	
70	Honduras	3.1	
71	Slovak Republic	3.0	
72	Argentina	2.9	
73	Zimbabwe	2.8	
74	Malaysia	2.8	
75	Bangladesh	2.5	

10.04 Capacity for innovation

Companies obtain technology: (1 = exclusively from foreign companies, 7 = by pioneering their own new products or processes)

RANK	COUNTRY	SCORE	MEAN: 3.8
1	Finland	6.4	
2	United States	5.9	
3	Japan	5.9	
4	France	5.9	
5	Sweden	5.8	
6	Israel	5.7	
7	Germany	5.7	
8	Switzerland	5.7	
9	Netherlands	5.5	
10	Denmark	5.5	
11	United Kingdom	5.1	
12	Italy	5.1	
13	Austria	5.1	
14	Belgium	4.8	
15	New Zealand	4.7	
16	Canada	4.7	
17	Norway	4.7	
18	Iceland	4.7	
19	Spain	4.7	
20	China	4.5	
21	Ireland	4.5	
22	Korea	4.4	
23	Australia	4.4	
24	Russian Federation	4.3	
25	Slovenia	4.3	
26	Singapore	4.2	
27	Taiwan	4.2	
28	South Africa	4.1	
29	Ukraine	4.1	
30	Costa Rica	3.9	
31	Trinidad and Tobago	3.8	
32	Poland	3.8	
33	Hong Kong SAR	3.7	
34	Lithuania	3.6	
35	Slovak Republic	3.6	
36	India	3.6	
37	Chile	3.6	
38	Brazil	3.6	
39	Bulgaria	3.5	
40	Colombia	3.5	
41	Paraguay	3.5	
42	Estonia	3.5	
43	Uruguay	3.4	
44	Panama	3.4	
45	Czech Republic	3.3	
46	Portugal	3.3	
47	Hungary	3.3	
48	Egypt	3.3	
49	Latvia	3.3	
50	Jamaica	3.2	
51	Ecuador	3.1	
52	Vietnam	3.1	
53	Romania	3.1	
54	Mexico	3.1	
55	Sri Lanka	3.1	
56	Indonesia	3.0	
57	Greece	3.0	
58	Dominican Republic	3.0	
59	Philippines	3.0	
60	Guatemala	2.9	
61	Venezuela	2.9	
62	Thailand	2.9	
63	Mauritius	2.8	
64	Nigeria	2.8	
65	Argentina	2.8	
66	Malaysia	2.7	
67	Peru	2.7	
68	Zimbabwe	2.6	
69	Bangladesh	2.6	
70	Bolivia	2.6	
71	Turkey	2.5	
72	El Salvador	2.5	
73	Jordan	2.5	
74	Nicaragua	2.4	
75	Honduras	2.2	

10.05 Uniqueness of product designs

Product designs are: (1 = copied or licensed from abroad, 7 = developed locally)

RANK	COUNTRY	SCORE	MEAN: 4.2
1	Finland	6.3	
2	Germany	6.0	
3	Denmark	6.0	
4	Sweden	6.0	
5	United States	5.9	
6	Japan	5.9	
7	France	5.9	
8	Italy	5.9	
9	Switzerland	5.7	
10	Netherlands	5.6	
11	Austria	5.4	
12	Israel	5.3	
13	United Kingdom	5.3	
14	Norway	5.2	
15	Belgium	5.1	
16	Spain	4.9	
17	Canada	4.9	
18	Russian Federation	4.8	
19	New Zealand	4.8	
20	Jamaica	4.8	
21	Iceland	4.8	
22	Ireland	4.6	
23	Latvia	4.6	
24	Slovenia	4.5	
25	Taiwan	4.5	
26	Estonia	4.4	
27	Australia	4.4	
28	Czech Republic	4.4	
29	Lithuania	4.4	
30	Korea	4.3	
31	South Africa	4.2	
32	China	4.1	
33	Trinidad and Tobago	4.1	
34	Singapore	4.0	
35	Bulgaria	4.0	
36	Mauritius	4.0	
37	Hong Kong SAR	4.0	
38	Poland	3.9	
39	Colombia	3.9	
40	Uruguay	3.8	
41	Brazil	3.8	
42	Costa Rica	3.8	
43	Vietnam	3.8	
44	Hungary	3.8	
45	Dominican Republic	3.7	
46	Ukraine	3.7	
47	Portugal	3.7	
48	Chile	3.7	
49	Egypt	3.7	
50	India	3.6	
51	Nigeria	3.6	
52	Ecuador	3.5	
53	Paraguay	3.5	
54	Guatemala	3.5	
55	Philippines	3.4	
56	Zimbabwe	3.4	
57	Romania	3.4	
58	Sri Lanka	3.4	
59	Slovak Republic	3.4	
60	Argentina	3.4	
61	Panama	3.3	
62	Thailand	3.3	
63	Greece	3.2	
64	Mexico	3.2	
65	Indonesia	3.2	
66	Nicaragua	3.1	
67	Jordan	3.1	
68	Bolivia	3.1	
69	Turkey	3.1	
70	El Salvador	3.0	
71	Peru	2.9	
72	Honduras	2.9	
73	Malaysia	2.9	
74	Venezuela	2.8	
75	Bangladesh	2.8	

10.06 Production process sophistication

Production processes generally: (1 = use obsolete technology, 7 = employ the world's best and most efficient technology)

RANK	COUNTRY	SCORE	MEAN: 4.7
1	Finland	6.7	
2	Germany	6.5	
3	Netherlands	6.4	
4	United States	6.4	
5	Switzerland	6.3	
6	Japan	6.3	
7	France	6.3	
8	Iceland	6.2	
9	Sweden	6.1	
10	Austria	6.1	
11	Singapore	6.0	
12	Denmark	5.9	
13	Italy	5.9	
14	Ireland	5.9	
15	Belgium	5.8	
16	United Kingdom	5.8	
17	Canada	5.8	
18	Israel	5.7	
19	Taiwan	5.6	
20	Norway	5.6	
21	Hong Kong SAR	5.4	
22	Spain	5.3	
23	Australia	5.3	
24	New Zealand	5.3	
25	Chile	5.0	
26	Mauritius	4.9	
27	Malaysia	4.9	
28	Hungary	4.8	
29	Korea	4.8	
30	Trinidad and Tobago	4.7	
31	Brazil	4.7	
32	South Africa	4.7	
33	Latvia	4.6	
34	Estonia	4.6	
35	Greece	4.5	
36	Turkey	4.4	
37	Slovenia	4.4	
38	Poland	4.4	
39	Thailand	4.4	
40	Costa Rica	4.3	
41	Portugal	4.3	
42	China	4.3	
43	Panama	4.3	
44	Philippines	4.3	
45	Mexico	4.3	
46	Egypt	4.3	
47	Jamaica	4.2	
48	Jordan	4.2	
49	Dominican Republic	4.1	
50	India	4.1	
51	Argentina	4.1	
52	Uruguay	4.1	
53	Lithuania	4.0	
54	Colombia	4.0	
55	Bangladesh	4.0	
56	Sri Lanka	3.9	
57	Indonesia	3.9	
58	Czech Republic	3.9	
59	Slovak Republic	3.8	
60	El Salvador	3.8	
61	Venezuela	3.7	
62	Peru	3.7	
63	Russian Federation	3.6	
64	Ecuador	3.6	
65	Romania	3.4	
66	Vietnam	3.4	
67	Paraguay	3.4	
68	Honduras	3.4	
69	Zimbabwe	3.4	
70	Nigeria	3.4	
71	Guatemala	3.3	
72	Ukraine	3.2	
73	Bolivia	3.0	
74	Bulgaria	2.9	
75	Nicaragua	2.8	

10.07 Extent of marketing

The extent of marketing in your country is: (1 = limited or primitive, 7 = high and among the world's most sophisticated)

RANK	COUNTRY	SCORE
1	United States	6.7
2	Netherlands	6.6
3	France	6.5
4	United Kingdom	6.4
5	Germany	6.2
6	Sweden	6.1
7	Switzerland	6.0
8	Canada	6.0
9	Hong Kong SAR	6.0
10	Australia	6.0
11	Finland	5.9
12	Italy	5.8
13	Japan	5.8
14	Austria	5.8
15	Denmark	5.8
16	Spain	5.6
17	New Zealand	5.6
18	Iceland	5.6
19	Belgium	5.5
20	South Africa	5.5
21	Ireland	5.5
22	Israel	5.4
23	Singapore	5.3
24	Norway	5.3
25	Brazil	5.3
26	Taiwan	5.3
27	Poland	5.2
28	Chile	5.0
29	Trinidad and Tobago	5.0
30	Jamaica	4.9
31	Panama	4.9
32	India	4.8
33	Argentina	4.8
34	Hungary	4.8
35	Philippines	4.7
36	Dominican Republic	4.7
37	Greece	4.7
38	Korea	4.7
39	Mexico	4.6
40	Portugal	4.5
41	Estonia	4.5
42	Venezuela	4.5
43	Thailand	4.5
44	Mauritius	4.4
45	Romania	4.4
46	Malaysia	4.4
47	Slovak Republic	4.4
48	Czech Republic	4.4
49	Uruguay	4.3
50	Slovenia	4.3
51	Costa Rica	4.3
52	Turkey	4.3
53	Indonesia	4.1
54	Sri Lanka	4.1
55	Latvia	4.1
56	Nigeria	4.0
57	Egypt	3.9
58	Peru	3.9
59	Colombia	3.9
60	Zimbabwe	3.8
61	El Salvador	3.8
62	Ecuador	3.7
63	Lithuania	3.6
64	Jordan	3.6
65	Paraguay	3.5
66	China	3.5
67	Bangladesh	3.5
68	Guatemala	3.4
69	Honduras	3.4
70	Ukraine	3.1
71	Bulgaria	3.0
72	Nicaragua	3.0
73	Russian Federation	2.9
74	Bolivia	2.9
75	Vietnam	2.8

MEAN: 4.7

10.08 Degree of customer orientation

Firms in your country: (1 = generally treat their customers badly, 7 = pay close attention to customer satisfaction)

RANK	COUNTRY	SCORE
1	United States	6.2
2	Japan	6.2
3	Switzerland	6.1
4	Finland	5.9
5	Iceland	5.9
6	Sweden	5.9
7	France	5.9
8	Austria	5.8
9	Netherlands	5.8
10	Taiwan	5.8
11	Denmark	5.8
12	Belgium	5.8
13	United Kingdom	5.8
14	Canada	5.7
15	Germany	5.6
16	Hong Kong SAR	5.6
17	Italy	5.5
18	Australia	5.5
19	Romania	5.5
20	Norway	5.5
21	New Zealand	5.4
22	Spain	5.4
23	Singapore	5.4
24	Ireland	5.3
25	Thailand	5.2
26	Estonia	5.1
27	Trinidad and Tobago	5.1
28	Korea	5.0
29	Latvia	5.0
30	Poland	5.0
31	Slovenia	4.9
32	Vietnam	4.9
33	Chile	4.9
34	Hungary	4.9
35	Ukraine	4.8
36	Brazil	4.8
37	Portugal	4.7
38	Philippines	4.7
39	Israel	4.7
40	Malaysia	4.6
41	Indonesia	4.6
42	Mauritius	4.6
43	Lithuania	4.6
44	Bangladesh	4.6
45	Jamaica	4.6
46	Greece	4.5
47	Colombia	4.5
48	Sri Lanka	4.5
49	Jordan	4.5
50	Mexico	4.5
51	Czech Republic	4.5
52	Nigeria	4.4
53	Panama	4.4
54	Uruguay	4.4
55	Turkey	4.3
56	Peru	4.3
57	India	4.3
58	China	4.2
59	Zimbabwe	4.2
60	Costa Rica	4.2
61	Russian Federation	4.2
62	Dominican Republic	4.2
63	South Africa	4.2
64	Egypt	4.1
65	El Salvador	4.1
66	Argentina	3.9
67	Bulgaria	3.8
68	Paraguay	3.8
69	Venezuela	3.6
70	Slovak Republic	3.6
71	Nicaragua	3.6
72	Guatemala	3.5
73	Honduras	3.4
74	Ecuador	3.3
75	Bolivia	2.7

MEAN: 4.8

425

10.09 Control of international distribution

International distribution and marketing from your country: (1 = takes place through foreign companies, 7 = is owned and controlled by local companies)

RANK	COUNTRY	SCORE
1	France	5.9
2	Japan	5.6
3	Netherlands	5.5
4	United States	5.5
5	Finland	5.4
6	Iceland	5.3
7	Germany	5.3
8	United Kingdom	5.2
9	Sweden	5.1
10	Denmark	5.1
11	Switzerland	5.0
12	Austria	5.0
13	Italy	4.8
14	Canada	4.8
15	Hong Kong SAR	4.7
16	Australia	4.7
17	Trinidad and Tobago	4.6
18	Korea	4.6
19	Taiwan	4.6
20	New Zealand	4.6
21	Slovenia	4.4
22	Singapore	4.4
23	Ireland	4.4
24	Belgium	4.4
25	Israel	4.4
26	South Africa	4.4
27	Norway	4.3
28	Jamaica	4.3
29	Spain	4.3
30	Chile	4.3
31	Jordan	4.2
32	Egypt	4.2
33	China	4.2
34	Indonesia	4.1
35	Mauritius	4.1
36	Brazil	4.1
37	Poland	4.0
38	Bulgaria	3.9
39	Lithuania	3.9
40	India	3.8
41	Portugal	3.8
42	Greece	3.8
43	Ukraine	3.8
44	Mexico	3.8
45	Peru	3.8
46	Panama	3.8
47	Philippines	3.7
48	Thailand	3.7
49	Argentina	3.7
50	Hungary	3.6
51	Estonia	3.6
52	Latvia	3.6
53	Uruguay	3.6
54	Colombia	3.6
55	Russian Federation	3.5
56	Sri Lanka	3.5
57	Paraguay	3.4
58	Dominican Republic	3.4
59	Turkey	3.4
60	Venezuela	3.4
61	Nigeria	3.3
62	Guatemala	3.3
63	Costa Rica	3.3
64	Bangladesh	3.3
65	Malaysia	3.3
66	Czech Republic	3.2
67	El Salvador	3.2
68	Slovak Republic	3.2
69	Zimbabwe	3.2
70	Vietnam	3.2
71	Honduras	3.1
72	Ecuador	3.1
73	Bolivia	3.0
74	Nicaragua	2.9
75	Romania	2.9

MEAN: 4.1

10.10 Extent of regional sales

Exports from your country to surrounding regions are: (1 = limited, 7 = substantial and growing)

RANK	COUNTRY	SCORE
1	Germany	6.6
2	Netherlands	6.5
3	France	6.4
4	Italy	6.4
5	Canada	6.3
6	Austria	6.3
7	Belgium	6.3
8	Finland	6.2
9	Denmark	6.2
10	Ireland	6.2
11	Singapore	6.2
12	United States	6.2
13	Switzerland	6.1
14	Japan	6.0
15	Trinidad and Tobago	6.0
16	Sweden	6.0
17	United Kingdom	5.9
18	Mexico	5.9
19	New Zealand	5.8
20	Australia	5.8
21	South Africa	5.8
22	Hong Kong SAR	5.7
23	Iceland	5.6
24	Taiwan	5.6
25	Chile	5.6
26	Spain	5.5
27	Uruguay	5.5
28	Turkey	5.5
29	Brazil	5.5
30	Norway	5.4
31	Slovenia	5.4
32	Greece	5.4
33	Portugal	5.3
34	Czech Republic	5.3
35	Malaysia	5.3
36	Korea	5.3
37	Colombia	5.3
38	Thailand	5.3
39	Egypt	5.2
40	El Salvador	5.2
41	Argentina	5.1
42	Jordan	5.1
43	Estonia	5.1
44	Indonesia	5.0
45	Costa Rica	4.9
46	Hungary	4.9
47	Latvia	4.8
48	Poland	4.8
49	China	4.7
50	Lithuania	4.6
51	Nigeria	4.5
52	India	4.4
53	Philippines	4.4
54	Vietnam	4.4
55	Sri Lanka	4.3
56	Jamaica	4.3
57	Panama	4.3
58	Guatemala	4.2
59	Slovak Republic	4.2
60	Mauritius	4.2
61	Zimbabwe	4.1
62	Bolivia	4.1
63	Ecuador	4.0
64	Bulgaria	4.0
65	Ukraine	4.0
66	Peru	3.9
67	Dominican Republic	3.9
68	Paraguay	3.8
69	Venezuela	3.8
70	Russian Federation	3.8
71	Honduras	3.5
72	Nicaragua	3.5
73	Bangladesh	3.0
74	Romania	2.5
75	Israel	2.3

MEAN: 5.0

10.11 Breadth of international markets

Exporting companies from your country sell: (1 = primarily in a few foreign markets, 7 = in virtually all international markets)

RANK	COUNTRY	SCORE
1	Germany	6.6
2	Netherlands	6.5
3	Japan	6.4
4	Finland	6.4
5	Sweden	6.3
6	Italy	6.3
7	United States	6.2
8	United Kingdom	6.1
9	Switzerland	6.0
10	France	6.0
11	Hong Kong SAR	5.9
12	Singapore	5.8
13	Denmark	5.8
14	Belgium	5.6
15	Taiwan	5.4
16	Ireland	5.4
17	Australia	5.4
18	New Zealand	5.3
19	Israel	5.3
20	Chile	5.3
21	Austria	5.2
22	Spain	5.1
23	Iceland	5.0
24	Korea	5.0
25	Turkey	4.8
26	Malaysia	4.8
27	Canada	4.8
28	Thailand	4.8
29	Norway	4.5
30	South Africa	4.5
31	Slovenia	4.4
32	Trinidad and Tobago	4.3
33	China	4.2
34	Indonesia	4.2
35	Hungary	4.1
36	Egypt	4.1
37	India	4.1
38	Poland	4.0
39	Brazil	4.0
40	Sri Lanka	3.9
41	Panama	3.9
42	Jamaica	3.8
43	Estonia	3.7
44	Czech Republic	3.7
45	Portugal	3.7
46	Costa Rica	3.7
47	Mexico	3.6
48	Russian Federation	3.6
49	Uruguay	3.6
50	Latvia	3.6
51	Jordan	3.6
52	Greece	3.5
53	Lithuania	3.5
54	Bangladesh	3.3
55	Ecuador	3.3
56	Argentina	3.3
57	Colombia	3.2
58	Vietnam	3.2
59	Philippines	3.1
60	Dominican Republic	3.1
61	Paraguay	3.0
62	Ukraine	3.0
63	Bulgaria	3.0
64	Guatemala	3.0
65	Peru	3.0
66	El Salvador	2.9
67	Zimbabwe	2.8
68	Mauritius	2.8
69	Nigeria	2.8
70	Venezuela	2.7
71	Slovak Republic	2.6
72	Romania	2.6
73	Honduras	2.4
74	Nicaragua	2.4
75	Bolivia	2.3

MEAN: 4.3

10.12 Extent of staff training

In your country, companies' general approach to human resources is to invest: (1 = little in training and development, 7 = heavily to attract, train, and retain staff)

RANK	COUNTRY	SCORE
1	Netherlands	6.1
2	Denmark	6.1
3	Sweden	6.0
4	United States	5.9
5	Switzerland	5.9
6	Finland	5.8
7	France	5.8
8	Germany	5.8
9	Japan	5.8
10	Singapore	5.7
11	Iceland	5.7
12	Belgium	5.5
13	Australia	5.4
14	Canada	5.4
15	United Kingdom	5.4
16	Norway	5.4
17	Austria	5.3
18	Ireland	5.2
19	Taiwan	4.9
20	Israel	4.8
21	New Zealand	4.8
22	Spain	4.7
23	Hong Kong SAR	4.6
24	Malaysia	4.6
25	Trinidad and Tobago	4.6
26	South Africa	4.5
27	Estonia	4.5
28	Brazil	4.3
29	Korea	4.3
30	Chile	4.3
31	Costa Rica	4.3
32	Hungary	4.3
33	Italy	4.2
34	Zimbabwe	4.2
35	Czech Republic	4.1
36	Latvia	4.1
37	Slovenia	4.1
38	Mauritius	4.1
39	Jamaica	4.0
40	Philippines	4.0
41	Indonesia	3.8
42	Panama	3.8
43	Jordan	3.8
44	Romania	3.8
45	Egypt	3.8
46	Poland	3.8
47	Portugal	3.8
48	Mexico	3.8
49	Greece	3.8
50	Thailand	3.7
51	Turkey	3.7
52	Sri Lanka	3.7
53	China	3.6
54	India	3.6
55	El Salvador	3.6
56	Uruguay	3.5
57	Dominican Republic	3.5
58	Colombia	3.5
59	Paraguay	3.5
60	Lithuania	3.4
61	Argentina	3.4
62	Nigeria	3.4
63	Vietnam	3.2
64	Slovak Republic	3.2
65	Peru	3.2
66	Guatemala	3.0
67	Venezuela	3.0
68	Nicaragua	3.0
69	Ukraine	3.0
70	Russian Federation	2.9
71	Ecuador	2.9
72	Honduras	2.7
73	Bolivia	2.5
74	Bulgaria	2.5
75	Bangladesh	2.5

MEAN: 4.2

10.13 Willingness to delegate authority

Willingness to delegate authority to subordinates is: (1 = generally low, 7 = generally high)

RANK	COUNTRY	SCORE
1	Sweden	6.4
2	Denmark	6.3
3	Finland	6.1
4	United States	5.9
5	Netherlands	5.9
6	Australia	5.8
7	Iceland	5.6
8	Canada	5.5
9	United Kingdom	5.5
10	Switzerland	5.5
11	Norway	5.4
12	Germany	5.4
13	New Zealand	5.3
14	Singapore	5.1
15	Belgium	5.1
16	Ireland	5.0
17	France	4.8
18	Austria	4.7
19	Taiwan	4.7
20	Israel	4.6
21	Hong Kong SAR	4.6
22	Estonia	4.5
23	Japan	4.4
24	Trinidad and Tobago	4.4
25	Spain	4.3
26	South Africa	4.3
27	Hungary	4.1
28	Jamaica	4.1
29	Zimbabwe	4.1
30	Brazil	4.1
31	Costa Rica	4.0
32	Malaysia	4.0
33	Ukraine	4.0
34	Slovenia	4.0
35	Korea	3.9
36	Chile	3.9
37	Philippines	3.8
38	Lithuania	3.8
39	Panama	3.8
40	Latvia	3.8
41	Egypt	3.8
42	Indonesia	3.8
43	Italy	3.7
44	El Salvador	3.7
45	Thailand	3.7
46	Mexico	3.6
47	Romania	3.6
48	Mauritius	3.5
49	India	3.5
50	Poland	3.5
51	Dominican Republic	3.4
52	Turkey	3.4
53	Sri Lanka	3.4
54	Argentina	3.4
55	Colombia	3.3
56	Jordan	3.3
57	Nicaragua	3.3
58	Portugal	3.3
59	Russian Federation	3.3
60	China	3.3
61	Greece	3.3
62	Nigeria	3.2
63	Paraguay	3.2
64	Peru	3.2
65	Slovak Republic	3.2
66	Uruguay	3.2
67	Czech Republic	3.2
68	Venezuela	3.1
69	Guatemala	3.0
70	Vietnam	2.9
71	Ecuador	2.8
72	Honduras	2.8
73	Bulgaria	2.7
74	Bolivia	2.6
75	Bangladesh	2.3

MEAN: 4.1

10.14 Extent of incentive compensation

Compensation of management in your country: (1 = is based exclusively on salary, 7 = includes substantial incentives in the form of bonuses and stock options)

RANK	COUNTRY	SCORE
1	United States	6.4
2	United Kingdom	5.8
3	Canada	5.7
4	Netherlands	5.6
5	Ireland	5.5
6	Hong Kong SAR	5.4
7	Singapore	5.4
8	Finland	5.4
9	Switzerland	5.4
10	Germany	5.4
11	Australia	5.3
12	Israel	5.3
13	Spain	5.3
14	South Africa	5.2
15	France	5.2
16	Belgium	5.2
17	Taiwan	5.2
18	Sweden	5.1
19	New Zealand	5.1
20	Italy	5.0
21	Brazil	4.8
22	Egypt	4.8
23	Zimbabwe	4.6
24	Hungary	4.6
25	Poland	4.6
26	Costa Rica	4.6
27	Austria	4.5
28	Panama	4.5
29	Estonia	4.5
30	Philippines	4.4
31	Iceland	4.4
32	Slovak Republic	4.4
33	Denmark	4.3
34	Ukraine	4.3
35	Portugal	4.3
36	Norway	4.2
37	Korea	4.2
38	El Salvador	4.2
39	Dominican Republic	4.2
40	Latvia	4.1
41	Jamaica	4.1
42	Trinidad and Tobago	4.0
43	Mexico	4.0
44	Argentina	4.0
45	Czech Republic	4.0
46	Greece	4.0
47	India	4.0
48	Honduras	3.9
49	Thailand	3.9
50	Malaysia	3.9
51	Japan	3.9
52	Slovenia	3.9
53	Nigeria	3.8
54	Uruguay	3.8
55	Peru	3.8
56	Sri Lanka	3.7
57	Guatemala	3.7
58	Nicaragua	3.7
59	Turkey	3.7
60	Mauritius	3.7
61	Indonesia	3.7
62	Chile	3.7
63	Vietnam	3.6
64	Venezuela	3.5
65	China	3.5
66	Lithuania	3.5
67	Russian Federation	3.3
68	Colombia	3.3
69	Paraguay	3.3
70	Ecuador	3.3
71	Jordan	3.2
72	Bolivia	2.9
73	Bulgaria	2.9
74	Romania	2.7
75	Bangladesh	2.4

MEAN: 4.3

10.15 Reliance on professional management

Senior management positions in your country: (1 = are often held by relatives, 7 = go only to skilled professionals)

RANK	COUNTRY	SCORE
1	Finland	6.5
2	Australia	6.3
3	Netherlands	6.3
4	United States	6.3
5	United Kingdom	6.2
6	New Zealand	6.1
7	Sweden	6.1
8	Canada	6.1
9	Denmark	6.0
10	Germany	5.9
11	Singapore	5.8
12	Switzerland	5.8
13	France	5.7
14	Norway	5.6
15	Ireland	5.5
16	Spain	5.5
17	Israel	5.5
18	Belgium	5.5
19	Romania	5.4
20	Austria	5.4
21	Estonia	5.4
22	South Africa	5.4
23	Taiwan	5.3
24	Brazil	5.3
25	Iceland	5.2
26	Japan	5.2
27	Trinidad and Tobago	5.1
28	Zimbabwe	5.1
29	Hungary	5.1
30	Malaysia	5.0
31	Hong Kong SAR	4.9
32	Chile	4.9
33	Philippines	4.8
34	Slovak Republic	4.8
35	Latvia	4.8
36	Jamaica	4.7
37	Argentina	4.7
38	Egypt	4.7
39	Poland	4.6
40	India	4.6
41	China	4.6
42	Nigeria	4.6
43	Czech Republic	4.5
44	Costa Rica	4.5
45	Italy	4.5
46	Russian Federation	4.5
47	Slovenia	4.5
48	Colombia	4.4
49	Sri Lanka	4.2
50	Portugal	4.2
51	Mexico	4.2
52	Venezuela	4.1
53	Lithuania	4.1
54	Thailand	4.0
55	Vietnam	3.9
56	Turkey	3.9
57	Peru	3.9
58	Korea	3.9
59	Jordan	3.9
60	Bangladesh	3.8
61	Ukraine	3.8
62	Mauritius	3.8
63	Uruguay	3.8
64	Greece	3.8
65	Indonesia	3.8
66	Panama	3.6
67	Guatemala	3.5
68	Dominican Republic	3.4
69	El Salvador	3.4
70	Nicaragua	3.2
71	Ecuador	3.0
72	Bulgaria	3.0
73	Honduras	3.0
74	Bolivia	3.0
75	Paraguay	2.9

MEAN: 4.7

10.16 Quality of management schools

Management schools in your country are: (1 = limited and of poor quality, 7 = among the world's best)

RANK	COUNTRY	SCORE
1	United States	6.6
2	France	6.3
3	Switzerland	6.1
4	Canada	6.1
5	Spain	5.9
6	United Kingdom	5.9
7	Netherlands	5.8
8	Sweden	5.8
9	Australia	5.8
10	Ireland	5.7
11	Finland	5.7
12	Singapore	5.7
13	Israel	5.5
14	Belgium	5.5
15	India	5.5
16	Chile	5.5
17	Costa Rica	5.4
18	Norway	5.4
19	South Africa	5.3
20	Iceland	5.3
21	Germany	5.3
22	Taiwan	5.2
23	Philippines	5.2
24	Denmark	5.2
25	New Zealand	5.1
26	Austria	5.1
27	Trinidad and Tobago	5.1
28	Hungary	5.0
29	Colombia	4.9
30	Estonia	4.9
31	Italy	4.8
32	Brazil	4.8
33	Slovenia	4.8
34	Portugal	4.7
35	Jamaica	4.7
36	Poland	4.7
37	Uruguay	4.7
38	Hong Kong SAR	4.7
39	Venezuela	4.7
40	Argentina	4.6
41	Mexico	4.6
42	Czech Republic	4.5
43	Thailand	4.4
44	Peru	4.4
45	Turkey	4.3
46	Latvia	4.2
47	Nicaragua	4.1
48	Korea	4.0
49	Japan	4.0
50	Lithuania	4.0
51	Dominican Republic	4.0
52	Nigeria	3.9
53	Russian Federation	3.8
54	Ukraine	3.8
55	Egypt	3.8
56	Jordan	3.8
57	Slovak Republic	3.8
58	Indonesia	3.8
59	Sri Lanka	3.7
60	Panama	3.7
61	Guatemala	3.6
62	China	3.6
63	Malaysia	3.5
64	Greece	3.4
65	Ecuador	3.3
66	Zimbabwe	3.2
67	Paraguay	3.2
68	Vietnam	3.2
69	El Salvador	3.1
70	Romania	3.1
71	Bolivia	3.1
72	Mauritius	3.0
73	Bulgaria	3.0
74	Bangladesh	2.8
75	Honduras	2.5

MEAN: 4.5

10.17 Efficacy of corporate boards

Corporate boards in your country are: (1 = controlled by management, 7 = powerful and represent outside shareholders)

RANK	COUNTRY	SCORE
1	Finland	5.9
2	United States	5.7
3	Sweden	5.6
4	Norway	5.5
5	Australia	5.5
6	United Kingdom	5.5
7	New Zealand	5.3
8	Switzerland	5.3
9	Germany	5.2
10	Denmark	5.2
11	Canada	5.2
12	Romania	5.1
13	South Africa	5.1
14	Spain	5.0
15	Netherlands	5.0
16	France	4.9
17	Singapore	4.8
18	Estonia	4.8
19	Iceland	4.8
20	Austria	4.8
21	Belgium	4.8
22	Taiwan	4.8
23	Hungary	4.7
24	Poland	4.7
25	Israel	4.7
26	Costa Rica	4.6
27	Ireland	4.6
28	Chile	4.5
29	Jamaica	4.5
30	Italy	4.4
31	Ukraine	4.3
32	Nigeria	4.2
33	Colombia	4.2
34	Zimbabwe	4.1
35	Vietnam	4.1
36	Argentina	4.0
37	Slovenia	4.0
38	Panama	4.0
39	Russian Federation	3.9
40	Hong Kong SAR	3.9
41	Thailand	3.9
42	Peru	3.8
43	Philippines	3.8
44	Latvia	3.8
45	Jordan	3.8
46	Slovak Republic	3.8
47	Uruguay	3.8
48	Lithuania	3.8
49	Trinidad and Tobago	3.8
50	Dominican Republic	3.7
51	Malaysia	3.7
52	Egypt	3.7
53	Portugal	3.6
54	India	3.5
55	Sri Lanka	3.5
56	Brazil	3.5
57	Paraguay	3.5
58	Nicaragua	3.5
59	Ecuador	3.5
60	El Salvador	3.5
61	Korea	3.5
62	Mexico	3.5
63	Indonesia	3.3
64	Venezuela	3.3
65	Bulgaria	3.3
66	Bolivia	3.3
67	China	3.3
68	Guatemala	3.3
69	Czech Republic	3.2
70	Greece	3.1
71	Japan	2.9
72	Turkey	2.8
73	Mauritius	2.6
74	Honduras	2.5
75	Bangladesh	2.2

MEAN: 4.1

10.18 Internet effects on business

To what extent has the Internet improved your firm's ability to coordinate with customers and suppliers to reduce inventory costs? (1 = no change, 7 = huge improvement)

RANK	COUNTRY	SCORE
1	Finland	5.2
2	United States	5.0
3	Germany	4.8
4	Taiwan	4.7
5	Singapore	4.6
6	Korea	4.5
7	Canada	4.5
8	Estonia	4.5
9	Iceland	4.5
10	France	4.4
11	Hong Kong SAR	4.3
12	Netherlands	4.3
13	Spain	4.2
14	Czech Republic	4.2
15	United Kingdom	4.2
16	South Africa	4.1
17	Japan	4.1
18	Panama	4.1
19	Ukraine	4.1
20	Austria	4.1
21	Ireland	4.0
22	Belgium	4.0
23	Sweden	4.0
24	Australia	4.0
25	Switzerland	4.0
26	New Zealand	3.9
27	Italy	3.9
28	Chile	3.8
29	Bolivia	3.8
30	Slovenia	3.8
31	Vietnam	3.8
32	Dominican Republic	3.8
33	Poland	3.7
34	Norway	3.7
35	Thailand	3.7
36	El Salvador	3.7
37	Mexico	3.7
38	Indonesia	3.7
39	Costa Rica	3.7
40	Peru	3.7
41	Honduras	3.6
42	Jamaica	3.6
43	Slovak Republic	3.6
44	Brazil	3.6
45	Romania	3.6
46	Malaysia	3.6
47	Jordan	3.6
48	Sri Lanka	3.6
49	Argentina	3.5
50	Ecuador	3.5
51	Latvia	3.5
52	Nicaragua	3.5
53	Denmark	3.5
54	Bangladesh	3.4
55	Portugal	3.4
56	Uruguay	3.4
57	Philippines	3.4
58	Israel	3.4
59	Venezuela	3.3
60	China	3.3
61	Egypt	3.3
62	Nigeria	3.3
63	Hungary	3.3
64	Guatemala	3.2
65	Lithuania	3.2
66	India	3.2
67	Colombia	3.2
68	Paraguay	3.1
69	Bulgaria	3.1
70	Trinidad and Tobago	3.1
71	Turkey	2.9
72	Mauritius	2.9
73	Russian Federation	2.8
74	Zimbabwe	2.8
75	Greece	2.5

MEAN: 3.7

10.19 Hiring and firing practices

Hiring and firing of workers is: (1 = impeded by regulations, 7 = flexibly determined by employers)

RANK	COUNTRY	SCORE
1	Romania	6.3
2	Hong Kong SAR	5.5
3	Peru	5.3
4	Singapore	5.3
5	Nigeria	5.3
6	United States	5.0
7	Denmark	4.9
8	Ukraine	4.8
9	Nicaragua	4.7
10	Russian Federation	4.7
11	Iceland	4.6
12	Trinidad and Tobago	4.5
13	Switzerland	4.4
14	Chile	4.3
15	Hungary	4.3
16	Israel	4.3
17	Turkey	4.2
18	Czech Republic	4.2
19	Argentina	4.2
20	Brazil	4.2
21	Guatemala	4.2
22	Dominican Republic	4.1
23	China	4.1
24	Canada	4.1
25	Costa Rica	4.0
26	Bangladesh	4.0
27	Vietnam	3.9
28	Bolivia	3.9
29	United Kingdom	3.9
30	El Salvador	3.9
31	Jamaica	3.9
32	Paraguay	3.8
33	Korea	3.8
34	Thailand	3.8
35	Taiwan	3.8
36	Estonia	3.7
37	Venezuela	3.7
38	Honduras	3.7
39	Jordan	3.7
40	Bulgaria	3.6
41	Japan	3.5
42	Colombia	3.5
43	Panama	3.5
44	Uruguay	3.5
45	Mexico	3.5
46	Malaysia	3.4
47	Latvia	3.4
48	Ireland	3.3
49	Spain	3.2
50	Ecuador	3.1
51	Philippines	3.0
52	Finland	2.9
53	Indonesia	2.9
54	Belgium	2.9
55	Australia	2.8
56	New Zealand	2.8
57	Egypt	2.8
58	Austria	2.8
59	Slovak Republic	2.8
60	Sri Lanka	2.7
61	Portugal	2.7
62	Lithuania	2.6
63	Poland	2.6
64	Netherlands	2.5
65	Greece	2.4
66	Slovenia	2.4
67	Sweden	2.3
68	Italy	2.3
69	South Africa	2.2
70	Norway	2.2
71	Mauritius	2.2
72	Germany	2.1
73	India	2.0
74	France	2.0
75	Zimbabwe	1.9

MEAN: 3.6

10.20 Employment rules

Companies can cut back workers' hours or get overtime labor without too much extra cost in your country. (1 = No, 7 = Yes)

RANK	COUNTRY	SCORE
1	Romania	5.6
2	Hong Kong SAR	5.1
3	Singapore	4.9
4	United States	4.9
5	Ukraine	4.9
6	Nigeria	4.7
7	Malaysia	4.6
8	Czech Republic	4.6
9	Iceland	4.5
10	Bangladesh	4.5
11	Peru	4.5
12	United Kingdom	4.5
13	Hungary	4.4
14	Thailand	4.4
15	Turkey	4.4
16	Canada	4.4
17	China	4.4
18	Trinidad and Tobago	4.3
19	Latvia	4.3
20	Denmark	4.2
21	Israel	4.1
22	Jordan	4.1
23	Switzerland	4.1
24	Korea	4.1
25	Bulgaria	4.1
26	Estonia	4.0
27	Australia	3.9
28	Argentina	3.8
29	Lithuania	3.7
30	Paraguay	3.7
31	Indonesia	3.7
32	New Zealand	3.6
33	Sri Lanka	3.6
34	Japan	3.5
35	Ireland	3.5
36	Vietnam	3.5
37	Russian Federation	3.5
38	Philippines	3.5
39	Netherlands	3.5
40	Egypt	3.4
41	Slovak Republic	3.4
42	Zimbabwe	3.4
43	Chile	3.3
44	Spain	3.3
45	Taiwan	3.3
46	Sweden	3.3
47	Bolivia	3.3
48	Austria	3.2
49	Jamaica	3.2
50	Nicaragua	3.1
51	India	3.1
52	Colombia	3.1
53	Finland	3.1
54	Mexico	3.0
55	Portugal	3.0
56	Mauritius	3.0
57	Slovenia	3.0
58	Poland	2.9
59	South Africa	2.9
60	Germany	2.9
61	Venezuela	2.8
62	Brazil	2.8
63	Norway	2.8
64	Belgium	2.7
65	Guatemala	2.6
66	Honduras	2.6
67	Dominican Republic	2.5
68	El Salvador	2.5
69	Greece	2.5
70	Ecuador	2.5
71	Uruguay	2.5
72	Italy	2.3
73	Panama	2.2
74	France	2.1
75	Costa Rica	1.9

MEAN: 3.6

431

10.21 Cooperation in labor-employer relations

Labor-employer relations in your country are: (1 = generally confrontational, 7 = generally cooperative)

RANK	COUNTRY	SCORE
		MEAN: 4.6
1	Singapore	6.4
2	Switzerland	6.2
3	Netherlands	6.1
4	Japan	6.1
5	Denmark	5.9
6	Sweden	5.8
7	Hong Kong SAR	5.8
8	Norway	5.8
9	Austria	5.8
10	Malaysia	5.7
11	Finland	5.6
12	Costa Rica	5.5
13	United Kingdom	5.4
14	Germany	5.3
15	Mauritius	5.2
16	Czech Republic	5.2
17	Iceland	5.2
18	Vietnam	5.1
19	Egypt	5.1
20	Estonia	5.0
21	United States	5.0
22	Hungary	5.0
23	El Salvador	5.0
24	Taiwan	4.9
25	New Zealand	4.9
26	Jordan	4.9
27	Ukraine	4.9
28	Dominican Republic	4.8
29	Thailand	4.8
30	Romania	4.8
31	Ireland	4.7
32	Peru	4.7
33	Belgium	4.7
34	Ecuador	4.7
35	Panama	4.7
36	Israel	4.7
37	Honduras	4.7
38	Spain	4.6
39	Chile	4.6
40	Portugal	4.5
41	Philippines	4.5
42	Mexico	4.5
43	Nicaragua	4.5
44	Latvia	4.5
45	China	4.5
46	Canada	4.4
47	Italy	4.4
48	Russian Federation	4.4
49	Colombia	4.4
50	Brazil	4.3
51	Australia	4.3
52	Argentina	4.3
53	Bangladesh	4.2
54	Zimbabwe	4.2
55	Slovenia	4.2
56	Guatemala	4.1
57	Greece	4.1
58	Trinidad and Tobago	4.1
59	Turkey	4.1
60	Indonesia	4.0
61	Lithuania	4.0
62	Bolivia	4.0
63	Jamaica	3.9
64	India	3.8
65	Poland	3.7
66	Bulgaria	3.7
67	Sri Lanka	3.7
68	Paraguay	3.7
69	Uruguay	3.6
70	Slovak Republic	3.6
71	South Africa	3.5
72	Korea	3.5
73	Nigeria	3.5
74	Venezuela	3.3
75	France	2.8

10.22 Union contributions to productivity

Labor unions in your country: (1 = prevent productivity improvements, 7 = contribute to productivity improvements)

RANK	COUNTRY	SCORE
		MEAN: 3.8
1	Singapore	5.9
2	Sweden	5.6
3	Japan	5.3
4	Finland	5.3
5	Switzerland	5.2
6	Netherlands	5.2
7	Norway	5.1
8	Iceland	5.1
9	Nigeria	4.9
10	Czech Republic	4.8
11	Austria	4.8
12	Vietnam	4.7
13	Jordan	4.7
14	China	4.7
15	Malaysia	4.6
16	Hong Kong SAR	4.6
17	United Kingdom	4.6
18	Denmark	4.6
19	Hungary	4.5
20	Zimbabwe	4.5
21	Romania	4.5
22	Italy	4.4
23	Taiwan	4.3
24	Ireland	4.3
25	Egypt	4.2
26	Belgium	4.2
27	Thailand	4.1
28	Ukraine	4.1
29	Germany	4.1
30	Estonia	4.0
31	New Zealand	3.9
32	Spain	3.9
33	Canada	3.9
34	Lithuania	3.8
35	Latvia	3.8
36	Peru	3.8
37	Slovenia	3.8
38	Turkey	3.8
39	Russian Federation	3.7
40	Trinidad and Tobago	3.7
41	Korea	3.7
42	Australia	3.7
43	United States	3.6
44	Philippines	3.6
45	Chile	3.6
46	Indonesia	3.5
47	Jamaica	3.5
48	Bulgaria	3.5
49	Israel	3.5
50	Mauritius	3.5
51	Portugal	3.4
52	Brazil	3.4
53	South Africa	3.3
54	Greece	3.3
55	India	3.3
56	Venezuela	3.2
57	Paraguay	3.1
58	Nicaragua	3.0
59	Dominican Republic	3.0
60	Mexico	2.9
61	Uruguay	2.9
62	Argentina	2.9
63	Panama	2.9
64	Sri Lanka	2.9
65	Bolivia	2.8
66	Poland	2.8
67	Colombia	2.8
68	France	2.6
69	Bangladesh	2.6
70	Costa Rica	2.5
71	El Salvador	2.4
72	Guatemala	2.2
73	Honduras	2.2
74	Ecuador	2.1
75	Slovak Republic	1.0

10.23 Pay and productivity

Pay in your country is: (1 = not related to worker productivity, 7 = strongly related to productivity)

RANK	COUNTRY	SCORE
1	Singapore	5.9
2	Hong Kong SAR	5.7
3	Vietnam	5.6
4	United States	5.4
5	United Kingdom	5.4
6	Taiwan	5.2
7	Estonia	5.1
8	Ukraine	5.1
9	Switzerland	5.0
10	Iceland	4.9
11	China	4.8
12	Latvia	4.8
13	Hungary	4.8
14	Russian Federation	4.7
15	Canada	4.7
16	Czech Republic	4.6
17	Lithuania	4.6
18	New Zealand	4.6
19	Malaysia	4.5
20	Chile	4.5
21	Finland	4.4
22	Denmark	4.4
23	Poland	4.3
24	Bulgaria	4.3
25	Australia	4.3
26	Ireland	4.3
27	Romania	4.2
28	Japan	4.2
29	Israel	4.2
30	Italy	4.2
31	Slovak Republic	4.2
32	Sweden	4.2
33	Trinidad and Tobago	4.2
34	Korea	4.2
35	El Salvador	4.2
36	Jordan	4.1
37	Thailand	4.1
38	Austria	4.1
39	Slovenia	4.1
40	Netherlands	4.1
41	Germany	4.1
42	Spain	4.0
43	Belgium	4.0
44	Philippines	3.9
45	Costa Rica	3.9
46	Panama	3.9
47	Brazil	3.8
48	Egypt	3.8
49	Dominican Republic	3.8
50	Norway	3.8
51	Mexico	3.7
52	France	3.6
53	Nicaragua	3.6
54	Nigeria	3.6
55	Turkey	3.6
56	Jamaica	3.6
57	Peru	3.5
58	India	3.5
59	Uruguay	3.5
60	Portugal	3.4
61	Argentina	3.4
62	South Africa	3.4
63	Greece	3.3
64	Sri Lanka	3.3
65	Guatemala	3.2
66	Bolivia	3.1
67	Indonesia	3.1
68	Paraguay	3.0
69	Zimbabwe	3.0
70	Colombia	2.9
71	Honduras	2.9
72	Bangladesh	2.8
73	Venezuela	2.7
74	Mauritius	2.6
75	Ecuador	2.4

MEAN: 4.1

Section XI: Environmental Policy

11.01 Air pollution regulations

The stringency of air pollution regulation in your country is: (1 = lax compared with most other countries, 7 = among the world's most stringent)

RANK	COUNTRY	SCORE
1	Germany	6.8
2	Netherlands	6.5
3	Sweden	6.5
4	Denmark	6.5
5	Finland	6.5
6	Austria	6.5
7	Switzerland	6.4
8	United States	6.2
9	Australia	6.0
10	Norway	5.9
11	Singapore	5.9
12	Iceland	5.9
13	Belgium	5.8
14	Italy	5.8
15	Japan	5.8
16	France	5.8
17	Canada	5.8
18	United Kingdom	5.7
19	New Zealand	5.5
20	Taiwan	5.3
21	Ireland	4.9
22	Czech Republic	4.8
23	Slovenia	4.7
24	Spain	4.6
25	Slovak Republic	4.6
26	Hungary	4.5
27	Portugal	4.5
28	Israel	4.4
29	Lithuania	4.3
30	Poland	4.3
31	Estonia	4.3
32	Korea	4.1
33	Latvia	4.1
34	Chile	4.0
35	Brazil	3.9
36	South Africa	3.8
37	Greece	3.8
38	Hong Kong SAR	3.8
39	Uruguay	3.7
40	Malaysia	3.7
41	Mexico	3.7
42	Jordan	3.6
43	Colombia	3.6
44	Romania	3.6
45	Costa Rica	3.6
46	Thailand	3.4
47	Turkey	3.4
48	Jamaica	3.4
49	Bulgaria	3.3
50	India	3.2
51	Mauritius	3.2
52	China	3.2
53	Russian Federation	3.2
54	Venezuela	3.1
55	Panama	3.1
56	Indonesia	3.0
57	Egypt	2.9
58	Zimbabwe	2.9
59	Argentina	2.8
60	Bolivia	2.7
61	Sri Lanka	2.7
62	Ukraine	2.6
63	Peru	2.6
64	Trinidad and Tobago	2.6
65	Philippines	2.5
66	Nicaragua	2.4
67	Dominican Republic	2.3
68	Honduras	2.3
69	Nigeria	2.2
70	Ecuador	2.2
71	Guatemala	2.2
72	Paraguay	2.1
73	Vietnam	2.1
74	El Salvador	1.9
75	Bangladesh	1.8

MEAN: 4.1

11.02 Water pollution regulations

The stringency of water pollution regulation in your country is: (1 = lax compared with most other countries, 7 = among the world's most stringent)

RANK	COUNTRY	SCORE
1	Finland	6.8
2	Germany	6.8
3	Austria	6.7
4	Denmark	6.7
5	Switzerland	6.7
6	Sweden	6.6
7	Netherlands	6.5
8	Iceland	6.4
9	United States	6.3
10	Australia	6.2
11	France	6.1
12	Singapore	6.1
13	United Kingdom	6.1
14	Belgium	6.0
15	Canada	6.0
16	Japan	6.0
17	New Zealand	6.0
18	Norway	5.9
19	Italy	5.5
20	Taiwan	5.2
21	Ireland	5.2
22	Spain	5.1
23	Czech Republic	4.9
24	Slovenia	4.7
25	Uruguay	4.6
26	Israel	4.6
27	Estonia	4.6
28	Portugal	4.5
29	Hungary	4.5
30	Slovak Republic	4.4
31	Lithuania	4.3
32	Poland	4.3
33	Jamaica	4.3
34	Chile	4.2
35	Korea	4.2
36	Latvia	4.1
37	Hong Kong SAR	4.1
38	South Africa	4.1
39	Jordan	4.0
40	Costa Rica	4.0
41	Greece	4.0
42	Malaysia	4.0
43	Brazil	3.8
44	Colombia	3.7
45	Panama	3.7
46	Thailand	3.7
47	Egypt	3.7
48	Romania	3.6
49	Mauritius	3.5
50	Indonesia	3.5
51	Mexico	3.5
52	Venezuela	3.5
53	Bulgaria	3.3
54	Turkey	3.3
55	China	3.2
56	Russian Federation	3.2
57	India	3.1
58	Sri Lanka	3.1
59	Argentina	3.0
60	Zimbabwe	2.9
61	Bolivia	2.9
62	Peru	2.8
63	Ukraine	2.6
64	Trinidad and Tobago	2.5
65	Philippines	2.5
66	Dominican Republic	2.4
67	Nicaragua	2.4
68	Honduras	2.4
69	Ecuador	2.3
70	Nigeria	2.2
71	Vietnam	2.2
72	Guatemala	2.1
73	Paraguay	2.1
74	El Salvador	2.0
75	Bangladesh	1.7

MEAN: 4.2

435

11.03 Toxic waste disposal regulations

The stringency of regulation concerning toxic waste disposal in your country is: (1 = lax compared to most other countries, 7 = among the world's most stringent)

RANK	COUNTRY	SCORE
1	Finland	6.9
2	Netherlands	6.8
3	Germany	6.8
4	Switzerland	6.7
5	Denmark	6.7
6	Sweden	6.6
7	Austria	6.6
8	Australia	6.4
9	United States	6.4
10	Iceland	6.3
11	Singapore	6.3
12	Belgium	6.2
13	Norway	6.1
14	Canada	6.1
15	United Kingdom	6.1
16	France	6.0
17	New Zealand	5.9
18	Japan	5.8
19	Italy	5.6
20	Taiwan	5.1
21	Spain	5.1
22	Slovak Republic	5.0
23	Ireland	5.0
24	Czech Republic	4.8
25	Slovenia	4.7
26	Estonia	4.7
27	Hungary	4.7
28	Portugal	4.6
29	Israel	4.5
30	Hong Kong SAR	4.3
31	Poland	4.3
32	Korea	4.3
33	Malaysia	4.3
34	South Africa	4.2
35	Lithuania	4.2
36	Jordan	4.2
37	Uruguay	4.1
38	Chile	4.0
39	Latvia	4.0
40	Greece	4.0
41	Egypt	3.8
42	Brazil	3.8
43	Jamaica	3.7
44	Costa Rica	3.7
45	Indonesia	3.7
46	Venezuela	3.6
47	Mexico	3.6
48	Thailand	3.6
49	Bulgaria	3.5
50	India	3.5
51	Turkey	3.4
52	Colombia	3.4
53	Mauritius	3.4
54	Romania	3.3
55	Zimbabwe	3.3
56	China	3.2
57	Sri Lanka	3.1
58	Argentina	3.1
59	Russian Federation	3.0
60	Panama	2.8
61	Ukraine	2.7
62	Philippines	2.6
63	Peru	2.5
64	Nigeria	2.5
65	Bolivia	2.4
66	Dominican Republic	2.4
67	Trinidad and Tobago	2.4
68	Honduras	2.4
69	Nicaragua	2.3
70	Vietnam	2.2
71	El Salvador	2.1
72	Ecuador	2.1
73	Paraguay	2.0
74	Guatemala	2.0
75	Bangladesh	1.8

MEAN: 4.2

11.04 Chemical waste regulations

In your country, the stringency of regulation concerning chemicals used in manufacturing is: (1 = lax compared with most other countries, 7 = among the world's most stringent)

RANK	COUNTRY	SCORE
1	Finland	6.9
2	Netherlands	6.7
3	Denmark	6.6
4	Germany	6.6
5	Sweden	6.5
6	Switzerland	6.5
7	Austria	6.4
8	United States	6.4
9	Norway	6.3
10	Australia	6.2
11	France	6.2
12	Iceland	6.2
13	Singapore	6.1
14	Canada	6.1
15	United Kingdom	6.1
16	Belgium	6.0
17	New Zealand	5.9
18	Japan	5.7
19	Italy	5.6
20	Ireland	5.2
21	Taiwan	5.1
22	Spain	5.0
23	Czech Republic	4.8
24	Slovenia	4.7
25	Hungary	4.6
26	Slovak Republic	4.6
27	Estonia	4.6
28	Malaysia	4.5
29	Poland	4.4
30	Hong Kong SAR	4.3
31	Korea	4.3
32	Israel	4.3
33	Portugal	4.3
34	Latvia	4.2
35	South Africa	4.1
36	Lithuania	4.1
37	Greece	4.1
38	Chile	4.0
39	Jordan	4.0
40	Uruguay	4.0
41	Brazil	4.0
42	Indonesia	3.9
43	Egypt	3.8
44	Costa Rica	3.8
45	Jamaica	3.8
46	Thailand	3.5
47	Mexico	3.5
48	Bulgaria	3.5
49	Colombia	3.5
50	Mauritius	3.4
51	India	3.4
52	China	3.3
53	Romania	3.2
54	Sri Lanka	3.2
55	Venezuela	3.2
56	Turkey	3.2
57	Zimbabwe	3.2
58	Russian Federation	3.1
59	Argentina	3.1
60	Panama	2.9
61	Ukraine	2.7
62	Philippines	2.7
63	Dominican Republic	2.7
64	Trinidad and Tobago	2.6
65	Ecuador	2.5
66	Peru	2.5
67	Bolivia	2.5
68	Honduras	2.5
69	Nigeria	2.4
70	Nicaragua	2.4
71	El Salvador	2.4
72	Paraguay	2.1
73	Vietnam	2.1
74	Guatemala	2.0
75	Bangladesh	1.9

MEAN: 4.2

11.05 Regulation of Genetically modified organisms (GMOs)

The stringency of regulation concerning genetically modified organisms in your country is: (1 = lax compared with most other countries, 7 = among the world's most stringent)

RANK	COUNTRY	SCORE
1	Netherlands	6.5
2	Germany	6.5
3	Denmark	6.5
4	Austria	6.5
5	France	6.3
6	Norway	6.1
7	Finland	6.1
8	Switzerland	6.0
9	Sweden	5.9
10	Italy	5.8
11	United Kingdom	5.6
12	Japan	5.6
13	New Zealand	5.6
14	Singapore	5.5
15	Belgium	5.5
16	Australia	5.5
17	Canada	5.4
18	Ireland	5.4
19	United States	5.2
20	Iceland	5.2
21	Spain	4.6
22	Taiwan	4.5
23	Czech Republic	4.4
24	Slovenia	4.4
25	Israel	4.3
26	Hungary	4.2
27	Brazil	4.2
28	Korea	4.1
29	Estonia	4.1
30	Uruguay	3.9
31	Lithuania	3.9
32	Egypt	3.8
33	Portugal	3.8
34	Slovak Republic	3.8
35	China	3.7
36	Bulgaria	3.7
37	South Africa	3.6
38	Hong Kong SAR	3.6
39	Greece	3.6
40	Jordan	3.5
41	Poland	3.5
42	Malaysia	3.5
43	Chile	3.5
44	Costa Rica	3.4
45	Latvia	3.3
46	Sri Lanka	3.2
47	Thailand	3.2
48	Indonesia	3.2
49	Mexico	3.1
50	Panama	3.1
51	Romania	3.1
52	Russian Federation	3.1
53	Ukraine	3.0
54	India	3.0
55	Turkey	2.9
56	Colombia	2.9
57	Jamaica	2.9
58	Argentina	2.8
59	Philippines	2.8
60	Zimbabwe	2.8
61	Trinidad and Tobago	2.7
62	Mauritius	2.6
63	Dominican Republic	2.5
64	Honduras	2.4
65	Nigeria	2.3
66	Nicaragua	2.3
67	Venezuela	2.3
68	El Salvador	2.1
69	Bolivia	2.1
70	Peru	2.1
71	Paraguay	2.1
72	Vietnam	2.1
73	Guatemala	1.9
74	Ecuador	1.9
75	Bangladesh	1.9

MEAN: 3.9

11.06 Stringency of environmental regulations

The stringency of overall environmental regulation in your country is: (1 = lax compared with most other countries, 7 = among the world's most stringent)

RANK	COUNTRY	SCORE
1	Netherlands	6.7
2	Germany	6.7
3	Denmark	6.7
4	Austria	6.6
5	Sweden	6.5
6	Finland	6.5
7	Switzerland	6.5
8	Norway	6.2
9	Iceland	6.2
10	France	6.2
11	Australia	6.2
12	United States	6.1
13	Belgium	6.1
14	Singapore	6.0
15	Canada	5.9
16	New Zealand	5.9
17	United Kingdom	5.8
18	Italy	5.7
19	Japan	5.7
20	Ireland	5.2
21	Taiwan	5.2
22	Czech Republic	5.1
23	Spain	4.9
24	Slovenia	4.8
25	Slovak Republic	4.8
26	Estonia	4.7
27	Hungary	4.6
28	Portugal	4.5
29	Israel	4.4
30	Latvia	4.4
31	Korea	4.2
32	Chile	4.2
33	Lithuania	4.2
34	Poland	4.2
35	Brazil	4.2
36	Turkey	4.1
37	South Africa	4.1
38	Jordan	4.1
39	Hong Kong SAR	4.1
40	Malaysia	4.1
41	Egypt	4.0
42	Costa Rica	4.0
43	Uruguay	4.0
44	Jamaica	3.9
45	Thailand	3.8
46	Greece	3.7
47	Indonesia	3.7
48	Colombia	3.7
49	Mexico	3.6
50	Bulgaria	3.5
51	Romania	3.4
52	China	3.4
53	India	3.4
54	Panama	3.3
55	Mauritius	3.3
56	Sri Lanka	3.3
57	Venezuela	3.2
58	Russian Federation	3.2
59	Argentina	3.1
60	Zimbabwe	3.1
61	Ukraine	3.0
62	Bolivia	2.9
63	Philippines	2.8
64	Trinidad and Tobago	2.6
65	Dominican Republic	2.6
66	Nigeria	2.5
67	Peru	2.5
68	Honduras	2.5
69	El Salvador	2.4
70	Ecuador	2.4
71	Nicaragua	2.4
72	Vietnam	2.3
73	Paraguay	2.2
74	Guatemala	2.2
75	Bangladesh	1.9

MEAN: 4.3

11.07 Subsidies for energy or materials

Government subsidies in your country: (1 = encourage inefficient use of energy or materials, 7 = are not provided for energy or materials usage)

RANK	COUNTRY	SCORE
1	Finland	5.9
2	France	5.9
3	New Zealand	5.7
4	Austria	5.6
5	Chile	5.6
6	Netherlands	5.5
7	Belgium	5.5
8	Sweden	5.4
9	Singapore	5.4
10	Bolivia	5.3
11	Germany	5.3
12	Switzerland	5.3
13	Hong Kong SAR	5.2
14	Canada	5.1
15	Italy	5.0
16	Iceland	5.0
17	Australia	5.0
18	Denmark	5.0
19	Mauritius	4.9
20	United Kingdom	4.9
21	United States	4.9
22	Peru	4.9
23	Panama	4.8
24	Argentina	4.8
25	Japan	4.8
26	Spain	4.7
27	Uruguay	4.7
28	Hungary	4.7
29	Ireland	4.6
30	Taiwan	4.6
31	Israel	4.6
32	South Africa	4.6
33	Jamaica	4.6
34	Norway	4.5
35	Brazil	4.5
36	El Salvador	4.5
37	Slovenia	4.5
38	Lithuania	4.5
39	Estonia	4.4
40	Costa Rica	4.4
41	Colombia	4.4
42	Turkey	4.4
43	Portugal	4.4
44	Czech Republic	4.4
45	Bulgaria	4.3
46	Poland	4.3
47	Latvia	4.3
48	Trinidad and Tobago	4.3
49	Vietnam	4.3
50	Jordan	4.2
51	China	4.2
52	Nicaragua	4.1
53	Greece	4.1
54	Korea	4.1
55	Zimbabwe	4.1
56	Egypt	4.0
57	Thailand	4.0
58	Philippines	4.0
59	Sri Lanka	3.9
60	Mexico	3.8
61	Honduras	3.8
62	Bangladesh	3.8
63	Venezuela	3.8
64	Malaysia	3.7
65	Russian Federation	3.7
66	India	3.7
67	Guatemala	3.7
68	Dominican Republic	3.7
69	Slovak Republic	3.4
70	Ukraine	3.3
71	Indonesia	3.3
72	Ecuador	2.9
73	Nigeria	2.9
74	Paraguay	2.8
75	Romania	2.6

MEAN: 4.4

11.08 Leadership in environmental policy

Compared with other countries, your country normally enacts environmental regulations: (1 = much later, 7 = ahead of most others)

RANK	COUNTRY	SCORE
1	Denmark	6.6
2	Sweden	6.5
3	Germany	6.5
4	Austria	6.4
5	Netherlands	6.4
6	Finland	6.3
7	Switzerland	6.0
8	Norway	5.9
9	United States	5.9
10	France	5.6
11	New Zealand	5.6
12	Canada	5.5
13	Belgium	5.4
14	United Kingdom	5.3
15	Japan	5.2
16	Australia	5.2
17	Singapore	5.2
18	Iceland	5.0
19	Italy	5.0
20	Taiwan	4.3
21	Spain	4.3
22	Latvia	4.2
23	Hungary	4.1
24	Ireland	4.1
25	Costa Rica	4.0
26	Czech Republic	4.0
27	Slovenia	4.0
28	Portugal	4.0
29	Jordan	3.9
30	Korea	3.9
31	Chile	3.9
32	Brazil	3.9
33	Hong Kong SAR	3.8
34	Poland	3.8
35	Slovak Republic	3.8
36	Malaysia	3.8
37	Estonia	3.8
38	Lithuania	3.7
39	Israel	3.7
40	Thailand	3.6
41	Jamaica	3.5
42	South Africa	3.5
43	Uruguay	3.4
44	Turkey	3.4
45	Egypt	3.3
46	India	3.3
47	Mexico	3.3
48	Romania	3.2
49	Greece	3.2
50	Indonesia	3.1
51	Trinidad and Tobago	2.9
52	Panama	2.9
53	Venezuela	2.9
54	Argentina	2.9
55	Mauritius	2.8
56	Colombia	2.8
57	China	2.8
58	Sri Lanka	2.8
59	Zimbabwe	2.8
60	Philippines	2.8
61	Bulgaria	2.7
62	Russian Federation	2.7
63	Ukraine	2.6
64	Nigeria	2.6
65	Bolivia	2.4
66	Peru	2.4
67	Dominican Republic	2.3
68	Nicaragua	2.2
69	Bangladesh	2.2
70	Paraguay	2.2
71	Vietnam	2.1
72	Guatemala	2.0
73	Ecuador	2.0
74	El Salvador	1.9
75	Honduras	1.9

MEAN: 3.8

11.09 Compliance with international agreements

Compliance with international environmental agreements is a high priority in your country's government. (1 = strongly disagree, 7 = strongly agree)

RANK	COUNTRY	SCORE	MEAN: 4.5
1	Finland	6.7	
2	Denmark	6.7	
3	Sweden	6.5	
4	Austria	6.3	
5	Germany	6.3	
6	Netherlands	6.2	
7	Norway	6.1	
8	Switzerland	5.9	
9	Iceland	5.9	
10	New Zealand	5.8	
11	Singapore	5.7	
12	United Kingdom	5.7	
13	France	5.7	
14	Canada	5.6	
15	Japan	5.5	
16	Belgium	5.5	
17	Australia	5.4	
18	Taiwan	5.4	
19	Estonia	5.4	
20	Italy	5.4	
21	Czech Republic	5.3	
22	United States	5.2	
23	China	5.0	
24	Hungary	5.0	
25	Hong Kong SAR	4.9	
26	Spain	4.9	
27	Ireland	4.8	
28	Slovak Republic	4.8	
29	Slovenia	4.7	
30	Poland	4.6	
31	Costa Rica	4.6	
32	Jordan	4.5	
33	Portugal	4.5	
34	Vietnam	4.5	
35	Korea	4.5	
36	Chile	4.5	
37	Latvia	4.5	
38	Egypt	4.4	
39	South Africa	4.3	
40	Lithuania	4.3	
41	Uruguay	4.3	
42	Brazil	4.2	
43	Romania	4.1	
44	Israel	4.0	
45	Malaysia	4.0	
46	Panama	4.0	
47	Thailand	4.0	
48	Mauritius	4.0	
49	Jamaica	4.0	
50	Mexico	3.9	
51	Turkey	3.9	
52	Bulgaria	3.9	
53	Colombia	3.8	
54	Dominican Republic	3.8	
55	Greece	3.7	
56	India	3.7	
57	Ukraine	3.7	
58	Indonesia	3.7	
59	Trinidad and Tobago	3.5	
60	Nigeria	3.4	
61	Bolivia	3.4	
62	Philippines	3.3	
63	Sri Lanka	3.3	
64	Venezuela	3.2	
65	Russian Federation	3.2	
66	Honduras	3.1	
67	Zimbabwe	3.1	
68	Argentina	3.1	
69	Peru	3.1	
70	Ecuador	3.1	
71	El Salvador	3.0	
72	Bangladesh	2.9	
73	Nicaragua	2.9	
74	Paraguay	2.8	
75	Guatemala	2.7	

11.10 Clarity and stability of regulations

Environmental regulations in your country are: (1 = confusing and frequently changing, 7 = transparent and stable)

RANK	COUNTRY	SCORE	MEAN: 4.2
1	Finland	6.7	
2	Singapore	6.2	
3	Switzerland	5.9	
4	Sweden	5.8	
5	Netherlands	5.6	
6	Iceland	5.6	
7	Austria	5.6	
8	Norway	5.5	
9	Japan	5.3	
10	Germany	5.3	
11	France	5.3	
12	Canada	5.2	
13	United Kingdom	5.1	
14	Denmark	5.0	
15	Hong Kong SAR	4.9	
16	United States	4.9	
17	Estonia	4.8	
18	Taiwan	4.8	
19	New Zealand	4.8	
20	Hungary	4.8	
21	Egypt	4.8	
22	Australia	4.7	
23	Ireland	4.7	
24	Belgium	4.6	
25	Spain	4.6	
26	Latvia	4.5	
27	Malaysia	4.5	
28	Jordan	4.4	
29	Slovenia	4.4	
30	Jamaica	4.4	
31	Uruguay	4.3	
32	Poland	4.3	
33	Slovak Republic	4.2	
34	Costa Rica	4.2	
35	South Africa	4.2	
36	Czech Republic	4.1	
37	Portugal	4.1	
38	Israel	4.0	
39	Thailand	4.0	
40	Korea	4.0	
41	Italy	3.9	
42	Brazil	3.9	
43	Turkey	3.9	
44	China	3.9	
45	Zimbabwe	3.8	
46	Mauritius	3.8	
47	Lithuania	3.8	
48	India	3.8	
49	Romania	3.7	
50	Chile	3.7	
51	Trinidad and Tobago	3.7	
52	Indonesia	3.7	
53	Bulgaria	3.6	
54	Philippines	3.6	
55	Panama	3.6	
56	Colombia	3.5	
57	Mexico	3.5	
58	Argentina	3.4	
59	Greece	3.4	
60	Sri Lanka	3.4	
61	Peru	3.3	
62	Nigeria	3.3	
63	Dominican Republic	3.2	
64	Vietnam	3.2	
65	Bolivia	3.2	
66	Russian Federation	3.2	
67	Paraguay	3.1	
68	Bangladesh	3.0	
69	Venezuela	3.0	
70	Ukraine	2.9	
71	El Salvador	2.8	
72	Nicaragua	2.7	
73	Ecuador	2.7	
74	Honduras	2.4	
75	Guatemala	2.4	

439

11.11 Flexibility of regulations

Environmental regulations in your country: (1 = offer no options for achieving compliance, 7 = are flexible and offer many options for achieving compliance)

RANK	COUNTRY	SCORE
1	Finland	5.4
2	Singapore	5.4
3	Sweden	5.0
4	United Kingdom	4.8
5	United States	4.8
6	Canada	4.8
7	Iceland	4.8
8	Hong Kong SAR	4.6
9	Ireland	4.5
10	Egypt	4.5
11	Estonia	4.5
12	Russian Federation	4.4
13	Malaysia	4.4
14	France	4.4
15	Trinidad and Tobago	4.4
16	Slovenia	4.4
17	Switzerland	4.4
18	Netherlands	4.4
19	Germany	4.3
20	New Zealand	4.3
21	Australia	4.3
22	Jordan	4.3
23	Uruguay	4.3
24	Japan	4.2
25	Austria	4.2
26	Israel	4.2
27	Slovak Republic	4.2
28	Czech Republic	4.2
29	Belgium	4.2
30	South Africa	4.2
31	Latvia	4.1
32	Jamaica	4.1
33	Denmark	4.1
34	Taiwan	4.1
35	Spain	4.1
36	Hungary	4.0
37	Brazil	4.0
38	Thailand	4.0
39	Korea	3.9
40	India	3.9
41	Indonesia	3.9
42	Norway	3.9
43	Panama	3.9
44	Poland	3.9
45	Portugal	3.9
46	Costa Rica	3.9
47	Colombia	3.8
48	Argentina	3.8
49	Romania	3.8
50	Zimbabwe	3.7
51	Vietnam	3.7
52	Chile	3.7
53	Peru	3.6
54	China	3.6
55	Mexico	3.6
56	Turkey	3.6
57	Sri Lanka	3.5
58	Dominican Republic	3.5
59	Mauritius	3.5
60	Ukraine	3.4
61	Bangladesh	3.4
62	Nigeria	3.4
63	Lithuania	3.3
64	Italy	3.3
65	Bulgaria	3.3
66	Philippines	3.2
67	Greece	3.2
68	Nicaragua	3.2
69	Venezuela	3.1
70	El Salvador	3.1
71	Bolivia	3.1
72	Paraguay	3.0
73	Honduras	3.0
74	Guatemala	2.8
75	Ecuador	2.6

MEAN: 4.0

11.12 Consistency of regulation enforcement

Environmental regulation in your country is: (1 = not enforced or enforced erratically, 7 = enforced consistently and fairly)

RANK	COUNTRY	SCORE
1	Finland	6.4
2	Singapore	6.2
3	Switzerland	6.0
4	Netherlands	5.9
5	Austria	5.7
6	Germany	5.7
7	Iceland	5.7
8	Denmark	5.6
9	Sweden	5.6
10	Australia	5.6
11	United States	5.6
12	United Kingdom	5.6
13	France	5.5
14	Canada	5.5
15	New Zealand	5.4
16	Japan	5.4
17	Norway	5.4
18	Belgium	5.1
19	Ireland	4.8
20	Taiwan	4.5
21	Hong Kong SAR	4.4
22	Hungary	4.3
23	Israel	4.3
24	Latvia	4.3
25	Malaysia	4.3
26	Italy	4.2
27	Spain	4.2
28	Poland	4.2
29	Slovenia	4.2
30	Korea	4.2
31	Estonia	4.1
32	Jordan	4.0
33	Lithuania	4.0
34	Slovak Republic	4.0
35	Chile	3.9
36	Brazil	3.9
37	Russian Federation	3.9
38	Portugal	3.9
39	Egypt	3.8
40	Uruguay	3.8
41	Thailand	3.7
42	Jamaica	3.7
43	Czech Republic	3.6
44	South Africa	3.6
45	Vietnam	3.6
46	Costa Rica	3.6
47	Indonesia	3.5
48	China	3.5
49	Colombia	3.5
50	Mexico	3.5
51	Bulgaria	3.4
52	Turkey	3.3
53	India	3.3
54	Panama	3.2
55	Greece	3.2
56	Mauritius	3.1
57	Trinidad and Tobago	3.1
58	Sri Lanka	3.1
59	Zimbabwe	3.1
60	Romania	3.0
61	Peru	2.9
62	Ukraine	2.8
63	Argentina	2.8
64	Philippines	2.8
65	Dominican Republic	2.7
66	Nigeria	2.7
67	Venezuela	2.7
68	Paraguay	2.5
69	Bolivia	2.4
70	Bangladesh	2.4
71	El Salvador	2.3
72	Nicaragua	2.3
73	Honduras	2.3
74	Ecuador	2.2
75	Guatemala	2.1

MEAN: 4.0

11.13 Effects of compliance on business

Complying with environmental standards in your country: (1 = hurts competitiveness, 7 = helps long-term competitiveness by prompting improvements in products and processes)

RANK	COUNTRY	SCORE
1	Finland	6.1
2	Singapore	6.0
3	Sweden	5.6
4	Switzerland	5.5
5	Japan	5.4
6	Austria	5.4
7	Netherlands	5.4
8	Iceland	5.3
9	Canada	5.2
10	France	5.2
11	United States	5.1
12	Egypt	5.0
13	Germany	5.0
14	Norway	4.9
15	Costa Rica	4.8
16	Jamaica	4.8
17	Panama	4.8
18	Denmark	4.8
19	Taiwan	4.8
20	Jordan	4.8
21	Ireland	4.8
22	United Kingdom	4.8
23	New Zealand	4.7
24	Malaysia	4.7
25	Belgium	4.7
26	Hungary	4.7
27	Dominican Republic	4.7
28	Spain	4.6
29	Hong Kong SAR	4.6
30	China	4.6
31	Nigeria	4.6
32	Uruguay	4.6
33	Australia	4.5
34	Ecuador	4.5
35	Brazil	4.5
36	Poland	4.5
37	South Africa	4.5
38	Estonia	4.5
39	Slovenia	4.4
40	Trinidad and Tobago	4.4
41	Slovak Republic	4.4
42	Mauritius	4.4
43	Nicaragua	4.4
44	Honduras	4.4
45	Korea	4.4
46	Colombia	4.4
47	Thailand	4.3
48	Portugal	4.3
49	Zimbabwe	4.3
50	Lithuania	4.3
51	Bangladesh	4.3
52	Latvia	4.3
53	Mexico	4.2
54	Vietnam	4.2
55	Israel	4.2
56	India	4.1
57	Czech Republic	4.1
58	Indonesia	4.1
59	Bulgaria	4.0
60	Peru	4.0
61	Chile	4.0
62	Greece	4.0
63	Turkey	3.9
64	Guatemala	3.9
65	Italy	3.9
66	El Salvador	3.8
67	Sri Lanka	3.8
68	Philippines	3.7
69	Bolivia	3.7
70	Ukraine	3.6
71	Romania	3.6
72	Argentina	3.6
73	Paraguay	3.5
74	Venezuela	3.5
75	Russian Federation	3.4

MEAN: 4.5

11.14 Political context of environmental gains

Environmental gains in your country are achieved through: (1 = adversarial and legal means, 7 = government-business cooperation and voluntary corporate action)

RANK	COUNTRY	SCORE
1	Singapore	5.9
2	Netherlands	5.5
3	Finland	5.4
4	Switzerland	5.3
5	Canada	5.1
6	Iceland	5.0
7	United Kingdom	5.0
8	Belgium	4.9
9	Sweden	4.9
10	Japan	4.8
11	Jamaica	4.8
12	New Zealand	4.7
13	Australia	4.7
14	Malaysia	4.7
15	Norway	4.6
16	Ireland	4.6
17	Panama	4.6
18	Spain	4.6
19	Taiwan	4.5
20	Hong Kong SAR	4.5
21	United States	4.5
22	Austria	4.4
23	Germany	4.4
24	France	4.4
25	Nigeria	4.4
26	Zimbabwe	4.4
27	South Africa	4.3
28	Denmark	4.3
29	Indonesia	4.3
30	Brazil	4.3
31	Jordan	4.3
32	Uruguay	4.3
33	Philippines	4.2
34	Costa Rica	4.2
35	Slovak Republic	4.2
36	China	4.2
37	Estonia	4.2
38	Thailand	4.2
39	Mauritius	4.1
40	Trinidad and Tobago	4.1
41	Colombia	4.1
42	Italy	4.0
43	Mexico	4.0
44	Korea	4.0
45	Poland	3.9
46	Portugal	3.9
47	Dominican Republic	3.8
48	Lithuania	3.8
49	Israel	3.8
50	Peru	3.8
51	Slovenia	3.8
52	Nicaragua	3.8
53	Bangladesh	3.8
54	Chile	3.8
55	Honduras	3.7
56	Guatemala	3.7
57	Latvia	3.7
58	Bulgaria	3.7
59	Ecuador	3.6
60	Hungary	3.6
61	Paraguay	3.6
62	Sri Lanka	3.5
63	Venezuela	3.5
64	Turkey	3.5
65	Greece	3.5
66	Egypt	3.4
67	Bolivia	3.4
68	Argentina	3.4
69	Czech Republic	3.3
70	India	3.3
71	Vietnam	3.3
72	El Salvador	3.0
73	Russian Federation	3.0
74	Ukraine	2.8
75	Romania	2.0

MEAN: 4.1

441

11.15 Prevalence of environmental management systems

How many companies in your country utilize environmental management systems such as ISO 14000? (1 = almost none, 7 = most companies)

RANK	COUNTRY	SCORE
1	Finland	5.7
2	Sweden	5.3
3	Netherlands	5.0
4	Germany	4.9
5	Canada	4.9
6	Australia	4.8
7	Switzerland	4.7
8	Singapore	4.7
9	Japan	4.7
10	Taiwan	4.6
11	Denmark	4.5
12	Austria	4.5
13	Belgium	4.4
14	United States	4.4
15	Korea	4.3
16	France	4.3
17	Italy	4.1
18	Norway	4.1
19	United Kingdom	4.1
20	Spain	4.1
21	Ireland	4.0
22	Brazil	3.9
23	Uruguay	3.8
24	New Zealand	3.8
25	Slovak Republic	3.8
26	South Africa	3.8
27	Thailand	3.7
28	Egypt	3.7
29	Czech Republic	3.6
30	Hungary	3.6
31	Nigeria	3.6
32	Zimbabwe	3.5
33	Israel	3.5
34	Iceland	3.5
35	Malaysia	3.4
36	Trinidad and Tobago	3.4
37	Slovenia	3.4
38	Jordan	3.3
39	China	3.3
40	Hong Kong SAR	3.3
41	Ukraine	3.2
42	India	3.2
43	Indonesia	3.2
44	Poland	3.2
45	Mauritius	3.1
46	Latvia	3.1
47	Jamaica	3.1
48	Vietnam	3.1
49	Philippines	3.1
50	Costa Rica	3.0
51	Mexico	3.0
52	Panama	3.0
53	Estonia	2.9
54	Portugal	2.9
55	Lithuania	2.9
56	Turkey	2.9
57	Argentina	2.9
58	Sri Lanka	2.7
59	Colombia	2.7
60	Chile	2.7
61	Bulgaria	2.7
62	Dominican Republic	2.6
63	Russian Federation	2.6
64	Honduras	2.5
65	Greece	2.5
66	Nicaragua	2.3
67	Ecuador	2.2
68	Peru	2.2
69	Guatemala	2.2
70	El Salvador	2.1
71	Bangladesh	2.1
72	Bolivia	2.0
73	Venezuela	2.0
74	Paraguay	1.8
75	Romania	1.3

MEAN: 3.4

Technical Notes and Sources

The data used in this *Report* represent the best available estimates from various national authorities, international agencies, and private sources at the time the *Report* was prepared (July/August 2001). It is possible that some data will have been revised or updated by national authorities after publication. Throughout the statistical tables in this publication, "n/a" denotes that the value is not available.

The following outlines some notes on sources for specific variables listed in the Data Tables of this *Report*. Not all of these variables are used in the calculations for the Growth Competitiveness Index or Current Competitive Index. For specific descriptions of the variables included in those indexes, see Chapters 1.1 and 1.2, respectively.

Section 1. Aggregate country performance indicators

1.01 Total GDP, 2000. Source: Gross domestic product (GDP) in current US dollars was taken from the International Monetary Fund's (IMF) *World Economic Outlook Database, May 2001*. Available online at http://www.imf.org/external/pubs/ft/weo/2001/01/data/index.htm.

1.02 Total population, 2000. Source: Population data were taken from the Economic Intelligence Unit's Country Data online (http://countrydata.bvdep.com) and national statistical offices.

1.03 GDP per capita (PPP), 2000. Source: Per capita GDP adjusted for purchasing power across countries was calculated by taking the 1999 GDP per capita (PPP) figures for all countries from the World Bank's *World Development Indicators 2001* and then multiplying each country's figure by the real per capita growth rate from 1999 to 2000 (see variable 1.04). These values were in turn scaled by the 1999 to 2000 US GDP implicit price deflator, as calculated from data posted by the US Department of Commerce's Bureau of Economic Analysis (http://www.bea.doc.gov/bea/dn/nipaweb/Index.htm).

1.04 Real growth in GDP per capita, 1999 to 2000. Source: IMF's online *World Economic Outlook Database, May 2001*. These values were constructed by calculating the year-on-year change in "Per Capita Gross Domestic Product, Constant Prices."

1.05 GDP per capita relative to the United States, 2000. Source: These values present the same underlying data as variable 1.03, but instead show GDP as a proportion of the United States' rather than at an absolute level.

1.06 GDP per capita relative to the United States, 1992. Source: Data come from the World Bank's *World Development Indicators 2001*. The transition economies for which 1995 ratios are listed instead of 1992 ratios are: Bulgaria, the Czech Republic, Estonia, Hungary, Latvia, Lithuania, Poland, Romania, Russia, the Slovak Republic, Slovenia, and Ukraine.

1.07 Change in GDP per capita relative to United States, 1992 to 2000. Source: Using the data listed in variables 1.05 and 1.06, average annual growth rates from 1992 (1995 for transition economies) to 2000 were calculated.

1.08 Unemployment rate, 2000. Source: the Economist Intelligence Unit's Country Data online, IMF Country Reports, and various national authorities. The data list the recorded official unemployment figures for 2000. Readers should note that, on this variable, strict comparison across all countries is particularly difficult due to countries' differing definitions of both labor force and unemployment. Measurement problems are often most acute in developing economies. The Economist Intelligence Unit reports, for instance, that China's official figure of 7 percent is widely believed to be a significant underestimate of the true unemployment level.

1.09 Employment to population ratio, 2000. Source: the Economist Intelligence Unit's Country Data online, IMF Country Reports, and various national authorities.

Section 2. Macroeconomic environment

2.23 Country credit rating, March 2001. Source: *The Institutional Investor Online*, accessed at http://www.iimagazine.com/premium/rr/countrycredit/ccr/2001.htm.

2.24 Government surplus/deficit, 2000. Source: IMF Country Reports, the Economist Intelligence Unit's Country Data online, and various national authorities. These figures are for general rather than central government budgets.

2.25 Government expenditure, 2000. Source: IMF Country Reports, the Economist Intelligence Unit's Country Data online, and various national authorities. These figures are for general rather than central government budgets.

2.26 National savings rate, 2000. Source: Economist Intelligence Unit's Country Data online and IMF Country Reports.

2.27 National investment rate, 2000. Source: Economist Intelligence Unit's Country Data online.

2.28 Inflation, 2000. Taken from the IMF's *World Economic Outlook Database, May 2001*. Data indicate annual percentage change averages for the year rather than end-of-period changes.

2.29 Real exchange rate, 2000. Using consumer price index data and period average annual (nominal) exchange rate data from the IMF's *International Financial Statistics, June 2001*, this variable was created by setting the average real exchange rate between 1990 and 1995 to 100 for most economies and the real exchange rate in 1995 to 100 for transition economies. The results thus show the relative appreciation, for numbers less than 100, or depreciation, for numbers greater than 100, of each currency relative to the US dollar up to 2000. The basis of the real exchange rate calculations was:

$$\left(\begin{array}{c} \text{period average exchange rate} \\ \text{(in national currency per US\$)} \end{array} \right) \times \left(\frac{\text{US Consumer Price Index}}{\text{national Consumer Price Index}} \right)$$

2.30 Interest rate spread, 2000. Source: IMF *International Financial Statistics, June 2001* and Economist Intelligence Unit's Country Data online. This variable is equal to the difference between the typical short-term lending and deposit rates over the 2000 period.

2.31 Average tariff rate, 2001. Source: O'Driscoll, Gerald P Jr, Kim Holmes, and Melanie Kirkpatrick. *2001 Index of Economic Freedom*. Washington, DC and New York, NY: The Heritage Foundation and Dow Jones and Company, 2001.

2.32 Corporate income tax rate, 2001. Source: O'Driscoll et al. *2001 Index of Economic Freedom*.

2.33 Value added tax rate, 2001. Source: O'Driscoll et al. *2001 Index of Economic Freedom*.

Section 3. Technological Innovation and Diffusion

3.15 Research and development spending. Source: World Bank, *World Development Indicators 2001*.

3.16 Utility patents in 2000. Source: United States Patent and Trademark Office, "Patent Counts by Country/State and Year: Utility Patents, January 1, 1963–December 31, 2000." Utility patents (ie, patents for invention) are recorded such that the origin of the patent is determined by the first-named inventor at the time of the grant. Patents per million population are calculated by dividing the number of patents granted to a country in 2000 by that country's population in the same year.

3.17 Utility patents in 1980s. Source: United States Patent and Trademark Office, as above in 3.16. Here the values listed are the average number of patents per million population from 1980 to 1989.

3.18 Secondary enrollment. Source: World Bank, *World Development Indicators 2001*. This is the net secondary enrollment ratio for 1997 or the most recent year available. According to the *World Development Indicators*, the net enrollment ratio is the ratio of the number of children of official school age (as defined by the national education system) who are enrolled in school relative to the population of the corresponding official school age. This measure is based on the International Standard Classification of Education, 1976 (ISCED76).

3.19 Tertiary enrollment. Source: World Bank, *World Development Indicators 2001* and World Bank Task Force on Education's *Higher Education in Developing Countries: Peril and Promise* (Washington, DC: World Bank, 2000), Table A. Figures are for 1997 wherever data are available for that year. Otherwise data are for the most recent available year (usually 1995). The gross tertiary enrollment rate is: "the ratio of total enrollment, regardless of age, to the population of the age group that officially corresponds to the level of education shown. Tertiary education, whether or not to an advanced research qualification, normally requires, as a minimum condition of admission, the successful completion of education at the secondary level" (from World Development Indicators CD-ROM definitions). Thus, a tertiary enrollment ratio could be greater than 100 if the number of students enrolled in tertiary education were greater than the population of the relevant age group.

3.20 Years of schooling. Source: Barro, Robert J and Jong-Wha Lee. "International Data on Educational Attainment: Updates and Implications," Center for International Development Working Paper no. 42, April 2000. Figures list Barro and Lee's calculations of average total years of schooling received by members of a country's population aged 15 and above. Data available for download at http://www.cid.harvard.edu/ciddata/ciddata.html.

3.21 Mathematics achievement. Source: 1999 Third International Mathematics and Science Study (TIMSS). *International Mathematics Report*. This table is listed only for reference, since less than half of the countries included in this *Report* participated in the most recent TIMSS study in 1999.

3.22 Science achievement. Source: 1999 Third International Mathematics and Science Study (TIMSS). *International Science Report*. This table is listed only for reference, since less than half of the countries included in this *Report* participated in the most recent TIMSS study in 1999.

3.23 Skill-based exports. Source: These data come from Statistics Canada's *World Trade Analyzer, 1980–1996* and from the International Trade Centre and United Nations Statistics Division's "COMTRADE" or *PC-TAS Trade Analysis System, 1995–1999*. The variable here lists the value of "skill-based exports" as a percentage of GDP. Skill-based exports are non-primary products or, more specifically, Standard Industrial Trade Classification codes 54—Medicinal and pharmaceutical products; 57—Plastics in primary forms; 58—Plastics in non-primary forms; 65—Textile yarn, fabrics, made-up articles not elsewhere specified (n.e.s.), and related products; 7—Machinery and transport equipment; 81—Prefabricated buildings; sanitary, plumbing, heating and lighting fixtures and fittings, n.e.s.; 82—Furniture, and parts thereof; bedding, mattresses, mattress supports, cushions and similar stuffed furnishings; 83—Travel goods, handbags and similar containers; 84—Articles of apparel and clothing accessories; 85—Footwear; 87—Professional, scientific and controlling instruments and apparatus, n.e.s.; 88—Photographic apparatus, equipment and supplies and optical goods, n.e.s.; watches and clocks; 893—Articles, n.e.s., of plastics; 894—Baby carriages, toys, games and sporting goods; 898—Musical instruments and parts and accessories thereof; records, tapes and other sound or similar recordings; 8996—Orthopedic appliances (including crutches, surgical belts and trusses); splints and other fracture appliances; artificial parts of the body; hearing-aids and other appliances which are worn or carried or implanted in the body, to compensate for a defect; and 95—Armored fighting vehicles and arms of war. Note that this term is closely linked to, but not the same as, the "technology in trade residual" in Chapter 1.1. The value here reflects the absolute level of skill-based exports, whereas the trade residual comes from a regression of these exports on population.

445

Section 4. Information and Communications Technology

4.13 Cellular telephones. Source: International Telecommunications Union indicators on cellular subscribers. Available at http://www.itu.int/ITU-D/ict/statistics/.

4.14 Internet users. Source: International Telecommunications Union Internet indicators. Available at http://www.itu.int/ITU-D/ict/statistics/.

4.15 Internet hosts. Source: International Telecommunications Union Internet indicators. Available at http://www.itu.int/ITU-D/ict/statistics/.

4.16 Telephone lines. Source: International Telecommunications Union basic indicators. Available at http://www.itu.int/ITU-D/ict/statistics/.

4.17 Personal computers. Source: International Telecommunications Union Internet indicators. Available at http://www.itu.int/ITU-D/ict/statistics/.

The World Economic Forum would like to thank KPMG for their support in making this *Report* possible.

KPMG is one of the world's largest professional services organizations, providing assurance and advisory services and tax solutions to leading businesses and organizations. The Firm serves clients in 159 countries and employs more than 100,000 people.

KPMG's services are focused and delivered along five industry lines of business, enabling the Firm to customize solutions to the individual needs of clients. Global innovation centers support product development, knowledge transfer, industry customization of solutions, and rapid deployment of products and services.

On a global basis, KPMG coordinates its national and local resources—people, ideas, solutions, technologies, and knowledge—through three operating regions, offering clients flexibility, faster responsiveness, and critical mass in a host of problem-solving disciplines. The Firm's extensive investments in knowledge management, training, and professional mobility enhance the work experience for KPMG professionals and ensure that it places the best professionals and technologies into work assignments that benefit clients.

The Global Competitiveness Report 2001–2002

World Economic Forum
2001 Executive Opinion Survey Results
on CD-ROM

Produced in collaboration with the Center for International Development at Harvard University and the Institute for Strategy and Competitiveness at Harvard Business School

This CD-ROM includes detailed survey results for all 75 economies included in *The Global Competitiveness Report 2001–2002*. The data are a product of the World Economic Forum's 2001 Executive Opinion Survey, and are organized into ten categories, including macroeconomic environment, technological innovation and diffusion, information and communications technology, and environmental policy. This includes many of the results used in the construction of the Growth Competitiveness Index and the Current Competitiveness Index.

Users can download the entire data file at once or use the built-in filtering mechanism to specified results for individual variables and countries. The data set is prepared in a user-friendly Microsoft Excel format, and can be run with any Microsoft Excel 97/2000 or Excel 5.0/95 software (Windows or Mac).

Hardware Requirements
Pentium 100 Mhz
32 MB RAM
CD-ROM drive

Software Requirements
Windows or Mac OS running
Microsoft Excel 97/2000 or Excel 5.0/95

Setup
The CD will autorun on systems running Windows 95/98/ME Windows NT/2000. For Windows 3.1, or if autorun is disabled, use Windows Explorer to browse the CD. Double click the file WEF_DATA.xls to open this Excel spreadsheet.
On Mac OS a window will open showing an Excel icon labeled WEF DATA. Double click on the icon to open this Excel spreadsheet.

To use from hard drive
Copy the WEF_DATA.xls file (approximately 1 MB) to your hard drive for use without the CD.

Navigating within the data file
Users can navigate between the Microsoft Excel worksheets either by clicking on the highlighted links within the opening pages or by clicking on the worksheet label tabs at the bottom of the screen.

Acknowledgment
This CD-ROM was prepared by CD\Works, 1266 Soldiers Field Road, Boston, MA 02135-1003, USA.
Tel: 1-800-CDWORKS
Website: http://www.cdworks.com
E-mail: sales@cdworks.com